TAKING SIDES

Clashing Views in

United States History, Volume 2, Reconstruction to the Present

FIFTEENTH EDITION

TAKING SIDES

Clashing Views in

United States History, Volume 2, Reconstruction to the Present

FIFTEENTH EDITION

Selected, Edited, and with Introductions by

Larry Madaras
Howard Community College

and

James M. SoRelle
Baylor University

Mc Graw Hill

Connect
Learn
Succeed™

TAKING SIDES: CLASHING VIEWS IN UNITED STATES HISTORY, VOLUME 2,
RECONSTRUCTION TO THE PRESENT, FIFTEENTH EDITION

Published by McGraw-Hill, a business unit of The McGraw-Hill Companies, Inc., 1221 Avenue of
the Americas, New York, NY 10020. Copyright ©2013 by The McGraw-Hill Companies, Inc. All
rights reserved. Printed in the United States of America. Previous edition(s) ©2011, 2009, and
2007. No part of this publication may be reproduced or distributed in any form or by any means,
or stored in a database or retrieval system, without the prior written consent of The McGraw-Hill
Companies, Inc., including, but not limited to, in any network or other electronic storage or
transmission, or broadcast for distance learning.

Some ancillaries, including electronic and print components, may not be available to customers
outside the United States.

This book is printed on acid-free paper.

Taking Sides® is a registered trademark of the McGraw-Hill Companies, Inc.
Taking Sides is published by the **Contemporary Learning Series** group within the McGraw-Hill
Higher Education division.

1 2 3 4 5 6 7 8 9 0 DOC/DOC 1 0 9 8 7 6 5 4 3 2

MHID: 0-07-8050464
ISBN: 978-0-07-8050466
ISSN: 2156-9452 (print)
ISSN: 2156-9460 (online)

Managing Editor: *Larry Loeppke*
Marketing Director: *Adam Kloza*
Marketing Manager: *Nathan Edwards*
Senior Developmental Editor: *Jill Meloy*
Lead Project Manager: *Jane Mohr*
Design Coordinator: *Brenda A. Rolwes*
Buyer: *Jennifer Pickel*
Cover Designer: *Rick Noel*
Senior Content Licensing Specialist: *Shirley Lanners*
Media Project Manager: *Sridevi Palani*

Compositor: MPS Limited
Cover Image: © Library of Congress Prints & Photographs Division [LC-USZ62-130684]

Editors/Academic Advisory Board

Members of the Academic Advisory Board are instrumental in the final selection of articles for each edition of TAKING SIDES. Their review of articles for content, level, and appropriateness provides critical direction to the editors and staff. We think that you will find their careful consideration well reflected in this volume.

TAKING SIDES: Clashing Views in UNITED STATES HISTORY, VOLUME 2, RECONSTRUCTION TO THE PRESENT

Fifteenth Edition

EDITORS

Larry Madaras
Howard Community College
and
James M. SoRelle
Baylor University

ACADEMIC ADVISORY BOARD MEMBERS

Editors/Academic Advisory Board continued

Preface

Since 1985, our aim has been to create an effective instrument to enhance classroom learning and to foster critical thinking in the subject area of U.S. history. Historical facts presented in a vacuum are of little value to the educational process. For students, whose search for historical truth often concentrates on *when* something happened rather than on *why,* and on specific events rather than on the *significance* of those events, *Taking Sides* is designed to offer an interesting and valuable departure. The understanding arrived at based on the evidence that emerges from the clash of views encourages the reader to view history as an *interpretive* discipline, not one of rote memorization. The success of the past 14 editions of *Taking Sides: Clashing Views in United States History* has encouraged us to remain faithful to its original objectives and methods, but previous users of this reader will notice several changes in the format of this new edition.

As in previous editions, the 18 issues and 36 selections that follow are arranged in chronological order and can be incorporated easily into any American history survey course. Each issue has an *Introduction,* which sets the stage for the debate that follows in the pro and con selections and provides historical and methodological background to the problem that the issue examines. For this new edition, each introduction has been expanded to focus more intentionally on *alternative perspectives* that are applicable to the question at hand in order to demonstrate that these issues contain a level of complexity that cannot be addressed fully in a simple Yes/No format. Additionally, each introduction is accompanied by a set of student-focused *Learning Outcomes,* which are designed to highlight what knowledge the reader should take away from reading and studying the issue.

The traditional *Postscript* from previous editions has been replaced by several new features. First, there are several questions that relate to the learning outcomes and to the material in the preceding selections that are designed to stimulate *Critical Thinking and Reflection.* Second, *Is There Common Ground?* attempts to encourage students to think more deeply about the issue by highlighting points shared by scholars on the subject at hand and tying the readings to alternative perspectives within the debate. Third, *Additional Resources* offers a brief annotated bibliography of important books and essays relating to the issue. Also, Internet site addresses (URLs), which should prove useful as starting points for further research, have been provided on the *Internet References* page that accompanies each unit opener.

Another new feature to this edition is the *Topic Guide,* a list of topics covered in the issues comprising this volume. At the back of the book, as in previous editions, is a listing of all the *contributors to this volume* with a brief biographical sketch of each of the authors whose views are debated here.

Changes to This Edition

In this edition, we have continued our efforts to maintain a balance between traditional political, diplomatic, and cultural issues and the new social history, which depicts a society that benefited from the presence of Native Americans, African Americans, women, and workers of various racial and ethnic backgrounds. With this in mind, we present nine new issues: Did a "New South" Emerge following Reconstruction? (issue 2); Were American Workers in the Gilded Age Conservative Capitalists? (issue 4); Did the Conservation Movement of the Early Twentieth Century Successfully Preserve the American Environment? (issue 7); Were the 1920s an Era of Social and Cultural Rebellion? (issue 9); Was the World War II Era a Watershed for the Civil Rights Movement? (issue 11); Was It Necessary to Drop the Atomic Bomb to End World War II? (issue 12); Did President John F. Kennedy Cause the Cuban Missile Crisis? (issue 14); Did the Activism of the 1960s Produce a Better Nation? (issue 15); and Were the 1980s a Decade of Affluence for the Middle Class? (issue 18).

A Word to the Instructor   An *Instructor's Resource Guide with Test Questions* (multiple-choice and essay) is available through the publisher for the instructor using *Taking Sides* in the classroom. A general guidebook, *Using Taking Sides in the Classroom,* which discusses methods and techniques for integrating the pro–con approach into any classroom setting, is also available. An online version of *Using Taking Sides in the Classroom* and a correspondence service for *Taking Sides* adopters can be found at www.mhhe.com/cls.

Acknowledgments   Many individuals have contributed to the successful completion of this edition. We appreciate the evaluations submitted to McGraw-Hill Contemporary Learning Series by those who have used *Taking Sides* in the classroom. Special thanks to those who responded with specific suggestions for past editions.

We are particularly indebted to Maggie Cullen, Cindy SoRelle, the late Barry Crouch, Virginia Kirk, Joseph and Helen Mitchell, and Jean Soto, who shared their ideas for changes, pointed us toward potentially useful historical works, and provided significant editorial assistance. Lynn Wilder performed indispensable typing duties connected with this project. Ela Ciborowski, James Johnson, and Sharon Glover in the library at Howard Community College provided essential help in acquiring books and articles on interlibrary loan. Finally, we are sincerely grateful for the commitment, encouragement, advice, and patience provided in recent years by Jill Meloy, senior development editor for the *Taking Sides* series, and the entire staff of McGraw-Hill Contemporary Learning Series.

Larry Madaras
Emeritus, Howard Community College

James M. SoRelle
Baylor University

Contents In Brief

Contents

LeeAnna Keith characterizes the assault on the Grant Parish courthouse in Colfax, Louisiana, on Easter Sunday in 1873 as a product of white racism and unwillingness by local whites to tolerate African American political power during the era of Reconstruction. Heather Cox Richardson argues that the failure of Radical Reconstruction was primarily a consequence of a national commitment to a free labor ideology, which opposed an expanding central government that legislated rights to African Americans that other citizens had acquired through hard work.

Edward L. Ayers, while conceding that some areas of the South remained tied to agriculture and that industrial development did not always match the rhetoric of New South boosters, insists that manufacturing and industrial production, funded by local capital, made impressive strides in the post-Reconstruction South and positively touched the lives of millions of southerners. James Tice Moore challenges the view that the white, Democratic political elite that ruled the post-Reconstruction South abandoned antebellum rural traditions in favor of business and commerce and concludes that these agriculturally oriented "Redeemers" actually represented a continuity of leadership from the Old South to the New South.

According to Howard Zinn, the new industrialists such as John D. Rockefeller, Andrew Carnegie, and J. P. Morgan adopted business practices that encouraged monopolies and used the powers of the government to control the masses from rebellion. John S. Gordon argues that the nineteenth-century men of big business such as John D. Rockefeller and Andrew Carnegie developed through the oil and steel industries' consumer products that improved the lifestyle of average Americans.

Issue 4.   Were American Workers in the Gilded Age Conservative Capitalists?   78

Historian Carl N. Degler maintains that the American labor movement accepted capitalism and reacted conservatively to the radical organizational changes brought about in the economic system by big business. Professor of history Herbert G. Gutman argues that from 1843 to 1893, American factory workers attempted to humanize the system through the maintenance of their traditional, artisan, and preindustrial work habits.

Issue 5.   Were Late Nineteenth-Century Immigrants "Uprooted"?   102

Oscar Handlin asserts that immigrants to the United States in the late nineteenth century were alienated from the cultural traditions of the homeland they had left as well as from those of their adopted country. Mark Wyman argues that as many as four million immigrants to the United States between 1880 and 1930 viewed their trip as temporary and remained tied psychologically to their homeland to which they returned once they had accumulated enough wealth to enable them to improve their status back home.

Issue 6.   Were the Populists Irrational Reactionaries?   126

According to Richard Hofstadter, the Populists created a conspiracy theory around the issues of industrialism and the "money question" that activated a virulent strain of nativism and anti-Semitism, and revealed their desire to return to a rural utopia that they associated with the early nineteenth century. Charles Postel characterizes the Populists as forward-thinking reformers who hoped to use the government to manage an increasingly modern, technologically sophisticated, and globally connected society for the benefit of ordinary citizens.

According to T.H. Watkins, Chief Forester Gifford Pinchot was a practical conservationist whose agency managed to balance the preservation of the environment with the "wise use of earth and its resources for the lasting good of men." According to Ted Steinberg, the conservationists often had negative effects on the ecosystem of America's forests, plants, and animals in their effort to bend nature to conform to the desire of mankind.

Professor John M. Cooper argues that the stroke that partially paralyzed Woodrow Wilson during his speaking tour in 1919 hampered the then president's ability to compromise with the Republicans over the terms of America's membership in the League of Nations if the Senate ratified the Treaty of Versailles. The late William G. Carleton believed that Woodrow Wilson understood better than any of his contemporaries the role that the United States would play in world affairs.

Gilman M. Ostrander portrays the 1920s as the beginning of an urbanization of American morals, which included dramatic changes in women's fashion and behavior and the emergence of a more affluent society and leisure class focused on mass consumer goods that encouraged Americans to live beyond their means, thereby undermining the traditional virtue of thriftiness. David A. Shannon asserts that the social and cultural changes described by many as revolutionary were actually superficial elements of which significance to the 1920s has been exaggerated; the real catalysts for change were the processes that expanded the American economy by ushering in prosperity through the creation of a mass consumer culture.

Professor Burton W. Folsom, Jr., argues the New Deal prolonged the Great Depression because its anti-free-market program of high taxes and special-interest spending to certain banks, railroads, farmers, and veterans created an antibusiness environment of regime uncertainty. Professor of history Roger Biles contends that, in spite of its minimal reforms and nonrevolutionary programs, the New Deal created a limited welfare state that implemented economic stabilizers to avert another depression.

Richard M. Dalfiume argues that the period from 1939 to 1945 marked a turning point in American race relations by focusing the attention of African Americans on their unequal status in American society and stimulating a mass militancy whose goals, tactics, and strategies sowed the seeds for the modern civil rights movement. Harvard Sitkoff challenges the "watershed" interpretation by pointing out that, after Pearl Harbor, militant African American protest against racial discrimination was limited by the constraints imposed on the nation at war, the dwindling resources for sustained confrontation, and the genuinely patriotic response by black Americans to dangers faced by the nation.

Professor of American history Robert James Maddox contends that the atomic bomb became the catalyst that forced the hard-liners in the

Japanese army to accept the emperor's plea to surrender, thus avoiding a costly, bloody invasion of the Japanese mainland. Professor of American history Tsuyoshi Hasegawa argues that the Soviet entrance into the war played a greater role in causing Japan to surrender than did the dropping of the atomic bombs.

American society and quickly discovered that, without a clear program, viable organizations, or a significant constituency, they were essentially powerless against the prevailing social order.

Former President Richard Nixon believes that the South Vietnamese government would not have lost the war to North Vietnam in 1975 if Congress had not cut off aid. According to Professor Larry Berman, President Nixon knew that the Paris Peace Accords of January 1973 were flawed, but he intended to bomb North Vietnamese troops to prevent the collapse of South Vietnam until he left office.

Writer and lecturer F. Carolyn Graglia argues that women should stay at home and practice the values of "true motherhood" because contemporary feminists have discredited marriage, devalued traditional homemaking, and encouraged sexual promiscuity. According to Professor Sara M. Evans, despite class, racial, religious, ethnic, and regional differences, women in the United States experienced major transformations in their private and public lives in the twentieth century.

According to Professor J. David Woodard, supply-side economics unleashed a wave of entrepreneurial and technological innovation that transformed the economy and restored America's confidence in the Golden Age from 1983 to 1992. Political Journalist Thomas Byrne Edsall argues that the Reagan Revolution brought about a policy realignment that reversed the New Deal and redistributed political power and economic wealth to the top 20 percent of Americans.

Correlation Guide

The *Taking Sides* series presents current issues in a debate-style format designed to stimulate student interest and develop critical thinking skills. Each issue is thoughtfully framed with an issue summary, an issue introduction, and a section on exploring the issue. The pro and con essays—selected for their liveliness and substance—represent the arguments of leading scholars and commentators in their fields.

Taking Sides: Clashing Views in United States History, Volume 2: Reconstruction to the Present, 15/e is an easy-to-use reader that presents issues on important topics such as *nineteenth-century immigrants, the conservation movement, the Cuban missile crisis, the Vietnam War,* and *women's liberation.* For more information on *Taking Sides* and other *McGraw-Hill Contemporary Learning Series* titles, visit www.mhhe.com/cls.

This convenient guide matches the issues in **Taking Sides: United States History, Volume 2, 15/e** with the corresponding chapters in two of our best-selling McGraw-Hill History textbooks by Brinkley and Davidson et al.

Taking Sides: United States History, Volume 2, 15/e	The Unfinished Nation: A Concise History of the American People, Volume 2, 7/e by Brinkley	Experience History, Volume 2: Since 1865, 7/e by Davidson et al.
Issue 1: Did Reconstruction Fail as a Result of Racism?	**Chapter 15:** Reconstruction and the New South	**Chapter 17:** Reconstructing the Union, 1865–1877
Issue 2: Did a "New South" Emerge Following Reconstruction?	**Chapter 15:** Reconstruction and the New South	**Chapter 17:** Reconstructing the Union, 1865–1877 **Chapter 18:** The New South & the Trans-Mississippi West, 1870–1914
Issue 3: Were the Nineteenth-Century Entrepreneurs "Robber Barons"?	**Chapter 17:** Industrial Supremacy **Chapter 18:** The Age of the City	**Chapter 19:** The New Industrial Order, 1870–1914 **Chapter 20:** The Rise of an Urban Order, 1870–1914
Issue 4: Were American Workers in the Gilded Age Conservative Capitalists?	**Chapter 17:** Industrial Supremacy	**Chapter 19:** The New Industrial Order, 1870–1914 **Chapter 20:** The Rise of an Urban Order, 1870–1914
Issue 5: Were Late Nineteenth-Century Immigrants "Uprooted"?	**Chapter 17:** Industrial Supremacy	**Chapter 19:** The New Industrial Order, 1870–1914 **Chapter 20:** The Rise of an Urban Order, 1870–1914 **Chapter 22:** The Progressive Era, 1890–1920
Issue 6: Were the Populists Irrational Reactionaries?	**Chapter 19:** From Crisis to Empire	**Chapter 21:** The Political System under Strain at Home and Abroad, 1877–1900
Issue 7: Did the Conservation Movement of the Early Twentieth Century Successfully Preserve the American Environment?	**Chapter 20:** The Progressives	**Chapter 19:** The New Industrial Order, 1870–1914 **Chapter 20:** The Rise of an Urban Order, 1870–1914 **Chapter 24:** The New Era, 1920–1929

Taking Sides: United States History, Volume 2, 15/e	The Unfinished Nation: A Concise History of the American People, Volume 2, 7/e by Brinkley	Experience History, Volume 2: Since 1865, 7/e by Davidson et al.
Issue 8: Was Woodrow Wilson Responsible for the Failure of the United States to Join the League of Nations?	**Chapter 21:** America and the Great War	**Chapter 22:** The Progressive Era, 1890–1920
Issue 9: Were the 1920s an Era of Social and Cultural Rebellion?	**Chapter 22:** The New Era **Chapter 23:** The Great Depression	**Chapter 22:** The Progressive Era, 1890–1920 **Chapter 23:** The United States and the Collapse of the Old World Order, 1901–1920 **Chapter 24:** The New Era, 1920–1929 **Chapter 25:** The Great Depression and the New Deal, 1929–1939
Issue 10: Did the New Deal Prolong the Great Depression?	**Chapter 23:** The Great Depression **Chapter 24:** The New Deal **Chapter 26:** America in a World at War	**Chapter 24:** The New Era, 1920–1929
Issue 11: Was the World War II Era a Watershed for the Civil Rights Movement?	**Chapter 28:** The Affluent Society	**Chapter 25:** The Great Depression and the New Deal, 1929–1939 **Chapter 26:** America's Rise to Globalism, 1927–1945 **Chapter 28:** The Suburban Era, 1945–1963 **Chapter 29:** Civil Rights & Uncivil Liberties, 1947–1969
Issue 12: Was It Necessary to Drop the Atomic Bomb to End World War II?	**Chapter 25:** The Global Crisis, 1921–1941 **Chapter 26:** America in a World at War	**Chapter 26:** America's Rise to Globalism, 1927–1945
Issue 13: Was President Truman Responsible for the Cold War?	**Chapter 26:** America in a World at War **Chapter 27:** The Cold War	**Chapter 27:** Cold War America, 1945–1954
Issue 14: Did President John F. Kennedy Cause the Cuban Missile Crisis?	**Chapter 28:** The Affluent Society **Chapter 29:** Civil Rights, Vietnam, and the Ordeal of Liberalism	**Chapter 28:** The Suburban Era, 1945–1963
Issue 15: Did the Activism of the 1960s Produce a Better Nation?	**Chapter 29:** Civil Rights, Vietnam, and the Ordeal of Liberalism **Chapter 30:** The Crisis of Authority	**Chapter 28:** The Suburban Era, 1945–1963 **Chapter 29:** Civil Rights & Uncivil Liberties, 1947–1969 **Chapter 30:** The Vietnam Era 1963–1975
Issue 16: Did President Nixon Negotiate a "Peace with Honor" in Vietnam in 1973?	**Chapter 29:** Civil Rights, Vietnam, and the Ordeal of Liberalism **Chapter 30:** The Crisis of Authority	**Chapter 30:** The Vietnam Era 1963–1975
Issue 17: Has the Women's Movement of the 1970s Failed to Liberate American Women?	**Chapter 30:** The Crisis of Authority	**Chapter 30:** The Vietnam Era 1963–1975 **Chapter 31:** The Conservative Challenge, 1976–1992
Issue 18: Were the 1980s a Decade of Affluence for the Middle Class?	**Chapter 31:** From "The Age of Limits" to the Age of Reagan **Chapter 32:** The Age of Globalization	**Chapter 31:** The Conservative Challenge, 1976–1992 **Chapter 32:** Nation of Nations in a Global Community, 1989–Present

Topic Guide

This topic guide suggests how the selections in this book relate to the subjects covered in your course. You may want to use the topics listed on these pages to search the web more easily. On the following pages a number of websites have been gathered specifically for this book. They are arranged to reflect the issues of this *Taking Sides* reader. You can link to these sites by going to www.mhhe.com/cls.

All issues and their articles that relate to each topic are listed below the bold-faced term.

African Americans

1. Did Reconstruction Fail as a Result of Racism?
11. Was the World War II Era a Watershed for the Civil Rights Movement?

Biography

3. Were the Nineteenth-Century Entrepreneurs "Robber Barons"?
8. Was Woodrow Wilson Responsible for the Failure of the United States to Join the League of Nations?
14. Did President John F. Kennedy Cause the Cuban Missile Crisis?
16. Did President Nixon Negotiate a "Peace with Honor" in Vietnam in 1973?

Economic

1. Did Reconstruction Fail as a Result of Racism?
2. Did a "New South" Emerge following Reconstruction?
3. Were the Nineteenth-Century Entrepreneurs "Robber Barons"?
4. Were American Workers in the Gilded Age Conservative Capitalists?
5. Were Late Nineteenth-Century Immigrants "Uprooted"?
10. Did the New Deal Prolong the Great Depression?
18. Were the 1980s a Decade of Affluence for the Middle Class?

Global

5. Were Late Nineteenth-Century Immigrants "Uprooted"?
8. Was Woodrow Wilson Responsible for the Failure of the United States to Join the League of Nations?

12. Was It Necessary to Drop the Atomic Bomb to End World War II?

Political

1. Did Reconstruction Fail as a Result of Racism?
2. Did a "New South" Emerge following Reconstruction?
6. Were the Populists Irrational Reactionaries?
10. Did the New Deal Prolong the Great Depression?
15. Did the Activism of the 1960s Produce a Better Nation?
18. Were the 1980s a Decade of Affluence for the Middle Class?

Religion

5. Were Late Nineteenth-Century Immigrants "Uprooted"?

Social

4. Were American Workers in the Gilded Age Conservative Capitalists?
5. Were Late Nineteenth-Century Immigrants "Uprooted"?
6. Were the Populists Irrational Reactionaries?
7. Did the Conservation Movement of the Early Twentieth Century Successfully Preserve the American Environment?
9. Were the 1920s and Era of Social and Cultural Rebellion?
11. Was the World War II Era a Watershed for the Civil Rights Movement?
15. Did the Activism of the 1960s Produce a Better Nation?
17. Has the Women's Movement of the 1970s Failed to Liberate American Women?

War and Diplomacy

8. Was Woodrow Wilson Responsible for the Failure of the United States to Join the League of Nations?
12. Was It Necessary to Drop the Atomic Bomb to End World War II?
13. Was President Truman Responsible for the Cold War?
14. Did President John F. Kennedy Cause the Cuban Missile Crisis?

16. Did President Nixon Negotiate a "Peace with Honor" in Vietnam in 1973?

Women

9. Were the 1920s an Era of Social and Cultural Rebellion?
17. Has the Women's Movement of the 1970s Failed to Liberate American Women?

Introduction

The Study of History

In a pluralistic society such as ours, the study of history is bound to be a complex process. How an event is interpreted depends not only on the existing evidence but also on the perspective of the interpreter. Consequently, understanding history presupposes the evaluation of information, a task that often leads to conflicting conclusions. An understanding of history, then, requires the acceptance of the idea of historical relativism. Relativism means the redefinition of our past is always possible and desirable. History shifts, changes, and grows with new and different evidence and interpretations. As is the case with the law and even with medicine, beliefs that were unquestioned 100 or 200 years ago have been discredited or discarded since.

Relativism, then, encourages revisionism. There is a maxim that "The past must remain useful to the present." Historian Carl Becker argued that every generation should examine history for itself, thus ensuring constant scrutiny of our collective experience through new perspectives. History, consequently, does not remain static, in part because historians cannot avoid being influenced by the times in which they live. Almost all historians commit themselves to revising the views of other historians by either disagreeing with earlier interpretations or creating new frameworks that pose different questions.

Schools of Thought

Three predominant schools of thought have emerged in American history since the first graduate seminars in history were given at The Johns Hopkins University in Baltimore, Maryland, in the 1870s. The *progressive* school dominated the professional field in the first half of the twentieth century. Influenced by the reform currents of populism, progressivism, and the New Deal, these historians explored the social and economic forces that energized America. The progressive scholars tended to view the past in terms of conflicts between groups, and they sympathized with the underdog.

The post–World War II period witnessed the emergence of a new group of historians who viewed the conflict thesis as overly simplistic. Writing against the backdrop of the Cold War, these *neoconservative* and *consensus*, historians argued that Americans possess a shared set of values and that the areas of agreement within our nation's basic democratic and capitalistic framework are more important than the areas of disagreement.

In the 1960s, however, the civil rights movement, women's liberation, and the student rebellion (with its condemnation of the war in Vietnam) fragmented the consensus of values upon which historians of the 1950s had centered their interpretations. This turmoil set the stage for the emergence of another group of scholars. *New Left* historians began to reinterpret the past once again. They emphasized the significance of conflict in American history, and they resurrected interest in those groups ignored by the consensus school. New Left history is still being written.

The most recent generation of scholars, however, focuses upon social history. Their primary concern is to discover what the lives of "ordinary Americans" were really like. These new social historians employ previously overlooked court and church documents, house deeds and tax records, letters and diaries, photographs, and census data to reconstruct the everyday lives of average Americans. Some employ new methodologies, such as quantification (enhanced by advanced computer technology) and oral history, whereas others borrow from the disciplines of political science, economics, sociology, anthropology, and psychology for their historical investigations.

The proliferation of historical approaches, which are reflected in the issues debated in this book, has had mixed results. On the one hand, historians have become so specialized in their respective time periods and methodological styles that it is difficult to synthesize the recent scholarship into a comprehensive text for the general reader. On the other hand, historians now know more about new questions or ones that previously were considered to be germane only to scholars in other social sciences. Although there is little agreement about the answers to these questions, the methods employed and the issues explored make the "new history" a very exciting field to study.

The topics that follow represent a variety of perspectives and approaches. Each of these controversial issues can be studied for its individual importance to American history. Taken as a group, they interact with one another to illustrate larger historical themes. When grouped thematically, the issues reveal continuing motifs in the development of American history.

Entrepreneurs, Laborers, Immigrants, African Americans, and Farm Workers

Issue 3 explores the dynamics of the modern economy through investigations of the nineteenth-century entrepreneurs. Were these industrial leaders "robber barons," as portrayed by contemporary critics and many history texts? Or were they industrial statesmen and organizational geniuses? The late radical historian Howard Zinn views the new industrialists as robber barons who adopted business practices that encouraged monopolies and use the power of government to control the masses from rebellion. But John Steele Gordon, a business historian, argues that men such as Rockefeller and Carnegie developed, through the oil and steel industries, consumer products that improved the lifestyle of average Americans.

In the wake of industrialization during the late 1800s, the rapid pace of change created working conditions for the labor class. How did laborers react to these new changes? Did they lose their autonomy in large corporations? Did they accept or reject the wage system? Were they pawns of the economic cycles of boom and bust, to be hired and fired at will? Did they look for an alternative to capitalism by engaging in strikes, establishing labor unions, or creating a socialist movement? In issue 4, Carl N. Degler maintains that American workers accepted capitalism and the changes that it brought forth. Degler argues that workers wanted to improve their lifestyle with better workplace conditions, shorter hours, better pay, and more benefits. Herbert G. Gutman sees the workers responding to the changing capitalist system in a different manner than Degler does. In the years 1843–1893, says Gutman, American factory workers attempted to humanize the system by maintaining their traditional artisan values. By the beginning of the twentieth century, however, the organizational innovations of John D. Rockefeller and the assembly-line techniques pioneered by Henry Ford had revolutionized American capitalism.

The vast majority of these factory workers came from the farms and cities of Europe. Massive immigration to the United States in the late nineteenth and early twentieth centuries introduced widespread changes in American society. Moreover, the presence of increasing numbers of immigrants from Southern or Eastern Europe, many of them Catholics and Jews, seemed to threaten native citizens, most of whom were Protestant and of Northern or Western European ancestry. Asian immigrants, mainly from China or Japan, added to nativist fears. In issue 5, Oscar Handlin argues that the immigrants were alienated from their Old World cultures as they adjusted to an unfamiliar and often hostile environment. But Professor Mark Wyman argues that immigrants never gave up the fight for their personal autonomy. He points out that many immigrants to the United States believed their stay in America would be temporary, a fact that limited their efforts as assimilation and reinforced ties to their original homelands to which many of them returned once they had acquired some wealth.

One section of the country that was different from the rest was the American South. Following the end of the Civil War and Reconstruction, did a "New South" emerge or was there continuity with the "Old South." In issue 2, Professor Edward L. Ayers argues that many southerners labored as industrial workers in the textile, tobacco, furniture, lumber, and mining industries. Moreover, although most southerners remained farmers, their lives too were impacted by industrial forces in the region. James Tice More, however, sees more continuity than change in the post-Reconstruction South. He insists that the Democratic political leaders who replaced the Radical Republicans in the South did not abandon their antebellum rural traditions in favor of business and commerce. Instead, they promoted policies that supported the interests of farmers far more than those benefiting a business-oriented elite.

With the end of slavery, one of the most controversial questions confronting those responsible for reconstructing the nation following the Civil War involved the future of African Americans. Perhaps no other period of American history has been subjected to more myths than has this postwar era. Even though most scholars today recognize that Reconstruction did not achieve its most enlightened economic and social goals, they differ in their explanations about the source of this failure. In issue 1, LeeAnna Keith relates the details of the Colfax massacre, an assault carried out by white Louisianans to eliminate Radical Republican rule in the state, which had empowered local African Americans. The military attack on the Grant Parish courthouse in Colfax on Easter Sunday 1873,

Keith says, was directed toward removing the all-black militia unit guarding the courthouse and reinstituting white supremacy in the Pelican State. Heather Cox Richardson, on the other hand, argues that the failure of Radical Reconstruction was primarily a consequence of a national commitment to a free-labor ideology that opposed an expanding central government that legislated rights to African Americans that other citizens had acquired through hard work.

Most African Americans were denied full political and economic rights until the 1960s. The starting point of the civil rights movement is traditionally dated with the *Brown* case of 1954, which mandated desegregated schools or the Montgomery boycott of the following year that challenged seating arrangements on local bus lines that disproportionately served black riders. Issue 11 challenges this traditional chronology by asking whether or not World War II served as the true "watershed" for the efforts to roll back Jim Crow laws that most associate with the 1950s and 1960s. In his seminal article written in 1968, Richard M. Dalfiume points out the hypocrisy and paradox of fighting for democracy abroad while denying full citizenship rights to African Americans at home. Prior to Pearl Harbor, African American leaders, such as labor leader A. Philip Randolph, threatened to march on the nation's capital unless the Roosevelt administration enforced equal employment opportunities in defense industries and took steps to desegregate American military forces. Randolph's approach clearly represented a commitment to black militancy, Dalfiume believes, that is more often associated with the leadership of Martin Luther King, Jr. Historian Harvard Sitkoff questions the degree to which African Americans practiced militant protest during the war. Recognizing evidence of mass protests by blacks during the 1930s, Sitkoff notes that once the United States entered the war in late 1941, most African American citizens and their leaders supported a united war effort to defeat the nation's enemies.

American Diplomacy in the Twentieth Century

As the United States developed a preeminent position in international affairs, the nation's politicians were forced to consider the proper relationship between their country and the rest of the world. To what extent, many asked, should the United States seek to expand its political, economic, and moral influence around the globe? Five issues in this volume illustrate the problems faced by the United States in grappling with the rest of the world.

The United States became a major participant in two world wars in the twentieth century. At the end of the World War I, President Woodrow Wilson attempted to enlarge the United States' role in world affairs by brokering the peace settlement and establishing the League of Nations to prevent the outbreak of another war. Issue 8 deals with the factors contributing to Wilson's failure to oversee U.S. membership in the League. John Milton Cooper, Wilson's leading contemporary biographer, is generally sympathetic to Wilson but believes that the debilitating stroke the President suffered while campaigning in support of the Treaty of Versailles prevented him from being able to negotiate effectively with his Republican opponents in the Senate. Professor William Carleton presents a passionate defense of Wilson and blames Senator Henry

Cabot Lodge and other Senate Republicans for sabotaging Wilson with their "self-centered" reservations, which they knew would doom the President's attempt to get the United States to join the League.

World War II brought the end of Nazi Germany and Imperial Japan. It was the war that was really supposed to end all wars. But this conflict produced two major unintended consequences. In a secret enclave in the desert in Los Alamos, New Mexico, thousands of scientists participating in the Manhattan Project sought to develop an atomic bomb. The first successful test of this weapon of mass destruction occurred two months after the war in Europe ended, but two bombs, named "Fat Man" and "Little Boy," were prepared for deployment against the Japanese. Were there alternatives to dropping atomic bombs on Japan to end the war in the Pacific? Were alternatives rejected to keep the Soviet Union out of the Asian phase of the war or to threaten the Russians and make them "more manageable" in postwar peace negotiations regarding political control in Eastern Europe? In the YES selection in issue 12, Robert James Maddox rejects these contentions and argues that military considerations were foremost in President Harry Truman's mind as he sought to shorten the war, to save American and Japanese lives, and to convince Japan's military hardliners to surrender because there were no acceptable alternatives. Professor Tsuyoshi Hasegawa plays down the role of the A-bombs in bringing about Japan's surrender. Based on a careful examination of Japanese, Russian, and American archives, he concludes that it was the Russian declaration of war, not the bombing at Hiroshima and Nagasaki, which forced the hand of the Japanese government who hoped to prevent the Soviet Union from occupying northern Japan after the war ended.

A second unintended consequence was the reemergence of the rivalry between the United States and the Soviet Union that we know as the Cold War. Was this conflict inevitable? Was one nation more responsible than the other for starting the Cold War? In issue 13, Professor Arnold A. Offner argues that President Truman was a parochial nationalist whose limited vision of foreign affairs precluded negotiations with the Russians over issues that distanced the two superpowers from one another. John Gaddis, the most prominent American scholar on this topic, insists that a half-century of research and writing has convinced him that Joseph Stalin was primarily responsible for the Cold War.

The nuclear arms' race produced the Cold War's greatest crisis in 1962 when Soviet Premier Nikita Khrushchev constructed and armed offensive nuclear weapon sites on the island of Cuba, less than 100 miles from the shores of Miami, Florida. How did President John F. Kennedy fare in his handling of the Cuban missile crisis? Historian Thomas Paterson argues in issue 14 that Kennedy mishandled the matter by adopting the tactic of military ultimatums recommended by his hastily organized decision-making committee of 14 experts instead of seeking less volatile diplomatic solutions. Colby University historian Robert Weisbrot, however, argues that sources uncovered over the past 20 years depict Kennedy as an anti-Communist Cold Warrior who nevertheless acted in a firm, rational, yet conciliatory, manner toward his opposing head of state in resolving the missile crisis.

No discussion of American foreign policy is complete without some consideration of the Vietnam War. Was America's escalation inevitable in 1965?

Did the U.S. government accomplish a "peace with honor" when it withdrew American troops from Vietnam in 1973 in exchange for the return of American POWs? In issue 16, former President Richard Nixon believes that the South Vietnamese government would not have lost the civil war in 1975, had not the United States Congress cut off aid. Professor Larry Berman argues that Nixon knew the Paris Peace Accords of 1973 were flawed, but he had intended to prevent the collapse of South Vietnam by bombing North Vietnamese troops. This plan was short-circuited, however, when Nixon was forced out of office in the wake of the Watergate scandal.

Political and Economic Changes

Populism, progressivism, the New Deal, and the decade of the 1960s represent major periods of reform in the United States over the past century. Issue 6 discusses the first major political and economic reform movement of the late nineteenth century. According to Richard Hofstadter, the Populists were not democratic reformers but rather reactionaries who created a conspiracy theory around the issues of industrialism and the "money question," which activated a virulent strain of nativism and anti-Semitism and revealed their desire to return to a rural utopia that they associated with the early nineteenth century. Charles Postel counters this view by characterizing the Populists as forward-thinking reformers who hoped to use the U.S. federal government to manage an increasingly modern, technologically sophisticated, and globally connected society for the benefit of ordinary citizens.

Historians have traditionally characterized the years from 1897 to 1917 as the Progressive Era. Whether the reformers of this period were successful in making significant alterations to the modern, urban-industrial society in their midst has been a subject of considerable debate through the years. Issue 7 focuses on a particular aspect of Progressive reform—the conservation movement. Did this movement successfully preserve the American environment? According to T.H. Watkins, Chief Forester Gifford Pinchot was a practical conservationist whose agency managed to balance the preservation of the environment with the "wise use of earth and its resources for the lasting good of men." Ted Steinberg disagrees with this conventional wisdom. He believes that the conservation movement often had negative effects on the ecosystem of the nation's forests, plants, and animals in its effort to bend nature to conform to the desire of human beings.

The Great Depression of the 1930s remains one of the most traumatic events in the U.S. history. The characteristics of that decade are deeply etched in American folk memory, but the remedies that were applied to those social and economic ills—known collectively as the New Deal—are not easy to evaluate. In Issue 10, Roger Biles contends that the economic stabilizers created by the New Deal programs prevented the recurrence of the Great Depression. Burton J. Folsom, Jr., on the other hand, criticizes the New Deal from a twenty-first century conservative perspective. In his view, because New Deal agencies were anti-business, they overregulated the economy and did not allow the free enterprise system to work out the depression that FDR's programs prolonged.

The American public experienced a shock in the late 1970s due to the normal expectations of constant growth. Rising oil prices, foreign economic competition, and double-digit interest and inflation rates created an economic recession. Issue 18 debates whether the 1980s was a decade of affluence or decline for middle-class Americans. According to Professor J. David Woodard, supply-side economics unleashed a wave of entrepreneurial and technological innovation that transformed the economy and restored America's confidence in the Golden Age from 1983 to 1992. Political Journalist Thomas Byrne Edsall argues that the Reagan revolution brought about a policy realignment that reversed the New Deal and redistributed political power and economic wealth to the tow 20 of percent of Americans.

Social and Cultural Rebellions

Significant political and economic changes in American history often have coincided with social and cultural transformations. Three issues in this volume treat some of these revolts in the twentieth century. Issue 9 asks, "Were the 1920s an era of social and cultural rebellion?" Gilman M. Ostrander's selection offers a resounding affirmative response. "The decade of the 1920s," he writes, "remains the watershed in the history of American morals." The fact that Ostrander made this observation at the end of the 1960s reinforces the extent to which he believes change was in the air in the "Roaring Twenties." In particular, Ostrander reaches his conclusions by focusing on the changing status and behavior of women in the 1920s and the role that mass-produced automobiles played in the challenge to American Victorian morality. David A. Shannon, however, asserts that the social and cultural changes described by many as revolutionary were actually superficial elements whose significance to the 1920s has been exaggerated; the real catalysts were the monumental processes that expanded the American economy by ushering in prosperity through the creation of a mass consumer culture with purchases of vacuum cleaners, electrical appliances, as well as automobiles, often financed through the installment plan.

In many ways the 1960s resembled the 1920s. Both decades were relatively prosperous; the music and the movies were more sexually explicit, as were dances such as the Charleston and the Twist. Both periods were characterized by a more influential youth culture, but political radicalism was far more prevalent in the sixties. Issue 15 asks whether the activism of the 1960s had positive consequences for the nation. Historian Terry Anderson believes "the tumultuous era cracked the cold war culture and the nation experienced a 'sea change'—a significant transformation in politics, society, culture and foreign policy." The civil rights movement served as a model for liberation movements that were designed to improve the status not only of African Americans but also of Latinos, Native Americans, and women. The biggest challenge to Cold War assumptions was the antiwar movement protesting U.S. involvement in Vietnam. The "sea change" interpretation has not gone unchallenged. Peter Clecak sees merit in the early New Left but argues that the later leftist coalitions fell apart as a result of the Black Power movement, the antiwar and counterculture movements, and the Women's Liberation Movement, all of which fragmented the Left and led to senseless nihilistic violence by remnants of the Students for a Democratic Society (SDS) in the late 1960s and early 1970s.

A direct lineage of the civil rights movement was the Women's Liberation Movement of the 1970s. Did it help or harm women? In issue 17, writer and lecturer F. Carolyn Graglia argues that women should stay at home and practice values of "true motherhood" because contemporary feminists have discredited marriage, devalued traditional homemaking, and encouraged sexual promiscuity. Feminist and activist scholar Sara M. Evans takes a much more positive view of the women's movement for suffrage and liberation over the past century. Despite their class, racial, religious, ethnic, and regional differences, Evans argues, women in the twentieth-century United States experienced major transformations in their private and public lives.

Conclusion

The process of historical study should rely more on thinking than on memorizing data. Once the basics of who, what, when, and where are determined, historical thinking shifts to a higher gear. Explanation, analysis, evaluation, comparison, and contrast take command. These skills not only increase our knowledge of the past, but also provide general tools for the comprehension of all the topics about which human beings think.

The diversity of a pluralistic society, however, creates some obstacles to comprehending the past. The spectrum of differing opinions on any particular subject eliminates the possibility of quick and easy answers. In the final analysis, conclusions often are built through a synthesis of several different interpretations, but even then they may be partial and tentative.

The study of history in a pluralistic society allows each citizen the opportunity to reach independent conclusions about the past. Since most, if not all, historical issues affect the present and future, understanding the past becomes necessary if society is to progress. Many of today's problems have a direct connection with the past. Additionally, other contemporary issues may lack obvious direct antecedents, but historical investigation can provide illuminating analogies. At first, it may appear confusing to read and to think about opposing historical views, but the survival of our democratic society depends on such critical thinking by acute and discerning minds.

Larry Madaras
Emeritus, Howard Community College

James M. SoRelle
Baylor University

Internet References . . .

Journal Sites

Important journal articles and book reviews that reflect the most recent scholarship on all the issues can be found on the following site:

www.h-net.org/

Freedmen's Bureau Online

This website contains more than 100 transcriptions of reports on murders, riots, and "outrages" (any criminal offense) that occurred in the former Confederate states from 1865 to 1868.

www.freedmensbureau.com/

John D. Rockefeller and the Standard Oil Company

This site, created by Swiss entrepreneur Francois Micheloud, provides a highly detailed history of the American oil industry, with John D. Rockefeller as a main focus.

www.micheloud.com/FXM/SO/rock.htm

World Wide Web Virtual Library

This site focuses on labor and business history.

www.socialhistory.org

International Channel

Immigrants helped to create modern America. Visit this interesting site to experience "the memories, sounds, even tastes of Ellis Island."

www.i-channel.com/

American Family Immigration History Center

Records on the more than 25 million passengers and crew members who passed through Ellis Island between 1892 and 1924 are available here.

www .ellisisland.org

(Gene) Autry National Center

Four thousand seven hundred Western Heritage Way, Los Angeles, CA 90027; phone (323) 667 2000. This site contains information about one of the most important museums and collections of western and Indian history.

www.autrynationalcenter.org

1896: The Presidential Campaign

The election of 1896 was one of the most contentious in the U.S. history. When Republican William McKinley defeated William Jennings Bryan on November 3, there were no fewer than six candidates on the ballot, and the country was in the throes of an economic depression. This website provides close to 100 political cartoons surrounding the elections campaigns.

http://projects.vassar.edu/1896/1896home.html

The Gilded Age

*E*conomic expansion and the seemingly unlimited resources available in the postbellum United States offered great opportunities and created new political, social, and economic challenges. After an initial burst of freedom, African Americans were disfranchised and segregated from mainstream America and limited in their opportunities for full citizenship. As the United States became more heavily industrialized in the years following the Civil War, the need for cheap labor to run the machinery of the Industrial Revolution created an atmosphere for potential exploitation, which was intensified by the concentration of wealth in the hands of a few entrepreneurs. Even the defeated South experienced the impact of industrialization, but questions remain as to how much the South remained tied to the political, economic, and social traditions of the Old South. In regions where industry thrived, the labor movement took root, with some elements calling for an overthrow of the capitalist system, whereas others sought to establish political power within the existing system. The formation of labor unions demanding rights of workers produced industrial warfare as management sought the support of the U.S. federal government to counter the efforts of strikers. Political freedom and economic opportunity provided incentives for immigration to the United States, but strains began to develop between immigrant and native workers. Some farmers responded to the industrial transformations in the nation by seeking collective change through the auspices of the Granger, Alliance, and Populist movements, the latter of which called upon the U.S. federal government to support reforms that would benefit the masses of American citizens, not just the wealthy few.

- Did Reconstruction Fail as a Result of Racism?
- Did a "New South" Emerge Following Reconstruction?
- Were the Nineteenth-Century Entrepreneurs "Robber Barons"?
- Were American Workers in the Gilded Age Conservative Capitalists?
- Were Late Nineteenth-Century Immigrants "Uprooted"?
- Were the Populists Irrational Reactionaries?

ISSUE 1

Did Reconstruction Fail as a Result of Racism?

YES: LeeAnna Keith, from *The Colfax Massacre: The Untold Story of Black Power, White Terror, and the Death of Reconstruction* (Oxford University Press, 2008)

NO: Heather Cox Richardson, from *The Death of Reconstruction: Race, Labor, and Politics in the Post-Civil War North, 1865–1901* (Harvard University Press, 2001)

Learning Outcomes

After reading this issue, you should be able to:

- Explain several factors that prevented the Reconstruction process from achieving greater success.
- Analyze the political, economic, and social implications of the era of Reconstruction.
- Evaluate the role played by race in the reaction to the Reconstruction governments in the South following the Civil War.
- Define free labor ideology and explain its influence on Reconstruction.

ISSUE SUMMARY

YES: LeeAnna Keith characterizes the assault on the Grant Parish courthouse in Colfax, Louisiana, on Easter Sunday in 1873 as a product of white racism and unwillingness by local whites to tolerate African American political power during the era of Reconstruction.

NO: Heather Cox Richardson argues that the failure of Radical Reconstruction was primarily a consequence of a national commitment to a free labor ideology, which opposed an expanding central government that legislated rights to African Americans that other citizens had acquired through hard work.

Given the complex issues of the post–Civil War years, it is not surprising that the era of Reconstruction (1865–1877) is enveloped in controversy. For the better part of the century following the war, historians typically characterized Reconstruction as a total failure that had proved detrimental to all Americans— northerners and southerners, whites and blacks. According to this traditional interpretation, a vengeful Congress, dominated by radical Republicans, imposed military rule upon the southern states; "carpetbaggers" from the North, along with traitorous white "scalawags," and their black accomplices in the South established coalition governments, which rewrote state constitutions, raised taxes, looted state treasuries, and disenfranchised former Confederates while extending the ballot to the freedmen. This era finally ended in 1877 when courageous southern white Democrats successfully "redeemed" their region from "Negro rule" by toppling the Republican state governments.

This portrait of Reconstruction dominated the historical profession until the 1960s. One reason behind this point of view is that white historians (both northerners and southerners) who wrote about this period operated from two basic assumptions: (1) the South was capable of solving its own problems without U.S. federal government interference; and (2) the former slaves were intellectually inferior to whites and incapable of running governments (much less one in which some whites would be their subordinates). African American historians, for example, W. E. B. Du Bois, wrote several essays and books that challenged this negative portrayal of Reconstruction, but their works seldom were taken seriously in the academic world and rarely were read by the general public. Still, these black historians foreshadowed the acceptance of revisionist interpretations of Reconstruction, which coincided with the successes of the civil rights movement (or "Second Reconstruction") in the 1960s.

Without ignoring obvious problems and limitations connected with this period, revisionist historians identified a number of accomplishments of the Republican state governments in the South and their supporters in Washington, DC. For example, revisionists argued that the state constitutions that were written during Reconstruction were the most democratic documents that the South had seen up to that time. Also, although taxes increased in the southern states, the revenues generated by these levies financed the rebuilding and expansion of the South's railroad network, the creation of a number of social service institutions, and the establishment of a public school system that benefited African Americans as well as whites. At the federal level, Reconstruction achieved the ratification of the Fourteenth and Fifteenth Amendments, which extended significant privileges of citizenship (including the right to vote) to African Americans, both North and South. Revisionist historians also placed the charges of corruption leveled by traditionalists against the Republican regimes in the South in a more appropriate context by insisting that political corruption was a *national* malady. Although the leaders of the Republican state governments in the South engaged in a number of corrupt activities, they were no more guilty than several federal officeholders in the Grant administration, or the members of New York City's notorious Tweed Ring (a Democratic urban political machine), or even the southern white Democrats (the

Redeemers), who replaced the radical Republicans in positions of power in the former Confederate states. Finally, revisionist historians sharply attacked the notion that African Americans dominated the reconstructed governments of the South.

There can be little doubt that racism played some role in the failure of the Radical Republicans to realize their most ambitious goals for integrating African Americans into the mainstream of American society in the years following the Civil War. After all, white supremacy was a powerful doctrine. At the same time, we should recognize some of the more positive conclusions reached by that first generation of revisionist historians who built upon Du Bois' characterization of Reconstruction as a "splendid failure." For example, Kenneth Stampp's *The Era of Reconstruction, 1865–1877* (Alfred A. Knopf, 1965) ends with the following statement: "The Fourteenth and Fifteenth Amendments, which could have been adopted only under the conditions of radical reconstruction, make the blunders of that era, tragic though they were, dwindle into insignificance. For if it was worth a few years of civil war to save the Union, it was worth a few years of radical reconstruction to give the American Negro the ultimate promise of equal civil and political rights." Eric Foner, too, recognizes something of a silver lining in the nation's post–Civil War reconstruction process. In *Reconstruction: America's Unfinished Revolution, 1863–1877* (Harper & Row, 1988), Foner claims that Reconstruction, while perhaps not all that radical, offered African Americans at least a temporary vision of a free society. Similarly, in *Nothing But Freedom: Emancipation and Its Legacy* (Louisiana State University Press, 1984), Foner advances his interpretation by comparing the treatment of ex-slaves in the United States with that of newly emancipated slaves in Haiti and the British West Indies. Only in the United States, he contends, were the freedmen given voting and economic rights. Although these rights had been stripped away from the majority of black southerners by 1900, Reconstruction had, nevertheless, created a legacy of freedom that inspired succeeding generations of African Americans to reclaim what had been gained and lost.

On the other hand, C. Vann Woodward, in "Reconstruction: A Counterfactual Playback," an essay in his thought-provoking *The Future of the Past* (Oxford University Press, 1988), challenges Foner's conclusions by insisting that former slaves were as poorly treated in the United States as they were in other countries. He also maintains that the confiscation of former plantations and the redistribution of land to the former slaves would have failed in the same way that the Homestead Act of 1862 failed to generate equal distribution of government lands to poor white settlers.

Thomas Holt's *Black Over White: Negro Political Leadership in South Carolina During Reconstruction* (University of Illinois Press, 1977) is representative of state and local studies that employ modern social science methodology to yield new perspectives. Although critical of white Republican leaders, Holt (who is African American) also blames freeborn mulatto politicians for the failure of Reconstruction in South Carolina, whose background distanced them economically, socially, and culturally from the masses of freedmen. Consequently, he argues, these political leaders failed to develop a clear and unifying ideology to challenge white South Carolinians who wanted to restore white supremacy.

In the YES and NO selections, LeeAnna Keith and Heather Cox Richardson present thought-provoking analyses of the influence racism had in the failure of Reconstruction. In the YES selection, Keith describes the events surrounding the military assault by white Louisianans on the Grant Parish courthouse located in the town of Colfax. Rumors had circulated for some time that such an attack would take place, and African American militiamen, who had been empowered by the Republican leaders in Louisiana, were prepared to protect the building that had become the symbol to whites of "Negro rule" in their region. The resulting massacre (most of the casualties occurred as a result of wholesale executions after a surrender had occurred) of over 150 blacks by southerners seeking to uphold the doctrine of white supremacy represented the deadliest incident of racial violence in U.S. history and paved the way for the end of Radical Reconstruction in Louisiana.

Heather Cox Richardson offers a post-revisionist interpretation of the failure of Reconstruction and contends that the key barrier to postwar assistance for African Americans was the nation's commitment to a free labor ideology. Believing that social equality derived from economic success, most Americans opposed legislation, such as the Civil Rights Act of 1875, which appeared to provide special interest legislation solely for the benefit of the former slaves.

YES  LeeAnna Keith

Battle of the Colfax Courthouse

The republican faction in control of the courthouse was prepared for trouble, but Jesse McKinney was not. McKinney tried to stay out of trouble—a goal that required a black man to steer clear of politics in general and to keep away from the town of Colfax in particular, after the seizure of the courthouse initiated its militarization. In the two weeks before his death, McKinney had observed the passage of armed men of both races from his home near the ferry crossing on Bayou Darrow. He stuck close to his wife and six young children. The family was watching on April 5, 1873 when the white men shot him in the head. They heard him scream—"like a pig," as a black neighbor remembered it—and they heard some of the white men asking if McKinney was killed. "Yes," came the answer, "he is dead as hell."

Republican commentators in Louisiana would later deplore the killing of a man at work, as they said, "peaceably building a fence around his property." In fact, in the charged environment of post—Civil War Louisiana, where black ownership seemed to threaten the social and economic order, the act of building a fence approximated a kind of defiance. McKinney had money. Like his father and brother, he acknowledged almost $500 in personal property in the 1870 census. Late in the season, his corn crib and pantries were fully stocked.

The white men who killed him were far from home. They needed food for their horses and water and provisions for their growing ranks. After they shot McKinney, they dismounted and "danced like mad" for two hours, then settled in to feed their horses out of his supply.

Jesse McKinney did not die instantly, but lingered for six or eight hours. Assisted by another woman, Eliza Smith, his wife Laurinda loaded him and the children into a wagon while the whites in the yard mocked them, hooting lecherously and calling them "bad names." Laurinda McKinney drove to her stepfather's house and laid her husband's body on the floor. At sundown, when he died, his wife found her way to Mirabeau Plantation to ask for a coffin and a safe place to sleep. All of her neighbors had fled. The body remained unburied, attracting so many turkey vultures by the end of the week that the roof of the house was covered with birds.

The raiding party at McKinney's farm brought together an unlikely handful of area whites. Among participants later identified by the widow and other eyewitnesses, representatives from distant parishes made up the party that pulled the trigger. Denis Lemoine, a rollicking Creole from 60 miles away in Avoyelles

From *The Colfax Massacre: the Untold Story of Black Power, White Terror, and the Death of Reconstruction* by Leeanna Keith, (Oxford University Press, 2008). Copyright © 2008 by Oxford University Press. Reprinted by permission of Oxford University Press (USA).

Parish, joined his cousins from the extensive Natchitoches clan of Lemoines. On April 5, Lemoine was riding with Bill Irwin, a poor farmer from the Rapides section of Grant Parish. Their unlikely company suggested the reach and strategy of the white supremacist organizations that planned the attack on the Colfax courthouse. In fact, the Knights of the White Camellia and a group calling itself the "Old Time Ku Klux Klan" played a major organizational role. Acting as scouts, Lemoine, Irwin, and their associates secured a site to feed and water the horses of a growing contingent of armed men. They would visit the abandoned McKinney house on patrol and make liaisons there until supplies ran out.

Like many who would join their ranks in the area around Colfax, Irwin and Lemoine were Confederate veterans. Apart from the killing of civilians and other excesses, white preparations betrayed a jaunty military spirit. Where former officers such as George Stafford and David Paul took the lead, volunteers formed "companies" and even designated ranks. Rapides Parishes offered three such units, under Captains Stafford, Paul, and Joseph W. Texada, all prominent planters and former slaveholders. Contingents from Catahoula, Concordia, and Winn Parishes traveled long distances under similar leadership. Others, such as Denis Lemoine, arrived as individuals or in small groups. Local residents offered directions and hospitality, putting up out-of-towners and providing meals as possible. Veterans figured prominently in the mix, but a significant number of young men joined in, including many, such as Stafford, who had lost older brothers and other relatives in the Civil War.

The talk around their campfires was of genocide. Many expressed the strong conviction that the seizure of the Colfax courthouse was the first step in a war of conquest to eradicate the white race.

> The Negroes at Colfax shouted daily across the river to our people that they intended killing every white man and boy, keeping only the young women to raise from them a new breed [explained the organizer of an elite Rapides Parish contingent]. On their part if ever successful, you may safely expect that neither age, nor sex, nor helpless infancy will be spared.

"[T]he open threats of the negroes were to kill the white men and violate the white women," remembered one participant. Another account suggested the participation of militant organizations in fanning the rumor.

> We were all startled and terrified at the news by a Courier who had just gotten in from our Parish Site, that the Negroes under the leadership of a few unprincipled white men had captured the Court House & driven all white inhabitants out of the Town, and were raiding stealing & driving the cattle out of the surrounding country. The Negro men making their brags that they would clean out the white men & then take their women folks for wifes.

Another fragment of the rhetoric of such claims referred in Klan-style idiom to the way the "Tytanic Black Hand was sweeping over the Red River Valley in 1873," and to the urgent response of white manhood in the state....

As Easter Sunday approached, the military character of the confrontation became increasingly pronounced. Blacks in Colfax drilled in formation and worked to stockpile ammunition, including homemade "blue whistlers" for bullets. With the assistance of the remaining Union veterans in the crowd. . . ., the men prepared three makeshift cannons using stovepipe and gunpowder and constructed shallow breastworks on two sides of the courthouse. . . .

Fortified by their faith in their rights as citizens, blacks in Colfax girded for the fight.

Whites made their own preparations, taking advantage of their control of the countryside surrounding Colfax to steal horses and mules from undefended black households. Creating army-style squadrons under the leadership of selected men, the whites assembled a version of a cavalry outfit. The white paramilitary patrolled constantly, assessing the strength of black defenses and scouting for the arrival of new recruits. . . . By Easter Sunday, according to their own estimate, the white line consisted of 140 men and teenage boys. . . .

Despite the intensity of the buildup on both sides, Easter Sunday started slowly in Colfax. A handful of lost stalwarts departed the radical camp in the morning. A prominent African American from Rock Island came to town to implore the men to surrender the fight. No formal observance of the holiday could be discerned. A bustle of activity, in contrast, occupied the white force as it prepared to move in concert from its network of campsites around the town. Riding to a designated spot on Bayou Darrow, the white captains paused to review the plan of attack. Captain Dave Paul read the muster roll and made a final address to the men.

"I close my eyes [and] his face and form comes before my mind just as he was that morning," wrote a participant, 50 years afterward. "Boys," said Paul, "there are one hundred and sixty-five of us to go into Colfax this morning; God knows how many will come out of it alive."

Upon the signal, the men swam their horses across the Bayou Darrow, crossing onto the Calhoun estate and initiating the hostile phase of their maneuvers. They rode in one company to the main road to Colfax and paused in battle formation where they could be seen from the courthouse and Smithfield Quarters. Christopher Columbus Nash—the former lieutenant—yielded military authority to Captains Paul, Stafford, and Wiggins but assumed formal responsibility for the fight as the Fusion ticket sheriff of the parish . . .. As such, Nash rode forward, accompanied by two men, to issue a final order for the blacks to disperse.

Bearing a white flag, Nash approached the Smithfield Quarters and asked for John Miles, a man later celebrated as a favorite of the white community. Miles would make the journey to the courthouse on Nash's behalf, walking out along the open road between the main positions of the armed rivals. Nash withdrew [within] seconds to a point forward of the white line and observed as a black man exited the courthouse and mounted a dappled gray horse.

Benjamin L. Allen—known locally as Levy, Levin, or Lev—identified himself as the commander of the courthouse defense. Allen was one of two Buffalo Soldiers to remain in the radical camp . . . Like the storekeeper, Peter Borland, who also chose to stay, Allen had long years of military experience, including the defense of stationary targets, such as garrisons and telegraph and railroad installations, against mounted Apaches on the Texas frontier. Though he never stood for office or played a visible role in Republican Party affairs, his commitment to preserving the possibility for black advancement in the parish was second to none. Allen had traveled the countryside during the buildup to the conflict, recruiting new men by appealing to the pride of their race. Even if he had no arms, he insisted, all black men should lend their hands to the defense. As for weapons, he said, "they could have his when he was killed."

The interview between Allen and Nash was dignified and brief, despite the breach of protocol that placed the black military commander, not the sheriff, as the counterpart of the would-be white officeholder. In fact, Sheriff Dan Shaw, the last of the white men in the courthouse defense, had headed for Mirabeau Plantation just as Nash and the others rode into view. Lev Allen himself had given Sheriff Shaw the go-ahead. "Old man," said Allen, "go away and save yourself, if you can." . . .

Having stated their cases, the two sides agreed to proceed with hostilities. Allen rode back to the courthouse redoubt, where he "received the approbation of the whole posse, the men all believing that the proposal of their assailants was a ruse to entrap them into disarming, that they might be incapable of resisting in case of a massacre."

Nash had agreed to give Allen 30 minutes to remove the women and children from the line of fire. Most headed for Mirabeau Plantation on the open road. Stragglers, a group that included the elderly and mothers of small children, became reluctant to enter the line of fire as the deadline approached. Scaling the riverbank, six to eight feet to a narrow shore, a contingent waited out the battle from just below the action.

A flanking maneuver brought one of the three white squadrons face to face with the noncombatants at the Red River shoreline, as a picked group of 30 men sought a new angle on the courthouse, some 75 yards from the riverbank. The encounter must have marked the interlude before the fighting with considerable tension down below, as the white men warned the gathering not to betray their location. No injuries or killings were reported, however, and the white squadron retained the element of surprise until the critical moment.

Up in the town, a kind of comic indolence set in as the warning period extended to about two hours. The improbability of the coming confrontation taxed the comprehension of men on both sides, the majority of whom knew one another by long acquaintance or at least reputation. In fact, the interlude of silence was repeatedly broken by shouted threats against specific individuals and their families, with most of the taunting emanating from the white side. Some of the white irregulars went into the Smithfield cabins, even helping themselves to hot lunches abandoned in haste. Another group played cards.

Black defenders showed defiance and disbelief (except for Baptiste Elzie, one of three local brothers in the fight, who had fallen asleep in the trench). A sniper on the courthouse roof took potshots in the vicinity of the card game, causing the whites to reform their ranks around 2 P.M. As the white line moved forward, firing a few shots, one man jumped to the top of the courthouse earthworks in a dramatic show of begging and pleading, "bowing his head and throwing up his hands several times, adding some expression, the precise words not being understood," as a white eyewitness remembered it. By some gesture, the black supplicant made clear that he was mocking them. Then the firing began in earnest.

The white offensive proceeded in three parts. Wheeling the cannon into action, a crew of artillerymen led by a northern-born white Union veteran fired on the courthouse, using a supply of iron slugs cut from two-by-two-inch bars in lieu of cannonballs. To protect the artillery charge, a squadron of men dismounted, approaching on foot in infantry formation. A mounted component, essentially disengaged from the action, maintained the rear.

Cannon fire penetrated the line of defenders in the courthouse earthworks, claiming the first fatality of the fight. According to the account of Baptiste Elzie, who described it years afterward, a slug cut across the abdomen of Adam Kimball, who was standing. His bowels torn open, Kimball ran inside the courthouse, where his intestines fell out. . . .

Some of the black defenders broke for the road, where they were shot. Others, such as Zach White, made their way to the river, where White swam a mile and a half to safety wearing clothes and carrying his shot pouch and powder horn. A white contingent led by Captain J.P.G. Hooe of Alexandria—who carried a sawed-off shotgun—awaited black militiamen who fled to the nearby black community of Cuny's Point. Those who ran for the woods—including Captain Lev Allen, who fled on horseback—fared best, capitalizing on the whites' uncertainty about black defenses that could not be seen. Allen freed his horse and found a hiding place with a view of the courthouse where he would remain until the fighting was done. Another handful of survivors spent the night up to their chins in a pond.

The largest contingent—an estimated 65 men—retreated into the courthouse, where accommodations for a siege had been prepared. Only one of the 25 Infantry veterans, the storekeeper Peter Borland, remained with the defense, which also included the local Union soldiers [Cuffy] Gaines, [Alabama] Mitchell, and [Edmund] Dancer. Shots from inside the courthouse felled the Yankee artilleryman, who survived, and fatally wounded a local man, Stephen Parish, also in the cannon crew. The black militia's jury-rigged artillery malfunctioned, but the brick walls and shuttered windows of the courthouse held firm against the last blasts of shrapnel. For the space of an hour, desultory gunshots (and the sound of shots fired in pursuit nearby) marked the standoff phase of the fight.

In their cleanup operations around town, the Fusionists and Klansmen had taken prisoner a handful of men in the warehouse and one hiding under a building nearby. From these, the captains chose a man named Pinkney Chambers and handed him a pole they had affixed to a saddle blanket doused in coal oil. "[Here's] a chance to save your life," they said; "we are going to light this and you must take it and put it on the roof." With "ten [double barrel] shotguns trained on him from his back, and I suppose 50 guns in front of him [in the courthouse]," as a white man remembered it, Chambers put the torch on the cypress shingles to start a lively fire.

The men inside the courthouse observed as Pinkney Chambers set the roof on fire, but did not shoot him. Instead, they tried to knock the burning cypress shingles from the roof from the building's rough upper story. The cause was hopeless, and many of the men inside began to despair.

> I warned our people not to go into the courthouse [a black participant told a reporter one month after the event]. I knowed it would be the end of 'em. But when the cannon went off we were all skeered, and huddled into the building like a herd of sheep. Then the burning roof began to fall on us, and every one was praying and shrieking and singing and calling on God to have mercy. The flesh of those furtherest from the door began to roast. I could smell it. . . . The hair bunt off our heads, our clothes burn [ed] and our skin roast[ed].

Among those fighting the fire on the second storey, a local man named Shack (or Jack or Jacques) White strayed too close to an open window. With the invaders deliberately shooting at the fire, providing cover as it grew, White took a bullet to the neck.

By this time, the white line had mostly dismounted and drawn close to the burning building. They were close enough for Shack White to recognize a friend among the men nearby. "Save me, Bill Irwin," he called from the window. Irwin replied that he owed him one, perhaps assuring him of the services of the surgeon and doctor in the company of whites. White tore the sleeve from his white shirt (some accounts say a large sheet of paper), put it out the window, and shouted, "We surrender!" Too late to save his life, he brought the courthouse siege to an unexpected halt.

Was he heard downstairs above the crackling of the fire on the roof? Could they know below about the improvised flag of truce? What they saw, within the incalculable space of time between two incidents, was the approach of armed white men to the door. The first, Sidney Harris, carrying a gun, opened the door. At his rear walked a man dressed in a sword and wearing the red rosette of his secret order, James West Hadnot.

Fast as thought, Harris was dead and Hadnot lay mortally wounded in the gut. . . .

The horror that gripped the body of whites at the courthouse—a group that included "Old Man" Hadnot's three young adult sons—turned the momentum of the fighting as if on a switch. By this time, a handful of black men had emerged from the courthouse and begun to stack their arms. They were overwhelmed by a blast of gunfire from the white side. With men pressing out of the burning building amid continuing fire, bodies fell in a stack by the door, including several who were slightly injured or not hurt. Using pistols and Bowie knives, the whites killed several in close combat. The door slammed. Those afraid to surrender hid under the floorboards. The cinders crackled overhead, as white men sorted out the living from the dead at the doorway and just beyond.

"Get up, old man, you're not dead," said a man. Benjamin Brimm was 56 years old, the father of four girls, a former slave. He was directed to the base of a pecan tree some distance from the courthouse and made to wait with other prisoners. Fifteen minutes later, he was told to go inside the burning courthouse to retrieve the last of the holdouts before it collapsed.

"They was under the floor in the little back room," he later testified. "[Y]'all had better come," he called. They agreed, all but one. "I might just as well to be burned up as to be shot," said the man, who burned to death some time in the next hour. The others, including Alabama Mitchell, emerged safely and were taken prisoner. A few dozen—28 or 48, in typical accounts—waited under the pecan tree to learn the final resolution of the fight.

After sunset it began to rain. The wounded blacks were moved to the porch of the nearby boardinghouse, while the remainder of the prisoners made do under the shelter of the tree. Black women, emboldened by the lack of gunfire, left their hiding places and moved within sight of the battlefield, staying well away from both the prisoners and the dead.

The armed force of whites was breaking up, with hungry men eager to make camp and others preparing for a long journey home. . . . The semblance of military discipline abated, as the remaining white chiefs discussed the fate of the last living black men in the town.

Nash wanted to set them free. "[N]ow boys," he asked Benjamin Brimm and the others, "if I take you all and send you home to your cotton, will you go to work?"

"I answered quick," remembered Brimm, "[as] I knowed Mr. Nash and he knowed me." Brimm promised he would.

A white man objected: "[B]y God, Nash . . . if you send these God Dam Negroes home you won't live to see two weeks." Having killed 50 or more in the courthouse fight and cleanup operations, many in the crowd may have feared reprisals, legal and personal, after the prisoners returned home. . . . Liquor whetted the appetite for violence in the group. One man said that he had ridden 60 miles to kill niggers, and was not yet prepared to stop. Overriding Nash's objections, the remainder of the white force decided to execute the prisoners. "Unless these niggers are killed," a Grant Parish man, Thomas Hickman, told Nash, "we will kill you.". . .

The white men told the remaining prisoners to line up and prepare to be marched to the sugarhouse, where they would spend the night and be set free in the morning. Luke Hadnot, whose dying father had recently departed on a boat to Alexandria, called out the names of five men. The five stepped forward; Hadnot lined them up in close ranks, and killed all five with two gunshots. Others likewise identified their victims of choice. Clement Penn, for example, selected and killed Etienne Elzie while Elzie's wife, Annie, stood by only a few feet away. "I was looking directly at Penn when he shot my husband," Annie Elzie later testified. "I heard him beg for his life.". . .

Chaos reigned in Colfax on Monday, when the excesses of the previous hours saw light of day. Scores of white men, including many who had not participated in the fight, came to town to witness the outcome of the struggle. The distribution of the bodies told much of the story. In the shallow breastworks around the courthouse, the bodies of the earliest victims could be seen. A significant number of corpses fanned out from the courthouse door, with piles on either side of the door in mute witness to the gunfire that greeted those trying to escape the fire. The ruins of the courthouse contained the smoldering remains of the man who feared to exit, and a few others were found killed beneath the warehouse and other buildings in the town.

Something special—still secret—could be found in the vicinity of the old pecan tree, which later became the object of special pride among area whites. According to some accounts, thirteen prisoners were hanged from its branches, and may have remained visible to visitors on April 14. By the time authorities arrived on Tuesday, however, the only bodies near the tree were the victims of gun violence. Most revealed gunshots to the head. One man's skull had been crushed. He had died with his hands still clasped in the act of begging for his life.

Whites in Colfax Monday attempted to count the number of dead, a task complicated by the pursuit of some black participants by men on horseback. At least three of the identifiable victims on April 13 had been killed outside the town, one more than ten miles downriver in Cotile, Louisiana. The removal and burial of some of the bodies on Monday further disrupted the count. Among those who attended to the numbers, the final tally varied on a wide range, with the most conservative reckoning the number of victims at 71. Whites may have indulged in exaggeration, but the most morbidly diligent white veteran historian of the massacre accepted the high number presented in Oscar Watson's reminiscences, "An Incident of My Boyhood Days":

Next morning myself & 8 or 10 others went back to look and count the dead[. A]fter making the rounds of the town 165 dead was reported within the entrenchment [and] no one will ever know how many met their fate further out[,] as some 25 or 30 men scoured the Country for 4 or 5 miles [and] no report ever reached us of how many they killed in this raid.

The black men had brought it on themselves, he reasoned.

[I]t was a sorry blunder the negroes made in [firing] on our men after surrender, for only their leaders would have been dealt with. [B]ut after their treachery the order went let none escape. The order was carried out.

Whether 70 or 165 or many more, the accepted number of victims was larger than any other incident of racial violence in American history (the only comparable number of casualties, the victims of the New York City Draft Riot of 1863, included large numbers of unfortunate whites). In surveying the damage, white men in Colfax were taking the measure of their terrible success.

White men also took liberties with the bodies of dead men and the possessions of those displaced by the violence. They mutilated the bodies, most often by shooting the corpses. In one awful case, mischief-makers used gunpowder or some other means to blow up the corpse of a local man known as Big Frank. One widow reported finding her husband's corpse with the pockets ripped open and wallet missing. Blacks in the area later complained about the theft of horses, mules, wagons, furniture, and money. "[Y]ea, even the clothes and shoes of the murdered men were taken and carried off," according to victims, "and this practice was being pursued for days after the massacre." W. R. Rutland, still aggrieved by his own loss of property in the burglary of his Colfax home, was seen riding a stolen horse around town.

Whites in Colfax sought to publicize their victory on Monday while most of the bodies remained unburied, encouraging blacks they encountered to go view the dead. "Go to town, if you want to see a mess of dead beeves," said a man to a woman whose husband was killed in the fight. Others used bad language, forced strangers to bury bodies or cook food, and taunted the widows with references to sexual favors.

Dorcas Pittman, the mother of one of the victims, arrived in Colfax on Monday to learn the fate of her son Lank, who had perished in the fight.

> When I went to Colfax the day after the fight I found my dead son's body; dogs were eating him; I took the remains home and buried them; I felt so bad that I didn't know what I did.

Whites permitted the removal of Lank Pittman's body because of the extreme circumstances, and may have allowed other burials as well. On the whole, however, they were satisfied to leave the bodies where they fell.

Their pride in display revealed the symbolic significance of the white raid on the town. Conceived as a lesson to those who advanced the black cause in politics, the rout of the courthouse defense served notice of white determination. The white men of Louisiana would unite to defeat their enemies within, killing and dying for white supremacy and home rule.

The Death of Reconstruction: Race, Labor, and Politics in the Post–Civil War North, 1865–1901

Civil Rights and the Growth of the National Government, 1870–1883

Northern Republican disillusionment with African-American attitudes toward social issues compounded the Northern association of Southern freedmen with labor radicals who advocated confiscation of wealth. Taking place during and immediately after the South Carolina tax crisis, the civil rights debates of the 1870s seemed to confirm that African-Americans were turning increasingly to legislation to afford them the privileges for which other Americans had worked individually. Civil rights agitation did more than simply flesh out an existing sketch of disaffected black workers, however; it suggested that advocates of African-American rights were actively working to expand the national government to cater to those who rejected the free labor ideal.

"Civil rights," in the immediate aftermath of the war, meant something different than it gradually came to mean over the next several years. *Harper's Weekly* distinguished between "natural rights" to life, liberty, and "the fruits of . . . honest labor," and "civil rights," which were critical to a freedperson's ability to function as a free worker. Civil rights, it explained, were "such rights as to sue, to give evidence, to inherit, buy, lease, sell, convey, and hold property, and others. Few intelligent persons in this country would now deny or forbid equality of natural and civil rights," it asserted in 1867. The 1866 Civil Rights Act, written by the man who had drafted the Thirteenth Amendment, Illinois senator Lyman Trumbull, was intended to secure to African-Americans "full and equal benefit of all laws and proceedings for the security of person and property as is enjoyed by white citizens." It guaranteed only that the legal playing field would be level for all citizens; state legislatures could not enact legislation endangering a black person's right to his life or his land. By 1867, hoping to woo conservative Republican voters into the Democratic camp and to undercut the justification for black suffrage, even moderate Democrats claimed to be willing to back civil rights for African-Americans "with every token of sincerity . . . from a free and spontaneous sense of justice."

"Social" equality was a different thing—it was a result of a person's economic success rather than a condition for it. It was something to be earned by whites and blacks alike. Directly related to economic standing, a man's social standing rose as he prospered. A good social position also required that a person possess other attributes that the community valued. A place in upwardly mobile American society required religious observance and apparently moral behavior, as well as the habits of thrift and economy dictated by a plan for economic success. This gradual social elevation became a mirror of gradual economic elevation through hard work as a traditional free laborer.

Immediately after the Civil War, as Democrats insisted that black freedom would usher in social mixing between races and intermarriage, almost all Northern Republicans emphatically denied that emancipation was intended to have any effect on social issues and reiterated that African-Americans must rise in society only through the same hard effort that had brought other Americans to prominence. In 1867, a correspondent to the radical *Cincinnati Daily Gazette* from Louisiana painted a complimentary portrait of Louisiana African-Americans, then concluded that they had neither the expectation nor the desire for "social equality, that favorite bugbear." They would ridicule any attempt to break down social distinctions by legislation, knowing that the government could give them only political equality, the writer claimed, quoting his informants as saying, "Our own brains, our own conduct, is what we must depend upon for our future elevation; each one of us striving for himself and laboring to improve his mental and moral condition." Adding credence to the correspondent's representations, the Georgia Freedmen's Convention of 1866 resolved, "We do not in any respect desire social equality beyond the transactions of the ordinary business of life, inasmuch as we deem our own race, equal to all our wants of purely social enjoyment."

As the Republicans enacted legislation promoting the interests of African-Americans, however, racist Democrats insisted they were forcing social interaction to promote African-Americans artificially, at the expense of whites. When the Civil Rights Act of 1866 took effect, Democrats charged that the Republican concept of black equality before the law meant Republicans believed that blacks and whites were entirely equal. The *New York World* predicted interracial marriages; the *Columbus (Ohio) Crisis* insisted that a black orator in Richmond had told his black audience to "vote for the man who will bring you into his parlor, who will eat dinner with you, and who, if you want her, will let you marry his daughter." In 1868, *De Bow's Review* argued that negro suffrage meant that African-Americans would "next meet us at the marriage altar and in the burial vault," where they would "order the white ancestors' bones to be disinterred and removed elsewhere, and their own transferred into these hitherto held sacred white family sepulchers."

In response to Democratic attacks, in 1868 the *New York Times* reiterated that Republicans planned only for African-Americans to share the rights and opportunities of typical free laborers. It maintained that "reconstruction did not fly in the face of nature by attempting to impose social . . . equality," it simply established political and legal equality. These rights would eventually "obliterate" social prejudices as white men sought black votes. The next year the *Times* approvingly reported that abolitionist agitator Wendell Phillips had said that "the social equality of the black race will have to be worked out by their own exertion." Frederick Douglass put out the best idea, it continued later, namely: "Let the negro alone."

⟫⟨⊚⟩⟪

Republican insistence that social equality would work itself out as freedpeople worked their way up to prosperity could not provide an answer for the overwhelming discrimination African-Americans faced. While many black and white Southerners accepted the established patterns of segregation, those practices meant that African-Americans' public life was inferior to that of their white counterparts. Black people could not sit on juries in most of the South, they could not be certain of transportation on railroads or accommodation at inns, their schools were poor copies of white schools. In addition to creating a climate of constant harassment for African-Americans, discrimination, especially discrimination in schooling, seemed to hamper their ability to rise economically. The Fourteenth and Fifteenth Amendments had made all Americans equal before the law, but they could not guarantee equal access to transportation, accommodations, or schools, and while many ex-slaves accepted conditions as an improvement on the past and dismissed civil rights bills as impractical, those African-Americans who had worked hard to become members of the "better classes" deeply resented their exclusion from public facilities. "Education amounts to nothing, good behavior counts for nothing, even money cannot buy for a colored man or woman decent treatment and the comforts that white people claim and can obtain," complained Mississippi Sheriff John M. Brown. Prominent African-Americans called for legislation to counter the constant discrimination they faced.

African-American proponents of a new civil rights law to enforce nondiscrimination in public services had a champion in the former abolitionist Senator Charles Sumner of Massachusetts. An exceedingly prominent man, the tall, aloof Sumner was the nation's leading champion of African-American rights after the war and had advocated a civil rights measure supplementary to the Civil Rights Act of 1866 since May 1870, when he introduced to the Senate a bill (S. 916) making the federal government responsible for the enforcement of equal rights in public transportation, hotels, theaters, schools, churches, public cemeteries, and juries.

But Sumner's sponsorship of a civil rights bill immediately made more moderate congressmen wary of it; his enthusiasm for black rights frequently made him advocate measures that seemed to remove African-Americans from the free labor system and make them favored wards of a government that was expanding to serve them. Only two months after the ratification of the fifteenth Amendment had reassured moderate Republicans and Democrats alike that they had done everything possible to make all men equal in America,

Sumner told the Senate that black men were not actually equal enough, but that his new bill would do the trick. When it passes, he said, "I [will] know nothing further to be done in the way of legislation for the security of equal rights in this Republic." . . .

◦◦◦

By 1874, most Republicans were ready to cut the freedpeople's ties to the government in order to force African-Americans to fall back on their own resources and to protect the government from the machinations of demagogues pushing special-interest legislation. When Mississippi Republicans asked President Grant in January 1874 to use the administration to shore up their state organization, the *Philadelphia Inquirer* enthusiastically reported his refusal. Grant "remove[d] his segar from his mouth and enunciate[d] a great truth with startling emphasis," according to a writer for the newspaper. The president said it was "time for the Republican party to unload." The party could not continue to carry the "dead weight" of intrastate quarrels. Grant was sick and tired of it, he told listeners. "This nursing of monstrosities has nearly exhausted the life of the party. I am done with them, and they will have to take care of themselves." The *Philadelphia Inquirer* agreed that the federal government had to cease to support the Southern Republican organizations of freedpeople and their demagogic leaders. The *New York Daily Tribune* approved Grant's similar hands-off policy in Texas, thrilled that "there [was] no longer any cause to apprehend that another State Government will be overturned by Federal bayonets."

Benjamin Butler's role as the House manager of the civil rights bill only hurt its chances, for he embodied the connection between freedpeople and a government in thrall to special interests. The symbol of the "corruption" of American government, Butler was popularly credited with strong-arming the House into recognizing the Louisiana representatives backed by the Kellogg government, which was generally believed to be an illegal creation of Louisiana's largely black Republican party, supported not by the people of the state but by federal officers. Honest men wanted to destroy "the principle which Mr. Butler and his followers represent," wrote the *New York Daily Tribune* and others. "The force in our politics of which he is the recognized exponent, and of which thousands of our politicians of less prominence are the creatures." "Butlerism" meant gaining power by promising an uneducated public patronage or legislation in their favor, and all but the stalwart Republicans and Democratic machine politicians hoped for the downfall of both Butler and what he represented.

Despite the fact that it was prosperous African-Americans who advocated the bill, it appeared to opponents that the civil rights bill was an extraordinary piece of unconstitutional legislation by which demagogues hoped to hold on to power in the South, and thus in the nation, by catering to the whims of disaffected African-Americans who were unwilling to work. The proposed law seemed to offer nothing to the nation but a trampled constitution, lazy freedpeople, and a growing government corrupted into a vehicle for catering to the undeserving.

The civil rights bill would probably never have passed the Senate had it not been for the sudden death of Charles Sumner on March 11, 1874. Before he died, Sumner charged fellow Massachusetts senator George F. Hoar to "take care of the civil-rights bill,—my bill, the civil-rights bill, don't let it fail." Even Republican enemies of the bill eulogized the "great man"; the *Chicago Tribune* reflected that "there is no man, friend or enemy, who does not pause to pay respect to the memory of Charles Sumner." African-Americans across the country mourned Sumner's death and called for the passage of his "last and grandest work," and on April 14, 1874, from the Committee on the Judiciary, Senator Frederick T. Frelinghuysen reported Sumner's civil rights bill protecting African-Americans from discrimination in public facilities, schools, and juries. The committee's amendments placed firmly in the national legal apparatus responsibility for overseeing violations of the proposed law. In caucus on May 8, some Republican senators objected to "certain features" of the bill but expressed a desire to act "harmoniously" on the measure. In the next caucus, the Republicans decided to support the bill without amendments.

After an all-night session of the Senate, a handful of African-American men in the galleries applauded as the Senate passed the bill on May 23, 1874, by a vote of twenty-nine to sixteen. Rumors circulated that the president had "some doubts about signing it" if it should pass the House, and many Republicans indicated they would not mind the loss of the bill. "Respect for the dead is incumbent on us all," snarled the *New York Times*, "—but legislation should be based on a careful and wise regard for the welfare of the living, not upon 'mandates,' real or fictitious, of the dead." Referring to the apparent African-American control of Southern governments, the *Times* asked whether the freedman "stands in need of protection from the white man, or the white man stands in need of protection from him." The House Judiciary Committee could not agree on its own civil rights measure and decided to replace its bill with the Senate's. The House then tabled the bill for the rest of the session, despite the continued urging of "leading colored men" that Benjamin Butler get it taken up and passed. . . .

The civil rights bill was rescued from oblivion only by Democratic wins in the 1874 elections. Republican congressmen's desire to consolidate Reconstruction before the Democrats arrived barely outweighed party members' fears that the measure was an attempt of corrupt politicians to harness the black vote by offering African-Americans extraordinary benefits that would undermine their willingness to work. When the lame-duck Congress reconvened in December 1874, House Republican leader Benjamin Butler tried to pass a bill protecting freedmen at the polls and an army appropriations bill to shore up stalwart Republicans in the South. Democrats filibustered. Butler was unable to get a suspension of the rules to maneuver around them as fifteen Republicans joined the opposition, worried that Butler's attempt to suspend the rules was simply a means "to get through a lot of jobbing measures under cover of Civil Rights and protection of the South." With his reputation as a special-interest broker, Butler had a terrible time getting the civil rights bill off the Speaker's table. Finally Republicans agreed to let Butler take it to the floor in late January.

The galleries were full as the House discussed the bill in early February. After omitting provisions for integrated schools, churches, and cemeteries, the House passed the bill on February 5 by a vote of 162 to 100. While African-Americans in favor of a civil rights bill were horrified at the sacrifice of the school clause, all but the most radical Republicans approved the omission. "The bill . . . is worthy [of] the support of every congressman who wishes to deal equitably with the citizens of the United States, white and black," wrote even the *Boston Evening Transcript*. "This measure simply provides for the education of the blacks, and does not force their children into association with white scholars," at the same time demanding that the schools be equal. "The Republicans can stand upon such a platform as that," the *Transcript* chided unwilling party members. "The great desire and solicitude of the people are to support 'civil rights' and so execute in good faith the constitutional pledges of the nation." After initial reluctance, the Senate passed the school amendment by a vote of 38 to 62, and despite Democratic plans to talk the bill to death, the Senate repassed the civil rights bill without further amendment on February 27, 1875, with Democrats in the opposition. Grant signed the civil rights bill into law on March 1, 1875.

While some radical papers like the *Boston Evening Transcript* defended the bill—wondering "[i]f the blacks and whites cannot shave and drink together . . . how can they remain tolerably peaceful in the same community?"—its passage drew fire from conservative and moderate Northern Republicans who still read into the measure a larger political story of the corruption of a growing government by those determined to advance through government support rather than through productive labor. The *New York Times* noted that Northern African-Americans were "quiet, inoffensive people who live for and to themselves, and have no desire to intrude where they are not welcome." In the South, however, it continued, "there are many colored men and women who delight in 'scenes' and cheap notoriety." It was these people, the "negro politician, . . . the ignorant field hand, who, by his very brutality has forced his way into, and disgraces, public positions of honor and trust—men . . . who have no feeling and no sensibility," who would "take every opportunity of inflicting petty annoyances upon their former masters." The author concluded that the law would not be enforceable, and that "it is a great mistake to seek to impose new social customs on a people by act of Congress." Noticing the immediate efforts of Southerners to circumvent the law by giving up public licenses and legislating against public disturbances, the *San Francisco Daily Alta California* agreed that the act was likely to produce more trouble than equality, and reiterated that social equality must be earned rather than enforced by law.

The true way for African-Americans to achieve equality, Republicans argued, was to work. The *New York Times* approvingly quoted an African-American minister in the South who reiterated the idea that laborers must rise socially only as they acquired wealth and standing. The *Times* recorded his warning that "character, education, and wealth will determine their position, and all the laws in the world cannot give them a high position if they are not worthy of it." Even a correspondent for the staunchly Republican *Cincinnati Daily Gazette* reflected that "Sambo . . . can go to the hotels, ride in first-class cars, and enjoy a box in the theater. To what good is all this? . . . He needs now, to be let alone, and let work out his own destiny, aided only as his wants make him an object of charity. . . .

  ◈

In 1883, the U.S. Supreme Court considered five civil rights cases, one each from Tennessee, New York, Kansas, Missouri, and California. On October 15, 1883, the court decided that the Civil Rights Act of 1875 was unconstitutional because federal authority could overrule only state institutional discrimination, not private actions; Justice John Marshall Harlan of Kentucky cast the only dissenting vote. With the decision, Northern Republicans stated that they had never liked the law, because it removed African-Americans from the tenets of a free labor society, using the government to give them benefits for which others had to work. The *New York Times* declared that African-Americans "should be treated on their merits as individuals precisely as other citizens are treated in like circumstances" and admitted that there was, indeed, "a good deal of unjust prejudice against" them. But the *Times* remained skeptical that legislation could resolve the problem. Even newspapers like the *Hartford Courant*, which supported the law, said it did so only because it proved that Americans were sincere in their quest for equal rights. Three days later that newspaper mused that the law had been necessary only for "the reorganization of a disordered society," and that freedpeople no longer needed its protection. The *Philadelphia Daily Evening Bulletin* agreed that public sentiment had changed so dramatically that the law was now unnecessary. Even the radical African-American *Cleveland Gazette*, which mourned the court's decision, agreed that the law was a dead letter anyway. The *New York Times* welcomed the decision, going so far as to charge the law with keeping "alive a prejudice against the negroes . . . which without it would have gradually died out."

Instead of supporting the Civil Rights Act, Republicans reiterated the idea that right-thinking African-Americans wanted to succeed on their own. The *New York Times* applauded the public address of the Louisville, Kentucky National Convention of Colored Men that concentrated largely on the needs of Southern agricultural labor and referred not at all to civil rights. That the convention had pointedly rejected chairman Frederick Douglass's draft address, which had included support for civil rights legislation, made the *Times* conclude that most attendees were "opposed to the extreme views uttered by Mr. Douglass," and that the great African-American leader should retire, since his "role as a leader of his race is about played out."

Despite the *Times*'s conclusion, African-Americans across the country protested the decision both as individuals and in mass meetings, reflecting, "It is a mercy that Charles Sumner is not alive to mourn for his cherished Civil Rights bill." At a mass meeting in Washington, D.C., Frederick Douglass admonished that the decision "had inflicted a heavy calamity on the 7,000,000 of colored people of this country, and had left them naked and defenceless against the action of a malignant, vulgar and pitiless prejudice." When the African Methodist Episcopal (AME) Church Conference of Western States, in session in Denver, discussed the decision, delegates made "incendiary" speeches and "[a] Bishop declared that if the negroes' rights were thus trampled upon a revolution would be the result." . . .

Republicans and Democrats agreed that the only way for African-Americans to garner more rights was to work to deserve them, as all others did in America's free labor system. The *Philadelphia Daily Evening Bulletin* repeated this view:

> [F]urther advancement depends chiefly upon themselves, on their earnest pursuit of education, on their progress in morality and religion, on their thoughtful exercise of their duties as citizens, on their persistent practice of industry, on their self-reliance, and on their determination to exalt themselves, not as proscribed or despised Africans, but as American men clothed with the privileges of citizenship in the one great republic of the earth. They have it in their power to secure for themselves, by their own conduct, more really important "rights" than can be given to them by any formal legislation of Congress.

The Democratic *Hartford Weekly Times* agreed, and asserted that true black leaders, "not men like Fred Douglass, who are 'professional' colored men, and who have been agitating something and been paid for it all of their lives," approved of the decision. "They say there is no such thing as social equality among white men, and that the colored man cannot get it by law, but by the way he conducts himself."

Republican and Democratic newspapers highlighted those African-Americans who cheerfully told their neighbors "to acquire knowledge and wealth as the surest way of obtaining our rights." From Baltimore came the news that "Mr. John F. Cook, a colored man of character, who deservedly enjoys the respect of this entire community, who has held and administered with marked ability for years the responsible office of Collector of Taxes for the District of Columbia," told a reporter that he had no fears of white reprisals after the decision, expecting whites to accord to African-Americans "what legislation could never accomplish." "These are golden words, and if all men of his race were like Mr. Cook there would never be any trouble on this subject," concluded the Republican *Philadelphia Daily Evening Bulletin.*

Even many Northern Democrats painted their own picture of an egalitarian free labor society that had no need of a civil rights law. First they restated the idea that Republican efforts for African-Americans had simply been a ploy to control the government by marshalling the black vote. Trying to make new ties to African-American voters, the Democratic *San Francisco Examiner* emphasized that Republicans had only wanted to use the black vote to create a Republican empire and that the reversal showed that Republicanism no longer offered advantages to black citizens. A reporter noted that members of the black community had said that "it was about time to shake off the Republican yoke and act in politics as American citizens, not as chattels of a party who cared but for their votes."

While the rhetoric of the *San Francisco Examiner* repeated long-standing Democratic arguments, it also reinforced the idea that some hardworking African-Americans had indeed prospered in America, and that these upwardly mobile blacks were fully accepted even in Democratic circles. In San Francisco, the paper noted, "there are . . . many intelligent and educated men and women of African descent." Using the Republican pattern of according prosperous African-Americans names, descriptions, and their own words, it interviewed the Reverend Alexander Walters, whom it described respectfully as an educated and well-traveled young man, and happily printed both his assertion that in cities across the nation and "in the West . . . race prejudice has died out," and his prediction that the court's decision would drive black voters from the Republican party. Similarly, it quoted P. A. Bell, "the veteran editor of the *Elevator*, the organ of the colored people," as saying that in California—a Democratic state—"we people are treated just as well as if there were fifty Civil Rights bills."

With the overturning of the 1875 Civil Rights Act, mainstream Republicans and Democrats, black and white, agreed that there must be no extraordinary legislation on behalf of African-Americans, who had to work their way up in society like everyone else. Stalwart Republicans who advocated additional protection for black citizens were seen as either political demagogues who wanted the black vote to maintain their power or misguided reformers duped by stories of white atrocities against freedpeople. Northern black citizens who advocated civil rights legislation, like Frederick Douglass, were either scheming politicians who, like their white counterparts, needed the votes of uneducated African-Americans, or they were disaffected workers who believed in class struggle and wanted to control the government in order to destroy capital.

Southern blacks seemed to be the worst of all these types. They appeared to want to increase the government's power solely in order to be given what others had earned, and to do so, they were corrupting government by keeping scheming Republican politicos in office.

EXPLORING THE ISSUE

Did Reconstruction Fail as a Result of Racism?

Critical Thinking and Reflection

1. What were the key factors that contributed to the Colfax massacre?
2. In what manner does an economic interpretation play a significant role in the essays by both Keith and Richardson?
3. In what way does a racial interpretation play a significant role in the essays by both Keith and Richardson?

Is There Common Ground?

The question posed in this issue assumes that Reconstruction policy ended in failure. Certainly, many of the goals formulated by the Radical Republicans in Congress remained unfulfilled by the time the Compromise of 1877 removed federal troops from the South. If the goal of Reconstruction was to bring the former Confederate states back into the Union, however, that task was accomplished despite the fact that relations between the North and South remained uneasy. If the goal was to rebuild the South economically, positive steps were taken in that direction as well. And coinciding with the end of Reconstruction were the efforts by some white southerners to demonstrate their willingness at reconciliation with the despised Yankees by attracting industrial and manufacturing interests to the "New" South as a means of diversifying the region's economy. In addition, state constitutions were democratized and public education was made available on a large scale for the first time.

For those few forward-thinking "Radicals" who envisioned a multiracial society in the South that extended full rights of citizenship to African Americans, many of whom had lived their entire lives in slavery until the end of the Civil War, failure was likely foreordained given the strength of the doctrine of white supremacy not only in the South but also nationally. Absent a firm economic foundation that could guarantee self-sufficiency, sustained access to the ballot box, and a broad-based commitment to equality of the races, African Americans in the South possessed little protection from poverty, political powerlessness, and the privilege of whiteness. Quiet, small victories would have to be crafted from within segregated black communities, while African Americans held out hope for future enforcement of the Fourteenth and Fifteenth Amendments.

Additional Resources

The study of the Reconstruction period benefits from an extensive bibliography. Traditional accounts of Reconstruction include William Archibald Dunning's *Reconstruction, Political and Economic, 1865–1877* (Harper & Brothers, 1907); Claude Bowers' *The Tragic Era: The Revolution after Lincoln* (Riverside Press, 1929); and E. Merton Coulter's, *The South During Reconstruction, 1865–1877* (Louisiana State University Press, 1947), the last major work written from the Dunning (or traditional) point of view. Some of the earliest revisionist views appeared in the scholarly works of African American historians such as W.E.B. Du Bois, *Black Reconstruction in America: An Essay Toward a History of the Part Which Black Folk Played in the Attempt to Reconstruct Democracy in America, 1860–1880* (Harcourt, Brace, 1935), a Marxist analysis, and John Hope Franklin, *Reconstruction: After the Civil War* (University of Chicago Press, 1961). Briefer overviews are available in Forrest G. Wood, *The Era of Reconstruction, 1863–1877* (Harlan Davidson, 1975) and Michael Perman, *Emancipation and Reconstruction, 1862–1879* (Harlan Davidson, 1987).

One of the best written studies of a specific episode during the Reconstruction years is Willie Lee Rose's *Rehearsal for Reconstruction: The Port Royal Experiment* (Bobbs-Merrill, 1964), which describes the failed effort at land reform in the sea islands of South Carolina. Richard Nelson Current's *Those Terrible Carpetbaggers: A Reinterpretation* (Oxford University Press, 1988) is a superb challenge to the traditional view of these much-maligned Reconstruction participants. Finally, for collections of interpretive essays on various aspects of the Reconstruction experience, see Staughton Lynd, ed., *Reconstruction* (Harper & Row, 1967); Seth M. Scheiner, ed., *Reconstruction: A Tragic Era?* (Holt, Rinehart and Winston, 1968); and Edwin C. Rozwenc, ed., *Reconstruction in the South* (2nd ed., Heath, 1972).

ISSUE 2

Did a "New South" Emerge Following Reconstruction?

YES: Edward L. Ayers, "Mill and Mine," from *The Promise of the New South: Life After Reconstruction* (Oxford University Press, 1992)

NO: James Tice Moore, from "Redeemers Reconsidered: Change and Continuity in the Democratic South, 1870–1900," *Journal of Southern History* (vol. 44, August 1978, pp. 357–378)

Learning Outcomes

After reading this issue, you should be able to:

- Define what scholars mean when they talk about a "New South" following the era of Reconstruction.
- Evaluate the extent to which the "New South" differed from the "Old South."
- Discuss the degree to which industrial processes were introduced into the southern economy after Reconstruction.
- Compare and contrast the characteristics of southern political leadership from the antebellum period to the late nineteenth century.
- Understand the concepts of "continuity" and "change" as they apply to historical processes in general and the realities of the post-Reconstruction South in particular.

ISSUE SUMMARY

YES: Edward L. Ayers, while conceding that some areas of the South remained tied to agriculture and that industrial development did not always match the rhetoric of New South boosters, insists that manufacturing and industrial production, funded by local capital, made impressive strides in the post-Reconstruction South and positively touched the lives of millions of southerners.

NO: James Tice Moore challenges the view that the white, Democratic political elite that ruled the post-Reconstruction South abandoned antebellum rural traditions in favor of business and commerce and concludes that these agriculturally oriented "Re-deemers" actually represented a continuity of leadership from the Old South to the New South.

One of the critical questions confronting those empowered to restore the former Confederate states to the Union following the Civil War was "What would the New South be like?" This rather large question can be broken down into several more specific parts: (1) "Who would take the reins of leadership in the South now that the war was over?" (2) "How would the southern economy differ, if at all, in light of the fact that the plantation system had been dealt a blow by the end of chattel slavery?" (3) "What would be the nature of race relations in the South in the wake of emancipation?" Over the course of the Reconstruction period, the Republican politicians who seized control of the southern state governments in the late 1860s sought to impose their image of America upon the vanquished South, but they confronted intense resistance from most white southerners, who railed against "Yankee oppression" and the imposition of "Negro rule." Most of the "radical Republican" governments fell quickly, and within a decade, conservative white Democrats had regained control of the South and were in a position to determine the economic and social meanings of the New South.

Prior to the Civil War, the southern economy had been based overwhelmingly on agricultural production dominated by the plantation-slave system. The South was not without its manufacturing operations, but as the sectional conflict began, the region lacked a sufficient industrial base to sustain a number of people at war. By the late 1870s, some influential white southerners realized that the economic future of the South, and their ultimate reconciliation with the North, depended upon their willingness to participate actively in the industrial expansion that was sweeping much of the nation north of the Mason-Dixon line. What would such a program entail? It would require the exploitation of the South's abundant natural resources of timber, coal, and iron; the establishment of local industries funded by local capital; the expansion of the southern railway system; the creation of new banks to extend credit; and the building of new towns as mercantile and industrial centers.

The proponents of the New South looked forward to the prospect that one day their region would support a business culture associated with cities, factories, and trade. Their supporting statements found robust voice in language that would have been unimaginable only a few years before, among a handful of southern newspaper editors who propagandized the goals of a diversified southern economy. Francis Dawson, editor of the *Charleston News and Courier*, wrote: "As for Charleston, the importation of about five hundred Yankees of the right stripe would put a new face on affairs, and make the whole place throb with life and vivid force." Henry Waterson of Louisville, Kentucky *Courier-Journal*, proclaimed that the "ambition of the South is to out-Yankee the Yankee." The most outspoken proponent of a New South, however, was

Henry Grady, editor of the *Atlanta Constitution*. Grady traveled widely to promote his vision of the New South, and in a speech to the New England Society of New York in 1886, he offered a message of regional reconciliation when he told his audience, "There was a South of slavery and secession—that South is dead. There is now a South of union and freedom—that South, thank God, is living, breathing, and growing every hour."

There was more than a rhetorical flourish to the idea of the New South; cotton textiles, iron and steel manufacturing, sulfur and phosphate production, and tobacco products made significant headway in diversifying the southern economy. For example, from 1880 to 1900, the number of spindles of cotton thread produced in the textile states of North and South Carolina, Georgia, and Alabama increased from 423,000 to 3,792,000. The capital invested in the textile industry alone increased from $17.4 million to $124.6 million, an increase of over 600 percent. Iron and steel manufacturing became major industries in the middle and lower South. This activity led Richard Edmonds, editor of the *Manufacturer's Record*, to report that "the easy-going days of the South have passed away, never to return." On another occasion, he proclaimed that throughout the South one could hear "a continuous and unbroken strain of what has been termed 'the music of progress'—the whir of the spindle, the buzz of the saw, the roar of the furnace and the throb of the locomotive." By 1914, the New South had become industrialized in ways that few Americans could have imagined at the end of the Civil War. More importantly, this was permanent change, despite the fact that the great majority of southerners (and other Americans for that matter) continued to earn their livelihoods from the soil. This industrial growth marked the beginning of the South's integration into the nation.

The first generation of professionally trained historians, many of them native southerners, was, along with propagandists such as Henry Grady, largely responsible for the pronouncement that a New South had emerged from the Civil War. For these scholars, the New South had reconciled with the North and become more urbanized and industrialized. Businessmen and manufacturers enjoyed a prominent place in southern society, but members of the antebellum planter aristocracy—the Bourbons—were most responsible for overthrowing the Reconstruction regimes and continued to wield significant economic and political power. This view of the post-Reconstruction Gilded Age remained largely intact until C. Vann Woodward published his monumental *The Origins of the New South, 1877–1913* (Louisiana State University Press, 1951). Woodward argued vigorously for a New South that had broken the back of the antebellum planter class. The architects of the elimination of Republican rule in the 1870s were "Redeemers"—white, conservative, business-oriented Democrats who, in Woodward's view, tried but failed to close the gap between the North and the South in terms of industrial production. At the same time, Woodward's Redeemers oversaw corrupt governments that failed to respond to the real needs of the southern population, especially African Americans, and pursued economic policies that ultimately left the South as little more than a colony of northeastern corporate interests. In the years since 1951, virtually every book and essay written about the South of the period from 1877 to 1913 has been crafted as a response to the "Woodward thesis." This is certainly the case in the YES and NO selections.

Edward Ayers recognizes Woodward's claim that southern industrialization did not match the exaggerated claims of many New South proponents, but he is convinced that southern manufacturing made impressive strides in numerous enterprises that rose to national prominence with the aid of local capitalization. Perhaps more importantly, this industrial activity touched the lives of millions of southerners, providing opportunities for them that might not otherwise have existed.

James Tice Moore focuses his attack on Woodward's depiction of the Redeemers. Where Woodward finds discontinuity in leadership from the antebellum period, Moore insists that the South's post-Reconstruction political elite were neither subservient to business interests nor willing to abandon the region's antebellum rural traditions. Southern politicians, he concludes, depended upon rural constituencies, held the same types of occupations as antebellum leaders, and are best characterized as members of an agricultural-oriented elite.

Mill and Mine

S... outhern manufacturing did not fit what we recognize as the general pattern of industrial development that transformed other Western countries in the nineteenth century. While the cigarette, furniture, and textile industries made impressive strides in the New South, most Southern industrial workers labored in forests and mines rather than in factories. Those extractive industries became increasingly dominant throughout the New South era, outstripping the growth of more heavily mechanized enterprises. Southern industry created relatively few salaried clerks and other officials and failed to fuel the widespread economic development of the sort experienced in the Midwest at the same time.

Given these very real limitations, many contemporaries and subsequent scholars have seen the Southern economy as essentially "colonial," producing new products for distant markets where the profitable finishing and use of the products took place. Some have ascribed the South's colonial position to the actions of the federal government, to the unfair policies of major corporations, to the selling-out of the region by its own political and business leaders, to the machinations of Northern capitalists, to the resistance of powerful planters. These critics stress, with good reason, the conscious decisions that shaped the industrial experience of the South and look for those to blame for the region's lack of long-term development.

It is misleading, though, to stop there. Whether or not Southern industry in the aggregate measured up to standards achieved elsewhere under more favorable circumstances, it touched the lives of a million people. Whether or not Southern industry measured up to the claims of the region's boosters— and it did not—it shaped the histories of hundreds of counties. The impact of industry in the New South needs to be measured in people's experience, not merely in numbers, not merely by debunking inflated rhetoric.

The North Carolina Piedmont provided the labor and the capital for the New South's first major growth industry—tobacco. The industry began to gather momentum soon after the end of the war, when Julian Carr, son of a Chapel Hill merchant, launched an advertising crusade for Bull Durham tobacco. Spending an unheard-of $300,000 a year for advertising, Carr spread the trademark of the bull from the East Coast to the West, even abroad into Egypt. Sign-painting crews followed railroad crews throughout the West and Southwest. Carr offered rewards to anyone who could invent machines that would make it possible to manufacture tobacco more quickly and more profitably and a series of Southerners came forward: one man devised a machine to fill bags with smoking tobacco, another concocted a machine to make bags fast enough to keep up with the first machine's ability to fill them, and then another developed a machine to tie and stamp the rapidly filled machine-made bags. By 1880, the red brick and granite factory, spread over fifteen acres in the center of Durham, drew on the power of over fifty steam-driven machines working in ten different departments. As early as 1883, Carr's Bull Durham smoking tobacco—having sold five million pounds that year alone—had become the biggest enterprise of its kind in the nation. He had to fight a constant battle to keep others from using the Durham or the Bull trademarks, from cashing in on his marketing savvy.

Meanwhile, a regional folk figure in the form of Washington Duke, yeoman farmer turned small tobacco producer turned industrial patriarch, was preparing to compete for this huge market. Duke offered a stark contrast to Julian Carr, who had inherited both money and commercial experience. Duke had returned to a desolate farm in 1865, when he was already forty-four years old, uncertain of what he would do to feed his family. Like some of his neighbors, he and his family began processing tobacco in barns and sheds on the farm to bring in needed cash. The business did well partly because the bright-leaf tobacco of North Carolina had been made newly popular by soldiers who had first tasted it while passing through Carolina in the late stages of the war; by 1873 the Dukes were selling 125,000 pounds of tobacco a year. Such volume allowed Duke to replace his own sons and daughters with a black work force and to replace the shed that had passed as a factory with a more suitable two-[storey] structure. Soon Duke moved the operation to Durham, where the factory benefited from steam power and proximity to the railroad.

Still the Dukes could not compete with Carr's Bull Durham. In 1880 Duke's son, James "Buck" Buchanan, decided that the only way to overtake their competitor was to go into a new line of business: cigarettes. Cigarettes were relatively new in America but were catching on fast; they offered the pleasures of tobacco in a form urban dwellers could enjoy—"clean, quick, and potent," as one historian has put it. Buck Duke sent to New York for a hundred recent Jewish immigrants to come to Durham to practice their craft and teach it to others. Meanwhile, the methods of advertising used so effectively by Carr were taken a step farther by the Dukes, who attached collectible pictures to each pack of cigarettes. Within four years, the company was selling four hundred thousand cigarettes a day.

The four cigarettes a minute that skilled workers could roll simply was not fast enough. A machine would have to be invented. In fact, an eighteen-year-old Virginia boy, James Bonsack, had invented such a machine four years earlier, but a Richmond manufacturer had given it a trial and deemed it unworkable. Buck Duke and a mechanic labored on the machine for months to get it into working order, however, and their efforts paid off when in 1884 the Bonsack machine managed to produce two hundred cigarettes per minute at less than half of what the skilled workers cost.

Meanwhile, other tobacco manufacturers in the South were specializing in other aspects of the trade and making similar, if less spectacular, advances. The older tobacco industry in Virginia still concentrated on chewing tobacco; Richmond, Lynchburg, and Petersburg turned out plug tobacco in enormous quantities in the 1880s and 1890s. Winston, North Carolina, using the newer and more expensive bright-leaf variety for its chewing tobacco, began to push aggressively in the smaller markets of the region. Furthermore, both Winston and Durham fought for and won additional rail lines that allowed them to ship to all parts of the country, and firms developed machinery to speed the manufacture of loose smoking tobacco. The aggressive entrepreneurs of North Carolina pulled every facet of manufacture under one roof. Factories produced their own tin, paper, cloth, and other packages, as well as the printing and lithography machinery for labels and advertising posters.

Small or old-fashioned manufactories could hardly compete on such a scale and started going out of business throughout the eighties and nineties. Virginia steadily lost ground to North Carolina, and any manufacturer off the railroad faced virtually insuperable odds. Duke made sure that no one else gained access to the Bonsack machine at such cheap rates and used the advantage and massive amounts of advertising to drive his competitors out of business by underselling them. He largely succeeded; in 1894, North Carolina had claimed 253 tobacco factories, but by 1904 that number had shrunk to 33—and they all belonged to Duke's American Tobacco Company, now based in New York.

The same years that saw the breathtaking emergence of the Southern tobacco industry also saw the furniture industry come to the South. Offering generous inducements to furniture manufacturers moving to places where wood was more plentiful, Southern communities attracted Northern superintendents who put up entire factories backed by Southern money. Factories were established in Tennessee, Virginia, Georgia, and North Carolina, with North Carolina passing the others after 1890. That state had only six factories in 1890, but claimed 44 a decade later. The town that soon passed all others in North Carolina was High Point, where 13 factories shipped out eight carloads of furniture every day. Much of the relatively simple and cheap furniture they produced went to the growing Southern market, but some manufacturers managed to penetrate the markets of the North and Midwest by the turn of the century.

Just as families throughout the South might well purchase their first piece of manufactured furniture from one of the firms in High Point, so might they build a home with products turned out by the new planing mills and building-supply firms of the region. Brick and tile manufactories were among the largest employers in Georgia, South Carolina, Tennessee, and Texas, providing essential materials for the red-brick buildings then held to be the symbols of substance and stability for any business enterprise. The "brickmaker of today is raised to the dignity of a manufacturer," one account pointed out in 1891, "carrying on his business the year round, employing steam by hundreds of horse-power, digging his clay by steam, carrying it to the machine-house by rail, dumping it into large hoppers, and performing all the various manipulations of screening, mixing, tempering, molding, drying, and burning without being exposed to weather, and never touching the clay with hands." Brickmaking businesses arose throughout the South to provide the materials to build the region's new towns and cities.

At the same time manufactured bricks became widely available, so did mass-produced moldings, window frames, doors, sashes, blinds, and other building products. As early as 1887, a farming journal assured its readers that the cheap and uniform versions of such materials rolling off the planes and mills of Southern factories were perfectly good and that it was no longer profitable to labor over these products themselves. Soon, buildings in even the most out-of-the-way corners of the region boasted machine-fabricated mantels, doors, windows, columns, and ornament, all available in sizes to suit. The residents of the company towns of the coal mines and textile mills often lived in houses built of prefabricated elements, their identical homes assembled on the spot. Railroads brought in dozens of carloads of lumber already cut to fit from nearby sawmills; manufactured nails, locks, and pipes from Richmond; precut shingles, plaster lathe, dressed floor planks, sashes, and doors from High Point; chimney flues from Greensboro. Even in the countryside, builders altered farmhouses to make room for fashionable gables and fancy moldings. The new rural houses of the late nineteenth century turned their adorned façades toward roads and railroads rather than toward the sun or water.

Thus, the South made an impressive showing in tobacco, furniture, and building supplies, using modern methods and local capital to build growing enterprises of national importance. The determination and cooperation of small investors built to the point where mechanization and competition could carry a business and an industry to wide geographic importance. These industries made insignificant villages into impressive towns, as High Point, Durham, and Winston prospered along with their industries into the twentieth century.

The New South had more than enough stories of great expectations followed by great disappointment, stories of boom and bust, stories of simple stagnation. One of these stories involved what must have seemed like a sure bet: the mining of phosphates on the coast of South Carolina, only a short distance by rail from the major market for such fertilizers, the older plantation districts of the Southeast. "Almost the whole country adjacent to the railroads in the South Atlantic States, is pervaded by the pungent fragrance of phosphates and other fertilizers," a reporter for the *Atlantic Monthly* wrote in 1882. "Travelers in the Pullman night coaches say they know when they are approaching a station by the potent odors which they encounter. Whole freight trains are laden with these substances, and hundreds of tons in sacks fill the freight platforms at all the stations."

The mining of phosphates began in the coastal areas around Charleston in the 1860s, flourished through the depression of the 1870s, and by the early 1880s was paying large dividends to the investors in the city. The amount of capital invested in the district's phosphate mining rose from $3.5 million in 1880 to $5.5 million in 1892, while the number of employees grew from 3,155 to 5,242. Nevertheless, those workers, almost all black men, performed distinctly old-fashioned back-breaking labor. For one kind of rock, they used a pick and shovel to dig pits from which the phosphate was extracted; for another, they simply waded into the rivers and used crowbars, picks, or oyster tongs to pry the phosphate loose; others dove for the rock in deeper water.

The black men in the phosphate mines, like others along the Carolina coast, refused to work in gangs. They insisted, instead, on working by the task, on getting paid for performing a certain amount of labor rather than for a set amount of time; they were more interested in controlling the pace of work and their daily wage than in making the maximum amount of money. Such preferences had characterized the Afro-American population of the coastal region for generations and had been the way they worked on the rice plantations before the phosphate boom began. The employers had to permit this labor arrangement if they were to get workers at all, for most of the laborers apparently preferred to work as independent farmers. Only steady wages, housing provided by the mine owners, health care, and credit (with its attendant indebtedness) could keep a labor force in the phosphate mines. When the industry went into decline in the 1890s, the black workers resumed the ways of making a living they had pursued before the mines opened.

Just as the labor force sought to conserve the ways of the past, so did the investors. The planters, cotton factors, and merchants who ran the mines used them mainly as a source of revenue to help maintain their accustomed way of life, not to create a New South. Charleston continued to pride itself on its conservatism, its aversion to the allure of progress. As a result of the city's resistance to new men and new money, in fact, businessmen and their capital fled Charleston. "The flower of Charleston's youth" left the city for the better chances of the textile mills in the upcountry or the stores and factories of Birmingham or Atlanta. When the phosphate magnates died, their wills showed that their money had not remained in their ancestral city with them. Iron foundries in Alabama, street cars in newer cities, mills in raw textile villages—those were the distant beneficiaries of the phosphate profits.

South Carolina's phosphate boom proved short-lived. A series of terrible storms wrecked the Carolina industry in the early 1890s, just when strong competition from Florida began. "Compare that little speck in South Carolina with the broad flowing band that sweeps through Florida—and then think of the millions of tons—yes probably billions of tons—of phosphate that has been mined and shipped in Charleston," a Tallahassee paper exulted soon after the discovery of phosphate in Florida in 1890. "Think of the millions of money it's brought into South Carolina and your knees will grow weak in attempting to calculate how many trillions of money the Florida phosphate beds will bring into our beloved and flower decked state."

Whereas the older Carolina mines had operated in an environment where generations of blacks and whites had evolved traditional ways of doing things and where men with capital remained quite conservative, the phosphate boom of Florida unleashed the far more typical New South feeding frenzy. "Trains were filled with prospecting parties armed with spades, chemicals, and camping apparatus. Thousands came by horseback, by wagon, and on foot," the industry's historian has written. "The open woods were tracked everywhere by buggy wheels and punctured like a sieve" by the twenty-foot-long steel sounding rods that prospectors used to locate phosphate beds. The few nearby hotels filled to overflowing, and livery stables raked in money renting out horses by the day. "Companies were formed hourly," one observer noted, and "gilt-edged stock" flooded the state.

All through the early 1890s, even through the depression, the boom continued. By 1891, two counties alone could claim eighteen mining companies worth $5 million; within another year, the state saw more than 215 companies in operation; by 1896 over 400 companies had arisen. A familiar pattern set in, though: harder times caused the smaller operations to fail, and larger companies consolidated or replaced them. By 1900, only 50 companies mined phosphate in Florida. The big companies brought in centrifugal pumps, driven by steam engines on dredge boats, that sucked the phosphate pebbles from the beds and dumped them on a revolving screen to separate them from the sand and clay. After the phosphate dried on the wood fires and was screened another time, it was ready to be sold for fertilizer. The mines used prodigious amounts of wood to dry the phosphate—often five hundred cords per day—and local whites cut cord wood by contract. The phosphate boom echoed deep into Florida, Georgia, and Alabama, as the mining companies recruited thousands of black laborers.

The promise of mineral wealth brought capitalists and workers to other places in the South. In the 1870s the transition to coke as a fuel to make pig iron allowed Chattanooga to surge ahead in the industry, and by 1885 the small Tennessee city claimed nine furnaces and seventeen foundries and machine shops. The iron industry was growing just as fast in Virginia and Alabama; the 205,000 tons of pig iron produced in the Southern mineral belt in 1880 had grown to 1,568,000 in 1892. Throughout the 1870s, Birmingham had been merely one of a host of towns between southwest Virginia and north Alabama trying to cash in on the bonanza. In the mid-1880s, though, the Tennessee Coal Iron and Railway Company threw its money and power behind Birmingham and that city rapidly left its Southern competitors behind. As the nation's and the region's cities installed miles of cast-iron pipe for their new utilities, most of it came out of Birmingham; in 1889, even Andrew Carnegie had come to believe that "the South is Pennsylvania's most formidable industrial enemy."

Indeed, Birmingham pig iron was beating Northern competition in Chicago and Cincinnati, in Philadelphia and New York, even in Britain. In one sense, Alabama succeeded too well, for the state's iron makers poured their capital and their energy into pig iron while most American iron producers converted to steel. The merchants and investors laboring to create new iron towns often held on to familiar and successful technologies rather than experimenting with expensive methods that had not yet been proven in the South.

Even the South's greatest drawing card for every industry—cheap and plentiful labor—hurt the iron and steel industry in the long run, delaying the adoption of new techniques. With plenty of black workers rushing into Birmingham to work in the mills at rates far below Northern wages, the mills had little incentive to adopt labor-saving machinery. Even when a mill superintendent invented an important machine in Birmingham in the mid-nineties, only advanced Northern mills bothered to install it; forty years passed before Southern mills adopted the advance. As a result, the South steadily fell behind in productivity.

Ironically, too, the natural attributes that so excited Alabama boosters proved to be deficient in the century of steel: the underground (rather than pit) mines, the erratic seams and topography, and the low iron and high phosphorous content of the ore made the switch to steel far more difficult in Alabama than in the North. Characteristics of the larger regional situation also worked against Alabama steel. The Southern iron industry's late start, its reliance on outside technical expertise, its need for vast sums of capital that could be acquired only outside the South, the relatively small and slowly growing Southern market for steel, and the neglect of the Southern industry by its Northern-oriented parent company, U.S. Steel—all these conspired to keep Birmingham from attaining what had seemed so close at hand in the early 1890s.

Even as iron and steel failed to live up to expectations, Southern cotton textile mills prospered. Although textiles, like iron, involved competition with mature international rivals and required sophisticated technology, they displayed important—and critical—differences from the metals industry. Textile mills could be built anywhere that there was power to run the machinery, and the Piedmont from Virginia through Alabama offered dozens of rivers and streams with an adequate flow of water. After the 1890s, when the production of the Southern coal fields made steam power feasible, textile mills could be located over a much broader area. Moreover, a textile mill required far less capitalization than an iron or steel mill, and most labor in a textile factory required little experience and little physical strength; even children would do for some jobs. Finally, the competition with other regions and countries was less harsh in textiles than in iron and steel, because mills could specialize in particular weaves or grades that other mills were not producing.

While the Southern iron and steel industry became concentrated in the Birmingham district after 1880, the Southern textile industry steadily spread over a large area. The 10,000 textile hands in the South of 1870 (the same number as in 1850 and 1860) grew to 17,000 by 1880, 36,000 by 1890, and 98,000 by 1900. In 1870, the South held only 8 percent of the nation's textile workers; by 1900, 32 percent. Although Georgia claimed twice as many textile operatives as any other Southern state in the 1870s—a continuation of its antebellum domination—in the 1880s both of the Carolinas closed the gap and in the 1890s raced ahead even as Georgia nearly doubled its own labor force. Of the nearly 100,000 people who labored in Southern mills by the turn of the century, a third worked in South Carolina, another third in North Carolina, and a fifth in Georgia; the rest were distributed throughout Alabama, Virginia, Tennessee, Mississippi, and Kentucky. Over a thousand textile workers appeared in Arkansas, Louisiana, and West Virginia, states not usually associated with the industry. The mills varied widely in size: in 1900, the average mill in South Carolina employed 377 workers, in Georgia 270, and in North Carolina 171; the regional average was 243. The larger mills tended to be located in or near cities and large towns, not in isolated enclaves.

The South's textile mills boasted the latest and most sophisticated machinery. While steam drove only 17 percent of Southern mills in 1880, the proportion increased to 47 percent in 1890 and to more than 60 percent by 1900; electricity powered a rapidly growing share of its own. By the 1890s electric lights illuminated some mills during the night shifts, and automatic sprinklers and humidifiers appeared in the more advanced factories. Southern manufacturers were among the first to adopt the latest in manufacturing equipment as well, including a new revolving card in the 1880s and an automatic loom in the 1890s. Of the 222,000 looms installed in American factories around the turn of the century, the South claimed 153,000. The most important innovation, the ring spindle—easily run and repaired, and doubling the output per spinner—operated in 90 percent of Southern mills in the 1890s but in only 70 percent of New England mills.

This rapid proliferation of up-to-date textile mills inspired much of the South's boosterism. Here was evidence, in county after county, state after state, that factories could prosper in the South. Here was an industry that used expensive and sophisticated machinery to manufacture products that could hold their own with those produced in Great Britain or Massachusetts. Here were products sought in China, India, and Latin America, for the South supplied 60 percent of all the American cloth sent abroad at the turn of the century. Here were factories that paid a profit early on and kept on paying for decades. Here were factories that tapped the South's great cotton crop at the source, that saved the expense of transporting the bulky fiber thousands of miles. Here were factories that prospered even during the depression of the 1890s, while virtually every other business in the country—including New England textile factories—suffered.

Perhaps most important for the South's perception of itself, the textile mills were built with local capital and employed local people. Until after the turn of the century, Northern capital played only a small role in building the Southern factories. The Northern capital that did arrive came through the companies that also supplied the machinery and marketing of the Southern crop—not, as in the case of Birmingham, from the owners and managers of competing firms in the North. Every property holder in and around the towns that built textile mills could reasonably expect to profit from the mill's arrival. "Impress this fact upon your merchants," an Atlanta man wrote to an associate in the small Georgia town of Ellijay trying to boost a mill, "a cotton factory means an increase in population with more money in circulation weekly, and means a high price paid farmers for the cotton, with an enlarged market for their produce. Factory operatives being unable to attend gardens buy their produce.". . .

The mill people were part of the unstable and rapidly evolving world of the New South, and we should not allow the images conjured up by the phrase "mill village" to obscure the connections between the mill operatives and the world beyond. New and larger mills appeared near towns and cities of considerable size; mill towns ringed cities such as Charlotte or Burlington. Company stores became less common as the years passed; only a third of the mill villages had such a store at the turn of the century, and that proportion declined as competing private stores grew up near the mills. Complex divisions developed among the mill workers, as those who owned their homes in a mill town distanced themselves from the more transient workers renting houses from the company.

Mill workers found it easy to visit nearby saloons or brothels as well as friends back on the farm or in town; mill families saw sons and daughters leave for work elsewhere or to establish families outside the mill village; many mill families took in boarders, kin and strangers; considerable numbers of mill workers farmed nearby, some of them owning land. Even after the mills became firmly established at the turn of the century, high cotton prices enticed enough workers back to the land to try farming again that employers complained of labor shortages. All these trends quickened with the accelerating growth of the industry in the nineties and after, although people then and ever since have tended to envision the villages as they were for a few years in the early 1880s: the embodiments of personal concern or personal domination. Instead, they were part of the much larger transformation of the South, a transformation that soon eroded any lingering paternalistic style. The mills were based on industrial work, on dependence upon friends and allies among one's own class, not a longing for a lost plantation ideal. . . .

James Tice Moore  **NO**

Redeemers Reconsidered: Change and Continuity in the Democratic South, 1870–1900

The political leaders of the post-Reconstruction South have experienced a curious fate at the hands of historians. Variously known as "Bourbons," "Redeemers," or "New Departure Democrats" (*Redeemers* is used in this essay), these men were lionized by scholars well into the twentieth century—only to suffer a sharp decline in their reputations from the 1920s to the 1950s. The sources of their initial popularity are readily apparent, for they had expelled the hated carpetbag governments from the South, reestablished white supremacy on the wreckage of a defunct Radicalism, and put an end to the humiliating military occupation of the region. Reflecting this favorable climate, historians in the first four or five decades after Reconstruction rarely questioned the motives or personal integrity of the Democratic leaders. Instead, scholars generally contented themselves with eulogies on the Redeemers' Confederate war records, their heroism and sagacity in the struggles against "Negro rule," and their ties in blood and sentiment to the chivalric aristocracy of antebellum days.

Occasional criticisms crept into these early analyses, to be sure; students of the period sometimes suggested that the region's Gilded Age Democrats had been too parsimonious in their spending policies and too conservative in their political outlook, too resistant to new men and new ideas. Even so, historians excused these short-comings because of the politicians' service on the battle-fields and in the legislative halls. Repeatedly hailed as the heirs and equals of the patriots of 1776, the Redeemers' place in history seemed assured. They were—in the eyes of scholars and public alike—the patrician saviors of their homeland, the natural leaders of the South.

This exalted image has not survived. Attacks on the post-Reconstruction leadership began to appear in the 1920s and became increasingly vitriolic for a generation. Inspired by Charles Austin Beard and other reformist historians of the Progressive Era, scholars . . . emphasized the negative aspects of the Redeemer establishment, and an image of the Democratic elite took shape that was far different from the heroic vision of previous years.

Where an earlier generation had perceived courage, self-sacrifice, and a sincere devotion to good government, the revisionist historians of the 1930s and 1940s by and large saw only intolerance, avarice, and a shocking indifference to

From *Journal of Southern History,* August 1978, pp. 357–363, 365, 367–369, 370–378. Copyright © 1978 by Journal of Southern History. Reprinted by permission.

popular needs. Many historians examined long-forgotten Democratic financial scandals and conflicts of interest, and they attacked the Redeemers' inadequate funding for schools, asylums, and prisons. Most important of all, students of the period questioned the social and economic origins of the post-Reconstruction leadership. Rejecting the previous emphasis on the Redeemers' "good blood" and patrician heritage, hostile scholars described the Democratic politicians of the 1870s and 1880s as an essentially new class of money-hungry townsmen, as upstart capitalists who had muscled their way to prominence in the turbulent post-Civil War era. This revisionist trend culminated in the 1951 publication of C. Vann Woodward's *Origins of the New South,* a work which brilliantly synthesized the findings of the preceding decades.

According to Woodward, the collapse of the carpetbaggers neither restored the South's prewar leaders to office nor revitalized the region's traditional values and beliefs. The secessionist firebrands of the planter class never regained their old preeminence, and the powers of government gravitated inexorably into the hands of urban-oriented parvenus, men who had enjoyed little influence in the antebellum years. Railroad executives, corporation lawyers, and speculators of various kinds set the political tone in Professor Woodward's New South. Revisionist historians also emphasized the importance of erstwhile Whigs in the Democratic hierarchy, and Woodward exploited this theme with particular effectiveness. He insisted that probusiness Whigs monopolized public offices in the Redeemer period, displacing the old-line adherents of Jefferson and Jackson. He described a Democratic elite that allegedly ignored the farmers' demands, lavished favors on the corporate interests, and aligned itself with northeastern capital on the great economic issues of the Gilded Age. In Woodward's opinion, therefore, the Redeemer hegemony represented fundamental, irreversible change. Parvenus presumably gained power over traditionalists, Whigs over Jacksonians, capitalists over agrarians. New men with new ideas clearly held sway in the revisionist South. . . .

In spite of its wide acceptance by historians, the revisionist appraisal, dominant for at least three decades, is now itself in need of revision. This claim is supported by the marked increase in historical research and writing on the Redeemer years since the publication of *Origins of the New South.* . . . This abundant new information should make possible a reassessment of the revisionist argument. Were the Democratic leaders in fact townsmen instead of farmers? Did parvenus take the place of aristocrats? Were old-line Jacksonians overshadowed by erstwhile Whigs? Did the Redeemers actually abandon antebellum traditions and favor industry and commerce at the expense of agriculture? The extent of change in the South's Gilded Age ruling class is obviously at issue, and this essay will attempt to gauge the strength of the contending forces of continuity and discontinuity, tradition and innovation.

As noted previously, revisionist scholars have concluded that the Redeemers were much more urban in occupation and attitude than were the prewar elite. Analysis of this claim suggests, however, that the evidence supporting it is too narrowly based to be conclusive. In 1922 Alex Mathews Arnett demonstrated that townsmen controlled the Georgia legislature and held almost all of the state's congressional seats in the 1870s and 1880s, but subsequent investigations have offered only the most tenuous proof of similar developments elsewhere. Revisionist arguments on this point have by and large been founded more on untested assumptions and sweeping generalizations than on substantive research.

C. Vann Woodward attempted to bolster the case for Redeemer urbanism, but his evidence was insufficient. Although Woodward cited examples of urban Democratic spokesmen throughout the region, including a number of governors and senators, he offered no systematic proof that these men were representative of the Redeemer leadership. On the contrary, much of the pertinent statistical data supports the concept of a continuing and potent agricultural influence. Publishing his findings in 1926, Francis Butler Simkins noted that farmers occupied most of the seats in South Carolina's legislature in the mid-1880s (several years before the upsurge of Tillmanite "agrarianism"), and Willie D. Halsell's 1945 analysis of Mississippi's "Bourbon" regime documented the predominance of rural lawmakers in that state as well. William Best Hesseltine in his 1950 survey of the post-Civil War careers of 656 former Confederate leaders—men whose activities shaped the economic and political life of the Gilded Age South—acknowledged that many of these prestigious individuals pursued new opportunities in the business world, but he also showed that the percentage of agriculturalists among them increased from 20 percent in the antebellum era to almost 30 percent after the war. The number of lawyers in the group, by contrast, actually declined, further indicating that the urban ascendancy over the countryside may have been less pronounced than historians have assumed. The argument that rural interests were eclipsed should be modified.

Approaching Redeemer urbanism from another direction, it is inaccurate to argue (as revisionists typically do) that the presence of a sizable group of lawyers or businessmen in a postwar southern legislature or congressional delegation constitutes *prima facie* evidence of a sharp break with antebellum or agrarian ideals, attitudes, or even personnel. Definitive statistical evidence on this point is lacking, but some of the "urban-oriented" Redeemer leaders may have emerged from the old plantation elite and borne its impress on their personal values and intellectual heritage. A planter or his son could move to the city and begin a new career with relative ease, but abandoning the ideological trappings of a lifetime was undoubtedly more difficult. Perhaps an even larger number of the postwar Democratic leaders lived in crossroads hamlets or courthouse towns. Although they were no longer planters, these Redeemer "urbanites" depended on rural constituencies for their livelihood and political preferment and were only little more independent of agricultural interests than the antebellum leadership had been. Such circumstances offer as great, if not greater, support for notions of continuity as for change in Gilded Age political patterns. To complicate the issue still further, Ralph Ancil Wooster has demonstrated that nonfarm occupational groups, especially lawyers, were already assuming dominant governmental roles in the upper South before the Civil War and held a smaller (though sizable) number of positions in the antebellum cotton states also. Developments in the 1870s and 1880s consequently represented, to some extent at least, a continuation of long-established trends.

In other words, evidence concerning Redeemers' occupations does not appear adequate in and of itself to sustain the concept of a sharp break with the prewar regime. . . .

The revisionists' stress on the emergence of new men in the Redeemer leadership appears at first glance to contradict another, more vital tenet of their interpretation—their emphasis on the continuing importance of Old Whigs in the southern Democratic regimes of the 1870s and 1880s. The Whigs had been a vigorous political force in the antebellum South, battling the Democrats on relatively even terms for a generation before the Civil War. The presence of many erstwhile Whigs in the Gilded-Age Democratic ranks (their own party having collapsed in the 1850s) would seem, therefore, to provide yet another link between antebellum and postbellum days, another evidence of continuity with the past. Accentuating change, however, Woodward and like-minded scholars have contended that former Whigs not only survived into the New South era but actually achieved a dominant role in the politics of the period—successfully imposing their nationalistic, capitalistic views on their old-line Democratic rivals. This dramatic upsurge of Whigs and Whiggery, according to the Woodward appraisal, thus further differentiated the New South from the Old. . . .

Professor Woodward's revisionist interpretation of Redeemer origins is itself in need of revision. City dwellers, parvenus, and persistent Whigs undoubtedly participated in Democratic politics in the 1870s and 1880s, but there is little evidence that they were numerically dominant in the party councils. Indeed, historical scholarship for the past three decades strongly supports the opposite conclusion. Recent state studies for the most part suggest that traditionalist, agriculturally oriented elites grasped the New South as firmly as they had the Old. William James Cooper provided the most forceful statement of this viewpoint in his analysis of Wade Hampton's South Carolina, but support for it can be found in other works as well. Allen Johnston Going and William Warren Rogers stressed the influence of black-belt planters in Redeemer Alabama, and Roger L. Hart wrote about the return to power of a similar group in Tennessee at the start of the 1880s. C. Alwyn Barr, Jr., emphasized the preeminence of cotton farmers, cattlemen, and other rural interests in post-Reconstruction Texas. William Ivy Hair and Edward Charles Williamson noted the continuing power of old-line "Bourbons" in Louisiana and Florida respectively, and Willie D. Halsell documented the influence of agricultural representatives in Mississippi's Redeemer government, especially in the state legislature. Jack P. Maddex, Jr., broke with the prevailing trend by accentuating the capitalistic, entrepreneurial character of Virginia's ruling elite in the 1870s. But Allen Wesley Moger argued instead that antebellum attitudes and values permeated the Old Dominion's Conservative regime.

These developments were paralleled in the other states. Indeed, only in the case of Georgia has the revisionist interpretation been fully sustained. In that state, according to Judson Clements Ward, Jr., the corporate interests set the political tone and controlled the operations of the Democratic machine. Elsewhere in the Redeemer South, by contrast, Whiggish innovators apparently continued to function as subordinate elements or junior partners—just as they had before the Civil War. Such findings necessarily point to the need for a reassessment of other aspects of the revisionist interpretation. If traditionalist groups dominated most of the post-Reconstruction Democratic regimes, it seems unlikely that those governments actually adopted the one-sidedly prourban and pro-industrial approach to the region's problems that Woodward describes. A new appraisal of Redeemer economic policies is, therefore, essential to a more accurate reinterpretation of the period.

Revisionist historians have devoted considerable attention to Redeemer economic programs, and, as noted previously, their findings have done little to enhance the image of the South's Democratic regimes. Exposés of pro-business bias fill their pages, and the evidence they advance to support their accusations is impressive. Seeking to attract capital investments, five of the post-Reconstruction state governments granted tax exemptions to new manufacturing enterprises. Legislatures and state constitutional conventions granted monopolies to such companies as the infamous Louisiana State Lottery, and the convict-lease system provided cheap labor for ambitious entrepreneurs, especially for owners of railroads, mines, and lumber camps. Railroads, in particular, became prime beneficiaries of Redeemer largesse. Democratic regimes in North Carolina and Virginia sold state-owned railroad properties to private interests at bargain prices, and the governments of Texas and Florida encouraged the construction of new lines with massive grants of government land. Further exploiting this Redeemer generosity, speculators purchased millions of additional acres of timber and mineral lands from state and federal governments at extremely low prices. Such developments, according to the revisionists, constituted nothing less than a southern-style "great barbecue," a wholesale plundering of the region's resources by avaricious capitalists.

This indictment of Redeemer economic policies is damning in tone and, for the most part, convincing in its main thrust. The Democratic regimes undoubtedly made numerous errors in their quest for economic growth. They squandered resources with little or no thought for the future and frequently confused private greed with public good. Even so, the revisionist argument is misleading in several significant respects. For one thing, the Woodward school employs this evidence of probusiness activity to support the concept of a radical break between New South and antebellum attitudes toward economic growth—a highly questionable assumption. Working essentially within the interpretive framework established by Charles A. Beard, the revisionists view the Redeemer program as marking the ascendancy of industry over agriculture in the region, the collapse of pre–Civil War agrarianism before the onslaughts of triumphant capitalism. . . .

In addition to exaggerating the innovative character of the Redeemer program, the dominant Woodward interpretation of New South economic policies suffers from another significant defect: the revisionists' stress on Democratic favoritism toward business led them for the most part to neglect Redeemer attempts to exact concessions from the corporate interests, to tap their financial resources for the public benefit. The post-Reconstruction politicians' efforts along these lines are evident in their revenue policies. Railroad magnates and other businessmen made handsome profits from the convict-lease system, as noted previously, but they also had to pay hundreds of thousands of dollars into southern state treasuries each year in return for the privilege. Louisiana derived forty thousand dollars annually from lottery interests in compensation for gambling rights, and South Carolina reaped even greater profits from its abundant phosphate beds. Allowing private contractors to mine the rich deposits, the state siphoned off mineral royalties which amounted to over $250,000 a year by 1890. Public-land sales, even at bargain prices, provided another source of funds for the Democratic regimes. Florida's Redeemer administration obtained a million dollars from one such sale during the 1880s, while Texas officials employed half the state's land receipts to support the public school system.

Revenues from these sources, however trifling by modern standards, constituted major windfalls at a time when a typical southern state's budget ranged from one to two million dollars a year. Carrying this approach still further, the Democratic leaders also demonstrated a willingness to exact license fees, sales taxes, and property taxes from the business community. Although liberal in their treatment of new factories and the railroads (many of which continued to enjoy tax exemptions under their original antebellum charters), the Redeemers showed much less consideration for the mercantile and professional classes. Southern legislatures imposed a bewildering variety of levies on storekeepers, insurance agents, traveling salesmen, liquor dealers, expressmen, money lenders, and other urban occupational groups. The enactment of such measures suggests a significant conclusion: the Redeemers were less subservient to business than has generally been assumed. They granted important concessions, but they expected those interests to pay part of the cost of providing public services.

The Democrats' pragmatic attitude toward businessmen was also expressed in their penchant for retracting privileges they had previously bestowed. The opportunism of South Carolina politicians in this respect is particularly notable. After witnessing the rapid expansion of the state's textile industry at the start of the 1880s, the Redeemers in 1885 repealed the tax exemption for new factories. Tax incentives in South Carolina rapidly gave way to tax levies. Southern Democrats also retreated from favoritism toward the railroads, especially after many of the lines fell under the control of Wall Street financiers during the depression of the 1870s. This northern takeover reignited old sectional antagonisms, and anti-railroad sentiment surged through the former Confederacy. Responding to this unrest, Redeemer legislatures passed laws requiring the rail corporations to maintain adequate depots, to fence their rights-of-way, and to compensate farmers for livestock killed by trains. Democratic regimes in Arkansas and Florida manifested the new hostility by defeating the rail lines in the courtroom, enabling them to raise the tax assessments on railroad property early in the 1880s—in the Florida case abolishing tax exemptions granted in 1855. Most important of all, the Redeemers joined with western politicians in pioneering the practice of governmental railroad regulation. Between 1877 and 1891 all the states of the former Confederacy except Arkansas and Louisiana established regulatory commissions of one sort or another. Significant rate cuts ensued, even though the commissions were frequently hampered by corporate intransigence and judicial conservatism. Not satisfied with these efforts, the region's Democrats played prominent roles in the struggle for federal railroad regulation as well. Texas Senator John H. Reagan led the fight to establish the Interstate Commerce Commission, and Alabama Redeemer Walter Lawrence Bragg, another champion of the regulatory cause, served as one of the original members of the new agency.

Paralleling these developments, moreover, Democratic attitudes toward the public lands underwent a similar transformation. Eager for economic growth, southerners had generally favored liberal land policies at the start of the Redeemer era. Northern lumber interests had bought timber tracts in the South in order to forestall potential competition, and other capitalists had purchased large acreages for purely speculative purposes, making no immediate effort to promote the region's prosperity. Misgivings arose about the land boom, and in 1888 southern congressmen led a successful movement to suspend cash sales of federal land, a maneuver which paved the way for reorganization of the entire public-land system along conservationist lines. Two Redeemers in Grover Cleveland's cabinet also worked to improve the management of natural resources. Secretary of the Interior Lucius Q. C. Lamar of Mississippi and Attorney General Augustus Hill Garland of Arkansas took action against illegal encroachments on the federal domain, and together they expelled speculators, ranchers, and railroads from an estimated 45,000,000 acres in the South and West. In land policies as well as railroad regulations, therefore, southern Democrats manifested an increasingly sophisticated attitude toward Gilded Age capitalism. Skepticism gradually supplanted gullibility; restrictions accompanied and sometimes overshadowed concessions.

Abounding in such ambiguities, the Redeemer economic program offered uncertain and tenuous encouragement for the entrepreneurial classes. Indeed, a case can be made that the Democratic elite provided more consistent and reliable support for farmers than for businessmen. Gathering most of their electoral strength from the countryside, Redeemer politicians generally reflected agrarian biases on such issues as debt scaling and railroad regulation, and their tax policies followed a similar pattern. As noted previously, they veered from one direction to another in their revenue demands on business. But they pursued a much more uniform and straightforward course with reference to property taxes—the exactions which fell most heavily on rural areas. Appalled by the high property levies of the Reconstruction years, Democratic leaders moved in the 1870s and 1880s to prevent the recurrence of such abuses. They wrote strict limits on property taxes into their state constitutions, severely curtailing the revenue-gathering authority of local as well as state governments. Southern legislatures accelerated this trend with numerous tax cuts, and the results were impressive. Mississippi set the pace for the entire region by slashing its state property levy from 14 mills in 1874 to 2.5 mills in 1882, a reduction of more than 80 percent. Alabama's less drastic adjustment from 7.5 mills in 1874 to 4 mills in 1889 was more typical, but substantial reductions occurred in state after state. These cuts, together with the South's traditionally low assessments of property values, offered massive tax savings for the agricultural population. The impact of these reforms was readily apparent, for millions of acres which had been forfeited for delinquent taxes during Reconstruction were reclaimed by farmers in the Redeemer era.

Applying political pressure through the Grange and Alliance, the rural interests derived many additional benefits from the Democratic regimes. Agricultural and mechanical colleges received increased funding, and the Redeemers established new land-grant schools in the Carolinas, Mississippi, and Virginia. Government-supported agricultural experiment stations proliferated as well. North Carolina pioneered the development of experimental farms in the 1870s, setting a pattern which the rest of the South followed during the next decade. Democratic legislatures provided another recognition of the farmers' importance by creating state departments of agriculture. Although hampered by inadequate budgets, these new agencies became increasingly innovative and efficient. By the 1880s state agriculture departments were inspecting commercial fertilizers, analyzing soil samples, conducting geological surveys, encouraging immigration, providing veterinary services, dispatching speakers to farm meetings, and collecting statistics on crop yields. In Alabama the Department of Agriculture eventually became the second most powerful agency in the state, enjoying an influence exceeded only by that of the governor.

Southern Democrats also demonstrated their support for farmers by sponsoring agricultural societies. Legislatures appropriated thousands of dollars each year to subsidize these groups (primarily to enable them to hold state fairs). Further belying the notion of the Redeemers' indifference to rural needs, the region's legislators passed hundreds of laws regarding the crop-lien system, the maintenance of fences and roads, and the conservation of fish and wildlife—all issues of concern to farm areas. These activities reflected an essential fact: the agriculturalists still constituted the most important interest group in the South, and they received due consideration from the Democratic elite.

The Redeemers' favoritism toward farmers also influenced developments at the national level, undermining another facet of the revisionist interpretation. According to Professor Woodward, investment-hungry southern congressmen generally subordinated the needs of their section and its people to the demands of the capitalistic, conservative Northeast. If this in fact was the case, the Democratic leaders manifested their subservience in an extremely curious way—by opposing the northern business interests on almost all the great economic issues of the Gilded Age. Southern crusades for federal railroad regulation and the conservation of the public domain have been noted previously, but the Redeemers assumed anticorporate stands in other national controversies as well. The great majority of the region's political leaders denounced protective tariffs and for decades battled to reinstitute the low duties of the antebellum years. Gaining particular prominence in these struggles, newspaper editor Henry Watterson of Kentucky, together with Senator Lamar of Mississippi, formulated the famous "tariff for revenue only" pledge in the 1880 Democratic platform, and House Ways and Means Chairman Roger Quarles Mills of Texas led the unsuccessful congressional fight for tariff reform in 1888. . . .

The Redeemers' commitment to an increased money supply also led them to criticize the restrictive policies of the national banking system. They opposed the rechartering of many of the national banks in the 1880s, and they urged the repeal of the federal government's prohibitive tax on state bank notes. Far from endorsing the Hamiltonian financial structure which had emerged during the Civil War, as revisionist historians have maintained, the southern Democrats were instead among the more persistent critics of that structure. Only with reference to federal aid to internal improvements did they find themselves in harmony with the prevailing system. Having witnessed the destruction of their ports, railroads, and levees by federal power during the war years, southerners requested federal money for rebuilding them. Even on this issue, surprisingly enough, the Redeemers' stand placed them in opposition to northern sentiment. Northeastern congressmen—Democrats and Republicans alike—had turned against government-financed internal improvements after the scandals of the Grant era, and the southerners were only able to vote the funds for their projects with the help of the West. On issue after issue, therefore, the Redeemers took sides against, not with, the masters of capital.

These national developments, together with similar trends at the state level, clearly point up inadequacies in the revisionist interpretation of Redeemer origins and views. Parvenus, urbanites, and persistent Whigs made their way into the Democratic leadership during the post–Civil War years, as Woodward and others have argued, but these potentially innovative groups proved either unable or unwilling to alter the entrenched patterns of southern government. Traditionalist forces enjoyed too much strength in both the electorate and the party hierarchy to permit any wholesale departure from established practices and policies. As a result the southern Democrats neither abandoned the farmers nor embraced Whiggery in the aftermath of Reconstruction. Indeed, their economic programs were more congruent with the ideals of Jefferson, Jackson, or even Calhoun than with those of Clay or Webster. Although they promoted limited industrial growth, the Redeemers continued to acknowledge and reward the primacy of agriculture in their region's life. Although they accepted the defeat of secession and the collapse of the slave system, most of them also continued to regard the capitalistic North with a deep-seated antagonism. . . . In the decisive economic clashes of the Gilded Age, . . . the Redeemer South consistently joined forces with the other great agricultural section of the United States, the West. Such facts lend further support to the notion of continuity between the Old and New Souths. All things had not changed with Appomattox, much less with the Compromise of 1877.

EXPLORING THE ISSUE

Did a "New South" Emerge Following Reconstruction?

Critical Thinking and Reflection

1. Based on the YES and NO selections, what is meant by the term "New South"?
2. How did the political leadership of the post-Reconstruction South differ from that of the antebellum period?
3. What impact did industrial production have on the South in the last quarter of the nineteenth century?
4. Based on your understanding of the YES and NO selections, to what extent did the economic and political character of the post-Reconstruction South represent continuity with the antebellum period?

Is There Common Ground?

Although the Civil War and Reconstruction clearly produced changes in the South, scholarly debates continue as to the extent of this change. For example, despite the introduction of impressive industrial processes, the vast majority of southerners continued to depend upon farming for their livelihoods. Moreover, Woodward recognizes that the South's postwar industries were tied to raw materials and natural resources extracted from southern lands. Even Woodward's argument in support of the discontinuity between the antebellum South and the postwar South suggests that the distinctions were not always complete. Whether or not the post-Reconstruction political leaders of the New South were "Bourbons" or "Redeemers," they still were white, conservative Democrats. In addition, the attitudes of post-Reconstruction politicians toward urban-industrial growth differed from state to state, making generalizations about change more difficult.

Another important aspect of this question, one that is not addressed in the YES and NO selections, is the social change in the post-Civil War South. Specifically, how different were patterns of race relations once the war had ended and slavery had been abolished? On the one hand, efforts by some Radical Republicans to promote a truly egalitarian society resulted in a framework to extend citizenship rights to African Americans through the Civil Rights Acts of 1866 and 1875 and the Fourteenth and Fifteenth Amendments. These actions held out the promise of a dramatic departure from the antebellum slave statutes or the quasi-freedom of the Black Codes in the immediate postwar South. On the other hand, the demise of the Reconstruction governments resulted in a general withdrawal of any commitment to advancing the status of black southerners and paved the way by the end of the century to firmly entrenched policies of peonage, political disfranchisement, and racial segregation. From the perspective of most black southerners, then, the prospect of fully participating in the benefits of American democracy seemed just as remote in 1900 as it had been in 1860.

Additional Resources

In addition to Woodward's *Origins of the New South*, perhaps the most important scholarly volume on the New South is Paul Gaston's *The New South Creed: A Study in Southern Mythmaking* (Alfred A. Knopf, 1970), which argues that the image of the New South crafted by the Redeemers was little more than an illusion. According to Gaston, "Unable to bequeath to the next generation of Americans a legacy of solid achievement, the New South spokesmen gave them instead a . . . mythic view of their own times that was as far removed from objective reality as the myth of the Old South."

The relationship between agricultural production and industrialization is explored in Pete Daniel, *Breaking the Land: The Transformation of Cotton, Tobacco, and Rice Cultures since 1880* (University of Illinois Press, 1985), which emphasizes the negative impact of mechanization on farmers; Roger L. Ransom and Richard Sutch, *One Kind of Freedom: The Economic Consequences of Emancipation* (Cambridge University Press, 1977), which focuses on the dominance of a new merchant class over planters; and Jonathan M. Wiener, *Social Origins of the New South, Alabama: 1860–1885* (Louisiana State University Press, 1978) and Jay Mandle, *The Roots of Black Poverty: The Southern Plantation After the Civil War* (Duke University Press, 1978), both of which insist that the planter aristocracy survived the Civil War and maintained a preeminent position through the creation of the sharecropping system. James C. Cobb, *Industrialization and Southern Society, 1877–1984* (University Press of Kentucky, 1984) and Gavin Wright, *Old South, New South: Revolutions in the Southern Economy Since the Civil War* (Basic Books, 1986) summarize economic development in the South in the century after Reconstruction, whereas Ronald Eller, *Miners, Millhands and Mountaineers: Industrialization of the Appalachian South, 1880–1930* (University of Tennessee Press, 1982) describes the transformative impact of industrialization in the mountain South. Woodward's characterization of post-Reconstruction political leaders as pro-business "new men" is directly challenged in William Cooper, *The Conservative Regime: South Carolina, 1877–1890* (Johns Hopkins Press, 1968).

The study of race relations in the New South also has been dominated by the work of C. Vann Woodward. His *The Strange Career of Jim Crow* (Oxford University Press, 1955), first published the year following the U. S. Supreme Court's *Brown v. Board of Education* decision, insisted that a full-blown system of legalized racial segregation had not emerged in the South until after 1890. Woodward's thesis generated numerous opposing responses from historians who argued for a much earlier appearance of segregation both in custom and in law. The best of these are Leon F. Litwack, *North of Slavery: The Negro in the Free States, 1790–1860* (University of Chicago Press, 1961); Richard C. Wade, *Slavery in the Cities: The South, 1820–1860* (Oxford University Press, 1964); Joel Williamson, *After Slavery: The Negro in South Carolina During Reconstruction, 1861–1877* (University of North Carolina Press, 1965); and Howard N. Rabinowitz, *Race Relations in the Urban South, 1865–1890* (Oxford University Press, 1978). Rabinowitz's argument is intriguing in that it posits that segregation replaced racial exclusion as the chief operating mode for southern race relations and, therefore, represented an improvement in the opportunities for African Americans in the South, particularly in light of the fact that full integration was not available as a viable alternative.

ISSUE 3

Were the Nineteenth-Century Entrepreneurs "Robber Barons"?

YES: **Howard Zinn**, from "Robber Barons and Rebels," in *A People's History of the United States* (HarperCollins, 1999)

NO: **John S. Gordon**, from "Was There Ever Such a Business!" in *An Empire of Wealth: The Epic History of American Economic Power* (Harper Perennial, 2004)

Learning Outcomes

After reading this issue, you should be able to:

- Identify and give the significance of the terms "robber baron," "entrepreneurial statesmen," and "organizational revolution."
- Critically analyze the strengths and weaknesses of the "entrepreneurial statesmen," "robber baron," and "organizational revolution" interpretations of the dominance of big business during the Gilded Age (1867–1900).
- Describe how the times we live in influence our interpretation of the rise of big business in the late nineteenth century.

ISSUE SUMMARY

YES: According to Howard Zinn, the new industrialists such as John D. Rockefeller, Andrew Carnegie, and J. P. Morgan adopted business practices that encouraged monopolies and used the powers of the government to control the masses from rebellion.

NO: John S. Gordon argues that the nineteenth-century men of big business such as John D. Rockefeller and Andrew Carnegie developed through the oil and steel industries' consumer products that improved the lifestyle of average Americans.

Between 1860 and 1914, the United States was transformed from a country of farms, small towns, and modest manufacturing concerns to a modern nation dominated by large cities and factories. During those years, the population tripled and the nation experienced astounding urban growth. A new proletariat emerged to provide the necessary labor for the country's developing factory system. In the period between the Civil War and World War I, the value of manufactured goods in the United States increased 12-fold, and the capital invested in industrial pursuits multiplied 22 times. In addition, the application of new machinery and scientific methods of agriculture produced abundant yields of wheat, corn, and other foodstuffs, despite the decline in the number of farmers.

Why did this industrial revolution occur in the United States during the last quarter of the nineteenth century? What factors contributed to the rapid pace of American industrialization? In answering these questions, historians often point to the first half of the 1800s and the significance of the "transportation revolution," which produced better roads, canals, and railroads to move people and goods more efficiently and cheaply from one point to another. Technological improvements such as the Bessemer process, refrigeration, electricity, and the telephone also made their mark in the nation's "machine age." Government cooperation with business, large-scale immigration from Europe and Asia, and the availability of foreign capital for industrial investments provided still other underpinnings for this industrial growth. Finally, American industrialization depended upon a number of individuals in the United States who were willing to organize and finance the nation's industrial base for the sake of anticipated profits. These, of course, were the entrepreneurs.

Regardless of how American entrepreneurs are perceived, there is no doubt that they constituted a powerful elite and were responsible for defining the character of society in the Gilded Age. For many Americans, these businessmen represented the logical culmination of the country's attachment to laissez-faire economics and rugged individualism. In fact, it was not unusual at all for the nation's leading industrialists to be depicted as the real-life models for the "rags-to-riches" theme epitomized in the self-help novels of Horatio Alger.

Closer examination of the lives of most of these entrepreneurs, however, reveals the mythical dimensions of this American idea. Simply put, the typical business executive of the late nineteenth century did not rise up from humble circumstances, a product of the American rural tradition or the immigrant experience, as frequently claimed. Rather, most of these big businessmen were of Anglo-Saxon origin and reared in a city by middle-class parents. According to one survey, over half of the leaders had attended college at a time when even the pursuit of a high school education was considered unusual. In other words, instead of having to pull themselves up by their own bootstraps from the bottom of the social heap, these individuals usually started their climb to success at the middle of the ladder or higher.

American public attitudes have reflected a schizophrenic quality with regard to the activities of the industrial leaders of the late nineteenth century. So much is this the case that the field of business history can be divided into three major interpretations: (1) the robber baron or anti-big business viewpoint; (2) the entrepreneurial statesman or pro-big business account; and (3) the organizational or bureaucratic functional framework, which deems the robber baron and entrepreneurial arguments irrelevant.

Although the "robber barons" stereotype emerged as early as the 1870s and was reinforced by the muckrakers of the Progressive Era (1897–1917) who were critical of the immoral methods used by businessmen such as J.J. Hill, John D. Rockefeller, and Andrew Carnegie to gain control over the railroads and the oil and steel processing industries, the book that did the most to fix the stereotype of the late nineteenth-century businessman as a predator was Matthew Josephson's *The Robber Barons: The Great American Capitalists, 1861–1901* (Harcourt Brace and World, 1934, 1962). Published in the midst of the Great Depression, Josephson admitted that large-scale production proved more efficient but concluded that the negative consequences far outweighed the positive. Some form of the "robber baron" interpretation continued to be found in high school and college texts through the 1960s. For example, New Left historians such as Gabriel Kolko in *The Triumph of Conservatism: A Reinterpretation of American History* (MacMillan, 1963) kept the interpretation alive as he blamed big business for the militarism, poverty, and racism, which still existed in the 1960s.

The Josephson interpretation did not go unchallenged. The Harvard Business School in the 1930s and writers such as the famous journalist and popular historian Allan Nevins, whose two-volume biography of John D. Rockefeller appeared in 1940 and was rewritten in 1953, stressed the oil mogul's positive attributes. Rockefeller was not a robber baron, maintained Nevins, but an entrepreneurial statesman who imposed upon American industry "a more rational and efficient pattern." Rockefeller and others like him were motivated not by wealth but by competition, achievement, and the "imposition of their will over a given environment." Through men like Rockefeller, the industries that developed in steel, oil, textiles, chemicals, and electricity gave the United States such a competitive advantage that the nation was able to win both world wars in the twentieth century.

The third school of business history was the organizational school. Led by Alfred D. Chandler, Jr., who almost single-handedly reshaped the way in which historians write about corporations, this view avoided the morality tale between robber barons and industrial statesmen and employed organizational theories of decision making borrowed from sociologists to stress how large-scale corporations in the United States vertically organized themselves with departments that stretched from production, accounting, marketing, sales, and distribution. Key to Chandler's view was the importance of the new national urban markets that had developed by 1900. The best place to start with Chandler is "The Beginning of 'Big Business' in American Industry," *Business History Review* (vol. 33, Spring 1959, pp. 1–31). See also *Strategy and Structure: Chapters in the History of American Industrial Enterprise* (MIT Press, 1962); *The Visible Hand: The Managerial Revolution in American Business* (Harvard University Press, 1977); and *Scale and Scope: The Dynamics of Industrial Capitalism* (Harvard University Press, 1990). Chandler's most important essays are collected in Thomas K. McCraw, ed., *The Essential Alfred Chandler: Essays Toward a Historical Theory of Big Business* (Harvard Business School Press, 1988). For an assessment of Chandler's approach and contributions, see Louis Galambos, "The Emerging Organizational Synthesis in Modern American History," *Business History Review* (Autumn 1970), and Thomas

K. McCraw, "The Challenge of Alfred D. Chandler, Jr.: Retrospect and Prospect," *Reviews in American History* (March 1987).

Chandler's critics have complained that he ignored the role of the individual entrepreneur in developing particular industries. In "Entrepreneurial Persistence Through the Bureaucratic Age," *Business History Review* (vol. 51, Winter 1977, pp. 415–443), Professor Harold C. Livesay tries to reconcile an organizational and entrepreneurial approach via case studies of Andrew Carnegie, Michigan National Bank President Howard Stoddard, and Henry Ford II and his post–World War II revival of the Ford Motor Company. Two important articles examine the main currents in business history today. Maury Klein, "Coming Full Circle: The Study of Big Business Since 1950," *Enterprise and Society* (vol. 2, September 2001, pp. 425–460), contrasts the broader external approach pushed by Professors Thomas C. Cochran and William Miller, *The Age of Enterprise: A Social History of Industrial America,* revised ed. (Harper & Row, 1961) with the internal bureaucratic approach of Chandler.

The YES and NO selections reveal the divergence of scholarly opinion as it applies to the nineteenth-century entrepreneurs who came to epitomize both the success and excess of corporate capitalism in the United States. In the YES selection, the late radical historian Howard Zinn portrays the economic environment of late nineteenth-century America in the tradition of Matthew Josephson. In brief, the new industrialists such as oil magnate John D. Rockefeller, steel baron Andrew Carnegie, and the financier J. P. Morgan adopted business and banking practices that encouraged monopolies and used the powers of the government to control the masses from rebellion. In Zinn's view, the state militia, the courts, the churches, and even the education system, both colleges and high schools, were designed to produce executives for the corporations and workers for the factories.

In the NO selection, independent scholar John Steele Gordon extols the virtues of the men of big business. He stresses the innovations in production and organization as well as the new technologies that entrepreneurs such as Rockefeller and Carnegie employed to improve the lifestyle of average Americans.

Robber Barons and Rebels

In the year 1877, the signals were given for the rest of the century: the blacks would be put back; the strikes of white workers would not be tolerated; the industrial and political elites of North and South would take hold of the country and organize the greatest march of economic growth in human history. They would do it with the aid of, and at the expense of, black labor, white labor, Chinese labor, European immigrant labor, female labor, rewarding them differently by race, sex, national origin, and social class, in such a way as to create separate levels of oppression—a skillful terracing to stabilize the pyramid of wealth.

Between the Civil War and 1900, steam and electricity replaced human muscle, iron replaced wood, and steel replaced iron (before the Bessemer process, iron was hardened into steel at the rate of 3 to 5 tons a day; now the same amount could be processed in 15 minutes). Machines could now drive steel tools. Oil could lubricate machines and light homes, streets, factories. People and goods could move by railroad, propelled by steam along steel rails; by 1900 there were 193,000 miles of railroad. The telephone, the typewriter, and the adding machine speeded up the work of business.

Machines changed farming. Before the Civil War it took 61 hours of labor to produce an acre of wheat. By 1900, it took 3 hours, 19 minutes. Manufactured ice enabled the transport of food over long distances, and the industry of meatpacking was born.

Steam drove textile mill spindles; it drove sewing machines. It came from coal. Pneumatic drills now drilled deeper into the earth for coal. In 1860, 14 million tons of coal were mined; by 1884 it was 100 million tons. More coal meant more steel, because coal furnaces converted iron into steel; by 1880 a million tons of steel were being produced; by 1910, 25 million tons. By now electricity was beginning to replace steam. Electrical wire needed copper, of which 30,000 tons were produced in 1880; 500,000 tons by 1910.

To accomplish all this required ingenious inventors of new processes and new machines, clever organizers and administrators of the new corporations, a country rich with land and minerals, and a huge supply of human beings to do the back-breaking, unhealthful, and dangerous work. Immigrants would come from Europe and China, to make the new labor force. Farmers unable to buy the new machinery or pay the new railroad rates would move to the cities.

From *A People's History of the United States: 1492–Present* by Howard Zinn (HarperCollins Twentieth Anniversary edition, 1999). Copyright © 1980 by Howard Zinn. Reprinted by permission of HarperCollins Publishers and Howard Zinn via The Balkan Agency.

Between 1860 and 1914, New York grew from 850,000 to 4 million, Chicago from 110,000 to 2 million, Philadelphia from 650,000 to 1½ million.

In some cases the inventor himself became the organizer of businesses—like Thomas Edison, inventor of electrical devices. In other cases, the businessman compiled other people's inventions, like Gustavus Swift, a Chicago butcher who put together the ice-cooled railway car with the ice- cooled warehouse to make the first national meatpacking company in 1885. James Duke used a new cigarette-rolling machine that could roll, paste, and cut tubes of tobacco into 100,000 cigarettes a day; in 1890 he combined the four biggest cigarette producers to form the American Tobacco Company.

While some multimillionaires started in poverty, most did not. A study of the origins of 303 textile, railroad, and steel executives of the 1870s showed that 90 percent came from middle- or upper-class families. The Horatio Alger stories of "rags to riches" were true for a few men, but mostly a myth, and a useful myth for control.

Most of the fortune building was done legally, with the collaboration of the government and the courts. Sometimes the collaboration had to be paid for. Thomas Edison promised New Jersey politicians $1,000 each in return for favorable legislation. Daniel Drew and Jay Gould spent $1 million to bribe the New York legislature to legalize their issue of $8 million in "watered stock" (stock not representing real value) on the Erie Railroad.

The first transcontinental railroad was built with blood, sweat, politics and thievery, out of the meeting of the Union Pacific and Central Pacific railroads. The Central Pacific started on the West Coast going east; it spent $200,000 in Washington on bribes to get 9 million acres of free land and $24 million in bonds, and paid $79 million, an overpayment of $36 million, to a construction company which really was its own. The construction was done by three thousand Irish and ten thousand Chinese, over a period of four years, working for one or two dollars a day.

The Union Pacific started in Nebraska going west. It had been given 12 million acres of free land and $27 million in government bonds. It created the Credit Mobilier company and gave them $94 million for construction when the actual cost was $44 million. Shares were sold cheaply to Congressmen to prevent investigation. This was at the suggestion of Massachusetts Congressman Oakes Ames, a shovel manufacturer and director of Credit Mobilier, who said: "There is no difficulty in getting men to look after their own property." The Union Pacific used twenty thousand workers—war veterans and Irish immigrants, who laid 5 miles of track a day and died by the hundreds in the heat, the cold, and the battles with Indians opposing the invasion of their territory.

Both railroads used longer, twisting routes to get subsidies from towns they went through. In 1869, amid music and speeches, the two crooked lines met in Utah.

The wild fraud on the railroads led to more control of railroad finances by bankers, who wanted more stability—profit by law rather than by theft. By the 1890s, most of the country's railway mileage was concentrated in six huge systems. Four of these were completely or partially controlled by the House of Morgan, and two others by the bankers Kuhn, Loeb, and Company.

J. P. Morgan had started before the war, as the son of a banker who began selling stocks for the railroads for good commissions. During the Civil War he bought five thousand rifles for $3.50 each from an army arsenal, and sold them to a general in the field for $22 each. The rifles were defective and would shoot off the thumbs of the soldiers using them. A congressional committee noted this in the small print of an obscure report, but a federal judge upheld the deal as the fulfillment of a valid legal contract.

Morgan had escaped military service in the Civil War by paying $300 to a substitute. So did John D. Rockefeller, Andrew Carnegie, Philip Armour, Jay Gould, and James Mellon. Mellon's father had written to him that "a man may be a patriot without risking his own life or sacrificing his health. There are plenty of lives less valuable."

It was the firm of Drexel, Morgan and Company that was given a U.S. government contract to float a bond issue of $260 million. The government could have sold the bonds directly; it chose to pay the bankers $5 million in commission.

On January 2, 1889, as Gustavus Myers reports:

> . . . a circular marked "Private and Confidential" was issued by the three banking houses of Drexel, Morgan & Company, Brown Brothers & Company, and Kidder, Peabody & Company. The most painstaking care was exercised that this document should not find its way into the press or otherwise become public. . . . Why this fear? Because the circular was an invitation . . . to the great railroad magnates to assemble at Morgan's house, No. 219 Madison Avenue, there to form, in the phrase of the day, an iron-clad combination . . . a compact which would efface competition among certain railroads, and unite those interests in an agreement by which the people of the United States would be bled even more effectively than before.

There was a human cost to this exciting story of financial ingenuity. That year, 1889, records of the Interstate Commerce Commission showed that 22,000 railroad workers were killed or injured.

In 1895 the gold reserve of the United States was depleted, while twenty-six New York City banks had $129 million in gold in their vaults. A syndicate of bankers headed by J. P. Morgan & Company, August Belmont & Company, the National City Bank, and others offered to give the government gold in exchange for bonds. President Grover Cleveland agreed. The bankers immediately resold the bonds at higher prices, making $18 million profit.

A journalist wrote: "If a man wants to buy beef, he must go to the butcher. . . . If Mr. Cleveland wants much gold, he must go to the big banker."

While making his fortune, Morgan brought rationality and organization to the national economy. He kept the system stable. He said: "We do not want financial convulsions and have one thing one day and another thing another day." He linked railroads to one another, all of them to banks, banks to insurance companies. By 1900, he controlled 100,000 miles of railroad, half the country's mileage.

Three insurance companies dominated by the Morgan group had a billion dollars in assets. They had $50 million a year to invest—money given by ordinary people for their insurance policies. Louis Brandeis, describing this in his book *Other People's Money* (before he became a Supreme Court justice), wrote: "They control the people through the people's own money."

John D. Rockefeller started as a bookkeeper in Cleveland, became a merchant, accumulated money, and decided that, in the new industry of oil, who controlled the oil refineries controlled the industry. He bought his first oil refinery in 1862, and by 1870 set up Standard Oil Company of Ohio, made secret agreements with railroads to ship his oil with them if they gave him rebates—discounts—on their prices, and thus drove competitors out of business.

One independent refiner said: "If we did not sell out. . . we would be crushed out. . . . There was only one buyer on the market and we had to sell at their terms." Memos like this one passed among Standard Oil officials: "Wilkerson & Co. received car of oil Monday 13th. . . . Please turn another screw." A rival refinery in Buffalo was rocked by a small explosion arranged by Standard Oil officials with the refinery's chief mechanic.

The Standard Oil Company, by 1899, was a holding company which controlled the stock of many other companies. The capital was $110 million, the profit was $45 million a year, and John D. Rockefeller's fortune was estimated at $200 million. Before long he would move into iron, copper, coal, shipping, and banking (Chase Manhattan Bank). Profits would be $81 million a year, and the Rockefeller fortune would total two billion dollars.

Andrew Carnegie was a telegraph clerk at seventeen, then secretary to the head of the Pennsylvania Railroad, then a broker in Wall Street selling railroad bonds for huge commissions, and was soon a millionaire. He went to London in 1872, saw the new Bessemer method of producing steel, and returned to the United States to build a million-dollar steel plant. Foreign competition was kept out by a high tariff conveniently set by Congress, and by 1880 Carnegie was producing 10,000 tons of steel a month, making $1½ million a year in profit. By 1900 he was making $40 million a year, and that year, at a dinner party, he agreed to sell his steel company to J. P. Morgan. He scribbled the price on a note: $492,000,000.

Morgan then formed the U.S. Steel Corporation, combining Carnegie's corporation with others. He sold stocks and bonds for $1,300,000,000 (about 400 million more than the combined worth of the companies) and took a fee of 150 million for arranging the consolidation. How could dividends be paid to all those stockholders and bondholders? By making sure Congress passed tariffs keeping out foreign steel; by closing off competition and maintaining the price at $28 a ton; and by working 200,000 men twelve hours a day for wages that barely kept their families alive.

And so it went, in industry after industry—shrewd, efficient businessmen building empires, choking out competition, maintaining high prices, keeping wages low, using government subsidies. These industries were the first beneficiaries of the "welfare state." By the turn of the century, American Telephone and telegraph had a monopoly of the nation's telephone system, International Harvester made 85 percent of all farm machinery, and in every other industry resources became concentrated, controlled. The banks had interests in so many of these monopolies as to create an interlocking network of powerful corporation directors, each of whom sat on the boards of many other corporations. According to a Senate report of the early twentieth century, Morgan at his peak sat on the board of forty-eight corporations; Rockefeller, thirty-seven corporations.

Meanwhile, the government of the United States was behaving almost exactly as Karl Marx described a capitalist state: pretending neutrality to maintain order, but serving the interests of the rich. Not that the rich agreed among themselves; they had disputes over policies. But the purpose of the state was to settle upper-class disputes peacefully, control lower-class rebellion, and adopt policies that would further the long-range stability of the system. The arrangement between Democrats and Republicans to elect Rutherford Hayes in 1877 set the tone. Whether Democrats or Republicans won, national policy would not change in any important way.

When Grover Cleveland, a Democrat, ran for President in 1884, the general impression in the country was that he opposed the power of monopolies and corporations, and that the Republican party, whose candidate was James Blaine, stood for the wealthy. But when Cleveland defeated Blaine, Jay Gould wired him: "I feel . . . that the vast business interests of the country will be entirely safe in your hands." And he was right.

One of Cleveland's chief advisers was William Whitney, a millionaire and corporation lawyer, who married into the Standard Oil fortune and was appointed Secretary of the Navy by Cleveland. He immediately set about to create a "steel navy," buying the steel at artificially high prices from Carnegie's plants. Cleveland himself assured industrialists that his election should not frighten them: "No harm shall come to any business interest as the result of administrative policy so long as I am President . . . a transfer of executive control from one party to another does not mean any serious disturbance of existing conditions."

The presidential election itself had avoided real issues; there was no clear understanding of which interests would gain and which would lose if certain policies were adopted. It took the usual form of election campaigns, concealing the basic similarity of the parties by dwelling on personalities, gossip, trivialities. Henry Adams, an astute literary commentator on that era, wrote to a friend about the election:

> We are here plunged in politics funnier than words can express. Very great issues are involved. . . . But the amusing thing is that no one talks about real interests. By common consent they agree to let these alone. We are afraid to discuss them. Instead of this the press is engaged in a most amusing dispute whether Mr. Cleveland had an illegitimate child and did or did not live with more than one mistress.

In 1887, with a huge surplus in the treasury, Cleveland vetoed a bill appropriating $100,000 to give relief to Texas farmers to help them buy seed grain during a drought. He said: "Federal aid in such cases . . . encourages the expectation of paternal care on the part of the government and weakens the sturdiness of our national character." But that same year, Cleveland used his gold surplus to pay off wealthy bondholders at $28 above the $100 value of each bond—a gift of $45 million.

The chief reform of the Cleveland administration gives away the secret of reform legislation in America. The Interstate Commerce Act of 1887 was supposed to regulate the railroads on behalf of the consumers. But Richard Olney, a lawyer for the Boston & Maine and other railroads, and soon to be Cleveland's Attorney General, told railroad officials who complained about the Interstate Commerce Commission that it would not be wise to abolish the Commission "from a railroad point of view." He explained:

> The Commission . . . is or can be made, of great use to the railroads. It satisfies the popular clamor for a government supervision of railroads, at the same time that that supervision is almost entirely nominal. . . . The part of wisdom is not to destroy the Commission, but to utilize it.

Cleveland himself, in his 1887 State of the Union message, had made a similar point, adding a warning: "Opportunity for safe, careful, and deliberate reform is now offered; and none of us should be unmindful of a time when an abused and irritated people . . . may insist upon a radical and sweeping rectification of their wrongs."

Republican Benjamin Harrison, who succeeded Cleveland as President from 1889 to 1893, was described by Matthew Josephson, in his colorful study of the post-Civil War years, *The Politicos*: "Benjamin Harrison had the exclusive distinction of having served the railway corporations in the dual capacity of lawyer and soldier. He prosecuted the strikers [of 1877] in the federal courts . . . and he also organized and commanded a company of soldiers during the strike. . . ."

Harrison's term also saw a gesture toward reform. The Sherman Anti-Trust Act, passed in 1890, called itself "An Act to protect trade and commerce against unlawful restraints" and made it illegal to form a "combination or conspiracy" to restrain trade in interstate or foreign commerce. Senator John Sherman, author of the Act, explained the need to conciliate the critics of monopoly: "They had monopolies . . . of old, but never before such giants as in our day. You must heed their appeal or be ready for the socialist, the communist, the nihilist. Society is now disturbed by forces never felt before. . . ."

When Cleveland was elected President again in 1892, Andrew Carnegie, in Europe, received a letter from the manager of his steel plants, Henry Clay Frick: "I am very sorry for President Harrison, but I cannot see that our interests are going to be affected one way or the other by the change in administration." Cleveland, facing the agitation in the country caused by the panic and depression of 1893, used troops to break up "Coxey's Army," a demonstration of unemployed men who had come to Washington, and again to break up the national strike on the railroads the following year.

Meanwhile, the Supreme Court, despite its look of somber, black-robed fairness, was doing its bit for the ruling elite. How could it be independent, with its members chosen by the President and ratified by the Senate? How could it be neutral between rich and poor when its members were often former wealthy lawyers, and almost always came from the upper class? Early in the nineteenth century the Court laid the legal basis for a nationally regulated economy by establishing federal control over interstate commerce, and the legal basis for corporate capitalism by making the contract sacred.

In 1895 the Court interpreted the Sherman Act so as to make it harmless. It said a monopoly of sugar refining was a monopoly in manufacturing, not commerce, and so could not be regulated by Congress through the Sherman Act (*U.S. v. E. C. Knight Co.*). The Court also said the Sherman Act could be used against interstate strikes (the railway strike of 1894) because they were in restraint of trade. It also declared unconstitutional a small attempt by Congress to tax high incomes at a higher rate (*Pollock v. Farmers' Loan & Trust Company*). In later years it would refuse to break up the Standard Oil and American Tobacco monopolies, saying the Sherman Act barred only "unreasonable" combinations in restraint of trade.

A New York banker toasted the Supreme Court in 1895: "I give you, gentlemen, the Supreme Court of the United States—guardian of the dollar, defender of private property, enemy of spoliation, sheet anchor of the Republic."

Very soon after the Fourteenth Amendment became law, the Supreme Court began to demolish it as a protection for blacks, and to develop it as a protection for corporations. However, in 1877, a Supreme Court decision (*Munn v. Illinois*) approved state laws regulating the prices charged to farmers for the use of grain elevators. The grain elevator company argued it was a person being deprived of property, thus violating the Fourteenth Amendment's declaration "nor shall any State deprive any person of life, liberty, or property without due process of law." The Supreme Court disagreed, saying that grain elevators were not simply private property but were invested with "a public interest" and so could be regulated.

One year after that decision, the American Bar Association, organized by lawyers accustomed to serving the wealthy, began a national campaign of education to reverse the Court decision. Its presidents said, at different times: "If trusts are a defensive weapon of property interests against the communistic trend, they are desirable." And: "Monopoly is often a necessity and an advantage."

By 1886, they succeeded. State legislatures, under the pressure of aroused farmers, had passed laws to regulate the rates charged farmers by the railroads. The Supreme Court that year (*Wabash v. Illinois*) said states could not do this, that this was an intrusion on federal power. That year alone, the Court did away with 230 state laws that had been passed to regulate corporations.

By this time the Supreme Court had accepted the argument that corporations were "persons" and their money was property protected by the due process clause of the Fourteenth Amendment. Supposedly, the Amendment had been passed to protect Negro rights, but of the Fourteenth Amendment cases brought before the Supreme Court between 1890 and 1910, nineteen dealt with the Negro, 288 dealt with corporations.

The justices of the Supreme Court were not simply interpreters of the Constitution. They were men of certain backgrounds, of certain interests. One of them (Justice Samuel Miller) had said in 1875: "It is vain to contend with Judges who have been at the bar the advocates for forty years of railroad companies, and all forms of associated capital. . . ." In 1893, Supreme Court Justice David J. Brewer, addressing the New York State Bar Association, said:

> It is the unvarying law that the wealth of the community will be in the hands of the few. . . . The great majority of men are unwilling to endure that long self-denial and saving which makes accumulations possible . . . and hence it always has been, and until human nature is remodeled always will be true, that the wealth of a nation is in the hands of a few, while the many subsist upon the proceeds of their daily toil.

This was not just a whim of the 1880s and 1890s—it went back to the Founding Fathers, who had learned their law in the era of *Blackstone's Commentaries*, which said: "So great is the regard of the law for private property, that it will not authorize the least violation of it; no, not even for the common good of the whole community."

Control in modern times requires more than force, more than law. It requires that a population dangerously concentrated in cities and factories, whose lives are filled with cause for rebellion, be taught that all is right as it is. And so, the schools, the churches, the popular literature taught that to be rich was a sign of superiority, to be poor a sign of personal failure, and that the only way upward for a poor person was to climb into the ranks of the rich by extraordinary effort and extraordinary luck.

In those years after the Civil War, a man named Russell Conwell, a graduate of Yale Law School, a minister, and author of best-selling books, gave the same lecture, "Acres of Diamonds," more than five thousand times to audiences across the country, reaching several million people in all. His message was that anyone could get rich if he tried hard enough, that everywhere, if people looked closely enough, were "acres of diamonds." A sampling:

> I say that you ought to get rich, and it is your duty to get rich. . . . The men who get rich may be the most honest men you find in the community. Let me say here clearly . . . ninety-eight out of one hundred of the rich men of America are honest. That is why they are rich. That is why they are trusted with money. That is why they carry on great enterprises and find plenty of people to work with them. It is because they are honest men. . . .
>
> I sympathize with the poor, but the number of poor who are to be sympathized with is very small. To sympathize with a man whom God has punished for his sins . . . is to do wrong . . . let us remember there is not a poor person in the United States who was not made poor by his own shortcomings. . . .

Conwell was a founder of Temple University. Rockefeller was a donor to colleges all over the country and helped found the University of Chicago. Huntington, of the Central Pacific, gave money to two Negro colleges, Hampton Institute and Tuskegee Institute. Carnegie gave money to colleges and to libraries. Johns Hopkins was founded by a millionaire merchant, and millionaires Cornelius Vanderbilt, Ezra Cornell, James Duke, and Leland Stanford created universities in their own names.

The rich, giving part of their enormous earnings in this way, became known as philanthropists. These educational institutions did not encourage dissent; they trained the middlemen in the American system—the teachers, doctors, lawyers, administrators, engineers, technicians, politicians—those who would be paid to keep the system going, to be loyal buffers against trouble.

In the meantime, the spread of public school education enabled the learning of writing, reading, and arithmetic for a whole generation of workers, skilled and semiskilled, who would be the literate or force of the new industrial age. It was important that these people learn obedience to authority. A journalist observer of the schools in the 1890s wrote: "The unkindly spirit of the teacher is strikingly apparent; the pupils, being completely subjugated to her will, are silent and motionless, the spiritual atmosphere of the classroom is damp and chilly."

Back in 1859, the desire of mill owners in the town of Lowell that their workers be educated was explained by the secretary of the Massachusetts Board of Education:

> The owners of factories are more concerned than other classes and interests in the intelligence of their laborers. When the latter are well-educated and the former are disposed to deal justly, controversies and strikes can never occur, nor can the minds of the masses be prejudiced by demagogues and controlled by temporary and factious considerations.

Joel Spring, in his book *Education and the Rise of the Corporate State*, says: "The development of a factory-like system in the nineteenth-century schoolroom was not accidental."

This continued into the twentieth century, when William Bagley's *Classroom Management* became a standard teacher training text, reprinted thirty times. Bagley said: "One who studies educational theory aright can see in the mechanical routine of the classroom the educative forces that are slowly transforming the child from a little savage into a creature of law and order, fit for the life of civilized society."

It was in the middle and late nineteenth century that high schools developed as aids to the industrial system, that history was widely required in the curriculum to foster patriotism. Loyalty oaths, teacher certification, and the requirement of citizenship were introduced to control both the educational and the political quality of teachers. Also, in the latter part of the century, school officials—not teachers—were given control over textbooks. Laws passed by the states barred certain kinds of textbooks. Idaho and Montana, for instance, forbade textbooks propagating "political" doctrines, and the Dakota territory ruled that school libraries could not have "partisan political pamphlets or books."

Against this gigantic organization of knowledge and education for orthodoxy and obedience, there arose a literature of dissent and protest, which had to make its way from reader to reader against great obstacles. Henry George, a self-educated workingman from a poor Philadelphia family, who became a newspaperman and an economist, wrote a book that was published in 1879 and sold millions of copies, not only in the United States, but all over the world. His book *Progress and Poverty* argued that the basis of wealth was land, that this was becoming monopolized, and that a single tax on land, abolishing all others, would bring enough revenue to solve the problem of poverty and equalize wealth in the nation. Readers may not have been persuaded of his solutions, but they could see in their own lives the accuracy of his observations:

> It is true that wealth has been greatly increased, and that the average of comfort, leisure and refinement has been raised; but these gains are not general. In them the lowest class do not share. . . . This association of poverty with progress is the great enigma of our times. . . . There is a vague but general feeling of disappointment; an increased bitterness among the working classes; a widespread feeling of unrest and brooding revolution. . . . The civilized world is trembling on the verge of a great movement. Either it must be a leap upward, which will open the way to advances yet undreamed of, or it must he a plunge downward which will carry us back toward barbarism. . . .

A different kind of challenge to the economic and social system was given by Edward Bellamy, a lawyer and writer from western Massachusetts, who wrote, in simple, intriguing language, a novel called *Looking Backward*, in which the author fells asleep and wakes up in the year 2000, to find a socialistic society in which people work and live cooperatively. *Looking Backward,* which described socialism vividly, lovingly, sold a million copies in a few years, and over a hundred groups were organized around the country to try to make the dream come true.

It seemed that despite the strenuous efforts of government, business, the church, the schools, to control their thinking, millions of Americans were ready to consider harsh criticism of the existing system, to contemplate other possible ways of living. They were helped in this by the great movements of workers and farmers that swept the country in the 1880s and 1890s. These movements went beyond the scattered strikes and tenants' struggles of the period 1830–1877. . . . They were nationwide movements, more threatening than before to the ruling elite, more dangerously suggestive. It was a time when revolutionary organizations existed in major American cities, and revolutionary talk was in the air.

John S. Gordon

Was There Ever Such a Business!

The industrial empires that were created by the robber barons appeared more and more threatening in their economic power as they merged into ever-larger companies. In the latter half of the 1890s, this trend toward consolidation accelerated. In 1897 there were 69 corporate mergers; in 1898 there were 303; the next year 1,208. Of the seventy-three "trusts" with capitalization of more than $10 million in 1900, two-thirds had been created in the previous three years.

In 1901 J. P. Morgan created the largest company of all, U.S. Steel, merging Andrew Carnegie's empire with several other steel companies to form a new company capitalized at $1.4 billion. The revenues of the federal government that year were a mere $586 million. The sheer size of the enterprise stunned the world. Even the *Wall Street Journal* confessed to "uneasiness over the magnitude of the affair," and wondered if the new corporation would mark "the high tide of industrial capitalism." A joke made the rounds where a teacher asks a little boy about who made the world. "God made the world in 4004 B.C.," he replied, "and it was reorganized in 1901 by J. P. Morgan."

But when Theodore Roosevelt entered the White House in September 1901, the laiseez-faire attitude of the federal government began to change. In 1904 the government announced that it would sue under the Sherman Antitrust Act—long thought a dead letter—to break up a new Morgan consolidation, the Northern Securities Corporation. Morgan hurried to Washington to get the matter straightened out.

"If we have done anything wrong," Morgan told the president, fully encapsulating his idea of how the commercial world should work, "send your man to my man and they can fix it up."

"That can't be done," Roosevelt replied.

"We don't want to fix it up," his attorney general, Philander Knox, explained. "We want to stop it."

From that point on, the federal government would be an active referee in the marketplace, trying—not always successfully, to be sure—to balance the needs of efficiency and economies of scale against the threat of overweening power in organizations that owed allegiance only to their stockholders, not to society as a whole.

In 1907 the federal government took on the biggest "trust" of all, Standard Oil. The case reached the Supreme Court in 1910 and was decided the following year, when the Court ruled unanimously that Standard Oil was a combination in restraint of trade. It ordered Standard Oil broken up into more than thirty separate companies.

The liberal wing of American politics hailed the decision, needless to say, but in one of the great ironies of American economic history, the effect of the ruling on the greatest fortune in the world was only to increase it. In the two years after the breakup of Standard Oil, the stock in the successor companies doubled in value, making John D. Rockefeller twice as rich as he had been before.

Nothing so epitomized the economy of the late nineteenth-century Western world as steel. Its production became the measure of a country's industrial power, and its uses were almost without limit. Its influence in other sectors of the economy, such as railroads and real estate, was immense. But steel was hardly an invention of the time. Indeed, it has been around for at least three thousand years. What was new was the cost of producing it.

Pig iron, the first step in iron and steel production, is converted into bar iron by remelting it and mixing it with ground limestone to remove still more impurities. Cast iron is then created by pouring this into molds, producing such items as frying pans, cookstoves, and construction members. Cast iron was widely used in urban construction in the antebellum period, but it had serious drawbacks. Extremely strong in compression, cast iron makes excellent columns. But, because it is very brittle, it is weak in tension, making it unsuitable for beams. For them, wrought iron was needed.

Wrought iron is made by melting pig iron and stirring it repeatedly until it achieves a pasty consistency and most of the impurities have been volatilized. The laborers who worked these furnaces were known as puddlers and were both highly skilled and highly paid. After the metal is removed from the puddling furnace, it is subjected to pressure and rolled and folded over and over—in effect, it is kneaded like bread dough—until it develops the fibrous quality that makes wrought iron much less brittle than cast iron and thus moderately strong in tension. Wrought iron is quite soft compared to cast iron but it is also ductile, able to be drawn out and hammered into various shapes, just as copper can be.

Wrought iron, of course, was much more expensive to produce than cast iron but could be used for making beams, bridges, ships, and, most important to the nineteenth-century economy after 1830, railroad rails. The Industrial Revolution simply could not have moved into high gear without large quantities of wrought iron.

Steel, which is iron alloyed with just the right amount of carbon under suitable conditions, has the good qualities of both cast and wrought iron. It is extremely strong and hard, like cast iron, while it is also malleable and withstands shock like wrought iron. And it is far stronger in tension than either, and thus makes a superb building material.

But until the mid-nineteenth century, the only way to make steel was in small batches from wrought iron, mixing the iron with carbon and heating it for a period of days. Thus its use was limited to very high-value items such as sword blades, razors, and tools, where its ability to withstand shock and take and hold a sharp edge justified its high cost. At mid-century, roughly 250,000 tons of steel were being made by the old methods in Europe, and only about 10,000 tons in the United States.

Then, in 1856, an Englishman named Henry Bessemer (later Sir Henry) invented the Bessemer converter, which allowed steel to be made directly and quickly from pig iron. As so often happens in the history of technological development, the initial insight was the result of an accidental observation. Bessemer had developed a new type of artillery shell, but the cast-iron cannons of the day were not strong enough to handle it. He began experimenting in hopes of developing a stronger metal, and one day a gust of wind happened to hit some molten iron. The oxygen in the air, combining with the iron and carbon in the molten metal, raised the temperature of the metal and volatilized the impurities. Most of the carbon was driven off. What was left was steel.

Bessemer, realizing what had happened, immediately set about designing an industrial process that would duplicate what he had observed accidentally. His converter was a large vessel, about ten feet wide by twenty feet high, with trunnions so that its contents could be poured. It was made of steel and lined with firebrick. At the bottom, air could be blasted through holes in the firebrick into the "charge," as the mass of molten metal in the crucible was called, converting it to steel in a stupendous blast of flame and heat. With the Bessemer converter, ten to thirty tons of pig iron could be turned into steel every twelve to fifteen minutes in what is one of the most spectacular of all industrial processes.

The labor activist John A. Fitch wrote in 1910 that "there is a glamor about the making of steel. The very size of things—the immensity of the tools, the scale of production—grips the mind with an overwhelming sense of power. Blast furnaces, eighty, ninety, one hundred feet tall, gaunt and insatiable, are continually gaping to admit ton after ton of ore, fuel, and stone. Bessemer converters dazzle the eye with their leaping flames. Steel ingots at white heat, weighing thousands of pounds, are carried from place to place and tossed about like toys. . . . [C]ranes pick up steel rails or fifty-foot girders as jauntily as if their tons were ounces. These are the things that cast a spell over the visitor in these workshops of Vulcan."

One of the visitors to Henry Bessemer's steelworks in Sheffield, England, in 1872, was a young Scottish immigrant to America, Andrew Carnegie. He was mightily impressed—so impressed, in fact, that in the next thirty years he would ride the growing demand for steel to one of the greatest American fortunes.

Carnegie had been born in Dunfermline, a few miles northwest and across the Firth of Forth from Edinburgh, in 1835. His father was a hand weaver who owned his own loom, on which he made intricately patterned damask cloth. Dunfermline was a center of the damask trade, and skilled weavers such as William Carnegie could make a good living at it.

But the Industrial Revolution destroyed William Carnegie's livelihood. By the 1840s power looms could produce cloth such as damask much more cheaply than handlooms. While there had been 84,560 handloom weavers in Scotland in 1840, there would be only 25,000 ten years later. William Carnegie would not be one of them.

The elder Carnegie sank into despair, and his far tougher-minded wife took charge of the crisis. She had gotten a letter from her sister, who had immigrated to America, settling in Pittsburgh. "This country's far better for the working man," her sister wrote, "than the old one, & there is room enough & to spare, notwithstanding the thousands that flock to her borders." In 1847, when Andrew was twelve, the Carnegie family moved to Pittsburgh.

The Carnegies were in the first wave of one of the great movements of people in human history, known as the Atlantic migration. At first most of the immigrants came from the British Isles, especially Ireland after the onset of the Great Famine of the 1840s. Later Germany, Italy, and Eastern Europe provided immigrants in huge numbers, more than two million in 1900 alone.

In its size and significance the Atlantic migration was the equal of the barbarian movements in late classic times that helped bring the Roman Empire to an end. But while many of the barbarian tribes had been pushed by those behind them, the more than thirty million people who crossed the Atlantic to settle in America between 1820 and 1914 were largely pulled by the lure of economic opportunity.

Many, such as the land-starved Scandinavians who settled in the Upper Middle West, moved to rural areas and established farms. But most, at least at first, settled in the country's burgeoning cities, in the fast-spreading districts that came to be called slums (a word that came into use, in both Britain and America, about 1825). For the first time in American history, a substantial portion of the population was poor. But most of the new urban poor were not poor for long.

These slums, by modern standards, were terrible almost beyond imagination, with crime- and vermin-ridden, sunless apartments that often housed several people, sometimes several families, to a room and had only communal privies behind the buildings. In the 1900 census, when conditions in the slums had much improved from mid-century, one district in New York's Lower East Side had a population of more than fifty thousand but only about five hundred bathtubs.

Such housing, however, was no worse—and often better—than what the impoverished immigrants left behind in Europe, and as Mrs. Carnegie's sister—and millions like her—reported back home, the economic opportunities were far greater. The labor shortage so characteristic of the American economy since its earliest days had not abated. So the average stay for an immigrant family in the worst of the slums was less than fifteen years, before they were able to move to better housing in better neighborhoods and begin the climb into the American middle class.

The migration of people to the United States in search of economic opportunity has never ceased, although legal limits were placed on it beginning in the early 1920s. And this vast migration did far more than help provide the labor needed to power the American economy. It has given the United States the most ethnically diverse population of any country in the world. And because of that, it has provided the country with close personal connections with nearly every other country on the globe, an immense economic and political advantage.

The Carnegies moved into two rooms above a workshop that faced a muddy alleyway behind Mrs. Carnegie's sister's house in Allegheny City, a neighborhood of Pittsburgh. Mrs. Carnegie found work making shoes, and Mr. Carnegie worked in a cotton mill. Andrew got a job there as well, as a bobbin boy earning $1.20 a week for twelve-hour days, six days a week.

Needless to say, it didn't take the bright and ambitious Andrew Carnegie fifteen years to start up the ladder. By 1849 he had a job as a telegraph messenger boy, earning $2.50 a week. This gave him many opportunities to become familiar with Pittsburgh and its business establishment, and Carnegie made the most of them. Soon he was an operator, working the telegraph himself and able to interpret it by ear, writing down the messages directly. His salary was up to $25 a month.

In 1853, in a classic example of Louis Pasteur's dictum that chance favors the prepared mind, Thomas A. Scott, general superintendent of the Pennsylvania Railroad, a frequent visitor to the telegraph office where Carnegie worked, needed a telegraph operator of his own to help with the system being installed by the railroad. He chose Carnegie, not yet eighteen years old. By the time Carnegie was thirty-three, in 1868, he had an annual income of $50,000, thanks to the tutelage of Thomas Scott and numerous shrewd investments in railway sleeping cars, oil, telegraph lines, and iron manufacturing. But after his visit to Bessemer's works in Sheffield, he decided to concentrate on steel.

⋅❦⋅

It had been pure chance that had brought the Carnegie family to Pittsburgh, but its comparative advantages would make it the center of the American steel industry.

Set where the Allegheny and Monongahela rivers join to form the Ohio and provide easy transportation over a wide area, Pittsburgh had been founded, as so many cities west of the mountains were, as a trading post. Shortly after the Revolution, Pittsburgh began to exploit the abundant nearby sources of both iron ore and coal and specialize in manufacturing. While the rest of the country still relied on wood, coal became the dominant fuel in Pittsburgh, powering factories that were turning out glass, iron, and other energy-intensive products. As early as 1817, when the population was still only six thousand, there were 250 factories in operation, and the nascent city, with already typical American boosterism, was calling itself the "Birmingham of America." Because of the cheap coal, Pittsburgh exploited the steam engine long before it began to displace water power elsewhere, and most of its factories were steam-powered by 1830.

There was, however, a price to be paid for the cheap coal, which produces far more smoke than does wood. About 1820, when Pittsburgh was still a relatively small town, a visitor wrote that the smoke formed "a cloud which almost amounts to night and overspreads Pittsburgh with the appearance of gloom and melancholy." By the 1860s even Anthony Trollope, London-born and no stranger to coal smoke, was impressed with the pall. Looked down on from the surrounding hills, Trollope reported, some of the tops of the churches could be seen, "But the city itself is buried in a dense cloud. I was never more in love with smoke and dirt than when I stood here and watched the darkness of night close in upon the floating soot which hovered over the house-tops of the city." As the Industrial Revolution gathered strength, other American cities became polluted with coal smoke and soot, but none so badly as Pittsburgh.

The most important coal beds in the Pittsburgh area were those surrounding the town of Connellsville, about thirty miles southeast of the city. What made Connellsville coal special was that it was nearly perfect for converting into coke. Indeed it is the best coking coal in the world.

Coke is to coal exactly what charcoal is to wood: heated in the absence of air to drive off the impurities, it becomes pure carbon and burns at an even and easily adjusted temperature. And either charcoal or coke is indispensable to iron and steel production. As the iron industry in Pittsburgh grew, it turned more and more to coke, the production of which was far more easily industrialized than was charcoal.

By the time Andrew Carnegie was moving into steel, Henry Clay Frick, who had been born in West Overton, Pennsylvania, not far from Connellsville, in 1849, was moving into coke. Like Carnegie, Frick was a very hardheaded businessman and willing to take big risks for big rewards. And like Carnegie, he was a millionaire by the time he was thirty. Unlike Carnegie, however, he had little concern with public opinion or the great social issues of the day. Carnegie always wanted to be loved and admired by society at large. Frick was perfectly willing to settle for its respect. Unlike Carnegie, he rarely granted newspaper interviews and never wrote articles for publication.

By the 1880s the Carnegie Steel Company and the H. C. Frick Company dominated their respective industries, and Carnegie was by far Frick's biggest customer. In late 1881, while Frick was on his honeymoon in New York, Carnegie, who loved surprises, suddenly proposed a merger of their companies at a family lunch one day. Frick, who had no inkling the proposal was coming, was stunned. So was Carnegie's ever-vigilant mother, now in her seventies. The silence that ensued was finally broken by what is perhaps the most famous instance of maternal concern in American business history.

"Ah, Andra," said Mrs. Carnegie in her broad Scots accent, "that's a very fine thing for Mr. Freek. But what do we get out of it?"

Needless to say, Carnegie had calculated closely what he would get out of it. First, the Carnegie Steel Company would get guaranteed supplies of coke at the best possible price; second, he would get the surpassing executive skills of Henry Clay Frick; and third, he would further the vertical integration of the steel industry in general and his company in particular.

Vertical integration simply means bringing under one corporation's control part or all of the stream of production from raw materials to distribution. It had been going on since the dawn of the Industrial Revolution (Francis Cabot Lowell had been the first to integrate spinning and weaving in a single building) but greatly accelerated in the last quarter of the nineteenth century as industrialists sought economies of scale as well as of speed to cut costs.

Carnegie and Frick shared a simple management philosophy: (1) Innovate constantly and invest heavily in the latest equipment and techniques to drive down operating costs. (2) Always be the low-cost producer so as to remain profitable in bad economic times. (3) Retain most of the profits in good times to take advantage of opportunities in bad times as less efficient competitors fail.

One such opportunity arose in 1889, by which time Frick was chairman of the Carnegie steel companies (Carnegie himself never held an executive position in the companies he controlled, but as the holder of a comfortable majority of the stock, he was always the man in charge). That year Frick snapped up the troubled Duquesne Steel Works, paying for it with $1 million in Carnegie company bonds due to mature in five years. By the time the bonds were paid off, the plant had paid for itself five times over.

Much of the technological advances that Carnegie was so quick to use came from Europe's older and more established steel industries, just as, nearly a century earlier, the American cloth industry had piggybacked on Britain's technological lead. As one of Carnegie's principal lieutenants, Captain W. M. Jones, explained to the British Iron and Steel Institute as early as 1881, "While your metallurgists as well as those of France and Germany, have been devoting their time and talents to the discovery of new processes, we have swallowed the information so generously tendered through the printed reports of the Institute, and we have selfishly devoted ourselves to beating you in output."

And beat them they did. In 1867 only 1,643 tons of Bessemer steel was produced in the United States. Thirty years later, in 1897, the tonnage produced was 7,156,957, more than Britain and Germany combined. By the turn of the century the Carnegie Steel Company alone would outproduce Britain. It would also be immensely profitable. In 1899 the Carnegie Steel Company, the low-cost producer in the prosperous and heavily protected American market, made $21 million in profit. The following year profits doubled. No wonder Andrew Carnegie exclaimed at one point, "Was there ever such a business!"

And steel was also transforming the American urban landscape. When stone was the principal construction material of large buildings, they could not rise much above six stories, even after the elevator was perfected in the 1850s, because of the necessary thickness of the walls. It was church steeples that rose above their neighbors and punctuated the urban skyline. But as the price of steel declined steadily as the industry's efficiency rose—by the 1880s the far longer-lasting steel railroad rails cost less than the old wrought-iron rails—more and more buildings were built with steel skeletons and could soar to the sky. Between the 1880s and 1913 the record height for buildings was broken as often as every year as "skyscrapers" came to dominate American urban skylines in an awesome display of the power of steel. . . .

While the late-nineteenth-century American economy was increasingly built by and with steel, it was increasingly fueled by oil. In 1859, the year Edwin Drake drilled the first well, American production amounted to only 2,000 barrels. Ten years later it was 4.25 million and by 1900, American production would be nearly 60 million barrels. But while production rose steadily, the price of oil was chaotic, sinking as low as 10 cents a barrel—far below the cost of the barrel itself—and soaring as high as $13.75 during the 1860s. One reason for this was the vast number of refineries then in existence. Cleveland alone had more than thirty, many of them nickel-and-dime, ramshackle operations.

Many people, while happy to exploit the new oil business, were unwilling to make large financial commitments to it for fear that the oil would suddenly dry up. The field in northwestern Pennsylvania was very nearly the only one in the world until the 1870s, when the Baku field in what was then southern Russia opened up. There would be no major new field in the United States until the fabulous Spindletop field in Texas was first tapped in 1902.

But a firm named Rockefeller, Flagler, and Andrews, formed to exploit the burgeoning market for petroleum products, especially kerosene, took the gamble of building top-quality refineries. Like Carnegie, it intended to exploit being the low-cost producer, with all the advantages of that position. The firm also began buying up other refineries as the opportunity presented itself.

The firm realized that there was no controlling the price of crude oil but that it could control, at least partly, another important input into the price of petroleum products: transportation. It began negotiating aggressively with the railroads to give the firm rebates in return for guaranteeing high levels of traffic. It was this arrangement that often allowed the firm to undersell its competitors and still make handsome profits, further strengthening the firm's already formidable competitive position.

In 1870 one of the partners, Henry Flagler, convinced the others to change the firm from a partnership to a corporation, which would make it easier for the partners to continue to raise capital to finance their relentless expansion while retaining control. The new corporation, named Standard Oil, was capitalized at $1 million and owned at that time about 10 percent of the country's oil refining capacity. By 1880 it would control 80 percent of a much larger industry.

The expansion of Standard Oil became one of the iconic stories of late-nineteenth-century America, as its stockholders became rich beyond imagination and its influence in the American economy spread ever wider. Indeed, the media reaction to Standard Oil and John D. Rockefeller in the Gilded Age is strikingly similar to the reaction to the triumph of Microsoft and Bill Gates a hundred years later. It is perhaps a coincidence that Rockefeller and Gates were just about the same age, their early forties, when they became household names and the living symbols of a new and, to some, threatening economic structure.

The image of Standard Oil that remains even today in the American folk memory was the product of a number of writers and editorial cartoonists who often had a political agenda to advance first and foremost. The most brilliant of these was Ida Tarbell, whose *History of the Standard Oil Company,* first published in *McClure's* magazine in 1902, vividly depicted a company ruthlessly expanding over the corporate bodies of its competitors, whose assets it gobbled up as it went.

That is by no means a wholly false picture, but it is a somewhat misleading one. For one thing, as the grip of Standard Oil relentlessly tightened on the oil industry, prices for petroleum products *declined* steadily, dropping by two-thirds over the course of the last three decades of the nineteenth century. It is simply a myth that monopolies will raise prices once they have the power to do so. Monopolies, like everyone else, want to maximize their profits, not their prices. Lower prices, which increase demand, and increased efficiency, which cuts costs, is usually the best way to achieve the highest possible profits. What makes monopolies (and most of them today are government agencies, from motor vehicle bureaus to public schools) so economically evil is the fact that, without competitive pressure, they become highly risk-aversive—and therefore shy away from innovation—and notably indifferent to their customers' convenience.

Further, Standard Oil used its position as the country's largest refiner not only to extract the largest rebates from the railroads but also to induce them to deny rebates to refiners that Standard Oil wanted to acquire. It even sometimes forced railroads to give it secret rebates not only on its own oil, but on that shipped by its competitors as well, essentially a tax on competing with Standard Oil. (This is about as close as the "robber barons" ever came to behaving like, well, robber barons.) It thus effectively presented these refiners with Hobson's choice: they could agree to be acquired, at a price set by Standard Oil, or they could be driven into bankruptcy by high transportation costs.

The acquisition price set, however, was a fair one, arrived at by a formula developed by Henry Flagler, and consistently applied. Sometimes, especially if the owners of the refinery being acquired had executive talents that Standard wished to make use of, the price was a generous one. Further, the seller had the choice of receiving cash or Standard Oil stock. Those who chose the latter—and there were hundreds—became millionaires as they rode the stock of the Standard Oil Company to capitalist glory. Those who took the cash often ended up whining to Ida Tarbell.

None of this, of course, was illegal, and that was the real problem. In the late nineteenth century people such as Rockefeller, Flagler, Carnegie, and J. P. Morgan were creating at a breathtaking pace the modern corporate economy, and thus a wholly new economic universe. They were moving far faster than society could fashion, through the usually slow-moving political process, the rules needed to govern that new universe wisely and fairly. But that must always be the case in democratic capitalism, as individuals can always act far faster than can society as a whole. Until the rules were written—largely in the first decades of the twentieth century—it was a matter of (in the words of Sir Walter Scott)

> *The good old rule, the simple plan*
> *That they should take who have the power*
> *And they should keep who can.*

Part of the problem is that there is a large, inherent inertia in any political system, and democracy is no exception. Politicians, after all, are in the reelection business, and it is often easier to do nothing than to offend one group or another. So while the American economy had changed profoundly since the mid-nineteenth century, the state incorporation laws, for instance, had not. As an Ohio corporation, Standard Oil was not allowed to own property in other states or to hold the stock of other corporations. As it quickly expanded throughout the Northeast, the country, and then across the globe, however, Standard Oil necessarily acquired property in other states and purchased other corporations.

The incorporation laws, largely written in an era before the railroads and telegraph had made a national economy possible, were no longer adequate to meet the needs of the new economy. To get around the outdated law, Henry Flager, as secretary of Standard Oil, had himself appointed as trustee to hold the property or stock that Standard Oil itself could not legally own. By the end of the 1870s, however, Standard owned dozens of properties and companies in other states, each, in theory, held by a trustee who was in some cases Flagler and in other cases other people. It was a hopelessly unwieldy corporate structure.

In all probability, it was Flagler—a superb executive—who found the solution. Instead of each subsidiary company having a single trustee, with these trustees scattered throughout the Standard Oil empire, the same three men, all at the Cleveland headquarters, were appointed trustees for all the subsidiary companies. In theory, they controlled all of Standard Oil's assets outside Ohio. In fact, of course, they did exactly what they were told.

Thus was born the business trust, a form that was quickly imitated by other companies that were becoming national in scope. The "trusts" would be one of the great bogeymen of American politics for the next hundred years, but, ironically, the actual trust form of organization devised by Henry Flagler lasted only until 1889. That year New Jersey—seeking a source of new tax revenue—became the first state to modernize its incorporation laws and bring them into conformity with the new economic realities. New Jersey now permitted holding companies and interstate activities, and companies flocked to incorporate there, as, later, they would flock to Delaware, to enjoy the benefits of a corporation-friendly legal climate. Standard Oil of New Jersey quickly became the center of the Rockefeller interests, and the Standard Oil Trust, in the legal sense, disappeared.

⋗⟨◉⟩⋖

With the growth of American industry, the nature of American foreign trade changed drastically. The United States remained, as it remains today, a formidable exporter of agricultural and mineral products. Two new ones were even added in the post-Civil War era: petroleum and copper. But it also became a major exporter of manufactured goods that it had previously imported. In 1865 they had constituted only 22.78 percent of American exports. By the turn of the twentieth century they were 31.65 percent of a vastly larger trade. The percentage of world trade, meanwhile, that was American in origin doubled in these years to about 12 percent of total trade.

Nowhere was this more noticeable than in iron and steel products, the cutting edge of late-nineteenth-century technology. Before the Civil War the United States exported only $6 million worth of iron and steel manufactures a year. In 1900 it exported $121,914,000 worth of locomotives, engines, rails, electrical machinery, wire, pipes, metalworking machinery, boilers, and other goods. Even sewing machines and typewriters were being exported in quantity. . . .

This country has never developed an aristocracy, because the concept of primogeniture, with the eldest son inheriting the bulk of the fortune, never took hold. Thus great fortunes have always been quickly dispersed among heirs in only a few generations. The American super rich are therefore always nouveau riche and often act accordingly, giving new meaning in each generation to the phrase *conspicuous consumption*. In the Gilded Age, they married European titles, built vast summer cottages and winter retreats that cost millions but were occupied only a few weeks a year. . . .

EXPLORING THE ISSUE

Were the Nineteenth-Century Entrepreneurs "Robber Barons"?

Critical Thinking and Reflections

1. Howard Zinn has been called a Marxist historian. What does this mean? How does his interpretation of the political and economic dynamics of nineteenth-century America fit a Marxist interpretation?

2. What is a "robber baron"? Describe and critically analyze Zinn's description of the monopolistic practices of the American businessmen John D. Rockefeller, J. P. Morgan, and Andrew Carnegie. Critically analyze how Zinn argues that the political system, religion, and education supported the monopolistic practices of the business elite.

3. Define vertical integration. Define horizontal integration. Explain how Rockefeller vertically integrated the oil industry. Explain how Carnegie integrated the steel industry.

4. What is more important in a successful business—organization or entrepreneurship? Critically discuss, using Rockefeller and Carnegie as examples.

5. Compare and contrast and critically evaluate the interpretations of Zinn and Gordon toward the nineteenth-century men of big business. Were they "robber barons" or "industrial statesmen"? Is it possible to reconcile the two viewpoints? Does Zinn provide enough evidence that the political, economic, judicial, and social climate of opinion was stacked against the worker? Critically discuss.

Is There Common Ground?

Questions concerning the characterization of late-nineteenth century entrepreneurs seldom fail to elicit strong student reaction. On one hand, Zinn draws upon the Josephson antibusiness tradition of the 1930s and his own New Left radical outlook of the 1960s and 1970s, which blamed business for the racism, poverty, and militarism, which infected American society. On the other hand, John Steele Gordon emphasizes the technological benefits in lifestyle—better homes, heating, food, automobiles—that the nineteenth-century industrial statesmen brought to the United States. Who is more persuasive—Zinn or Gordon? Critics have faulted Zinn's interpretation as too one-sided and lacking an appreciation for the divisions between small and large businessmen and small and large farmers or the pressures put upon Congress, the Justice Department that staffed the Antitrust Division in charge of enforcing the Sherman Act, and the members of the Interstate Commerce Commission who were supposed to regulate the railroads. Critics of the entrepreneurial statesmen point of view have challenged Gordon's rosy picture of development and questioned whether management paid workers a living wage and provided a clean and safe working environment at the same time they produced a creative and dynamic economy. Could a nation of pre-1880s small entrepreneurs competing with each other have produced the consumer-oriented society with its munificent lifestyle enjoyed by middle-class and upper-class Americans? Is monopoly or managed or mismanaged capitalism the best system?

Additional Resources

Discussions of the competing interpretations regarding late-nineteenth century entrepreneurs can be followed in "Should History Be Rewritten? A Debate Between Allan Nevins and Matthew Josephson," *Saturday Review* (February 6, 1954, pp. 7–10, 44–49); Hal Bridges, "The Robber Baron Concept in American History," *Business History Review* (vol. 32, Spring 1958, pp. 1–13); and Maury Klein's critique of Josephson, "A Robber Historian," *Forbes* (October 26, 1987). Biographies of the titans of industry remain popular with the general public, and the authors are typically sympathetic to their subjects. See Joseph Frazier Wall, *Andrew Carnegie* (New York, 1970); Harold C. Livesay, *American Made: Men Who Shaped the American Economy* (Little, Brown & Co., Boston, 1986) and *Andrew Carnegie and the Rise of Big Business* (Library of American Biography, Boston, 1975, 1990); James T. Baker, *Andrew Carnegie: Robber Baron as Hero* (Wadsworth, Thompson Learning, 2003); Ron Chernow, *Titan: The Life of John D. Rockefeller, Sr.* (Random House, 1998); Jean Strouse, *Morgan: American Financier* (HarperCollins, New York, 1999); and Robert Sobel and David B. Sicilia, *The Entrepreneurs: An American Adventure* (Houghton Mifflin, Boston, 1986).

Labor historian Steve Fraser offers a critical review of T.J. Stiles, *The First Tycoon* (Knopf, 2009) in "The Misunderstood Robber Baron," *The Nation* (November 30, 2009). If Cornelius Vanderbilt, builder of the Erie Railroad, was lionized as a great entrepreneur, Fraser asks, how much concern did he show for the thousands of workers who were killed building the railroad because they worked excessively long hours for paltry wages? See also the exchange between Stiles and Fraser in letters to the editor, *The Nation* (December 14, 2009).

For a very detailed and sophisticated article useful for history majors with a business emphasis, see Naomi R. Lamoreaux, Daniel M. G. Raff, and Peter Temin, "Beyond Markets and Hierarchies: Toward a New Synthesis of Business History," *American Historical Review* (April 2003, pp. 404–433). The authors argue that some of Chandler's vertically integrated corporations lost control of their markets in the 1980s and, therefore, more flexible frameworks need to be developed to explain current and past behaviors of corporations.

ISSUE 4

Were American Workers in the Gilded Age Conservative Capitalists?

YES: Carl N. Degler, from *Out of Our Past,* 3rd ed. (Harper & Row, 1984)

NO: Herbert G. Gutman, from *Work, Culture, and Society in Industrializing America* (Alfred A. Knopf, 1976)

Learning Outcomes

After reading this issue, you should be able to:

- Understand why the organizational changes brought about by big business marked a radical transformation of capitalism.
- Understand that workers formed unions to adjust to the changes brought about by big business.
- Understand that American factory workers—whether union or nonunion—tried to humanize the system and control the work environment in the years from the 1840s to the depression of 1893.
- Understand why the United States never developed a full-fledged socialist movement.

ISSUE SUMMARY

YES: Historian Carl N. Degler maintains that the American labor movement accepted capitalism and reacted conservatively to the radical organizational changes brought about in the economic system by big business.

NO: Professor of history Herbert G. Gutman argues that from 1843 to 1893, American factory workers attempted to humanize the system through the maintenance of their traditional, artisan, and preindustrial work habits.

The two major labor unions that developed in the late nineteenth century were the Knights of Labor and the American Federation of Labor (AFL). Because of the hostility toward labor unions, the Knights of Labor functioned for 12 years as a secret organization. Between 1879 and 1886 the strength of Knights of Labor grew from 10,000 to 700,000 members. Idealistic in many of its aims, the union supported social reforms such as equal pay for men and women, the prohibition of alcohol, and the abolition of convict and child labor. Economic reforms included the development of workers' cooperatives, public ownership of utilities, and a more moderate, eight-hour workday. The Knights declined after 1886 for several reasons. Although it was opposed to strikes, the union received a black eye (as did the whole labor movement) when it was blamed for the bombs that were thrown at the police during the 1886 Haymarket Square riot in Chicago. According to most historians, other reasons that are usually associated with the decline of the Knights include the failure of some cooperative businesses, conflict between skilled and unskilled workers, and, most important, competition from the AFL. By 1890, the Knights' membership had dropped to 100,000. It died in 1917.

A number of skilled unions got together in 1896 and formed the AFL. Samuel Gompers was elected its first president, and his philosophy permeated the AFL during his 37 years in office. He pushed for practical reforms—better hours, wages, and working conditions. Unlike the Knights, the AFL avoided associations with political parties, workers' cooperatives, unskilled workers, immigrants, and women. Decision-making power was in the hands of locals rather than the central board. Gompers was heavily criticized by his contemporaries, and later by historians, for his narrow craft unionism. But despite the depression of the 1890s, membership increased from 190,000 to 500,000 by 1900, to 1,500,000 by 1904, and to 2,000,000 by the eve of World War I.

Gompers's cautiousness is best understood in the context of his times. The national and local governments were in the hands of men who were sympathetic to the rise of big business and hostile to the attempts of labor to organize. Whether it was the railroad strike of 1877, the Homestead steel strike of 1892, or the Pullman car strike of 1894, the pattern of repression was always the same. Companies would cut wages, workers would go out on strike, scab workers would be brought in, fights would break out, companies would receive court injunctions, and the police and state and federal militia would beat up the unionized workers. After a strike was broken, workers would lose their jobs or would accept pay cuts and longer workdays.

On the national level, Theodore Roosevelt became the first president to show any sympathy for the workers. As a police commissioner in New York City and later as governor of New York, Roosevelt observed firsthand the deplorable occupational and living conditions of the workers. Although he avoided recognition of the collective bargaining rights of labor unions, Roosevelt forced the anthracite coal owners in Pennsylvania to mediate before an arbitration board for an equitable settlement of a strike with the mine workers.

In 1905 a coalition of socialists and industrial unionists formed America's most radical labor union: the Industrial Workers of the World (IWW).

There were frequent splits within this union and much talk of violence. But in practice, the IWW was more interested in organizing unskilled workers into industrial unions than in fighting, as were the earlier Knights of Labor and the late Congress of Industrial Organizations. Strikes were encouraged to improve the daily conditions of the workers through long-range goals, which included reducing the power of the capitalists by increasing the power of the workers.

For the past 35 years historians have been studying the social and cultural environment of the American working class. The approach is modeled after Edward P. Thompson's highly influential and sophisticated Marxist analysis (*The Making of the English Working Class* (Vintage Books, 1966)), which is the capstone of an earlier generation of British and French social historians. The father of the "new labor history" in the United States is the late Herbert G. Gutman, who was the first to discuss American workers as a group separate from the organized union movement. Gutman's distinction between preindustrial and industrial values laid the groundwork for a whole generation of scholars who have produced case studies of both union and nonunion workers in both urban and rural areas of the United States. Such works have proliferated in recent years but should be sampled first in the following collections of articles: Daniel J. Leab and Richard B. Morris, eds., *The Labor History Reader* (University of Illinois Press, 1985); Charles Stephenson and Robert Asher, eds., *Life and Labor: Dimensions of American Working-Class History* (State University of New York Press, 1986); and Milton Cantor, ed., *American Working Class Culture: Explorations in American Labor and Social History* (Greenwood, 1979).

Carl Degler agrees with the traditional labor historians that the American worker accepted capitalism and wanted a bigger piece of the pie. But he reverses the radical-conservative dichotomy as applied to the conflict between the worker and the businessman. In his view, the real radicals were the industrialists who created a more mature system of capitalism. Labor merely fashioned a conservative response to the radical changes brought about by big business. The system led to its demise. Its place was taken by the AFL, whose long-time leader Samuel Gompers was famous for his acceptance of the wage system and American capitalism. The AFL adopted practical goals; it strove to improve the day-to-day lives of a lot of workers by negotiating for better hours, wages, and working conditions. "In an age of big business," says Degler, "Samuel Gompers made trade unionism a business, and his reward was the survival of his Federation."

In explaining the failure of socialism in the United States, Degler argues that Americans lacked a working-class consciousness because they believed in real mobility. Also, a labor party failed to emerge because Americans developed their commitment to the two-party system before the issues of the industrial revolution came to the forefront. The influx of immigrants from a variety of countries created the heterogeneous labor force, and animosities between rival ethnic groups appeared more real than class antagonisms. "In the final reckoning," says Degler, "the failure of socialism in America is to be attributed to the success of capitalism."

Gutman's framework differs from mainstream American historians' more traditional approach in several ways. Gutman abandons the division of American history at the Civil War/Reconstruction fault line. He proposes a threefold division for free, white workers: (1) the premodern early industrial period from 1815 to 1843; (2) the transition to capitalism, which encompasses the years 1843–1893; and (3) the development of a full-blown industrial system, which took place from the late 1890s through World War I. Gutman's unique periodization enables us to view the evolution of the free, white nonunion worker, whose traditional values withstood the onslaughts of an increasingly large-scale dehumanized factory system that emphasized productivity and efficiency until the depression of 1893.

Gutman also challenges the view that workers were helpless pawns of the owners and that they were forced to cave in every time a strike took place. He shows that on a local level in the 1880s, immigrant workers not only joined unions but also usually won their strikes. This is because small shopkeepers and workers in other industries often supported those who were out on strike. Gutman also argues from census data of the 1880s that immigrant families were more stable and less prone to divorce and desertion than native families.

Were the American workers of the Gilded Age conservative supporters of American capitalism? In the YES selection, Carl N. Degler argues in the affirmative. He concludes that, led by the bread-and-butter leader of the AFL, Samuel Gompers, the American worker sought a larger slice of the profits in the form of better hours, wages, and benefits. In the NO selection, however, Herbert G. Gutman argues that in the Gilded Age, the American worker tried to humanize the factory system through the maintenance of traditional, cultural, artisan, preindustrial work habits.

YES

Carl N. Degler

Out of Our Past

The Workers' Response

To say that the labor movement was affected by the industrialization of the postwar years is an understatement; the fact is, industrial capitalism created the labor movement. Not deliberately, to be sure, but in the same way that a blister is the consequence of a rubbing shoe. Unions were labor's protection against the forces of industrialization as the blister is the body's against the irritation of the shoe. The factory and all it implied confronted the working-man with a challenge to his existence as a man, and the worker's response was the labor union.

There were labor unions in America before 1865, but, as industry was only emerging in those years, so the organizations of workers were correspondingly weak. In the course of years after Appomattox, however, when industry began to hit a new and giant stride, the tempo of unionization also stepped up. It was in these decades, after many years of false starts and utopian ambitions, that the American labor movement assumed its modern shape.

Perhaps the outstanding and enduring characteristic of organized labor in the United States has been its elemental conservatism, the fantasies of some employers to the contrary notwithstanding. Indeed, it might be said that all labor unions, at bottom, are conservative by virtue of their being essentially reactions against a developing capitalism. Though an established capitalist society views itself as anything but subversive, in the days of its becoming and seen against the perspective of the previous age, capitalism as an ideology is radically subversive, undermining and destroying many of the cherished institutions of the functioning society. This dissolving process of capitalism is seen more clearly in Europe than in America because there the time span is greater. But, as will appear later, organized labor in the United States was as much a conservative response to the challenge of capitalism as was the European trade union movement.

Viewed very broadly, the history of modern capitalism might be summarized as the freeing of the three factors of production—land, labor, and capital—from the web of tradition in which medieval society held them. If capitalism was to function, it was necessary that this liberating process take place.

Only when these basic factors are free to be bought and sold according to the dictates of the profit motive can the immense production which capitalism promises be realized. An employer, for example, had to be free to dismiss labor when the balance sheet required it, without being compelled to retain workers because society or custom demanded it. Serfdom, with its requirement that the peasant could not be taken from the land, was an anachronistic institution if capitalism was to become the economic ideology of society. Conversely, an employer needed to be unrestricted in his freedom to hire labor or else production could not expand in accordance with the market. Guild restrictions which limited apprenticeships were therefore obstacles to the achievement of a free capitalism.

The alienability of the three factors of production was achieved slowly and unevenly after the close of the Middle Ages. By the nineteenth century in most nations of the West, land had become absolutely alienable—it could be bought and sold at will. With the growth of banking, the development of trustworthy monetary standards, and finally the gold standard in the nineteenth century, money or capital also became freely exchangeable. Gradually, over the span of some two centuries, the innovating demands of capitalism stripped from labor the social controls in which medieval and mercantilistic government had clothed it. Serfdom as an obstacle to the free movement of labor was gradually done away with; statutes of laborers and apprenticeships which fixed wages, hours, and terms of employment also fell into disuse or suffered outright repeal. To avoid government interference in the setting of wage rates, the English Poor Law of 1834 made it clear that the dole to the unemployed was always to be lower than the going rate for unskilled labor. Thus supply and demand would be the determinant of wage levels. Both the common law and the Combination Acts in the early nineteenth century in England sought to ensure the operation of a free market in labor by declaring trade unions to be restraints on trade.

Like land and capital, then, labor was being reduced to a commodity, freely accessible, freely alienable, free to flow where demand was high. The classical economists of the nineteenth century analyzed this long historical process, neatly put it together, and called it the natural laws of economics.

To a large extent, this historical development constituted an improvement in the worker's status, since medieval and mercantilist controls over labor had been more onerous than protective. Nevertheless, something was lost by the dissolution of the ancient social ties which fitted the worker into a larger social matrix. Under the old relationship, the worker belonged in society; he enjoyed a definite if not a high status; he had a place. Now he was an individual, alone; his status was up to him to establish; his urge for community with society at large had no definite avenue of expression. Society and labor alike had been atomized in pursuit of an individualist economy. Herein lay the radical character of the capitalist ideology.

That the workingman sensed the radical change and objected to it is evident from what some American labor leaders said about their unions. Without rejecting the new freedom which labor enjoyed, John Mitchell, of the Mine Workers, pointed out that the union "stands for fraternity, complete and absolute." Samuel Gompers' eulogy of the social microcosm which was the trade union has the same ring. "A hundred times we have said it," he wrote, "and we say it again, that trade unionism contains within itself the potentialities of working class regeneration." The union is a training ground for democracy and provides "daily object lessons in ideal justice; it breathes into the working classes the spirit of unity"; but above all, it affords that needed sense of community. The labor union "provides a field for noble comradeship, for deeds of loyalty, for self-sacrifice beneficial to one's fellow-workers." In the trade union, in short, the workers could obtain another variety of that sense of community, of comradeship, as Gompers put it, which the acid of individualistic capitalism had dissolved.

And there was another objection to the transformation of labor into an exchangeable commodity. The theoretical justification for the conversion of the factors of production into commodities is that the maximum amount of goods can be produced under such a regime. The increased production is deemed desirable because it would insure greater amounts of goods for human consumption and therefore a better life for all. Unfortunately for the theory, however, labor cannot be separated from the men who provide it. To make labor a commodity is to make the men who provide labor commodities also. Thus one is left with the absurdity of turning men into commodities in order to give men a better life! . . .

Seen in this light, the trade union movement stands out as a truly conservative force. Almost instinctively, the workers joined labor unions in order to preserve their humanity and social character against the excessively individualistic doctrines of industrial capitalism. Eventually, the workers' organizations succeeded in halting the drive to the atomized society which capitalism demanded, and in doing so, far from destroying the system, compelled it to be humane as well as productive.

The essential conservatism of the labor movement is to be seen in particular as well as in general. The organizations of American labor that triumphed or at least survived in the course of industrialization were conspicuous for their acceptance of the private property, profit-oriented society. They evinced little of the radical, anticapitalist ideology and rhetoric so common among European trade unions. Part of the reason for this was the simple fact that all Americans—including workers—were incipient capitalists waiting for "the break." But at bottom it would seem that the conservatism of American labor in this sense is the result of the same forces which inhibited the growth of socialism and other radical anticapitalist ideologies. . . .

"The overshadowing problem of the American labor movement," an eminent labor historian has written, "has always been the problem of staying organized. No other labor movement has ever had to contend with the fragility so characteristic of American labor organizations." So true has this been that even today the United States ranks below Italy and Austria in percentage of workers organized (about 25 per cent as compared, for instance, with Sweden's 90 per cent). In such an atmosphere, the history of organized labor in America has been both painful and conservative. Of the two major national organizations of workers which developed in the latter half of the nineteenth century, only the cautious, restrictive, pragmatic American Federation of Labor

[A.F. of L.] lived into the twentieth century. The other, the Knights of Labor, once the more powerful and promising, as well as the less accommodating in goals and aspirations, succumbed to Selig Perlman's disease of fragility.

Founded in 1869, the Noble Order of the Knights of Labor recorded its greatest successes in the 1880s, when its membership rolls carried 700,000 names. As the A.F. of L. was later to define the term for Americans, the Knights did not seem to constitute a legitimate trade union at all. Anyone who worked, except liquor dealers, bankers, lawyers, and physicians, could join, and some thousands of women workers and Negroes were members in good standing of this brotherhood of toilers. But the crucial deviation of the Knights from the more orthodox approach to labor organization was its belief in worker-owned producers' co-operatives, which were intended to make each worker his own employer. In this way, the order felt, the degrading dependence of the worker upon the employer would be eliminated. "There is no good reason," Terence V. Powderly, Grand Master Workman of the order, told his followers, "why labor cannot, through co-operation, own and operate mines, factories and railroads."

In this respect the order repudiated the direction in which the America of its time was moving. It expressed the small-shopkeeper mentality which dominated the thinking of many American workers, despite the obvious trend in the economy toward the big and the impersonal. As the General Assembly of 1884 put it, "our Order contemplates a radical change, while Trades' Unions . . . accept the industrial system as it is, and endeavor to adapt themselves to it. The attitude of our Order to the existing industrial system is necessarily one of war." Though the order called this attitude "radical," a more accurate term, in view of the times, would have been "conservative" or "reactionary."

In practice, however, the Knights presented no more of a threat to capitalism than any other trade union. Indeed, their avowed opposition to the strike meant that labor's most potent weapon was only reluctantly drawn from the scabbard. The Constitution of 1884 said, "Strikes at best afford only temporary relief"; members should learn to depend on education, co-operation, and political action to attain "the abolition of the wage system."

Though the order officially joined in political activity and Grand Master Workman Powderly was at one time mayor of Scranton, its forays into politics accomplished little. The experience was not lost on shrewd Samuel Gompers, whose American Federation of Labor studiously eschewed any alignments with political parties, practicing instead the more neutral course of "rewarding friends and punishing enemies."

In a farewell letter in 1893, Powderly realistically diagnosed the ills of his moribund order, but offered no cure: "Teacher of important and much-needed reforms, she has been obliged to practice differently from her teachings. Advocating arbitration and conciliation as first steps in labor disputes she has been forced to take upon her shoulders the responsibilities of the aggressor first and, when hope of arbitrating and conciliation failed, to beg of the opposing side to do what we should have applied for in the first instance. Advising against strikes we have been in the midst of them. While not a political party we have been forced into the attitude of taking political action."

For all its fumblings, ineptitude, and excessive idealism, the Knights did organize more workers on a national scale than had ever been done before. At once premature and reactionary, it nonetheless planted the seeds of industrial unionism which, while temporarily overshadowed by the successful craft organization of the A.F. of L., ultimately bore fruit in the C.I.O. [Committee for Industrial Organization]. Moreover, its idealism, symbolized in its admission of Negroes and women, and more in tune with the mid-twentieth century than the late nineteenth, signified its commitment to the ideals of the democratic tradition. For these reasons the Knights were a transitional type of unionism somewhere between the utopianism of the 1830s and the pragmatism of the A.F. of L. It seemed to take time for labor institutions to fit the American temper.

In the course of his long leadership of the American Federation of Labor, Samuel Gompers welcomed many opportunities to define the purposes of his beloved organization. . . .

"The trade unions are the business organizations of the wage-earners," Gompers explained in 1906, "to attend to the business of the wage-earners." Later he expressed it more tersely: "The trade union is not a Sunday school. It is an organization of wage-earners, dealing with economic, social, political and moral questions." As Gompers' crossing of swords with Hillquit demonstrated, there was no need or place for theories. "I saw," the labor leader wrote years later, in looking back on his early life in the labor movement, "the danger of entangling alliances with intellectuals who did not understand that to experiment with the labor movement was to experiment with human life. . . . I saw that the betterment of workingmen must come primarily through workingmen."

In an age of big business, Samuel Gompers made trade unionism a business, and his reward was the survival of his Federation. In a country with a heterogeneous population of unskilled immigrants, reviled and feared Negroes, and native workers, he cautiously confined his fragile organization to the more skilled workers and the more acceptable elements in the population. The result was a narrow but lasting structure.

Though never ceasing to ask *for* "more," the A.F. of L. presented no threat to capitalism. "Labor Unions are for the workingman, but against no one," John Mitchell of the United Mine Workers pointed out. "They are not hostile to employers, not inimical to the interests of the general public. . . . There is no necessary hostility between labor and capital," he concluded. Remorselessly pressed by Morris Hillquit as Gompers was, he still refused to admit that the labor movement was, as Hillquit put it, "conducted against the interests of the employing people." Rather, Gompers insisted, "It is conducted for the interests of the employing people." And the rapid expansion of the American economy bore witness to the fact that the Federation was a friend and not an enemy of industrial capitalism. Its very adaptability to the American scene— its conservative ideology, if it was an ideology at all—as Selig Perlman has observed, contained the key to its success. "The unionism of the American Federation of Labor 'fitted' . . . because it recognized the virtually inalterable conservatism of the American community as regards private property and private initiative in economic life."

This narrow conception of the proper character of trade unionism—job consciousness, craft unionism, lack of interest in organizing the unskilled, the eschewing of political activity—which Gompers and his Federation worked out for the American worker continued to dominate organized labor until the earthquake of the depression cracked the mold and the Committee for Industrial Organization issued forth.

Nobody Here But Us Capitalists

"By any simple interpretation of the Marxist formula," commented Socialist Norman Thomas in 1950, "the United States, by all odds the greatest industrial nation and that in which capitalism is most advanced, should have had long ere this is a very strong socialist movement if not a socialist revolution. Actually," he correctly observed, "in no advanced western nation is organized socialism so weak." Nor was this the first time Socialists had wondered about this. Over eighty years ago, in the high noon of European socialism, Marxist theoretician Werner Sombart impatiently put a similar question: *"Warum gibt es in den Vereinigten Staaten keinen Sozialismus?"*

The failure of the American working class to become seriously interested in socialism in this period or later is one of the prominent signs of the political and economic conservatism of American labor and, by extension, of the American people as a whole. This failure is especially noteworthy when one recalls that in industrialized countries the world over—Japan, Italy, Germany, Belgium, to mention only a few—a Socialist movement has been a "normal" concomitant of industrialization. Even newly opened countries like Australia and New Zealand have Labour parties. Rather than ask, as Americans are wont to do, why these countries have nurtured such frank repudiators of traditional capitalism, it is the American deviation from the general pattern which demands explanation.

In large part, the explanation lies in the relative weakness of class consciousness among Americans. Historically, socialism is the gospel of the *class-conscious* working class, of the workingmen who feel themselves bound to their status for life and their children after them. It is not accidental, therefore, that the major successes of modern socialism are in Europe, where class lines have been clearly and tightly drawn since time immemorial, and where the possibility of upward social movement has been severely restricted in practice if not in law. Americans may from time to time have exhibited class consciousness and even class hatred, but such attitudes have not persisted, nor have they been typical. As Matthew Arnold observed in 1888, "it is indubitable that rich men are regarded" in America "with less envy and hatred than rich men in Europe." A labor leader like Terence Powderly was convinced that America was without classes. "No matter how much we may say about classes and class distinction, there are no classes in the United States. . . . I have always refused to admit that we have classes in our country just as I have refused to admit that the labor of a man's hand or brain is a commodity." And there was a long line of commentators on American society, running back at least to Crèvecoeur, to illustrate the prevalence of Powderly's belief.

The weakness of American class consciousness is doubtless to be attributed, at least in part, to the fluidity of the social structure. Matthew Arnold, for example, accounted for the relative absence of class hatred on such grounds, as did such very different foreign observers as Werner Sombart and Lord Bryce. The British union officials of the Mosely Commission, it will be recalled, were convinced of the superior opportunities for success enjoyed by American workers. Stephan Thernstrom in his study of Newburyport gave some measure of the opportunities for economic improvement among the working class when he reported that all but 5 per cent of those unskilled workers who persisted from 1850 to 1900 ended the period with either property or an improvement in occupational status.

Men who are hoping to move upward on the social scale, and for whom there is some chance that they can do so, do not identify themselves with their present class. "In worn-out, king-ridden Europe, men stay where they are born," immigrant Charles O'Conor, who became an ornament of the New York bar, contended in 1869. "But in America a man is accounted a failure, and certainly ought to be, who has not risen about his father's station in life." So long as Horatio Alger means anything to Americans, Karl Marx will be just another German philosopher.

The political history of the United States also contributed to the failure of socialism. In Europe, because the franchise came slowly and late to the worker, he often found himself first an industrial worker and only later a voter. It was perfectly natural, in such a context, for him to vote according to his economic interests and to join a political party avowedly dedicated to those class interests. The situation was quite different in America, however, for political democracy came to America prior to the Industrial Revolution. By the time the industrial transformation was getting under way after 1865, all adult males could vote and, for the most part, they had already chosen their political affiliations without reference to their economic class; they were Republicans or Democrats first and workers only second—a separation between politics and economics which has become traditional in America. "In the main," wrote Lord Bryce about the United States of the 1880s, "political questions proper have held the first place in a voter's mind and questions affecting his class second." Thus, when it came to voting, workers registered their convictions as citizens, not as workingmen. (In our own day, there have been several notable failures of labor leaders to swing their labor vote, such as John L. Lewis' attempt in 1940 and the C.I.O.'s in 1950 against Senator Taft and the inability of union leaders to be sure they could hold their members to support Hubert Humphrey in the Presidential election of 1968.) To most workers, the Socialist party appeared as merely a third party in a country where such parties are political last resorts.

Nor did socialism in America gain much support from the great influx of immigration. It is true that many Germans came to this country as convinced Socialists and thus swelled the party's numbers, but they also served to pin the stigma of "alien" upon the movement. Even more important was the fact that the very heterogeneity of the labor force, as a result of immigration, often made animosities between ethnic groups more important to the worker than class antagonism. It must have seemed to many workers that socialism, with its central concern for class and its denial of ethnic antagonism, was not dealing with the realities of economic life.

In the final reckoning, however, the failure of socialism in America is to be attributed to the success of capitalism. The expanding economy provided opportunities for all, no matter how meager they might appear or actually be at times. Though the rich certainly seemed to get richer at a prodigious rate, the poor, at least, did not get poorer—and often got richer. Studies of real wages between 1865 and 1900 bear this out. Though prices rose, wages generally rose faster, so that there was a net gain in average income for workers during the last decades of the century. The increase in real wages in the first fifteen years of the twentieth century was negligible—but, significantly, there was no decline. The high wages and relatively good standard of living of the American worker were patent as far as the twenty-three British labor leaders of the Mosely Commission were concerned. The American is a "better educated, better housed, better clothed and more energetic man than his British brother," concluded the sponsor, Alfred Mosely, a businessman himself.

But America challenged socialism on other grounds than mere material things. Some years ago an obscure Socialist, Leon Samson, undertook to account for the failure of socialism to win the allegiance of the American working class; his psychological explanation merits attention because it illuminates the influence exercised by the American Dream. Americanism, Samson observes, is not so much a tradition as it is a doctrine; it is "what socialism is to a socialist." Americanism to the American is a body of ideas like "democracy, liberty, opportunity, to all of which the American adheres rationalistically much as a socialist adheres to his socialism—because it does him good, because it gives him work, because, so he thinks, it guarantees him happiness. America has thus served as a substitute for socialism."

Socialism has been unable to make headway with Americans, Samson goes on, because "every concept in socialism has its substitutive counterconcept in Americanism." As Marxism holds out the prospect of a classless society, so does Americanism. The opportunities for talent and the better material life which socialism promised for the future were already available in America and constituted the image in which America was beheld throughout the world. The freedom and equality which the oppressed proletariat of Europe craved were a reality in America—or at least sufficiently so to blunt the cutting edge of the Socialist appeal. Even the sense of mission, of being in step with the processes of history, which unquestionably was one of the appeals of socialism, was also a part of the American Dream. Have not all Americans cherished their country as a model for the world? Was not this the "last, best hope of earth"? Was not God on the side of America, as history, according to Marx, was on the side of socialism and the proletariat?

Over a century ago, Alexis de Tocqueville predicted a mighty struggle for the minds of men between two giants of Russia and the United States. In the ideologies of socialism and the American Dream, his forecast has been unexpectedly fulfilled.

Herbert G. Gutman

 **NO**

Work, Culture, and Society in Industrializing America

The traditional imperial boundaries (a function, perhaps, of the professional subdivision of labor) that have fixed the territory open to American labor historians for exploration have closed off to them the study of such important subjects as changing work habits and the culture of work. Neither the questions American labor historians usually ask nor the methods they use encourage such inquiry. With a few significant exceptions, for more than half a century American labor history has continued to reflect both the strengths and the weaknesses of the conceptual scheme sketched by its founding fathers, John R. Commons and others of the so-called Wisconsin school of labor history. Even their most severe critics, including the orthodox "Marxist" labor historians of the 1930s, 1940s, and 1950s and the few New Left historians who have devoted attention to American labor history, rarely questioned that conceptual framework. Commons and his colleagues asked large questions, gathered important source materials, and put forth impressive ideas. Together with able disciples, they studied the development of the trade union as an institution and explained its place in a changing labor market. But they gave attention primarily to those few workers who belonged to trade unions and neglected much else of importance about the American working population. Two flaws especially marred this older labor history. Because so few workers belonged to permanent trade unions before 1940, its overall conceptualization excluded most working people from detailed and serious study. More than this, its methods encouraged labor historians to spin a cocoon around American workers, isolating them from their own particular subcultures and from the larger national culture. An increasingly narrow "economic" analysis caused the study of American working-class history to grow more constricted and become more detached from larger developments in American social and cultural history and from the writing of American social and cultural history itself. After 1945 American working-class history remained imprisoned by self-imposed limitations and therefore fell far behind the more imaginative and innovative British and Continental European work in the field. . . .

[T]he focus in these pages is on free white labor in quite different time periods: 1815–1843, 1843–1893, 1893–1919. The precise years serve only as guideposts to mark the fact that American society differed greatly in each period. Between 1815 and 1843, the United States remained a predominantly preindustrial society and most workers drawn to its few factories were the products of rural and village preindustrial culture. Preindustrial American society was not premodern in the same way that European peasant societies were, but it was, nevertheless, premodern. In the half-century after 1843 industrial development radically transformed the earlier American social structure, and during this Middle Period (an era not framed around the coming and the aftermath of the Civil War) a profound tension existed between the older American preindustrial social structure and the modernizing institutions that accompanied the development of industrial capitalism. After 1893 the United States ranked as a mature industrial society. In each of these distinctive stages of change in American society, a recurrent tension also existed between native and immigrant men and women fresh to the factory and the demands imposed upon them by the regularities and disciplines of factory labor. That state of tension was regularly revitalized by the migration of diverse premodern native and foreign peoples into an industrializing or a fully industrialized society. The British economic historian Sidney Pollard has described well this process whereby "a society of peasants, craftsmen, and versatile labourers became a society of modern industrial workers." "There was more to overcome," Pollard writes of industrializing England,

> than the change of employment or the new rhythm of work: there was a whole new culture to be absorbed and an old one to be traduced and spurned, there were new surroundings, often in a different part of the country, new relations with employers, and new uncertainties of livelihood, new friends and neighbors, new marriage patterns and behavior patterns of children within the family and without.

That same process occurred in the United States. Just as in all modernizing countries, the United States faced the difficult task of industrializing whole cultures, but in this country the process was regularly repeated, each stage of American economic growth and development involving different first-generation factory workers. The social transformation Pollard described occurred in England between 1770 and 1850, and in those decades premodern British cultures and the modernizing institutions associated primarily with factory and machine labor collided and interacted. A painful transition occurred, dominated the ethos of an entire era, and then faded in relative importance. After 1850 and until quite recently, the British working class reproduced itself and retained a relative national homogeneity. New tensions emerged but not those of a society continually busy (and worried about) industrializing persons born out of that society and often alien in birth and color and in work habits, customary values, and behavior. "Traditional social habits and customs," J. F. C. Harrison reminds us, "seldom fitted into the patterns of industrial life, and they had . . . to be discredited as hindrances to progress." That happened regularly in the United States after 1815 as the nation absorbed and worked to transform new groups of preindustrial peoples, native whites among them. The result however, was neither a static tension nor the mere recurrence of similar cycles, because American society itself changed as did the composition of its laboring population. But the source of the tension remained the same, and conflict often resulted. It was neither the conflict emphasized by the older Progressive historians (agrarianism versus capitalism, or sectional disagreement) nor that emphasized by recent critics of that early twentieth-century synthesis (conflict between competing elites). It resulted instead from the fact that the American working class was continually altered in its composition by infusions, from within and without the nation, of peasants, farmers, skilled artisans, and casual day laborers who brought into industrial society ways of work and other habits and values not associated with industrial necessities and the industrial ethos. Some shed these older ways to conform to new imperatives. Others fell victim or fled, moving from place to place. Some sought to extend and adapt older patterns of work and life to a new society. Others challenged the social system through varieties of collective associations. But for all—at different historical moments—the transition to industrial society, as E. P. Thompson has written, "entailed a severe restructuring of working habits—new disciplines, new incentives, and a new human nature upon which these incentives could bite effectively."

Much in the following pages depends upon a particular definition of culture and an analytic distinction between culture and society. Both deserve brief comment. "Culture" as used here has little to do with Oscar Lewis's inadequate "culture of poverty" construct and has even less to do with the currently fashionable but nevertheless quite crude behavioral social history that defines class by mere occupation and culture as some kind of a magical mix between ethnic and religious affiliations. Instead this [selection] has profited from the analytic distinctions between culture and society made by the anthropologists Eric Wolf and Sidney W. Mintz and the exiled Polish sociologist Zygmunt Bauman. Mintz finds in culture "a kind of resource" and in society "a kind of arena," the distinction being "between sets of historically available alternatives or forms on the one hand, and the societal circumstances or settings within which these forms may be employed on the other." "Culture," he writes, "is *used;* and any analysis of its use immediately brings into view the arrangements of persons in societal groups for whom cultural forms confirm, reinforce, maintain, change, or deny particular arrangements of status, power, and identity.". . .

Despite the profound economic changes that followed the American Civil War, Gilded Age artisans did not easily shed stubborn and time-honored work habits. Such work habits and the life-styles and subcultures related to them retained a vitality long into these industrializing decades. Not all artisans worked in factories, but some that did retained traditional craft skills. Mechanization came in different ways and at different times to diverse industries. Samuel Gompers recollected that New York City cigarmakers paid a fellow craftsman to read a newspaper to them while they worked, and Milwaukee cigarmakers struck in 1882 to retain such privileges as keeping (and then selling) damaged cigars and leaving the shop without a foreman's permission. "The difficulty with many cigarmakers," complained a New York City manufacturer in 1877, "is this. They come down to the shop in the morning; roll a few cigars and then go to a beer saloon and play pinnocio or some other game, . . . working probably only two or three hours a day." Coopers felt new machinery "hard and insensate," not a blessing but an evil that "took a great deal of joy out of life" because machine-made barrels undercut a subculture of work and leisure. Skilled coopers "lounged about" on Saturday (the regular payday), a "lost day" to their employers. A historian of American cooperage explained:

> Early on Saturday morning, the big brewery wagon would drive up to the shop. Several of the coopers would club together, each paying his proper share, and one of them would call out the window to the driver, "Bring me a Goose Egg," meaning a half-barrel of beer. Then others would buy "Goose Eggs," and there would be a merry time all around. . . . Little groups of jolly fellows would often sit around upturned barrels playing poker, using rivets for chips, until they had received their pay and the "Goose Egg" was dry.
>
> Saturday night was a big night for the old-time cooper. It meant going out, strolling around the town, meeting friends, usually at a favorite saloon, and having a good time generally, after a week of hard work. Usually the good time continued over into Sunday, so that on the following day he usually was not in the best of condition to settle down to the regular day's work.
>
> Many coopers used to spend this day [Monday] sharpening up their tools, carrying in stock, discussing current events, and in getting things in shape for the big day of work on the morrow. Thus, "Blue Monday" was something of a tradition with the coopers, and the day was also more or less lost as far as production was concerned.
>
> "Can't do much today, but I'll give her hell tomorrow," seemed to be the Monday slogan. But bright and early Tuesday morning, "Give her hell" they would, banging away lustily for the rest of the week until Saturday which was pay day again, and its thoughts of the "Goose Eggs."

Such traditions of work and leisure—in this case, a four-day work week and a three-day weekend—angered manufacturers anxious to ship goods as much as worried Sabbatarians and temperance reformers. Conflicts over life- and work-styles occurred frequently and often involved control over the work process and over time. The immigrant Staffordshire potters in Trenton, New Jersey, worked in "bursts of great activity" and then quit for "several days at a time." "Monday," said a manufacturer, "was given up to debauchery." After the potters lost a bitter lockout in 1877 that included torchlight parades and effigy burnings, *Crockery and Glass Journal* mockingly advised:

> Run your factories to please the crowd. . . . Don't expect work to begin before 9 a.m. or to continue after 3 p.m. Every employee should be served hot coffee and a bouquet at 7 a.m. and allowed the two hours to take a free perfumed bath. . . . During the summer, ice cream and fruit should be served at 12 p.m. to the accompaniment of witching music.

Hand coopers (and potters and cigarmakers, among others) worked hard but in distinctly preindustrial styles. Machine-made barrels pitted modernizing technology and modern habits against traditional ways. To the owners of competitive firms struggling to improve efficiency and cut labor costs, the Goose Egg and Blue Monday proved the laziness and obstinacy of craftsmen as well as the tyranny of craft unions that upheld venerable traditions. To the skilled cooper the long weekend symbolized a way of work and life filled with almost ritualistic meanings. Between 1843 and 1893, compromise between such conflicting interests was hardly possible.

Settled premodern work habits existed among others than those employed in nonfactory crafts. Owners of already partially mechanized industries complained of them, too. "Saturday night debauches and Sunday carousels though they be few and far between," lamented the *Age of Steel* in 1882, "are destructive of modest hoardings, and he who indulges in them will in time become a striker for higher wages." In 1880 a British steelworker boasted that native Americans never would match immigrants in their skills: "adn't the 'ops, you know." Manufacturers, when able, did not hesitate to act decisively to end such troubles. In Fall River new technology allowed a print cloth manufacturer to settle a long-standing grievance against his stubborn mule spinners. "On Saturday afternoon after they had gone home," a boastful mill superintendent later recollected, "we started right in and smashed a room full of mules with sledge hammers. . . . On Monday morning, they were astonished to find that there was not work for them. That room is now full of ring frames run by girls." Woolen manufacturers also displaced handjack spinners with improved machinery and did so because of "the disorderly habits of English workmen. Often on a Monday morning, half of them would be absent from the mill in consequence of the Sunday's dissipation." Blue Monday, however, did not entirely disappear. Paterson artisans and factory hands held a May festival on a Monday each year ("Labor Monday") and that popular holiday soon became state law, the American Labor Day. It had its roots in earlier premodern work habits.

The persistence of such traditional artisan work habits well into the nineteenth century deserves notice from others besides labor historians, because those work habits did not exist in a cultural or social vacuum. If modernizing technology threatened and even displaced such work patterns, diverse nineteenth-century subcultures sustained and nourished them. "The old nations of the earth creep on at a snail's pace," boasted Andrew Carnegie in *Triumphant Democracy* (1886), "the Republic thunders past with the rush of an express." The articulate steelmaster, however, had missed the point. The very rapidity of the economic changes occurring in Carnegie's lifetime meant that many, unlike him, lacked the time, historically, culturally, and psychologically, to be separated or alienated from settled ways of work and life and from relatively fixed beliefs. Continuity not consensus counted for much in explaining working-class and especially artisan behavior in those decades that witnessed the coming of the factory and the radical transformation of American society. Persistent work habits were one example of that significant continuity. But these elements of continuity were often revealed among nineteenth-century American workers cut off by birth from direct contact with the preindustrial American past, a fact that has been ignored or blurred by the artificial separation between labor history and immigration history. In Gilded Age America (and afterward in the Progressive Era despite the radical change in patterns of immigration), working-class and immigration history regularly intersected, and that intermingling made for powerful continuities. In 1880, for example, 63 of every 100 Londoners were native to that city, 94 coming from England and Wales, and 98 from Great Britain and Ireland. Foreign countries together contributed only 1.6 percent to London's massive population. At that same moment, more than 70 of every 100 persons in San Francisco (78), St. Louis (78), Cleveland (80), New York (80), Detroit (84), Milwaukee (84), and Chicago (87) were immigrants or the children of immigrants, and the percentage was just as high in many smaller American industrial towns and cities. "Not every foreigner is a workingman," noticed the clergyman Samuel Lane Loomis in 1887, "but in the cities, at least, it may almost be said that every workingman is a foreigner." And until the 1890s most immigrants came from Northern and Western Europe, French- and English-speaking Canada, and China. In 1890, only 3 percent of the nation's foreign-born residents—290,000 of 9,200,000 immigrants—had been born in Eastern or Southern Europe. (It is a little recognized fact that most North and West European immigrants migrated to the United States after, not before, the American Civil War.) When so much else changed in the industrializing decades, tenacious traditions flourished among immigrants in ethnic subcultures that varied greatly among particular groups and according to the size, age, and location of different cities and industries. ("The Irish," Henry George insisted, "burn like chips, the English like logs.") Class and occupational distinctions within a particular ethnic group also made for different patterns of cultural adaptation, but powerful subcultures thrived among them all.

Suffering and plain poverty cut deeply into these ethnic working-class worlds. In reconstructing their everyday texture there is no reason to neglect or idealize such suffering, but it is time to discard the notion that the large-scale uprooting and exploitative processes that accompanied industrialization caused little more than cultural breakdown and social anomie. Family, class, and ethnic ties did not dissolve easily. "Almost as a matter of definition," the sociologist Neil Smelzer has written, "we associate the factory system with the decline of the family and the onset of anonymity." Smelzer criticized such a view of early industrializing England, and it has just as little validity for nineteenth-century industrializing America. Family roles changed in important ways, and strain was widespread, but the immigrant working-class family held together. Examination of household composition in sixteen census enumeration districts in Paterson in 1880 makes that clear for this predominantly working-class immigrant city, and while research on other ethnic working-class communities will reveal significant variations, the overall patterns should not differ greatly. The Paterson immigrant (and native white) communities were predominantly working class, and most families among them were intact in their composition. For this population, at least (and without accounting for age and sex ratio differences between the ethnic groups), a greater percentage of immigrant than native white households included two parents. Ethnic and predominantly working-class communities in industrial towns like Paterson and in larger cities, too, built on these strained but hardly broken familial and kin ties. Migration to another country, life in the city, and labor in cost-conscious and ill-equipped factories and workshops tested but did not shatter what the anthropologist Clifford Geertz has described as primordial (as contrasted to civic) attachments, "the 'assumed' givens . . . of social existence: immediate contiguity and kin connections mainly, but beyond them, the givenness that stems from being born into a particular religious community, speaking a particular language, and following particular social patterns." Tough familial and kin ties made possible that transmission and adaptation of European working-class cultural patterns and beliefs to industrializing America. As late as 1888, residents in some Rhode Island mill villages figured their wages in British currency. Common rituals and festivals bound together such communities. Paterson silk weavers had their Macclesfield wakes, and Fall River cotton mill workers their Ashton wakes. British immigrants "banded together to uphold the popular culture of the homeland" and celebrated saints' days: St. George's Day, St. Andrew's Day, and St. David's Day. Even funerals retained an archaic flavor. Samuel Sigley, a Chartist house painter, had fled Ashton-under-Lyne in 1848, and built American trade unions. When his wife died in the late 1890s a significant ritual occurred during the funeral: some friends placed a chaff of wheat on her grave. Mythic beliefs also cemented ethnic and class solidarities. The Irish-American press, for example, gave Martin O'Brennan much space to argue that Celtic had been spoken in the Garden of Eden, and in Paterson Irish-born silk, cotton, and iron workers believed in the magical powers of that town's "Dublin Spring." An old resident remembered:

> There is a legend that an Irish fairy brought over the water in her apron from the Lakes of Killarney and planted it in the humble part of that town. . . . There were dozens of legends connected with the Dublin Spring and if a man drank from its precious depository. . . he could never leave Paterson [but] only under the fairy influence, and the wand of the nymph would be sure to bring him back again some time or other.

When a "fairy" appeared in Paterson in human form, some believed she walked the streets "as a tottering old woman begging with a cane." Here was a way to assure concern for the elderly and the disabled.

Much remains to be studied about these cross-class but predominantly working-class ethnic subcultures common to industrializing America. Relations within them between skilled and unskilled workers, for example, remain unclear. But the larger shape of these diverse immigrant communities can be sketched. More than mythic beliefs and common work habits sustained them. Such worlds had in them what Thompson has called "working-class intellectual traditions, working-class community patterns, and a working-class structure of feeling," and men with artisan skills powerfully affected the everyday texture of such communities. A model subculture included friendly and benevolent societies as well as friendly local politicians, community-wide holiday celebrations, an occasional library (the Baltimore Journeymen Bricklayer's Union taxed members one dollar a year in the 1880s to sustain a library that included the collected works of William Shakespeare and Sir Walter Scott's Waverley novels), participant sports, churches sometimes headed by a sympathetic clergy, saloons, beer gardens, and concert halls or music halls and, depending upon circumstances, trade unionists, labor reformers, and radicals. The

Massachusetts cleric Jonathan Baxter Harrison published in 1880 an unusually detailed description of one such ethnic, working-class institution, a Fall River music hall and saloon. About fifty persons were there when he visited it, nearly one-fourth of them young women. "Most of those present," he noticed, were "persons whom I had met before, in the mills and on the streets. They were nearly all operatives, or had at some time belonged to that class." An Englishman sang first, and then a black whose songs "were of many kinds, comic, sentimental, pathetic, and silly. . . . When he sang 'I got a mammy in the promised land,' with a strange, wailing refrain, the English waiter-girl, who was sitting at my table, wiped her eyes with her apron, and everybody was very quiet." Harrison said of such places in Fall River:

> All the attendants. . . had worked in the mills. The young man who plays the piano is usually paid four or five dollars per week, besides his board. The young men who sing receive one dollar per night, but most of them board themselves. . . . The most usual course for a man who for any reason falls out of the ranks of mill workers (if he loses his place by sickness or is discharged) is the opening of a liquor saloon or drinking place.

Ethnic ties with particular class dimensions sometimes stretched far beyond local boundaries and even revealed themselves in the behavior of the most successful practitioners of Gilded Age popular culture. In 1884, for example, the pugilist John L. Sullivan and the music-hall entertainers Harrigan and Hart promised support to striking Irish coal miners in the Ohio Hocking Valley. Local ties, however, counted for much more and had their roots inside and outside of the factory and workshop. Soon after Cyrus H. McCormick, then twenty-one, took over the management of his father's great Chicago iron machinery factory (which in the early 1880s employed twelve hundred men and boys), a petition signed by "Many Employees" reached his hands:

> It only pains us to relate to you . . . that a good many of our old hands is not here this season and if Mr. Evarts is kept another season a good many more will leave. . . . We pray for you . . . to remove this man. . . . We are treated as though we were dogs. . . . He has cut wages down so low they are living on nothing but bread. . . . We can't talk to him about wages if we do he will tell us to go out side the gate. . . . He discharged old John the other day he has been here seventeen years. . . . There is Mr. Church who left us last Saturday he went about and shook hands with every old hand in the shop . . . this brought tears to many men's eyes. He has been here nineteen years and has got along well with them all until he came to Mr. Evarts the present superintendent.

Artisans, themselves among those later displaced by new technology, signed this petition, and self-educated artisans (or professionals and petty enterprisers who had themselves usually risen from the artisan class) often emerged as civic and community leaders. "Intellectually," Jennie Collins noticed in Boston in the early 1870s, "the journeymen tailors . . . are ever discussing among themselves questions of local and national politics, points of law, philosophy, physics, and religion."

Such life-styles and subcultures adapted and changed over time. In the Gilded Age piece-rates in nearly all manufacturing industries helped reshape traditional work habits. "Two generations ago," said the Connecticut Bureau of Labor Statistics in 1885, "time-work was the universal rule." "Piece-work" had all but replaced it, and the Connecticut Bureau called it "a moral force which corresponds to machinery as a physical force." Additional pressures came in traditional industries such as shoe, cigar, furniture, barrel, and clothing manufacture, which significantly mechanized in these years. Strain also resulted where factories employed large numbers of children and young women (in the 1880 manuscript census 49.3 percent of all Paterson boys and 52.1 percent of all girls aged eleven to fourteen had occupations listed by their names) and was especially common among the as yet little-studied pools of casual male laborers found everywhere. More than this, mobility patterns significantly affected the structure and the behavior of these predominantly working-class communities. A good deal of geographic mobility, property mobility (home ownership), and occupational mobility (skilled status in new industries or in the expanding building trades, petty retail enterprise, the professions, and public employment counted as the most important ways to advance occupationally) reshaped these ethnic communities as Stephan Thernstrom and others have shown. But so little is yet known about the society in which such men and women lived and about the cultures which had produced them that it is entirely premature to infer "consciousness" (beliefs and values) only from mobility rates. Such patterns and rates of mobility, for example, did not entirely shatter working-class capacities for self-protection. The fifty-year period between 1843 and 1893 was not conducive to permanent, stable trade unions, but these decades were a time of frequent strikes and lockouts and other forms of sustained conflict.

Not all strikes and lockouts resulted in the defeat of poorly organized workers. For the years 1881 to 1887, for example, the New Jersey Bureau of Labor Statistics collected information on 890 New Jersey industrial disputes involving mostly workers in the textile, glass, metal, transportation, and building trades: 6 percent ended in compromise settlements; employers gained the advantage in 40 percent; strikers won the rest (54 percent). In four of five disputes concerning higher wages and shorter hours, New Jersey workers, not their employers, were victorious. Large numbers of such workers there and elsewhere were foreign-born or the children of immigrants. More than this, immigrant workers in the mid-1880s joined trade unions in numbers far out of proportion to their place in the labor force. Statistical inquiries by the Bureau of Labor Statistics in Illinois in 1886 and in New Jersey in 1887 make this clear. Even these data may not have fully reflected the proclivity of immigrants to seek self-protection. (Such a distortion would occur if, for example, the children of immigrants apparently counted by the bureaus as native-born had remained a part of the ethnic subcultures into which they had been born and joined trade unions as regularly as the foreign-born). Such information from Illinois and New Jersey suggests the need to treat the meaning of social mobility with some care. So does the sketchy outline of Hugh O'Donnell's career. By 1892, when he was twenty-nine years old, he had already improved his social status a great deal. Before the dispute with Andrew Carnegie and Henry Clay Frick culminated in the bitter Homestead lockout that year, O'Donnell had voted Republican, owned a home, and had in it a Brussels carpet and even a piano. Nevertheless this Irish-American skilled worker led the Homestead workers and was even indicted under a Civil War treason statute never before used. The material improvements O'Donnell had experienced mattered greatly to him and suggested significant mobility, but culture and tradition together with the way in which men like O'Donnell interpreted the transformation of Old America defined the value of those material improvements and their meaning to him.

Other continuities between 1843 and 1893 besides those rooted in artisan work habits and diverse ethnic working-class subcultures deserve brief attention as important considerations in understanding the behavior of artisans and other workers in these decades. I have suggested in other writings that significant patterns of opposition to the ways in which industrial capitalism developed will remain baffling until historians re-examine the relationship between the premodern American political system and the coming of the factory along with the strains in premodern popular American ideology shared by workers and large numbers of successful self-made Americans (policemen, clergymen, politicians, small businessmen, and even some "traditional" manufacturers) that rejected the legitimacy of the modern factory system and its owners. One strain of thought common to the rhetoric of nineteenth-century immigrant and native-born artisans is considered here. It helps explain their recurrent enthusiasm for land and currency reform, cooperatives, and trade unions. It was the fear of dependence, "proletarianization," and centralization, and the worry that industrial capitalism threatened to transform "the Great Republic of the West" into a "European" country. In 1869, the same year that saw the completion of the transcontinental railroad, the chartering of the Standard Oil Company, the founding of the Knights of Labor, and the dedication of a New York City statue to Cornelius Vanderbilt, some London workers from Westbourne Park and Notting Hill petitioned the American ambassador for help to emigrate. "Dependence," they said of Great Britain, "not independence, is inculcated. Hon. Sir, this state of things we wish to fly from . . . to become citizens of that great Republican country, which has no parallels in the world's history." Such men had a vision of Old America, but it was not a new vision. Industrial transformation between 1840 and 1890 tested and redefined that vision. Seven years after their visit, the New York *Labor Standard,* then edited by an Irish socialist, bemoaned what had come over the country: "There was a time when the United States was the workingman's country, . . . the land of promise for the workingman. . . . We are now in an *old country.*" This theme recurred frequently as disaffected workers, usually self-educated artisans, described the transformation of premodern America. "America," said the Detroit *Labor Leaf* "used to be the land of promise to the poor. . . . The Golden Age is indeed over—the Age of Iron has taken its place. The iron law of necessity has taken the place of the golden rule." We need not join in mythicizing preindustrial American society in order to suggest that this tension between the old and the new helps give a coherence to the decades between 1843 and 1893 that even the trauma of the Civil War does not disturb.

EXPLORING THE ISSUE

Were American Workers in the Gilded Age Conservative Capitalists?

Critical Thinking and Reflection

1. The four factors of production in any economic system are land, labor, capital, and entrepreneurship. Explain how the freeing up of these factors of production made capitalism a dynamic economic system.
2. Describe the emergence of worker activism as reflected in the major strikes that took place in late nineteenth-century United States. Discuss the reaction of employers, the government, and the public to this new worker activism.
3. Compare and contrast the membership, goals, strategies, successes, and failure of the Knights of Labor and of the American Federation of Labor (AFL).
4. Explain what Degler means when he argues that the American labor movement was a conservative response to the radical changes brought about by the industrial revolution.
5. Explain why Degler argues that the AFL succeeded where the Knights of Labor failed.
6. List four reasons cited by Degler that the United States failed to develop a strong socialist movement.
7. Explain how Gutman's treatment of workers is different from that of traditional labor historians.
8. Explain what Gutman means by culture. How does he distinguish culture from society? When do culture and society intersect?
9. Distinguish the major characteristics of the three time periods of the free white worker: 1815–1843, 1843–1893, and 1893–1919.
10. Discuss how Gutman's time frame differs from the traditional Civil War/Reconstruction dividing line in American history.
11. Critically evaluate what British social historian Edward P. Thompson called the "working-class intellectual traditions, working-class community patterns, and a working-class structure of feeling," which Gutman finds in the factories and communities of the Gilded Age.
12. Compare the factory system of the Gilded Age with the factory system that emerged after 1893. Use examples from the NO selection to illustrate the differences.

Is There Common Ground?

Professor Carl Degler argues that workers were conservatives who accepted capitalism but wanted their fair share of the pie in the form of better hours, wages, benefits, and working conditions. How does this argument differ from Professor Herbert Gutman's view that in the early stages of industrialism, workers' attempts at controlling the system achieved a number of successes in developing a more humane environment? The turning point, says Gutman, came after the depression of the 1890s when the distinction between workers and owners in the large steel and oil factories became more fully pronounced with an emphasis on productivity and efficiency.

Is it possible that the factory system could have developed in the twentieth century in a more humane way similar to the relationship between workers and owners in the 1870s and 1880s? Or was it inevitable that the giant-sized corporations such as U.S. Steel meant that a more impersonal system with clashes between owners and workers was inevitable?

Additional Resources

To learn more about the rise and fall of the Knights of Labor, see the case studies in Leon Fink's *Workingmen's Democracy: The Knights of Labor and American Politics* (University of Illinois Press, 1983). See also Fink's collection of articles, *In Search of the Working Class* (University of Illinois Press, 1994). Two other noteworthy books on the Knights of Labor are Robert E. Weir, *Beyond Labor's Veil: The Culture of the Knights of Labor* (Penn State University Press, 1996) and Kim Voss, *The Making of American Exceptionalism: The Knights of Labor and Class Formation in the Nineteenth Century* (Cornell University Press, 1993), and Bruce Laurie, *Artisans Into Workers: Labor in Nineteenth-Century America* (Hill and Wang, 1989).

Two journals have devoted entire issues to the American labor movement: the Fall 1989 issue of *The Public Historian* and the February 1982 issue of *Social Education*. Students who wish to sample the diverse scholarship on the American workers should consult "A Round Table: Labor, Historical Pessimism, and Hegemony," *Journal of American History* (June 1988).

The question of why the United States never developed a major socialist movement or labor party has been the subject of much speculation. A good starting point is John H. Laslett and Seymour Martin Lipset, eds., *Failure of a Dream? Essays in the History of American Socialism* (University of California Press, 1974), a collection of articles that generally reinforces Degler's arguments. Political scientist Theodore J. Lowi argues that the U.S. political system of federalism prevented a socialist movement in "Why Is There No Socialism in the United States?" *Society* (January/February 1985). Historian Eric Foner tears down all explanations and asks "Why Has There Been No Socialist Transformation in Any Advanced Capitalist Society?" *History Workshop* (Spring 1984). Finally, see Rick Halpern and Jonathan Morris, eds., *American Exceptionalism? U.S. Working-Class Formation in an International Context* (St. Martin's Press, 1997).

ISSUE 5

Were Late Nineteenth-Century Immigrants "Uprooted"?

YES: Oscar Handlin, from *The Shock of Alienation,* 2nd ed. (Little, Brown and Company, 1973)

NO: Mark Wyman, from *The America Trunk Comes Home* (Cornell University Press, 1993)

Learning Outcomes

After reading this issue, you should be able to:

- Describe the difficulties of immigrants relating both to their former homeland and to the United States.
- Evaluate the changing attitudes of native Americans toward immigrants during the nineteenth century.
- Assess the challenges attached to the assimilation of immigrants to American ways.
- Analyze the role of social workers in the lives of immigrants to the United States.
- Explain a broader range of short-term and long-range goals exhibited by those who immigrated to the United States between 1880 and 1930.

ISSUE SUMMARY

YES: Oscar Handlin asserts that immigrants to the United States in the late nineteenth century were alienated from the cultural traditions of the homeland they had left as well as from those of their adopted country.

NO: Mark Wyman argues that as many as four million immigrants to the United States between 1880 and 1930 viewed their trip as temporary and remained tied psychologically to their homeland to which they returned once they had accumulated enough wealth to enable them to improve their status back home.

Immigration has been one of the most powerful forces shaping the development of the United States since at least the early seventeenth century. In fact, it should not be overlooked that even the ancestors of the country's native population were migrants to this "New World" some 37,000 years ago. There can be little doubt that the United States is a nation of immigrants, a reality reinforced by the motto "E Pluribus Unum" (One from Many), which is used on the Great Seal of the United States and on several U.S. coins.

The history of immigration to the United States can be organized into four major periods of activity: 1607–1830, 1830–1890, 1890–1924, and 1968 to the present. During the first period, the seventeenth and eighteenth centuries, there were a growing number of European migrants who arrived in North America, mostly from the British Isles, as well as several million Africans who were forced to migrate to colonial America as a consequence of the Atlantic slave trade. Although increased numbers of non-English immigrants arrived in America in the eighteenth century, it was not until the nineteenth century that large numbers of immigrants from other northern and western European countries, as well as from China, arrived and created significant population diversity. Two European groups predominated during this second major period: as a result of the potato famine, large numbers of Irish Catholics emigrated in the 1850s; and, for a variety of religious, political, and economic reasons, so did many Germans. Chinese immigration increased, and these immigrants found work in low-paying service industries, such as laundries and restaurants, and as railroad construction workers.

The Industrial Revolution of the late nineteenth century sparked a third wave of immigration. Millions of the newcomers, attracted by the unskilled factory jobs that were becoming more abundant, began pouring into the United States. Migration was encouraged by various companies whose agents distributed handbills throughout Europe advertising the ready availability of good-paying jobs in America. This phase of immigration, however, represented something of a departure from previous ones as most of these "new immigrants" came from Southern and Eastern Europe. This flood continued until World War I, after which mounting xenophobia culminated in the passage by Congress in 1924 of the National Origins Act, which restricted the number of immigrants into the country to 150,000 annually, and which placed quotas on the numbers permitted from each foreign country. By 1882, Congress already had curtailed Asian immigration with the Chinese Exclusion Act, a measure that remained in effect until its repeal in 1943.

In the aftermath of World War II, restrictions were eased for several groups, especially those who survived the Nazi death camps or who sought asylum in the United States in the wake of the aggressive movement into Eastern Europe by the Soviet Union after the war. But many other restrictions were not lifted until the Immigration Reform Act of 1965, which set in motion a fourth phase of immigration history. In contrast to earlier migrations, the newest groups entering the United States in large numbers have come from Latin America, the Middle East, and South and Southeast Asia.

Efforts to curb immigration to the United States reflect an anxiety and ambivalence that many Americans have long held with regard to "foreigners." Anxious to benefit from the labor of these newcomers but still hesitant to accept the immigrants as full-fledged citizens entitled to the same rights and privileges as native residents, Americans have on a number of occasions discovered that they had an "immigrant problem." Harsh anti-immigrant sentiment based on prejudicial attitudes toward race, ethnicity, or religion has periodically boiled over into violence and calls for legislation to restrict immigration, as is the case today in response to fears of international terrorism and concerns over the presence of illegal aliens drawing upon the nation's resources.

These concerns are by no means unique to contemporary society. In 1890, Jacob Riis, a Danish immigrant who had arrived in the United States 20 years earlier, published an exposé of the living conditions of the poor, most of them immigrants, in New York City. Riis had served as a police reporter for the New York *Tribune* and in that capacity had gained an awareness of the squalid living conditions in the city's Lower East Side. His book, *How the Other Half Lives* replete with photographic evidence of slum conditions, pioneered in the form of investigative reporting that his friend Theodore Roosevelt labeled "muckraking." Primarily directed at middle-class audiences whose influence could possibly demand reform of New York's worst tenements, almost every reader of this classic today would cringe at the numerous stereotypical depictions of the subjects whose circumstances Riis hoped to improve. He described the Italian as a "born gambler"; of Eastern European Jews, he wrote, "Money is their God"; and he comments on the "sensuality and . . . lack of moral accountability" of African Americans living in Harlem. Riss' greatest hostility, however, was directed at the Chinese who, despite their "scrupulous neatness," would "rather gamble than eat any day" and who, he claimed, were guilty of luring young white women into opium dens, hooking them on drugs, and turning them to a life of prostitution.

The traditional welcome and appreciation for immigrants in American society became particularly harsh during difficult economic times. Not long after the publication of *How the Other Half Lives,* the American economy began to sink into the worst economic depression in the nation's history up to that time. The Panic of 1893 unleashed anxieties that produced a backlash against the millions of new immigrants who had poured into the United States during the previous decade. It was not unusual, as indicated in the quotation from Jacob Riis cited above, that this antagonism occasionally took the form of religious hostility. For example, the American Protective Association (APA), an anti-Catholic secret society established in 1887, became particularly active in the 1890s. Requiring its members never to employ, work for, or vote for a Catholic, the leaders of the APA in 1893 circulated a bogus document allegedly written by Pope Leo XIII imploring the Catholic faithful in the United States to begin preparations for an invasion of the United States by a papal army for the purpose of overthrowing the U.S. federal government and imposing Catholic rule over the nation. While the Pope's military force never showed up, the APA's actions stirred up significant hysteria in some parts of the country and produced a wave of anti-Catholicism, much of which was directed at recent Catholic immigrants.

What effect did these kinds of attitudes have on those who migrated to the United States in search of a life better than the one they experienced in their native lands? What happened to their Old World customs and traditions? How fully did immigrants assimilate into the new culture they encountered in the United States? Was the United States, in fact, a melting pot for immigrants, as some have suggested?

The first historian to give significant attention to the subject of immigration to the area that became the United States was Marcus Lee Hansen. A student of the noted American historian Frederick Jackson Turner, Hansen called for systematic research on the various aspects of the immigrant experience. In *The Atlantic Migration, 1607–1860* (Harvard University Press, 1940), Hansen, himself the son of immigrant parents, focused on the European conditions and forces that had stimulated early migration to America.

Oscar Handlin (1915–2011) was perhaps the most influential scholar of American immigration history. His doctoral dissertation, published as *Boston's Immigrants: A Study in Acculturation* (Harvard University Press, 1941) when he was only 26 years old, won the Dunning Prize from the American Historical Association as the best historical study by a young scholar. This was the first study of immigration to integrate sociological concepts within a historical framework, but a decade later, Handlin published *The Uprooted* (Little, Brown, 1951) in which he combined an interdisciplinary framework with a personal narrative of the immigrants' history. Although many historians criticized this approach, the book earned Handlin a Pulitzer Prize.

John Bodnar's *The Transplanted,* while offering a contrasting metaphor for the immigration experience to the United States, shares with Handlin's work an attempt to present a general account of that experience, to portray the immigrants in a sympathetic light, and to employ an interdisciplinary approach by borrowing concepts from the social sciences. Handlin and Bodnar, however, differ in their perspectives about America's ethnic past. Handlin viewed the immigrants as people who were removed from their particular Old World cultures and who assimilated into the New World value system within two generations. In contrast, Bodnar argues that some first-generation immigrants may have shed their traditional culture quickly upon arrival in the United States, but more continued to maintain a viable lifestyle in their adopted homeland that focused upon the family household and the neighboring ethnic community. "Not solely traditional, modern or working class," writes Bodnar of this immigrant experience, "it was a dynamic culture, constantly responding to changing needs and opportunities and grounded in a deep sense of pragmatism and mutual assistance."

In the YES and NO selections, Oscar Handlin argues that the immigrants were uprooted from their Old World cultures as they attempted to adjust to an unfamiliar and often hostile environment in the United States. Mark Wyman points out that many immigrants to the United States believed that their stay in America would be temporary, a fact that limited their efforts at assimilation and reinforced ties to their original homelands.

YES

Oscar Handlin

The Shock of Alienation

... **A**s the passing years widened the distance, the land the immigrants had left acquired charm and beauty. Present problems blurred those they had left unsolved behind; and in the haze of memory it seemed to these people they had formerly been free of present dissatisfactions. It was as if the Old World became a great mirror into which they looked to see right all that was wrong with the New. The landscape was prettier, the neighbors more friendly, and religion more efficacious; in the frequent crises when they reached the limits of their capacities, the wistful reflection came: *This would not have happened there.*

The real contacts were, however, disappointing. The requests—that back there a mass be said, or a wise one consulted, or a religious medal be sent over—those were gestures full of hope. But the responses were inadequate; like all else they shrank in the crossing. The immigrants wrote, but the replies, when they came, were dull, even trite in their mechanical phrases, or so it seemed to those who somehow expected these messages to evoke the emotions that had gone into their own painfully composed letters. Too often the eagerly attended envelopes proved to be only empty husks, the inner contents valueless. After the long wait before the postman came, the sheets of garbled writing were inevitably below expectations. There was a trying sameness to the complaints of hard times, to the repetitious petty quarrels; and before long there was impatience with the directness with which the formal greeting led into the everlasting requests for aid.

This last was a sore point with the immigrants. The friends and relatives who had stayed behind could not get it out of their heads that in America the streets were paved with gold. *Send me for a coat. . . . There is a piece of land here and if only you would send, we could buy it. . . . Our daughter could be married, but we have not enough for a dowry. . . . We are ashamed, everyone else gets . . . much more frequently than we.* Implicit in these solicitations was the judgment that the going-away had been a desertion, that unfulfilled obligations still remained, and that the village could claim assistance as a right from its departed members.

From the United States it seemed there was no comprehension, back there, of the difficulties of settlement. It was exasperating by sacrifices to scrape together the remittances and to receive in return a catalogue of new needs, as if there were not needs enough in the New World too. The immigrants never

From *The Uprooted: The Epic Story of the Great Migrations That Made the American People,* 2nd ed. by Oscar Handlin (Little, Brown and Company, 1951, 1973), excerpts from pp. 260–266, 270–274, 279–285. Copyright © 1951, 1973 by Oscar Handlin. Reprinted by permission of Little, Brown and Company/Hachette Book Group USA and the author.

shook off the sense of obligation to help; but they did come to regard their Old Countrymen as the kind of people who depended on help. The trouble with the Europeans was, they could not stand on their own feet.

The cousin green off the boat earned the same negative appraisal. Though he be a product of the homeland, yet here he cut a pitiable figure; awkward manners, rude clothes, and a thoroughgoing ineptitude in the new situation were his most prominent characteristics. The older settler found the welcome almost frozen on his lips in the face of such backwardness.

In every real contact the grandeur of the village faded; it did not match the immigrants' vision of it and it did not stand up in a comparison with America. When the picture came, the assembled family looked at it beneath the light. This was indeed the church, but it had not been remembered so; and the depressing contrast took some of the joy out of remembering.

The photograph did not lie. There it was, a low building set against the dusty road, weather-beaten and making a candid display of its ill-repair. But the recollections did not lie either. As if it had been yesterday that they passed through those doors, they could recall the sense of spaciousness and elevation that sight of the structure had always aroused.

Both impressions were true, but irreconcilable. The mental image and the paper representation did not jibe because the one had been formed out of the standards and values of the Old Country, while the other was viewed in the light of the standards and values of the New. And it was the same with every other retrospective contact. Eagerly the immigrants continued to look back across the Atlantic in search of the satisfactions of fellowship. But the search was not rewarded. Having become Americans, they were no longer villagers. Though they might willingly assume the former obligations and recognize the former responsibilities, they could not recapture the former points of view or hold to the former judgments. They had seen too much, experienced too much to be again members of the community. It was a vain mission on which they continued to dispatch the letters; these people, once separated, would never belong again.

Their home now was a country in which they had not been born. Their place in society they had established for themselves through the hardships of crossing and settlement. The process had changed them, had altered the most intimate aspects of their lives. Every effort to cling to inherited ways of acting and thinking had led into a subtle adjustment by which those ways were given a new American form. No longer Europeans, could the immigrants then say that they belonged in America? The answer depended upon the conceptions held by other citizens of the United States of the character of the nation and of the role of the newcomers within it.

In the early nineteenth century, those already established on this side of the ocean regarded immigration as a positive good. When travel by sea became safe after the general peace of 1815 and the first fresh arrivals trickled in, there was a general disposition to welcome the movement. The favorable attitude persisted even when the tide mounted to the flood levels of the 1840s and 1850s. The man off the boat was then accepted without question or condition.

The approval of unlimited additions to the original population came easily to Americans who were conscious of the youth of their country. Standing at the edge of an immense continent, they were moved by the challenge of empty land almost endless in its extension. Here was room enough, and more, for all who would bend their energies to its exploitation. The shortage was of labor and not of acres; every pair of extra hands increased the value of the abundant resources and widened opportunities for everyone.

The youth of the nation also justified the indiscriminate admission of whatever foreigners came to these shores. There was high faith in the destiny of the Republic, assurance that its future history would justify the Revolution and the separation from Great Britain. The society and the culture that would emerge in this territory would surpass those of the Old World because they would not slavishly imitate the outmoded forms and the anachronistic traditions that constricted men in Europe. The United States would move in new directions of its own because its people were a new people.

There was consequently a vigorous insistence that this country was not simply an English colony become independent. It was a nation unique in its origins, produced by the mixture of many different types out of which had come an altogether fresh amalgam, the American. The ebullient citizens who believed and argued that their language, their literature, their art, and their polity were distinctive and original also believed and argued that their population had not been derived from a single source but had rather acquired its peculiar characteristics from the blending of a variety of strains.

There was confidence that the process would continue. The national type had not been fixed by its given antecedents; it was emerging from the experience of life on a new continent. Since the quality of men was determined not by the conditions surrounding their birth, but by the environment within which they passed their lives, it was pointless to select among them. All would come with minds and spirits fresh for new impressions; and being in America would make Americans of them. Therefore it was best to admit freely everyone who wished to make a home here. The United States would then be a great smelting pot, great enough so that there was room for all who voluntarily entered; and the nation that would ultimately be cast from that crucible would be all the richer for the diversity of the elements that went into the molten mixture.

The legislation of most of the nineteenth century reflected this receptive attitude. The United States made no effort actively to induce anyone to immigrate, but neither did it put any bars in the way of their coming. Occasional laws in the four decades after 1819 set up shipping regulations in the hope of improving the conditions of the passage. In practice, the provisions that specified the minimum quantities of food and the maximum number of passengers each vessel could carry were easily evaded. Yet the intent of those statutes was to protect the travelers and to remove harsh conditions that might discourage the newcomers.

Nor were state laws any more restrictive in design. The seaports, troubled by the burdens of poor relief, secured the enactment of measures to safeguard their treasuries against such charges. Sometimes the form was a bond to guarantee that the immigrant would not become at once dependent upon public support; sometimes it was a small tax applied to defray the costs of charity. In either case there was no desire to limit entry into the country; and none of these steps had any discernible effect upon the volume of admissions.

Once landed, the newcomer found himself equal in condition to the natives. Within a short period he could be naturalized and acquire all the privileges of a citizen. In some places, indeed, he could vote before the oath in court so transformed his status. In the eyes of society, even earlier than in the eyes of the law, he was an American. . . .

As the nineteenth century moved into its last quarter, a note of petulance crept into the comments of some Americans who thought about this aspect of the development of their culture. It was a long time now that the melting pot had been simmering, but the end product seemed no closer than before. The experience of life in the United States had not broken down the separateness of the elements mixed into it; each seemed to retain its own identity. Almost a half-century after the great immigration of Irish and Germans, these people had not become indistinguishable from other Americans; they were still recognizably Irish and German. Yet even then, newer waves of newcomers were beating against the Atlantic shore. Was there any prospect that all these multitudes would ever be assimilated, would ever be Americanized?

A generation earlier such questions would not have been asked. Americans of the first half of the century had assumed that any man who subjected himself to the American environment was being Americanized. Since the New World was ultimately to be occupied by a New Man, no mere derivative of any extant stock, but different from and superior to all, there had been no fixed standards of national character against which to measure the behavior of newcomers. The nationality of the new Republic had been supposed fluid, only just evolving; there had been room for infinite variation because diversity rather than uniformity had been normal.

The expression of doubts that some parts of the population might not become fully American implied the existence of a settled criterion of what was American. There had been a time when the society had recognized no distinction among citizens but that between the native and the foreign-born, and that distinction had carried no imputation of superiority or inferiority. Now there were attempts to distinguish among the natives between those who really belonged and those who did not, to separate out those who were born in the United States but whose immigrant parentage cut them off from the truly indigenous folk.

It was difficult to draw the line, however. The census differentiated after 1880 between natives and native-born of foreign parents. But that was an inadequate line of division; it provided no means of social recognition and offered no basis on which the *true Americans* could draw together, identify themselves as such.

Through these years there was a half-conscious quest among some Americans for a term that would describe those whose ancestors were in the

United States before the great migrations. Where the New Englanders were, they called themselves Yankees, a word that often came to mean non-Irish or non-Canadian. But Yankee was simply a local designation and did not take in the whole of the old stock. In any case, there was no satisfaction to such a title. Its holders were one group among many, without any distinctive claim to Americanism, cut off from other desirable peoples prominent in the country's past. Only the discovery of common antecedents could eliminate the separations among the really American.

But to find a common denominator, it was necessary to go back a long way. Actually no single discovery was completely satisfactory. Some writers, in time, referred to the civilization of the United States as Anglo-Saxon. By projecting its origins back to early Britain, they implied that their own culture was always English in derivation, and made foreigners of the descendants of Irishmen and Germans, to say nothing of the later arrivals. Other men preferred a variant and achieved the same exclusion by referring to themselves as "the English-speaking people," a title which assumed there was a unity and uniqueness to the clan which settled the home island, the Dominions, and the United States. Still others relied upon a somewhat broader appellation. They talked of themselves as Teutonic and argued that what was distinctively American originated in the forests of Germany; in this view, only the folk whose ancestors had experienced the freedom of tribal self-government and the liberation of the Protestant Reformation were fully American.

These terms had absolutely no historical justification. They nevertheless achieved a wide currency in the thinking of the last decades of the nineteenth century. Whatever particular phrase might serve the purpose of a particular author or speaker, all expressed the conviction that some hereditary element had given form to American culture. The conclusion was inescapable: to be Americanized, the immigrants must conform to the American way of life completely defined in advance of their landing.

⸱❦⸱

There were two counts to the indictment that the immigrants were not so conforming. They were, first, accused of their poverty. Many benevolent citizens, distressed by the miserable conditions in the districts inhabited by the laboring people, were reluctant to believe that such social flaws were indigenous to the New World. It was tempting, rather, to ascribe them to the defects of the newcomers, to improvidence, slovenliness, and ignorance rather than to inability to earn a living wage.

Indeed to those whose homes were uptown the ghettos were altogether alien territory associated with filth and vice and crime. It did not seem possible that men could lead a decent existence in such quarters. The good vicar on a philanthropic tour was shocked by the moral dangers of the dark unlighted hallway. His mind rushed to the defense of the respectable young girl: *Whatever her wishes may be, she can do nothing—shame prevents her from crying out.* The intention of the reformer was to improve housing, but the summation nevertheless was, *You cannot make an American citizen out of a slum.*

The newcomers were also accused of congregating together in their own groups and of an unwillingness to mix with outsiders. The foreign-born flocked to the great cities and stubbornly refused to spread out as farmers over the countryside; that alone was offensive to a society which still retained an ideal of rusticity. But even the Germans in Wisconsin and the Scandinavians in Minnesota held aloofly to themselves. Everywhere, the strangers persisted in their strangeness and willfully stood apart from American life. A prominent educator sounded the warning: *Our task is to break up their settlements, to assimilate and amalgamate these people and to implant in them the Anglo-Saxon conception of righteousness, law, and order.*

It was no simple matter to meet this challenge. The older residents were quick to criticize the separateness of the immigrant but hesitant when he made a move to narrow the distance. The householders of Fifth Avenue or Beacon Street or Nob Hill could readily perceive the evils of the slums but they were not inclined to welcome as a neighbor the former denizen of the East Side or the North End or the Latin Quarter who had acquired the means to get away. Among Protestants there was much concern over the growth of Catholic, Jewish, and Orthodox religious organizations, but there was no eagerness at all to provoke a mass conversion that might crowd the earlier churches with a host of poor foreigners. When the population of its neighborhood changed, the parish was less likely to try to attract the newcomers than to close or sell its building and move to some other section.

Indeed there was a fundamental ambiguity to the thinking of those who talked about "assimilation" in these years. They had arrived at their own view that American culture was fixed, formed from its origins, by shutting out the great mass of immigrants who were not English or at least not Teutonic. Now it was expected that those excluded people would alter themselves to earn their portion in Americanism. That process could only come about by increasing the contacts between the older and the newer inhabitants, by sharing jobs, churches, residences. Yet in practice, the man who thought himself an Anglo-Saxon found proximity to the other folk just come to the United States uncomfortable and distasteful and, in his own life, sought to increase rather than to lessen the gap between his position and theirs.

There was an escape from the horns of this unpleasant dilemma. It was tempting to resolve the difficulty by arguing that the differences between Americans on the one hand and Italians or Jews or Poles on the other were so deep as to admit of no conciliation. If these other stocks were cut off by their own innate nature, by the qualities of their heredity, then the original breed was justified both in asserting the fixity of its own character and in holding off from contact with the aliens. . . .

The fear of everything alien instilled by the First World War brought to fullest flower the seeds of racist thinking. Three enormously popular books by an anthropologist, a eugenist, and a historian revealed to hundreds of thousands of horrified Nordics how their great race had been contaminated by contact with lesser breeds, dwarfed in stature, twisted in mentality, and ruthless in the pursuit of their own self-interest.

These ideas passed commonly in the language of the time. No doubt many Americans who spoke in the bitter terms of race used the words in a figurative sense or in some other way qualified their acceptance of the harsh doctrine. After all, they still recognized the validity of the American tradition of equal and open opportunities, of the Christian tradition of the brotherhood of man. Yet, if they were sometimes troubled by the contradiction, nevertheless enough of them believed fully the racist conceptions so that five million could become members of the Ku Klux Klan in the early 1920s. . . .

◦◦◦

The activities of the Klan were an immediate threat to the immigrants and were resisted as such. But there was also a wider import to the movement. This was evidence, at last become visible, that the newcomers were among the excluded. The judgment at which the proponents of assimilation had only hinted, about which the racist thinkers had written obliquely, the Klan brought to the open. The hurt came from the fact that the mouthings of the Kleagle were not eccentricities, but only extreme statements of beliefs long on the margin of acceptance by many Americans. To the foreign-born this was demonstration of what they already suspected, that they would remain as alienated from the New World as they had become from the Old.

Much earlier the pressure of their separateness had begun to disturb the immigrants. As soon as the conception of Americanization had acquired the connotation of conformity with existing patterns, the whole way of group life of the newcomers was questioned. Their adjustment had depended upon their ability as individuals in a free society to adapt themselves to their environment through what forms they chose. The demand by their critics that the adjustment take a predetermined course seemed to question their right, as they were, to a place in American society.

Not that these people concerned themselves with theories of nationalism, but in practice the hostility of the "natives" provoked unsettling doubts about the propriety of the most innocent actions. The peasant who had become a Polish Falcon or a Son of Italy, in his own view, was acting as an American; this was not a step he could have taken at home. To subscribe to a newspaper was the act of a citizen of the New World, not of the Old, even if the journal was one of the thousand published by 1920 in languages other than English. When the immigrants heard their societies and their press described as un-American they could only conclude that they had somehow become involved in an existence that belonged neither in the old land nor in the new.

Yet the road of conformity was also barred to them. There were matters in which they wished to be like others, undistinguished from anyone else, but they never hit upon the means of becoming so. There was no pride in the surname, which in Europe had been little used, and many a new arrival was willing enough to make a change, suitable to the new country. But August Björkegren was not much better off when he called himself Burke, nor the Blumberg who became Kelly. The Lithuanians and Slovenes who moved into the Pennsylvania mining fields often endowed themselves with nomenclature of the older settlers, of the Irish and Italians there before them. In truth, these people found it difficult to know what were the "American" forms they were expected to take on.

What they did know was that they had not succeeded, that they had not established themselves to the extent that they could expect to be treated as if they belonged where they were.

If he was an alien, and poor, and in many ways helpless, still he was human, and it rankled when his dignity as a person was disregarded. He felt an undertone of acrimony in every contact with an official. Men in uniform always found him unworthy of respect; the bullying police made capital of his fear of the law; the postmen made sport of the foreign writing on his letters; the streetcar conductors laughed at his groping requests for directions. Always he was patronized as an object of charity, or almost so.

His particular enemies were the officials charged with his special oversight. When misfortune drove him to seek assistance or when government regulations brought them to inspect his home, he encountered the social workers, made ruthless in the disregard of his sentiments by the certainty of their own benevolent intentions. Confident of their personal and social superiority and armed with the ideology of the sociologists who had trained them, the emissaries of the public and private agencies were bent on improving the immigrant to a point at which he would no longer recognize himself.

The man who had dealings with the social workers was often sullen and unco-operative; he disliked the necessity of becoming a case, of revealing his dependence to strangers. He was also suspicious, feared there would be no understanding of his own way of life or of his problems; and he was resentful, because the powerful outsiders were judging him by superficial standards of their own. The starched young gentleman from the settlement house took stock from the middle of the kitchen. Were there framed pictures on the walls? Was there a piano, books? He made a note for the report: *This family is not yet Americanized; they are still eating Italian food.*

The services are valuable, but taking them is degrading. It is a fine thing to learn the language of the country; but one must be treated as a child to do so. *We keep saying all the time, This is a desk, this is a door. I know it is a desk and a door. What for keep saying it all the time? My teacher is a very nice young lady, very young. She does not understand what I want to talk about or know about.*

The most anguished conflicts come from the refusal of the immigrants to see the logic of their poverty. In the office it seems reasonable enough: people incapable of supporting themselves would be better off with someone to take care of them. It is more efficient to institutionalize the destitute than to allow them, with the aid of charity, to mismanage their homes. But the ignorant poor insist on clinging to their families, threaten suicide at the mention of the Society's refuge, or even of the hospital. What help the woman gets, she is still not satisfied. Back comes the ungrateful letter. *I don't ask you to put me in a poorhouse where I have to cry for my children. I don't ask you to put them in a home and eat somebody else's bread. I can't live here without them. I am so sick for them. I could live at home and spare good eats for them. What good did you give me to send me to the poorhouse? You only want people to live like you but I will not listen to you no more.*

A few dedicated social workers, mostly women, learned to understand the values in the immigrants' own lives. In some states, as the second generation became prominent in politics, government agencies came to co-operate with and protect the newcomers. But these were rare exceptions. They scarcely softened the rule experience everywhere taught the foreign-born, that they were expected to do what they could not do—to live like others.

For the children it was not so difficult. They at least were natives and could learn how to conform; to them the settlement house was not always a threat, but sometimes an opportunity. Indeed they could adopt entire the assumption that national character was long since fixed, only seek for their own group a special place within it. Some justified their Americanism by discovery of a colonial past; within the educated second generation there began a tortuous quest for eighteenth-century antecedents that might give them a portion in American civilization in its narrower connotation. Others sought to gain a sense of participation by separating themselves from later or lower elements in the population; they became involved in agitation against the Orientals, the Negroes, and the newest immigrants, as if thus to draw closer to the truly native. Either course implied a rejection of their parents who had themselves once been green off the boat and could boast of no New World antecedents.

The old folk knew then they would not come to belong, not through their own experience nor through their offspring. The only adjustment they had been able to make to life in the United States had been one that involved the separateness of their group, one that increased their awareness of the differences between themselves and the rest of the society. In that adjustment they had always suffered from the consciousness they were strangers. The demand that they assimilate, that they surrender their separateness, condemned them always to be outsiders. In practice, the free structure of American life permitted them with few restraints to go their own way, but under the shadow of a consciousness that they would never belong. They had thus completed their alienation from the culture to which they had come, as from that which they had left.

Mark Wyman  **NO**

The America Trunk Comes Home

The emigrant who once boarded a ship for America was returning, and with him came the "America trunk" that had been loaded so carefully for the outgoing voyage. In Finland, this *American arkku* was filled when it came home with everything from glass dishes to locks from a baby's first haircut to such prized American objects as a phonograph player or double-bitted axe. Its contents were the talk of the neighborhood, valued for decades as mementos.

The America trunk is an apt symbol of both emigration and remigration, of immigrants coming to America and returning to their homelands. The symbol persists, for the trunk occupies hallowed positions today in homes of third-generation Americans who cling to an image of their ancestral saga; in many European homes, similarly, the chest that came back is still revered as a remnant, a piece of that dream which once drew an emigrant across the seas.

But there was more, much more, symbolized in the America trunk. Within its recesses were tools or clothes that carried memories of hard struggles abroad. It provided a continuing connection with America, and because the United States increasingly played a leading role in international affairs, remigrants would be called on to interpret that role. They became *americani* and "Yanks"; America's importance raised their importance. And the items they valued enough to carry back in trunks would provide clues to what America's impact would be: was it tools the returners brought? or books on political theory, nationalist aspirations, labor organization, new churches? Or were the contents of the America trunk to be used to impress neighbors, perhaps to be sold to help purchase a shop or an extra piece of land? Modern students of immigration who seek answers to such questions are no different than Charles Dickens, who gazed at the emigrants returning home to Europe on his ship in 1842 and admitted that he was "curious to know their histories, and with what expectations they had gone out to America, and on what errands they were going home, and what their circumstances were.". . .

The Ubiquitous Remigrant

The trunks were but one small part, like the tip of an iceberg, of the enormity of the movement of people, objects, and ideas back to Europe.

Percentage rates of return ranged from 30 to 40 percent for such groups as the Italians, down to 10 percent among the Irish. Using these as a rough

From *Round Trip to America: The Immigrants Return to Europe, 1880–1930* by Mark Wyman (Cornell University Press, 1993), pp. 189, 191–197, 204–209. Copyright © 1993 by Cornell University. Reprinted by permission of Cornell University Press.

guide, it is possible to estimate that the total return to Europe may have been as high as four million repatriated emigrants during the 1880–1930 era of mass immigration into North America.

Examined within individual countries, these massive totals mean that one in twenty residents of Italy was a returned emigrant at the time of World War I, and shortly thereafter in a Norwegian county of heavy emigration it was found that one-fourth of all males over age fifteen had lived at least two years in America. Such high numbers signify that for the next sixty years visitors to European villages would encounter former residents of Scranton or Cleveland or Detroit, happy to describe their American experiences, wanting to know how the baseball pennant race was shaping up. . . .

A More-Reachable America

The years 1880–1930 stand out in the immigrant experience. Europeans crossed to North America in ever-increasing numbers as major improvements appeared in transportation. For generations before, however, an extensive pattern of short-term, work-seeking migration had existed in most areas of Europe, from Macedonians heading out to jobs around the Mediterranean to Irishmen and women crossing to England and Scotland for farm work. These nearby treks continued into the era of mass transatlantic emigration, as was evident in Polish totals: at the peak of Polish emigration to the United States in 1912–13, 130,000 left for America—compared to 800,000 heading for sea- sonal work elsewhere in Europe. It is true that development of the oceango- ing steamship, coupled with an increasing flow of news and publicity about American jobs, helped shift the destinations of many short-term migrants to the West, across the Atlantic. North and South America were becoming more closely fitted into the Atlantic economy and, if this meant that midwestern pork could now be packed for consumers in Germany, it also signified that Germans from those same consuming areas, and Poles, Italians, and Finns, could easily travel to find employment in those same U.S. packing plants.

These developments welded mass migration closely to the variations, booms, and busts of American industry. To these immigrants, America became basically the site of factory employment, gang labor on a railroad section, a job underground following a coal seam. One Italian could talk of his American experiences only in terms of trains, rails, and crossties, "as if all of America was nothing but a braid of tracks," a countryman reported.

As the trio of concerns of *journey, job hunt, and employment* became more predictable, less dangerous, the trip to America could then be viewed as some- thing other than a lifetime change. Like short-term labor migration within Europe, it became a means to improve life at home, through earning enough to achieve a higher status or more solid position in the village. It was not so much the start of a new life as another step in the process of social mobility. These factors in turn dictated that life in the American "workshop" would be temporary for many.

. . . In all, it is impossible to know what percentage of immigrants planned to return home, but it is not reaching far beyond the evidence to estimate that a majority in the 1880–1930 period initially expected to turn their backs on life and labor overseas once they had accumulated some wealth. Various things caused most to change their minds: in the United States these included realizing that opportunities in America outstripped those at home, gaining a better job, becoming accustomed to a higher standard of living, the arrival of news from abroad that removed the necessity for return, or gradual Americanization through learning the language, acquiring American friends, falling in love with a local girl.

Sometimes the shifts in expectations could be traced through a progression of names, as in the case of a Lithuanian immigrant couple who lived in coal towns in Pennsylvania and Illinois, always planning to return to Lithuania until they moved on to Oklahoma and decided to settle down. Their first two children were born in 1896 and 1900, when they still expected to go back to Europe, and were accordingly named Gediminas and Juozas. The third arrived in 1912, when they had become Americans. They named him Edwin.

But until that decision was made, until the carefully plotted return plans were finally abandoned, then every act, every expenditure had to be undertaken with an eye toward repatriation. This fact dawned gradually on an American in 1903 as he traveled about Italy and found that returned emigrants were much different, better persons at home; they had lived in brutal conditions in the United States because of "a feeling among them that they were merely temporizing . . .; that they had come to America to make a few hundred dollars to send or take back to Italy; and that it did not make much difference what they ate, wore or did, just so long as they got the money and got back." Their day-to-day existence in the United States would not improve until they were "drawn into the real American life" and changed their minds about going back to Europe.

Dreams of the village were especially strong among such persons; their thoughts were directed eastward toward home, even while they lived and worked in the West. This longing made assimilation difficult, and ethnic identities were further maintained by life in immigrant enclaves, blocking or discouraging connections with American institutions. Such isolation drew the fire of many Americans and settled members of the Old Immigration. Angered at the spectacle of U.S. dollars being carried overseas, they were also appalled by living conditions among those expecting to return. Labor unions suffered from the influx of these low-wage immigrants who often rejected invitations to join their fight for better wages and conditions. For years the unions approached the newcomers from two directions, often at the same time: seeking to organize the aliens while attacking them as strikebreakers and cheap competition. And the continued exodus of remigrants added to the pressure on union leaders to side with the restrictionist movement. . . .

As these immigrants held back from identifying with their new country of residence, many became part of a subculture within their own immigrant culture; that is, the temporary immigrant did even less than other immigrants to learn English, adapt to American ways, join American organizations. This reluctance further stimulated nativist attacks, which reached a climax with the restriction legislation of the postwar 1920s. Remigrants were not the only cause of the nativist surge, but their lifestyles in America helped fuel the restrictionist drive and they became one of the nativists' easiest targets.

Praise and Scorn at Home

As they returned to Europe the remigrants found a mixed welcome. Constructing new-style houses of brick rather than wood, many wore fancy clothes and endeavored to climb the social ladder. But villagers often looked askance at these people who seemed all too often to be putting on airs. One critic was the father of later emigrant Stoyan Christowe, who observed the well-dressed remigrants parading around their Bulgarian village and spat out, "An ox is an ox even if you put golden horns on him."

Their stories were often too fantastic, too farfetched. Norwegians began referring to them as *Amerikaskroner*—"tall tales from America." One man recalled his uncle's return to Norway in 1929 and his strange revelations about the things he had seen: "He told us about the Christmas trees that went round and round, he talked about streetcars, he talked of electric lights, he told of huge buildings, skyscrapers, he told us how they built them, he talked about the communications, railroads that went to every corner in the land, he told us about an industrial society which was so different from what we knew that it was like a completely different world." Was it all believable? Perhaps not. More recently, a returned emigrant showed his Norwegian grade school pupils a U.S. postcard with a photo graph of a giant Pacific Northwest log on a logging truck, the driver standing proudly on top. When he translated the postcard's legend, "Oregon Toothpick," one child retorted, "I've always heard that Americans have big mouths."

Their money was a reality that could not be denied, however. The cash carried home, together with the vast sums mailed back by those still toiling across the ocean, helped stabilize the economies of Europe and served as a stimulus for local booms. Business experience and connections became the most obvious gains from remigration in many districts, especially in Germany. Land, apartment houses, taverns, shops, and other firms were purchased by those coming home with "golden horns." For a time in Bydgoszcz, a Polish city in Pomerania, seventy agencies worked primarily to help remigrants obtain or sell properties. Two generations later the flow of retirees back from America would stimulate similar activities through their Social Security checks and factory pensions.

Most who returned in the 1880–1930 era went into agriculture, and this activity was at the center of much of the debate over their impact. Certainly agriculture was extremely backward in many areas; one estimate by returning Norwegians was that farming in Norway was fifty years behind that in the United States. But would returned emigrants be the ones to launch the required changes? Remigrants rushed to buy farmland, and large-scale commercialization of land became one of the most noted results of the vast emigration and return. But early evidence indicated that remigrants then continued or even expanded traditional and backward farming practices.

In contrast, areas such as Prussia and the English Midlands, where farm progress was extensive in the late nineteenth century, featured either the growth of larger land units with major investments of capital or the contrary development of smaller but more specialized farms that used the latest in farm technology and benefited from growing consumer demand. A student of the transformation of British agriculture notes increased farming complexity through use of artificial manures and new seeds and livestock breeds and adds that this "no doubt . . . also required flexibility of mind." But flexibility of mind regarding agricultural improvements may have been missing among many remigrants coming back to traditional farming in such areas as southern Italy or Poland. Few had worked on American farms, and this fact alone predicted that their impact on the Continent's agriculture would be minimal. Sporadic improvements and changes were widely publicized, but these were unusual, like the tomatoes planted by some Finns or the new flowers appearing in Polish gardens. Only in certain areas, such as parts of Scandinavia, could it be said that the remigrants were a definite mainstay of drives to modernize agriculture.

But in other occupations and situations, where emigrants had been able to learn American methods, improvements were obvious. To begin with, more vigorous work habits were widely noted. Also, many carried home sewing machines, which led to improvements in clothing, and holiday garb began to be worn more regularly. Homemaking benefited: when Irish women returned, they refused to continue traditional hearth cooking because it only permitted meat to be boiled; soon they installed grates or bought ranges. Personal hygiene improved, and a Hungarian report indicated that remigrants even kept their windows open at night, rejecting the traditional belief that night air held evils.

Many threw themselves into various campaigns for government change: Irish Home Rulers sought to throw off British control, Slovaks and Croatians pushed for separate nations, some Finns who had attended the Duluth Work People's College wanted to destroy capitalism. Others agitated for the development of public schools, and the remigrants' presence helped spread English through Gaelic-speaking areas of Ireland and in many other districts across Europe. Returned emigrants began to appear as members of village councils, school boards, even national legislatures; three of them became prime ministers, of Norway, Latvia, and Finland. . . .

Conclusions

In an examination of the remigrant from 1880 to 1930, before leaving Europe, at work in America, and after the return home, nine broad conclusions emerge:

1. The temporary immigrant was in truth far different from the immigrant who planned to stay. The expectations of any immigrant were all-important in directing his or her job-seeking, assimilation, and adjustment to American life, and the immigrant who stepped onto American soil planning permanent residence saw these goals differently than did the short-term industrial migrant. The latter was basically a *sojourner,* defined by sociologists as a deviant form

of the stranger, who remains psychologically in his homeland while living somewhere else, culturally isolated, tied physically but not mentally to a job. He may have changed his mind eventually, but until that point he lived the life of one who saw his future back in Europe.

Employment became the critical part of the remigrant's American existence. Like a New England girl arriving to work briefly in the Lowell mills in the 1830s, or a Turkish *Gastarbeiter* in Germany today, the temporary industrial migrant in the 1880–1930 period saw the world through different eyes than did (or does) the worker planning to remain. To ignore this fact and its implications is to miss a major facet of immigration's impact and an important explanation of immigrants' failure to assimilate despite lengthy residence abroad. Failing to take it into account would also make it difficult to understand why so many who returned home took up farming rather than the industrial occupations they had known overseas. If one task of the historian is to see the past from different angles, then following the contrary path of the temporary immigrant can provide an important new perspective.

2. The American immigration story becomes less unified, more diverse, when remigrants are considered within the broad picture of the peopling of a continent. There was little in common between the Bohemian family settling the Nebraska prairies in the 1890s and Bohemian men arriving for a year's work in a Chicago stockyard. Assimilation was soon forced on those farming in Nebraska; it was not even a remote goal of most of those lining up for their wages each fortnight in Chicago. One immigrant is not always equal to another—an obvious fact, but one made both more apparent and more significant when the remigrant experience is considered. . . .

3. There were many Americas contained within the broad vision of the United States by the 1880s, but America as the symbol of economic opportunity increasingly became uppermost for immigrants, especially those planning a temporary stay. Democracy was of little importance to a sojourner dreaming of adding to his piece of earth in the Mezzogiorno. When economic opportunity and democracy were seen as two branches of the same trunk, however, one could buttress the other in forming an image of the nation. But a remigrant who had witnessed few examples of democracy in his twelve-hour days in a steel mill would consider America in a different light than would another new resident escaping from religious unrest and finding herself in the competitive free-for-all of U.S. church denominations. Economic opportunity became the representative American symbol to millions.

4. The basis of American nativism was not opposition to return migration, but it gained several major arguments in the course of reacting to temporary immigrants. Nativists began to erupt in anger as thousands and thousands of short-term residents avoided assimilation and escaped abroad with their American earnings. The exodus goaded many Americans into ever stronger condemnations of immigration in general, and the identification of European remigrants with Chinese sojourners became complete. This provided an opening for earlier, permanent immigrants to condemn later arrivals and to become in effect immigrant nativists. Anti-foreign sentiment among U.S. labor groups leaned especially hard on the temporary immigrant.

5. The striving for status—to hold onto a vanishing position, or even to climb higher—emerges as one of the main forces behind remigration as well as emigration. Remigrants often left Europe to seek a higher status at home; they did not seek a permanent existence and better status in America. The New World may have represented a horn of plenty, but its wealth would be more useful back in Europe. Basic subsistence could be met, and after that the possibility of becoming landowners of importance in the village. Immigrants knew enough about life in the United States to understand the saying, "America for the oxen, Europe for the peasant." It was in Europe, not America, that the opportunity to reach a new level of existence waited.

6. The remigrant's importance in stimulating further immigration may have eclipsed even that of the much-maligned steamship agent. A large-scale exodus developed mainly from European areas where there had been an earlier emigration, which had produced a return flow of successes with money to purchase land and to construct "American houses." These acts promoted America with more impact than did handbills posted on village walls. There is also evidence of what might be called "emigration families," providing members from each generation who spent time in the United States and then returned, their tales handed down to stimulate others to try America later. The process was then repeated, generation after generation, and the remigrant ancestors became long-term role models. Their example competed with the emigrant letter as the chief propagandist of emigration. And the picture of America as a horn of plenty became indelibly fastened on a people who grew up hearing American stories around the winter hearth.

7. The return flow must be counted as a major reason that Europe's enormous exodus to America did not result in a net loss for the home society. Some form of general decline might have been expected for a continent that lost 36 million of its most active and future-oriented citizens to the United States from 1820 to 1975. The same could have been predicted for other regions that sent their people to America; one might even apply it to Mexico and the Caribbean nations today. But instead of causing a deterioration, the era of mass emigration proved overall to be one of general advance and progress for the people of many nations. This pattern continues. Certainly many things, tangible and intangible, have contributed to this result, but one is the extensive return flow of people, money, and ideas. As a Polish priest concluded from his study of the emigration from Miejsce parish in 1883, the returns from America meant that the exodus was "not a loss but a gain for this province." It could be said for most of Europe.

The Continent benefited as well from the return of organizational and political skills, as men and women of all ideologies and aspirations came back to launch labor unions and community organizations and to become involved in political affairs. Churches were challenged and new philosophies began to circulate. When Finland and Latvia achieved independence amid scenes of enormous chaos, leadership in each new country fell to those already experienced in labor and political struggles in America. Norway also chose a remigrant as its prime minister to lead the country through the dark days of depression and World War II. Many others coming back occupied government posts in municipalities as well as in national regimes.

The remigrants brought change in many forms. New words were carried home: modern Finnish has been enriched by many remigrant words and phrases, according to recent studies. Beyond this, many of those returning to Europe displayed an openness, an attitude that shook off the old and helped transform the peasant world. And remigration contributed further to a mingling of cultures which encouraged change as well as helping bring a gradual integration of the cultures of Europe and America.

The United States is more than just people transferred from Europe; Europe is guided by more than influences from America. But the two-way exchange was one crucial factor in the historical development of both, and the remigrant helped in both directions, a continuing link between two cultures.

8. American "exceptionalism," the view that the American experience has been unique and that developments in the United States were basically different from those elsewhere, is dealt a further blow by the remigration story. The United States was not a land where every immigrant came to stay; it was a country seen by many foreigners as a means rather than an end. As such, the American immigration pageant contained many scenes known elsewhere, for temporary stays as well as permanent moves have long been part of human migrations.

Parallels are numerous. Just as was often the case in the United States, temporary migrants were unpopular in the Ruhr, where German unions fought Poles, employers put aliens in the dirtiest jobs, and officials sought their removal. Swiss workers assaulted Italians in 1896, the government meanwhile blocked their naturalization, and welfare groups refused to give aid. This was nativism run wild. Riots erupted against Italian workers in France from the 1880s on; in 1893, fifty Italians were killed and 150 wounded during an attack by French miners at the Aigues-Mortes salt-works. There was physical violence in the United States, but as in Europe the opposition to those planning to return usually took other forms: unions sought their dismissal, politicians argued for bans on their employment, and editorial writers aimed darts at those who carried off national wealth. . . .

9. Finally, the story of the returned immigrant brings the historian face to face with the importance of human feelings, human emotions, in world events. Scholars often stress impersonal forces when discussing developments involving masses of people. But the fact that several million immigrants could turn around and leave a land with a higher standard of living and all the glitter of modernization, to cross the ocean again and return to a backward peasant village, with its distinctive culture and traditions, stands as supreme testimony to the pull of kin and home.

The Psalmist cried, "How shall we sing the Lord's song in a strange land?" And the longing to be within the family circle, in the familiar pathways and fields of home, has always been part of the human condition. The human heart must be given equal rank here with cold economic statistics and the pleadings of steamship agents. For the sense of being lost, away from moorings, left thousands of immigrants with the feeling that nothing seemed right in the New World—not holidays, not religious rites, not even the summer sunrise. They like the Psalmist felt lost in a strange land. The Swedish novelist of emigration, Vilhelm Moberg, reflected on these feelings in his autobiographical novel *A Time on Earth:*

> Man must have a root in the world; he must belong somewhere. He cannot abandon the land where he was born and adopt another country as his birthplace. Prattle about old and new mother countries is prattle only, and a lie. Either I have a country of my own, or I have not. Mother country is singular, never plural.
>
> The country you knew as child and young man was the country you left. That was your fate; you could never find another homeland.

In the final analysis, the story of the returned immigrants is a record of the endurance of home and family ties. It provides further evidence that, for many, immigration demonstrated the strength and unity of the family—both in going to America and in returning—rather than the family's weakening or destruction. For it was to rejoin their people, to walk again on their own land, to sit in the parish church once more, that the temporary immigrants repacked their America trunks and booked passage again, this time for home. The journey to America had been round-trip. And as they had helped shape life in the United States, its world of work, its image of itself and of foreigners, now they would affect the lives of their own families, their villages, their homelands. It would be a different future on both continents because of the returned immigrants.

EXPLORING THE ISSUE

Were Late Nineteenth-Century Immigrants "Uprooted"?

Critical Thinking and Reflection

1. Compare and contrast the YES and NO selections by Handlin and Wyman in terms of the way that immigrants identified with their native homelands and their adopted country.
2. Based upon your reading of the YES and NO selections, what problems did immigrants to the United States face in assimilating to American ways?
3. Given your understanding of the immigrant experience in the United States, to what extent is it appropriate to describe late nineteenth-century American society as a "melting pot"?
4. What does Mark Wyman's NO selection suggest about the geographical mobility of immigrants in the United States?
5. Why does Wyman believe that the portrait he paints of the immigrant experience challenges the notion of American exceptionalism?
6. Identify and summarize the nine conclusions that emerge from Wyman's argument.

Is There Common Ground?

It is very difficult for a country recognized and defined as a "nation of immigrants" not to appreciate the contributions made to the historical development of the nation by peoples who have migrated from other lands. Nevertheless, the ongoing debate over illegal aliens and national immigration policy threatens to undermine that reality. One wonders if a similar debate might have taken place among native Americans five centuries ago as Europeans began disembarking from their ships to plant colonies in what they considered to be a vast New World wilderness.

The newest immigrants to America have always occupied the position of "outsider," "foreigner," or "other" in the eyes of those claiming to be "native." All of those immigrants left something behind, but unless they were coerced by capture, as was the case with Africans and some indentured servants, or came as children with little voice in the matter, they made a conscious decision to leave their homeland in search of economic opportunity, political or religious freedom, or adventure—in short, a better life. They often faced hardship, a sense of alienation, and/or prejudice in one form or another. Still, they most endured, and remained rooted themselves in the soil of their adopted society and at some point made the transition from alien to citizen. For some Americans, that immigrant experience occurred centuries ago; for others, it has just begun.

Additional Resources

Stephan Thernstrom and Oscar Handlin, eds., *The Harvard Encyclopedia of American Ethnic Groups* (Harvard University Press, 1980) is a valuable collection of articles on every ethnic group in the United States. It also contains 29 thematic essays on such subjects as prejudice, assimilation, and folklore. Also useful and more manageable is Stephanie Bernardo, *The Ethnic Almanac* (Doubleday, 1981), purpose of which is to "amuse, inform and entertain you with facts about your heritage and that of your friends, neighbors and relatives." Leonard Dinnerstein and David Reimers's *Ethnic Americans: A History of Immigration and Assimilation,* 2nd ed. (Harper & Row, 1982) is a short but accurate text, whereas Joe R. Feagan's, *Racial and Ethnic Relations,* 2nd ed. (Prentice Hall, 1985) is a useful sociological text that examines the major ethnic groups through assimilationist and power-conflict models.

One of Oscar Handlin's staunchest critics was Rudolph Vecoli, who complained of the many inaccuracies in *The Uprooted* and faulted Handlin for failing to appreciate the different experiences of various groups of immigrants. These views are best expressed in Vecoli's "Contadini in Chicago: A Critique of *The Uprooted," Journal of American History* (vol. 51, December 1964). Maldwyn Allen Jones, *American Immigration* (University of Chicago Press, 1960) recognized the different experiences of different immigrant groups but discounted the significance of those distinctions and went so far as to ignore the traditional distinction between "old" and "new" immigrants.

In the last generation, dozens of studies have focused on the experiences of particular immigrant groups in the United States. See, for example, Moses Rischin, *The Promised City: New York's Jews, 1870–1914* (Harvard University Press, 1962); Jack Chen, *The Chinese in America* (Harper & Row, 1980); Ronald Takaki, *Strangers from a Different Shore: A History of Asian Americans* (Little, Brown, 1989); Matt S. Meier and Feliciano Rivera, *The Chicanos: A History of Mexican Americans* (Hill and Wang, 1972); Humbert Nelli, *Italians in Chicago, 1880–1930: A Study of Ethnic Mobility* (Oxford University Press, 1970); and Thomas Kessner, *The Golden Door: Italian and Jewish Immigrant Mobility in New York City, 1880–1915* (Oxford University Press, 1977). John Higham's *Strangers in the Land: Patterns of American Nativism, 1860–1925* (Rutgers University Press, 1955) is still considered the best work on anti-immigrant prejudice in this time period.

ISSUE 6

Were the Populists Irrational Reactionaries?

YES: **Richard Hofstadter,** from *The Folklore of Populism* (Alfred A. Knopf, 1955 and 1972)

NO: **Charles Postel,** from *The Populist Vision* (Oxford University Press, 2007)

Learning Outcomes

After reading this issue, you should be able to:

- Discuss the strengths and weaknesses of the Populist movement.
- Evaluate whether or not the Populists were primarily nostalgic for the agrarian past of the early republic.
- Compare and contrast Populism with the characteristics of Jacksonian democracy.
- Evaluate some scholars' interpretation that the Populists' world view centered on a conspiracy theory of history in which society was dominated by an international money power of Jewish bankers.
- Analyze the extent to which the Populists constituted a modern reform movement.
- Compare and contrast the reforms sought by Populists and Progressives in a modern industrial society.

ISSUE SUMMARY

YES: According to Richard Hofstadter, the Populists created a conspiracy theory around the issues of industrialism and the "money question" that activated a virulent strain of nativism and anti-Semitism, and revealed their desire to return to a rural utopia that they associated with the early nineteenth century.

NO: Charles Postel characterizes the Populists as forward-thinking reformers who hoped to use the government to manage an increasingly modern, technologically sophisticated, and globally connected society for the benefit of ordinary citizens.

Industrialism produced significant changes and affected every major group in American society. Manufacturers and laborers obviously experienced the impact of these new forces, but industrial influences were felt beyond the confines of the nation's growing cities. Industrialism also altered the lives of rural Americans who depended upon the soil for their livelihoods. Although they hoped to benefit from new markets and increased prosperity, the reality for most American farmers was greater poverty. After 1815, the independent, self-sufficient farmer began his retreat into American mythology in the wake of the relentless advance of commercial agriculture.

Between 1860 and 1900, American farmers confronted a steady downward spiral of agricultural prices, especially among major cash crops like wheat, corn, and cotton. Greater efficiency created higher production levels, which in turn drove prices to lower levels. Meanwhile, farmers and their families had to purchase manufactured goods, many of which were inflated artificially in price by existing tariff schedules. Purchasing new land and better machinery to offset declining prices only compounded the problem and created a new one—the difficulty of repaying credit extended by the nation's banks. By 1890, many farmers were losing their lands to foreclosure and were forced into tenancy or sharecropping; others abandoned the countryside for the city. The independent yeoman farmer, once described by Thomas Jefferson as the backbone of the nation, seemed to be losing everything.

The discontent bred by these factors led American farmers to conclude that the best solution lay in organization. This was a momentous decision on the part of a group of citizens who for generations had expressed a commitment to individualism of the most rugged sort. But with industrialists forming managers' associations and urban workers pushing for the recognition of their unions, many farmers decided to follow suit. Initial attempts to organize resulted in the National Grange of the Patrons of Husbandry in the 1860s, essentially a social group, and the Alliance movement of the 1870s and 1880s. Finally, farmers attempted to organize an effective political movement in the 1890s, which culminated in the People's, or Populist, Party. The Populists mounted opposition to the forces that threatened to make beggars of agricultural and urban workers alike, but with the defeat of William Jennings Bryan in the presidential election of 1896, Populism passed quickly from the scene. Nevertheless, many of the ideas and programs advanced by the People's Party subsequently were secured by reformers in the twentieth century.

Who were the Populists? How were their goals and ideology molded by the times in which they lived? As advocates of measures that would improve the status of the American farmer, how did the Populist Party react to the urban, industrial values that seemed to be dominating American society in the late nineteenth century? Did they oppose the modern processes of industrialization? Was the revolt of the Populists in large part an effort to return American society to the simpler, traditional agrarian utopia that they believed had characterized the United States in the early 1800s?

The first comprehensive scholarly study of Populism appeared, not surprisingly, in the midst of the Great Depression with the publication of John D. Hicks' *The Populist Revolt: A History of the Farmers' Alliance and the People's Party* (University of Minnesota Press, 1931). Hicks viewed Populism in a positive light as a response to hard economic times that served as a precursor to the Progressive movement of the early twentieth century and contributed to the nation's commitment to freedom and democracy.

In the 1950s, Hicks' positive interpretation met challenges from several scholars who emphasized what historian Robert McMath, Jr., has called "the dark side of Populism." Leading the charge was Richard Hofstadter who characterized the Populists as nostalgic, irrational, intolerant anti-Semites who associated all of their very real economic hardships with an illusory international banking conspiracy. Political scientist Victor C. Ferkiss extended this critique in "Populist Influences in American Fascism," *Western Political Quarterly* (June 1957), where he argued that the Populists, by encouraging majority rule over governmental institutions, committed themselves to a "plebiscitary democracy" very similar to that proposed for Germany by Adolf Hitler.

Walter T. K. Nugent, *The Tolerant Populists: Kansas Populism and Nativism* (University of Chicago Press, 1963) sought to rehabilitate the Populist image by insisting that the agrarian reformers he studied in Kansas were not xenophobic, anti-Semitic, or consumed by the bugaboo of a conspiracy of the "moneyed interests." According to Nugent, "The Populists have been accused of nativism . . .; instead, they were friendlier and more receptive to foreign persons and foreign institutions than the average of their contemporary political opponents. They have been accused of 'conspiracy-mindedness'; for them, however, tangible fact quite eclipsed neurotic fiction. They have been accused of anti-Semitism . . .; instead they consistently . . . refrained from extending their dislike of certain financiers, who happened to be Jews, to Jews in general." Similarly, Norman Pollack, *The Populist Response to Industrial America* (Harvard University Press, 1962), depicted the Populists as forward-thinking radicals who were receptive to mechanization and offered concrete remedies to meet existing difficulties.

The first treatment since Hicks to study Populism in its entirety was Lawrence Goodwyn's impressive *Democratic Promise: The Populist Moment in America* (Oxford University Press, 1976). Rather than focusing on the Midwest as did Hicks and others, Goodwyn argued that Populism developed out of the Southern Farmers' Alliance originating in Texas. Emphasizing the call for farmers' cooperatives and the development of a "movement culture," Goodwyn concluded that Populism was a truly democratic mass movement of which demise was followed quickly by the triumph of corporate capitalism.

In the YES and NO selections, Richard Hofstadter credits the Populist Party for being the first to seriously attack the problems associated with industrialization and for being the first political movement to insist upon federal responsibility for the common good of American society. At the same time, Hofstadter claims, Populism was provincial, nationalistic, nativistic, and anti-Semitic, characteristics that he ascribes to a group of reactionary agrarians living uncomfortably in a modern, rapidly industrializing nation.

According to Charles Postel, the Populists were neither irrational nor reactionary. Their vision for the United States involved the use of an active federal government as an agency of the majority, rather than the corporate and wealthy elite, in order to ensure fair access to the benefits of modernity. In short, they were far more forward-looking than their opponents in either of the two major national political parties.

   **Richard Hofstadter**

The Folklore of Populism

The Two Nations

For a generation after the Civil War, a time of great economic exploitation and waste, grave social corruption and ugliness, the dominant note in American political life was complacency. Although dissenting minorities were always present, they were submerged by the overwhelming realities of industrial growth and continental settlement. The agitation of the Populists, which brought back to American public life a capacity for effective political indignation, marks the beginning of the end of this epoch. In the short run the Populists did not get what they wanted, but they released the flow of protest and criticism that swept through American political affairs from the 1890s to the beginning of the first World War.

Where contemporary intellectuals gave the Populists a perfunctory and disdainful hearing, later historians have freely recognized their achievements and frequently overlooked their limitations. Modern liberals, finding the Populists' grievances valid, their programs suggestive, their motives creditable, have usually spoken of the Populist episode in the spirit of Vachel Lindsay's bombastic rhetoric:

> Prairie avenger, mountain lion,
> Bryan, Bryan, Bryan, Bryan,
> Gigantic troubadour, speaking like a siege gun,
> Smashing Plymouth Rock with his boulders from the West.

There is indeed much that is good and usable in our Populist past. While the Populist tradition had defects that have been too much neglected, it does not follow that the virtues claimed for it are all fictitious. Populism was the first modern political movement of practical importance in the United States to insist that the federal government has some responsibility for the common weal; indeed, it was the first such movement to attack seriously the problems created by industrialism. The complaints and demands and prophetic denunciations of the Populists stirred the latent liberalism in many Americans and startled many conservatives into a new flexibility. Most of the "radical" reforms in the Populist program proved in later years to be either harmless or useful. In at least one important area of American life a few Populist leaders

From *The Age of Reform: From Byron to F.D.R.* by Richard Hofstadter (Alfred A. Knopf 1955, 1972), pp. 60–65, 70, 75–83, 91–93 (notes omitted). Copyright © 1955, 1972 by Richard Hofstadter. Reprinted by permission of Alfred A. Knopf, a division of Random House, Inc. For on-line information about other Random house, Inc. books and authors: www.randomhouse.com

in the South attempted something profoundly radical and humane—to build a popular movement that would cut across the old barriers of race—until persistent use of the Negro bogy distracted their following. To discuss the broad ideology of the Populists does them some injustice, for it was in their concrete programs that they added most constructively to our political life, and in their more general picture of the world that they were most credulous and vulnerable. Moreover, any account of the fallibility of Populist thinking that does not acknowledge the stress and suffering out of which that thinking emerged will be seriously remiss. But anyone who enlarges our portrait of the Populist tradition is likely to bring out some unseen blemishes. In the books that have been written about the Populist movement, only passing mention has been made of its significant provincialism; little has been said of its relations with nativism and nationalism; nothing has been said of its tincture of anti-Semitism.

The Populist impulse expressed itself in a set of notions that represent what I have called the "soft" side of agrarianism. These notions, which appeared with regularity in the political literature, must be examined if we are to re-create for ourselves the Populist spirit. To extract them from the full context of the polemical writings in which they appeared is undoubtedly to oversimplify them; even to name them in any language that comes readily to the historian of ideas is perhaps to suggest that they had a formality and coherence that in reality they clearly lacked. But since it is less feasible to have no labels than to have somewhat too facile ones, we may enumerate the dominant themes in Populist ideology as these: the idea of a golden age; the concept of natural harmonies; the dualistic version of social struggles; the conspiracy theory of history; and the doctrine of the primacy of money. . . .

The utopia of the Populists was in the past, not the future. According to the agrarian myth, the health of the state was proportionate to the degree to which it was dominated by the agricultural class, and this assumption pointed to the superiority of an earlier age. The Populists looked backward with longing to the lost agrarian Eden, to the republican America of the early years of the nineteenth century in which there were few millionaires and, as they saw it, no beggars, when the laborer had excellent prospects and the farmer had abundance, when statesmen still responded to the mood of the people and there was no such thing as the money power. What they meant—though they did not express themselves in such terms—was that they would like to restore the conditions prevailing before the development of industrialism and the commercialization of agriculture. It should not be surprising that they inherited the traditions of Jacksonian democracy, that they revived the old Jacksonian cry: "Equal Rights for All, Special Privileges for None," or that most of the slogans of 1896 echoed the battle cries of 1836. General James B. Weaver, the Populist candidate for the presidency in 1892, was an old Democrat and Free-Soiler, born during the days of Jackson's battle with the United States Bank, who drifted into the Greenback movement after a short spell as a Republican, and from there to Populism. His book, *A Call to Action,* published in 1892, drew up an indictment of the business corporation which reads like a Jacksonian polemic. Even in those hopeful early days of the People's Party, Weaver projected no grandiose plans for the future, but lamented the course of recent history, the growth of economic oppression, and the emergence of great contrasts of wealth and poverty, and called upon his readers to do "All in [their] power to arrest the alarming tendencies of our times."

Nature, as the agrarian tradition had it, was beneficent. The United States was abundantly endowed with rich land and rich resources, and the "natural" consequence of such an endowment should be the prosperity of the people. If the people failed to enjoy prosperity, it must be because of a harsh and arbitrary intrusion of human greed and error. "Hard times, then," said one popular writer, "as well as the bankruptcies, enforced idleness, starvation, and the crime, misery, and moral degradation growing out of conditions like the present, being unnatural, not in accordance with, or the result of any natural law, must be attributed to that kind of unwise and pernicious legislation which history proves to have produced similar results in all ages of the world. It is the mission of the age to correct these errors in human legislation, to adopt and establish policies and systems, in accord with, rather than in opposition to divine law." In assuming a lush natural order whose workings were being deranged by human laws, Populist writers were again drawing on the Jacksonian tradition, whose spokesmen also had pleaded for a proper obedience to "natural" laws as a prerequisite of social justice.

Somewhat akin to the notion of the beneficence of nature was the idea of a natural harmony of interests among the productive classes. To the Populist mind there was no fundamental conflict between the farmer and the worker, between the toiling people and the small businessman. While there might be corrupt individuals in any group, the underlying interests of the productive majority were the same; predatory behavior existed only because it was initiated and underwritten by a small parasitic minority in the highest places of power. As opposed to the idea that society consists of a number of different and frequently clashing interests—the social pluralism expressed, for instance, by Madison in the *Federalist*—the Populists adhered, less formally to be sure, but quite persistently, to a kind of social dualism: although they knew perfectly well that society was composed of a number of classes, for all practical purposes only one simple division need be considered. There were two nations. "It is a struggle," said Sockless Jerry Simpson, "between the robbers and the robbed." "There are but two sides in the conflict that is being waged in this country today," declared a Populist manifesto. "On the one side are the allied hosts of monopolies, the money power, great trusts and railroad corporations, who seek the enactment of laws to benefit them and impoverish the people. On the other are the farmers, laborers, merchants, and all other people who produce wealth and bear the burdens of taxation. . . . Between these two there is no middle ground." "On the one side," said Bryan in his famous speech against the repeal of the Sherman Silver Purchase Act, "stand the corporate interests of the United States, the moneyed interests, aggregated wealth and capital, imperious, arrogant, compassionless. . . . On the other side stand an unnumbered throng, those who gave to the Democratic party a name and for whom it has assumed to speak." The people versus the interests, the public versus the plutocrats, the toiling multitude versus the money power—in various phrases this central antagonism was expressed. From this simple social classification it seemed to follow that once the techniques of misleading the people were exposed, victory over the money power ought to be easily accomplished, for in sheer numbers the people were overwhelming. "There is no power on earth that can defeat us," said General Weaver during the optimistic days of the campaign of 1892. "It is a fight between labor and capital, and labor is in the vast majority." . . .

History as Conspiracy

. . . There was something about the Populist imagination that loved the secret plot and the conspiratorial meeting. There was in fact a widespread Populist idea that all American history since the Civil War could be understood as a sustained conspiracy of the international money power. . . .

Wherever one turns in the Populist literature of the nineties one can find this conspiracy theory expressed. It is in the Populist newspapers, the proceedings of the silver conventions, the immense pamphlet literature broadcast by the American Bimetallic League, the Congressional debates over money; it is elaborated in such popular books as Mrs. S. E. V. Emery's *Seven Financial Conspiracies which have Enslaved the American People* or Gordon Clark's *Shylock: as Banker, Bondholder, Corruptionist, Conspirator.*

Mrs. Emery's book, first published in 1887, and dedicated to "the enslaved people of a dying republic," achieved great circulation, especially among the Kansas Populists. According to Mrs. Emery, the United States had been an economic Garden of Eden in the period before the Civil War. The fall of man had dated from the war itself, when "the money kings of Wall Street" determined that they could take advantage of the wartime necessities of their fellow men by manipulating the currency. "Controlling it, they could inflate or depress the business of the country at pleasure, they could send the warm life current through the channels of trade, dispensing peace, happiness, and prosperity, or they could check its flow, and completely paralyze the industries of the country." With this great power for good in their hands, the Wall Street men preferred to do evil. Lincoln's war policy of issuing greenbacks presented them with the dire threat of an adequate supply of currency. So the Shylocks gathered in convention and "perfected" a conspiracy to create a demand for their gold. The remainder of the book was a recital of a series of seven measures passed between 1862 and 1875 which were alleged to be a part of this continuing conspiracy, the total effect of which was to contract the currency of the country further and further until finally it squeezed the industry of the country like a hoop of steel.

Mrs. Emery's rhetoric left no doubt of the sustained purposefulness of this scheme—described as "villainous robbery," and as having been "secured through the most soulless strategy." She was most explicit about the so-called "crime of 1873," the demonetization of silver, giving a fairly full statement of the standard greenback-silverite myth concerning that event. As they had it, an agent of the Bank of England, Ernest Seyd by name, had come to the United States in 1872 with $500,000 with which he had bought enough support in Congress to secure the passage of the demonetization measure. This measure was supposed to have greatly increased the value of American four per cent bonds held by British capitalists by making it necessary to pay them in gold only. To it Mrs. Emery attributed the panic of 1873, its bankruptcies, and its train of human disasters: "Murder, insanity, suicide, divorce, drunkenness and all forms of immorality and crime have increased from that day to this in the most appalling ratio."

"Coin" Harvey, the author of the most popular single document of the whole currency controversy, *Coin's Financial School,* also published a novel, *A Tale of Two Nations,* in which the conspiracy theory of history was incorporated into a melodramatic tale. In this story the powerful English banker Baron Rothe plans to bring about the demonetization of silver in the United States, in part for his own aggrandizement but also to prevent the power of the United States from outstripping that of England. He persuades an American Senator (probably John Sherman, the *bête noire* of the silverites) to co-operate in using British gold in a campaign against silver. To be sure that the work is successful, he also sends to the United States a relative and ally, one Rogasner, who stalks through the story like the villains in the plays of Dion Boucicault, muttering to himself such remarks as "I am here to destroy the United States—Cornwallis could not have done more. For the wrongs and insults, for the glory of my own country, I will bury the knife deep into the heart of this nation." Against the plausibly drawn background of the corruption of the Grant administration, Rogasner proceeds to buy up the American Congress and suborn American professors of economics to testify for gold. He also falls in love with a proud American beauty, but his designs on her are foiled because she loves a handsome young silver Congressman from Nebraska who bears a striking resemblance to William Jennings Bryan!

One feature of the Populist conspiracy theory that has been generally overlooked is its frequent link with a kind of rhetorical anti-Semitism. The slight current of anti-Semitism that existed in the United States before the 1890s had been associated with problems of money and credit. During the closing years of the century it grew noticeably. While the jocose and rather heavy-handed anti-Semitism that can be found in Henry Adams's letters of the 1890s shows that this prejudice existed outside Populist literature, it was chiefly Populist writers who expressed that identification of the Jew with the usurer and the "international gold ring" which was the central theme of the American anti-Semitism of the age. The omnipresent symbol of Shylock can hardly be taken in itself as evidence of anti-Semitism, but the frequent references to the House of Rothschild make it clear that for many silverites the Jew was an organic part of the conspiracy theory of history. Coin Harvey's Baron Rothe was clearly meant to be Rothschild; his Rogasner (Ernest Seyd?) was a dark figure out of the coarsest anti-Semitic tradition. "You are very wise in your way," Rogasner is told at the climax of the tale, "the commercial way, inbred through generations. The politic, scheming, devious way, inbred through generations also." One of the cartoons in the effectively illustrated *Coin's Financial School* showed a map of the world dominated by the tentacles of an octopus at the site of the British Isles, labeled: "Rothschilds." In Populist demonology, anti-Semitism and Anglophobia went hand in hand.

The note of anti-Semitism was often sounded openly in the campaign for silver. A representative of the New Jersey Grange, for instance, did not hesitate to warn the members of the Second National Silver Convention of 1892 to watch out for political candidates who represented "Wall Street, and the Jews of Europe." Mary E. Lease described Grover Cleveland as "the agent of Jewish bankers and British gold." Donnelly represented the leader of the governing Council of plutocrats in *Cæsar's Column,* one Prince Cabano, as a powerful Jew, born Jacob Isaacs; one of the triumvirate who lead the Brotherhood of Destruction is also an exiled Russian Jew, who flees from the apocalyptic carnage with a hundred million dollars which he intends to use to "revive the ancient splendors of the Jewish race, in the midst of the ruins of the world." One of the more elaborate documents of the conspiracy school traced the power of the Rothschilds over America to a transaction between Hugh McCulloch, Secretary of the Treasury under Lincoln and Johnson, and Baron James Rothschild. "The most direful part of this business between Rothschild and the United States Treasury was not the loss of money, even by hundreds of millions. It was the resignation of the country itself as England had long been resigned into the hands of."

Such rhetoric, which became common currency in the movement, later passed beyond Populism into the larger stream of political protest. By the time the campaign of 1896 arrived, an Associated Press reporter noticed as "one of the striking things" about the Populist convention at St. Louis "the extraordinary hatred of the Jewish race. It is not possible to go into any hotel in the city without hearing the most bitter denunciation of the Jews as a class and of the particular Jews who happen to have prospered in the world." This report may have been somewhat overdone, but the identification of the silver cause with anti-Semitism did become close enough for Bryan to have to pause in the midst of his campaign to explain to the Jewish Democrats of Chicago that in denouncing the policies of the Rothschilds he and his silver friends were "not attacking a race; we are attacking greed and avarice which know no race or religion."

It would be easy to misstate the character of Populist anti-Semitism or to exaggerate its intensity. For Populist anti-Semitism was entirely verbal. It was a mode of expression, a rhetorical style, not a tactic or a program. It did not lead to exclusion laws, much less to riots or pogroms. There were, after all, relatively few Jews in the United States in the late 1880s and early 1890s, most of them remote from the areas of Populist strength. It is one thing, however, to say that this prejudice did not go beyond a certain symbolic usage, quite another to say that a people's choice of symbols is of no significance. Populist anti-Semitism does have its importance—chiefly as a symptom of a certain ominous credulity in the Populist mind. It is not too much to say that the Greenback-Populist tradition activated most of what we have of modern popular anti-Semitism in the United States. From Thaddeus Stevens and Coin Harvey to Father Coughlin, and from Brooks and Henry Adams to Ezra Pound, there has been a curiously persistent linkage between anti-Semitism and money and credit obsessions. A full history of modern anti-Semitism in the United States would reveal, I believe, its substantial Populist lineage, but it may be sufficient to point out here that neither the informal connection between Bryan and the Klan in the twenties nor Thomas E. Watson's conduct in the Leo Frank case were altogether fortuitous. And Henry Ford's notorious anti-Semitism of the 1920s, along with his hatred of "Wall Street," were the foibles of a Michigan farm boy who had been liberally exposed to Populist notions.

The Spirit Militant

The conspiratorial theory and the associated Anglophobic and Judophobic feelings were part of a larger complex of fear and suspicion of the stranger that haunted, and still tragically haunts, the nativist American mind. This feeling, though hardly confined to Populists and Bryanites, was none the less exhibited by them in a particularly virulent form. Everyone remote and alien was distrusted and hated—even Americans, if they happened to be city people. The old agrarian conception of the city as the home of moral corruption reached a new pitch. Chicago was bad; New York, which housed the Wall Street bankers, was farther away and worse; London was still farther away and still worse. This traditional distrust grew stronger as the cities grew larger, and as they were filled with immigrant aliens. As early as 1885 the Kansas preacher Josiah Strong had published *Our Country,* a book widely read in the West, in which the cities were discussed as a great problem of the future, much as though they were some kind of monstrous malignant growths on the body politic. Hamlin Garland recalled that when he first visited Chicago, in the late 1880s, having never seen a town larger than Rockford, Illinois, he naturally assumed that it swarmed with thieves. "If the city is miles across," he wondered, "how am I to get from the railway station to my hotel without being assaulted?" While such extreme fears could be quieted by some contact with the city, others were actually confirmed—especially when the farmers were confronted with city prices. Nativist prejudices were equally aroused by immigration, for which urban manufacturers, with their insatiable demand for labor, were blamed. "We have become the world's melting pot," wrote Thomas E. Watson. "The scum of creation has been dumped on us. Some of our principal cities are more foreign than American. The most dangerous and corrupting hordes of the Old World have invaded us. The vice and crime which they have planted in our midst are sickening and terrifying. What brought these Goths and Vandals to our shores? The manufacturers are mainly to blame. They wanted cheap labor: and they didn't care a curse how much harm to our future might be the consequence of their heartless policy." . . .

As we review these aspects of Populist emotion, an odd parallel obtrudes itself. Where else in American thought during this period do we find this militancy and nationalism, these apocalyptic forebodings and drafts of world-political strategies, this hatred of big businessmen, bankers, and trusts, these fears of immigrants and urban workmen, even this occasional toying with anti-Semitic rhetoric? We find them, curiously enough, most conspicuous among a group of men who are in all obvious respects the antithesis of the Populists. During the late 1880s and the '90s there emerged in the eastern United States a small imperialist elite representing, in general, the same type that had once been Mugwumps, whose spokesmen were such solid and respectable gentlemen as Henry and Brooks Adams, Theodore Roosevelt, Henry Cabot Lodge, John Hay, and Albert J. Beveridge. While the silverites were raging openly and earnestly against the bankers and the Jews, Brooks and Henry Adams were expressing in their sardonic and morosely cynical private correspondence the same feelings, and acknowledging with bemused irony their kinship at this point with the mob. While Populist Congressmen and newspapers called for war with England or Spain, Roosevelt and Lodge did the same, and while Mrs. Lease projected her grandiose schemes of world partition and tropical colonization, men like Roosevelt, Lodge, Beveridge, and Mahan projected more realistic plans for the conquest of markets and the annexation of territory. While Populist readers were pondering over Donnelly's apocalyptic fantasies, Brooks and Henry Adams were also bemoaning the approaching end of their type of civilization, and even the characteristically optimistic T. R. could share at moments in "Brooks Adams' gloomiest anticipations of our gold-ridden, capitalist-bestridden, usurer-mastered future." Not long after Mrs. Lease wrote that "we need a Napoleon in the industrial world who, by agitation and education, will lead the people to a realizing sense of their condition and the remedies," Roosevelt and Brooks Adams talked about the threat of the eight-hour movement and the danger that the country would be "enslaved" by the organizers of the trusts, and played with the idea that Roosevelt might eventually lead "some great outburst of the emotional classes which should at least temporarily crush the Economic Man."

Not only were the gentlemen of this imperialist elite better read and better fed than the Populists, but they despised them. This strange convergence of unlike social elements on similar ideas has its explanation, I believe, in this: both the imperialist elite and the Populists had been bypassed and humiliated by the advance of industrialism, and both were rebelling against the domination of the country by industrial and financial capitalists. The gentlemen wanted the power and status they felt due them, which had been taken away from their class and type by the *arriviste* manufacturers and railroaders and the all-too-potent banking houses. The Populists wanted a restoration of agrarian profits and popular government. Both elements found themselves impotent and deprived in an industrial culture and balked by a common enemy. On innumerable matters they disagreed, but both were strongly nationalistic, and amid the despairs and anxieties of the nineties both became ready for war if that would unseat or even embarrass the moneyed powers, or better still if it would topple the established political structure and open new opportunities for the leaders of disinherited farmers or for ambitious gentlemen. But if there seems to be in this situation any suggestion of a forerunner or analogue of modern authoritarian movements, it should by no means be exaggerated. The age was more innocent and more fortunate than ours, and by comparison with the grimmer realities of the twentieth century many of the events of the nineties take on a comic-opera quality. What came in the end was only a small war and a quick victory; when the farmers and the gentlemen finally did coalesce in politics, they produced only the genial reforms of Progressivism; and the man on the white horse turned out to be just a graduate of the Harvard boxing squad, equipped with an immense bag of platitudes, and quite willing to play the democratic game.

Charles Postel  **NO**

The Populist Vision

"**Y**ou shall not crucify mankind upon a cross of gold." With this indictment of the financial establishment, William Jennings Bryan, a young congressman from Nebraska, electrified the delegates to the Democratic Convention gathered under the hot roof of the Chicago Coliseum in July of 1896. On the fifth ballot, Bryan won a surprise nomination as the presidential candidate. The nomination marked a historic shift in party alignment, with the Democratic party embracing a platform of minting silver, a federal income tax, and other reforms demanded by rural and labor constituencies. Two weeks later, at its convention in St. Louis, the People's party also endorsed Bryan for president.

For Republicans, and a considerable number of "sound money" Democrats, the Populist endorsement confirmed their worst fears about the Bryan campaign. They viewed the Populists and their reckless currency doctrines as instruments of "anarchy" and "lawlessness." Theodore Roosevelt, the police commissioner of New York City at the time, believed that the Populists were "plotting a social revolution," and to check their efforts at "subversion" he proposed lining up twelve Populist leaders against a wall and "shooting them dead." Similarly apocalyptic and fearful language characterized the hard-fought election campaign that pitted the Democratic-Populist Bryan against the "goldbug" Republican William McKinley.

Bryan's loss that November inflicted wounds on the People's party from which it never recovered. Populism failed in presidential politics. It failed to sustain a viable presence at the polls. And it failed to maintain any semblance of cohesion, as the movement slid into rancorous discord over who was to blame. "Middle-of-the-road" Populists accused the architects of "fusion" with the Democrats of betraying principles. The "fusionists" accused their critics of failing to recognize political realities. The faithful of both camps continued to keep the People's party name alive into the twentieth century. But their small numbers only confirmed that what had once been a powerful social and political movement was no longer so. Populism failed, leaving in its wake the question of why.

Lawrence Goodwyn has provided the most stirring explanation: the "democratic promise" of Populism fell victim to an insidious and Judas-like "shadow movement" ("fusionists") that betrayed honest and straight "middle-of-the-road" Populism to the tender mercies of corporate power. Such a rendering makes for gripping tragedy. However, it has little to do with the interior fault lines of Populist politics and ideology. It also fails to take into account the external obstacles that the movement faced. Among other things, the Populists had to break the formidable grip in which the two established parties held the political system. This presented a challenge that the People's party came as close to meeting as any third party had since prior to the Civil War. That the Populists realized the electoral strength that they did is at least partly attributable to their innovative melding of "middle-of-the-road" and "fusionist" tactics. Such flexibility was facilitated by the Populists' distrust of partyism, a distrust that also contributed to the Populists' undoing.

Goodwyn's tragedy fits within the larger narrative of the defeat of traditional society by modernity: Populism failed because the wheels of history rolled over it. When social and cultural historians portray late nineteenth-century social movements as expressions of resistance to the market and modernity, it is difficult to avoid the conclusion that such movements, despite the heroism and humanity they may have revealed, were doomed from the outset by an inexorable historical process. In a provocative dissent, James Livingston recognizes comedy where others see tragedy. For Livingston, . . . Populism represented the premodern and republican past. But, unlike the others, he rejects the notion that the destruction of that past frames the tragic narrative of the twentieth century. Modernity offered democratic and progressive possibilities, Livingston contends, and farm and labor movements—with their soft-money doctrines and fear of "concentrated market power"—opposed the advent of the modern market society. The demands of modernity, Livingston implies, required the "eradication of Populism."

The setbacks suffered by the People's party at the polls, however, must not be read as extended referenda on the historical rights or wrongs of the Populist program. Populist electoral setbacks said little about the historic necessity, much less inevitability, of gold or silver, greenbacks or subtreasury loans. Summing up the defeat of the Populists and other late nineteenth-century reform movements, Gretchen Ritter writes that their loss was not determined by either destiny or nature. Their defeat "was not dictated by the anonymous forces of historical progress and economic modernity." Rather, she concludes, "political choice, structural constraints, and historical contingency shaped the fate of the antimonopolists."

Nor did the Populists lose because their views were unrealistic. True, their rhetoric could be far-fetched. Their discussion of the currency, for example, although grounded in plausible assumptions about the benefits of inflation, could also be utopian, paranoid, or apocalyptic. This, however, cannot explain the movement's failures, because the movement had no monopoly on delusional thinking. If anything, the Populists were outdone in this respect by academic and corporate elites who convinced themselves of numerous absurdities. Gold standard advocates, for example, could match any contenders when it came to absurd and paranoid arguments, as they dogmatically insisted that any deviation from a gold-based currency would immediately dispatch civilization to the hell fires of anarchy. Such flights of fancy—"superstition" as the Populists rightly called it—circulated as profound wisdom among American scholars and business leaders. As C. Vann Woodward noted, "The political crisis of the nineties evoked hysterical responses and apocalyptic delusions in more than one quarter." The Populist electoral failure therefore provides for a poor measure of the fanciful or overwrought. But it does say a great deal about which quarter had what political resources in terms of political machinery, mass media, bribery, and fraud—and the will to energetically use such resources.

Populism's failure must also be viewed in light of what came after. In the wake of the defeat of the People's party, a wave of reform soon swept the country. Progressive Era legislation in the first years of the new century expanded the role of government in American life and laid the foundations of modern political development. Populism provided an impetus for this modernizing process, with many of their demands co-opted and refashioned by progressive Democrats and Republicans. By a turn of fate, Populism proved far more successful dead than alive. At the same time, the process of co-optation and refashioning produced a reconfiguration of the social dynamics of reform. The Populist vision for a modern America was increasingly eclipsed by a corporate vision. . . .

The passage of the Federal Reserve Act of 1913 pointed to the direction of the shifting nexus of reform. Aroused to action by the financial panic of 1907, a wide range of banking, industrial, farming, and other business leaders sought to modernize America's archaic and patchwork monetary and financial systems. The banking establishment sought to protect the prerogatives of corporate managers and their control over the new system. The farm lobby and reform Democrats from the West and the South sought to ensure that rural constituencies would be given equitable access. The final product reflected concessions to all parties. Provisions long sought by rural reform included a more elastic currency to facilitate circulation and economic expansion. Later in the twentieth century, the need for such elasticity was well established in financial orthodoxy, although in 1913 some members of the financial establishment continued to denounce the notion as Populist financial heresy. The Federal Reserve Act also provided for a regulated and standardized system of rural lending, making a reality of farmers' demands for access to reliable lines of credit.

In significant ways, however, the Federal Reserve Act represented the eclipse of Populist ideals. The money question, as the Farmers' Alliance Committee on the Monetary System had explained, was ultimately about the "levers of power" and who controlled them. People's party leader Herman Taubeneck had expressed the same idea: "Who shall issue the necessary paper money and control its volume? This is the pivot upon which the money question revolves. It is the pith, the marrow, the alpha and omega of this great subject." To put the levers of control in the hands of the public, the Populists believed, required centralization. It meant replacing the federally chartered and corporately owned banks of the National Banking System with a federal subtreasury system and other institutions centered in the Treasury and Post Office departments in Washington. Alternative proposals circulated within the Farmers' Alliance, including a scheme for regional centralization with a "Cotton States Bank" and a "Grain States Bank" under the direction of regional "Mother Banks." The

People's party, however, insisted on centralizing the power to issue money and credit in the national bureaucracy in Washington.

In this regard, the Populists were no less "centralizers" than their corporate opponents. James Livingston argues that only the corporate elite and their intellectual allies favored monetary centralization because they alone represented modernity, whereas the Populist coalition of farmers and laborers stood for premodern "dispersed assets." But simply because the corporate elite claimed that their views were the only ones that conformed to the requirements of modernity did not necessarily make it so. The Populists were equally committed, if not more committed, to centralization as a means to rationalize and modernize the nation's monetary and credit systems. They looked to the Bank of France as a model, a system that was centralized, rationalized, bureaucratic, and modern, and that formed quite independently of corporate industry. If monetary centralization provides a test of modernity, then the Populists were at least a step ahead of most of their adversaries.

In terms of the levers of power, however, the Federal Reserve System bore little resemblance to the Populist ideal. The problem lay not with centralization, but in the structural distribution of control. If anything, the devolution of responsibilities to regional reserve banks only weakened the possibility of public accountability. The requirement that gave bankers and their business allies a majority on the regional boards of directors did the same. Most strikingly, the enormous power conferred on an unelected Federal Board of Directors epitomized how far monetary "science" had evolved toward an exclusive enterprise. Populists believed that the regulation of the money supply could and must be understood by the people whose business interests and livelihoods were affected by it. Expert statisticians and economists provided an essential service. But when properly compiled and presented, "any mechanic" could understand the essential rules governing currency volume, production, and demand. Gathered in their meeting lodges, farmers and laborers could master the "science of money" and thereby wrest the levers of monetary power from the corporate elite. Such was the Populist vision that faded into memory as a handful of financial wizards took the reins at the Federal Reserve.

The Country Life Movement reflected a change in the social dynamics of rural reform. In the 1880s and 1890s, rural modernization was largely driven by rural people. In the first years of the new century, urban people—government officials, academics, ministers, business leaders—grew alarmed at what they perceived as rural backwardness. The Roosevelt administration set up a Commission on Country Life to explore paths to "better farming, better business, and better living on the farm." The Commission's 1909 report warned that the "incubus of ignorance and inertia is so heavy and widespread" in rural America "as to constitute a national danger." The report pointed to stagnant farm productivity, crude business methods, appalling sanitation and hygiene, overworked women, poor schools, and primitive churches. Country Life reformers looked for remedies. They exuded a sublime self-confidence that through education and regulation, social ills could be healed and those deemed dangerously on the margins could be safely integrated into the progressive society. Much as upper- and middle-class

Progressives had set their sights on "cleaning up" the urban slums, now they would also bring modernity to the rural districts.

The recommendations of the Country Life Commission translated into policy that, for the most part, enjoyed support among rural constituencies. The Smith-Lever Act of 1914 formalized a national system of agricultural extension services to help farmers apply scientific and business methods. Federal and state agencies committed resources to fact-finding surveys and to a broad campaign to improve rural homes, schools, and churches. Progressive Era urban reformers focused on many of the goals of rural modernization that rural Populism had articulated a generation before—a fact that was both the greatest strength and the most glaring weakness of the Country Life Movement.

A number of farm reformers resented what they perceived as an act of usurpation. They pointed out that for years farm organizations had pointed to the same rural deficiencies and the same needs for reform the Country Life Commission presented as new discoveries. Nahum J. Bachelder of the national Grange caustically noted that the Grange itself was a "country life commission," and one with greater knowledge of rural conditions. Bachelder suggested that perhaps the Grange should set up a "commission on city life" to study deficiencies in urban life. Farm reformers who had spent their lives toiling in the traces of rural modernization often resented the paternalistic assumptions that inspired the Country Life Movement.

Country Life reformers paid special attention to improving the lot of rural women. Their proposals closely resembled those heard in the Farmer's Alliance in the 1880s and 1890s to modernize women's lives. They sought to place women's work in the home and garden on systematic and business lines, to boost efficiency by equipping kitchens and laundries with the latest appliances, and to improve women's cultural, social, and economic opportunities. However, when rural women and men discussed these issues among themselves in their suballiance meetings, it carried a different meaning from the concerted campaign of university professors, trained ministers, and other perceived outsiders. Despite their best efforts to reassure their rural subjects of their good intentions, the urban-based reformers often appeared as zealous missionaries seeking, as the Country Life Commission put it, "to teach persons how to live." Farmwomen at times responded coolly to expert lectures on hygiene and health. After wearing themselves out scrubbing and cleaning, they had reason to resent the exhortations from learned professors about clean homes and the civilizing effects of "combating dirt."

Urban reformers expressed similarly paternalistic and condescending attitudes toward the rural church. Again, the agrarian reformers of the previous generation had addressed the same deficiencies of the country churches that the Country Life reformers did. They, too, had criticized the "intense sectarian consciousness" that tended to put doctrine and creed above the social needs of the farmers. As the Country Life Commission put it, the country church failed as "effective agents in the social evolution of their communities." The Populists had felt similarly, and many of them had abandoned the church in search of other avenues of spiritual expression. The Country Life Movement, however, looked to reorganize the country church on the urban model, as urban professors and ministers tried to replace the small rural church with a new, modern, and consolidated church.

Predictably, the urban-based campaign for rural modernization opened fissures of distrust. Although rural people tended to support Progressive Era reforms, they also questioned the intentions of academics, urban ministers, and state and federal government agents seeking to refashion their homes, schools, and churches. Skepticism occasionally led to resistance. Historians have noted that the 1925 Tennessee law against teaching evolution in the public schools, for example, was driven less by ideological objections to Darwin than by an effort to reassert majority will over matters of education and religion in the face of intervention by perceived outsiders.

Meanwhile, academics, church officials, and government experts undertook extensive surveys of "rural problems." Among the problems they sought to resolve was why farmers responded with such ambivalence to urban efforts at rural uplift. Part of the explanation lay with farmers' skepticism about the intentions of their self-appointed urban benefactors. At the same time, a working assumption of the burgeoning field of rural sociology was the need to look deeper into the peculiar features of the rural environment and rural mind that led farmers to resist innovation, science, and progress. For modernity to come to the American countryside, it would take the concerted efforts of scientific experts and state agencies to convince the farmers to go along.

As the influence of urban-based elites in rural reform grew, the reform impulse was channeled along a narrower and more exclusive path. The Farmers' Alliance had originally promised to organize cotton, wheat, and other producers as a class. Rich and poor farmers alike would find strength in business organization. Alliance enterprises quickly demonstrated, however, that such organization was far more accessible to prosperous and land-owning farmers than cash-poor and debt-strapped small farmers and tenants. The Progressive Era system of business organization tilted even more sharply in favor of the former, and largely excluded the latter. The broad Populist "confederation of industrial orders" gave way to a narrower coalition of the propertied and the exclusively white. . . .

The Progressive reformers of the early twentieth century saw themselves uplifting the human condition, shaping popular modes of thought, and engineering the society of the future. The efforts of the Country Life Movement to remake rural life reflected a vision that agrarian scholar James C. Scott describes in a broader context as "high modernism." The concept of "high modernism," Scott writes, is "best conceived as a strong (one might even say muscle-bound) version of the beliefs in scientific and technical progress that were associated with industrialization in Western Europe and in North America from roughly 1830 until World War I." It displayed "a supreme self-confidence about continued lineal progress" and "increasing control over nature." "High modernism," Scott concludes, was a "sweeping vision of how the benefits of technical and scientific progress might be applied—usually through the state— in every field of human activity."

Bringing Scott's concept to bear on American rural history, Deborah Fitzgerald writes that "high modernist" urban leaders of the 1920s and 1930s persuaded reluctant farmers to "become modern." By her account agricultural college professors, government agents, bankers, and other business leaders sought "to bring agriculture kicking and screaming into the modern world." In other words, modernity was imposed from the outside on a largely static rural environment.

Fitzgerald's narrative poses a number of outstanding questions, especially about earlier developments. What does it say about late nineteenth-century social conflict and the historic role of Populism and similar movements? Would the term "high modernism" apply to the Populist vision, at least as Scott defines it? No less than their industrial counterparts, Leonidas Polk, Charles Macune, Mary Elizabeth Lease, Marion Cannon, Reuben Kolb, Herman Taubeneck, Marion Butler, Thomas Nugent, Marion Todd, William Peffer, and a host of other Populist leaders displayed a "muscle-bound" belief in progress, science, and technology. Their "evolutionary imagination" gave them enormous self-confidence that the course of progress was both lineal and knowable. They believed in the human capacity, through government action and otherwise, to harness nature and cure a broad range of society's ills. And they acted accordingly as agricultural commissioners, politicians, state appointees, and executives of powerful farm organizations.

Yet, if the Populist leaders counted among the "high modernists" of their day, they were of a special type. Unlike the Country Life Movement of the early twentieth century, rural Populism grew from rural roots. These roots were evident in the network of men and women—Populism's "organic intellectuals"—that sustained the movement's systems of lectures and rural newspapers and brought a modernizing vision to farmers' homes and meeting lodges. Where the Country Life Movement looked to improve the lot of others, the Populists were modernizers from within. They spoke in the language of self-help and sought improvements on the principle of self-activation.

The Populists incorporated into their modernizing vision mass organizations enrolling millions of common working people. In late nineteenth- and twentieth-century Europe, Asia, Latin America, and Africa "high modernists" of various types—socialists, radicals, nationalists, populists—built their modern systems on labor, peasant, and other mass organizations. In the United States, the Populists took extraordinary strides toward making mass organizations of farmers and laborers the mainspring of their vision of social reconstruction. The Farmers' Alliance and associated "industrial orders" gave flesh to the majoritarian, if not entirely democratic, principles that Populism pursued.

Where the Country Life leaders may have felt most comfortable in the university laboratory or business board meeting, the Macunes and Polks of Populism were at home in gatherings of people with callused hands and sunburned necks. Manual labor was part of the ethos that shaped the possibilities for a broad and inclusive coalition. Many rural Populists disapproved of strikes and labor boycotts and erected walls of hostility against immigrant and Chinese workers in particular. Yet the emergence of labor Populism within the ranks of railway employees, miners, and other sections of the working class revealed that Populism had the potential of an expansive organizational alliance.

As social engineers, the Populists were second to none in terms of earnest commitment and scope of vision. The Populist movement contained too many diverse and contradictory elements to speak of a single Populist social blueprint.

Some of these elements, such as Bellamy's Nationalism, represented influential mental constructs more than a practical system of reform. Other elements were not unique to the Populists at all but were broadly pursued by modernizers among business, academic, and political leaders. This was especially true in regard to race, with all of the ominous implications that entailed.

Nonetheless, the sum of Populist strivings leaves a distinct outline of what their "cooperative commonwealth" might have looked like. In regard to the nation's business, the Populists hoped to take the materials at hand—the latest technologies and organizational systems—and use them to rationalize markets and regulate and centralize the channels of commerce and finance. Their vision involved a complex and dynamic combination of public and private, cooperative and corporate, municipal and nationalized property relations. Progressive Era models contained elements of this complexity. However, the Populist version was more flexible in terms of encroachments on private and corporate prerogatives. This included a major role for the self-organization of labor within the management and structure of the economy, a role that American corporate managers would fiercely—and successfully—resist.

The Populists wanted an active government to ensure fair access to the benefits of modernity. By way of the referendum and the initiative and other political reforms, Populists sought to reshape government as an agency of the majority rather than of the corporate and wealthy minority. A federal income tax on high incomes was part of the Populist goal of checking the concentration of wealth and spreading the abundance of farm and factory to those who produced it. But there was a reason why so much of the Populist imagination focused on publicly owned and subsidized systems of postal delivery, telecommunications, railways, and the perfection of the public system of education. The Populist republic would squarely and equitably place even the rural "clodhopper" on the national and international grid of modern culture and knowledge.

For the 1892 electoral canvass, Thomas Watson published a campaign book under the title *Not a Revolt; It Is a Revolution*. Populism would usher in "a new order of things," "re-mark the lines of life," and bring a complete "revolution in the old systems." In the fever of electoral warfare, both friends and foes of the third-party movement tended to accept similar terms: for better or for worse, a Populist victory at the polls meant a momentous transformation of American society. Through the prism of time, it is apparent that a Populist triumph would have been less of a revolution than advertised. A Populist United States would have taken evolutionary steps to reform and rationalize the capitalist system. Perhaps it would have placed American institutions on paths akin to those of Canada or even Denmark—significant changes but hardly the overthrow of existing conditions. Yet, Populism did indeed represent something momentous. It mobilized millions of ordinary men and women in an effort to steer the political and economic institutions of an increasingly modern, technologically sophisticated, and globally connected society. The significance of this movement lay in the act of trying.

EXPLORING THE ISSUE

Were the Populists Irrational Reactionaries?

Critical Thinking and Reflection

1. What were the major goals of the Populists, and how effective were they in realizing those goals?
2. Compare and contrast the assessments of the Populists offered by Hofstadter and Postel. Which author makes the most persuasive argument?
3. What evidence does Hofstadter present that the Populists were anti-Semitic?
4. What is the relationship between Populism and Progressivism?
5. Based on your reading of the YES and NO selections, did the Populists fail? If so, why?

Is There Common Ground?

If one looks at the Progressive movement that was developing at the local and state levels contemporaneously with Populism in the 1890s, it is clear that, although the participants among these two groups of reformers came from different backgrounds, they nevertheless shared notions that the political, economic, and social climate of the United States was in need of change. By 1920, most of the planks of the Populists' 1892 Omaha Platform had been enacted into law by the Progressives. Moreover, both the Populists and Progressives were motivated by a desire to use the federal government as an influential instrument to promote a more just, democratic society. With that in mind, it is important to understand that many individuals and groups in contemporary America who define themselves as "Populists" and who are more notable for challenging the legitimacy of U.S. federal government activism are not necessarily operating within the ideological tradition of the late nineteenth-century Populists.

Additional Resources

The origins of the farmers' revolt of the late nineteenth century are explored in D. Sven Nordin, *Rich Harvest: A History of the Grange, 1867–1900* (University Press of Mississippi, 1974); Robert C. McMath, Jr., *Populist Vanguard: A History of the Southern Farmers' Alliance* (University of North Carolina Press, 1975); Michael Schwartz, *Radical Protest and Social Structure: The Southern*

Farmers' Alliance and Cotton Tenancy, 1880–1890 (Academic, 1976); Stephen Hahn, *The Roots of Southern Populism: Yeoman Farmers and the Transformation of the Georgia Upcountry, 1850–1890* (Oxford University Press, 1983); and Donna Barnes, *Farmers in Rebellion: The Rise and Fall of the Southern Farmers' Alliance and People's Party in Texas* (University of Texas Press, 1984).

Agricultural History (April 1965) published the results of a symposium on Populism in the form of essays by several revisionists and their critics. For an insightful analysis of Hofstadter's rendering of Populism within the context of the historian's craft, see Robert M. Collins, "The Originality Trap: Richard Hofstadter on Populism," *Journal of American History* (vol. 76, June 1989, pp. 150–167). Interested students also should consult two historiographical collections—Theodore Saloutos, ed., *Populism: Reaction or Reform?* (Holt, Rinehart and Winston, 1968) and William F. Holmes, ed., *American Populism* (D.C. Heath, 1994)—as well as Worth Robert Miller, "A Centennial Historiography of American Populism," *Kansas History* (vol. 16, Spring 1993, pp. 54–69). Norman Pollack offers a valuable collection of primary sources in *The Populist Mind* (Bobbs-Merrill, 1967). Also of importance is his *The Just Polity: Populism, Law, and Human Welfare* (University of Illinois Press, 1987). Bruce Palmer, *"Man Over Money": The Southern Populist Critique of American Capitalism* (1980), offers divergent views of some of the themes developed by Goodwyn. More recently, Gene Clanton's *Populism: The Humane Preference in America, 1890–1900* (Twayne, 1991) and Robert C. McMath, Jr.'s *American Populism: A Social History, 1877–1898* (Hill and Wang, 1993) have surveyed the entire Populist movement.

The relationship between African Americans and southern white Populists was enormously complex. C. Vann Woodward's classic biography *Tom Watson: Agrarian Rebel* (Oxford University Press, 1938) and Lawrence Goodwyn's "Populist Dreams and Negro Rights: East Texas as a Case Study," *American Historical Review* (December 1971) emphasize the success of black–white coalitions. Gerald H. Gaither, *Blacks and the Populist Revolt: Ballots and Bigotry in the "New South"* (University of Alabama Press, 1977), challenges the optimistic biracial portrayals of Woodward and Goodwyn. Gregg Cantrell, *Kenneth and John B. Rayner and the Limits of Southern Dissent* (University of Illinois Press, 1993), represents one of the few biographical studies of a black Populist leader.

Robert F. Durden, *The Climax of Populism: The Election of 1896* (University of Kentucky Press, 1966) and Paul W. Glad, *McKinley, Bryan, and the People* (J. B. Lippincott, 1964) are competent studies of the Populists' electoral defeat. William Jennings Bryan's involvement in Populist goals is covered in Glad, *The Trumpet Soundeth: William Jennings Bryan and His Democracy, 1896–1912* (University of Nebraska Press, 1960) and in the early chapters of Robert W. Cherny, *A Righteous Cause: The Life of William Jennings Bryan* (Little, Brown, 1985). Finally, for an intriguing argument that blends history with popular culture, see Henry M. Littlefield, "The Wizard of Oz: Parable of Populism," *American Quarterly* (Spring 1964).

Internet References . . .

Gilded Age and Progressive Era Resources

General resources on the Gilded Age and Progressive Era.

www2.tntech.edu/history/gilprog.html

The Roaring 20s and the Great Depression

An extensive anthology of web links to sites on the roaring 1920s and the Great Depression.

www.snowcrest.net

New Deal Network

Offering more than 20,000 items, this website focuses on objects, documents, and images relevant to the New Deal. "Document Library" contains more than 900 newspaper and journal articles, speeches, letters, reports, advertisements, and other textual materials that treat a broad array of subjects.

http://newdeal.feri.org/

Work Progress Administration/Folklore Project

Open this home page of the Folklore Project of the Works Progress Administration (WPA) Federal Writers' Project to gain access to thousands of documents on the life histories of ordinary Americans from all walks of life during the Great Depression.

http://lcweb2.loc.gov/ammem/wpaintro/wpahome.html

Remembering Jim Crow

Created as a companion to a National Public Radio (NPR) documentary on segregation in the South, the website presents legal, social, and cultural aspects of segregation, the black community, and black resistance to the Jim Crow way of life.

http://americanradioworks.publicradio.org/features/remembering/laws.html

World War II WWW Sites

Visit this site as a starting point to find research links for World War II, including topics specific to the United States' participation and the impact on the country.

http://besthistorysites.net/index.php/ww2

Hiroshima Archive

The Hiroshima Archive was originally set up to join the online effort made by people all over the world to commemorate the 50th anniversary of the atomic bombing. It is intended to serve as a research and educational guide to those who want to gain and expand their knowledge of the atomic bombing.

www.lclark.edu/~history/HIROSHIMA/

The Enola Gay

The official website of Brig. Gen. Paul W. Tibbets, Jr (Ret.). This site offers a wealth of historical analysis and photographs of the events surrounding the use of atomic weapons on Japan in 1945.

www.theenolagay.org/index.html

Reform, Depression, and War

*F*rom 1897 to 1917, the country enacted a series of political and economic reforms collectively known as the Progressive Movement. The Progressives brought about major domestic reforms to ameliorate the worst abuses of rapid industrial growth and urbanization. One of the most lasting of these reforms was the environmental movement led by then President Theodore Roosevelt.

In the 1920s, tensions rose between the values of the nation's rural past and the new social and cultural values of modern America. There was controversy over the impact of prohibition schools teaching evolution, the rise of a new Ku Klux Klan, the emergence of "flappers," jazz, and the social consequences of the automobile.

The onset of a more activist federal government by the Progressives accelerated with the Great Depression. With more than one-quarter of the workforce unemployed, Franklin D. Roosevelt (FDR) was elected on a promise to give Americans a "New Deal." Every sector of the economy was affected by the proliferation of the Alphabet Soup New Deal agencies. Big business, agriculture, and banking continued to receive their share of government handouts, but working-class Americans also were given government help. Historians continue to debate whether the New Deal measures ameliorated or prolonged the Great Depression.

The emergence of a conservative Congress and the impending world war killed the New Deal by 1939. With the fall of France to the Germans in 1940, FDR tried to abandon the traditional foreign policy of isolationism by aiding allies in Europe and Asia without involvement in the war. The effort failed, and on December 7, 1941, the Japanese attacked Pearl Harbor. At home, African Americans connected the struggle for democracy abroad to their own efforts to secure full citizenship rights in their own country. The war framed a debate over the status of blacks in the United States, whereas the end of the war through the introduction of weapons of mass destruction not only introduced the world to the Atomic Age, but also produced a controversy involving the moral efficacy of deploying such weapons.

- Did the Conservation Movement of the Early Twentieth Century Successfully Preserve the American Environment?
- Was Woodrow Wilson Responsible for the Failure of the United States to Join the League of Nations?
- Were the 1920s an Era of Social and Cultural Rebellion?
- Did the New Deal Prolong the Great Depression?
- Was the World War II Era a Watershed for the Civil Rights Movement?
- Was It Necessary to Drop the Atomic Bomb to End World War II?

ISSUE 7

Did the Conservation Movement of the Early Twentieth Century Successfully Preserve the American Environment?

YES: T.H. Watkins, from "Father of the Forests (Gifford Pinchot)," *American Heritage* (vol. 52, February/March 1991)

NO: Ted Steinberg, from *Conservation Reconsidered* (Oxford University Press, 2002)

Learning Outcomes
After reading this issue, you should be able to:
• Understand why the conservation movement began in the late nineteenth century.
• Distinguish between the preservationists, conservationists, and the utilitarian conservationists.
• Evaluate the successes and failures of Chief Forester Gifford Pinchot as a utilitarian conservationist.
• Critically evaluate what some writers consider the negative effects of conservation on our ecological system of forests, rivers, lakes, and farm land.

ISSUE SUMMARY

YES: According to T.H. Watkins, Chief Forester Gifford Pinchot was a practical conservationist whose agency managed to balance the preservation of the environment with the "wise use of earth and its resources for the lasting good of men."

NO: According to Ted Steinberg, the conservationists often had negative effects on the ecosystem of America's forests, plants, and animals in their effort to bend nature to conform to the desire of mankind.

On April 22, 1970, "Earth Day" was celebrated as protesters temporarily shifted their demonstrations from the Vietnam War to a concern for the environment. In the following decade gas prices at the pump rose from $.38 per gallon to $2.50 per gallon when the Organization of the Petroleum Exporting Countries (OPEC) cartel created oil shortages because of a disagreement with the United States' pro-Israel policy. Think tanks held seminars on topics such as "Global Warming" and "The Limits of Growth." Middle school children were pleading with their parents to stop smoking not only for health reasons but also because of its "ecological" effects on the environment. Thus was born America's second conservation movement.

It was not always this way. For most of this nation's history there was an anticonservationist ethic. In the seventeenth century, the English colonists were attracted to the New World because of the abundance of resources—water, timber, fish, animals—and most of all good climate and a limitless supply of land. A myth of "inexhaustibility" prevailed wherein the earth's supplies would never run out. The notion of unlimited growth with infinite resources ran opposite to the idea of conservation.

The idea of unlimited growth was given an additional boost in the nineteenth century when two treaties stretched the boundaries of the United States from the Mississippi River to the Pacific Ocean. The Louisiana Purchase of 1803 pushed the nation's boundaries north of Texas to the Rocky Mountains below Canada. The Treaty of Guadalupe Hidalgo, which ended the Mexican War in 1848, brought the United States the future southwestern states and, most importantly, California. When Thomas Jefferson acquired the Louisiana Territory, he thought it would take 300 years to populate the territory. But by the 1850s, when the southwestern territories were acquired, a new form of transportation—the railroads—had arrived and fostered migration across the country before the twentieth century arrived.

After the Civil War, there was a gradual shift to a concern for the environment. The Industrial Revolution and the flood of immigrants into the nation's factories and large urban centers created health problems beyond the scope of what the founding fathers had foreseen. Clearly, the end of the frontier with its unlimited supply of land and resources had been reached by 1900. There was a gradual recognition of the change, and this was reflected in the way Americans' views and policies toward the supply of trees and water reflected a desire to preserve these natural resources.

This *preservation* goal manifested itself in the national park idea, which had received support in the 1840s and 1850s from the philosopher and writer Henry David Thoreau. He was uneasy about the impending passing of the frontier, which he viewed as the mainstay of civilization. National parks, he believed, would not only protect animals and native Americans but also act as sanctuaries for civilization. Several states—Arkansas and California—had parceled out areas as sanctuaries, but it was not until 1872 that President Ulysses S. Grant designated over two million acres of northwestern Wyoming as Yellowstone National Park. Today the national parks such as Yellowstone remain incredibly popular as millions of tourists visit them to enjoy the natural beauty contained within, but the preservation movement represents only one phase of the conservation ideal.

Utilitarian conservation, or the scientific and efficient use of the nation's forests, represented a second characteristic of the conservation movement. In 1891, the Forest Reserve Act empowered the President to create "national forests" from the unappropriated public domain. The purpose of the act was to control the actions of the lumber companies from recklessly cutting down trees without any plans to replace them. "By the time the United States Forest Service was organized in 1905," says Roderick Nash, "it was clear that the national forests were not synonymous with national parks. Lumbering, grazing, and mining were appropriate uses of the former; the parks' purpose was preservation."

In 1901, the assassination of President William McKinley brought Theodore Roosevelt to the presidency. The youngest president to hold office at age 43, Theodore Roosevelt put the conservation movement in the national spotlight. A former rancher, big game hunter, and collector of rare species, Roosevelt also established 51 wildlife refuges, added land to several existing national parks, and created new ones in Crater Lake in Oregon, Mesa Verde in Utah, Platt in Oklahoma, and Wind Cave in South Dakota. He even spent 4 days camping in the Sierras with John Muir, America's leading preservationist.

Roosevelt's aggressive stance in favor of scientific conservation created a gulf between himself and the more conservative, business-oriented wing of his party. Both sides supported the Newlands Act of 1902 because it provided federal funds for the construction of dams, reservoirs, and canals in the West (which years later would provide new lands for cultivation and cheap electric power such as the Hoover Dam). But when Congress restricted its power over public lands in 1907, Roosevelt and his chief forester, Gifford Pinchot, seized all the forests and many of the power sites before the bill became law.

In 1898, Pinchot became the head of the Forest Division, a nondescript, powerless agency in the Department of Agriculture with 11 employees and a tiny budget of $28,000. With the help of President Roosevelt, Pinchot transformed the Forest Division into a powerful well-run government agency. First, he hired and trained a loyal cadre of workers who would manage specific areas of the national forest. Second, he worked with the President in establishing an ad hoc national conservation policy with the passage of the Forest Transfer Act of 1905 that shifted more than 63 million acres of land from the Interior Department into the Agriculture Department. By 1909 its domain had increased to 148 million acres. Pinchot and his associates were in charge of enforcing new laws, which charged fees for cutting timber and grazing cattle and sheep.

The fight between preservationists and utilitarian conservationists came to a head in the Hetch Hetchy controversy. Residents of San Francisco, worried about finding enough water for their growing population, saw the Hetch Hetchy Valley in Yosemite National Park as an ideal place for a dam. Support for the dam increased after the 1906 San Francisco earthquake and fire severely damaged the city. President Roosevelt and Chief Forester Pinchot agreed with the city's residents who voted in favor of a dam in a 1908 referendum.

Opposition to the dam came from the naturalist John Muir. A preservationist to the core and the founder of the Sierra Club, this Scottish immigrant had devoted his life to maintaining the nation's rivers, valleys, and mountains in their pristine state. Nevertheless, after many delays the dam's construction was completed in the 1920s.

Modern historians such as Roderick Nash tend to favor the preservationists in their interpretation of the conservation movement. More recently, however, historians such as T.H. Watkins and Char Miller have given Gifford Pinchot his historical due. In the YES and NO selections Watkins and Ted Steinberg debate the consequences of efforts to preserve the nation's natural resources during the Progressive era. In the YES selection, T.H. Watkins provides a complimentary biographical sketch of Gifford Pinchot, "who knew more about the woodlands than any man in America." Watkins praises Pinchot's ability to balance efforts to protect the nation's natural beauty with a utilitarian reform goal of meeting the needs of the American people, even when it meant incurring the wrath of strict preservationists such as John Muir.

In the NO selection, Ted Steinberg is less concerned about the arguments and philosophies of the utilitarian conservationists and preservationists and more interested in the effects that government conservation measures had "on the ecosystems that were the target of this important reform impulse." Steinberg complains that teaching the arguments between the conservationists and preservationists without discussing the outcomes of the government's policies is similar to studying the Civil War without mentioning who won the war. Steinberg's major argument is that the conservationists were so intent on controlling and managing the resources of the wilderness—be they trees, natural fires, or animals—that Pinchot and his disciples "failed to fully comprehend or chose to ignore the interdependency of the forest." Eliminating all the moths, for example, meant destroying the food supply of different species of wasps, flies, spiders, and birds. Finally, Professor Steinberg argues that the massive destruction of coyotes, wolves, bears, prairie dogs, and gophers, which ate the settlers' crops, caused a proliferation of deer to overpopulate, whereas hordes of mice literally took over the town of Taft, California, in 1924.

YES

T. H. Watkins

Father of the Forests
(Gifford Pinchot)

Like most public officials, Gov. Gifford Pinchot of Pennsylvania could not answer all his mail personally. Much of it had to be left to aides, but not all of these realized the character of their boss. When a citizen wrote in 1931 to complain angrily about one of the governor's appointments, Pinchot was not pleased to find the following prepared for his signature: "I am somewhat surprised at the tone of your letter. . . . It has been my aim since I became Governor to select the best possible person for each position. . . . I hope time will convince you how greatly you have erred."

The governor was not given to such mewlings and forthwith composed his own letter: "Either you are totally out of touch with public sentiment, or you decline to believe what you hear. . . . To say that I was not attempting to do right when I made these appointments is nonsense. I was doing the best I knew how, and my confidence that I did so is by no means impaired by your letter." That was more like it—and more like the man too.

Gifford Pinchot passed through nearly six decades of American public life like a Jeremiah, the flames of certitude seeming to dance behind his dark eyes. "Gifford Pinchot is a dear," his good friend and mentor Theodore Roosevelt once said of him, "but he is a fanatic, with an element of hardness and narrowness in his temperament, and an extremist."

The complaint was legitimate, but the zealot in question also was the living expression of an idea shared by much of an entire generation (indeed, shared by Roosevelt himself): the conviction that men and women could take hold of their government and shape it to great ends, great deeds, lifting all elements of American life to new levels of probity, grace, freedom, and prosperity. The urge was not entirely selfless; the acquisition and exercise of power have gratifications to which Pinchot and his kind were by no means immune. But at the forefront was a solemn and utterly earnest desire that the lot of humanity should be bettered by the work of those who were equipped by circumstance, talent, and training to change the world. It had something to do with duty and integrity and honesty, and if it was often marred by arrogance, at its best it was just as often touched by compassion.

And the world, in fact, was changed.

I have . . . been a Governor, every now and then, but I am a forester all the time—have been, and shall be, all my working life." Gifford Pinchot made this pronouncement in a speech not long before his death at the age of eighty-one, and repeated it in *Breaking New Ground,* his account of the early years of the conservation movement and his considerable place in it. It was true enough, but it could just as legitimately be said of him that he had been a forester every now and then but was a politician, had been and would be, all his working life.

It could also be said that it was forestry that taught him his politics. Pinchot was born on August 11, 1865, into the sort of environment that would normally have pointed him in the direction of nothing more exotic than law or one of the other gentlemanly persuasions. His father, James, a self-made man of the classic stripe, had acquired so much money as a dry goods merchant in New York City that he had been able to retire to the pursuit of good works at the age of forty-four. His mother, Mary, was the daughter of Amos Eno, a Manhattan real estate tycoon whose Fifth Avenue Hotel was so valuable a property that his estate was able to sell it after his death for the staggering figure of $7,250,000.

The Pinchots figured prominently, if sedately, in society and traveled ambitiously in England and on the Continent. Giffodd, his younger brother, Amos, and their sister, Antoinette, all grew up able to speak French and snatches of German at early ages, and Antoinette, in fact, would become Lady Johnstone, wife of the British consul in Copenhagen.

Altogether it seemed an unlikely background for a man who was to spend much of his adult life with trees. There was not at the time a single American-born man and precious few men of any nationality in this country practicing anything that could remotely be described as forestry. Nevertheless, "How would you like to be a forester?" Pinchot's father asked him in the summer of 1885, as the young man prepared to enter Yale. "It was an amazing question for that day and generation," he remembered, "how amazing I didn't begin to understand at the time." In his travels the elder Pinchot had become an admirer of the kind of scientific forestry practiced in France, Germany, and Switzerland and had even written a few articles on the subject.

The son proved open to his father's enthusiasm. From childhood Pinchot had been active in the outdoors, fond of hiking, camping, and, especially, trout fishing. Since there was nowhere yet in the United States to study his chosen profession, after graduating from Yale he took himself back to Europe, where for more than a year he studied forest management at the French Forestry School in Nancy and put in a month of fieldwork under Forstmeister ("Chief Forester") Ulrich Meister in the city forest of Zurich, Switzerland.

Back in this country he was hired by George W. Vanderbilt in 1892 to manage the five-thousand-acre forest on his Biltmore estate in North Carolina, a ragged patchwork of abused lands purchased from numerous individual farmers. While nursing this wrecked acreage back to health, the young forester persuaded Vanderbilt to expand his holdings by an additional one hundred thousand acres of nearly untouched forest land outside the estate. This new enterprise became known as the Pisgah Forest, and it was there in 1895 that

Pinchot introduced what were almost certainly the first scientific logging operations ever undertaken in this country.

By then the young man had made a secure reputation in the field; indeed, he *was* the field. In December 1893 he opened an office in Manhattan as a "consulting forester." Over the next several years, while continuing his work for Vanderbilt in North Carolina, he provided advice and research work on forest lands in Michigan, Pennsylvania, and New York State—including the six-millionacre Adirondack Park and Forest Preserve, established in 1895 as the largest state-owned park in the nation. He could—and doubtless did—take satisfaction from a description given of him by a newspaper columnist as early as 1892: "Contrast the career of this Yale graduate with that of certain young men of Gotham who flatten their noses against club windows in the morning, and soften their brains with gossip, champagne and the unmentionables at other periods of the day and night."

There was nothing soft in this graduate's brain, and since he lived most of his time at home with his mother and father, there was even less that could be called unmentionable in his behavior or experience (his first fiancée died in 1894, an event that so devastated him he did not marry until twenty years later, after his mother's own death). By the turn of the century he was fully equipped by temperament and experience to assume the task that would soon be given him: the intelligent management of more forest land than had ever been placed in the control of any single individual.

It would be difficult to find a more convenient symbol for the dark side of American enterprise than the state of the nation's forest lands in the last quarter of the nineteenth century. Restrained only by the dictates of the marketplace, the timber industry had enjoyed a free hand for generations, and the wreckage was considerable. Most of the best forest land east of the Mississippi had long since been logged out—sometimes twice over—and while generally humid conditions had allowed some of the land to recover in second and third growth, erosion had permanently scarred many areas. Unimpeded runoff during seasonal rains had caused such ghastly floods as that leading to the destruction of Johnstown, Pennsylvania, in 1889.

The land of the Mississippi and Ohio valleys was almost entirely privately owned; west of the Mississippi most of the land belonged to the nation. It was called the public domain, its steward was the federal government, as represented by the General Land Office, and for years it had been hostage to the careless enthusiasm of a tradition that looked upon land as a commodity to be sold or an opportunity to be exploited, not a resource to be husbanded. About two hundred million acres of this federal land were forested, and much of it, too, had been systematically mutilated. In addition to legitimate timber companies that consistently misused the various land laws by clear-cutting entire claims without even bothering to remain around long enough to establish final title, many "tramp" lumbermen simply marched men, mules, oxen, and sometimes donkey engines onto an attractive (and vacant) tract of public forest land, stripped it, and moved out, knowing full well that apprehension and prosecution were simply beyond the means or interest of the understaffed, overcommitted, and largely corrupt General Land Office. As early as

1866 such instances of cheerful plunder had gutted so many forests of the public domain that the surveyors general of both Washington Territory and Colorado Territory earnestly recommended to the General Land Office that the forest lands in their districts be sold immediately, while there was something left to sell.

The forests were not sold, nor did they vanish entirely, but they did remain vulnerable to regular depredation. It was not until 1891 and passage of an obscure legislative rider called the Forest Reserve Clause that the slowly growing reform element in the executive branch was enabled to do anything about it. Armed with the power of this law, President Benjamin Harrison withdrew thirteen million acres of public forest land in the West from uses that would have been permitted by any of the plethora of lenient land laws then on the books, and at the end of his second term, President Grover Cleveland added another twenty-one million acres. Since there was virtually no enforcement of the new law, however, withdrawal provided little protection from illegal use; at the same time, it specifically disallowed legitimate use of public timber and grasslands. In response to the howl that arose in the West and to give some semblance of protection and managed use, Congress passed the Forest Organic Act of June 1897, which stipulated that the forest reserves were intended "to improve and protect the forest . . . for the purpose of securing favorable conditions of water flow, and to furnish a continuous supply of timber for the use and necessities of citizens of the United States."

Gifford Pinchot, the young "consulting forester," was the author of much of the language of the act. In the summer of 1896 he had distinguished himself as the secretary of the National Forest Commission, a body formed by President Cleveland to investigate conditions in the nation's public forests and to recommend action for their proper use and protection, and it was the commission that had put forth the need for an organic act. No one knew more about American forests than Pinchot did, and he seemed the only logical choice to head the Department of Agriculture's Forestry Division when the position of director fell vacant in May 1898.

On the face of it, Pinchot's new post was less than prestigious. The Forestry Division was housed in two rooms of the old red-brick Agriculture Building on the south side of the Mall in Washington, D.C. It enjoyed a total of eleven employees and an annual appropriation of $28,500. And since the forest reserves remained under the jurisdiction of the Interior Department, the Forestry Division had little to do beyond advising private landowners on the proper management of their wood lots and forests. This was anathema to an activist like Pinchot, and he was soon honing the skills that would make him one of the most persistent and effective lobbyists who ever prowled the cloakrooms and cubbyholes of Congress.

His ambition was not a small one: He wanted nothing less than to get the forest reserves transferred to Agriculture and placed under his care in the Forestry Division and then to build the division into the first effective agency for the management and conservation of public lands in the history of the nation. It did not hurt his chances when he became intimate with another early American conservationist—Theodore Roosevelt.

Roosevelt had spent much of his youth killing and stuffing birds and was to spend much of his adult life shooting bigger and better animals, which he had other people stuff for him. Nevertheless, when he assumed the Presidency in 1901, he became the first Chief Executive to play an informed and active role in the conservation movement. With George Bird Grinnell (editor of *Forest and Stream* magazine) he had been a cofounder of the Boone and Crockett Club, an exclusive gathering of conservation-minded hook-and-bullet men whose influence had gone a long way toward preserving the wildlife in Yellowstone National Park and toward slowing the wholesale commercial slaughter that had exterminated the passenger pigeon and was well on its way toward wiping out several other species. During his Presidency Roosevelt would establish the first federal wildlife refuges, support the expansion of the national park system, back passage of the Reclamation Act of 1902, and use the full power of the Antiquities Act of 1906 to designate no fewer than eighteen national monuments, including the Grand Canyon, in Arizona.

Nor was Roosevelt indifferent to forests. "The American had but one thought about a tree," he once wrote, "and that was to cut it down." While governor of New York, he had sought forestry advice from Pinchot, and they had hit it off from the start. "There has been a peculiar intimacy between you and Jim [James R. Garfield, his Secretary of the Interior] and me," Roosevelt wrote Pinchot in later years, "because all three of us have worked for the same causes, have dreamed the same dreams, have felt a substantial identity of purpose as regards many of what we three deemed the most vital problems of today." Pinchot's own feelings bordered on adulation, although Roosevelt maintained that the younger man admired his predatory instincts above all else. "He thinks," he told Archie Butt, his personal assistant, "that if we were cast away somewhere together and we were both hungry, I would kill him and eat him, *and*," he had added with that carnivore's grin of his, "*I would, too.*"

The two men combined almost immediately in an effort to get the forest reserves into Pinchot's care. The public lands committees of both the House and Senate, however, were dominated by Westerners, many of whom had vested interests in the status quo, and it took more than three years of public campaigning and artful cajolery, Roosevelt himself bringing the full weight of the Presidency to bear on the point, before Pinchot was given his heart's desire: passage of the Forest Transfer Act, on February 1, 1905. In addition to bringing over the forests—which now totaled more than sixty-three million acres—the new law provided for the charging of fees for cutting timber and grazing cattle and sheep, and this was followed by the Agricultural Appropriation Act of March 3, a section of which gave federal foresters "authority to make arrests for the violation of laws and regulations relating to the forest reserves. . . ."

The government was now in the tree business with a vengeance. Shortly the name of the reserves was changed to that of national forests, the Forestry Division to that of the U.S. Forest Service, and Gifford Pinchot was solidly in place as the nation's first chief forester, a position he would hold officially only until his resignation in 1910 but would hold in his heart for the rest of his life.

With his President's blessing, Pinchot crafted the young agency into a public body whose dedication to the ideal of service to the public was nearly unique for its time (or our own, for that matter). It came directly out of Pinchot's own convictions. "It is the first duty of a public officer to obey the law," he wrote in *The Fight for Conservation,* in 1910. "But it is his second duty, and a close second, to do everything the law will let him do for the public good. . . ."

It was an elite corps that Pinchot created, built on merit and merit alone, one in which both competence and stupidity were swiftly rewarded—and little went unnoticed by the chief forester ("I found him all tangled up," Pinchot wrote to a lieutenant about one hapless employee, "and generally making an Ass of himself, with splendid success"). William R. Greeley, one of the twenty-five hundred foresters who served under Pinchot (and who later became chief forester himself), caught the spirit of Pinchot's influence precisely: "He made us . . . feel like soldiers in a patriotic cause."

The system this exemplary body of men administered was carefully structured by the chief forester. Individual forests were divided up into man-agement units, each with its own ranger or ranger force, and administrative headquarters were established in the six districts across the West where most of the forests were grouped, from Missoula, Montana, to Portland, Oregon. Pinchot gave his district supervisors a great deal of autonomy and encouraged them to give their rangers similarly loose reins in the field—whether selecting stands of harvestable trees, supervising a timber sale, regulating the number of cows or sheep that might be allowed on a piece of grazing land, or fighting fires. The first step in proper administration, he said, "was to find the right man and see that he understood the scope and limits of his work, and just what was expected of him"; then "the next step was to give him his head and let him use it."

The chief forester did not remain aloof. He was given to unannounced field trips, poking his prominent nose into every nook and cranny of the sys-tem to see what was what, and he maintained a body of field inspectors who reported regularly to him and him alone. "To get results," he remembered, "we had to revise, common-sensitize, and make alive the whole attitude and action of the men who had learned the Land Office way of handling the Reserves. . . . We had to drive out red tape with intelligence, and unite the office and the field. Next . . . we had to bring about a fundamental change in the attitude and action of the men who lived in or near the Reserves and used them. We had to get their cooperation by earning their respect."

That respect did not come easily. Those individuals and corporations that had become accustomed to unrestricted access to Western resources did not remain silent during all this, nor did their politicians. At one point in 1908 the *Rocky Mountain News* featured a cartoon showing "Czar Pinchot and His Cossack Rangers." Others declared that the Forest Service was subverting the pioneering instinct that had built the country. "While these chiefs of the Bureau of Forestry sit within their marble halls," Sen. Charles W. Fulton of Oregon intoned in 1907, "and theorize and dream of waters conserved, forests and streams protected and preserved throughout the ages and the ages, the lowly pioneer is climbing the mountain side where he will erect his humble cabin, and within the shadow of the whispering pines and the lofty firs of the forest engage in the laborious work of carving out for himself and his loved ones a home and a dwelling place."

Despite such cavils, by the time Roosevelt left office in March 1909, the national forest system had been enlarged to 148 million acres, and the Forest Service had become one of the most respected government services in the nation—reason enough for the historian M. Nelson McGeary's encomium of 1960: "Had there been no Pinchot to build the U.S. Forest Service into an exceptionally effective agency, it would hardly have been possible to report in 1957 that 'most' of the big lumber operators had adopted forestry as a policy; or that the growth of saw timber has almost caught up with the rate of drain on forest resources from cutting, fire, and natural losses. . . ."

Nor, it is safe to say, would there have been much left of the forests themselves. The principles Pinchot put to work would inform the management of the public lands throughout most of the twentieth century and become one of the roots of the sensibility we call environmentalism. It was called conservation then, and Pinchot always claimed that he was the first to put that use upon the word. "Conservation," he wrote, "means the wise use of the earth and its resources for the lasting good of men. Conservation is the foresighted utilization, preservation, and/or renewal of forests, waters, lands, and minerals, for the greatest good of the greatest number for the longest time."

Wise use was the cornerstone, and Pinchot and his followers had little patience with the still-embryonic notion that the natural world deserved preservation quite as much for its own sake as for the sake of the men and women who used it. John Muir, a hairy wood sprite of a naturalist whom Pinchot had met and befriended as early as 1896, personified this more idealistic instinct, tracing the roots of his own inspiration back to Henry David Thoreau's declaration that "in Wildness is the preservation of the World." For a time, the two men were allies in spite of their differences, but the friendship disintegrated after 1905, when Pinchot lent his support to the efforts of the city of San Francisco to dam the Hetch Hetchy Valley in Yosemite National Park for a public water-and-power project in order to free the city from a private power monopoly.

Muir, whose writings about Yosemite had brought him a measure of fame, had founded the Sierra Club in 1892 largely as a tool to protect the glorious trench of the Yosemite Valley and other pristine areas in the Sierra Nevada. Among these was the Hetch Hetchy Valley, which these early preservationists maintained was the equal of Yosemite itself in beauty. The reservoir that would fill up behind the proposed dam on the Tuolumne River would obliterate that beauty. But this was exactly the sort of public power-and-water project that spoke most eloquently to the deepest pragmatic instincts of Pinchot and his kind, who argued that every measure of conservation as they understood it would be fulfilled by approval of the project. "Whoever dominates power," Pinchot wrote, "dominates all industry."

Both sides in the argument faced off energetically in this first major conflict between the utilitarian and the preservationist wings of the conservation movement, and it took nearly ten years, the approval of two Presidents, and the passage of special legislation by Congress in 1913 before San Francisco obtained permission to build its dam. "The destruction of the charming groves and gardens, the finest in all California," Muir wrote to a friend, "goes to my heart. But in spite of Satan & Co., some sort of compensation must surely come out of this dark damn-dam damnation." Pinchot had no doubts and no regrets.

Pinchot's devotion to the principles of conservation went beyond the immediate question of use versus preservation. Monopoly was evil personified, and monopoly, he believed, stemmed directly from the control of the natural world. "Monopoly of resources," he wrote in *Breaking New Ground,* "which prevents, limits, or destroys equality of opportunity is one of the most effective of all ways to control and limit human rights, especially the right of self-government." With this conviction to guide him, it did not take him long to find his way from the world of conservation to the world of politics, where, like thousands of his class, he found his imagination seized by Progressive Republicanism. . . .

The movement had been distilled from more than forty years of what the historian Howard Mumford Jones called "exuberance and wrath" following the Civil War. Its followers saw themselves and their values caught in a vise: threatened on one side by an increasingly violent and potentially revolutionary uprising on the part of the great unwashed—largely represented by the Democratic party—and on the other by a cynical plutocratic brotherhood—largely represented by the regular Republican party—which brutally twisted and subverted American institutions for purposes of personal greed and power.

Imperfectly but noisily, Theodore Roosevelt had given these people in the middle a voice and a symbol to call their own, and when he chose not to run for a third term in 1908, they felt abandoned. Prominent among them was Gifford Pinchot, and there is some evidence to suggest that he engineered his own dismissal as chief forester by President William Howard Taft, whom Roosevelt had groomed as his own chosen successor. The opportunity came in 1909, when Pinchot learned that Taft's Secretary of the Interior, Richard Ballinger, was determined to honor a number of coal-mining claims on lands in Alaska that Roosevelt had earlier withdrawn from such uses.

When Taft backed his Interior Secretary, Pinchot chose to see it as the beginning of a wholesale repudiation of all that Roosevelt had done to champion the public interest. He made no secret of his conclusions, and Taft was certain that more than bureaucratic integrity was behind Pinchot's loudly voiced concerns. "I am convinced," he wrote his brother, "that Pinchot with his fanaticism and his disappointment at my decision in the Ballinger case plans a coup by which I shall be compelled to dismiss him and he will be able to make out a martyrdom and try to raise opposition against me."

Taft resisted as long as he reasonably could, but when Pinchot violated the President's direct orders to maintain silence by writing an open letter to a Senate committee investigating the Ballinger matter, he decided he had no choice. Calling the letter an example of insubordination "almost unparalleled in the history of the government," Taft fired the chief forester of the United States on January 7, 1910. Pinchot rushed home with the letter of dismissal and waved it at his mother, crying, "I'm fired!." "My Mother's eyes flashed," he remembered, in *Breaking New Ground;* "she threw back her head, flung one hand high above it, and answered with one word: 'Hurrah!'"

Despite these memories of triumph, the most effective and reward-ing part of Pinchot's career had come to an end. It certainly would not have seemed so to him at the time, however, as he joined in his friend Roosevelt's 1912 campaign to unseat Taft as a third-party candidate. Pinchot had been promised the State Department if Roosevelt won, but Roosevelt lost and, los-ing, split the Republican party and gave the Presidency to Woodrow Wilson. All Pinchot got was the satisfaction of seeing Taft humiliated—which nonethe-less was "something to be proud and happy about," he crowed.

There followed years of politicking, all with his old vigor, but with mixed results and mostly confined to the state of Pennsylvania, where he served a couple of stormy, largely unproductive terms as governor.

It all took him too far from the forests that were his abiding interests. He had never lost sight of them, of course. In 1937, at the age of seventy-two, he undertook a five-thousand-mile trip sponsored by the Forest Service through the national forests of Montana, Idaho, Oregon, and California, sleeping out in the open, flying in Forest Service planes, and generally re-creating the delights of his youthful days on the old Forest Commission. "What I saw gave me the greatest satisfaction," he wrote upon his return. "The service is better than it was when I left and everywhere the forests are coming back. What more could a man ask?"

He was a good deal less mellow when FDR's Secretary of the Interior, his old friend and colleague Harold L. Ickes, opened a campaign to have the national forests taken out of the Department of Agriculture and placed back in Interior—an effort that earlier Interior Secretaries had supported and to which Pinchot had taken predictable umbrage. This time, however, the invective he launched against the idea was more than matched by that of the self-described curmudg-eon Ickes, as the two old Progressives attempted to outdo each other in vitriol.

"What is behind all this?" Pinchot asked the assembled members of the Izaak Walton League in April 1937. "The man who has been my friend for more than a quarter of a century has allowed his ambition to get away with his judgement," and Ickes's great power had "bred the lust of greater power." Ickes countered that "Gifford Pinchot, who is a persistent fisherman in politi-cal waters, exemplifies more than anyone else in American public life how the itch for public office can break down one's intellectual integrity." The charac-ter of the debate between the two men rarely rose above this level until the beginning of World War II rendered the question moot. The forests stayed in the Department of Agriculture.

Appropriately, much of Pinchot's remaining years were spent in the writing of *Breaking New Ground,* which remains one of the central documents of the Amer-ican conservation movement. That was a legacy worth the offering, and it is a pity that he did not live to see its publication before his death on October 4, 1946.

But the essential legacy of this committed, driven man, this public serv-ant, this prince of rectitude, is the national forests themselves. There are 191 million acres of them now, spreading over the mountain slopes and river val-leys of the West like a great dark blanket, still the center of controversy, still threatened and mismanaged and nurtured and loved as they were when the son of a dry goods merchant first walked in an American wood and wondered what could be done to save it for the future.

Conservation Reconsidered

One of the ranchers who watched the blizzard of 1887 wipe out his herd of cattle was Theodore Roosevelt. In the early 1880s, Roosevelt, a New Yorker, built a ranch in North Dakota's Badlands, stocked it with animals, and hired two cowboys to oversee his venture. In the spring of 1887, he headed west to check on the status of his 85,000-dollar investment, arriving in the Little Missouri valley only to find that death had beaten him there. He saw cattle carcasses—23 in just a single little spot—and found his once glorious herd reduced to just "a skinny sorry-looking crew." The ground itself was in no better shape. "The land was a mere barren waste; not a green thing could be seen; the dead grass eaten off till the country looked as if it had been shaved with a razor."

In the fall of 1887, Roosevelt returned once again to the Badlands, this time on a hunting trip. Not much had improved since his last visit. The region's prairie grass had lost the battle with ranchers, ever eager to stock the range with more animals than it could reasonably have been expected to bear. The remaining grass fell victim to desperate cattle seeking whatever little forage they could find in the wake of the death-dealing blizzard of 1887. An eerie silence spread out over the land. Four years earlier, on a visit to this spot, Roosevelt found few, if any, buffalo. In 1885, he lamented the loss of wild sheep and antelope. In 1886, he worried about the disappearance of migratory birds. By 1887, then, the Badlands must have offered a melancholy sight, and Roosevelt proposed to do something about it. He returned to New York to invite 12 of his animal-loving friends over for a meal and in January 1888 they established the Boone & Crockett Club, named in honor of Daniel Boone and Davy Crockett, legendary frontiersmen whom Roosevelt worshipped. The club was one of the first organizations in this country dedicated to saving big-game animals. And it was the work of a man who would go on to become president of the United States, a man whose name has become synonymous with the American conservation movement.

The story generally told about conservation goes something like this. President Roosevelt, an avid outdoor enthusiast, believed the government needed to intervene to save the nation's forests, streams, and other natural resources from rapacious loggers, ranchers, and market hunters alike. To carry out this mission, Roosevelt named Gifford Pinchot to head the newly formed

U.S. Forest Service in 1905[,] Pinchot and his colleagues in the conservation movement, many drawn from fields such as forestry, geology, and hydrology, felt that a rational plan for organizing the nation's use of its natural resources was in order. Business leaders, driven by unrestrained competition for timber, water, and grass, they held, would have to cede authority to expert government planners, with their scientific background, who would see to the most efficient use of the country's natural wealth. Roosevelt, Pinchot, and other conservationists thus were not interested so much in preserving nature untouched as in standing guard to make sure it was used in the wisest, most efficient way possible.

Opposing the "efficient use" brand of conservation, in this story, were the preservationists, the most famous of whom was John Muir. Born in 1838 in Dunbar, Scotland, and brought by his parents to Wisconsin when he was 11, Muir, who experienced a devout upbringing, would go on to found what was by all rights his own religion. It was based on the idea that we are "all God's people"— "we" referring not just to human beings but to foxes, bears, plants, indeed, all elements of the natural world. Humans had no more right to exist than other species of life did. Often touted as the founder of the environmental movement, Muir strongly disagreed with Pinchot and the practical philosophy that informed his view of conservation. He proposed instead that wilderness areas enriched human life, existing as sacred refuges, antidotes to the stresses of modern society. "Climb the mountains and get their good tidings," he once remarked. Muir, who founded the Sierra Club in 1892, felt government had a moral responsibility to preserve nature, not simply to use it wisely in the name of industry. He urged the nation's political leaders to lock away America's wilderness areas and throw the key as far from business as humanly possible, though he came to modify that stance as he was increasingly drawn into the practical world of politics.

In the early years of the twentieth century, these two philosophies— utilitarianism versus preservationism—collided in the beautiful Hetch Hetchy valley in California's Sierra Nevada. In the aftermath of a devastating earthquake and fire in 1906, the city of San Francisco to the south proposed a dam to bring water to the growing metropolis, flooding the valley in the process. Pinchot supported the project on practical grounds. He faced off against the preservation-minded John Muir, who lost the battle. The dam was built and the valley inundated, as human impulse trumped natural beauty.

The problem with this portrayal, as it is rendered, for instance, in most American history textbooks, is that conservation, in both its guises, is primarily viewed as a battle over *ideas* about nature. Little is said about the effect of conservation measures—such as the establishment of national parks, forests, and wildlife preserves—on the ecosystems that were the target of this important reform impulse. And yet, to consider policies aimed at conserving nature without exploring what happened on the ground—to the natural world (and the people who depended on it for food)—is like teaching the Civil War without mentioning the outcome. Perhaps nature succumbed at Hetch Hetchy, but elsewhere the results of conservation policy were far more complicated. Oftentimes the West's plants, trees, and animals simply thumbed their noses at the supposed experts sent to manage them. Conservationists found themselves unable to fully grasp the complexity of ecological forces and erroneously took steps that caused nature to strike back with devastating wildfires and game explosions.

Another problem with the conventional story is that it tends to mask the fact that both strains of conservation thinking—Pinchot's and Muir's—sought to bend nature to conform to the desires of humankind. Both, in other words, contained strong doses of anthropocentrism, not just the utilitarian variety. Even more important, both visions of how to go about conserving nature favored some groups of people over others. As the federal government moved in to try its hand at managing the forests and range in the name of tourism, ranching, and logging, Indians and poor whites, who had depended on such lands for food, found their interests shoved to the side. Conservation for some meant fines and jail time, and empty bellies for others.

Taylor-Made Forests

While the conservationists were off dreaming up ways of reining in laissez-faire capitalism, engineer Frederick Taylor was busy inventing a strategy for bringing efficiency to the workplace. Rarely spoken of in the same breath, the two developments ought to be. Taylorism tried to help employers streamline production by eliminating the chaos present on the shop floor, prevailing on workers to use the most efficient set of motions necessary to complete any given task, to yield before the expert and his stopwatch. Conservation, meanwhile, at least in the form that Pinchot espoused, tried to rid not the shop floor but the forests of the very same disorderly tendencies, seeking the most efficient way of producing not steel, but crops of timber and animals. Taylorism controlled workers, conservation controlled nature, and both relied on the principles of scientific management to do so. Frederick Taylor and Gifford Pinchot, in short, were cut from the same mold.

Before Pinchot's view of conservation rose to dominance, an ecologically informed group of foresters had tried to understand the forest on its own terms. Bernard Fernow, for example, one of the early scientific foresters, believed that forests did more than simply serve the economic needs of the American people. As interdependent entities, the woods, if managed properly, could help fend off floods and soil erosion. Forestland, he once wrote, played an important part "in the great economy of nature." Early conservationists, concerned with the overall ecology of federal forestland, evinced an anti-industry stance, opposing the timber companies in their disastrous quest for short-term profits. Conservation, in other words, got off to a promising start.

Eager to please the timber companies, however, Pinchot, who replaced Fernow as chief of the Department of Agriculture's Division of Forestry in 1898, elevated economics over ecology. "The first principle of conservation is development," he wrote in 1910, "the use of the natural resources now existing on this continent for the benefit of the people who live here now." Pinchot felt that his first loyalty was to his own generation of Americans "and afterward the welfare of the generations to follow." Like Fernow, he opposed the unrestrained destruction of the nation's vast forest reserves. But unlike Fernow, he aimed to replace that approach with a scientifically grounded one that emphasized renewal of the resource as a way of serving economic—not ecological—ends.

Pinchot had no intention then of simply putting the woods off limits to loggers. He was far too practical-minded for that. The forests existed to serve the economic demands of the nation, he believed, and to do that the lumber industry needed to cede authority to the experts at the Forest Service, who would tell them when it was time to cut a tree down. "The job," as Pinchot put it, "was not to stop the axe, but to regulate its use." Trees, in this view, were just like any other resource, human or natural. Frederick Taylor studied the behavior of workers in order to find the most efficient path to more production; Pinchot and his colleagues studied trees with the same end in mind. The woods could yield a constant source of timber if its trees were harvested at the proper time and then replanted, creating a second-growth forest even more manageable and in tune with the needs of the American economy than the original stands it replaced.

At the outset, Pinchot galvanized the American public behind his forest initiative by calling their attention to an impending resource scarcity. By the turn of the century, the nation's timber frontier was coming to a close, as lumbermen ventured to the Pacific Northwest, having already cleared vast portions of the Great Lakes states and South. In 1906, lumber consumption reached 46 billion board feet, a record that has yet to be broken. With prices rising, Pinchot and Roosevelt both raised the prospect of a wood shortage. "A timber famine in the future is inevitable," Roosevelt declared in 1905. Clearly the nation's original forest cover had decreased, from 850 million acres in the early seventeenth century to roughly 500 million acres by the dawn of the twentieth century. Famine or not, the context was ripe for intervention, a point Pinchot clearly sensed.

"Forestry is handling trees so that one crop follows another," Pinchot was fond of saying. What he meant, reduced to its essence, was that left to its own devices, nature was far too inefficient to serve the demands of a modern, industrial economy. Nothing irritated Pinchot and his fellow foresters more than the sight of an old-growth forest, filled with mature, dead, and diseased trees. Those old and disorderly forests needed to come down to make room for a new crop of timber. "To the extent to which the overripe timber on the national forests can not be cut and used while merchantable, public property is wasted," intoned Henry Graves, who followed Pinchot as chief of the Forest Service. Like a worker prone to loafing and distraction, the forest too became the target of the efficiency experts.

Anything that got in the way of a speedup in forest production—old growth, disease, insects, and fire—had to be extinguished. But what Pinchot and his disciples either failed to fully comprehend or chose to ignore was the complexity and, above all, the interdependency of the forest. The various elements that made up the woods—trees, plants, insects, and animals—functioned as a unit. Small changes could have enormous impact. A change to one element in the mix—removing a dead tree or ridding the forest of an insect—had consequences that ramified throughout an ecosystem, at times, ironically, even interfering with the business-oriented goals of the conservationists to boot. A species of moth, for instance, fed on the needles of Oregon's Douglas fir trees, a sight that drove the Forest Service wild. But behind the scenes hundreds of different species of wasps, flies, spiders, and birds were eating the moths, providing the agency with a free extermination treatment. When federal foresters in Oregon's Blue Mountains tried to eliminate the moths early in the twentieth century, the insect's predators lost out and died too. The moths then bounced back with a vengeance to devour the trees once again.

A dead tree, an obstruction in the eyes of an efficiency-minded forester, was a viable habitat from the perspective of an insect. Thus removing fallen trees eliminated a food source for thousands of carpenter ants, preventing them from carrying out their duties on the forest floor: decomposing dead wood and returning it to the soil. The Forest Service eventually wound up interfering with the cycle of death and decomposition on which the future health of the woods rested.

Pinchot's brand of conservation did even more damage when it came to the issue of fire. Fire had, of course, long been a major component of the West's, indeed of North America's, ecological mosaic, and early foresters remained fully aware of this fact. In much of the South as well as large parts of California, people set fire to the woods to reduce brush and encourage the growth of pasturage. In 1910, one timber man went so far as to call on the government to make burning mandatory in the Golden State. But it was not an auspicious year for incendiarism, not with fires in the northern Rockies raging out of control. The spring of 1910 was the driest month on record in the northwestern United States. That fact, combined with the buildup of slash, as logging increased and Indian burning of the land declined, led to one of the greatest wildfire disasters in American history. Conflagrations raged across the states of Idaho, Montana, Washington, and Oregon, sending smoke as far east as New England.

The fires left a legacy on government policy as enduring as the effect they had on the ground. Specifically, the 1910 fires worked to elevate the policy of fire suppression into a veritable religion at the Forest Service. Pinchot laid the intellectual groundwork for such a policy change. "I recall very well indeed," he wrote in 1910, "how, in the early days of forest fires, they were considered simply and solely as acts of God, against which any opposition was hopeless and any attempt to control them not merely hopeless but childish. It was assumed that they came in the natural order of things, as inevitably as the seasons or the rising and setting of the sun. Today we understand that forest fires are wholly within the control of men."

In 1910, at precisely the same time that Pinchot argued for suppression, the eminent ecologist Frederic Clements confirmed the views of foresters like Fernow, who viewed fire as a creative and positive environmental force. But Pinchot and those who came after him in the Forest Service remained unimpressed with such thinking. In keeping with the guiding spirit of efficiency and control at the heart of his brand of conservation, Pinchot feared the disorder and chaos that fire produced, especially if the conflagration in question was set on purpose. In 1898, he wrote, "forest fires encourage a spirit of lawlessness and a disregard of property rights." Those who burned the forest, for whatever reason, were no better than criminals, outlaws engaged in what federal foresters would soon call "incendiarism" or "woods arson."

In the year following the 1910 calamity, Congress passed the Weeks Act, which allowed the federal government to purchase as much as 75 million acres of land and led to a consensus among federal and state officials on the need for fire suppression. Suppressing forest fires—a major preoccupation of the Forest Service for the bulk of the twentieth century—proved in the end both misguided and self-defeating. Fires aid the decomposition of forest litter and help recycle nutrients through an ecosystem. Without them growth slows down. Worse still, by suppressing fires, the Forest Service allowed fuels to build up, increasing the possibility for catastrophic conflagrations. Once again, nature had the last laugh, as Pinchot's brand of conservation centered on economic imperatives and anxiety over lawless behavior trumped an earlier, more broad-minded concern with the forest's noneconomic functions.

Revenge of the Varmints

There is a dark side to conservation, although one would never know it from reading a U.S. history textbook. Roosevelt and Pinchot swooping in to rescue the wanton destruction being carried out across the landscape, planting trees and giving birth to a new and improved forest—none of this smacks of anything cold-blooded in the least. Left out of this rosy scenario, however, is the fact that conservation, because it was founded on the most productive use of the land, sometimes ventured into the realm of death and destruction. It is no coincidence that the most destructive period in the nation's wildlife history— replete with the ruthless and systematic annihilation of some entire animal species—coincided with the decades when conservation gripped the nation's political imagination. Efficiency and extermination went hand in hand.

Taking their cue from Pinchot's philosophy of making trees over into harvestable crops, game managers in the early twentieth century tried to do the same for animals, cultivating those species favored by sport hunters and tourists such as elk, bison, waterfowl, and especially deer. By the 1880s, overhunting and habitat loss had caused the populations of these animal groups to plummet. To revitalize them, federal and state wildlife managers pushed for laws regulating hunting and setting up refuges. In 1903, Roosevelt designated Pelican Island in Florida as the first such federal wildlife preserve. Five years later came the National Bison Range in Montana on an old Indian reservation. Tourists queued up to see what amounted to the pathetic remnants of the once abundant and glorious species.

Conserving some species, however, meant killing others. In 1915, Congress set up a new division within the Department of Agriculture's Bureau of Biological Survey, the arm of the government (founded in 1905) responsible for game management. It had an ominous title: Predatory Animal and Rodent Control Service. Its mission was to exterminate those creatures that preyed on the rancher's cattle and sheep and the sport hunter's elk and deer. In the eyes of the conservation-minded, mountain lions, wolves, coyotes, and bobcats, among other species, became the Satans of the animal kingdom. "Large predatory mammals destructive to livestock and game no longer have a place in our advancing civilization," was how one biologist at the bureau put it.

There were 40 million sheep in the West by the last decade of the nineteenth century, in addition to vast numbers of cattle. All were defenseless before the predators that roamed the plains looking for some substitute fare now that the buffalo had been driven off the land. Wolves proved especially destructive to livestock; indeed, it would be hard to overestimate the hatred ranchers had for the species. Cowboys commonly strung a captured wolf between two horses to tear it apart. But poison, mainly strychnine, was the preferred method of dispatching them.

Bounties, established by a number of western states during the late nineteenth century, spurred hunters to kill predatory animals. But it took the intervention of the federal government with its extermination program to put an end to the predator problem. The ruthlessness of the campaign—steel traps, guns, and strychnine in hand—is hard to fathom. An astonishing 40,000 animals were killed in Wyoming alone between 1916 and 1928—coyotes, wolves, bears, bobcats, lynxes, and mountain lions, plus prairie dogs, gophers, squirrels, and jack rabbits, which had the annoying habit of eating the settlers' crops. "Bring Them in Regardless of How," went the slogan coined by one hunters' newsletter. It was allout war and when it was over—by 1926, no wolves existed in Arizona—the West's ranchers, farmers, and sport hunters could rest easier at night.

Life in western America seemed to be moving along swimmingly in the post-predatory age until it began to dawn on some people that such species as wolves, coyotes, and mountain lions actually served a purpose in life. An object lesson on the importance of predators unfolded on Arizona's Kaibab Plateau. In 1906, Roosevelt set aside a portion of the area as a wildlife refuge known as the Grand Canyon National Game Preserve. Roughly 4,000 deer lived in the refuge in the year it was founded. Enter the federal hunters, who between 1916 and 1931 took 4,889 coyotes, 781 mountain lions, and 554 bobcats. Victory, went the shout, as the deer proliferated, swelling to perhaps as many as 100,000 by 1924, a gain in productivity to end all gains. But two winters later, the deer population crashed, reduced by some 60 percent, as the animals starved for lack of forage. When such predators as coyotes and mountain lions are not around to hold down their numbers, deer will reproduce almost endlessly, populating their habitat beyond what it can bear and dying in classic Malthusian style.

While deer overran the Kaibab Plateau, hordes of mice were marching on the town of Taft, California. In 1924, the Bureau of Biological Survey had launched, to the glee of farmers, an all-out effort to eradicate coyotes, hawks, and other predators from Kern County. Two years later, the rodents, their numbers now unchecked, descended in droves. "The mice," one report had it, "invaded beds and nibbled the hair of horrified sleepers, chewed through the sides of wooden storehouses to get at food supplies, and crawled boldly into children's desks at Conley School." Passing cars crushed the mice that littered the road, making some highways too slick for safe travel. Farmers resorted to mechanical harvesters to fend off the rodents. Eventually the Bureau of Biological Survey was called in to exterminate the varmints it had poisoned into existence in the first place. Conservation had more than a few such ironic moments.

Park Rules

Managing game was one thing, but administering it to attract thousands of big game-loving tourists was something yet again. The setting aside of national parks in the late nineteenth century raised a host of problems for the nation's conservationists. Chief among these was how to rationalize game in the interests of tourism—that is, to create and preserve a wilderness experience where visitors could be sure to find elk, bison, and other large animals. In carrying out their mission, the managers of wildlife ran up against a number of obstacles. Native Americans and rural whites—inclined to view the creatures more as a food source than as curiosities—did not appreciate the restrictions the managers imposed on hunting. Complicating matters further, delineating an arbitrary park boundary and using it to contain wild species with biological needs for food that sent them outside the park, left government officials forever playing the role of traffic cop.

The national park movement stemmed, in part, from a change in American attitudes toward wilderness. Back in the colonial period, the word referred to desolate, wild places untouched, as yet, by civilisation. There was little, if anything, positive about wilderness areas in the minds of the first settlers, who diligently set about improving—fencing and farming—the raw material of nature. By the late nineteenth century, however, the meaning of the word had undergone a sea change. Wilderness areas were no longer thought to be worthless; in fact, just the reverse was the case: They were increasingly viewed as places of virginal natural beauty in need of the most zealous care.

Not that the economic impulse that informed the early idea of wilderness disappeared completely. In setting aside the first national parks, Congress made a point of looking for worthless lands—regions with limited agricultural and ranching prospects and no sign of valuable minerals—possessed of monumental grandeur. Unlike European countries, the United States, a much younger nation by comparison, had few cultural icons to match the castles and cathedrals that gave Old World states unique national identities. With the country emerging from the divisive Civil War, its status as a unified nation still quite fragile, congressmen searched the landscape for awe-inspiring physical features—stunning mountain scenery, vast and colorful canyons, spectacular geysers—for its citizens to rally around.

In 1872, Congress settled on a rectangular piece of land some two million acres in extent where Wyoming, Idaho, and Montana come together, an improbable place for agriculture, averaging some 6,000 feet in altitude and prone to frost, but containing hundreds of geysers, mud pots, and other geothermal wonders. Here was a picture-perfect spot to knit together the fledgling nation, North and South, East and West, a place so majestic and so capable of uniting the country under God that Congress purchased a painting of the area done by artist Thomas Moran to hang in the Capitol. "This will be the grandest park in the world—the grand, instructive museum of the grandest Government on Earth," proclaimed the *Nevada Territorial Enterprise*. To congressmen such as Henry Dawes of Massachusetts, who worked to establish the park, Yellowstone represented nature in its most pristine state, a beautiful but harsh wilderness environment so formidable that not even Indians, he asserted, could live there, a place seemingly without history.

It would be wrong, however, to see the establishment of Yellowstone, the nation's first national park, as simply the work of Congress. The railroads played a major role as well—financiers such as Jay Cooke and Frederick Billings and their Northern Pacific company, a corporation that stood to gain immensely from the passenger traffic that the park would bring. As Billings once remarked, "commerce could serve the cause of conservation by bringing visitors to a site worthy of preservation." In 1883, the Northern Pacific completed its route across the country, the second transcontinental railroad in the nation's history, putting Yellowstone within reach of tourists nationwide. That same year the nation went on standard time to accommodate railroad travel, a key development in the streamlining of modern life that perhaps also explains the fascination tourists had with the scheduled eruptions of Yellowstone's most famous geyser, Old Faithful, which as one observer remarked, "played by the clock."

Advocates for Yellowstone may have thought they were preserving a wilderness area. But it is more accurate to say that they were inventing it. In Yellowstone's case, creating wilderness meant rendering the Native Americans, who laid claim to the area, invisible when, in fact, they had long used it for hunting, fishing, and other means of survival. Preservation of the country's national parks and Indian removal proceeded in lock-step motion. Treaties and executive orders signed between 1855 and 1875 effectively consigned the Bannock, Shoshone, Blackfeet, and Crow Indians to reservations, where they would be less likely to interfere with tourists headed for Yellowstone. Park supporters rationalized the removal of Indians by relying on a time-tested strategy first used in the colonial period. The Indians, they pointed out, made no agricultural improvements to the area; use it or lose it, went the boosters' logic. The rugged physical environment of the park, inhospitable to farming and other economic uses, helped support this supposition, as did the view of park officials such as Philetus Norris, who explained that Indians avoided the Yellowstone area because they held its geothermal features in "superstitious awe."

As late as 1962, one historian observed that only "deteriorating, half-miserable-animal, half-miserable-man" types inhabited the park prior to its creation. This was little more than park and railroad propaganda masquerading as facts. Park officials were quite aware of the Native American presence in Yellowstone and its potential to frighten tourists. As Superintendent Moses Harris explained in 1888, "the mere rumor of the presence of Indians in the park is sufficient to cause much excitement and anxiety." The Northern Pacific Railroad, meanwhile, did what it could to allay such fears. It recommended that tourists visit the Little Big Horn (where George Armstrong Custer and his troops went down to defeat in 1876) on their way to Yellowstone, safe in knowing that the Plains Indians no longer posed any threat.

The year following Custer's defeat, the U.S. Army waged war against the Nez Perce Indians, at one point chasing them straight through Yellowstone National Park. The Nez Perce, according to accounts written at the time, were lost and frightened by the park's geothermal sites. But as Yellow Wolf recalled years after the battle, the Indians "knew that country well before passing through there in 1877. The hot smoking springs and high-shooting water were nothing new to us."

In fact, a number of Native American groups were intimately familiar with the park and its offerings. The Shoshones, for example, hunted buffalo, fished, and gathered various plants, activities that depending on the season could lead them into the area eventually designated as parkland. Aided by horses, even more distant Indian groups descended on the park to trap beaver and hunt elk. Perhaps not surprisingly, the decline of the buffalo beginning in the 1870s only made Indians more dependent on the park's wildlife for food. And in an ironic turn of events, the displacement of Native Americans onto reservations may actually have increased their visits to the park. Denied adequate rations in the government camps, such groups as the Crows and Shoshones made up the balance by setting off to hunt on unoccupied public lands, a right granted to them in an 1868 treaty. As the agent for Idaho's Fort Hall Reservation explained, "Being short-rationed and far from self-supporting according to the white man's methods, they [Bannocks and Shoshones] simply follow their custom and hunt for the purpose of obtaining sustenance."

The prospect of Indians taking game found within the confines of Yellowstone was long a bone of contention between native groups and park officials. In 1889, Superintendent Moses Harris called Indian hunting an "unmitigated evil" and lamented that it would be impossible to protect the park's remaining game if Yellowstone continued "to afford summer amusement and winter sustenance to a band of savage Indians." Locals who acted as guides to well-off hunters from the East also resented Indian poaching of game because it instilled fear in their clients while decreasing the likelihood of a successful outing.

In 1896, the U.S. Supreme Court in the leading case of *Ward* v. *Race Horse* overturned the protection the 1868 treaty granted Indians to hunt on unoccupied government land in a seven-to-one decision. Even though it was common knowledge that the Shoshone and Bannock Indians hunted game to feed themselves and, moreover, that insufficient rations on the Fort Hall Reservation left many malnourished and more inclined to hunt on their own, Justice Edward White asserted that hunting was a privilege "given" to the tribes by the U.S. government, one that could be revoked when called for by "the necessities of civilization." In his dissenting opinion, Justice Henry Brown pointed out that "the right to hunt on the unoccupied lands of the United States was a matter of supreme importance to them [the Indians]. . . . It is now proposed to take it away from them, not because they have violated a treaty, but because the State of Wyoming desires to preserve its game." The case effectively upheld a 1895 Wyoming law regulating the taking of wildlife, making it illegal for

Indians to hunt on public land during seasons closed to hunting and under-mining the centuries-old subsistence practices of the Yellowstone area's Native American groups. But unlike the well-known *Plessy* v. *Ferguson* case decided in the same year (establishing "separate but equal" segregation), Word, although heavily criticized then and since, has not been systematically overturned, remaining to this day a legally influential opinion.

The only thing as annoying to park officials as an Indian taking down one of Yellowstone's grand four-legged creatures was the sight of a rural white doing so. The founding of Gardiner, Montana, in 1883, on Yellowstone's north-ern border gave whites seeking game a base from which to launch their forays into the park. "In the town of Gardiner there are a number of men, armed with rifles, who toward game have the gray-wolf quality of mercy," wrote the eminent conservationist William Hornaday. Whites also gathered wood from the park and grazed cattle, creating a situation so chaotic that the U.S. govern-ment was forced to call ' on the military to restore order in the wilderness. In 1886, the cavalry moved in and stayed more than 30 years, until 1916 when the National Park Service took over the administration of Yellowstone.

EXPLORING THE ISSUE

Did the Conservation Movement of the Early Twentieth Century Successfully Preserve the American Environment?

Critical Thinking and Reflection

1. Critically analyze the role played by Gifford Pinchot in managing the nation's forest reserves.
2. Critically evaluate the relationship between President Theodore Roosevelt and Chief Forester Gifford Pinchot in the development of effective conservation policies.
3. Compare and contrast the preservationist ethic of John Muir with the utilitarian conservationist policies of Gifford Pinchot.
4. Critically examine "the effect of conservation measures—such as the establishment of national parks, forests, wildlife preserves—on the ecosystems that were the target of this important reform impulse."
5. Critically evaluate the impact of the national park system on native Americans, poor white Western farmers, and middle-class tourists.
6. Critically evaluate the struggle between the preservationists and utilitarian conservationists to establish a dam to supply water to San Francisco in the Hetch Hetchy Valley.

Is There Common Ground?

Has Professor Steinberg gone overboard in his criticisms of both Pinchot and Muir, who were the leaders of both sides of the conservation movement? Could they foresee the negative consequences of the movement? Or is Watkins correct in his view of Gifford Pinchot as the most important figure who started the current conservation movement? The portrayal of the Hetch Hetchy controversy pits two contrasting philosophies of the conservation movement against one another: the utilitarian practical conservationism of Gifford Pinchot versus the idealistic preservationist views of John Muir. At different times do their views converge? For example, Pinchot's biographers and his own autobiography *Breaking New Ground: Commemorative Edition* (Island Press, 1998), completed shortly before his death in 1946, discuss the many field trips Pinchot took to observe the wonders of nature. In addition, a new study by Robert W. Righter, *The Battle Over Hetch Hetchy: America's Most Controversial Dam and the Birth of Modern Environmentalism* (Oxford University Press, 2005) disagrees with the standard interpretation as expressed in Roderick Nash's classic, *Wilderness and the American Mind* (Yale University Press, 1967, 1973, 1983, 2001) that the defenders of the valley did not want to preserve a wilderness. Instead, according to Righter, "the defenders of the valley consistently advocated development, including roads, hotels, winter sports amenities, and the infrastructure to support legions of visitors. The land use battle joined over one question: Would the valley be used for water storage or nature tourism?" (pp. 5–6).

Additional Resources

Ted Steinberg's *Down to Earth: Nature's Role in American Society* (Oxford University Press, 2002) is highly opinionated, but it is the best written, comprehensive overview of the environmental movement by a scholar. The two best scholarly articles that are easily accessible are John Steele Gordon, "The American Environment," *American Heritage* (October 1993) and Stuart L. Udall, "How the Wilderness Was Won," *American Heritage* (February/March 2000). Roderick Frazier Nash's *Wilderness and the American Mind*, 4th ed. (Yale University Press, 2001) is the classic intellectual history of the subject. The latest summary that is less controversial than Steinberg's work is Thomas R. Wellock, *Preserving the Nation: The Conservation and Environmental Movements, 1870–2000* (Harlan Davidson, 2007).

J. Leonard Bates, "Fulfilling American Democracy: The Conservation Movement, 1907–1921," *Mississippi Valley Historical Review* (vol. 44, June 1957, pp. 29–57) is a good overview of the traditional view of the progressive movement and conservation, but Samuel P. Hay's *Conservation and the Gospel of Efficiency* (Harvard University Press, 1959) created a new framework in viewing conservation as a "scientific movement" of which "essence was rational planning to promote efficient development and use of all natural resources." Two important biographies of the leading figures of the twentieth century conservation movement are Stephen Fox, *John Muir and His Legacy: The American Conservation Movement* (Little, Brown , 1981) and Char Miller, *Gifford Pinchot and the Making of Modern Environmentalism* (Island Press, Shearwater Books, 2001).

President Theodore Roosevelt was our first conservation president. Two books stand out in their discussions of this aspect of Theodore Roosevelt's policies: Paul Russell Cutright, *The Making of a Conservationist* (University of Illinois Press, 1985) remains a classic because it is brief, pointed, and well researched; Douglas Brinkley, *The Wilderness Warrior: Theodore Roosevelt and the Crusade for America* (Harper Collins, 2009) is massive and informative but at times makes the reader feel he is in the wilderness. Mark Harvey, "A Massive and Valuable Study of Theodore Roosevelt and Conservation," *Theodore Roosevelt Association Journal* (vo. 32, Winter-Spring 2011) is an extensive, highly critical review, which among other points claims Brinkley "oversimplifies and at times caricatures conservation opponents." A brief summary of Roosevelt's conservation record can be found in Tweed Roosevelt, "Theodore Roosevelt: The Mystery of the Unrecorded Environmentalist," *Theodore Roosevelt Association Journal* (vol. 35, 2002).

Seth Shteir, "To Dare Mighty Things: A Celebration of Theodore Roosevelt and His National Parks Legacy, 150 Years After His Birth," *National Parks* (vol. 82, Fall 2008) is brief and a good starting point. Glen Sussman and Byron W. Daynes, "Spanning the Century: Theodore Roosevelt, Franklin Roosevelt, Richard Nixon, Bill Clinton, and the Environment," *White House Studies* (vol. 4, no. 3, pp. 337–354), considers these four as model environmental presidents.

Bill McKibben has edited *Environmental Writing Since Thoreau: American Earth* (N.Y.: Literary Classics of the United States, 2008). For purposes of this issue, there are primary source selections from John Muir, Gifford Pinchot, and Theodore Roosevelt.

ISSUE 8

Was Woodrow Wilson Responsible for the Failure of the United States to Join the League of Nations?

YES: John M. Cooper, Jr., from *Breaking the Heart of the World* (Cambridge University Press, 2001)

NO: William G. Carleton, from "A New Look at Woodrow Wilson," *The Virginia Quarterly Review* (Autumn 1962)

Learning Outcomes

After reading this issue you should be able to:

- Discuss how Woodrow Wilson performed in various presidential roles.
- Distinguish between the realist approach and the idealist approach to foreign policy.
- Evaluate whether Wilson was a realist or an idealist?
- Determine whether Wilson was psychologically or physically impaired during the treaty fight in the Senate.
- Conclude whether Wilson or Senator Henry Cabot Lodge killed the Treaty of Versailles.
- Determine whether Wilson was ahead of his times and American public opinion during the treaty fight.

ISSUE SUMMARY

YES: Professor John M. Cooper argues that the stroke that partially paralyzed Woodrow Wilson during his speaking tour in 1919 hampered the then president's ability to compromise with the Republicans over the terms of America's membership in the League of Nations if the Senate ratified the Treaty of Versailles.

NO: The late William G. Carleton believed that Woodrow Wilson understood better than any of his contemporaries the role that the United States would play in world affairs.

The presidential polls of Arthur Schlesinger in 1948 and 1962 as well as the 1983 Murray-Blessing poll have ranked Woodrow Wilson among the top 10 presidents. William Carleton considers him the greatest twentieth-century president, only two notches below Jefferson and Lincoln. Yet, among his biographers, Wilson has been treated ungenerously. They carp at him for being naive, overly idealistic, and too inflexible. It appears that Wilson's biographers respect the man but do not like the person.

Wilson's own introspective personality may be partly to blame. He was, along with Jefferson and to some extent Theodore Roosevelt, America's most intellectual president. He spent nearly 20 years as a history and political science teacher and scholar at Bryn Mawr, Wesleyan, and at his alma mater, Princeton University. Although his multivolume *History of the United States* appears dated as it gathers dust on musty library shelves, his Ph.D. dissertation on *Congressional Government*, written as a graduate student at Johns Hopkins, remains a classic statement of the weakness of leadership in the American constitutional system.

There is one other reason why Wilson has been so critically analyzed by his biographers. Certainly, no president before or since Wilson has had less formal political experience than Wilson. Apparently, academic work does not constitute the proper training for the presidency. Yet, in addition to working many years as a college professor and a short stint as a lawyer, Wilson served 8 distinguished years as the president of Princeton University. He turned it into one of the outstanding universities in the country. He introduced the preceptorial system, widely copied today, which supplemented course lectures with discussion conferences led by young instructors. He took the lead in reorganizing the university's curriculum. He lost two key battles. The alumni became upset when he tried to replace the class-ridden eating clubs with his "Quadrangle Plan," which would have established smaller colleges within the university system. What historians most remember about his Princeton career, however, was his losing fight with the Board of Trustees and Dean Andrew West concerning the location and eventual control over the new graduate school. Wilson resigned when it was decided to build a separate campus for the graduate school.

Shortly after Wilson left Princeton in 1910, he ran for governor of New Jersey and won his only political office before he became the president. As a governor, he gained control over the state Democratic Party and pushed through the legislature a litany of progressive measures—a primary elections law, a corrupt practices act, workmen's compensation, utilities regulation, school reforms, and an enabling act that allowed certain cities to adopt the commission form of government. When he was nominated on the 46th ballot at the Democratic convention in 1912, Wilson had enlarged the power of the governor's office in New Jersey and foreshadowed the way in which he would manage the presidency.

If one uses the standard categories of the late Professor Clinton Rossiter, Wilson ranks very high as a textbook president. No one, with the exception of Franklin Roosevelt and perhaps Ronald Reagan, performed the ceremonial role of the presidency as well as Wilson. His speeches rang with oratorical brilliance and substance. No wonder he abandoned the practice of Jefferson and his successors by delivering the president's annual State of the Union Address to Congress in person rather than in writing.

During his first 4 years, he also fashioned a legislative program rivaled only by Franklin D. Roosevelt's later "New Deal." The "New Freedom" pulled together conservative and progressive, rural and urban, as well as southern and northern Democrats in passing such measures as the Underwood-Simmons Tariff, the first bill to significantly lower tariff rates since the Civil War, and the Owens-Keating Child Labor Act. It was through Wilson's adroit maneuvering that the Federal Reserve System was established. This banking measure, the most significant in United States history, established the major agency that regulates money supply in the country today. Finally, President Wilson revealed his flexibility when he abandoned his initial policy of rigid and indiscriminate trust busting for one of regulating big business through the creation of the Federal Trade Commission.

More controversial were Wilson's presidential roles as commander-in-chief of the armed forces and chief diplomat. Some have argued that Wilson did not pay enough attention to strategic issues in the war, whereas other writers have said that he merged the proper dose of force and diplomacy.

Thomas A. Bailey's *Woodrow Wilson and the Lost Peace* (Macmillan, 1944) and *Woodrow Wilson and the Great Betrayal* (Macmillan, 1945) were written as guidance for President Franklin Roosevelt to avoid the mistakes that Wilson made at home and abroad in his failure to gain ratification to the Treaty of Versailles. Specifically, Bailey blamed Wilson for failing to compromise with Senator Henry Cabot Lodge. Similarly, Wilson found himself the target of diplomat George F. Kennan whose chapter in *American Diplomacy, 1900–1950* (Mentor Books, 1951) protested vehemently about the "legalistic–moralistic" streak that he believed permeated Wilson's foreign policy. More recently, former Secretary of State Henry Kissinger, in his scholarly history *Diplomacy* (Simon & Schuster, 1994), insisted that Wilson was excessively moralistic and naive, in telling the American people that they were entering the war to "bring peace and safety to all nations and make the world itself at last free."

Many recent historians agree with David F. Trask that Wilson developed realistic and clearly articulated goals and coordinated his larger diplomatic aims with the use of force better than any other wartime U.S. president. See his essay "Woodrow Wilson and the Reconciliation of Force and Diplomacy, 1917–1918," *Naval War College Review* (January/February 1975). John Milton Cooper, Jr., *The Warrior and the Priest: Woodrow Wilson and Theodore Roosevelt* (Harvard University Press, 1984), presents Wilson as the realist and Theodore Roosevelt as the idealist. Even George Kennan acknowledged that his earlier criticism of Wilson had to be viewed within the context of the Cold War. "I now view Wilson," he wrote in 1991, "as a man who, like so many other people of broad vision and acute sensitivities, was ahead of his time, and did not live long enough to know what great and commanding relevance his ideas would acquire before this century was out." See Thomas J. Knock, "Comments on the Paper Entitled 'Kennan Versus Wilson'" in John Milton Cooper et al., eds., *The Wilson Era: Essays in Honor of Arthur S. Link* (Harlan Davison, 1991).

The issue here is whether or not Wilson bears the responsibility for the failure of the United States to join the League of Nations. In the YES selection, John M. Cooper gives a qualified yes. Had Wilson stayed home and negotiated with the Republicans as he did on other occasions, he might have gotten his peace treaty. But the debilitating stroke he suffered in 1919 after his return from Paris accelerated a stubborn streak that limited his negotiation skills. Cooper characterizes Lodge's reservations as part of his responsibility as the loyal opposition and, in the end, lays most of the blame for the failure of the United States to ratify the Treaty of Versailles and enter the League of Nations at Wilson's feet.

In the NO selection, the late William G. Carleton presents an impassioned defense both of Wilson's policies at Versailles and their implications for the future of American foreign policy. Carleton responds to the two main charges historians continue to level against Wilson: his inability to compromise and his naive idealism. In contrast to Cooper, Carleton excoriates Lodge, who served as the chairman of the Senate Foreign Relations Committee, for adding "nationally self-centered" reservations that he knew would emasculate the League of Nations and most likely would cause other nations to seek their own amendments to the Treaty of Versailles. Wilson, according to Carleton, was a true realist when he refused to consider the Lodge reservations that were politically motivated to embarrass the President and to kill the treaty in the Senate. In rejecting the view of Wilson as a naive idealist, Carleton maintains: "He recognized the emergence of the anti-imperialist revolutions . . . the importance of social politics in the international relations of the future . . . the implications for future world politics of the technological revolutions in war, of total war, and of the disintegration of the old balance of power."

YES

John M. Cooper, Jr.

Breaking the Heart of the World

... **W**hat did it all mean? Did the outcome of the League fight do what Wilson said it would do? Did the failure of the United States to join the League "break the heart of the world"? Or were the obstacles to peacemaking so great, were the odds stacked so heavily against the restoration of world order, that it was an exercise in futility? Did those obstacles and odds make it, in the words of Shakespeare's Macbeth, "full of sound and fury, signifying nothing"? These questions define the two poles in the argument that lasted for the first four or five decades after the League fight.

Unlike most great historical arguments with lasting relevance, this one has led to broad agreement. Since the middle of the twentieth century, few historians or other analysts have doubted that the second set of answers to the question about what the League fight meant is the right one. The near consensus that has emerged around those answers usually employs a more polite phrasing than "sound and fury." It also includes a bow or two toward marginal differences that American membership in the League might have made. But, at bottom, few writers have challenged the notion that the course of American foreign policy and international relations would have been much the same regardless of the outcome of League fight.[1]

Ironically, Wilson's posthumous apotheosis in the 1940s and the sense of having belatedly heeded his warnings have contributed more than anything else to the prevalence of this view of the meaning of the League fight. As usually stated, the prevailing argument boils down to three interlocking propositions. First, Wilson was ahead of his time. Second, Americans were not ready after World War I to make the full-scale commitment to collective security and international enforcement that Wilson demanded. Third, it took World War II to drive home the lessons that Wilson had tried to teach. These propositions need to be examined both separately and together. Separately, each one reveals different assumptions about why the League fight turned out the way it did and what its lasting repercussions were. Together, they provide answers to the question of whether the outcome of the League fight did indeed break the heart of the world.

Each of these propositions is like the face of a three-sided pyramid. Each one takes its shape from the central question of what the League fight meant, yet at the same time each one presents its own distinctive aspect. The first proposition—that Wilson was ahead of his time—speaks directly to his personal role. That role has long since come to be judged as pivotal. Without Wilson, the League fight almost certainly would not have arisen in the first place. A less bold and visionary leader—one who was not ahead of his or her time—would not have attempted to do so much. Likewise, without Wilson, the League fight would almost certainly have ended in some kind of compromise. His unbending insistence upon joining an essentially political international organization with firm obligations under Article X ruled out any halfway house between that position and rejection of membership. In short, the correctness of Winston Churchill's early pronouncement about "this man's mind and spirit" seems incontrovertible.

But there is more to the proposition that Wilson was ahead of his time, and this is where controversy persists. At issue are the value and meaning placed upon his being ahead of his time. In one way, any strong leader must have the capacity for anticipating events and forecasting opportunities and dangers. This capacity is what Shakespeare meant by recognizing the "tide in the affairs of men which, taken at the flood, leads on to fortune" and what Bismarck meant by hearing the distant hoofbeat of the horse of history. Conversely, leaders must retain an appreciation of how willing and able their followers are to accompany them in great leaps forward. Most interpreters of Wilson in the League fight have stressed the negative aspect of his being ahead of his time. "Too far ahead" is the prevailing judgment, and the controversy revolves around why this appears to have been the case.

Two broad schools of interpretation have arisen to account for this perceived fault. One school is cultural and psychological; the other is circumstantial and physiological. The key word for the first school is "messianic." That word, in its view, captures Wilson's religiously based affliction with delusions of divine revelation and chosenness. He believed, so this argument goes, that he and he alone had both the capacity and the message to save the world. This is a cultural view of Wilson for two reasons. First, it sees him as a product of his own culture—the Anglo-American Protestant middle-class world that flourished in the second half of the nineteenth century. Second, this view grows out of the culture of those who have held it, the twentieth century "modernist" dispensation that arose in Europe before World War I and took firm hold there and in America starting in the 1920s. As applied to Wilson, this view found earliest expression in Keynes's depiction of him in *The Economic Consequences of the Peace* and was soon followed by similar treatment at the hands of Mencken and other "debunkers" of that decade.

The psychological side of this school also flowered early. Starting with the American literary critic Edmund Wilson in the mid-1920s, various writers have attributed Woodrow Wilson's alleged messianism to psychological deformations. As viewed through their Freudian lenses, Wilson emerged from his childhood with a severely damaged ego and unresolved oedipal conflict. Further, those maladjustments bred in him messianic delusions and compulsions toward figuratively mortal conflicts with father figures. This happened first in his academic career and later in politics, where Lodge in the League fight played the part of the last of these adversaries. In fact, Sigmund Freud himself painted just such a portrait of Wilson, in collaboration with the defector from the American delegation to the peace conference, William Bullitt. Their contribution did not come to light, however, until the 1960s. In the meantime, this essentially Freudian interpretation had already entered the mainstream of American political interpretation, in general through the writings of Harold Lasswell and in particular application to Wilson through the work of Alexander and Juliette George.[2]

This school of interpretation has several shortcomings. The main defect of the cultural interpretation is—to reverse Mark Twain's celebrated crack about Wagner's music ("It's not as bad as it sounds")—it is not as good as it sounds. This interpretation was present though not greatly developed in Keynes's depiction of Wilson in the *Economic Consequences of the Peace* and found fuller expression in the late 1930s in E. H. Carr's *The Twenty Years' Crisis*. More recently, others have stressed racial, gendered, and ethnocentric biases that supposedly crippled him in dealing with the more diverse and disorderly world of the twentieth century. Wilson, in these views, was the exponent of culture-bound, antiquated, hegemonic notions of order ill suited to the realities of the twentieth century.[3]

The main response to this interpretation is—at the risk of impoliteness—so what? Where else except from his own cultural background was Wilson going to get his ideas about world order? It is blatantly presentist and ahistorical to expect anything else. More important, do the origins and limitations of his ideas necessarily invalidate them? Perhaps so, but perhaps not. The alternatives to his vision of order, "pluralism" and "disorder," entailed ethnic and national conflicts, genocides, and world wars. Viewed in that light, Wilson's time-bound views do not look so bad, especially because his insistence upon flexible application of them and adjustment over time left room for growth and change.

Likewise, the stress on Wilson's psychological flaws has three major flaws of its own. First and most clearly, any reading of what Wilson said at almost any time during the League fight makes it difficult to sustain the allegation of messianism. For example, he never uttered the phrase "war to end all wars." That came from Lloyd George, as did "self-determination" as both a phrase and a general principle. Wilson, by contrast, made a limited and circumspect case for his program, as he had done earlier with the Fourteen Points and as he continued to do throughout the League fight. He stressed that the League marked only the indication of the direction and the beginning of the journey toward a more just and peaceful world. He called the League "a living thing," and he expected and wanted it to evolve over time. He repeatedly claimed that he would welcome a better alternative if his opponents could come up with one. To be sure, that was a rhetorical offer, but at a deeper level Wilson meant it sincerely. In laying stress on the obligation under Article X, he revealed that he cared far less about the particular provisions of the treaty and the Covenant and far more about ensuring his nation's commitment to an active role in preserving peace. The only way to reconcile such sophisticated, self-critical arguments with messianism is to impute fantastic deviousness and insincerity to Wilson. This requires a psychological stretch that only a few of his worst enemies in the League fight were willing to make.

The second flaw in this psychological interpretation is that it resembles the biblical parable of the mote and the beam. It detects and pounces on Wilson's supposed shortcomings while remaining oblivious to its own greater limitations. Its own "modernist" assumptions limit and disable this psychological interpretation. Those assumptions stress the supremacy of unconscious and emotional forces, combined with racial, class, and gendered biases. Thereby, Wilson and figures like him—who drew their assumptions from orthodox religious creeds and believed in disinterestedness and the power of reason—have become literally incomprehensible to this modernist sensibility. In fact, it was Wilson's grounding in that very culture of his time, especially his youthful immersion in some of the most sophisticated religious thinking of that day, that inoculated him against the messianic tendencies that did afflict others in the atmosphere of supercharged idealism and evangelism that suffused much of American political life from 1900 to 1920.[4]

The final flaw in this psychological interpretation is its downgrading of physiological factors. The need to see the "real" Wilson in his refusal to compromise during the League fight requires adherents to this school to scoff at suggestions that other circumstances in 1919 and 1920 may also have played an important role. Leaving aside the question of whether anyone's behavior at a particular time can reveal the "real" person, this refusal to give consideration to the major stroke that Wilson suffered appears willful or even perverse. How could such a devastating illness *not* have affected his behavior? How could the worst crisis of presidential disability in American history *not* have affected the outcome of the League fight? These objections become particularly acute when they are set against the events of January and February 1920. Then, virtually every League advocate and every member of the president's inner circle, including Tumulty, Dr. Grayson, and Mrs. Wilson, tried to persuade him to compromise. To imagine that a healthier Wilson would not have tried to bring the League fight to a better, more pleasant, more constructive conclusion requires another psychological stretch. It demands an insistence upon personality-warped messianism that borders on the ludicrous.[5]

The other broad school of interpretation of Wilson's being ahead of his time—the one that stresses circumstantial factors—answers that last, health-based objection to the cultural-psychological interpretation. But this second school of interpretation did not originate as a response to the first one. Rather, it initially stressed not his health, but other circumstances, as part of the Wilsonian position during and right after the League fight. Wilson was ahead of his time, this view holds, chiefly because so many of his contemporaries in the nation's political leadership refused to keep up with him. This view shifts the onus for an unsatisfactory outcome to the League fight over to the Republicans, particularly Lodge and, to a lesser degree, Root. These men stand accused of putting personal dislike of Wilson and pursuit of partisan advantage ahead of the greater good of the nation and the world. By contrast, Taft and others in the LEP stand as paragons of enlightenment and bipartisan harmony.[6]

The flaws in such a circumstantial case are not hard to see. Like the opposing school, this one also imputes hidden and ignoble motives to the actors whom it dislikes. It gives little credence to the sincerity and rationality of Lodge or Root when they raised what they regarded as practical and principled objections to Wilson's program. It also fails to recognize that, given their inconstancy in supporting that program, Taft, Lowell, and the Thirty-One Republicans of October 1920, were not so different from their fellow partisans. Furthermore, to deplore partisanship and exalt bipartisanship, as this school does, is to misunderstand the essentially adversarial nature of the American two-party system. Like this country's legal system, the two-party system demands vigorous conflict between the two sides, whereas bipartisanship usually requires abdication by one of the adversaries. This system has built-in limitations. These limitations become particularly acute in harnessing diverse coalitions within one or the other of only two parties and in processes that require supermajorities in one or both houses of Congress, such as the two-thirds needed for approval of constitutional amendments or consent to treaties. But to blame the outcome of the League fight on partisanship is like blaming the weather. To blame Lodge, Root, and others for acting like partisans is to blame them for doing what they were supposed to do.

The most serious flaw in this circumstantial interpretation is that it does not square with the facts of the League fight. In one way, the more culpable partisans were the Democrats. Many of them bowed to Wilson's dictation against their better judgment. Republican senators were scoring partisan points when they leveled such charges at their colleagues across the aisle before the votes on the treaty, but they were largely correct. On the Republican side, what seems noteworthy is not how staunchly the non-Irreconcilable senators opposed Wilson but how far, by their lights, they went to meet him. After the Round Robin and the Foreign Relations Committee's effort to amend the treaty, the Lodge reservations represented a considerable retreat for many of them. As for Lodge, despite his manifest negativism toward the League and hostile stance toward Wilson, he showed much greater flexibility than most interpreters have given him credit for or than he himself cared to remember. Both his dealings with Stephen Bonsal in November 1919 and even more his conduct in the bipartisan talks in January 1920 revealed a wavering in his total rejection of Article X and some openness toward compromise. Lodge did not come away from the League fight a beloved figure, but he was not at all the wily, underhanded villain of contemporary and later caricature.[7]

What this circumstantial view does stress correctly is that others besides Wilson contributed to his being ahead of his time. This view also correctly calls attention to the excessive heat of partisan conflict in 1919 and 1920. Much of that heat stemmed from the emotions that had been whipped up during the war and had not abated after the abrupt end of the fighting in November 1918. Simultaneously with the League fight, those emotions and other discontents were exploding into race riots and lynchings, massive labor strikes, and the Red Scare of 1919 and 1920. Much of the partisan heat of those years also stemmed from the uneasy position of both parties. Thanks largely to their own earlier internecine conflicts, the once-dominant Republicans had endured banishment from the White House and congressional majorities for the longest period in their party's history. Their victory in the 1918 elections raised their hopes, but they gained control of Congress only by narrow margins, and their best presidential prospect, Roosevelt, died in January 1919. By the same token, the Democrats approached the postwar situation with mingled hope and apprehension, and few of them had any stomach for questioning the leadership of their only president to win reelection since Andrew Jackson. In short, these political circumstances would have taxed the resources of even the ablest, healthiest leader who tried to pull off a foreign policy coup like Wilson's.

Clearly, the weightiest circumstance of all was that Wilson was not the healthiest of leaders during the League fight. Whether he was the ablest leader available is a different question and one that cannot be answered apart from considerations of his health. With the exception of Thomas A. Bailey, those who developed the circumstantial interpretation of Wilson's performance did not pay much attention to his health. Only with the work of Edwin Weinstein, a trained neurologist, in the 1970s did anyone confront head-on the question of what impact illness in general and the 1919 stroke in particular had on Wilson's behavior. The leading Wilson scholar and editor of *The Papers of Woodrow Wilson*, Arthur Link, soon joined Weinstein in promoting a more physiological interpretation of his life and career. Several of the published volumes of this series came to include extensive notes and appendixes both by Link and his fellow editors and by medical experts about the likely influences of his physical condition at different times but most significantly during the peace conference and the League fight.[8]

Such attention was long overdue in interpreting why Wilson behaved as he did in 1919 and 1920. Moreover, the emphasis on his health throughout his life broadened the inquiry beyond the narrow question of whether the stroke was responsible for his failure to compromise. Unfortunately, in their zeal to pursue their medical interpretation, Weinstein and Link gratuitously attacked the psychological school and provoked a series of furious rejoinders by the Georges, who enlisted a medical expert of their own. The ensuing melee showed neither side at its best, but when the dust had settled some agreement did emerge about the likely influences of Wilson's cardiovascular and neurological condition in 1919 and 1920. The most important area of agreement lay in examining his condition prior to as well as following the stroke. "Cerebrovascular accidents," especially ones such as Wilson suffered, have an antecedent pathology, which often includes "small strokes" and which, even without those, often affects the victim's personality and behavior. That pathology, together with the impact of age and fatigue, underscores the conclusion that Wilson was operating at a level far below his best standard of performance in the White House.[9]

Unfortunately, this stress on his health and the controversy with the psychological school created the impression that Link and Weinstein were putting all their interpretative eggs in one basket and that they were seeking to exculpate Wilson. That was not the case. Weinstein, in particular, mixed his medical interpretations with a psychological portrait of Wilson that differed in tone but not much in content from earlier views. This was a surpassingly important point that went unnoticed in the scholarly fracas. Whatever the impact of Wilson's stroke, its antecedent pathology, and its subsequent effects, that impact could only have occurred in conjunction with his psychological makeup. Put another way, a different person would have reacted differently to an illness like this.

It might seem tempting to try to reconcile the psychological and physiological interpretations by claiming that the stroke and its surrounding neurological condition simply accentuated his personality deformations and exacerbated his messianic tendencies. But such an attempt at reconciliation would only make a bad interpretation worse. The one sound element in that blending of views is the neurologists' finding that such strokes often exaggerate their victims' personality traits. Clearly, this was true with Wilson. Combined with the ill effects of his isolation from outside contacts, his stroke appears to have destroyed previously exercised compensations for tendencies toward self-righteousness and stubbornness. But the psychological injuries inflicted by the stroke did not turn him into a would-be messiah. Rather, the stroke, its treatment, and perhaps its preceding neurological effects operated on a different aspect of Wilson's personality. His condition rendered him incapable of compromise only partly because of stubbornness and self-righteousness and not at all from messianic delusions.

The best adjective to describe the aspect of Wilson's personality that was most significantly affected by his health is "promethean." He resembled the character in ancient Greek mythology, Prometheus, who defied the gods in order to steal fire from Olympus and bring it back as a gift to his fellow mortals. The promethean traits of boldness and willingness to gamble for great stakes formed central aspects of Wilson's character at least from middle age onward. Without such boldness, Wilson would have been an ordinary college president, not the most exciting academic innovator of his time. Without such boldness, he would not have gone into politics at all, rather than running for office for the first time at the age of fifty-three. Without such boldness, he might have become a humdrum governor, rather than a leading reformer ranked alongside such contemporary state-level "progressive" titans as La Follette and Hiram Johnson, as well as his party's presidential nominee within two years. Without such boldness, he might have been a cautious domestic president who felt his way slowly, instead of one of the three greatest legislative leaders in the White House in the twentieth century. Without such boldness, he might have pursued a cautious neutrality throughout the world war, instead of finally, for better or worse, intervening with full force in order to try to shape the postwar international order.[10]

Even without his role in the League fight, Wilson ranks as one of the most daring presidents in American history. Public images to the contrary notwithstanding, he moved much more boldly in the White House than his great rival Theodore Roosevelt had done. He may even have surpassed Franklin Roosevelt in his willingness to gamble for great stakes at home and abroad. Unquestionably, Wilson's biggest gamble was his basically political conception of the League of Nations combined with a strong American commitment to international enforcement. The promethean quality of his personality shone through more brightly there than anywhere else. His decision to go to Europe and stay for the whole peace conference, his refusal to take along senators or big-name Republicans who might get in his way, his seizing the moment to whip together the Draft Covenant with Article X at its heart, his defiance of the Round Robin, his speaking tour in September—all these actions bespoke the promethean character of Wilson's role in the League fight. Finally, tragically, even his fate was promethean. The gods punished Prometheus by chaining him for eternity to a rock, while vultures pulled out his innards. Both the physical disability and the psychological imbalance that the stroke inflicted were mortal equivalents to such divine punishment.

Whether such a promethean approach was wise in the abstract is a pertinent question. It is another way of asking whether Wilson got too far ahead of his time and, if so, whose fault that was. More concretely, it needs to be asked whether this was a wise approach given the state of Wilson's health. One who seeks to play the part of Prometheus had better be in possession of every possible strength and ability. Wilson was nowhere near such fighting trim. Even before his stroke, the flare-up at the Round Robin, the failure of the speech presenting the treaty to the Senate, the inability to reach out to sympathetic Republican senators, the slowness in hitting his oratorical stride, and the faltering on the speaking tour—all these sprang in some measure from failing health. Such physical shortcomings and their likely psychological effects would have hampered any leader at any time, but they proved devastating for a would-be promethean figure at such a critical juncture.

The stroke appears to have exacerbated this promethean trait by rendering Wilson literally incapable of compromise. With his stroke-warped judgment, he could not view his gamble on the League and Article X as anything but an all-or-nothing proposition. Half a loaf looked like poison to him. His delusions about some sort of "referendum" and running for a third term, together with the threat to withdraw from the peace treaty in the diplomatic note about Fiume, attested to his willingness to lose everything rather than settle for an inconclusive outcome to the League fight. Pride and convictions about the righteousness of his cause also gripped the stroke-plagued Wilson when he scorned compromise after compromise, but it was the gambler rather than the would-be messiah who found total, clearcut defeat better than an unsatisfying, muddled draw. Wilson could not do what he had once exhorted others to do. He could not accept "peace without victory."

The second proposition in the prevailing answer to questions about the meaning of the League fight—that the American people were not ready to assume Wilson's commitments—is a corollary to the first proposition about his being ahead of his time. This second proposition shifts attention from leaders to followers. Of these three propositions, this one has stirred the least controversy. Few interpreters have doubted that, indeed, the American people in 1919 and 1920 were unwilling to take up the burden that Wilson wanted to thrust upon them. . . .

Consideration of where the public stood during the League fight leads logically to the third proposition about its meaning—that it took World War II to get Americans to heed the Wilsonian message. This third proposition requires acceptance of the preceding one, and it strikes closest to the central question of what the League fight really meant. Agreeing with these two propositions requires believing that the League fight meant comparatively little. This belief assumes further that American membership in the League and greater participation in world politics would not have done much to forestall the breakdown of international order in the 1930s. A different outcome to the League fight, so this answer holds, would not have prevented World War II. Failure to follow Wilson did not "break the heart of the world." Here is the heart of the matter. The basic question remains: Is this so?

The strongest argument in support of this third proposition is the observation that things did happen that way. World War II evidently did induce near universal and lasting support for Wilsonian commitments to maintain international order and peace. Two questions immediately arise about this proposition. First, could anything else have induced such support? Second, what were the nature and consequences of the support that World War II did induce? . . .

One last consideration needs to be noted in answering the overriding Question of what the League meant. This is the matter of what was at stake.

The stakes that Wilson strove to win in the League fight were nothing less than to prevent a recurrence of the carnage that had raged from 1914 through 1918. Even without seeing with his own eyes, he grasped how truly death-dealing and calamitous modern industrial-technological warfare had become. He also recognized that death and wounding and destruction did not comprise the sum of this kind of war's evil effects. He saw that order had broken down not only among nations but also within them, releasing terrible passions that might feed into lurid ideologies.

Wilson does not need to be exalted to the status of a secular prophet in order to appreciate his vision. He understood Communism only dimly, although he recoiled from the Bolsheviks' revolutionary violence. He did not foresee Fascism and Nazism, although he feared the nationalist passions that he saw unleashed in Europe and elsewhere. He did not foresee nuclear weapons, although he did envision how conventional warfare could become even more terribly destructive, as it did in World War II, Korea, and Vietnam. Wilson did not need to be a prophet. It was enough for him to be a sensitive man who had glanced into the abyss that yawned ahead if people and nations did not mend their ways. He never claimed to be a messiah or to have surefire solutions. As he said repeatedly on his speaking tour for the League, he was offering only some insurance against a repetition of what had just ravaged the world. But, he insisted, any insurance, even limited, partial insurance, was better than none. This was the same man who had cried out to Frank Cobb of the New York *World* in March 1917, as he agonized over whether to intervene in the war, "If there is any alternative, for God's sake let's take it."

Did the outcome of the League fight "break the heart of the world"? Of course it did. It is not necessary to claim that a different outcome would have prevented the rise of Hitler, the Holocaust, World War II, or the dropping of the atomic bomb. Just to list those events and to remember other things that have occurred between the end of World War I and the last decade of the twentieth century is to gain an appreciation of what the stakes in the League fight really were. Just to recall those events is to see that Wilson was absolutely right to grasp at any insurance against such things happening. Decent and reasonable people disagreed with him. They did not see the stakes the way Wilson did, and they believed that what he was asking was excessive and dangerous. Wilson failed to be as flexible and persuasive as he should have been, and his illness turned him into the biggest obstacle to a more-constructive outcome. But two facts remain incontrovertible. For all their decency and intelligence, Wilson's opponents were wrong. For all his flaws and missteps, Wilson was right. He should have won the League fight. His defeat did break the heart of the world. . . .

Notes

1. For a recent expression of this view, see Ninkovich, *Wilsonian Century: U.S. Foreign Policy since 1900* (Chicago, 1999), p. 76.

2. See Sigmund Freud and William Bullitt, *Thomas Woodrow Wilson: A Psychological Study* (Boston, 1967); and Alexander George and Juliette George, *Woodrow Wilson and Colonel House: A Personality Study* (New York, 1956). Appropriately, the Georges were students of Lasswell's at the University of Chicago.

3. See E. H. Carr, The Twenty Years' Crisis (London, 1939), esp. 102–112. Two able recent presentations of this view of Wilson are in Lloyd E. Ambrosius, *Woodrow Wilson and the American Diplomatic Tradition: The Treaty Fight in Perspective* (New York, 1987); and David Steigerwald, *Wilsonian Idealism in America* (Ithaca, N.Y., 1994).

4. Examples of Wilson's contemporaries who can fairly be accused of messianic tendencies include not only that paragon of evangelical and conservative Protestantism, Bryan, but also such apparent religious skeptics as La Follette and Roosevelt. On Wilson's religious upbringing and prepresidential political thought, see John M. Mulder, *Woodrow Wilson: The Years of Preparation* (Princeton, N.J., 1978); and Niels Aage Thorsen, *The Political Thought of Woodrow Wilson, 1875–1910* (Princeton, N.J., 1988).

5. To be fair to those who downgrade the influence of the stroke in particular, it should be noted that none other than Arthur Link once stated, "It is, therefore, possible, even probable, that Wilson would have acted as he did even had he not suffered his breakdown, for it was not in his nature to compromise away the principles in which he believed." Arthur S. Link, *Wilson the Diplomatist: A Look at His Major Foreign Policies* (Baltirnore, 1957), 155. When he wrote those words, Link had evidently not completely discarded the critical, sometimes even harsh, view of Wilson that he expressed in the first volume of his biography, *Wilson: The Road to the White House* (Princeton, N.J., 1947), and in *Woodrow Wilson and the Progressive Era, 1910–1917* (New York, 1954). He later modified most of those criticisms of Wilson and reversed his evaluation of the effect of the stroke on Wilson's refusal to compromise in the League fight.

6. The stress on the nefarious influence of partisanship is one of the few points on which I disagree with the otherwise estimable and incisive treatment of the League fight in Thomas A. Bailey, *Woodrow Wilson and the Great Betrayal* (New York, 1945).

7. Although I am less sympathetic toward Lodge, I do agree in the main with the assessments of him in William Widenor's excellent *Henry Cabot*

Lodge and the Search for an American Foreign Policy (Berkeley, Calif., 1980), especially when he says, "We may reasonably assume that Lodge would have swallowed the League had he seen therein the means of securing a Republican victory" (309) and Lodge "had to be less forthright in expressing his views, had to be all things to all men" (322).

8. See Edwin Weinstein, "Woodrow Wilson's Neurological Illness," *Journal of American History,* LVII (Sept. 1970), 324–351, and *Woodrow Wilson: A Medical and Psychological Biography* (Princeton, N.J., 1981). Relevant notes and appendixes to the *Papers of Wilson* are cited above in the notes relating to Wilson's behavior in the summer of 1919 and the impact of the stroke.

9. On the controversy, see Edwin Weinstein, James William Anderson, and Arthur S. Link, "Woodrow Wilson's Political Personality: A Reappraisal," *Political Science Quarterly,* XCIII (Winter 1978–79), 585–598; George and George, "Woodrow Wilson and Colonel House: A Reply to Weinstein, Anderson, and Link," ibid., XCVI (Winter 1981–82), 641–643; George and George, "Issues in Wilson Scholarship: References to Early Strokes in the Papers of Woodrow Wilson," *Journal of American History,* LXX (March 1984), 845–853; Arthur S. Link, David W. Hirst, John Wells Davidson, and John E. Little, "Communication," ibid., 945–955. Alexander George, Michael T. Marmor, and Juliette George, "Communication," ibid., 955–956. For an appraisal of Weinstein's book and the first two items in this battle of the articles, see Dorothy Ross, "Woodrow Wilson and the Case for Psychohistory," ibid., LXIX (Dec. 1982), 639–668; and Lloyd E. Ambrosius, "Woodrow Wilson's Health and the Treaty Fight," *International History Review,* IX (February 1987), 73–84.

10. A remark that revealed this side of Wilson's personality came in 1910 when he told his brother-in-law Stockton Axson, after his defeat in the graduate school controversy at Princeton, "I am not interested in simply administering a club. Unless I can develop something I cannot get thoroughly interested." Axson memoir, "Princeton Controversy," Ray Stannard Baker Papers, Box 99.

William G. Carleton

 **NO**

A New Look at Woodrow Wilson

All high-placed statesmen crave historical immortality. Woodrow Wilson craved it more than most. Thus far the fates have not been kind to Wilson; there is a reluctance to admit him to as great a place in history as he will have.

Congress has just gotten around to planning a national memorial for Wilson, several years after it had done this for Theodore Roosevelt and Franklin D. Roosevelt. Wilson is gradually being accepted as one of the nation's five or six greatest Presidents. However, the heroic mold of the man on the large stage of world history is still generally unrecognized.

There is a uniquely carping, hypercritical approach to Wilson. Much more than other historical figures he is being judged by personality traits, many of them distorted or even fancied. Wilson is not being measured by the yardstick used for other famous characters of history. There is a double standard at work here.

What are the common errors and misrepresentations with respect to Wilson? In what ways is he being judged more rigorously? What are the reasons for this? Why will Wilson eventually achieve giant stature in world history?

There are two criticisms of Wilson that go to the heart of his fame and place in history. One is an alleged inflexibility and intransigence, an inability to compromise. The other is that he had no real understanding of world politics, that he was a naïve idealist. Neither is true.

If Wilson were indeed as stubborn and adamant as he is often portrayed he would have been a bungler at his work, for the practice and art of politics consist in a feeling for the possible, a sense of timing, a capacity for give-and-take compromise. In reality, Wilson's leadership of his party and the legislative accomplishments of his first term were magnificent. His performance was brilliantly characterized by the very qualities he is said to have lacked: flexibility, accommodation, a sense of timing, and a willingness to compromise. In the struggles to win the Federal Reserve Act, the Clayton Anti-Trust Law, the Federal Trade Commission, and other major measures of his domestic program, Wilson repeatedly mediated between the agrarian liberals and the conservatives of his party, moving now a little to the left, now to the right, now back to the left. He learned by experience, cast aside pride of opinion,

From *Virginia Quarterly Review,* vol. 38, no. 4 (Autumn 1962), pp. 545–566. Copyright © 1962 by University of Virginia. Reprinted by permission.

accepted and maneuvered for regulatory commissions after having warned of their danger during the campaign of 1912, and constantly acted as a catalyst of the opposing factions of his party and of shifting opinion.

The cautious way Wilson led the country to military preparedness and to war demonstrated resiliency and a sense of timing of a high order. At the Paris Conference Wilson impressed thoughtful observers with his skill as a negotiator; many European diplomats were surprised that an "amateur" could do so well. Here the criticism is not that Wilson was without compromise but that he compromised too much.

Actually, the charge that Wilson was incapable of compromise must stand or fall on his conduct during the fight in the Senate over the ratification of the League of Nations, particularly his refusal to give the word to the Democratic Senators from the South to vote for the Treaty with the Lodge Reservations, which, it is claimed, would have assured ratification. Wilson, say the critics, murdered his own brain child. It is Wilson, and not Lodge, who has now become the villain of this high tragedy.

Now, would a Wilsonian call to the Southerners to change their position have resulted in ratification? Can we really be sure? In order to give Southerners time to readjust to a new position, the call from the White House would have had to have been made several weeks before that final vote. During that time what would have prevented Lodge from hobbling the League with still more reservations? Would the mild reservationists, all Republicans, have prevented this? The record shows, I think, that in the final analysis the mild reservationists could always be bamboozled by Lodge in the name of party loyalty. As the fight on the League had progressed, the reservations had become more numerous and more crippling. Wilson, it seems, had come to feel that there simply was no appeasing Lodge.

During the Peace Conference, in response to the Senatorial Round Robin engineered by Lodge, Wilson had reopened the whole League question and obtained the inclusion of American "safeguards" he felt would satisfy Lodge. This had been done at great cost, for it had forced Wilson to abandon his position as a negotiator above the battles for national advantages and to become a suppliant for national concessions. This had resulted in his having to yield points in other parts of the Treaty to national-minded delegations from other countries. When Wilson returned from Paris with the completed Treaty, Lodge had "raised the ante," the Lodge Reservations requiring the consent of other signatory nations were attached to the Treaty, and these had multiplied and become more restrictive in nature as the months went by. Would not then a "final" yielding by Wilson have resulted in even stiffer reservations being added? Was not Lodge using the Reservations to effect not ratification but rejection, knowing that there was a point beyond which Wilson could not yield?

Wilson seems honestly to have believed that the Lodge Reservations emasculated the League. Those who read them for the first time will be surprised, I think, to discover how nationally self-centered they were. If taken seriously, they surely must have impaired the functioning of the League. However, Wilson was never opposed to clarifying or interpreting reservations which would not require the consent of the other signatories. Indeed, he him-self wrote the Hitchcock Reservations.

Even had the League with the Lodge Reservations been ratified, how cer-tain can we really be that this would have meant American entrance into the League? Under the Lodge Reservations, every signatory nation had to accept them before the United States could become a member. Would all the signa-tories have accepted every one of the fifteen Lodge Reservations? The United States had no monopoly on chauvinism, and would not other nations have interposed reservations of their own as a condition to their acceptance of the Lodge Reservations?

At Paris, Wilson had personally experienced great difficulty getting his own mild "reservations" incorporated into the Covenant. Now, at this late date, would Britain have accepted the Lodge Reservation on Irish self-determination? In all probability. Would Japan have accepted the Reservation on Shantung? This is more doubtful. Would the Latin American states have accepted the stronger Reservation on the Monroe Doctrine? This is also doubtful. Chile had already shown concern, and little Costa Rica had the temerity to ask for a defini-tion of the Doctrine. Would the British Dominions have accepted the Reserva-tion calling for one vote for the British Empire or six votes for the United States? Even Lord Grey, who earlier had predicted that the signatories would accept the Lodge Reservations, found that he could not guarantee acceptance by the Dominions, and Canada's President of the Privy Council and Acting Secretary for External Affairs, Newton W. Rowell, declared that if this Reservation were accepted by the other powers Canada would withdraw from the League.

By the spring of 1920, Wilson seems to have believed that making the League of Nations the issue in the campaign of 1920 would afford a better opportunity for American participation in an effective League than would further concessions to Lodge. To Wilson, converting the Presidential election into a solemn referendum on the League was a reality. For months, because of his illness, he had lived secluded in the White House, and the memories of his highly emotional reception in New York on his return from Paris and of the enthusiasm of the Western audiences during his last speaking trip burned vividly bright. He still believed that the American people, if given the chance, would vote for the League without emasculating reservations. Does this, then, make Wilson naïve? It is well to remember that in the spring of 1920 not even the most sanguine Republican envisaged the Republican sweep that would develop in the fall of that year.

If the strategy of Wilson in the spring of 1920 was of debatable wisdom, the motives of Lodge can no longer be open to doubt. After the landslide of 1920, which gave the Republicans the Presidency and an overwhelming majority in a Senate dominated by Lodge in foreign policy, the Treaty was never resurrected. The Lodge Reservations, representing months of gruelling legislative labor, were cavalierly jettisoned, and a separate peace was made with Germany.

What, then, becomes of the stock charge that Wilson was intolerant of opposition and incapable of bending? If the truth of this accusation must rest on Wilson's attitude during the Treaty fight, and I think it must, for he showed remarkable adaptability in other phases of his Presidency, then it must fall. The situation surrounding the Treaty fight was intricately tangled, and there is certainly as much evidence on the side of Wilson's forbearance as on the side of his obstinacy.

A far more serious charge against Wilson is that he had no realistic understanding of world politics, that he was an impractical idealist whose policies intensified rather than alleviated international problems. Now what American statesman of the period understood world politics better than Wilson—or indeed in any way as well as he? Elihu Root, with his arid legalism? Philander Knox, with his dollar diplomacy? Theodore Roosevelt or Henry Cabot Lodge? Roosevelt and Lodge had some feel for power politics, and they understood the traditional balance of power, at least until their emotions for a dictated Allied victory got the better of their judgment: but was either of them aware of the implications for world politics of the technological revolution in war and the disintegration of the old balance of power? And were not both of them blind to a new force in world politics just then rising to a place of importance—the anti-imperialist revolutions, which even before World War I were getting under way with the Mexican Revolution and the Chinese Revolution of Sun Yat-sen?

Wilson is charged with having no understanding of the balance of power, but who among world statesmen of the twentieth century better sated the classic doctrine of the traditional balance of power than Wilson in his famous Peace Without Victory speech? And was it not Theodore Roosevelt who derided him for stating it? With perfectly straight faces Wilson critics, and a good many historians, tell us that TR, who wanted to march to Berlin and saddle Germany with a harsh peace, and FDR, who sponsored unconditional surrender, "understood" the balance of power, but that Wilson, who fought to salvage a power balance by preserving Germany from partition, was a simple-simon in world politics—an illustration of the double standard at work in evaluating Wilson's place in history.

Wilson not only understood the old, but with amazing clarity he saw the new, elements in world politics. He recognized the emergence of the anti-imperialist revolutions and the importance of social politics in the international relations of the future. He recognized, too, the implications for future world politics of the technological revolution in war, of total war, and of the disintegration of the old balance of power—for World War I had decisively weakened the effective brakes on Japan in Asia, disrupted the Turkish Empire in the Middle East and the Austro-Hungarian Empire in Europe, and removed Russia as a make-weight for the foreseeable future. Wilson believed that a truncated Germany and an attempted French hegemony would only add to the chaos, but he saw too that merely preserving Germany as a power unit would not restore the old balance of power. To Wilson, even in its prime the traditional balance of power had worked only indifferently and collective security would have been preferable, but in his mind the revolutionary changes in the world of 1919 made a collective-security system indispensable.

Just what is realism in world politics? Is it not the ability to use purposefully many factors, even theoretically contradictory ones, and to use them not singly and consecutively but interdependently and simultaneously, shifting the emphasis as conditions change? If so, was not Wilson a very great realist in world politics? He used the old balance-of-power factors, as evidenced by his fight to save Germany as a power unit and his sponsoring of a tripartite alliance of the United States, Britain, and France to guarantee France from any German aggression until such time as collective security would become effective. But he labored to introduce into international relations the new collective-security factors to supplement and gradually supersede in importance the older factors, now increasingly outmoded by historical developments. To label as doctrinaire idealist one who envisaged world politics in so broad and flexible a way is to pervert the meaning of words. . . .

Ranking the Presidents has become a popular game, and even Presidents like to play it, notably Truman and Kennedy. In my own evaluation, I place Wilson along with Jefferson and Lincoln as the nation's three greatest Presidents, which makes Wilson our greatest twentieth-century President. If rated solely on the basis of long-range impact on international relations, Wilson is the most influential of all our Presidents.

What are the achievements which entitle Wilson to so high a place? Let us consider the major ones, although of course some of these are more important than others.

. . . [B]etter than any responsible statesman of his day, Wilson understood and sympathized with the anti-imperialist revolutions and their aspirations for basic internal reforms. He withdrew American support for the Bankers' Consortium in China, and the United States under Wilson was the first of the great powers to recognize the Revolution of Sun Yat-sen. Early in his term he had to wrestle with the Mexican Revolution. He saw the need for social reform; avoided the general war with Mexico that many American investors, Catholics, and professional patriots wanted; and by refusing to recognize the counter-revolution of Huerta and cutting Huerta off from trade and arms while allowing the flow of arms to Carranza, Villa, and Zapata, he made possible the overthrow of the counter-revolution and the triumph of the Revolution. What merciless criticism was heaped on Wilson for insisting that Latin Americans should be positively encouraged to institute reforms and develop democratic practices. Yet today Americans applaud their government's denial of Alliance-for-Progress funds to Latin American countries which refuse to undertake fundamental economic and social reforms and flout democracy.

. . . [C]onfronted with the stupendous and completely novel challenge of having to mobilize not only America's military strength but also its civilian resources and energies in America's first total war, the Wilson Administration set up a huge network of administrative agencies, exemplifying the highest imagination and creativity in the art of practical administration. FDR, in his New Deal and in his World War II agencies, was to borrow heavily from the Wilson innovations.

. . . Wilson's Fourteen Points and his other peace aims constituted war propaganda of perhaps unparalleled brilliance. They thrilled the world. They gave high purpose to the peoples of the Allied countries and stirred their war efforts. Directed over the heads of the governments to the enemy peoples themselves, they produced unrest, helped bring about the revolutions that overthrew the Sultan, the Hapsburgs, and the Hohenzollerns, and hastened the end of the war.

. . . [T]he Treaty of Versailles, of which Wilson was the chief architect, was a better peace than it would have been (considering, among other things, the imperialist secret treaties of the Allies) because of Wilson's labors for a just peace. The League of Nations was founded, and this was to be the forerunner of the United Nations. To the League was assigned the work of general disarmament. The mandate system of the League, designed to prepare colonial peoples for self-government and national independence, was a revolutionary step away from the old imperialism. The aspirations of many peoples in Europe for national independence were fulfilled. (If the disruption of the Austro-Hungarian Empire helped destroy the old balance of power, it must be said that in this particular situation Wilson's doctrine of national autonomy only exploited an existing fact in the interest of Allied victory, and even had there been no Wilsonian self-determination the nationalities of this area were already so well developed that they could not have been denied independence after the defeat of the Hapsburgs. Wilson's self-determination was to be a far more *creative* force among the colonial peoples than among the Europeans.) The Treaty restrained the chauvinism of the Italians, though not as much as Wilson would have liked. It prevented the truncating of Germany by preserving to her the Left Bank of the Rhine. The war-guilt clause and the enormous reparations saddled on Germany were mistakes, but Wilson succeeded in confining German responsibility to civilian damage and the expenses of Allied military pensions rather than the whole cost of the war; and had the United States ratified the Treaty and participated in post-war world affairs, as Wilson expected, the United States would have been in a position to join Britain in scaling down the actual reparations bill and in preventing any such adventure as the French seizure of the Ruhr in 1923, from which flowed Germany's disastrous inflation and the ugly forces of German nihilism. (There is poignancy in the broken Wilson's coming out of retirement momentarily in 1923 to denounce France for making "waste paper" of the Treaty of Versailles.) Finally, if Shantung was Wilson's Yalta, he paid the kind of price FDR paid and for precisely the same reason—the collapse of the balance of power in the immediate area involved.

. . . [T]he chief claim of Wilson to a superlative place in history—and it will not be denied him merely because he was turned down by the United States Senate—is that he, more than any other, formulated and articulated the ideology which was the polestar of the Western democracies in World War I, in World War II, and in the decades of Cold War against the Communists. Today, well past the middle of the twentieth century, the long-time program of America is still a Wilsonian program: international collective security, disarmament, the lowering of economic barriers between nations (as in America's support for the developing West European community today), anti-colonialism, self-determination of nations, and democratic social politics as an alternative to Communism. And this was the program critics of Wilson called "anachronistic," a mere "throw-back" to nineteenth-century liberalism!

America today is still grappling with the same world problems Wilson grappled with in 1917, 1918, and 1919, and the programs and policies designed to meet them are still largely Wilsonian. But events since Wilson's time have made his solutions more and more prophetic and urgent. The sweep of the anti-imperialist revolutions propels us to wider self-determination and social politics. The elimination of space, the increasing interdependence of the world, the further disintegration of the balance of power in World War II, and the nuclear revolution in war compel us to more effective collective security and to arms control supervised by an agency of the United Nations.

There will be more unwillingness to identify Wilson with social politics abroad than with the other policies with which he is more clearly identified. Historians like to quote George L. Record's letter to Wilson in which he told Wilson that there was no longer any glory in merely standing for political democracy, that political democracy had arrived, that the great issues of the future would revolve around economic and social democracy. But Wilson stood in no need of advice on this score. Earlier than any other responsible statesman, Wilson had seen the significance of the Chinese Revolution of Sun Yat-sen and of the Mexican Revolution, and he had officially encouraged both. Wilson believed that economic and social reform was implicit in the doctrine of self-determination, especially when applied to the colonial peoples. He recognized, too, that the Bolshevist Revolution had given economic and social reform a new urgency in all parts of the world. He was also well aware that those who most opposed his program for a world settlement were the conservative and imperialist elements in Western Europe and Japan, that socialist and labor groups were his most effective supporters. He pondered deeply how closely and openly he could work with labor and socialist parties in Europe without cutting off necessary support at home. (This—how to use social democracy and the democratic left to counter Communism abroad and still carry American opinion—was to be a central problem for every discerning American statesman after 1945.) Months before he had received Record's letter, Wilson himself had expressed almost the same views as Record. In a long conversation with Professor Stockton Axson at the White House, Wilson acknowledged that his best support was coming from labor people, that they were in touch with world movements and were international-minded, that government ownership of some basic resources and industries was coming, even in the United States, and that it was by a program of social democracy that Communism could be defeated.

In 1918 two gigantic figures—Wilson and Lenin—faced each other and articulated the contesting ideologies which would shake the world during the century. Since then, the lesser leaders who have succeeded them have added little to the ideology of either side. We are now far enough into the century to see in what direction the world is headed, provided there is no third world war. It is not headed for Communist domination. It is not headed for an American hegemony. And it is not headed for a duality with half the world Communist and the other half capitalist. Instead, it is headed for a new pluralism. The emerging new national societies are adjusting their new industrialism to their own conditions and cultures; and their developing economies will be varying mixtures of privatism, collectivism, and welfarism. Even the Communist states differ from one another in conditions, cultures, stages of revolutionary development, and degrees of Marxist "orthodoxy" or "revisionism." And today, all national states, old and new, Communist and non-Communist, join the United Nations as a matter of course.

There will be "victory" for neither "side," but instead a world which has been historically affected by both. Lenin's international proletarian state failed to materialize, but the evolving economies of the underdeveloped peoples are being influenced by his collectivism. However, the facts that most of the emerging economies are mixed ones, that they are working themselves out within autonomous national frameworks, and that the multiplying national states are operating internationally through the United Nations all point to a world which will be closer to the vision of Wilson than to that of Lenin. For this reason Wilson is likely to become a world figure of heroic proportions, with an acknowledged impact on world history more direct and far-reaching than that of any other American.

EXPLORING THE ISSUE

Was Woodrow Wilson Responsible for the Failure of the United States to Join the League of Nations?

Critical Thinking and Reflection

1. Compare and contrast the roles of President Wilson and Senator Lodge in bringing about the defeat of the Treaty of Versailles in the Senate. Who should bear responsibility for this failure?
2. Critically analyze how Carleton defends Wilson from the charges of (1) inflexibility and (2) naïve optimism. Do you agree or disagree with these criticisms? Why?
3. Compare and contrast the interpretations of Cooper and Carleton regarding Wilson's approach to foreign policy.
4. Given Cooper's interpretation, do you think Wilson would have compromised on the treaty with Senator Lodge had he not suffered a severe stroke? Discuss.
5. Who does Cooper blame for the failure of the United States to ratify the Treaty of Versailles? Do you agree with his interpretation?
6. Discuss the realist/idealist debate in American foreign policy in the 1950s. Was Wilson a naive idealist or, according to Professors Carleton and Cooper, the true realist? Discuss.
7. Cooper spends a lot of time discussing the psychological makeup versus the physiological makeup of President Wilson. Lay out the major arguments of both proponents (the Georges) versus opponents (Link/Weinstein). Critically analyze whether it was Wilson's health or psychological makeup that influenced his arguments with Congress over the treaty issue.
8. Historians and political scientists now discuss *Wilsonianism* as a major component of American current foreign policy. What do they mean by this?

Is There Common Ground?

Both Carleton and Cooper make strong cases for their points of view. Carleton blames the Republicans, in particular, the chairman of the Senate Foreign Relations Committee, Henry Cabot Lodge, for stalling votes on the treaty by reading its provisions to an empty Senate for nearly 2 weeks. He also rejects the Freudian interpretation, which argues that Wilson was incapable of compromise.

Cooper, on the other hand, blames Wilson more than Lodge for killing the treaty and the opportunity for the United States to enter and influence the League of Nations. Had Wilson not been physically damaged by his stroke, he might have struck a deal with Republicans as he had done previously on passing his New Freedom legislative program. Perhaps Cooper best hits the mark when he argues that Wilson was ahead of his times and the American people went, not willingly, to overthrow their traditional isolationist views and to join an international league of nations.

Additional Resources

Professor John Milton Cooper's monumental and massive *Woodrow Wilson: A Biography* (Knopf, 2009) is now the definitive biography of the current generation of historians. The most recent scholarship on Wilson can be found in two collections: John Milton Cooper, Jr., ed., *Reconsidering Woodrow Wilson: Progressivism, Internationalism, War and Peace* (Woodrow Wilson Center Press and Johns Hopkins University Press, 2008), where the editor characterizes Wilson as "one of the greatest legislators to sit in the White House." See also Cooper, Jr., "Whose League of Nations? Theodore Roosevelt, Woodrow Wilson, and World Order," in William N. Tilchin and Charles E. New, eds., *Artists of Power: Theodore Roosevelt, Woodrow Wilson, and Their Enduring Impact on U.S. Foreign Policy* (Praeger Security International, 2006). Arthur S. Link, co-editor of the *Papers of Woodrow Wilson, vol. 60* (Princeton, 1966–1993), gives a point-by-point response to Kennan in a series of revised lectures presented at Johns Hopkins University and reprinted in *Woodrow Wilson: Revolution, War, and Peace* (Harlan Davison, 1979).

Wilson's health has received serious scrutiny. In the early 1930s, Sigmund Freud and William C. Bullitt, a former diplomat, wrote a scathing and highly inaccurate biography of *Thomas Woodrow Wilson*, published posthumously in 1967 by Houghton Mifflin. The book was poorly received and scathingly reviewed by Arthur S. Link, "The Case for Woodrow Wilson," *The Higher Realism of Woodrow Wilson* (Vanderbilt University Press, 1971). The major controversy seems to be of those who stress psychological difficulties—see, for example, Alexander and Juliette George, *Woodrow Wilson and Colonel House: A Personality Study* (Dover Press, 1956, 1964)—versus medical illnesses—see Edwin A. Weinstein, *Woodrow Wilson: A Medical and Psychological Biography* (Princeton University, 1981). For the best summaries of the controversy, see Thomas T. Lewis, "Alternative Psychological Interpretations of Woodrow Wilson," *Mid-America* (vol. 45, 1983); and Lloyd E. Ambrosius, "Woodrow Wilson's Health and the Treaty Fight, 1919–1920," *The International History Review* (February 1987). Phyllis Lee Levin, *Edith and Woodrow: The White House Years* (Scribners, 2001) and Robert J. Maddox, "Mrs. Wilson and the Presidency," *American History* (February 1973) make the case that we have already had America's first woman president.

Four of the best bibliographies of Wilson include the introduction to Lloyd E. Ambrosius's *Wilsonianism: Woodrow Wilson and His Legacy in American Foreign Relations* (Palgrave Macmillan, 2002), which is a collection of articles from the leading realist Wilsonian scholar; British scholar John A. Thompson's up-to-date analysis of the Wilson scholarship in *Woodrow Wilson* (Pearson Education, 2002), a short, scholarly sympathetic study in the "Profiles in Power" series designed for student use; David Steigerwald's, "The Reclamation of Woodrow Wilson," *Diplomatic History* (Winter 1999), most appropriate for advanced undergraduates; and Francis J. Gavin, "The Wilsonian Legacy in the Twentieth Century," *Orbis* (Fall 1997).

ISSUE 9

Were the 1920s an Era of Social and Cultural Rebellion?

YES: Gilman M. Ostrander, from "The Revolution in Morals" in John Braeman, Robert H. Bremner, and David Brody, eds., *Change and Continuity in Twentieth-Century America: The 1920s* (Ohio State University Press, 1968)

NO: David A. Shannon, from *American Society and Culture in the 1920s* (Houghton Mifflin, 1965)

Learning Outcomes

After reading this issue, you should be able to:

- Evaluate ways in which the decade of the 1920s marked either a continuity with or contrast from the preceding decade.
- Discuss the economic changes that dominated the 1920s.
- Analyze the changing status of women in the 1920s.
- Describe the social, cultural, and economic impacts of mass-produced consumer goods in the decade following World War I.
- Assess the extent to which Americans were affected by "revolutionary" social and cultural changes in the 1920s.

ISSUE SUMMARY

YES: Gilman M. Ostrander portrays the 1920s as the beginning of an urbanization of American morals, which included dramatic changes in women's fashion and behavior and the emergence of a more affluent society and leisure class focused on mass consumer goods that encouraged Americans to live beyond their means, thereby undermining the traditional virtue of thriftiness.

NO: David A. Shannon asserts that the social and cultural changes described by many as revolutionary were actually superficial elements of which significance to the 1920s has been exaggerated; the real catalysts for change were the processes that expanded the American economy by ushering in prosperity through the creation of a mass consumer culture.

Americans, including many journalists and scholars, have never been shy about attaching labels to their history, and frequently they do so to characterize particular years or decades in their distant or recent past. It is doubtful, however, that any period in America's history has received as many catchy appellations as has the decade of the 1920s. Described at various times as "the Jazz Age," the "Roaring Twenties," the "dry decade," the "prosperity decade," the "age of normalcy," or simply the "New Era," these are years that obviously have captured the imagination of the American public, including the chroniclers of the nation's past.

In 1920, the Great War was over, and President Woodrow Wilson received the Nobel Peace Prize, despite his inability to persuade the United States Senate to adopt the Covenant of the League of Nations. The "Red Scare," culminating in the Palmer raids conducted by the Justice Department, came to an embarrassingly fruitless halt, and Republican Warren Harding won a landslide victory in the campaign for the presidency, an election in which women, buoyed by the ratification of the Nineteenth Amendment, exercised their suffrage rights for the first time in national politics. In Pittsburgh, the advent of the radio age was symbolized by the broadcast of election results on KDKA, the nation's first commercial radio station. F. Scott Fitzgerald and Sinclair Lewis each published their first important novels and helped to usher in the most significant American literary renaissance since the early nineteenth century.

During the next 9 years, Americans witnessed a number of amazing events: the rise and fall of the Ku Klux Klan; the trial, conviction, and execution of anarchists Nicola Sacco and Bartolomeo Vanzetti on murder charges and subsequent legislative restrictions on immigration into the United States; continuation of prohibition laws and emergence of the illicit manufacture and trade of alcohol controlled by mob bosses such as Alphonse "Scarface Al" Capone; battles over teaching of evolution in the schools epitomized by rhetorical clashes between William Jennings Bryan and Clarence Darrow during the Scopes trial in Dayton, Tennessee; the Harding scandals; "talking" motion pictures; and, in 1929, collapse of the New York Stock Exchange, symbolizing the beginning of the Great Depression and bringing a startling end to the euphoric claims of business prosperity that had dominated the decade.

For many historians the 1920s marked an era of change in the United States, from international involvement and war to isolationism and peace, from the feverish reform of the Progressive era to the conservative political retrenchment of "Republican ascendancy," from entrenched values of Victorian America to the cultural rebellion identified with the proliferation of "flivvers," "flappers," and hip flasks. In 1931, Frederick Lewis Allen focused on these changes in his popular account of the decade, *Only Yesterday*. In a chapter entitled "The Revolution of Morals and Manners," Allen established a widely accepted image of the 1920s as a period of significant social and cultural rebellion.

The themes of Allen's journalistic account received attention from the scholarly community both at the time and later. For example, in their classic sociological study of the values of a group of "typical" Americans of the 1920s residing in Muncie, Indiana, Robert and Helen Lynd, in *Middletown:*

A Study in Contemporary American Culture (Harcourt, Brace, 1929), provided a cultural anthropological portrait that characterized the town's residents as focused heavily upon the economic climate of business prosperity. As beneficiaries of a mass consumer society, these citizens exhibited the attitudes of self-satisfaction and complacency that author Sinclair Lewis had satirized in his novels *Main Street* (1920) and *Babbitt* (1922). In Middletown, Lynn concluded, "no other accompaniment of getting a living approaches in importance the money received for their work. It is more this future, instrumental aspect of work, rather than the intrinsic satisfaction involved, that keeps Middletown working so hard as more and more of the activities of living are coming to be strained through the bars of the dollar sign."

Thirty years later, historian William Leuchtenburg provided a scholarly corroboration of Lewis Allen's interpretation of the 1920s. According to Leuchtenburg in his book *The Perils of Prosperity, 1914–32* (University of Chicago Press, 1958), traditional religious sanctions dissolved in the 1920s in the face of growing secularization and reduced stability of the family. The "new woman" of the decade, politically empowered by the Nineteenth Amendment, rebelled against traditional domestic roles ascribed to her and demanded sexual and economic freedom. Young Americans, in particular, participated in a self-indulgent hedonism that challenged the authority of traditional social and cultural institutions.

The degree to which one views the 1920s as a rebellious decade may very well depend on the extent to which World War I is interpreted as a watershed event in American history. How much did American society in the 1920s differ from its prewar counterpart? The argument for change is widespread. For example, Henry May has characterized the years from 1912 to 1917 as marking "the end of American innocence." Similarly, the literary and artistic members of the "lost generation" were certain that the war had created a much different world from the one they had occupied previously. A different political climate seemed to exist in the 1920s in which a business-oriented conservatism deflated the momentum for reform that had dominated the first two decades of the twentieth century.

In the YES and NO selections the validity of these perceptions is evaluated. Gilman M. Ostrander supports the notions of social and cultural rebellion presented earlier by Allen and Leuchtenburg. Ostrander describes the "urbanization of morals" in which many Americans commonly resided beyond their means in an affluent and democratic leisure class. This society also witnessed significant changes in the status and behavior of women and greater mobility for a larger portion of the population as a consequence of the mass production of the automobile at a price many Americans could afford.

David A. Shannon insists that the interpretation presented by Ostrander exaggerates the importance of several factors that really had little relevance to Americans in the 1920s. The crucial changes for most Americans, he says, were economic, not social or cultural. The prosperity of an expanding industrial economy, with its increased productivity, per capita income, and readily available consumer goods, was the most significant change in the post–World War I United States. The emergence of the "mass man," not the "flapper," therefore, was of greatest consequence to most Americans in the decade.

YES

Gilman M. Ostrander

The Revolution in Morals

... Though it was the "lost generation" of intellectuals who made articulate the repudiation of the old moral order, it was their despised Philistine America that gave body to the new concepts in the age of the flapper. The younger generation had already started on its way to freedom before the war, although it was by no means as far along in revolt as were the intellectuals. The most evident symptom was the much-discussed "dance craze," for ragtime was in vogue in the northern cities even before the wartime closing of the New Orleans brothels sent jazz musicians on their way to Chicago and New York. In 1911 Irving Berlin had written "Alexander's Ragtime Band," the waltz had suddenly faded in popularity, and the dance craze was on. There were the Fox Trot, the Horse Trot, the Grizzly Bear, and many others. One girl, according to a popular song of 1912, declared that "mother said I shouldn't dare/To try and do the grizzly bear," but girls nevertheless did try to do it. Of these new dances, the Bunny Hug was singled out by critics for special censure.

Young women were already divesting themselves of some of the clothing their parents had worn. Skirts rose from the ground to the ankle, and some undergarments were shucked off altogether. The president of the New York Cotton Exchange announced in 1912 that these changes in dress had "reduced consumption of cotton fabrics by at least twelve yards of finished goods for each adult female inhabitant." By 1915 the evolution of the new American woman had advanced sufficiently for H. L. Mencken to herald her arrival and bestow upon her the name of flapper.

> Observe, then, this nameless one, this American Flapper. Her skirts have just reached her very trim and pretty ankles; her hair, newly coiled upon her skull, has just exposed the ravishing whiteness of her neck. . . .
>
> Life, indeed, is almost empty of surprises, mysteries, horrors to this Flapper of 1915. . . . She knows exactly what the Wassermann reaction is, and has made up her mind that she will never marry a man who can't show an unmistakable negative . . . is inclined to think that there must be something in this new doctrine of free motherhood. She is opposed to the double standard of morality, and favors a law prohibiting it. . . .

Then the war came for America, with its excitement, confusion, social disorientation, and call for service. Several million American men and a good many women went overseas to England and France. Mademoiselle from Armentièrs may not have made a lasting impression on most of them, but the whole violent disruption of their lives had an enduring effect. On the home front, bands played, lovers said good-bye, women went into war work, and everybody knew that everything was different and that life must be led according to new rules. Then, just as all was started, it all stopped. Armistice was declared, the boys came home, and a great deal of adrenalin, which was to have been used up on the enemy, was expended during the next few years domestically.

There followed a postwar period of disillusionment that remained a matter for puzzled comment by foreign observers, especially as it was reflected in American literature of the 1920s. Compared to Europe, America had been lightly touched by the war; yet the cynicism arising out of the war and its conclusion seemed to be more deeply felt in America than in the European nations that the war had ravaged. Americans loudly and rudely repudiated the moralistic idealism of the Wilsonian war aims along with the moralistic idealism of Wilsonian progressivism. The fighting war had directly touched relatively few Americans, but the mood that received its classic expression in Hemingway's *A Farewell to Arms* and *The Sun Also Rises* was widely shared. After the war the flapper almost at once made herself the flaming symbol of this cynical spirit.

Within the space of a half-dozen years, women's skirts rose from the ankle to the knee. The number of inches between the hemline and the ankle was rightly taken as the index of the revolutionary change in morals and manners that accompanied and followed the war, and responsible elements in the nation moved to check the revolution by putting women back into their old clothes. Fashion writers warned that the American woman had "lifted her skirts beyond any modest limitation," and they decreed that she should drop them the next year. The YWCA issued a national "Modesty Appeal" and reported that it was getting good results. Bills were introduced in the Utah legislature fixing skirts at three inches above the ankle and in the Virginia legislature fixing necklines to within three inches of the upper part of the throat, but the girls went right ahead with what they were wearing.

Some of them took to smoking publicly and conspicuously, and proprietors of public places, who would have ejected them five years earlier, retreated. Then they were overrunning the speak-easies. The pre-Prohibition saloons had been male sanctuaries where primarily beer had been dispensed. In the speak-easies mixed drinking of mixed drinks was the rule, the women bellying up to the bar with the men, skirts short, stockings rolled below the knees, and corsets sometimes checked at the cloak room. Many young women who did not frequent the speak-easies nevertheless felt obliged to school themselves in social drinking in their own homes and in those of their friends. Drinking, formerly proscribed for middle- and upper-middle-class women, became, under the pressure of Prohibition, socially mandatory in many of those circles.

The girls were petting also, and the "petting question" was anxiously discussed on and on in the ladies' magazines and elsewhere. The rule earlier had been that a nice girl did not allow a man to kiss her unless they were engaged to be married. By the early 1920s the polling of coeds showed that fairly indiscriminate petting was the rule. When it came to the question of extramarital sexual intercourse, fewer of these coeds were inclined to give their unqualified approval, but that question also was much mooted and in a spirit of open-mindedness that was frightening to fathers and mothers.

In sex as in other matters the girls were determined to demolish the double standard. They did not approve of a society in which men were free to wander back and forth across the tracks while women had to choose their side and stay there. In this wish they had been abetted by progressive reformers and later, during the war, by the Navy and War departments, which had fought against the red-light districts. The wartime antivice campaign had been highly successful, and thereafter the era of the roaring red-light district was substantially at an end except in some larger cities and some industrial and mining towns.

The war opened up unprecedented career opportunities to American women, and these opportunities were eagerly taken advantage of. In 1900 about one out of five American women was gainfully employed, but most of these were miserably victimized in sweatshops. Among the better people at that time it had been a matter for sorrow and concern that a girl one knew was reduced in circumstances to the point where she was obliged to take employment as a schoolmistress. The war turned the working girl into a patriot and opened up many opportunities to her, the single most important field being secretarial work. At the war's end women fought with some success to retain these positions and to enter new lines of activity formerly closed to them.

The American housewife was freed for outside activities as never before. The tendency in the twenties was to move to smaller houses or to apartments, and at the time when immigration restriction laws reduced the supply of servants, the much more manageable electrical household appliances took their place. Throughout American history the number-one killer of women had been childbearing. Advocates of birth control, led by Margaret Sanger, had long fought their cause against bitter official and unofficial opposition. Opposition continued throughout the 1920s, but the average size of families declined rapidly during the same period.

That the emancipated women in the 1920s did not know quite where to go with their new freedom was indicated in the styles, which combined short skirts and make-up with bobbed hair and boyish figures. Nevertheless, the flapper was the symbol of the Jazz Age. So far as men were concerned, alterations in morals and manners were in large measure forced upon them by the new relationship they found themselves in with respect to the new American woman.

The flapper as a type was on the way out even before the coming of the depression, giving way to the siren. Mothers had followed the fashions set by their daughters early in the decade. Then in the late 1920s both mother and daughter let their hair grow a little longer and dropped the hemline of their skirts five or six inches below the knee. They did not do this under social pressure, however; by the end of the decade the issues aroused by petting and short skirts had ceased to burn brightly, which is to say that the women had won that battle.

By 1930 the United States had become statistically an urban nation. More than half of its population was living in communities of 2,500 or more, and the automobile had made the city readily accessible to the farming regions. In almost all of the major cities first- and second-generation immigrants still made up a majority of the population. In most cities native American Protestants continued to control business and to set the social tone, but this differed from city to city. On the one hand, Boston retained, rather desperately, a properly Bostonian air amid the welter of newer immigrants. On the other hand, San Francisco's ruling class had been made up largely of non-Anglo-Saxons since the days of the gold rush, and the personality of the city was as cosmopolitan as that of Boston was provincial.

Like San Francisco, St. Louis and New Orleans had been non-Anglo-Saxon in origin and had retained something of their old Gallic flavor, and Cincinnati and Milwaukee continued to be influenced by their sizeable German populations. Los Angeles, by extreme contrast, was the most Protestant of any sizeable American city, and it was very mindful of its heritage of American Puritanism. A booster for the city had written that "it is a city of churches and schools and civic bodies, deeply interested in the best. The type is that of the highest moral and ethical citizenship." Willard Huntington Wright, one-time editor of the *Smart Set*, agreed. The city had been formed, he wrote, by the "rural pietist obsessed with the spirit of village fellowship, of suburban respectability. . . . Hypocrisy, like a vast fungus, has spread over the city's surface. . . . Los Angeles is overrun with militant moralists, connoisseurs of sin, experts on biological purity."

In most cities where the non-Protestants outnumbered the Protestants, the newer immigrants had been effectively segregated into ghettos and kept down by bad wages, and their social influence had thereby been minimized. In the 1920s, however, Congress passed two enactments that, in their consequences, did much to reconcile many among the older Protestant population to the more recent immigrants: the Volstead Act, passed to enforce prohibition, and the National Origins Act, passed to limit severely further immigration from southern and eastern Europe.

The National Origins Act of 1924 was illiberal and racist in intent, but in its consequences it proved enormously beneficial to the recent immigrant groups against whose former countrymen it was directed. These recent immigrants had formerly been despised and feared by older generations of Americans as the vanguard of an endless army of foreign rabble that threatened to subvert American society. Following immigration restriction, however, these recent immigrants became part of an exclusive American community. They came to see themselves in this light, and they came increasingly to be so viewed by the older Americans. When that happened, there developed a greater appreciation for their contributions to American culture, and American culture became more cosmopolitan than it had formerly been.

More than anything else it was Prohibition that brought many older Americans to the conclusion that these newer arrivals were not such bad fellows after all. Drinkers and drys alike had supposed that Prohibition, once written into the Constitution, would be generally obeyed by a law-abiding nation, but such proved to be not remotely the case. Only during the first year of the experiment was Prohibition even moderately successful. Then it absolutely collapsed. Systems were perfected for smuggling, moonshining, and bootlegging; and soon almost anybody who wanted his tipple could obtain it easily, even out in the countryside. The bootleggers and the proprietors of speakeasies were drawn mainly from the newer immigrant population, and these became minor heroes to the people they served. The blustering and ineffectual Anti-Saloon League became an object of fun for many Americans, including many who had soberly advocated Prohibition in the first place. There emerged a distinctly anticlerical sentiment among urban middle-class Americans, such as had already been voiced by American intellectuals. Thus protected by immigration restriction and harassed by Prohibition, middle-class, urban Protestant Americans began to blur the distinctions that formerly had set them apart in their own minds from the newer arrivals. (Some among the newer arrivals who involved themselves in the bootlegging industry, meanwhile, took advantage of Prohibition to organize nation-wide crime syndicates that have remained a part of the American moral structure ever since.)

Probably most Americans in the twenties were convinced that the chief contribution of the United States to civilization lay in the fields of business enterprise and technology, and they were not by any means alone in this opinion. Teams of experts came from the corners of the earth to see how this miracle had been achieved. The Germans coined a word for it, *Fordismus*. In Russia, it was said, Henry Ford was honored above all other foreigners. From the coming of the Puritans through the rise of democracy, America has always had a message for the world. Of all America's messages, this materialistic one was the message that has been most eagerly received.

American intellectuals confused creative achievement in the realm of material things with materialism of the spirit. They lumped them together and damned them without qualification and without a second thought. Other Americans took an exalted and idealistic view of their nation's achievement. What it had accomplished had been no less than the democratization of the way of life that in other nations was restricted to the privileged few. It had created an affluent society and a democratic leisure class.

In the 1920s millions of Americans became part of the carriage trade. The carriage had always been a hallmark of gentility (for the American businessman had not invented materialism), and in the early years of the century this had been true of the automobile, which had been custom-made and very expensive. It had been the view of Woodrow Wilson that nothing had done more to advance socialism in America than the automobile. Henry Ford had had a different idea, however, and in the 1920s millions of Americans owned their own mass-produced Model T's, which at one point could be purchased for less than $300. One of the most startling sights in America, in the view of foreign observers, was the factory parking lot filled with workmen's cars.

The American majority was also given the leisure time to enjoy its new opportunities. In the nineteenth century the working day had commonly been from dawn to dusk, six days a week, the seventh day presumably being reserved for rest and prayer. The ten-hour day had been the best that the worker could hope for. In 1890 the average work week was estimated at 60 hours. In 1926 it was estimated at 49.8, and Americans at last had time on their hands. Real wages had risen substantially in the meantime, so Americans had more money in their pockets than ever before.

What would this do to their morals? Employers had long followed the pious practice of keeping wages down for the reason that the added money would simply go down the rum hole. Employers had also always defended long working hours as the only means of keeping the lower classes out of trouble. The 1920s was, among other things, the first experiment in the history of modern civilization, except during periods of depression, in mass leisure.

Perhaps surprisingly, the increased time and money, instead of debauching the working classes, proved an elevating influence, at least by the rum-hole standard. Where the old saloon had been known as the poor man's club, the speakeasy's clientele was drawn to a greater extent from the middle and upper-middle classes; and intoxication, so far as it manifested itself in public, was afflicting "a better class than formerly and a much younger class," according to the chief supervisor of dance halls in San Francsico.

What appears to have been the case is that blue-collar workers, untrained in the art of leisure, spent most of their free time working around the house and yard and listening to the radio with their families. Beyond that, sports provided them with their chief recreation. Fishing and hunting were the two sports in which they themselves participated to any great extent. Otherwise they remained spectators of baseball, football, boxing, and horse racing. They memorized baseball statistics and followed the exploits of Red Grange and Babe Ruth. This gave them plenty to talk about when they got together in their idle hours, as is still the case.

Public-spirited persons of cultured taste hoped that the people would take advantage of their increased leisure by doing more reading, and they did. Newspaper circulation increased greatly, and in 1919 Bernard McFadden launched *True Story Magazine*, which achieved a circulation of almost two million by 1926. Asserting that "its foundation is the solid rock of truth," it featured such articles as "The Primitive Lover," "Her Life Secret," "How to Keep the Thrill in Marriage," and "What I Told My Daughter the Night before Her Marriage." Women have always made up the main reading public in the United States, and the two most popular themes for them have always been those of religion and seduction. The social developments of the twenties did not greatly alter this. To the extent that change is to be seen in that era, the change was in the direction of a greater interest in literary works.

The "lost generation" of writers enjoyed thinking of themselves as alien to the Philistine American majority. Sinclair Lewis, upon receiving the Nobel Prize for Literature in 1930, delivered an acceptance speech entitled "The American Fear of Literature," in which he criticized his fellow Americans for failing to support their creative artists. This was the same Lewis whose *Main*

Street had sold more than 400,000 copies in 1920 to rival *The Sheik* as the best-selling book of the year and whose subsequent novels had all sold just about as briskly in his native land. Lewis had enjoyed greater success than most other serious-minded writers. It is, neverthless, true that America in the 1920s supported its best writers as it had never done previously.

Happily, the new technology created new forms of popular entertainment at the same time that it created the new leisure class. Chief among these were the radio, the phonograph, motion pictures, and the automobile. In 1890 theater-goers in Muncie, [Indiana,] were limited to the Opera House, where performances were irregular. The theater would be dark for as much as a month at a time. In 1924 Muncie supported nine motion-picture houses, operating daily the year around. The western was the staple at five of the theaters, but movies with sex appeal drew the largest crowds. Patrons were attracted in large numbers to "*Alimony*—Brilliant men, beautiful jazz babies, champagne baths, midnight revels, petting parties in the purple dawn, all ending in one terrific smashing climax that makes you gasp." Others such as *Sinners in Silk*, *Women Who Give*, and *Rouged Lips* similarly tried for gasps. Opinions varied widely as to the influence these movies exerted on their audiences, composed mainly of children and women; but to the extent that they were influential, the direction is evident.

The impact of the automobile upon morals in America was undoubtedly greater than that of the movies and is easier to determine. By the end of 1923 there were two cars for every three families in Muncie, a good many of the car-owners being without bathtubs in their homes. The automobile had replaced the house as the chief status symbol in the community, and car-owners declared themselves willing to go without food or decent clothing rather than give up their automobiles.

One of the revolutionary results of the automobile was the institution of instalment buying, which established itself in the twenties. The traditional American virtue of thrift was undermined systematically and with great success by the advertising companies, and a finance-company officer in Muncie estimated that between 75 and 90 per cent of automobiles purchased locally were bought on the instalment plan. Living beyond one's means, a sin to previous generations, became the thing to do.

There were those who argued that the automobile served to keep the family together by providing a diversion the whole family could share together. The opposite opinion, however, was the one more frequently expressed. Methods of courtship changed. In the days before the automobile, courtship might very likely consist of a boy and a girl attending a church social and then walking back to the girl's house to sit on the sofa and talk to her parents. What the automobile did, as Frederick Lewis Allen pointed out, was to take that sofa out of the parlor and put it on wheels and move it off into the woods. A judge in Muncie declared that of thirty girls brought before his court during a year for "sex crimes," nineteen had committed their acts in automobiles. And whether it was used for sex purposes or for more conventionally acceptable diversions, the car, and who was going to get to use it, became a major source of family conflict.

Cicero in the first century B.C. was worried that the younger generation was going to the dogs, and spokesmen for the older generation have frequently been of this opinion since then. A lot was said to that point by members of the older generation in the twenties, and during that decade there was much in what they said. It is no doubt true that every generation rebels to some extent against its elders, and it is also of course true that many young people in the twenties did not. The decade of the 1920s, nevertheless, remains the watershed in the history of American morals. It was the grandmothers of the present generation who hiked up their skirts, bobbed their hair, put on lipstick, and went out in the car with the boys to the speak-easy to drink bootleg liquor and do the Black Bottom. The twenties was the decade when there occurred, to some extent in the country as well as the city, the urbanization of American morals.

David A. Shannon  **NO**

American Society and Culture in the 1920s

Journalists, scenario writers, even professional historians (usually a rather solemn bunch) who normally make a serious effort to deal with the problems that confront society and individuals in their relations with one another are prone to get a little giddy when they approach the social and cultural history of the 1920s and prattle joyously but aimlessly about "the jazz age." To judge from some accounts, Americans did little else from 1920 until 1929 but make millions in the stock market, dance the Charleston and the Black Bottom, dodge gangster bullets, wear raccoon coats, and carry hip flasks. "Flapper," "saxophone," "bathtub gin," and "speakeasy" are the key words in this special genre of popular historical writing, and the interpretation of the era, usually only implied, is that America went on a hedonistic binge for approximately a decade. Obviously, such a characterization of an epoch is shallow and exaggerated once one thinks about it critically and looks into the epoch more searchingly, but that style of social history for the postwar decade persists and thrives.

Probably the great change in the conditions of society and the mood of the people after 1929 [is] the root cause of this curious historiographical aberration. The grimness, despair, and drabness of America in the 1930s probably prompted writers to look back at the previous decade with a kind of nostalgia for a more carefree existence and led them to look too fondly and too long at what were actually superficialities. An extraordinarily skillful popular historian, Frederick Lewis Allen, set the style with his *Only Yesterday*, which appeared in 1931, a gray year indeed. The book was a delight to read and still is, and Allen's feat was all the more remarkable for having done it so soon after the fact. A careful reading of *Only Yesterday* reveals that Allen was often concerned with more than the superficialities of the 1920s, but he nevertheless put an unusual emphasis upon the bizarre and transitory aspects of the 1920s that contrasted sharply with the 1930s.

The thesis of this chapter is not to declaim that there were no flappers, no saxophones, no jazz age. The chapter will suggest that there were other aspects of the 1920s—as the previous two chapters have already indicated—that are more useful to examine if we wish to understand the era and the way that it helped to shape our own contemporary society. In other words, the flappers were not a myth, but we will do well to look beyond the flappers, which have already been written about more than sufficiently.

Prosperity and Economic Change

Prosperity was a basic fact of the 1920s, one that shaped and conditioned many aspects of life outside the economic realm. A generally expanding economy underlay a generally expansive view about life, as happened again in the generation after World War II. To say that the economy was healthy would be to ignore the almost fatal illness that struck it low in 1929, but it was clearly prosperous.

The path of the economy even during its boom years was not entirely smooth, however. Although relatively brief, the postwar depression that hit in mid-1920 was as steep and as sudden as any American economy had ever experienced. The year 1921 was a hard one. Unemployment went up to 4,750,000, and national income was down 28 per cent from the previous year. Farm prices were far too low to enable most farmers to meet their costs of production. But in 1922 the economy came back strong, and by the end of the year it was buzzing along in better shape than it had been when the depression hit. There were minor dips in the business cycle in 1924 and 1927, but they were not serious.

Besides cyclical fluctuations there were other blemishes on prosperity's record. Some economic activities did not share in the general prosperity. Agriculture never really recovered from the postwar depression, and low farm prices were the root of farmer discontent that manifested itself in McNary-Haugenism. Some industries were in bad shape throughout the period. The world market for textiles declined when women's styles changed. A dress in 1928 required less than one-half the material that a seamstress needed to make a dress in 1918. Furthermore, many clothes in the 1920s were made of synthetic fibers. Rayon became very popular. Consequently the textile industry was unable to pay wages consistent with the rising standard of living. The industry continued its long-range shift of operations from New England to the South, particularliy to the southern Appalachians, where wage rates were lower. Coal was another sick industry. As home owners shifted gradually to other fuels for space heating and as automobiles and trucks gradually displaced the railroads, once a major market for coal, the total coal market shrank slightly. There was approximately 10 per cent less coal mined at the end of the decade than there had been at the beginning. New mining technology enabled mine operators to get along with a smaller labor force. Almost one fourth of the nation's coal miners at work in 1923 were out of the pits by 1929, and since most miners lived in isolated communities where there were almost no other employment opportunities, the economic hardship in the mining towns was acute. Even employed miners worked at hourly wage rates that were 14 per cent lower in 1929 than they had been in 1923.

But despite cyclical downswings and generally depressed conditions in agriculture, textiles, and coal, prosperity was strong. One has only to look at the statistics. Real per-capita income increased almost one third from 1919 to 1929. (Real per-capita income is total national income divided by population and adjusted for price changes.) The mythical average person—not worker, but all people, men, women; and children—received $716 in 1929. In 1919 he had received just $543, measured in 1929 dollars. Manufacturing industries increased their output by almost two thirds, but because of a tremendous increase in labor productivity due to technological advances there were actually fewer people engaged in manufacturing in 1929 than there had been in 1919. A large number of these displaced production workers went into service industries, where many of the jobs were "white collar." Furthermore, there was a shift in the nature of industrial production that tended to improve the lot of the consumer. Since the early days of American industry a large part of production had been capital goods, that is, products that were used to produce further wealth rather than be consumed by the people. Much American production, for example, had gone into building a vast railroad network, the biggest and most intricate rail system that any nation in the world had found it necessary to develop. The number of miles of railroad track began actually to decrease slightly after 1920. When any industrial economy matures it reaches a point at which a significantly higher proportion of production may go to consumer goods, and the American economy reached this level in the postwar decade. This is not to say that capital production ceased, which would have been calamitous for long-range growth—indeed, it even increased in absolute terms—but a larger proportion of annual production was in the form of articles that ordinary people could use, such as washing machines, radios, and motor cars. The number of such durable consumer goods in use was small compared to what it would be by midcentury, but still more people than ever before enjoyed their convenience. In fact, because of increased national production, relatively stable price levels, and increased production of consumer goods, most Americans lived better in the 1920s than ever before.

To a considerable degree the prosperity of the 1920s was due to the vast expansion of a few relatively new industries and to increased construction, much of which was actually due to the new industries. Road building, for example, was a major enterprise during the decade, and the roads were necessary because of the relatively new automobile industry.

In 1915, soon after Henry Ford developed the Model T, there were about 2.5 million cars on the roads of America. By 1920 there were over 9 million and the industry's growth had only started. By 1925 there were nearly 20 million cars registered, and in 1929 there were 26.5 million. In that last year of the boom the industry produced 5,622,000 motor vehicles. Ford had made the big break-through with his mass-produced, inexpensive Model T, but later decisions of the industry similarly broadened the market. In 1923 the major car manufacturers abandoned open cars except for a few sports models and concentrated on closed vehicles. Many a family that had resisted getting one of the older and colder models succumbed to the lure of relatively comfortable transportation. The auto industry also soon discovered that to tap a really mass market it had to develop a credit system. It developed an auto financing system which remains largely the same today. By 1925 over two thirds of the new cars purchased each year were bought on credit. Installment buying, which became general in other fields as well, did not increase the purchasing power of any given family income. In fact, it reduced it by as much as the interest charges amounted to. But it did greatly stimulate new car purchases, and the purchases had a stimulating effect upon the economy in general.

The auto industry statistics were impressive. In 1929 automobiles accounted for over one eighth of the total dollar value of all manufacturing in the nation. Over 7 per cent of all wage earners engaged in manufacturing worked for automobile companies. The industry took 15 per cent of national steel production. When one considers the effect that auto production had on the manufacture and distribution of tires, oil and gasoline, and glass it has been estimated that the industry provided jobs for about 3.7 million workers, roughly one tenth of the nonagricultural labor force.

Motor vehicles were the most spectacular new industry, but chemicals and electric appliances also had a very large growth. Before World War I the American chemical industry had been rather small, unable to compete with German firms for most items. The war shut off German imports and the federal government confiscated German patents and sold them to domestic corporations. By the end of the 1920s the American chemical industry had grown roughly 50 per cent larger than it had been before the outbreak of the war in Europe. The electric appliance industry became economically significant as more and more American homes gained access to electric power. In 1912 roughly one sixth of America's families had electricity in their homes; by 1927 almost two thirds of them had electric power. The first use that families put the new power to was lighting, but they quickly began to use it to lighten their work. By 1925; 80 per cent of the homes with electricity had electric irons, 37 per cent had vacuum cleaners, and 25 per cent had washing machines. Most families continued to use ice for food storage. Radio was intimately connected with the electric industry, although especially in the early 1920s many of the sets manufactured were operated by storage batteries, big things that weighed over twenty-five pounds and were nothing like the dry cells that power today's transistor radios. The home radio industry was altogether new. The first commercial radio station was KDKA, operated by the Westinghouse Electric Company from East Pittsburgh, in 1920. By 1924 there were over five hundred commercial radio stations. By 1929 sales of radios amounted to over $400 million and roughly two fifths of the families of America owned one. Without these new industries, which were based primarily upon new inventions or improved technology, it is doubtful if the 1920s would have been any more prosperous than the prewar period.

Trade unions usually increase in membership strength during periods of prosperity. More workers are employed, thereby increasing trade-union potential, and employers, optimistic about the prospect of profits, usually want labor stability and are willing to make concessions to unions in order to prevent disruption of production. But trade unions in the 1920s departed from this general rule; they actually decreased in membership and influence during the decade. Total union membership in 1920 was roughly five million; by the end of the decade it had declined to about three and one-half million.

There were three main reasons for failure of trade unions in the 1920s: a strong counterattack against them by employers, in which government cooperated; cautious and complacent union leadership; and widespread lack of interest in unions among unorganized workers. During the postwar depression, an opportune time, many employers engaged in a fierce and somewhat successful anti-union drive. Their campaign was for the open shop, which they called "the American plan" in an effort to associate union-ism with un-Americanism. (In an open shop no employee is under any compulsion to join a union. If a union exists in the shop, nonmembers receive whatever wages and hours union members have, which puts the union at a disadvantage in getting new members. In a closed shop the employer agrees to hire only union members. In a union shop the employer hires as he chooses but the employees must join the union.) The open-shop campaign was strong even in some industries where unionism had been well established, such as printing and building construction. Some building contractors were under pressure to break unions. The president of the Bethlehem Steel Company announced in late 1920 that his firm would not sell steel to contractors in New York and Philadelphia who consented to keep their established closed-shop policy. Also in the 1920s employers embarked upon a program to extend what came to be called welfare capitalism. A rather nebulous concept, welfare capitalism ran the gamut from employee stock-purchase plans (usually nonvoting stock) to athletic and social programs for employees and better toilets and locker rooms. Welfare capitalism programs tended to make employees identify their welfare with the company rather than a union and to remove some of the annoyances that sometimes erupt into union-management conflict.

Despite the intensity of the employers' attack it is likely that more vigorous and imaginative union leadership would have enabled the unions to hold their own. Samuel Gompers, the primary founder of the American Federation of Labor and its president for all but one year of its existence during his lifetime, was seventy years old in 1920, hardened in his approach to unionism, and lacking in the vigor which he had displayed at the beginning of the century. William Green, successor to the AFL presidency after Gompers' death in 1924, was depressingly cautious and almost completely without imagination. Whatever forward motion the labor movement made from Green's accession to the AFL presidency in 1924 to his death in the 1950s was made despite Green rather than because of him. The fundamental difficulty in union leadership from World War I until the early 1930s was that the AFL had no real interest in getting the unorganized into unions except for those in skilled trades. Not until labor leaders eager to organize unskilled workers in basic industry came to the fore in the 1930s did the unions get off the ground. There was one major exception that proved the generalization: in the needle trades David Dubinsky and Sidney Hillman adopted new techniques and ideas. Their innovations were successful, and their organizations thrived while the rest of labor stagnated and shriveled.

Many workers in basic industry in the 1920s were apathetic or hostile to unionism, not only because of their employers' attitudes and the failure of union leadership to excite them but because they lived better than ever they had before and because they had formed their social ideas in a preindustrial society. There is no question but that most industrial workers were better off materially in the 1920s than they had been earlier. Real wages (the relationship of money wages to the cost of living) in 1919 were at 105 on a scale in which 1914 was 100. By 1928 the figure stood at 132, a truly significant increase. Many an industrial worker's social ideas and assumptions earned him the unionist's contemptuous term "company man." Especially in the new industries like autos and electric appliances a large part of the labor force was composed of men who had begun their lives in small towns or on the farm, where there had been no big employers and where the terms of work were laid down by the employer on a take-it-or-leave-it basis or settled by each individual employee bargaining with the employer. Individualistic social attitudes formed in a rural society were difficult to shake, even when a man lived the anything but individualistic life of a city worker on a production line, the employee of a vast and complex corporation. It took the depression of the next decade to shock many workers from a rural background into modifying their views about the relationship of capital and labor sufficiently to join a union and make it a countervailing power to the corporation.

There are no statistics that reveal precisely how many industrial workers in the 1920s were originally from urban areas, but the population statistics reveal a vast growth of the cities during the decade. Many rural counties continued to grow, but urban counties grew much more rapidly. The general pattern of migration was from the farm or small town to the small city of the same region and thence to a big city, often out of the region. The biggest growths were in New York City, the industrial cities on or near the Great Lakes, the San Francisco area, and Los Angeles. California tended to draw its new population from the West and the Midwest. New York's growth came from all over the nation, but the bulk of it came from the East and the Southeast. The burgeoning cities of the Midwest grew from rural-to-urban movement within the region and from migration from the South.

Great numbers of the migrants from the South were Negro. Negro migration to the North first became numerically significant during World War I. In 1910 more than 90 per cent of the Negroes of the United States lived in states that had been slave areas in 1860. The census of that year showed only 850,000 Negroes living outside the South. The census of 1920 showed 1,400,000 in the North and West, most of them having migrated after 1917. The movement continued, even expanded, during the 1920s. In the 1930 census, 2,300,000 Negroes were living outside the South. The day was rapidly coming when the typical American Negro would not be a southern sharecropper but a northern or western urban wage earner.

This movement from rural to urban areas, for both Negroes and whites, came about for essentially economic reasons. Agriculture languished; industry flourished. Economic conditions pushed people off the farms and out of the small towns; better economic conditions in the cities pulled them into population clusters.

The Effects of Affluence

America in the 1920s was a relatively affluent society. Affluence made it possible for Americans to change significantly the way they lived, to buy a car and a radio, to go to movies, to improve their schools and send their children to school for more years than they themselves had attended. These effects of affluence in turn had their own effects, some of them very far-reaching.

Foreign visitors to the United States in the late 1920s who had not seen the nation for a decade or two were impressed most of all by the numbers of automobiles they saw and the changes that the automobile had wrought in society. In 1929 there were between one fifth and one sixth as many cars in the United States as there were people, a far higher proportion than that of any other country except Canada. It was physically possible for everyone in America to be rolling on automobile wheels simultaneously, and in some of the traffic jams of summer weekends it appeared that the nation had actually tried to perform the feat.

Any attempt to enumerate all the effects of widespread automobile ownership would bog down in superficial relationships, but some of the major effects are evident. The very appearance of the country changed. Merchants and manufacturers could not resist trying to profit from the captive audiences that traveled the main highways and erected billboards on the land that only a few generations back had been a wilderness. Short-order restaurants and gasoline stations lined the roads approaching towns and cities. Tourist cabins, the predecessors of motels, clustered around the main points of tourist interest. Towns and cities began their sprawl into the countryside as the automobile enabled workers to live a great distance from their employment. Cities such as Los Angeles, which experienced most of their growth after the coming of the automobile age, tended not to have the central business area traditional in older American, and European cities.

The social effects of the automobile have been the subject of a great deal of speculation. Many observers have asserted that the car changed courtship patterns by making young people more mobile and removing them from the supervision of their elders. Certainly every community by the end of the 1920s had a secluded area known as "lovers' lane[,] where cars parked on summer nights, but this whole theory of changed courtship patterns tends to underestimate the ingenuity of young people of the pre-automobile age. "Lovers' lanes" once had buggies parked beside them, and because of the superiority of horse intelligence to that of an automobile a buggy driver could pay less attention to his driving than could a car driver. Still, there are other, more important, and better documented social effects of the automobile.

By the end of the 1920s thousands of families took long vacation trips by car and quite obviously the American public knew more of its nation's geography at first hand than had earlier and less mobile generations. In 1904 a Chicago lawyer made a trip by auto from New York to San Francisco, and his trip was so unusual that he wrote a book about his experiences. By 1929, however, families that had taken such trips found it difficult even to interest their neighbors in their tales of travel.

Perhaps one of the most far-reaching changes brought by the automobile, or the bus, was the change in rural schools. Before the day of cars each rural township operated a grade school, some of them through grade six, more often through grade eight. Most of these rural schools had one room and one teacher. Despite the sentimental nostalgia of some people in a later age, these schools did not offer good education. The teachers were poorly prepared; most of them had not been to college at all. With a room full of children of various sizes and ages, most teachers were able to do little more than maintain a degree of discipline. The products of these schools were ill equipped for living anywhere but on the farm and were not particularly well educated even for that. The school bus made consolidated rural schools possible, and farm youngsters of high-school age for the first time began to go beyond the eighth grade in significant numbers. Many of the new consolidated rural schools were a long way from being ideal educational institutions, but they were clearly an improvement over the ungraded one-room school. At last, rural children were receiving substantially the same kind of education as urban children.

Indeed, the automobile and the radio tended to blur the distinction between rural and urban life. The farmer went to town for his entertainment (usually the movies) and listened to the same radio programs as the city dweller. His children attended schools like those in urban centers. He read a city newspaper. The farmer frequently even took a job in the city, at least for part of the year, and continued to live on the land. Because of the generally depressed conditions of agriculture during the 1920s and the greater amount of capital necessary to begin profitable farming that came as a result of farm mechanization, most of the farmer's children became wage earners in town or city. There still remained a great difference in the ways of life of the small town and the big city, but no longer, except in the most primitive, poorest, and most isolated parts of the nation, did the farmer live significantly differently from the small-town dweller.

Affluence changed the education of the city youngster just as it and the automobile had changed rural schooling. The greatest change was in the number of students in high school. High-school enrollments in 1920 totaled 2.2 million; by 1930 almost exactly twice as many students were in the nation's secondary schools. An increase in the population was part of the reason for the increased enrollments, but more important was an increase in the percentage of high-school-age boys and girls who went on past the eighth grade. In 1930 roughly one half of the population between the ages of fourteen and eighteen was in school.

The main reason why more young people stayed in school instead of dropping out to go to work was that their families, for the first time, could afford to continue without the youngsters' wages. Failure to recognize the fact that children's wages were needed at home was the chief flaw in the reasoning of earlier opponents of child labor. In the first Wilson administration reformers had put a law through Congress prohibiting child labor, and the Supreme Court had in 1918 declared the act unconstitutional. The reformers then set about amending the Constitution, getting an amendment through Congress but never getting it ratified by a sufficient number of states. Enforcement of compulsory school-attendance laws in the 1920s (usually to age fifteen or sixteen) succeeded in accomplishing most of what the reformers had desired, but not even the school laws could be enforced well when public opinion opposed them. When employers wanted to hire children, when parents wanted children to go to work to help on the family income, and when the children themselves wanted to leave school—and this was the situation in many of the textile towns of the Appalachian South throughout the decade—truant officers were unable really to enforce the law. But the attendance laws were enforced where public opinion supported them. Affluence rather than law kept children in school and off the labor market. By 1929 most urban young people at least started to high school. Finishing high school became almost universal in the middle classes, and most of the children from working-class homes finished high school if they had at least average academic ability.

The great number of high-school students had a profound effect on the nature of the high school. At one time, secondary education had been primarily preparation for the college and university. Now in the 1920s the high schools were filled with young people who had no intention whatsoever of going on to college. Furthermore, many of the students lacked the intelligence or the desire or both to cope with the conventional high-school curriculum of literature, mathematics, science, and foreign language. A number of educators argued that trigonometry and Latin did not have much relevance for students who were going to stop their formal education after high school to go to work and that the schools should provide these young people with other training. Many schools never solved the problem in a satisfactory manner; most of them watered down the conventional curriculum to accommodate the new kind of student and created vocational courses which often had little more relevance than did Latin. But despite educational deficiencies—and we must not assume that the secondary schools of the era before World War I were paragons of intellectual virtue—increasing numbers of young people insisted upon a high-school education and they probably profited from their high-school years.

Colleges and universities also were swollen during the 1920s, their enrollments increasing from about 600,000 in 1920 (larger than usual with soldiers returning from World War I) to about 1,200,000 in 1930. The greatest increase in college enrollments came in the vocational fields, teacher preparation, engineering, and business administration. Undergraduate schools of business were something new in higher education, but it was not surprising that in the business civilization of the 1920s hundreds of young men studied such vocational subjects as salesmanship and advertising. . . .

By 1929 the typical American had become a mass man. He worked for a huge industrial corporation; he bought mass-produced articles made by the large corporation; he more than likely lived in an apartment house or in a small residence that differed little from thousands of others; he read a mass newspaper; he attended Metro-Goldwyn-Mayer movies and listened to national radio programs; he avidly followed the athletic exploits of Babe Ruth and Red Grange—and, wondrously, he voted for Herbert Hoover because the Great Engineer praised "rugged individualism." He was the new mass man of the New Era and all seemed rosy. But he and the New Era were soon to receive a jolt of unprecedented force and power.

EXPLORING THE ISSUE

Were the 1920s an Era of Social and Cultural Rebellion?

Critical Thinking and Reflection

1. How did the status and behavior of American women change in the 1920s?
2. What impact did the availability of mass-produced consumer goods have on the lives of Americans of all classes in the 1920s?
3. What economic changes most dramatically influenced changes in American society following World War I?
4. Is it appropriate to think of the decade of the 1920s as a "new era"?

Is There Common Ground

In making a case for revolutionary changes in the 1920s, several questions deserve our attention. First, who participated in this alleged rebellion? Second, are their ways to join the arguments of Ostrander and Shannon to conclude that a much broader set of changes was put in motion that included social, cultural, *and* economic changes of great consequence? Third, to what extent did the nature of politics in the United States mark a significant break with the past?

Clearly, there were signs of revolt in the 1920s that challenged traditional commitments to order and decorum. The enfranchisement of women coincided with a youth rebellion that challenged Victorian moral values in the 1920s, much as young Americans challenged mainstream values in the 1960s. The popularity of jazz and the new dances of the 1920s deeply troubled parents and arbiters of high culture. Americans across generational, gender, and racial lines joined in defying the prohibition laws that remained in effect throughout the decade. Still, most Americans adhered to the more conservative and respectable mores associated by the Lynds with the residents in "Middletown."

The transition from a producer to a mass consumer society had a tremendous impact on postwar America, and both Ostrander and Shannon recognize this reality. Ostrander's discussion of the automobile as affecting the nation's methods of courtship does not mean that we should not also recognize mass-produced cars as a striking symbol of the success of American capitalism.

Finally, one of the great paradoxes of the 1920s is that during the time of significant social and cultural change, American national politics was characterized as essentially conservative in that the nation's leaders resisted the types of progressive reform that had dominated the first two decades of the twentieth century. And yet, by championing business-minded values of American capitalism, which Shannon found most impressive, these leaders contributed to the economic expansion that produced the affluent, urban nation depicted by Ostrander.

Additional Resources

There are a number of important overviews of the 1920s that treat the topics raised by Ostrander and Shannon. Among the more useful are John D. Hicks, *Republican Ascendancy, 1921–1933* (Harper & Row, 1960), a volume in The New American Nation Series; Roderick Nash, *The Nervous Generation: American Thought, 1917–1930* (Rand McNally, 1970); two volumes by Paul Carter, *The Twenties in America*, 2nd ed. (Harlan Davidson, 1975) and *Another Part of the Twenties* (Columbia University Press, 1977); and Lynn Dumenil, *The Modern Temper: American Culture and Society in the 1920s* (Hill & Wang, 1995). For a discussion of youth in the 1920s, see Paula S. Fass, *The Damned and the Beautiful: American Youth in the 1920s* (Oxford University Press, 1979).

The economic history of the decade is discussed in George Soule, *Prosperity Decade: From War to Depression, 1917–1929* (Holt, Rinehart & Winston, 1947); Peter Fearon, *War, Prosperity, and Depression* (University of Kansas Press, 1987); and John Kenneth Galbraith, *The Great Crash, 1929*, rev. ed. (Houghton Mifflin, 1989). For a critical biography of the decade's most notable business leader, see Keith Sward, *The Legend of Henry Ford* (Rinehart, 1948).

The status of women in the decade after suffrage receives general treatment in William H. Chafe, *The Paradox of Change: American Women in the 20th Century* (Oxford University Press, 1991) and, more thoroughly, in Dorothy M. Brown, *Setting a Course: American Women in the 1920s* (Twayne, 1987). Discussions of feminism in the 1920s are competently presented in William L. O'Neill, *Everyone Was Brave: The Rise and Fall of Feminism in America* (University of Illinois Press, 1973); Susan D. Baker, *The Origins of the Equal Rights Amendment: Feminism Between the Wars* (Greenwood Press, 1981); and Nancy F. Cott, *The Grounding of Feminism* (Yale University Press, 1987). Cott's study argues that the diversity within the women's movement created important paradoxes. For example, although feminists in the 1920s desired equality with men, unity among themselves, and gender consciousness, they also focused upon their differences from men, the diversity of women, and the elimination of constraining gender roles. David M. Kennedy, *Birth Control in America: The Career of Margaret Sanger* (Yale University Press, 1970) examines an important issue that attracted the interest of many women's groups in the 1920s, whereas Jacqueline Dowd Hall, *Revolt Against Chivalry: Jessie Daniel Ames and the Women's Campaign Against Lynching* (Columbia University Press, 1979) explores the role of women in the area of race relations.

Race is also the focal point of several studies of the Harlem Renaissance. The best of these works include Nathan Irvin Huggins, *Harlem Renaissance* (Oxford University Press, 1971); David Levering Lewis, *When Harlem Was in Vogue* (Alfred A. Knopf, 1981); and Cary D. Wintz, *Black Culture and the Harlem Renaissance* (Rice University Press, 1988).

The history of the prohibition experiment during the 1920s is presented effectively in Andrew Sinclair, *Prohibition: The Era of Excess* (Harper & Row, 1962); Norman H. Clark, *Deliver Us from Evil: An Interpretation of American Prohibition* (W. W. Norton, 1976); Thomas R. Pegram, *Battling Demon Rum: The Struggle for a Dry America, 1800–1933* (Ivan R. Dee, 1998); and Daniel Okrent, *Last Call: The Rise and Fall of Prohibition* (Scribners, 2011).

Recent scholarship on the Ku Klux Klan in the 1920s has focused on its grass-roots participation in local and state politics. Klan members are viewed less as extremists and more as political pressure groups whose aims were to gain control of various state and local governmental offices. The best overview of this perspective is Shawn Lay, ed., *The Invisible Empire in the West: Toward a New Historical Appraisal of the Ku Klux Klan of the 1920s* (University of Illinois Press, 1992). Nancy MacLean, *Behind the Mask of Chivalry: The Making of the Second Ku Klux Klan* (Oxford University press, 1994), offers an economic interpretation in which the Klan's prominence resulted from middle-class anxieties generated by the hard times of the early 1920s. Two recent studies, Kelly J. Baker, *Gospel According to the Klan: The KKK's Appeal to Protestant America, 1915–1930* (University Press of Kansas, 2011) and Thomas Pegram, *One Hundred Percent American: The Rebirth and Decline of the Ku Klux Klan in the 1920s* (Ivan R. Dee, 2011), debate the history of the Klan in the 1920s as a "mainstream" organization.

ISSUE 10

Did the New Deal Prolong the Great Depression?

YES: Burton W. Folsom, Jr., from *New Deal or Raw Deal? How FDR's Economic Legacy Has Damaged America* (Simon & Schuster, 2008)

NO: Roger Biles, from *A New Deal for the American People* (Northern Illinois University Press, 1991)

Learning Outcomes

After reading this issue, you should be able to:

- Describe the major programs of the New Deal.
- Analyze the major arguments supporting the positive aspects of the New Deal.
- Describe Keynesian economics.
- Analyze the major free-market critiques of the New Deal.
- Critically discuss whether World War II brought about the nation's economic recovery.

ISSUE SUMMARY

YES: Professor Burton W. Folsom, Jr., argues the New Deal prolonged the Great Depression because its anti–free-market program of high taxes and special-interest spending to certain banks, railroads, farmers, and veterans created an antibusiness environment of regime uncertainty.

NO: Professor of history Roger Biles contends that, in spite of its minimal reforms and nonrevolutionary programs, the New Deal created a limited welfare state that implemented economic stabilizers to avert another depression.

T he catastrophe triggered by the 1929 Wall Street debacle crippled the American economy, deflated the optimistic future most Americans assumed to be their birthright, and ripped apart the values by which the country's businesses, farms, and governments were run. During the next decade, the inertia of the Great Depression stifled their attempts to make ends meet.

The world depression of the 1930s began in the United States. The United States had suffered periodic economic setbacks—in 1873, 1893, 1907, and 1920—but those slumps had been limited and temporary. The omnipotence of American productivity, the ebullient American spirit, and the self-deluding thought, "it can't happen here" blocked out any consideration of an economic collapse that might devastate the capitalist economy and threaten U.S. democratic government.

All aspects of American society trembled from successive jolts; there were 4 million unemployed people in 1930 and 9 million more by 1932. Those who had not lost their jobs took pay cuts or worked for scrip. There was no security for those whose savings were lost forever when banks failed or stocks declined.

Manufacturing halted, industry shut down, and farmers destroyed wheat, corn, and milk rather than selling them at a loss. Worse, there were millions of homeless Americans—refugees from the cities roaming the nation on freight trains, victims of the drought or the Dust Bowl seeking a new life farther west, and hobo children estranged from their parents.

Business and government leaders alike seemed immobilized by the economic giant that had fallen to its knees. Herbert Hoover, the incumbent president at the start of the Great Depression, attempted some relief programs, but they were ineffective considering the magnitude of the unemployment, hunger, and distress. The then president's attempts at voluntary cooperation between business and labor to avoid layoffs or pay increases broke down by the severity of the depression in mid-1931. Hoover went further than previous presidents in using the power of the U.S. federal government to make loans to ailing businesses, railroads, banks, and farmers, but they were too small and too late.

As governor of New York, Franklin D. Roosevelt (who was elected president in 1932) had introduced some relief measures, such as industrial welfare and a comprehensive system of unemployment remedies, to alleviate the social and economic problems facing the citizens of the state. Yet, his campaign did little to reassure his critics that he was more than a rich man who wanted to be the president. In light of later developments, Roosevelt may have been the only presidential candidate to deliver more programs than he actually promised.

The New Deal attempted to jump-start the economy with dozens of recovery and relief measures. On inauguration day, FDR told the nation "the only thing we have to fear is fear itself." A bank holiday was immediately declared. Congress passed the Emergency Banking Act, which pumped Federal Reserve notes into the major banks and stopped the wave of bank failures. Later banking acts separated commercial and investment institutions, and the Federal Deposit Insurance Corporation (FDIC) guaranteed people's savings from a loss of up to $2,500 in member banks. A number of relief agencies were set up that provided work for youth and able-bodied men on various state and local building projects. Finally, the Tennessee Valley Administration (TVA) was created to provide electricity in rural areas not serviced by private power companies.

In 1935 the Supreme Court ended the First New Deal by declaring both the Agriculture Adjustment Act and National Recovery Act unconstitutional. In response to critics on the left who felt that the New Deal was favoring the large banks, big agriculture, and big business, FDR shifted his approach in 1935. The Second New Deal created the Works Project Administration (WPA), which became the nation's largest employer in its eight years of operation. Social Security was passed, and the government guaranteed monthly stipends for the aged, the unemployed, and dependent children. Labor pressured the administration for a collective bargaining bill. The Wagner Act established a National Labor Relations Board to supervise industry-wide elections. The steel, coal, automobile, and some garment industries were unionized as membership tripled from 3 million in 1933 to 9 million in 1939.

Roosevelt was beloved by the average American. "He understands that my boss is a 'son-of-a-bitch,'" said one person to a pollster. In 1936, FDR was reelected by the largest popular majority in history attaining 60 percent of the popular vote and carrying 46 of 48 states.

By the summer of 1937, the economy had almost recovered to 1929 levels. But Roosevelt, himself, never a Keynesian, cut spending in order to cut the deficit. The "Roosevelt recession" followed with 1.6 million WPA workers losing their jobs as well as 4 million others: industrial production dropped by more than 34 percent. With economic conditions reverting back to 1932 levels, Roosevelt asked Congress for an additional $5 billion for public works and relief programs in April 1938. Later in the year, Congress passed the Fair Labor Standards Act, which set up a 40-hour work week, a national minimum wage, and severely restricted child labor.

By the late 1930s, however, the New Deal, for all practical purposes, was over. Several factors hurt Roosevelt politically and stymied further domestic reform: (1) Roosevelt's attempt to expand the size of the Supreme Court in order to have the opportunity to nominate liberal justices made him appear devious; (2) his campaign in the South against anti–New Deal Democrats backfired and, along with the Court-packing scheme produced a sizable conservative coalition of southern Democrats and Republicans that blocked progressive legislation; and (3) the outbreak of World War II in Europe in 1939 diverted the then president's attention to foreign affairs.

The YES and NO selections debate whether or not the New Deal prolonged the Great Depression. Professor Burton Folsom argues that the New Deal created an antibusiness environment that rejected free-market capitalism with special-interest spending financed by high taxes. He argues that both the Hoover and Roosevelt administrations abandoned free-market economics by passing the Smooth-Hawley Tariff Act in 1930 that created high tariffs on 3,218 goods American industries needed for their production, increased prices to the American consumer, and prevented European nations from paying off their debts. Meanwhile, the Federal Reserve System continued to raise interest rates making it harder for businesses to borrow money. Folsom also challenges the notion that underconsumption and overproduction of consumer goods were major problems in the 1920s. He goes on to argue that the New Deal bureaucracy prevented the country from ending the depression more quickly.

Folsom's critique is based on the arguments used by Roosevelt's Republican opponents in the 1930s as well as the conservative assumptions of the well-known free-market advocates Milton Friedman and Anna Jacobson Schwartz, who argue in *A Monetary History of the United States, 1867–1960* (Princeton University Press, 1963) that the Great Depression was a government failure, brought on primarily by Federal Reserve policies that abruptly cut the money supply. This view runs counter to those of Peter Temin, *Did Monetary Forces Cause the Depression?* (Norton, 1976); Michael A. Bernstein, *The Great Depression: Delayed Recovery and Economic Change in America* (Cambridge University Press, 1987); and the lively account of John Kenneth Galbraith, *The Great Crash* (Houghton Mifflin, 1955), which argues that the crash exposed various structural weaknesses in the economy that caused the economic crisis.

Historian Roger Biles argues in the NO selection that, compared to the economic and political changes that were taking place in Soviet Russia, Fascist Italy, and Nazi Germany, the New Deal was not particularly revolutionary in scope. This analysis basically agrees with the British historian Anthony J. Badger who argues in *The New Deal* (Hill and Wang, 1989) that FDR's domestic legislation represented a "holding operation" until the World War II created the "political economy of modern America." Both Biles and Badger note that once the immediate crisis of 1933 subsided, the opposition to the New Deal came from big business, conservative congressmen, and local government officials who resisted the increasing power of the U.S. federal government. Although the recovery did not come about until World War II, Biles recognizes that the New Deal changed the relationship between the U.S. federal government and the people, stabilized the banking industry and stock exchange, ameliorated the relationship of workers with business, and through social security provided a safety net for the aged, the unemployed, and the disabled. In politics, urbanization and immigration cemented a new coalition that sustained itself until the 1980s, when racial issues and the maturing of a new suburban middle class fractured the Democratic majority.

YES

Burton W. Folsom, Jr.

New Deal or Raw Deal? How FDR's Economic Legacy Has Damaged America

The Making of the Myth: FDR and the New Deal

On May 9, 1939, Henry Morgenthau, Jr., the secretary of the treasury and one of the most powerful men in America, had a startling confession to make. He made this remarkable admission before the influential Democrats who ran the House Ways and Means Committee. As he bared his soul before his fellow Democrats, Morgenthau may have pondered the irony of his situation.

Here he was—a major cabinet head, a man of great authority. The source of his power, of course, was his intimate friendship with President Franklin Delano Roosevelt. Morgenthau was the president's longtime neighbor, close confidant, and—would be for over a decade—his loyal secretary of the treasury. Few men knew the president better, talked with him more, or defended him more faithfully. Eleanor Roosevelt once said Morgenthau was one of only two men who could tell her husband "categorically" that he was wrong and get away with it. Roosevelt and Morgenthau liked to banter back and forth at cabinet meetings, pass each other secret notes, meet regularly for lunch, and talk frequently on the phone. Morgenthau cherished a photo of himself and the president in a car, side by side, friends forever, with Roosevelt's inscription: "To Henry," it read, "from one of two of a kind."

But in May 1939, Morgenthau had a problem. The Great Depression—the most devastating economic catastrophe in American history—was not only persisting, in some ways it was getting worse. Unemployment, for example, the previous month had again passed the 20 percent mark. Here was Morgenthau, the secretary of the treasury, an expert on finance, a fount of statistics on the American economy during the 1930s; his best friend was the president of the United States and the author of the New Deal; key public policy decisions had to go through Morgenthau to get a hearing. And yet, with all this power, Morgenthau felt helpless. After almost two full terms of Roosevelt and the New Deal, here are Morgenthau's startling words—his confession—spoken candidly before his fellow Democrats on the House Ways and Means Committee:

We have tried spending money. We are spending more than we have ever spent before and it does not work. And I have just one interest, and if I am wrong . . . somebody else can have my job. I want to see this country prosperous. I want to see people get a job. I want to see people get enough to eat. We have never made good on our promises. . . . I say after eight years of this Administration we have just as much unemployment as when we started. . . . And an enormous debt to boot!

In these words, Morgenthau summarized a decade of disaster, especially during the years Roosevelt was in power. Indeed average unemployment for the whole year in 1939 would be higher than that in 1931, the year before Roosevelt captured the presidency from Herbert Hoover. Fully 17.2 percent of Americans, or 9,480,000, remained unemployed in 1939, up from 16.3 percent, or 8,020,000 in 1931. On the positive side, 1939 was better than 1932 and 1933, when the Great Depression was at its nadir, but 1939 was still worse than 1931, which at that time was almost the worst unemployment year in U.S. history. No depression, or recession, had ever lasted even half this long.

Put another way, if the unemployed in 1931 under Hoover would have been lined up one after the other in three separate lines side by side, they would have extended from Los Angeles across the country to the border of Maine. In 1939, eight years later, the three lines of unemployed Americans would have lengthened, heading from the border of Maine south to Boston, then to New York City, to Philadelphia, to Washington, D.C., and finally into Virginia. That line of unemployed people from the border of Maine into Virginia was mostly added when Roosevelt was president.

We can visualize this hypothetical line of unemployed Americans, but what about the human story of their suffering. Who were some of them, and what were they thinking? In the line at Chicago, we would encounter salesman Ben Isaacs. "Wherever I went to get a job, I couldn't get no job," Isaacs said of the prolonged depression. "I went around selling razor blades and shoe laces. There was a day I would go over all the streets and come home with fifty cents, making a sale. That kept going until 1940, practically." Letters to President Roosevelt tell other stories. For example, in Chicago, a twelve-year-old Chicago boy wrote the president, "We haven't paid the gas bill, and the electric bill, haven't paid grocery bill for 3 months. . . . My father he staying home. All the time he's crying because he can't find work. I told him why are you crying daddy, and daddy said why shouldn't I cry when there is nothing in the house." In our hypothetical unemployment line at Latrobe, Pennsylvania, we might see the man who wrote in 1934, "No home, no work, no money. We cannot go along this way. They have shut the water supply from us. No means of sanitation. We cannot keep the children clean and tidy as they should be." From Augusta, Georgia, in 1935 came this letter to the president: "I am eating flour bread and drinking water, and no grease and nothing in the bread. . . . I aint even got bed[d]ing to sleep on. . . ." But even he was better off than the man from Beaver Dam, Virginia, who wrote the president, "We right now, have no work, no winter bed clothes. . . . Wife don't even have a winter coat. What are we going to do through these cold times coming on? Just looks we will have to freeze and starve together."

High unemployment was just one of many tragic areas that made the 1930s a decade of disaster. The *Historical Statistics of the United States,* compiled by the Census Bureau, fills out the rest of the grim picture. The stock market, which picked up in the mid-1930s, had a collapse later in the decade. The value of all stocks dropped almost in half from 1937 to 1939. Car sales plummeted one-third in those same years, and were lower in 1939 than in any of the last seven years of the 1920s. Business failures jumped 50 percent from 1937 to 1939; patent applications for inventions were lower in 1939 than for any year of the 1920s. Real estate foreclosures, which did decrease steadily during the 1930s, were still higher in 1939 than in any year during the next two decades.

Another disaster sign in the 1930s was the spiraling national debt. The United States had budget surpluses in 1930 and 1931, but soon government spending ballooned and far outstripped revenue from taxes. The national debt stood at $16 billion in 1931; by the end of the decade the debt had more than doubled to more than $40 billion. Put another way, the national debt during the last eight years of the 1930s, less than one decade, grew more than it had in the previous 150 years of our country's existence. From 1776 to 1931, the spending to support seven wars and at least five recessions was more than off-set by the debt acquired during the 1930s. Put yet another way, if Christopher Columbus, on that October day when he discovered the New World, could have arranged to put $100 a minute in a special account to defray the American debt, by 1939 his account would not yet have accumulated enough cash to pay for just the national debt acquired in the 1930s alone. In other words, if we were to pay $100 a minute (in 1930s dollars) into a special '30s debt account, we would need more than 450 years to raise enough money to pay off the debt of that decade.

The economic travail of the New Deal years can also be seen in the seven consecutive years of unbalanced trade from 1934 to 1940. Much of our government spending during the decade went to prop up prices of wheat, shirts, steel, and other exports, which in turn, because of the higher prices, made them less desirable as exports to other countries. From 1870 to 1970, only during the depression years plus the year 1888 did the United States have an unfavorable balance of trade.

Hard times are often followed by social problems. The United States in the 1930s was no exception. For example, the American birthrate dropped sharply, and the country's population increased only 7 percent in that decade. During the more prosperous 1920s, by contrast, the birthrate was higher and the country's population increased 16 percent.

For many Americans, the prolonged Great Depression of the 1930s became a time of death. As one eighty-year-old wrote, "Now [December 1934] there are a lot of us [who] will choose suicide in preference to being herded into the poor house." Apparently, thousands of Americans agreed with her, because suicides increased from 1929 to 1930 and remained high throughout the 1930s. Equally sad were the people who gave up on life after prolonged despair and took their lives more subtly, through an accidental fall, reckless driving, or being hit by a train. All three of these categories hit record numbers of deaths per capita during the New Deal years.

The loss of the will to live was also reflected in <u>life expectancy</u> during the 1930s. When Franklin Roosevelt became president in 1933, life expectancy in the United States was 63.3 years. Since 1900, it had steadily increased sixteen years—almost half a year each year of the first third of the twentieth century. In 1940, however, after more than seven years of the New Deal, life expectancy had dropped to 62.9 years. Granted, the slight decline during these years was not consistent—two of the seven years showed an increase over 1933. But the steady increase in life expectancy from 1900 to 1933 and from 1940 to the end of the century was clearly interrupted only during the New Deal years.

The halt in improved life expectancy hit blacks even harder than whites. In 1933, black Americans could expect to live only 54.7 years, but in 1940 that had dropped to 53.1 years. Both before and after the Great Depression, the gap in life expectancy between blacks and whites had narrowed, but from 1933 to 1940 it actually widened. Strong indications are that blacks suffered more than whites during Roosevelt's first term as president.

Someone might survey the wreckage from the 1930s and say, "Okay, maybe the whole decade of the thirties was a disaster. But since the Great Depression was a worldwide catastrophe, doesn't that diminish America's blame for its bad numbers?" The Great Depression did, of course, rock most of the world, but some nations performed better than others in limiting damage and restoring economic growth. Fortunately, the League of Nations collected data from many nations throughout the 1930s on industrial production, unemployment, national debt, and taxes. How did the United States compare with other countries? The answer: in all four of these key indexes the U.S. did very poorly, almost worse than any other nation studied. Most nations of Europe weathered the Great Depression better than the United States did.

In a decade of economic disaster, such as the 1930s, a <u>decline in morality</u> is a significant danger. If record numbers of people are hungry, out of jobs, and taxed higher than ever before, will the charity, honesty, and integrity necessary to hold a society together begin to crumble as well? The *Historical Statistics of the United States* offers some help in answering this question. Homicides increased slightly during the 1930s. There were more than 10,000 murders a year only seven times from 1900 to 1960, and all seven years were in the 1930s. Arrests during this decade roughly doubled: almost 300,000 were made in 1932, and this steadily increased, reaching a peak of almost 600,000 in 1939. Divorce rates increased as well, especially during the late 1930s, and the number of cases of syphilis treated almost doubled, although cases of gonorrhea were roughly constant.

Statistics can't tell the whole story of the changing mores of the 1930s. Many persons openly threatened to steal—or thought about stealing—to make ends meet during the Great Depression. Joblessness also led to "jumping trains" either to find work elsewhere or just to roam the country. R. S. Mitchell of the Missouri Pacific Railroad testified before the U.S. Senate that young men who jumped trains often encountered "hardened criminals" on these rides, who were a "bad influence" on the character of these youths. The *Historical*

Statistics further shows that deaths to trespassers on railroads were at their highest ever during the depression years of 1933 to 1936.

Roosevelt and the Historians

Did the New Deal, rather than helping to cure the Great Depression, actually help prolong it? That is an important question to ask and ponder. Almost all historians of the New Deal rank Roosevelt as a very good to great president and the New Deal programs as a step in the right direction. With only a few exceptions, historians lavish praise on Roosevelt as an effective innovator, and on the New Deal as a set of programs desperately needed and very helpful to the depressed nation.

An example of this adulation is the appraisal by Henry Steele Commager and Richard B. Morris, two of the most distinguished American historians of the twentieth century. Commager, during a remarkable career at Columbia University and Amherst College, wrote over forty books and became perhaps the bestselling historian of the century. From the first year of Roosevelt's presidency, Commager lectured and wrote articles in defense of the New Deal. Richard Morris, his junior partner at Columbia, was a prolific author and president of the American Historical Association. Here is Commager and Morris's assessment of Roosevelt and the New Deal:

> The character of the Republican ascendancy of the twenties had been pervasively negative; the character of the New Deal was overwhelmingly positive. "This nation asks for action, and action, now," Roosevelt said in his first inaugural address, and asked for "power to wage war against the emergency." . . .
>
> It is the stuff of good history, this—a leadership that was buoyant and dynamic; a large program designed to enable the government to catch up with a generation of lag and solve the problems that crowded upon it; a people quickened into resolution and self-confidence; a nation brought to realize its responsibilities and its potentialities. How it lends itself to drama! The sun rises on a stricken field; the new leader raises the banner and waves it defiantly at the foe; his followers crowd about him, armies of recruits emerge from the shadows and throng into the ranks; the bands play, the flags wave, the army moves forward, and soon the sound of battle and the shouts of victory are heard in the distance. In perspective we can see that it was not quite like that, but that was the way it seemed at the time.

Commager and Morris's assessment highlights four main points of defense for Roosevelt and the New Deal that have been adopted by most historians for the last seventy years: first, the 1920s were an economic disaster; second, the New Deal programs were a corrective to the 1920s, and a step in the right direction; third, Roosevelt (and the New Deal) were very popular; and fourth, Roosevelt was a good administrator and moral leader.

These four points constitute what many historians call "the Roosevelt legend." Since the works of Arthur M. Schlesinger, Jr., and William Leuchtenburg have been essential in shaping and fleshing out this view of Roosevelt, I will quote from them liberally. . . .

In fact, the most recent Schlesinger poll (1996) ranks Roosevelt and Lincoln as *the* greatest presidents in U.S. history. He and his New Deal have become American idols. As Conlin writes, "From the moment F. D. R. delivered his ringing inaugural address—the clouds over Washington parting on cue to let the March sun through, it was obvious that he was a natural leader." Even before Roosevelt died, Conlin notes, "he was ranked by historians as among the greatest of the chief executives. . . . No succeeding generation of judges has demoted him." Leuchtenburg concludes, "Few would deny that Franklin Delano Roosevelt continues to provide the standard by which every successor has been, and may well continue to be, measured."

Of course, historians are often nigglers and all students of Roosevelt and his presidency have some complaints. What's interesting is that most of these complaints are that Roosevelt should have done more than he did, not less. "The havoc that had been done before Roosevelt took office," Leuchtenburg argues, "was so great that even the unprecedented measures of the New Deal did not suffice to repair the damage." Therefore, to Leuchtenburg and others, the New Deal was only "a halfway revolution" that should have gone further. Some historians say FDR should have done more deficit spending during the recession of 1937; some chide him for not supporting civil rights more strongly; some point to abuse or corruption in some of the programs; and some say he should have done much more to redistribute wealth. The New Deal was, many historians conclude, a conservative revolution that saved capitalism and preserved the existing order. Some New Deal historians of the 1980s, 1990s, and 2000s—loosely called the "constraints school"—argue that the New Deal did promote many needed changes, but that Roosevelt was constrained in what he could accomplish and therefore he did as much reform as circumstances would permit.

These recent criticisms of Roosevelt and the New Deal slightly alter but do not diminish the Roosevelt legend. The four points of defense are currently intact, and are usually found in most histories of the New Deal and in virtually all of the American history textbooks today. . . .

After his 1996 presidential poll, Schlesinger was more confident in Roosevelt than ever. Of the thirty-two experts consulted, thirty-one gave FDR the highest rating of "Great" and one ranked him "Near Great," the second highest rating. "For a long time FDR's top standing enraged many who had opposed his New Deal," Schlesinger wrote. "But now that even Newt Gingrich pronounces FDR the greatest president of the century, conservatives accept FDR at the top with stoic calm." Along these lines, historian David Hamilton, who edited a book of essays on the New Deal, observed, "Conservative critiques [of the New Deal] have drawn less attention in recent years. . . ." In other words, according to Schlesinger and many historians, the debate is over as the Roosevelt legend is established even among conservative historians.

The historical literature tends to support Schlesinger. The books and articles on Roosevelt and the New Deal are now so extensive, however, that it is almost impossible to read it all. Historian Anthony Badger has come as close as any modern historian to mastering the New Deal literature, and his book *The*

New Deal: The Depression Years, 1933–1940 is an essential tool to the modern historian trying to sort out all the writing on the subject. Badger looks fondly at Schlesinger and Leuchtenburg, the two key historians to shape the historical writing on the New Deal:

> At a time when there were few specialist monographs, both authors [Schlesinger and Leuchtenburg] displayed a remarkably sure touch in identifying the critical issues at stake in the most diverse New Deal activities. Both demonstrated an enviable mastery of a vast range of archival material. No one is ever likely to match the richness of Schlesinger's dramatic narrative. No one is ever likely to produce a better one volume treatment of the New Deal than Leuchtenburg's.

Thus, the Roosevelt legend seems to be intact. And as long as it is intact, the principles of public policy derived from the New Deal will continue to dominate American politics. As historian Ray Allen Billington noted, the New Deal "established for all time the principle of positive government action to rehabilitate and preserve the human resources of the nation." Yet, as we have seen, there is that nagging observation in 1939 by Henry Morgenthau, the secretary of the treasury, the friend of Roosevelt's and the man in the center of the storm. With great sadness, he confessed, "We are spending more than we have ever spent before and it does not work. . . . We have never made good on our promises."

Since national unemployment during the previous month of April 1939 was 20.7 percent, Morgenthau's admission has the ring of truth to it.

Is it possible that the Roosevelt legend is really the Roosevelt myth?. . .

What Finally Did End the Great Depression

If Roosevelt's New Deal programs did not break the Great Depression, then what did? Most historians have argued that America's entry into World War II was the key event that ended it. Federal spending drastically increased as twelve million U.S. soldiers went to war, and millions more mobilized in the factories to make war material. As a result, unemployment plummeted and, so the argument goes, the Great Depression receded.

William Leuchtenburg, who has written the standard book on the New Deal, claims, "The real impetus to recovery was to come from rapid, large-scale spending." Roosevelt, according to Leuchtenburg, was reluctant to take this step. When, at last, Pearl Harbor was bombed, "The war proved that massive spending under the right conditions produced full employment."

Recently, David M. Kennedy, in his Pulitzer Prize-winning book on Roosevelt, echoed Leuchtenburg's argument. "Roosevelt," Kennedy insisted, "remained reluctant to the end of the 1930s to engage in the scale of compensatory spending adequate to restore the economy to pre-Depression levels, let alone expand it." At the end of his book, Kennedy concluded, "It was a war that had brought [Americans] as far as imagination could reach, and beyond, from the ordeal of the Great Depression. . . ." More specifically, "The huge expenditures for weaponry clinched the Keynesian doctrine that government spending could underwrite prosperity. . . ."]

[Economists, Keynes notwithstanding, have always been less willing to believe this theory than historians.]F. A. Hayek, who won the Nobel Prize in economics, argued against this view in 1944 in *The Road to Serfdom*. Economist Henry Hazlitt, who wrote for the *New York Times* during the Roosevelt years, observed, "No man burns down his own house on the theory that the need to rebuild it will stimulate his energies." And yet, as historians and others viewed World War II, "they see almost endless benefits in enormous acts of destruction. They tell us how much better off economically we all are in war than in peace. They see 'miracles of production' which it requires a war to achieve." Thus, in Hazlitt's argument, the United States merely shifted capital from private markets, where it could have made consumer goods, to armament factories, where it made tanks, bombs, and planes for temporary use during war.

Along these lines, economist Robert Higgs has observed, "Unemployment virtually disappeared as conscription, directly and indirectly, pulled more than 12 million potential workers into the armed forces and millions of others into draft-exempt employment, but under the prevailing conditions, the disappearance of unemployment can hardly be interpreted as a valid index of economic prosperity." A supporting point for this idea is that real private investment and real personal consumption sharply declined during the war. Stock market prices, for example, in 1944 were still below those of 1939 in real dollars.

If not World War II, what did end the Great Depression? This question is still open to research and original thinking. [Higgs argues," It is time for economists and historians to take seriously the hypothesis that the New Deal prolonged the Great Depression by creating an extraordinarily high degree of regime uncertainty in the minds of investors."]Roosevelt, as we have seen, regularly attacked business and steadily raised income tax rates, corporate tax rates, and excise taxes during the 1930s. He added the undistributed profits tax and conducted highly publicized tax cases that sent many investors to prison. During World War II, Roosevelt softened his rhetoric against businessmen, whom he needed to wage the war, [but he did issue an executive order for a 100 percent tax on all personal income over $25,000.] When Roosevelt died, and Truman became president, the hostile rhetoric toward businessmen further declined and no new tax hikes were added. [During the war, in fact, Roosevelt had switched from attacking rich people to letting big corporations monopolize war contracts. Under Truman, businessmen were even more optimistic. They expanded production, and the U.S. economy was thus able to absorb the returning soldiers and those who had previously worked to make war equipment.]

That, in a nutshell, is Higgs's thesis, and he has two persuasive pieces of evidence on his side. First, many leading industrialists of the 1930s openly explained how the president's efforts to tax and regulate were stifling the nation's economic expansion. For example, Lammot Du Pont, who revolutionized the textile industry in the 1940s with the invention of nylon, was one of many businessmen who complained about Roosevelt's policies. "Uncertainty rules the tax situation, the labor situation, the monetary situation, and practically every legal condition under which industry must operate," Du Pont protested in 1937. "Are new restrictions to be placed on capital, new limits on profits? . . . It is impossible to even guess at the answers."

Second, Higgs cites poll data that show a sharp increase in optimism about business after Roosevelt died and Truman became president. For example, the American Institute of Public Opinion (AIPO) did solid polling of attitudes on business and its findings are impressive. In March 1939, for example, AIPO asked a national sample, "Do you think the attitude of the Roosevelt administration toward business is delaying business recovery?" More than twice as many respondents said "yes" as said "no." In May 1945, however, one month after Roosevelt's death, the AIPO pollsters asked, "Do you think Truman will be more favorable or less favorable toward business than Roosevelt was?" On this poll, Truman had eight times more yeses than nos. *Forbes* and *Fortune* also did polls of businessmen and found similar results. What that meant was that after the war, American businessmen expanded production and thereby absorbed into the workforce the returning soldiers. The Great Depression was over at last.

Other nations recovered from the Great Depression more quickly than did the United States. During the late 1930s, the League of Nations collected statistics from the United States and from many other nations on industrial recovery. Much of that data support the idea that Roosevelt's New Deal created economic uncertainty and was in fact uniquely unsuccessful as a recovery program. In the table below, we can see some of the aftermath of the depression within a depression in 1937, when the stock market lost one-third of its value. During late 1938, the United States had some recovery, but in early 1939 recovery again lagged. By May 1939, unemployment again reached 20 percent, industrial production had fallen about 10 percent from the first of the year, and Henry Morgenthau confessed, "We are spending more than we have ever spent before and it does not work."

. . . The U.S. economy was in a tailspin six years after FDR became president and the country suffered more unemployment than most of the other ones studied by the League of Nations.

Some historians, trying to defend Roosevelt, point out that unemployment in the United States slightly dropped each year from 1933 to 1937, which suggests some progress in fighting the Depression. Unemployment was 25.2 percent in 1933, 22 percent in 1934, 20.3 percent in 1935, 17 percent in 1936, and 14.3 percent in 1937. That 14.3 percent, however, is alarmingly high and—outside of the 1930s—was only exceeded for a brief period in all of American history during the Panic of 1893. What's worse, the business uncertainty during Roosevelt's second term stifled that modest recovery of his first term.

To be fair, if we describe the downward move of unemployment during Roosevelt's first term, we must present the steady upward move of unemployment during most of his second term. Unemployment was 15.0 percent in September 1936, 15.1 percent in January 1937, 17.4 percent in January 1938, 18.7 percent in January 1939, and 20.7 percent in April 1939. Thus, more than six years after Roosevelt took office, and almost ten years after the stock market crash of 1929, unemployment topped the 20 percent mark. The League of

Industrial Production in the United States *Date (1929 = 100)*	
June 1938	65
December 1938	87
January 1939	85
February 1939	82
March 1939	82
April 1939	77
May 1939	77
June 1939	81

Sources: League of Nations, *World Economic Survey, 1938/39* (Geneva, 1939), 110–11.

Nations study, which tried to explain the poor performance of the U.S. economy, cited the "uneasy relations between business and the [Roosevelt] Administration." As Yale economist Irving Fisher bluntly wrote Roosevelt, "You have also delayed recovery."

Why was the performance of the U.S. economy—especially relative to other nations—so miserable? What were some of the ingredients in America's unique "regime uncertainty"? The first place to start is tax policy. One reason that the United States lagged behind other countries in recovery from the Great Depression is that Roosevelt strongly emphasized raising revenue by excise taxes. According to another League of Nations study, the U.S. increased its revenue from excise taxes more rapidly than did any of the other nine nations surveyed. Britain and France, for example, decreased their dependency on excise taxes from 1929 to 1938. Japan, Germany, Italy, and Hungary did increase their excise revenues, but only slightly. The United States, however, had a whopping 328 percent increase in excise revenue from 1929 to 1938. "The very large increases of yield [in tax revenue] which are shown in the case of Belgium [310 percent] and the United States [328 percent] are due to substantial increases in the rate of duty," the study concluded. Since these taxes fell heavier on lower incomes, that may have contributed to the poorer rate of recovery from the Great Depression by the United States.

Other tax problems contributed to "regime uncertainty." Corporate taxes went up, the estate tax was increased to a top rate of 70 percent, and the United States alone among nations passed an undistributed profits tax. Businessmen watched the top rate of the federal income tax increase from 24 to 63 percent in 1932 under Hoover and then to 79 percent in 1935 under Roosevelt. The president regularly castigated businessmen and threatened to raise rates further. On April 27, 1942, Roosevelt issued an executive order that would tax all personal income over $25,000 at 100 percent. All "excess income," the president argued/should go to win the war." Furthermore, Roosevelt's use of the IRS to prosecute wealthy Americans, especially Republicans, created incentives for businessmen to shift their investments into areas of lesser taxation. All of this created "regime uncertainty," and the Great Depression persisted throughout the 1930s. As we have seen in the League of Nations study, in 1929 the United States had the lowest level of unemployment of any of the sixteen nations surveyed. The U.S. dropped to eighth place by 1932, eleventh place in 1937, and then to thirteenth place in 1938.

In retrospect, we can see that Roosevelt's special-interest spending created insatiable demands by almost all groups of voters for special subsidies. That, in itself, created regime uncertainty. Under the RFC, for example, the federal government made special loans to banks and railroads; then the AAA had price supports for farmers; soon the operators of silver mines were demanding special high prices for their product. At one level, as we have seen, Roosevelt used these subsidies as political tools to reward friends and punish enemies. But beyond that, where would the line be drawn? Who would get special taxpayer subsidies and who would not? As Walter Waters, who led the veterans' march on Washington in 1932, observed, "I noticed, too, that the highly organized lobbies in Washington for special industries were producing results: loans were being granted to their special interests and these lobbies seemed to justify their existence. Personal lobbying paid, regardless of the justice or injustice of their demand."

Roosevelt became trapped in a debt spiral of special-interest spending. He often did not try to escape because of the political benefits received when he supported subsidy bills to targeted interest groups. In 1935, when the veterans came clamoring again for a special subsidy, Roosevelt cast only a tepid veto—how could he justify the cash to all the other groups, but deny the veterans? Therefore, an obliging Congress voted the veterans a special bonus of $2 billion—a sum exceeding 6 percent of the entire national debt. As the *St. Louis Post-Dispatch* observed, "Here is a superb example of how a powerful minority, in this case the veterans' organizations, has been able . . . to win Congress over to a proposition in defiance of logic, good sense and justice." Such an unwarranted subsidy was, the editor feared, a "grave defect in our system." We can better understand Henry Morgenthau's frustration in May 1939. He could just as easily have said, "We have tried spending and it creates frantic lobbying and a never-ending cycle of more spending."

 **NO**

A New Deal for the American People

At the close of the Hundred Days, Franklin D. Roosevelt said, "All of the proposals and all of the legislation since the fourth day of March have not been just a collection of haphazard schemes, but rather the orderly component parts of a connected and logical whole." Yet the president later described his approach quite differently. "Take a method and try it. If it fails admit it frankly and try another. But above all, try something." The impetus for New Deal legislation came from a variety of sources, and Roosevelt relied heavily at various times on an ideologically diverse group of aides and allies. His initiatives reflected the contributions of, among others, Robert Wagner, Rexford Tugwell, Raymond Moley, George Norris, Robert LaFollette, Henry Morgenthau, Marriner Eccles, Felix Frankfurter, Henry Wallace, Harry Hopkins, and Eleanor Roosevelt. An initial emphasis on recovery for agriculture and industry gave way within two years to a broader-based program for social reform; entente with the business community yielded to populist rhetoric and a more ambiguous economic program. Roosevelt suffered the opprobrium of both the conservatives, who vilified "that man" in the White House who was leading the country down the sordid road to socialism, and the radicals, who saw the Hyde Park aristocrat as a confidence man peddling piecemeal reform to forestall capitalism's demise. Out of so many contradictory and confusing circumstances, how does one make sense of the five years of legislative reform known as the New Deal? And what has been its impact on a half century of American life?[1]

A better understanding begins with the recognition that little of the New Deal was new, including the use of federal power to effect change. Nor, for all of Roosevelt's famed willingness to experiment, did New Deal programs usually originate from vernal ideas. Governmental aid to increase farmers' income, propounded in the late nineteenth century by the Populists, surfaced in Woodrow Wilson's farm credit acts. The prolonged debates over McNary-Haugenism in the 1920s kept the issue alive, and Herbert Hoover's Agricultural Marketing Act set the stage for further federal involvement. Centralized economic planning, as embodied in the National Industrial Recovery Act, flowed directly from the experiences of Wilson's War Industries Board; not surprisingly, Roosevelt chose Hugh Johnson, a veteran of the board, to head the National Recovery Administration. Well established in England and Germany before the First World War, social insurance appeared in a handful of states—notably Wisconsin—before

From *A New Deal for the American People* by Roger Biles (Northern Illinois University Press, 1991). Copyright © 1991 by Northern Illinois University Press. Reprinted by permission.

the federal government became involved. Similarly, New Deal labor reform took its cues from the path-breaking work of state legislatures. Virtually alone in its originality, compensatory fiscal policy seemed revolutionary in the 1930s. Significantly, however, Roosevelt embraced deficit spending quite late after other disappointing economic policies and never to the extent Keynesian economists advised. Congress and the public supported the New Deal, in part, because of its origins in successful initiatives attempted earlier under different conditions.

Innovative or not, the New Deal clearly failed to restore economic prosperity. As late as 1938 unemployment stood at 19.1 percent and two years later at 14.6 percent. Only the Second World War, which generated massive industrial production, put the majority of the American people back to work. To be sure, partial economic recovery occurred. From a high of 13 million unemployed in 1933, the number under Roosevelt's administration fell to 11.4 million in 1934, 10.6 million in 1935, and 9 million in 1936. Farm income and manufacturing wages also rose, and as limited as these achievements may seem in retrospect, they provided sustenance for millions of people and hope for many more. Yet Roosevelt's resistance to Keynesian formulas for pump priming placed immutable barriers in the way of recovery that only war could demolish. At a time calling for drastic inflationary methods, Roosevelt introduced programs effecting the opposite result. The NRA restricted production, elevated prices, and reduced purchasing power, all of which were deflationary in effect. The Social Security Act's payroll taxes took money from consumers and out of circulation. The federal government's $4.43 billion deficit in fiscal year 1936, impressive as it seemed, was not so much greater than Hoover's $2.6 billion shortfall during his last year in office. As economist Robert Lekachman noted, "The 'great spender' was in his heart a true descendant of thrifty Dutch Calvinist forebears." It is not certain that the application of Keynesian formulas would have sufficed by the mid-1930s to restore prosperity, but the president's cautious deflationary policies clearly retarded recovery.[2]

Although New Deal economic policies came up short in the 1930s, they implanted several "stabilizers" that have been more successful in averting another such depression. The Securities and Exchange Act of 1934 established government supervision of the stock market, and the Wheeler-Rayburn Act allowed the Securities and Exchange Commission to do the same with public utilities. Severely embroiled in controversy when adopted, these measures have become mainstays of the American financial system. The Glass–Steagall Banking Act forced the separation of commercial and investment banking and broadened the powers of the Federal Reserve Board to change interest rates and limit loans for speculation. The creation of the Federal Deposit Insurance Corporation (FDIC) increased government supervision of state banks and significantly lowered the number of bank failures. Such safeguards restored confidence in the discredited banking system and established a firm economic foundation that performed well for decades thereafter.

The New Deal was also responsible for numerous other notable changes in American life. Section 7(a) of the NIRA, the Wagner Act, and the Fair Labor Standards Act transformed the relationship between workers and business and breathed life into a troubled labor movement on the verge of total extinction.

In the space of a decade government laws eliminated sweatshops, severely curtailed child labor, and established enforceable standards for hours, wages, and working conditions. Further, federal action eliminated the vast majority of company towns in such industries as coal mining. Although Robert Wagner and Frances Perkins dragged Roosevelt into labor's corner, the New Deal made the unions a dynamic force in American society. Moreover, as Nelson Lichtenstein has noted, "by giving so much of the working class an institutional voice, the union movement provided one of the main political bulwarks of the Roosevelt Democratic party and became part of the social bedrock in which the New Deal welfare state was anchored."[3]

Roosevelt's avowed goal of "cradle-to-grave" security for the American people proved elusive, but his administration achieved unprecedented advances in the field of social welfare. In 1938 the president told Congress: "Government has a final responsibility for the well-being of its citizenship. If private co-operative endeavor fails to provide work for willing hands and relief for the unfortunate, those suffering hardship from no fault of their own have a right to call upon the Government for aid; and a government worthy of its name must make fitting response." The New Deal's safety net included low-cost housing; old-age pensions; unemployment insurance; and aid for dependent mothers and children, the disabled, the blind, and public health services. Sometimes disappointing because of limiting eligibility requirements and low benefit levels, these social welfare programs nevertheless firmly established the principle that the government had an obligation to assist the needy. As one scholar wrote of the New Deal, "More progress was made in public welfare and relief than in the three hundred years after this country was first settled."[4]

More and more government programs, inevitably resulting in an enlarged administrative apparatus and requiring additional revenue, added up to a much greater role for the national government in American life. Coming at a time when the only Washington bureaucracy most of the people encountered with any frequency was the U.S. Postal Service, the change seemed all the more remarkable. Although many New Deal programs were temporary emergency measures, others lingered long after the return of prosperity. Suddenly, the national government was supporting farmers, monitoring the economy, operating a welfare system, subsidizing housing, adjudicating labor disputes, managing natural resources, and providing electricity to a growing number of consumers. "What Roosevelt did in a period of a little over 12 years was to change the form of government," argued journalist Richard L. Strout. "Washington had been largely run by big business, by Wall Street. He brought the government to Washington." Not surprisingly, popular attitudes toward government also changed. No longer willing to accept economic deprivation and social dislocation as the vagaries of an uncertain existence, Americans tolerated—indeed, came to expect—the national government's involvement in the problems of everyday life. No longer did "government" mean just "city hall."[5]

The operation of the national government changed as well. For one thing, Roosevelt's strong leadership expanded presidential power, contributing to what historian Arthur Schlesinger, Jr., called the "imperial presidency." Whereas Americans had in previous years instinctively looked first to Capitol Hill, after Roosevelt the White House took center stage in Washington. At the same time, Congress and the president looked at the nation differently. Traditionally attentive only to one group (big business), policymakers in Washington began responding to other constituencies such as labor, farmers, the unemployed, the aged, and to a lesser extent, women, blacks, and other disadvantaged groups. This new "broker state" became more accessible and acted on a growing number of problems, but equity did not always result. The ablest, richest, and most experienced groups fared best during the New Deal. NRA codes favored big business, and AAA benefits aided large landholders; blacks received relief and government jobs but not to the extent their circumstances merited. The long-term result, according to historian John Braeman, has been "a balkanized political system in which private interests scramble, largely successfully, to harness governmental authority and/or draw upon the public treasury to advance their private agendas."[6]

Another legacy of the New Deal has been the Roosevelt revolution in politics. Urbanization and immigration changed the American electorate, and a new generation of voters who resided in the cities during the Great Depression opted for Franklin D. Roosevelt and his party. Before the 1930s the Democrats of the northern big-city machines and the solid South uneasily coexisted and surrendered primacy to the unified Republican party. The New Deal coalition that elected Roosevelt united behind common economic interests. Both urban northerners and rural southerners, as well as blacks, women, and ethnic immigrants, found common cause in government action to shield them from an economic system gone haywire. By the end of the decade the increasing importance of the urban North in the Democratic party had already become apparent. After the economy recovered from the disastrous depression, members of the Roosevelt coalition shared fewer compelling interests. Beginning in the 1960s, tensions mounted within the party as such issues as race, patriotism, and abortion loomed larger. Even so, the Roosevelt coalition retained enough commitment to New Deal principles to keep the Democrats the nation's majority party into the 1980s.[7]

Yet for all the alterations in politics, government, and the economy, the New Deal fell far short of a revolution. The two-party system survived intact, and neither fascism, which attracted so many followers in European states suffering from the same international depression, nor communism attracted much of a following in the United States. Vital government institutions functioned without interruption and if the balance of powers shifted, the nation remained capitalistic; free enterprise and private ownership, not socialism, emerged from the 1930s. A limited welfare state changed the meld of the public and private but left them separate. Roosevelt could be likened to the British conservative Edmund Burke, who advocated measured change to offset drastic alterations—"reform to preserve." The New Deal's great achievement was the application of just enough change to preserve the American political economy.

Indications of Roosevelt's restraint emerged from the very beginning of the New Deal. Rather than assume extraordinary executive powers as Abraham Lincoln had done in the 1861 crisis, the president called Congress into special session. Whatever changes ensued would come through normal governmental activity. Roosevelt declined to assume direct control of the economy, leaving the nation's resources in the hands of private enterprise. Resisting the blandishments of radicals calling for the nationalization of the banks, he provided the means for their rehabilitation and ignored the call for national health insurance and federal contributions to Social Security retirement benefits. The creation of such regulatory agencies as the SEC confirmed his intention to revitalize rather than remake economic institutions. Repeatedly during his presidency Roosevelt responded to congressional pressure to enact bolder reforms, as in the case of the National Labor Relations Act, the Wagner-Steagall Housing Act, and the FDIC. The administration forwarded the NIRA only after Senator Hugo Black's recovery bill mandating 30-hour workweeks seemed on the verge of passage.

As impressive as New Deal relief and social welfare programs were, they never went as far as conditions demanded or many liberals recommended. Fluctuating congressional appropriations, oscillating economic conditions, and Roosevelt's own hesitancy to do too much violence to the federal budget left Harry Hopkins, Harold Ickes, and others only partially equipped to meet the staggering need. The president justified the creation of the costly WPA in 1935 by "ending this business of relief." Unskilled workers, who constituted the greatest number of WPA employees, obtained but 60 to 80 percent of the minimal family income as determined by the government. Roosevelt and Hopkins continued to emphasize work at less than existing wage scales so that the WPA or PWA never competed with free labor, and they allowed local authorities to modify pay rates. They also continued to make the critical distinction between the "deserving" and "undeserving" poor, making sure that government aided only the former. The New Deal never challenged the values underlying this distinction, instead seeking to provide for the growing number of "deserving" poor created by the Great Depression. Government assumed an expanded role in caring for the disadvantaged, but not at variance with existing societal norms regarding social welfare.

The New Deal effected no substantial redistribution of income. The Wealth Tax Act of 1935 (the famous soak-the-rich tax) produced scant revenue and affected very few taxpayers. Tax alterations in 1936 and 1937 imposed no additional burdens on the rich; the 1938 and 1939 tax laws actually removed a few. By the end of the 1930s less than 5 percent of Americans paid income taxes, and the share of taxes taken from personal and corporate income levies fell below the amount raised in the 1920s. The great change in American taxation policy came during World War II, when the number of income tax payers grew to 74 percent of the population. In 1942 Treasury Secretary Henry Morgenthau noted that "for the first time in our history, the income tax is becoming a people's tax." This the New Deal declined to do.[8]

Finally, the increased importance of the national government exerted remarkably little influence on local institutions. The New Deal seldom dictated and almost always deferred to state and local governments—encouraging, cajoling, bargaining, and wheedling to bring parochial interests in line with national objectives. As Harry Hopkins discovered, governors and mayors angled to obtain as many federal dollars as possible for their constituents but with no strings attached. Community control and local autonomy, conditions thought to be central to American democracy, remained strong, and Roosevelt understood the need for firm ties with politicians at all levels. In his study of the New Deal's impact on federalism, James T. Patterson concludes: "For all the supposed power of the New Deal, it was unable to impose all its guidelines on the autonomous forty-eight states. . . . What could the Roosevelt administration have done to ensure a more profound and lasting impression on state policy and politics? Very little."[9]

Liberal New Dealers longed for more sweeping change and lamented their inability to goad the president into additional action. They envisioned a wholesale purge of the Democratic party and the creation of a new organization embodying fully the principles of liberalism. They could not abide Roosevelt's toleration of the political conservatives and unethical bosses who composed part of the New Deal coalition. They sought racial equality, constraints upon the southern landholding class, and federal intrusion to curb the power of urban real estate interests on behalf of the inveterate poor. Yet to do these things would be to attempt changes well beyond the desires of most Americans. People pursuing remunerative jobs and the economic security of the middle class approved of government aiding the victims of an unfortunate economic crisis but had no interest in an economic system that would limit opportunity. The fear that the New Deal would lead to such thoroughgoing change explains the seemingly irrational hatred of Roosevelt by the economic elite. But, as historian Barry Karl has noted, "it was characteristic of Roosevelt's presidency that he never went as far as his detractors feared or his followers hoped."[10]

The New Deal achieved much that was good and left much undone. Roosevelt's programs were defined by the confluence of forces that circumscribed his admittedly limited reform agenda—hostile judiciary; powerful congressional opponents, some of whom entered into alliances of convenience with New Dealers and some of whom awaited the opportunity to build on their opposition; the political impotence of much of the populace; the pugnacious independence of local and state authorities; the strength of people's attachment to traditional values and institutions; and the basic conservatism of American culture. Obeisance to local custom and the decision to avoid tampering with the fabric of American society allowed much injustice to survive while shortchanging blacks, women, small farmers, and the "unworthy" poor. Those who criticized Franklin Roosevelt for an unwillingness to challenge racial, economic, and gender inequality misunderstood either the nature of his electoral mandate or the difference between reform and revolution—or both.

If the New Deal preserved more than it changed, that is understandable in a society whose people have consistently chosen freedom over equality. Americans traditionally have eschewed expanded government, no matter how efficiently managed or honestly administered, that imposed restraints on personal success—even though such limitations redressed legitimate grievances or righted imbalances. Parity, most Americans believed, should not be purchased with the loss of liberty. But although the American dream has always entailed individual success with a minimum of state interference, the profound shock of capitalism's near demise in the 1930s undermined numerous previously unquestioned beliefs. The inability of capitalism's "invisible hand" to stabilize the market and the failure of the private sector to restore prosperity enhanced the consideration of stronger executive leadership and centralized planning. Yet with the collapse of democratic governments and their replacement by totalitarian regimes, Americans were keenly sensitive to any threats to liberty. New Deal programs, frequently path breaking in their delivery of federal resources outside normal channels, also retained a strong commitment to local government and community control while promising only temporary disruptions prior to the return of economic stability. Reconciling the necessary authority at the federal level to meet nationwide crises with the local autonomy desirable to safeguard freedom has always been one of the salient challenges to American democracy. Even after New Deal refinements, the search for the proper balance continues.

Notes

1. Otis L. Graham, Jr., and Meghan Robinson Wander, eds., *Franklin D. Roosevelt, His Life and Times: An Encyclopedic View* (Boston: G. K. Hall, 1985), p. 285 (first quotation); Harvard Sitkoff, "Introduction," in Sitkoff, *Fifty Years Later,* p. 5 (second quotation).

2. Richard S. Kirkendall, "The New Deal as Watershed: The Recent Literature," *Journal of American History* 54 (March 1968), p. 847 (quotation).

3. Graham and Wander, *Franklin D. Roosevelt, His Life and Times,* p. 228 (quotation).

4. Leuchtenburg, "The Achievement of the New Deal," p. 220 (first quotation); Patterson, *America's Struggle against Poverty, 1900–1980,* p. 56 (second quotation).

5. Louchheim, *The Making of the New Deal: The Insiders Speak,* p. 15 (quotation).

6. John Braeman, "The New Deal: The Collapse of the Liberal Consensus," *Canadian Review of American Studies* 20 (Summer 1989), p. 77.

7. David Burner, *The Politics of Provincialism: The Democratic Party in Transition, 1918–1932* (New York: Alfred A. Knopf, 1968).

8. Mark Leff, *The Limits of Symbolic Reform,* p. 287 (quotation).

9. James T. Patterson, *The New Deal and the States: Federalism in Transition* (Princeton: Princeton University Press, 1969), p. 202.

10. Barry D. Karl, *The Uneasy State: The United States from 1915 to 1945* (Chicago: University of Chicago Press, 1983), p. 124.

EXPLORING THE ISSUE

Did the New Deal Prolong the Great Depression?

Critical Thinking and Reflection

1. Biles calls the New Deal a limited revolution, a movement of "reform to preserve" (quoting the famous British conservative politician Edmund Burke).

   (a) Explain what he means by this.
   (b) Explain what was old and what was new about the New Deal.
   (c) Explain which New Deal programs preserved the status quo or were regressive, and which ones were truly reformist.
   (d) Explain the political and ideological obstacles to bringing about a real liberal or socialist reform movement in the 1930s.

2. List the accomplishments of the New Deal, according to Biles, in the following areas: (a) banking; (b) the power of big business; (c) agriculture; (d) housing; (e) unions; (f) jobs; (g) welfare; (h) taxes; and (i) politics.

3. Folsom argues, like President Herbert Hoover and most conservatives of his day, that the New Deal worsened and prolonged the depression. Critically analyze the argument by a specific examination of most New Deal legislation passed between 1933 and 1938.

4. If you were a conservative businessman between 1933 and 1938, describe your situation and offer suggestions for ending the depression.

5. Compare, contrast, and critically evaluate the view of Folsom regarding the New Deal. In your answer, consider the following: (a) the values of both authors as regards democracy and capitalism; (b) the changing role of government toward the economy; (c) the impact of the New Deal on American politics; (d) the severity of the depression at home and abroad; and (e) the social impact of the New Deal.

6. Explain how the New Deal altered the role of the national government. Do you think the United States will ever revert to a system where states are more important than the national government? Will the business community dominate the national government? Critically analyze your arguments.

7. Compare your hometown or state as it existed in 1931 and 1941. Describe and analyze the changes that took place during those 10 years as a result of the New Deal.

Is There Common Ground?

Historians and economists disagree on the causes of the Great Depression. This is because the modern fights between liberals and conservatives stem from the economic philosophies pro and con during the New Deal. Should government intervene in the economy? Yes, say modern liberals whose political hero is FDR. No, say modern conservatives who evoke the legacy of President Ronald Reagan, where there is a consensus that it was World War II and not the New Deal that brought the United States out of the Great Depression. Again there is disagreement. Liberals argue that if Franklin Roosevelt had run deficits in the 1930s as large as the government did during the war, the United States would have come out of the depression earlier. But conservatives stay steadfast and blame the excessive spending of government programs for intimidating businesses with an uncertain climate for recovery.

Additional Resources

A number of books in the past two decades have adopted the free-market argument against the New Deal. See Gary Dean Best, *Pride, Prejudice and Politics: Roosevelt versus Recovery, 1933–1938* (Praeger, 1990); Robert Eden, ed., *The New Deal and its Legacy: Critique and Reappraisal* (Greenwood Press, 1989); and Jim Powell, *FDR's Folly: How Roosevelt and His New Deal Prolonged the Great Depression* (Crown Forum, 2003). *Wall Street Journal* writer Amity Shlaes wrote *The Forgotten Man* (Harper Collins, 2007), a highly publicized and widely reviewed controversial critique of New Deal programs. Finally, Robert Higgs has a short, concise essay criticizing the New Deal among other liberal programs in *Against Leviathan: Government Power and a Free Society* (The Independent Institute, 2004). See also Higgs' important essay used by Folsom, "Regime Uncertainty: Why the Great Depression Lasted So Long and Why Prosperity Resumed after the War," *Independent Review* (vol. 1, Spring 1997).

Two of the most recent studies sympathetic to the New Deal are David M. Kennedy, *Freedom from Fear: The American People in Depression and War, 1929–1945* (Oxford University Press, 1999); and George McJimsey, *The Presidency of Franklin Delano Roosevelt* (University Press of Kansas, 2000). In *A Commonwealth of Hope: The New Deal Response to Crisis* (The Johns Hopkins University Press, 2006), Alan Lawson identifies ideas in which New Deal planners attempted to implant a "cooperative commonwealth" in the country, thus challenging the ad hoc pragmatic approach usually attributed to FDR. Out of vogue but still worth reading are the pro-Roosevelt studies of the New Deal by William Leuchtenburg, *Franklin D. Roosevelt and the New Deal* (Harper and Row, 1963) and his interpretative essays written over 30 years in *The FDR Years: On Roosevelt and His Legacy* (Columbia University Press, 1985). See also the beautifully written second and third volumes of Arthur M. Schlesinger, Jr.'s never-to-be-completed *The Age of Roosevelt: The Coming of the New Deal* (Houghton Mifflin, 1959) and *The Politics of Upheaval* (Houghton Mifflin, 1960), which advance the interpretation of the first and second New Deals found in most American history survey textbooks. Steve Fraser and Gary Gerstle have edited a series of social and economic essays, which they present in *The Rise and Fall of the New Deal Order, 1930–1980* (Princeton University Press, 1989). Two important collections of recent writings are David E. Hamilton, ed., *Major Problems in American History, 1920–1945* (Houghton Mifflin, 1999). A recent annotated bibliography is Robert F. Himmelbert, *The Great Depression and the New Deal* (Greenwood Press, 2001).

ISSUE 11

Was the World War II Era a Watershed for the Civil Rights Movement?

YES: Richard M. Dalfiume, from "The 'Forgotten Years' of the Negro Revolution," *Journal of American History* (vol. 55, 1968, pp. 90–106)

NO: Harvard Sitkoff, from "African American Militancy in the World War II South: Another Perspective," in Neil R. McMillen, ed., *Remaking Dixie: The Impact of World War II on the American South* (University Press of Mississippi, 1997, pp. 70–92)

Learning Outcomes

After reading this issue, you should be able to:

- Explain what historians mean when they speak of a "watershed" event.
- Discuss the concept of the "long civil rights movement."
- Analyze the impact of World War II on the African American freedom struggle.
- Identify the key leaders and organizations that worked during the war to advance the cause of civil rights for black Americans.
- Describe the attitudes of African Americans toward the U.S. involvement in World War II.
- Understand the relationship between the U.S. federal government and civil rights initiatives during World War II.

ISSUE SUMMARY

YES: Richard M. Dalfiume argues that the period from 1939 to 1945 marked a turning point in American race relations by focusing the attention of African Americans on their unequal status in American society and stimulating a mass militancy whose goals, tactics, and strategies sowed the seeds for the modern civil rights movement.

NO: Harvard Sitkoff challenges the "watershed" interpretation by pointing out that, after Pearl Harbor, militant African American protest against racial discrimination was limited by the constraints imposed on the nation at war, the dwindling resources for sustained confrontation, and the genuinely patriotic response by black Americans to dangers faced by the nation.

Historians have long sought to identify and write about specific moments in the past that produced a major shift in the political, economic, social, or diplomatic fortunes of a particular nation or group of people. As a result, extensive scholarship has been devoted to "revolutions," "turning points," and "sea changes," following which conditions were markedly different from what they had been previously. These "watershed" events that mark a change of course from the past can be positive or negative, depending upon one's point of view, and U.S. history is filled with them: the American Revolution, the Civil War, the Great War (World War I), the Great Depression, World War II, the Cold War, or 9/11.

For students of the modern American civil rights movement, there are several events that appear to serve the purpose of a watershed moment: the U.S. Supreme Court's landmark decision in the *Brown* case that overturned *Plessy v. Ferguson* and set the stage for the dismantling of legally supported racial segregation; Rosa Parks' refusal to relinquish her seat on a Montgomery city bus in December 1955, which precipitated a year-long boycott and served as a springboard to Dr. Martin Luther King's rise to national prominence; the actions of four African American college students in Greensboro, North Carolina who had grown weary of a contradictory Jim Crow system that allowed them to purchase products in a Woolworth's store but not sit down at the lunch counter for service in the rear of the same establishment. Each of these events altered the trajectory of African American activism in important ways and cleared the path for what many scholars characterize as the most successful social movement in American history.

Over the course of the past two decades, however, historians have begun to take a broader look at the African American freedom struggle and to identify significant precursors to the movement that many previously had placed within the chronological time frame of 1954–1968. For example, see Jacqueline Dowd Hall, "The Long Civil Rights Movement and the Political Uses of the Past," *Journal of American History* (vol. 91, March 2005, pp. 1233–1263), who argues for a much earlier starting point for the civil rights struggle and insists that the search for watershed events must be moved back farther in the twentieth century. In the hands of such scholars, the key historical moments came in World War II, as the United States and its Allies combated a fascist dictatorship firmly committed to an ideology of extermination; or during the Great Depression as Franklin Roosevelt's New Deal produced a much larger role for government to play in the lives of the American people; or as a consequence of the Wilson Administration's effort to make the world safe for democracy while maintaining strict segregation of the races in his own nation. Still others claim that it is not unreasonable to push back the timeline of the civil rights movement to cover the intense anti-lynching efforts of Ida B. Wells–Barnett or to the Reconstruction period with its efforts to establish citizenship rights for African Americans who, while freed from the bonds of slavery at war's end, remained captive to Chief Justice Roger Taney's dictum in the Dred Scott case (1857) that peoples of African descent possessed no rights that whites were bound by law to respect.

The story of the United States' involvement in World War II involves much more than a delineation of military engagements in Europe and the Pacific. The war occurred on the heels of a devastating depression and helped to turn the economy around with nearly to full production and employment. The war possessed significant social implications for many Americans, including women and ethnic and racial minorities, a subject that has received general scholarly attention from prominent historians Richard Polenberg, *War and Society: The United States, 1941–1945* (J. B. Lippincott, 1972); John Morton Blum, *V Was for Victory: Politics and American Culture During World War II* (Harcourt Brace Jovanovich, 1976); and Allan M. Winkler, *Home Front U.S.A.: America during World War II*, 2nd ed. (Harlan Davidson, 2000). The present issue examines the impact of World War II on efforts by black Americans to demonstrate their loyalty to the United States while at the same time insisting upon the same citizenship rights accorded white Americans.

In the YES and NO selections, historians Richard Dalfiume and Harvard Sitkoff debate the degree to which World War II deserves to be considered a watershed event in the history of the American civil rights movement. Dalfiume pioneered the point of view that scholars had overlooked World War II as a period in which African Americans aggressively combined patriotism and a challenge to Jim Crow. During these "forgotten years," Dalfiume argues, civil rights organizations such as the National Association for the Advancement of Colored People (NAACP) and A. Philip Randolph's March on Washington Movement (MOWM) applied pressure on the Roosevelt Administration to eliminate discrimination in the military and in defense industry hiring practices. In doing so, mass militancy became a major strategy among blacks during the war and sowed the seeds for the civil rights revolution of the postwar period.

Harvard Sitkoff, who interestingly once had been a proponent of the conclusions reached by Dalfiume, now questions the validity of the "watershed" interpretation. He makes a clear distinction between the views expressed by African Americans before Pearl Harbor and the ideas they articulated after December 7, 1941, and concludes that black militancy declined sharply following the attack on the American fleet in Hawaii. Even African American Communists, he reports, softened their attacks on American racism during the war. According to Sitkoff, the types of black militancy that were evident prior to the Pearl Harbor attack were now inhibited by the constraints imposed by a nation at war, dwindling resources for sustained protest, and the patriotic response by blacks to the dangers faced by the United States.

YES

Richard M. Dalfiume

The "Forgotten Years" of the Negro Revolution

A recent president of the American Sociological Society addressed himself to a puzzling question about what we know as the Civil Rights Revolution: "Why did social scientists—and sociologists in particular—not foresee the explosion of collective action of Negro Americans toward full integration into American society?" He pointed out that "it is the vigor and urgency of the Negro demand that is new, not its direction or supporting ideas." Without arguing the point further, the lack of knowledge can be attributed to two groups—the ahistorical social scientists, and the historians who, until recently, have neglected modern Negro history.

The search for a "watershed" in recent Negro history ends at the years that comprised World War II, 1939–1945. James Baldwin has written of this period: "The treatment accorded the Negro during the Second World War marks, for me, a turning point in the Negro's relation to America. To put it briefly, and somewhat too simply, a certain hope died, a certain respect for white Americans faded." Writing during World War II, Gunnar Myrdal predicted that the war would act as a "stimulant" to Negro protest, and he felt that "There is bound to be a redefinition of the Negro's status in America as a result of this War." The Negro sociologist E. Franklin Frazier states that World War II marked the point where "The Negro was no longer willing to accept discrimination in employment and in housing without protest." Charles E. Silberman writes that the war was a "turning point" in American race relations, in which "the seeds of the protest movements of the 1950s and 1960s were sown." While a few writers have indicated the importance of these years in the recent Negro protest movement, the majority have failed to do so. Overlooking what went before, most recent books on the subject claim that a Negro "revolution" or "revolt" occurred in 1954, 1955, 1960, or 1963. Because of the neglect of the war period, these years of transition in American race relations comprise the "forgotten years" of the Negro revolution.

To understand how the American Negro reacted to World War II, it is necessary to have some idea of the discrimination he faced. The defense build-up begun by the United States in 1940 was welcomed by Negroes who were disproportionately represented among the unemployed. Employment discrimination

From *Journal of American History*, June 1968, pp. 90–94, 96–106. Copyright © 1968 by Organization of American Historians. Reprinted by permission of Oxford University Press Journals via the Copyright Clearance Center.

in the revived industries, however, was rampant. When Negroes sought jobs at aircraft factories where employers begged for workers, they were informed that "the Negro will be considered only as janitors and in other similar capacities. . . ." Government financed training programs to overcome the shortages of skilled workers discriminated against Negro trainees. When government agencies issued orders against such discrimination, they were ignored.

Increasing defense preparations also meant an expansion of the armed forces. Here, as in industry, however, Negroes faced restrictions. Black Americans were assigned a minimal role and rigidly segregated. In the navy, Negroes could enlist only in the all-Negro messman's branch. The marine and the air corps excluded Negroes entirely. In the army, black Americans were prevented from enlisting, except for a few vacancies in the four regular army Negro units that had been created shortly after the Civil War; and the strength of these had been reduced drastically in the 1920s and 1930s.

Although the most important bread-and-butter issue for Negroes in this period was employment discrimination, their position in the armed forces was an important symbol. If one could not participate fully in the defense of his country, he could not lay claim to the rights of a full-fledged citizen. The NAACP organ, the *Crisis*, expressed this idea in its demand for unrestricted participation in the armed forces: "this is no fight merely to wear a uniform. This is a struggle for status, a struggle to take democracy off of parchment and give it life." Herbert Garfinkel, a student of Negro protest during this period, points out that "in many respects, the discriminatory practices against Negroes which characterized the military programs . . . cut deeper into Negro feelings than did employment discrimination."

Added to the rebuffs from industry and the armed services were a hundred others. Negroes, anxious to contribute to the Red Cross blood program, were turned away. Despite the fact that white and Negro blood is the same biologically, it was deemed inadvisable "to collect and mix caucasian and Negro blood indiscriminately." When Negro citizens called upon the governor of Tennessee to appoint some black members to the state's draft boards, he told them: "This is a white man's country. . . . The Negro had nothing to do with the settling of America." At a time when the United States claimed to be the last bulwark of democracy in a war-torn world, the legislature of Mississippi passed a law requiring different textbooks for Negro schools: all references to voting, elections, and democracy were to be excluded from the black student's books.

The Negro's morale at the beginning of World War II is also partly explained by his experience in World War I. Black America had gone into that war with high morale, generated by the belief that the democratic slogans literally meant what they said. Most Negroes succumbed to the "close ranks" strategy announced by the crusading NAACP editor, W. E. B. Du Bois, who advocated subduing racial grievances in order to give full support to winning the war. But the image of a new democratic order was smashed by the race riots, lynchings, and continued rigid discrimination. The result was a mass trauma and a series of movements among Negroes in the 1920s which were characterized by a desire to withdraw from a white society which wanted little to do with them. When the war crisis of the 1940s came along, the bitter memories of World War I were recalled with the result that there was a built-in cynicism among Negroes toward the democratic slogans of the new war.

Nevertheless, Negroes were part of the general population being stimulated to come to the defense of democracy in the world. When they responded and attempted to do their share, they were turned away. The result was a widespread feeling of frustration and a general decline of the Negro's morale toward the war effort, as compared with the rest of American society. But paradoxically, the Negro's general morale was both low and high.

While the morale of the Negro, as an American, was low in regard to the war effort, the Negro, as a member of a minority group, had high morale in his heightened race consciousness and determination to fight for a better position in American society. The same slogans which caused the Negro to react cynically also served to emphasize the disparity between the creed and the practice of democracy as far as the Negro in America was concerned. Because of his position in society, the Negro reacted to the war both as an American and as a Negro. Discrimination against him had given rise to "a sickly, negative attitude toward national goals, but at the same time a vibrantly positive attitude toward racial aims and aspirations."

When war broke out in Europe in 1939, many black Americans tended to adopt an isolationist attitude. Those taking this position viewed the war as a "white man's war." George Schuyler, the iconoclastic columnist, was a typical spokesman for this view: "So far as the colored peoples of the earth are concerned," Schuyler wrote, "it is a toss-up between the 'democracies' and the dictatorships. . . . [W]hat is there to choose between the rule of the British in Africa and the rule of the Germans in Austria?" Another Negro columnist claimed that it was a blessing to have war so that whites could "mow one another down" rather than "have them quietly murder hundreds of thousands of Africans, East Indians and Chinese. . . ." This kind of isolationism took the form of anti-colonialism, particularly against the British. There was some sympathy for France, however, because of its more liberal treatment of black citizens.

Another spur to isolationist sentiment was the obvious hypocrisy of calling for the defense of democracy abroad while it was not a reality at home. The NAACP bitterly expressed this point:

> THE CRISIS is sorry for brutality, blood, and death among the peoples of Europe, just as we were sorry for China and Ethiopia. But the hysterical cries of the preachers of democracy for Europe leave us cold. We want democracy in Alabama and Arkansas, in Mississippi and Michigan, in the District of Columbia—*in the Senate of the United States.*

The editor of the Pittsburgh *Courier* proclaimed that Negroes had their "own war" at home "against oppression and exploitation from without and against disorganization and lack of confidence within"; and the Chicago *Defender* thought that "peace at home" should be the main concern of black Americans. . . .

Cynicism and hope existed side by side in the Negro mind. Cynicism was often the attitude expressed after some outrageous example of discrimination. After Pearl Harbor, however, a mixture of hope and certainty—great changes favorable to the Negro would result from the war and things would never be the same again—became the dominant attitude. Hope was evident in the growing realization that the war provided the Negro with an excellent opportunity to prick the conscience of white America. "What an opportunity the crisis has been . . . for one to persuade, embarrass, compel and shame our government and our nation . . . into a more enlightened attitude toward a tenth of its people!" the Pittsburgh *Courier* proclaimed. Certainty that a better life would result from the war was based on the belief that revolutionary forces had been released throughout the world. It was no longer a "white man's world," and the "myth of white invincibility" had been shattered for good.

There was a growing protest against the racial status quo by black Americans; this was evidenced by the reevaluation of segregation in all sections of the country. In the North there was self-criticism of past acceptance of certain forms of segregation. Southern Negroes became bolder in openly questioning the sacredness of segregation. In October 1942, a group of southern Negro leaders met in Durham, North Carolina, and issued a statement on race relations. In addition to endorsing the idea that the Negro should fight for democracy at home as well as abroad, these leaders called for complete equality for the Negro in American life. While recognizing the "strength and age" of the South's racial customs, the Durham meeting was "fundamentally opposed to the principle and practice of compulsory segregation in our American society." In addition, there were reports of deep discontent among southern Negro college students and evidence that political activity among the blacks of the South, particularly on the local level, was increasing.

The American Negro, stimulated by the democratic ideology of the war, was reexamining his position in American society. "It cannot be doubted that the spirit of American Negroes in all classes is different today from what it was a generation ago," Myrdal observed. Part of this new spirit was an increased militancy, a readiness to protest loud and strong against grievances. The crisis gave Negroes more reason and opportunity to protest. Representative of all of the trends of black thought and action—the cynicism, the hope, the heightened race consciousness, the militancy—was the March on Washington Movement (MOWM).

The general idea of exerting mass pressure upon the government to end defense discrimination did not originate with A. Philip Randolph's call for a march on Washington, D.C., in early 1941. Agitation for mass pressure had grown since the failure of a group of Negro leaders to gain any major concessions from President Franklin D. Roosevelt in September 1940. Various organizations, such as the NAACP, the Committee for Participation of Negroes in the National Defense, and the Allied Committees on National Defense, held mass protest meetings around the country in late 1940 and early 1941. The weeks passed and these efforts did not seem to have any appreciable impact on the government; Walter White, Randolph, and other Negro leaders could not even secure an appointment to see the President. "Bitterness grew at an alarming pace throughout the country," White recalled.

It remained, however, for Randolph to consolidate this protest. In January 1941, he wrote an article for the Negro press which pointed out the failure of committees and individuals to achieve action against defense discrimination. "Only power can effect the enforcement and adoption of a given policy," Randolph noted; and "Power is the active principle of only the organized masses, the masses united for a definite purpose." To focus the weight of the black masses, he suggested that 10,000 Negroes march on Washington, D.C., with the slogan: "We loyal Negro-American citizens demand the right to work and fight for our country."

This march appeal led to the formation of one of the most significant—though today almost forgotten—Negro protest movements. The MOWM pioneered what has become the common denominator of today's Negro revolt—"the spontaneous involvement of large masses of Negroes in a political protest." Furthermore, as August Meier and Elliott Rudwick have recently pointed out, the MOWM clearly foreshadowed "the goals, tactics, and strategy of the mid-twentieth-century civil rights movement." Whites were excluded purposely to make it an all-Negro movement; its main weapon was direct action on the part of the black masses. Furthermore, the MOWM took as its major concern the economic problems of urban slum-dwellers.

Randolph's tactic of mass pressure through a demonstration of black power struck a response among the Negro masses. The number to march on Washington on July 1, 1941, was increased to 50,000, and only Roosevelt's agreement to issue an executive order establishing a President's Committee on Fair Employment Practices led to a cancellation of the march. Negroes then, and scholars later, generally interpreted this as a great victory. But the magnitude of the victory is diminished when one examines the original MOWM demands: an executive order forbidding government contracts to be awarded to a firm which practiced discrimination in hiring, an executive order abolishing discrimination in government defense training courses, an executive order requiring the United States Employment Service to supply workers without regard to race, an executive order abolishing segregation in the armed forces, an executive order abolishing discrimination and segregation on account of race in all departments of the federal government, and a request from the President to Congress to pass a law forbidding benefits of the National Labor Relations Act to unions denying Negroes membership. Regardless of the extent of the success of the MOWM, however, it represented something different in black protest. Unlike the older Negro movements, the MOWM had captured the imagination of the masses.

Although overlooked by most recent writers on civil rights, a mass militancy became characterisitic of the American Negro in World War II. This was symbolized by the MOWM and was the reason for its wide appeal. Furthermore, older Negro organizations found themselves pushed into militant stands. For example, the NAACP underwent a tremendous growth in its membership and became representative of the Negro masses for the first time in its history. From 355 branches and a membership of 50,556 in 1940, the NAACP grew to 1,073 branches with a membership of slightly less than 450,000 in 1946. The editors of the Pittsburgh *Courier* recognized that a new spirit was present in black America. In the past, Negroes

> made the mistake of relying entirely upon the gratitude and sense of fair play of the American people. Now we are disillusioned. We have neither faith in promises, nor a high opinion of the integrity of the American people, where race is involved. Experience has taught us that we must rely primarily upon our own efforts. . . . That is why we protest, agitate, and demand that all forms of color prejudice be blotted out. . . .

By the time of the Japanese attack on Pearl Harbor, many in America, both inside and outside of the government, were worried over the state of Negro morale. There was fear that the Negro would be disloyal. The depth of white ignorance about the causes for the Negro's cynicism and low morale is obvious from the fact that the black press was blamed for the widespread discontent. The double victory attitude constantly displayed in Negro newspapers throughout the war, and supported by most black Americans, was considered as verging on disloyalty by most whites. White America, ignorant of the American Negroes' reaction to World War I, thought that black citizens should subdue their grievances for the duration.

During World War II, there was pressure upon the White House and the justice department from within the federal government to indict some Negro editors for sedition and interference with the war effort. President Roosevelt refused to sanction this, however. There was also an attempt to deny newsprint to the more militant Negro newspapers, but the President put an end to this when the matter was brought to his attention. The restriction of Negro newspapers from military installations became so widespread that the war department had to call a halt to this practice in 1943. These critics failed to realize that, although serving to unify black opinion, the Negro press simply reflected the Negro mind.

One of the most widely publicized attacks on the Negro press was made by the southern white liberal, Virginius Dabney, editor of the Richmond *Times Dispatch*. He charged that "extremist" Negro newspapers and Negro leaders were "demanding an overnight revolution in race relations," and as a consequence they were "stirring up interracial hate." Dabney concluded his indictment by warning that "it is a foregone conclusion that if an attempt is made forcibly to abolish segregation throughout the South, violence and bloodshed will result." The Negro press reacted vigorously to such charges. Admitting that there were "all-or-nothing" Negro leaders, the Norfolk *Journal and Guide* claimed they were created by the "nothing-at-all" attitude of whites. The Chicago *Defender* and Baltimore *Afro-American* took the position that they were only pointing out the shortcomings of American democracy, and this was certainly not disloyal. The NAACP and the Urban League claimed that it was patriotic for Negroes to protest against undemocratic practices, and those who sought to stifle this protest were the unpatriotic ones.

The Negro masses simply did not support a strategy of moderating their grievances for the duration of the war. After attending an Office of Facts and Figures conference for Negro leaders in March 1942, Roy Wilkins of the NAACP wrote:

> . . . it is a plain fact that no Negro leader with a constituency can face his members today and ask full support for the war in the light of the atmosphere the government has created. Some Negro educators who are responsible only to their boards or trustees might do so, but the heads of no organized groups would dare do so.

By 1942, the federal government began investigating Negro morale in order to find out what could be done to improve it. This project was undertaken by the Office of Facts and Figures and its successor, the Office of War Information. Surveys by these agencies indicated that the great amount of national publicity given the defense program only served to increase the Negro's awareness that he was not participating fully in that program. Black Americans found it increasingly difficult to reconcile their treatment with the announced war aims. Urban Negroes were the most resentful over defense discrimination, particularly against the treatment accorded black members of the armed forces. Never before had Negroes been so united behind a cause: the war had served to focus their attention on their unequal status in American society. Black Americans were almost unanimous in wanting a show of good intention from the federal government that changes would be made in the racial status quo.

The government's inclination to take steps to improve Negro morale, and the Negro's desire for change, were frustrated by the general attitude of white Americans. In 1942, after two years of militant agitation by Negroes, six out of ten white Americans felt that black Americans were satisfied with things the way they were and that Negroes were receiving all of the opportunities they deserved. More than half of all whites interviewed in the Northeast and West believed that there should be separate schools, separate restaurants, and separate neighborhoods for the races. A majority of whites in all parts of the country believed that the Negro would not be treated any better after the war than in 1942 and that the Negro's lesser role in society was due to his own shortcomings rather than anything the whites had done. The white opposition to racial change may have provided the rationale for governmental inactivity. Furthermore, the white obstinance must have added to the bitterness of black Americans.

Although few people recognized it, the war was working a revolution in American race relations. Sociologist Robert E. Park felt that the racial structure of society was "cracking," and the equilibrium reached after the Civil War seemed "to be under attack at a time and under conditions when it is particularly difficult to defend it." Sociologist Howard W. Odum wrote from the South that there was "an unmeasurable and unbridgeable distance between the white South and the reasonable expectation of the Negro." White southerners opposed to change in the racial mores sensed changes occurring among "their" Negroes, "Outsiders" from the North, Mrs. Franklin Roosevelt, and the Roosevelt Administration were all accused of attempting to undermine segregation under the pretense of wartime necessity.

Racial tensions were common in all sections of the country during the war. There were riots in 1943. Tensions were high because Negro Americans were challenging the status quo. When fourteen prominent Negroes, conservatives and liberals, southerners and northerners, were asked in 1944 what they thought the black American wanted, their responses were almost unanimous. Twelve of the fourteen said they thought that Negroes wanted full political equality, economic equality, equality of opportunity, and full social equality with the abolition of legal segregation. The war had stimulated the race consciousness and the desire for change among Negroes.

Most American Negroes and their leaders wanted the government to institute a revolutionary change in its race policy. Whereas the policy had been acquiescence in segregation since the end of Reconstruction, the government was now asked to set the example for the rest of the nation by supporting integration. This was the demand voiced by the great majority of the Negro leaders called together in March 1942 by the Office of Facts and Figures. *Crisis* magazine summarized the feelings of many black Americans: Negroes have "waited thus far in vain for some sharp and dramatic notice that this war is not to maintain the status quo here."

The White House, and it was not alone, failed to respond to the revolutionary changes occurring among the nation's largest minority. When the Fraternal Council of Negro Churches called upon President Roosevelt to end discrimination in the defense industries and armed forces, the position taken was that "it would be very bad to give encouragement beyond the point where actual results can be accomplished." Roosevelt did bestir himself over particularly outrageous incidents. When Roland Hayes, a noted Negro singer, was beaten and jailed in a Georgia town, the President dashed off a note to his attorney general: "Will you have someone go down and check up . . . and see if any law was violated. I suggest you send a northerner."

Roosevelt was not enthusiastic about major steps in the race relations field proposed by interested individuals within and without the government. In February 1942 Edwin R. Embree of the Julius Rosenwald Fund, acutely aware of the growing crisis in American race relations, urged Roosevelt to create a commission of experts on race relations to advise him on what steps the government should take to improve matters. FDR's answer to this proposal indicates that he felt race relations was one of the reform areas that had to be sacrificed for the present in order to prosecute the war. He thought such a commission was "premature" and that "we must start winning the war . . . before we do much general planning for the future." The President believed that "there is a danger of such long-range planning becoming projects of wide influence in escape from the realities of war. I am not convinced that we can be realists about the war and planners for the future at this critical time."

After the race riots of 1943, numerous proposals for a national committee on race relations were put forward; but FDR refused to change his position. Instead, the President simply appointed Jonathan Daniels to gather information from all government departments on current race tensions and what they were doing to combat them. This suggestion for what would eventually become a President's Committee on Civil Rights would have to wait until a President recognized that a revolution in race relations was occurring and that action by the government could no longer be put off. In the interim, many would share the shallow reasoning of Secretary of War Stimson that the cause of racial tension was "the deliberate effort . . . on the part of certain radical leaders of the colored race to use the war for obtaining . . . race equality and interracial marriages. . . ."

The hypocrisy and paradox involved in fighting a world war for the four freedoms and against aggression by an enemy preaching a master race ideology, while at the same time upholding racial segregation and white supremacy, were too obvious. The war crisis provided American Negroes with a unique opportunity to point out, for all to see, the difference between the American creed and practice. The democratic ideology and rhetoric with which the war was fought stimulated a sense of hope and certainty in black Americans that the old race structure was destroyed forever. In part, this confidence was also the result of the mass militancy and race consciousness that developed in these years. When the expected white acquiescence in a new racial order did not occur, the ground was prepared for the civil rights revolution of the 1950s and 1960s; the seeds were indeed sown in the World War II years.

Harvard Sitkoff

African American Militancy in the World War II South: Another Perspective

It is now commonplace to emphasize the Second World War as a watershed in the African American freedom struggle, as a time of mass black militancy, and as the direct precursor to the civil rights protest movement of the late 1950s and 1960s. Even most textbooks today dramatize the wartime bitterness of African American protests against racial discrimination in the defense industry and the military, and highlight the phenomenal growth of the National Association for the Advancement of Colored People and the beginnings of the Congress of Racial Equality, which practiced direct-action civil disobedience to desegregate places of public accommodation. They quote the sardonic statement, supposedly popular during the war, of a black man, just drafted, who seethed: "Write on my tombstone—Here lies a black man, killed fighting a yellow man, for the protection of a white man." The individual military experience of a Jackie Robinson or a Medgar Evers is portrayed as representative of the turning point for African Americans as a whole; and virtually all devote the lion's share of space on blacks in the war to A. Philip Randolph's March-on-Washington Movement. Commonly described as the foremost manifestation of wartime mass black militancy, and singularly credited with forcing a reluctant President Franklin Roosevelt to issue Executive Order 8802 banning racial discrimination in defense and government employment, the MOWM is invariably pictured as the forerunner of the later Black Freedom Struggle's tactics and strategy. Most accounts also assert that the African American press during World War II was militantly demanding in a way it had never before been, and that the black masses, who actively, aggressively, even violently confronted Jim Crow, were yet far more militant. The war years, in sum, are depicted as a time when mass militancy became characteristic of the African American, when blacks belligerently assaulted the racial status quo, and when this watershed in black consciousness and behavior ignited the Negro Revolution that would later blaze.

Perhaps. Maybe. It is comforting to think that the destructiveness of mass warfare can have redeeming virtues; it is good to have forebears to admire and emulate. But if by a watershed in militancy we mean a crucial turning point in the aggressiveness of black actions, a far greater combativeness than previously exhibited, then the evidence to prove this argument conclusively has yet to appear; and major questions concerning this interpretation remain unanswered. This is especially so concerning the South, particularly the rural South, where most African Americans continued to live during World War II. Total war did, of course, generate major ruptures and upheavals in American life. Japan's sudden attack on the U.S. Pacific fleet at Pearl Harbor on December 7, 1941, evoked a widespread wave of patriotism and national purpose. Few Americans, black or white, dissented from the war spirit, intensified by media publicity and government-orchestrated campaigns to rally 'round the flag. Support for the war effort placed a premium on loyalty and unity. Even those who wished to protest had to tread carefully.

The angry demonstrations by African Americans against racial discrimination in the defense industry and in the armed services, the flurry of petitions and protests, so common in 1940 and 1941, diminished after the United States entered the war, and received decreasing attention as the war dragged on. In fact, the most militant editorials in the Negro press, the virulent threats by African American protest leaders and protest organizations, the indignant portents of black disloyalty or of tepid support by blacks for the Allied cause, almost without exception came *before* Pearl Harbor, *before* the United States entered the war. Pre-war actions are not instances of *wartime* militancy.

Indeed, soon after the attack on Pearl Harbor, Edgar G. Brown, director of the National Negro Council [,] telegraphed President Roosevelt that all African Americans pledge 100 percent loyalty to the United States. The National Urban League promised total support for the war effort. The Southern Negro Youth Congress raised money for defense bonds, sponsored an Army Welfare Committee to establish a USO Center for Negroes, and created its own Youth V for Victory Committee. W. E. B. Du Bois and A. Philip Randolph spoke at "Victory Through Unity" conferences. Father Divine donated a hotel to the Navy, and Paul Robeson travelled to training camps to entertain the troops. Dr. Charles Drew, whose research made blood transfusions possible, proclaimed that the priority of all Americans, "whether black or white, is to get on with the winning of the war" despite the scientifically unwarranted decision of the Red Cross to segregate the blood of black and white donors. Joe Louis promised the entire profits of his next two fights to the Army and Navy relief funds. Langston Hughes wrote plays for the War Writers Board and jingles for the Treasury Department. Josh White sang "Are You Ready?" promising to batter the Japanese "ratter till his head gets flatter," and Doc Clayton sounded a call for revenge in his "Pearl Harbor Blues." African Americans working in Hollywood formed a Victory Committee, headed by Hattie McDaniel. Richard Wright, who had earlier denounced American involvement in the war, immediately offered his literary services to the government for "the national democratic cause," and African Americans in the Communist Party hierarchy sought to aid the war effort by ordering that the attacks on racism in the script for the Broadway play based on Wright's *Native Son* be toned down.

The first issues of the Negro press after Pearl Harbor proclaimed in banner headlines "Mr. President, Count on Us," and "The Black Tenth is Ready." Major newspapers that had once excoriated Du Bois for penning his First World War

"Close Ranks" editorial now repeated his very imagery to restate his plea that Negroes put aside their special grievances for the duration. The Norfolk *Journal and Guide* called upon African Americans to "close ranks and join with fervent patriotism in this battle for America." "The hour calls for a closing of ranks, for joining of hands, not for a widening of the racial gap" echoed the Chicago *Defender*. The California *Eagle* promised to shift its campaign from full citizenship rights to full citizenship duties. A study of twenty-four Negro newspapers in the first several months of the war found that only three harped on the grievances and complaints of African Americans; the other twenty-one stressed the necessity of racial cooperation to avenge Pearl Harbor and the common goal of both blacks and whites of defeating the United States' foreign enemies. Columnists who before the attack on Pearl Harbor had accentuated the similarities between Nazism and American racism, stressed their differences after Pearl Harbor; essayists who had trumpeted that the Black Yanks Are Not Coming changed their tune to the Need to Do Everything to Win the War. And the Negro Newspaper Publishers Association, at its first meeting after the entry of the United States into the war, unanimously pledged its unequivocal loyalty to the nation and to the president. . . .

Instead of militant protest, the dominant theme of African American organizations and journals during the Second World War was that patriotic duty and battlefield bravery would lead to the Negro's advancement. The notion that blacks would gain from the war, not as a gift of white goodwill but because the nation needed the loyalty and manpower of African Americans, had been sounded in every one of America's previous armed conflicts, and it continued to reverberate throughout World War II. "War may be hell for some," columnist Joseph Bibb exulted, "but it bids fair to open up the portals of heaven for us." Whites will respond positively to the needs of African Americans if Negroes do their part as 100 percent loyal Americans declared Lester Granger. In order for African Americans to benefit later they must fight for the United States now, "segregation and Jim Crowism to the contrary notwithstanding," announced the New York *Age*. Full participation in the defense of the nation, claimed the Baltimore *Afro-American*, is the path to eventual equality. And the NAACP declared the slogan for its mid-1942 convention to be "Victory is Vital to Minorities."

In this vein, African Americans took up the call of the Pittsburgh *Courier* for a "Double V" campaign. Originating with a letter to the editor from James G. Thompson of Wichita, Kansas, who sought to join the army "to take his place on the fighting front for the principles which he so dearly loved," the *Courier* urged blacks to "fight for the right to fight" because wartime performance would determine postwar status. Opposing the war effort, or sitting on the sidelines, argued the *Courier*, would be the worst possible course for blacks to follow. Rather than calling for a massive attack on the Jim Crow system, the *Courier* added, African-Americans must join in the defense of their country. "The more we put in," argued columnist J. A. Rogers, "the more we have a right to claim." That notion was re-stated in hundreds of ways, as the *Courier* and the Negro press overall harped on the necessity of African Americans serving fully and faithfully so that they could prove their patriotism and later gain concessions. With cause, the Socialist Workers Party denounced the Double V as "a cover for unqualified support of the war." Yet even a fight for the right to fight could be misunderstood, and the space devoted to the Double V in the *Courier* declined by half between April and August 1942. By the end of 1942 the Double V campaign had been wholly superceded by less ambiguous, more positive, declarations of African American patriotism; and the *Courier* would go on to urge black soldiers to "insist on combat duty." "The most significant achievement of the Negro press during this crisis, in our estimation," bragged African American publishers in 1944, "lies in the fact that the Negro newspapers have brought home to the Negro people of America that this is their war and not merely 'a white man's war.'"

However much the great majority of African Americans desired the end of racial discrimination and segregation in American life, only a minority thought that their fight for rights should take precedence over defeating Germany and Japan, and far fewer flirted with militant protests that might be considered harmful to the war effort. Thus A. Philip Randolph's March-on-Washington Movement, generally depicted as the epitome of mass black militancy during the war, truly held center-stage in the Negro community only for a few months in 1941, before American entry into the war, and then gradually withered away. Shunned as "unpatriotic" by many of the mainstream Negro organizations and newspapers that had earlier supported it, Randolph's group labored in vain to rebut accusations of employing the "most dangerous demagoguery on record" and of "Marching Against the War Effort." Polls in the Negro press during 1942. revealed a steady diminution of black support for a March on Washington to demand a redress of grievances. When Randolph called for mass marches on city halls in 1942, no blacks marched. When he called for a week of non-violent civil disobedience and non-cooperation to protest Jim Crow school and transportation systems in 1943, a poll indicated that more than 70 percent of African Americans opposed the campaign, and no blacks engaged in such activities. And when he called upon the masses to come to his "We Are Americans, Too!" conference in Chicago in the summer of 1943, virtually no blacks other than members of his Sleeping Car Porters union attended. By then, as Randolph admitted, the March-on-Washington Movement was "without funds." Unable to pay the rent for an office or for the services of an executive secretary, the organization existed only on paper.

Asa Philip Randolph's brief shining moment had passed quickly. The March-on-Washington Movement ended with Randolph having never led a wartime mass march or a civil disobedience campaign. When he described the program of his organization in Rayford Logan's *What the Negro Wants* (1944), Randolph barely discussed mass militant protests. Instead, most of his essay was devoted to attacking American Communists, to explaining why racial change in the South must be gradual and piecemeal, and to advocating race relations committees that would take the necessary measures to prevent or stop race riots. Quite at odds with the image of the wartime Randolph in most current accounts, his wartime agenda for the March-on-Washington Movement in fact differed tittle from that of the NAACP. Randolph, moreover, devoted the greatest amount of his time and energy during the war to criticizing discrimination within the American Federation of Labor and heading the National Council for a Permanent Fair Employment Practices Commission, a traditional legislative lobby which never advocated mobilizing the masses and which was controlled by an elite group of mainly white New York socialists and labor leaders. Penning the moribund March-on-Washington Movement's epitaph in 1945, Adam Clayton Powell, Jr., described it as an "organization with a name that it does not live up to, an announced program that it does not stick to, and a philosophy contrary to the mood of the times." Its former headquarters in Harlem had already been converted into a bookshop.

The Congress of Racial Equality suffered much the same fate as the March-on-Washington Movement during the war, but it did so in relative obscurity. The white media barely mentioned it, and the Negro press did so even less. A tiny interracial, primarily white, elite group of pacifist and socialist followers of A. J. Muste, CORE mainly engaged in efforts to counter discrimination in places of public accommodation and recreation in northern cities where those practices were already illegal. It did little to try to desegregate schools and housing, or to expand job opportunities for African Americans, or to influence civil rights legislation, and its wartime efforts proved negligible. Because its dozen or so local chapters took to heart the reconciliatory aspects of Gandhian non-violence, the vital importance of changing the consciousness of those engaged in racist practices, few of its Christian pacifist members went beyond negotiations to direct action in the streets. CORE's hopes of becoming a mass, broad-based movement lingered as only a dream during the war, and blacks at Howard University and in St. Louis who, independent of each other, thought they were inventing the sit-in in 1944, did not even know that CORE, too, sought to employ the tactics of the CIO's famous "sit-down" strikes to the fight against Jim Crow. Faced with public apathy, unstable chapters, and a budget of less than $100 a month for its national office, CORE did not even contemplate, entering the upper South until 1947, when eight blacks and eight whites decided to test the compliance with the Supreme Court's 1946 ruling in the Irene Morgan case, declaring segregation in interstate carriers unconstitutional. Even then, CORE would not try to establish a chapter in the South for another decade.

The NAACP, on the other hand, saw its membership grow from 50,556 and 355 branches in 1940 to over half a million and more than a thousand branches in 1946. Yet, it essentially remained middle-class in orientation and bureaucratic in structure, abhoring radical tactics and adhering to a legalistic approach that did not countenance collective action. This was especially so in the South, the site of three-quarters of the new wartime branches. None of the southern branches sanctioned confrontations, direct action, or extra-legal tactics. Ella Baker, who visited local chapters of the NAACP throughout the wartime South, first as an assistant field secretary of the Association and then as its national director of branches, never ceased hectoring the national office that most of those branches were little more than social clubs with no interest whatsoever in pursuing local protests. Thurgood Marshall also chafed at the reluctance of the southern branch officers to attack Jim Crow, and their tendency to devote themselves solely to teacher-salary equalization suits. Such suits "aroused little excitement, even in the Deep South," maintains George B. Tindall: "The tedious pace, the limited results, the manifest equity of the claim" muted white alarm. And that suited the NAACP's southern leadership of black academics, businessmen, and ministers just fine. The issue of inequitable salaries for Negro public school teachers would remain their top priority even in the immediate postwar years. The pursuit of traditional objectives by restrained tactics remained the hallmark of the Association in the South. As they had in the 1930s, the wartime southern branches lobbied and litigated against the poll tax, the white primary, and lynching, and requested a more equitable share of educational facilities and funds.

Continuity also characterized the work of the seven southern affiliates of the National Urban League. They held firm to their social work orientation and to their reliance on negotiations to expand employment, recreational, and housing opportunities for African Americans. Such matters as African American juvenile delinquency and family disorganization took precedence over the fight for equal rights. Their wariness toward demonstrations and protests reflected their fear of losing funding from the Community Chest and local philanthropies, their faith in being able to make progress by working in conventional channels, and their hostility toward the NAACP—which they viewed as a competitor for financial contributions. Confrontation and disruption, even harsh talk, did not fit the Urban League's pursuit of gradual and limited racial change. When Benjamin Bell, the newly appointed executive secretary of the Urban League in Memphis, angered white politicians and businessmen by denouncing Jim Crow, the national office quickly replaced him with someone more compliant.

Much as southern black leaders did not support direct action protests or forthright attacks on segregation during the war, the editorials of southern Negro newspapers rarely echoed the demands for racial equality of those in the North. Several African American newspapers in the South followed the wartime lead of the Savannah *Tribune in* discontinuing the practice of reprinting editorials from northern black newspapers. Most of the southern Negro press had never done so, and they continued, as did most southern black church and community leaders during the war, to stay on the sidelines of the civil rights struggle, to advocate upright behavior and individual economic advancement within the existing order, and to preach paternalism and "civility." Even when calling for "fair play" or an end to disfranchisement, they did so in a manner that posed no clear and present danger to white supremacy. Lest criticism be construed as unpatriotic, they accentuated African American loyalty and contributions to the war effort above all else. Surveying the Negro press in Mississippi during the war, Julius Thompson concluded: "Submission to the system was the watchword."

. . . African American Communists soft-pedaled their censure of racism in the United States during the war. Executing an about-face from the period of the Nazi-Soviet Pact, when they took the lead in exposing Jim Crow in the armed forces, the Communists opposed efforts by blacks to embarrass the military after Germany invaded the Soviet Union in June 1941. They even sought to prevent African American legal challenges against discrimination from coming before the courts. The party's wartime policy was to do nothing that might erode the unity necessary for prosecuting the war. Ben Davis vigorously denounced both the March-on-Washington Movement and the NAACP for placing the interests of blacks above the needs for "national unity, maximum war production, and the highest possible morale in the armed forces." Having opposed civil disobedience by blacks and mass protests against racism, and defended the military against its civil rights critics, Davis confessed after the war that he had "often lost sight of" the black liberation struggle. Communist leader and social scientist John Williamson later concurred. "Neglect of the problems of the Negro people," Williamson wrote, "and the cessation of organizing efforts in the South undoubtedly slowed the pace of the freedom movement which arose later.

As did most black Communists, Georgian Angelo Herndon and his *Negro Quarterly* followed Earl Browders wartime policy of refraining from public censure of Jim Crow. Its articles and editorials downplayed racial militancy, emphasized the need for patriotic unity, dispelled the "dangerous fallacy" that this is "a white man's war," and subordinated all racial issues to victory over fascist aggression. Similarly, chapters of the National Negro Congress metamorphosed into Negro Labor Victory Committees; Southern Negro Youth Congress cadre mainly worked within NAACP and CIO affiliates to promote victory abroad; and local party members in St. Louis hounded that city's March-on-Washington Movement and accused it of "disrupting the war effort" when it attempted to organize a demonstration to get more blacks jobs in defense plants. The response of the *Daily Worker* to the race riot in Detroit was to condemn the NAACP for making such a fuss and to urge everyone to get back to work quickly. . . .

With so many former allies in the fight for equal rights now counseling "go slow," most African American advocates of aggressive tactics to achieve fundamental racial change either trimmed their sails or foundered. Battling Hitler largely terminated the encouragement to black asseertiveness that had been supplied in the 1930s by the Communists, militant labor union activists, supportive progressive government officials, and by the beliefs and sympathies spurred by the reform liberalism of the Great Depression-New Deal era. During the 1930s, at least ten cities had experienced NAACP-supported school boycotts protesting segregation. To demand employment, African Americans, with the support of major community leadership, had mounted sustained campaigns of picketing and boycotting retail establishments in at least thirty-five cities, including Atlanta, Baltimore, Durham, Houston, Memphis, New Orleans, and Richmond. In Charlotte, Greensboro, and Norfolk, as well as in Chicago, Philadelphia, and New York, blacks had sat-in at relief bureaus, conducted rent strikes, and led mass hunger marches. They had engaged in direct action protests against racial discrimination at restaurants, hotels, beaches, and theaters in both the South and North. In comparison, there was only one boycott against school segregation during the war, in Hillburn, New York, and not another one in the South until 1951; there were just a handful of direct action protests against Jim Crow in public accommodations, primarily by the largely white CORE in Chicago and Denver; and there were no sustained boycotts or mass demonstrations against job discrimination in World War II. As Meier and Rudwick state, in the only study to enumerate African American protest activities: the Depression—not the war—is the "watershed in Afro-American direct action." Militant black activism in the Thirties "achieved a salience in black protest that would not be equalled or surpassed until the late 1950s and 1960s." Indeed, they conclude, there "was less actual use of direct action tactics during World War II than in the 1930s"; the number of protest "demonstrations declined sharply during World War II compared to the 1930s"; and, overall, "the amount of direct action was minor compared to the Depression era."

These facts do not in the least suggest that African Americans wanted equal rights any less in 1944 than in 1937; or that blacks during the war complacently accepted second-class status. Discontent is ever-present among those who are discriminated against and oppressed. Indeed, as has been amply described, the war against Hitlerism intensified the civil rights consciousness of the New Deal years, raised the expectations of blacks considerably, and had a significant impact on American racial opinions, especially in heightening perceptions of the discrepancy between the democratic ideals of the United States and its undemocratic racial practices. But compared to the Depression decade, and far more to the 1960s, blacks in World War II faced greater resistance to change, in a milieu less hospitable to disruptive protests, with reduced internal wherewithal and external support. The constraints imposed by a nation at war, the dwindling resources for sustained confrontation, and the genuinely patriotic response of most African Americans to the dangers their nation faced all inhibited militant protest activity. . . .

Militant protest never entirely abated during the war, but it never assumed dominance in either black strategy or action. To the extent that it is now possible to gauge the amount and strength of the rupture, or the transformation, in civil rights protest activities, World War II does not appear to be a watershed. Change, of course, occurred. But in a limited manner. The status and protest cognition of southern blacks in 1945, their organizations, leadership, language, and strategies for reform were neither exactly the same nor fundamentally different than they had been in 1940. The goals considered a distant dream in the 1930s had not suddenly appeared attainable. The traditional tactics of African American protest groups had not suddenly become unacceptable, nor had new, more disruptive ones come into widespread use. "Why? In part, because the nearly million young black men who might have been expected to be in the forefront of more militant forays against racist practices had been uprooted from their communities to serve in an armed forces which cramped organized protests. In part, because the optimism of African Americans for postwar progress, induced by the sudden prosperity of those who left mule and plow or domestic work for a job in a defense plant and by the din of democratic propaganda during the war, mitigated against a radical turn in practices. And, certainly in part, because wartime America proved an infertile ground for the seeds of protest planted in the 1930s. The needs of war came first. Period. The domestic unity, as well as manpower and production efficiency, required for victory took precedence over all else, for the Roosevelts, and for virtually every prominent African American, labor leader, white liberal, and progressive proponent of civil rights. And if that meant holding the color line, defusing conflicts, eschewing confrontation for compromise, well, the expected rewards for African Americans would come after the war. Furthermore, social, economic, and demographic alterations, no matter how vast or rapid, in and of themselves do not generate mass movements for social change by the aggrieved or oppressed. The resources for sustained mass confrontations with the Jim Crow system in the South were gestating but still embryonic, and the political climate that would facilitate rather than inhibit militant collective action had not yet emerged. The war had driven old Dixie downward, but not down and out.

The hopes of some, and dire warnings of others, "that a New Negro will return from the war," willing to fight and die rather than accept the traditional structure of white dominance in southern society, proved premature. Indeed, it appears that many of those southern African Americans most "modernized" by military service soon left the South in the greatest numbers to pursue their individual ambitions in northern cities, or re-enlisted in the armed forces, depleting the pool of potential southern black activists. The insurgent struggle for racial justice to come in the South would eventually draw sustenance from the many fundamental transformations in American life and world affairs catalyzed by the Second World War, but that mass movement would hardly be just an extension, a continuation, of previous civil rights reform efforts. Those militantly fighting for change in the 1960s would not look to the agenda and actions of World War II blacks and racial organizations as models to emulate.

EXPLORING THE ISSUE

Was the World War II Era a Watershed for the Civil Rights Movement?

Critical Thinking and Reflection

1. Discuss in detail the major complaints confronting African Americans in the World War II era.
2. Evaluate the success or failure of civil rights organizations in their efforts to improve the status of black Americans during the war.
3. Who was A. Philip Randolph, and how did he hope to advance the interests of African Americans during the war? How successful was he?
4. In what ways do Dalfiume and Sitkoff disagree in their assessment of black militancy in the period from 1939 to 1945?
5. Based on your reading of the YES and NO selections, was World War II a watershed event in the African American freedom struggle?

Is There Common Ground?

Although the Roosevelt administration demonstrated considerable reluctance in positively addressing the concerns of African Americans during the war, FDR's decision to issue Executive Order 8802, in response to the threat by A. Philip Randolph to stage a march on the nation's capital, did pave the way for a federal commitment to eliminate employment discrimination in the nation's defense industries and to end segregation in the armed forces. Absent this level of black militancy, it is difficult to imagine Roosevelt acting on his own initiative to address these concerns within the African American community. With Roosevelt's death in 1945, it remained for Harry Truman, surprisingly but forthrightly, to carry these commitments to the end of the war and beyond.

Dalfiume also is correct in pointing out that African Americans during the war developed goals, tactics, and strategies of protest that typically are associated with Dr. Martin Luther King, Jr., in the 1950s and 1960s. Despite the tendency to attribute the development of nonviolent direct action techniques to Dr. King, this strategy was derivative of techniques pioneered by Randolph and the Congress of Racial Equality (CORE) in the 1940s. Similarly, it is important to keep in mind the prominent role played by the NAACP and its leaders, especially Walter White and Roy Wilkins, not only in lobbying the Roosevelt administration on civil rights issues but also for conducting a legal action strategy that resulted in numerous Supreme Court civil rights victories, during the 1940s, in the areas of housing, public education, and political enfranchisement.

Finally, the positive impact on the civil rights movement is evident in the lives of many African American veterans who returned from fighting fascism abroad and launched their own attacks to erase the limitations to full freedom in their local communities. Among the most well known of these World War II veterans were Medgar and Charles Evers, Amzie Moore, Oliver Brown, Robert F. Williams, and Ralph Abernathy. In the lives of these individuals, we see a direct connection between World War II and the modern civil rights movement.

Additional Resources

The literature of the "long civil rights movement" is growing. Among the best are: Mark Robert Schneider, *"We Return Fighting": The Civil Rights Movement in the Jazz Age* (Northeastern University Press, 2002); Glenda Elizabeth Gilmore, *Defying Dixie: The Radical Roots of Civil Rights, 1919–1950* (W. W. Norton, 2008); Harvard Sitkoff, *A New Deal for Blacks: The Emergence of Civil Rights as a National Issue: The Depression Decade* (Oxford University Press, 1978); Patricia Sullivan, *Days of Hope: Race and Democracy in the New Deal Era* (University of North Carolina Press, 1996); and John Egerton, *Speak Now Against the Day: The Generation Before the Civil Rights Movement in the South* (University of North Carolina Press, 1994).

Harvard Sitkoff's views on this topic clearly have evolved over time. In "Racial Militancy and Interracial Violence in the Second World War," *Journal of American History* (vol. 58, December 1971, pp. 661–681), he offered corroboration for Dalfiume's earlier work. His transitioning ideas were being worked through in "American Blacks in World War II: Rethinking the Militancy-Watershed Hypothesis," in James Titus, ed., *The Home Front and War in the Twentieth Century* (U.S. Air Force Academy, 1984, pp. 147–156), and then culminated in the essay in this issue. The interpretational line presented by Sitkoff also is followed in the essays collected in Kevin M. Kruse and Stephen Tuck, eds., *Fog of War: The Second World War and the Civil Rights Movement* (Oxford University Press, 2012).

For African American veterans who became actively involved in the civil rights movement upon their return home, see Christopher S. Parker, *Fighting For Democracy: Black Veterans and the Struggle Against White Supremacy in the Postwar South* (Princeton University Press, 2009); John Dittmer, *Local People: The Struggle for Civil Rights in Mississippi* (University of Illinois Press, 1994), especially chapter 1 and 2; Timothy B. Tyson, *Robert F. Williams and the Roots of Black Power* (University of North Carolina Press, 1999); and Ralph David Abernathy, *And the Walls Came Tumbling Down: An Autobiography* (Harper & Row, 1989).

The World War II era as a fertile ground for civil rights activity is reinforced by a number of scholarly works. The NAACP's legal action campaign on several fronts is documented in Patricia Sullivan, *Lift Every Voice: The NAACP and the Making of the Civil Rights Movement* (The New Press, 2009), c.apter 7;

Mark V. Tushnet, *Making Civil Rights Law: Thurgood Marshall and the Supreme Court, 1936--1961* (Oxford University Press, 1994); Clement E. Vose, *Caucasians Only: The Supreme Court, the NAACP, and the Restrictive Covenant Cases* (University of California Press, 1967); and Darlene Clark Hine, *Black Victory: The Rise and Fall of the White Primary in Texas* (KTO Press, 1979). The best history of the Congress of racial equality is August Meier and Elliott Rudwick, *CORE: A Study in the Civil Rights Movement, 1942–1968* (Oxford University Press, 1973). For A. Philip Randolph protest activities in the 1940s, see Cornelius L. Bynum, *A. Philip Randolph and the Struggle for Civil Rights* (University of Illinois Press, 2010) and Herbert Garfinkel, *When Negroes March: The March On Washington Movement in the Organizational Politics for FEPC* (The Free Press, 1959).

ISSUE 12

Was It Necessary to Drop the Atomic Bomb to End World War II?

YES: Robert James Maddox, from "The Biggest Decision: Why We Had to Drop the Atomic Bomb," *American History* (May/June 1995)

NO: Tsuyoshi Hasegawa, from *Racing the Enemy: Stalin, Truman and the Surrender of Japan* (The Belknap Press of Harvard University Press, 2005)

Learning Outcomes

After reading this issue, you should be able to:

- Determine whether the atomic bomb was dropped for military or political reasons.
- Explain whether it was necessary to drop the atomic bomb in order to end the war against Japan.
- List three alternatives considered in place of dropping the atomic bomb. Explain why these alternatives were rejected.
- Consider whether the atomic bomb would have been dropped on Germany if the war in Europe was still going on, or were the allies willing to deploy the weapon only on a nonwhite nation.
- Critically examine whether Japan surrendered in response to the two atomic bombs, the Russian declaration of war, or both.

ISSUE SUMMARY

YES: Professor of American history Robert James Maddox contends that the atomic bomb became the catalyst that forced the hard-liners in the Japanese army to accept the emperor's plea to surrender, thus avoiding a costly, bloody invasion of the Japanese mainland.

NO: Professor of American history Tsuyoshi Hasegawa argues that the Soviet entrance into the war played a greater role in causing Japan to surrender than did the dropping of the atomic bombs.

America's development of the atomic bomb began in 1939 when a small group of scientists led by well-known physicist Albert Einstein called President Franklin D. Roosevelt's attention to the enormous potential uses of atomic energy for military purposes. In his letter, Einstein warned Roosevelt that Nazi Germany was already experimenting in this area. The program to develop the bomb, which began very modestly in October 1939, soon expanded into the $2 billion Manhattan Project, which combined the talents and energies of scientists (many of whom were Jewish refugees from Hitler's Nazi Germany) from universities and research laboratories across the country. The Manhattan Project was the beginning of the famed military–industrial–university complex that we take for granted today.

Part of the difficulty in reconstructing the decision to drop the atomic bomb lies in the rapidity with which events moved in the spring of 1945. On May 7, 1945, Germany surrendered. Almost a month earlier the world was stunned by the death of FDR, who was succeeded by Harry Truman, a former U.S. senator who was chosen as a compromise vice-presidential candidate in 1944. The man from Missouri had never been a confidant of Roosevelt. Truman did not even learn of the existence of the Manhattan Project until 12 days after he became president, at which time Secretary of War Henry L. Stimson advised him of a "highly secret matter" that would have a "decisive" effect upon America's postwar foreign policy.

Because Truman was unsure of his options for using the bomb, he approved Stimson's suggestion that a special committee of high-level political, military, and scientific policymakers be appointed to consider the major issues. The committee recommended unanimously that "the bomb should be used against Japan as soon as possible . . . against a military target surrounded by other buildings . . . without prior warning of the nature of the weapon."

A number of scientists disagreed with this report. They recommended that the weapon be tested on a deserted island in front of representatives of the United Nations and that an ultimatum be sent to Japan warning of the destructive power of the bomb. These young scientists suggested that the bomb be used if the Japanese would reject the warning, and only "if sanction of the United Nations (and of public opinion at home) was obtained."

A second scientific committee created by Stimson rejected both the test demonstration and warning alternatives. This panel believed that if the bomb failed to work during the demonstration, there would be political repercussions both at home and abroad.

Thus, by the middle of June 1945, the civilian leaders were unanimous that the atomic bomb should be used. During the Potsdam Conference in July, Truman learned that the bomb had been successfully tested in New Mexico. The big three—Truman, British Prime Minister Clement Atlee, and Joseph Stalin— issued a warning to Japan to surrender or suffer prompt and utter destruction. When the Japanese equivocated in their response, the United States replied by dropping an atomic bomb on Hiroshima on August 6, which killed 100,000 people. On August 8, Russia declared war on Japan, and a second bomb was dropped the following day leveling the city of Nagasaki. During this time, the emperor pleaded with the Japanese military to end the war. On August 14, the Japanese accepted the terms of surrender with the condition that the emperor not be treated as a war criminal.

Why atomic bombs were dropped has been subject to two different interpretations: an "official or "traditional" interpretation and a revisionist point of view. The "official" history defends the use of the atomic bombs against Japan. After some early doubts by some publicists and church leaders, the hardening Cold War with Russia after 1947 caused the decision makers to defend their policy. The atomic bombs were dropped for military reasons. It forced the Japanese to end the war quickly and saved both Japanese and American lives. In a much quoted article, "The Decision to Use the Atomic Bomb," *Harper's Magazine,* February 1947, former Secretary of Defense Henry L. Stimson asserted that the two proposed land invasions of Kyushu and Honshu might be expected to cost over a million casualties to American forces. Although the real military estimates for the invasions are disputed by historians today, Truman's ghost writers in his *Memoirs: Volume I, Year of Decisions* (Doubleday, 1955) estimated casualties at 500,000.

The official interpretation was basically unchallenged until the 1960s when a revisionist school emerged, which blamed the Americans rather than the Russians for the Cold War. In a series of articles and a published doctoral dissertation published as *Atomic Diplomacy: Hiroshima and Potsdam* (Simon and Schuster, 1965, rev. ed. 1985), Gar Alperovitz argued that President Truman reversed Roosevelt's policy of cooperation with our Russian allies, rejected alternatives such as a test demonstration, blockade, or a specific warning, and dropped the bombs to make the Russians more manageable in Eastern Europe. Not all historians, even revisionists, accepted Alperovitz's view of the bomb as a trump card against the Soviet Union. Critics argued that Alperovitz had too narrow a perspective and did not see the continuity in policy between the Roosevelt and Truman administrations. Alperovitz also was selective in his use of sources and quoted from participants whose memory was faulty or self-serving. He especially relied on the diary of Secretary of War Stimson, a 77-year-old career diplomat whom Truman respected but whose advice he rejected. Finally, Alperovitz made Truman appear to be more decisive in making decisions than he really was and characterized the Japanese government as united and willing to surrender if the Americans allowed the imperial dynasty to survive.

Most revisionists did not go so far as Alperovitz in arguing that the bombs were dropped primarily for political reasons. Moderate revisionists such as Barton J. Bernstein, who has written at least two dozen articles on the subject, accept the premise that although military objectives were important, there was a diplomatic "bonus" whereby sole possession of the bomb gave the United States military superiority over the Russians. This edge lasted until the fall of 1949 when the Russians successfully tested their own A-bomb.

The new orthodoxy among historians is a moderate revisionist interpretation of both military and political objectives, but general public opinion has not followed suit. When the Smithsonian Institute tried to host a historically balanced 50th anniversary exhibit of the events surrounding the A-bomb, a huge controversy developed. Under pressure from the Air Force Associated, the American Legion, and Congress, the original exhibit was canceled. Only the *Enola Gay,* the plane that dropped the first bomb on Hiroshima, was displayed with minimal comment. For a full-scale analysis of the controversy and the development of A-bomb historiography, see Barton J. Bernstein, "Afterward: The Struggle over History: Defining the Hiroshima Narrative," in Philip Nobile, ed., *Judgment at the Smithsonian* (Marlowe, 1995), and Michael J. Hogan, ed., *Hiroshima as History and Memory* (Cambridge University Press, 1996). See also Barton J. Bernstein, "The Atomic Bombings Reconsidered," *Foreign Affairs* (January/February 1995), where he argues that the distinction between civilian and military casualties became blurred with the saturation bombing of enemy targets in World War II.

Was it necessary to drop atomic bombs on Japan in order to end the war? Robert James Maddox, a long-time critic of Cold War revisionist history, argues that Truman believed that the use of the atomic bomb would shorten the war and save lives, particularly American ones. Maddox also asserts that the bombs at Hiroshima and Nagasaki allowed the emperor to plead successfully with army hard-liners to end the war. Maddox makes a compelling case for the military circumstances surrounding the decision to drop the atomic bomb on Japan. The Americans had suffered 50,000 casualties in the capture of the island of Okinawa in the spring of 1945. This was considered a preview of the impending invasion of Japan. Maddox points out that estimates of casualties were mere guesswork at a given time and that Army Chief of Staff George C. Marshall himself increased these numbers considerably when he realized that the Japanese were stationing hundreds of thousands of troops on their main islands. A long review essay by Donald Kagan on "Why America Dropped the Bomb," *Commentary* (September 1995) and "Letters from Readers" in the December 1995 issue thank Maddox and make similar points.

Professor Tsuyoshi Hasegawa casts the use of the atomic bomb in a wider setting. Based on his extensive research in Russian, Japanese, and American archives, he argues that Truman never seriously considered other options to dropping the bomb because he wanted to avenge the sneak attack at Pearl Harbor. Unlike most revisionists, however, Hasegawa is just as critical of the policies of the Russians and the Japanese. Stalin had his own expansionist aims. He was determined to recover the territories promised him at the Yalta Conference of February 1945 in exchange for his entrance into the Asian war once Germany was defeated. After the first bomb was dropped, Stalin rushed his entry into the Asian war by a week and proceeded to seize the Northern Sakhalin Islands, which was not part of the Yalta agreements. Hasegawa is also one of the few historians to seriously explore the Japanese decision-making process. Although most Japanese view the emperor as a hero who broke the deadlock between hard-liners and moderates in ending the war, Hasegawa views the emperor's intervention in the deadlock not as a "noble" decision to end the war, but simply as an attempt "to preserve the imperial house." Hasegawa's most controversial contention, however, is that Truman ordered deployment of atomic weapons to force Japan's surrender before the Soviet Union could further expand its military presence into Asia.

YES

Robert James Maddox

The Biggest Decision: Why We Had to Drop the Atomic Bomb

On the morning of August 6, 1945, the American B-29 Enola Gay dropped an atomic bomb on the Japanese city of Hiroshima. Three days later another B-29, *Bock's Car,* released one over Nagasaki. Both caused enormous casualties and physical destruction. These two cataclysmic events have preyed upon the American conscience ever since. The furor over the Smithsonian Institution's *Enola Gay* exhibit and over the mushroom-cloud postage stamp last autumn are merely the most obvious examples. Harry S. Truman and other officials claimed that the bombs caused Japan to surrender, thereby avoiding a bloody invasion. Critics have accused them of at best failing to explore alternatives, at worst of using the bombs primarily to make the Soviet Union "more manageable" rather than to defeat a Japan they knew already was on the verge of capitulation.

By any rational calculation Japan was a beaten nation by the summer of 1945. Conventional bombing had reduced many of its cities to rubble, blockade had strangled its importation of vitally needed materials, and its navy had sustained such heavy losses as to be powerless to interfere with the invasion everyone knew was coming. By late June advancing American forces had completed the conquest of Okinawa, which lay only 350 miles from the southernmost Japanese home island of Kyushu. They now stood poised for the final onslaught.

Rational calculations did not determine Japan's position. Although a peace faction within the government wished to end the war—provided certain conditions were met—militants were prepared to fight on regardless of consequences. They claimed to welcome an invasion of the home islands, promising to inflict such hideous casualties that the United States would retreat from its announced policy of unconditional surrender. The militarists held effective power over the government and were capable of defying the emperor, as they had in the past, on the ground that his civilian advisers were misleading him.

Maddox, Robert James. From *American Heritage,* May/June 1995, pp. 71–74, 76–77. Copyright © 1995 American Heritage, Inc. Reprinted by permission of American Heritage Publishing and the author.

Okinawa provided a preview of what invasion of the home islands would entail. Since April 1 the Japanese had fought with a ferocity that mocked any notion that their will to resist was eroding. They had inflicted nearly 50,000 casualties on the invaders, many resulting from the first large-scale use of kamikazes. They also had dispatched the superbattleship *Yamato* on a suicide mission to Okinawa, where, after attacking American ships offshore, it was to plunge ashore to become a huge, doomed steel fortress. *Yamato* was sunk shortly after leaving port, but its mission symbolized Japan's willingness to sacrifice everything in an apparently hopeless cause.

The Japanese could be expected to defend their sacred homeland with even greater fervor, and kamikazes flying at short range promised to be even more devastating than at Okinawa. The Japanese had more than 2,000,000 troops in the home islands, were training millions of irregulars, and for some time had been conserving aircraft that might have been used to protect Japanese cities against American bombers.

Reports from Tokyo indicated that Japan meant to fight the war to a finish. On June 8 an imperial conference adopted "The Fundamental Policy to Be Followed Henceforth in the Conduct of the War," which pledged to "prosecute the war to the bitter end in order to uphold the national polity, protect the imperial land, and accomplish the objectives for which we went to war." Truman had no reason to believe that the proclamation meant anything other than what it said.

Against this background, while fighting on Okinawa still continued, the President had his naval chief of staff, Adm. William D. Leahy, notify the Joint Chiefs of Staff (JCS) and the Secretaries of War and Navy that a meeting would be held at the White House on June 18. The night before the conference Truman wrote in his diary that "I have to decide Japanese strategy—shall we invade Japan proper or shall we bomb and blockade? That is my hardest decision to date. But I'll make it when I have all the facts."

⚬⟨❀⟩⚬

Truman met with the chiefs at three-thirty in the afternoon. Present were Army Chief of Staff Gen. George C. Marshall, Army Air Force's Gen. Ira C. Eaker (sitting in for the Army Air Force's chief of staff, Henry H. Arnold, who was on an inspection tour of installations in the Pacific), Navy Chief of Staff Adm. Ernest J. King, Leahy (also a member of the JCS), Secretary of the Navy James Forrestal, Secretary of War Henry L. Stimson, and Assistant Secretary of War John J. McCloy. Truman opened the meeting, then asked Marshall for his views. Marshall was the dominant figure on the JCS. He was Truman's most trusted military adviser, as he had been President Franklin D. Roosevelt's.

Marshall reported that the chiefs, supported by the Pacific commanders Gen. Douglas MacArthur and Adm. Chester W. Nimitz, agreed that an invasion of Kyushu "appears to be the least costly worthwhile operation following Okinawa." Lodgment in Kyushu, he said, was necessary to make blockade and bombardment more effective and to serve as a staging area for the invasion of Japan's main island of Honshu. The chiefs recommended a target date of November 1 for the first phase, code-named Olympic, because delay would give the Japanese more time to prepare and because bad weather might postpone the invasion "and hence the end of the war" for up to six months. Marshall said that in his opinion, Olympic was "the only course to pursue." The chiefs also proposed that Operation Cornet be launched against Honshu on March 1, 1946.

⚜

Leahy's memorandum calling the meeting had asked for casualty projections which that invasion might be expected to produce. Marshall stated that campaigns in the Pacific had been so diverse "it is considered wrong" to make total estimates. All he would say was that casualties during the first thirty days on Kyushu should not exceed those sustained in taking Luzon in the Philippines—31,000 men killed, wounded, or missing in action. "It is a grim fact," Marshall said, "that there is not an easy, bloodless way to victory in war." Leahy estimated a higher casualty rate similar to Okinawa, and King guessed somewhere in between.

King and Eaker, speaking for the Navy and the Army Air Forces respectively, endorsed Marshall's proposals. King said that he had become convinced that Kyushu was "the key to the success of any siege operations." He recommended that "we should do Kyushu now" and begin preparations for invading Honshu. Eaker "agreed completely" with Marshall. He said he had just received a message from Arnold also expressing "complete agreement." Air Force plans called for the use of forty groups of heavy bombers, which "could not be deployed without the use of airfields on Kyushu." Stimson and Forrestal concurred.

Truman summed up. He considered "the Kyushu plan all right from the military standpoint" and directed the chiefs to "go ahead with it." He said he "had hoped that there was a possibility of preventing an Okinawa from one end of Japan to the other," but "he was clear on the situation now" and was "quite sure" the chiefs should proceed with the plan. Just before the meeting adjourned, McCloy raised the possibility of avoiding an invasion by warning the Japanese that the United States would employ atomic weapons if there were no surrender. The ensuing discussion was inconclusive because the first test was a month away and no one could be sure the weapons would work.

In his memoirs Truman claimed that using atomic bombs prevented an invasion that would have cost 500,000 American lives. Other officials mentioned the same or even higher figures. Critics have assailed such statements as gross exaggerations designed to forestall scrutiny of Truman's real motives. They have given wide publicity to a report prepared by the Joint War Plans Committee (JWPC) for the chiefs' meeting with Truman. The committee estimated that the invasion of Kyushu, followed by that of Honshu, as the chiefs proposed, would cost approximately 40,000 dead, 150,000 wounded, and 3,500 missing in action for a total of 193,500 casualties.

That those responsible for a decision should exaggerate the consequences of alternatives is commonplace. Some who cite the JWPC report profess to see more sinister motives, insisting that such "low" casualty projections call into question the very idea that atomic bombs were used to avoid heavy losses. By discrediting that justification as a cover-up, they seek to bolster their contention that the bombs really were used to permit the employment of "atomic diplomacy" against the Soviet Union.

The notion that 193,500 anticipated casualties were too insignificant to have caused Truman to resort to atomic bombs might seem bizarre to anyone other than an academic, but let it pass. Those who have cited the JWPC report in countless op-ed pieces in newspapers and in magazine articles have created a myth by omitting key considerations: First, the report itself is studded with qualifications that casualties "are not subject to accurate estimate" and that the projection "is admittedly only an educated guess." Second, the figures never were conveyed to Truman. They were excised at high military echelons, which is why Marshall cited only estimates for the first thirty days on Kyushu. And indeed, subsequent Japanese troop buildups on Kyushu rendered the JWPC estimates totally irrelevant by the time the first atomic bomb was dropped.

e◈

Another myth that has attained wide attention is that at least several of Truman's top military advisers later informed him that using atomic bombs against Japan would be militarily unnecessary or immoral, or both. There is no persuasive evidence that any of them did so. None of the Joint Chiefs ever made such a claim, although one inventive author has tried to make it appear that Leahy did by braiding together several unrelated passages from the admiral's memoirs. Actually, two days after Hiroshima, Truman told aides that Leahy had "said up to the last that it wouldn't go off."

Neither MacArthur nor Nimitz ever communicated to Truman any change of mind about the need for invasion or expressed reservations about using the bombs. When first informed about their imminent use only days before Hiroshima, MacArthur responded with a lecture on the future of atomic warfare and even after Hiroshima strongly recommended that the invasion go forward. Nimitz, from whose jurisdiction the atomic strikes would be launched, was notified in early 1945. "This sounds fine," he told the courier, "but this is only February. Can't we get one sooner?" Nimitz later would join Air Force generals Carl D. Spaatz, Nathan Twining, and Curtis LeMay in recommending that a third bomb be dropped on Tokyo.

Only Dwight D. Eisenhower later claimed to have remonstrated against the use of the bomb. In his *Crusade in Europe,* published in 1948, he wrote that when Secretary Stimson informed him during the Potsdam Conference of plans to use the bomb, he replied that he hoped "we would never have to use such a thing against any enemy," because he did not want the United States to be the first to use such a weapon. He added, "My views were merely personal and immediate reactions; they were not based on any analysis of the subject."

Eisenhower's recollections grew more colorful as the years went on. A later account of his meeting with Stimson had it taking place at Ike's headquarters in Frankfurt on the very day news arrived of the successful atomic test in New Mexico. "We'd had a nice evening at headquarters in Germany," he remembered. Then, after dinner, "Stimson got this cable saying that the bomb had been perfected and was ready to be dropped. The cable was in code . . . 'the lamb is born' or some damn thing like that." In this version Eisenhower claimed to have protested vehemently that "the Japanese were ready to surrender and it wasn't necessary to hit them with that awful thing." "Well," Eisenhower concluded, "the old gentleman got furious."

The best that can be said about Eisenhower's memory is that it had become flawed by the passage of time. Stimson was in Potsdam and Eisenhower in Frankfurt on July 16, when word came of the successful test. Aside from a brief conversation at a flag-raising ceremony in Berlin on July 20, the only other time they met was at Ike's headquarters on July 27. By then orders already had been sent to the Pacific to use the bombs if Japan had not yet surrendered. Notes made by one of Stimson's aides indicate that there was a discussion of atomic bombs, but there is no mention of any protest on Eisenhower's part. Even if there had been, two factors must be kept in mind. Eisenhower had commanded Allied forces in Europe, and his opinion on how close Japan was to surrender would have carried no special weight. More important, Stimson left for home immediately after the meeting and could not have personally conveyed Ike's sentiments to the President, who did not return to Washington until after Hiroshima.

On July 8 the Combined Intelligence Committee submitted to the American and British Combined Chiefs of Staff a report entitled "Estimate of the Enemy Situation." The committee predicted that as Japan's position continued to deteriorate, it might "make a serious effort to use the USSR [then a neutral] as a mediator in ending the war." Tokyo also would put out "intermittent peace feelers" to "weaken the determination of the United Nations to fight to the bitter end, or to create inter-allied dissension." While the Japanese people would be willing to make large concessions to end the war, "For a surrender to be acceptable to the Japanese army, it would be necessary for the military leaders to believe that it would not entail discrediting warrior tradition and that it would permit the ultimate resurgence of a military Japan."

Small wonder that American officials remained unimpressed when Japan proceeded to do exactly what the committee predicted. On July 12 Japanese Foreign Minister Shigenori Togo instructed Ambassador Naotaki Sato in Moscow to inform the Soviets that the emperor wished to send a personal envoy, Prince Fuminaro Konoye, in an attempt "to restore peace with all possible speed." Although he realized Konoye could not reach Moscow before the Soviet leader Joseph Stalin and Foreign Minister V. M. Molotov left to attend a Big Three meeting scheduled to begin in Potsdam on the fifteenth, Togo sought to have negotiations begin as soon as they returned.

American officials had long since been able to read Japanese diplomatic traffic through a process known as the MAGIC intercepts. Army intelligence (G-2) prepared for General Marshall its interpretation of Togo's message the next day. The report listed several possible constructions, the most probable being that the Japanese "governing clique" was making a coordinated effort to "stave off defeat" through Soviet intervention and an "appeal to war weariness in the United States." The report added that Undersecretary of State Joseph C. Grew, who had spent ten years in Japan as ambassador, "agrees with these conclusions."

Some have claimed that Togo's overture to the Soviet Union, together with attempts by some minor Japanese officials in Switzerland and other neutral countries to get peace talks started through the Office of Strategic Services (OSS), constituted clear evidence that the Japanese were near surrender. Their sole prerequisite was retention of their sacred emperor, whose unique cultural/religious status within the Japanese polity they would not compromise. If only the United States had extended assurances about the emperor, according to this view, much bloodshed and the atomic bombs would have been unnecessary.

A careful reading of the MAGIC intercepts of subsequent exchanges between Togo and Sato provides no evidence that retention of the emperor was the sole obstacle to peace. What they show instead is that the Japanese Foreign Office was trying to cut a deal through the Soviet Union that would have permitted Japan to retain its political system and its prewar empire intact. Even the most lenient American official could not have countenanced such a settlement.

⋅◆⋅

Togo on July 17 informed Sato that "we are not asking the Russians' mediation in *anything like unconditional surrender* [emphasis added]." During the following weeks Sato pleaded with his superiors to abandon hope of Soviet intercession and to approach the United States directly to find out what peace terms would be offered. "There is . . . no alternative but immediate unconditional surrender," he cabled on July 31, and he bluntly informed Togo that "your way of looking at things and the actual situation in the Eastern Area may be seen to be absolutely contradictory." The Foreign Ministry ignored his pleas and continued to seek Soviet help even after Hiroshima.

"Peace feelers" by Japanese officials abroad seemed no more promising from the American point of view. Although several of the consular personnel and military attachés engaged in these activities claimed important connections at home, none produced verification. Had the Japanese government sought only an assurance about the emperor, all it had to do was grant one of these men authority to begin talks through the OSS. Its failure to do so led American officials to assume that those involved were either well-meaning individuals acting alone or that they were being orchestrated by Tokyo. Grew characterized such "peace feelers" as "familiar weapons of psychological warfare" designed to "divide the Allies."

Some American officials, such as Stimson and Grew, nonetheless wanted to signal the Japanese that they might retain the emperorship in the form of a constitutional monarchy. Such an assurance might remove the last stumbling block to surrender, if not when it was issued, then later. Only an imperial rescript would bring about an orderly surrender, they argued, without which Japanese forces would fight to the last man regardless of what the government in Tokyo did. Besides, the emperor could serve as a stabilizing factor during the transition to peacetime.

There were many arguments against an American initiative. Some opposed retaining such an undemocratic institution on principle and because they feared it might later serve as a rallying point for future militarism. Should that happen, as one assistant Secretary of State put it, "those lives already spent will have been sacrificed in vain, and lives will be lost again in the future." Japanese hard-liners were certain to exploit an overture as evidence that losses sustained at Okinawa had weakened American resolve and to argue that continued resistance would bring further concessions. Stalin, who earlier had told an American envoy that he favored abolishing the emperorship because the ineffectual Hirohito might be succeeded by "an energetic and vigorous figure who could cause trouble," was just as certain to interpret it as a treacherous effort to end the war before the Soviets could share in the spoils.

There were domestic considerations as well. Roosevelt had announced the unconditional surrender policy in early 1943, and it since had become a slogan of the war. He also had advocated that peoples everywhere should have the right to choose their own form of government, and Truman had publicly pledged to carry out his predecessor's legacies. For him to have formally *guaranteed* continuance of the emperorship, as opposed to merely accepting it on American terms pending free elections, as he later did, would have constituted a blatant repudiation of his own promises.

Nor was that all. Regardless of the emperor's actual role in Japanese aggression, which is still debated, much wartime propaganda had encouraged Americans to regard Hirohito as no less a war criminal than Adolf Hitler or Benito Mussolini. Although Truman said on several occasions that he had no objection to retaining the emperor, he understandably refused to make the first move. The ultimatum he issued from Potsdam on July 26 did not refer specifically to the emperorship. All it said was that occupation forces would be removed after "a peaceful and responsible" government had been established according to the "freely expressed will of the Japanese people." When the Japanese rejected the ultimatum rather than at last inquire whether they might retain the emperor, Truman permitted the plans for using the bombs to go forward.

Reliance on MAGIC intercepts and the "peace feelers" to gauge how near Japan was to surrender is misleading in any case. The army, not the Foreign Office, controlled the situation. Intercepts of Japanese military communications, designated ULTRA, provided no reason to believe the army was even considering surrender. Japanese Imperial Headquarters had correctly guessed that the next operation after Okinawa would be Kyushu and was making every effort to bolster its defenses there.

General Marshall reported on July 24 that there were "approximately 500,000 troops in Kyushu" and that more were on the way. ULTRA identified new units arriving almost daily. MacArthur's G-2 reported on July 29 that "this threatening development, if not checked, may grow to a point where we attack on a ratio of one (1) to one (1) which is not the recipe for victory." By the time the first atomic bomb fell, ULTRA indicated that there were 560,000 troops in southern Kyushu (the actual figure was closer to 900,000), and projections for November 1 placed the number at 680,000. A report, for medical purposes, of July 31 estimated that total battle and non-battle casualties might run as high as 394,859 *for the Kyushu operation alone.* This figure did not include those men expected to be killed outright, for obviously they would require no medical attention. Marshall regarded Japanese defenses as so formidable that even after Hiroshima he asked MacArthur to consider alternate landing sites and began contemplating the use of atomic bombs as tactical weapons to support the invasion.

The thirty-day casualty projection of 31,000 Marshall had given Truman at the June 18 strategy meeting had become meaningless. It had been based on the assumption that the Japanese had about 350,000 defenders in Kyushu and that naval and air interdiction would preclude significant reinforcement. But the Japanese buildup since that time meant that the defenders would have nearly twice the number of troops available by "X-day" than earlier assumed. The assertion that apprehensions about casualties are insufficient to explain Truman's use of the bombs, therefore, cannot be taken seriously. On the contrary, as Winston Churchill wrote after a conversation with him at Potsdam, Truman was tormented by "the terrible responsibilities that rested upon him in regard to the unlimited effusions of American blood."

Some historians have argued that while the first bomb *might* have been required to achieve Japanese surrender, dropping the second constituted a needless barbarism. The record shows otherwise. American officials believed more than one bomb would be necessary because they assumed Japanese hard-liners would minimize the first explosion or attempt to explain it away as some sort of natural catastrophe, precisely what they did. The Japanese minister of war, for instance, at first refused even to admit that the Hiroshima bomb was atomic. A few hours after Nagasaki he told the cabinet that "the Americans appeared to have one hundred atomic bomb . . . they could drop three per day. The next target might well be Tokyo."

Even after both bombs had fallen and Russia entered the war, Japanese militants insisted on such lenient peace terms that moderates knew there was no sense even transmitting them to the United States. Hirohito had to intervene personally on two occasions during the next few days to induce hard-liners to abandon their conditions and to accept the American stipulation that the emperor's authority "shall be subject to the Supreme Commander of the Allied Powers." That the militarists would have accepted such a settlement before the bombs is farfetched, to say the least.

Some writers have argued that the cumulative effects of battlefield defeats, conventional bombing, and naval blockade already had defeated Japan. Even without extending assurances about the emperor, all the United States had to do was wait. The most frequently cited basis for this contention is the *United States Strategic Bombing Survey,* published in 1946, which stated that Japan would have surrendered by November 1 "even if the atomic bombs had not been dropped, even if Russia had not entered the war, and even if no invasion had been planned or contemplated." Recent scholarship by the historian Robert P. Newman and others has demonstrated that the survey was "cooked" by those who prepared it to arrive at such a conclusion. No matter. This or any other document based on information available only after the war ended is irrelevant with regard to what Truman could have known at the time.

❦

What often goes unremarked is that when the bombs were dropped, fighting was still going on in the Philippines, China, and elsewhere. Every day that the war continued thousands of prisoners of war had to live and die in abysmal conditions, and there were rumors that the Japanese intended to slaughter them if the homeland was invaded. Truman was Commander in Chief of the American armed forces, and he had a duty to the men under his command not shared by those sitting in moral judgment decades later. Available evidence points to the conclusion that he acted for the reason he said he did: to end a bloody war that would have become far bloodier had invasion proved necessary. One can only imagine what would have happened if tens of thousands of American boys had died or been wounded on Japanese soil and then it had become known that Truman had chosen not to use weapons that might have ended the war months sooner.

 **NO**

Racing the Enemy: Stalin, Truman and the Surrender of Japan

Assessing the Roads Not Taken

The end of the Pacific War was marked by the intense drama of two races: the first between Stalin and Truman to see who could force Japan to surrender and on what terms; and the second between the peace party and the war party in Japan on the question of whether to end the war and on what conditions. To the very end, the two races were inextricably linked. But what if things had been different? Would the outcome have changed if the key players had taken alternative paths? Below I explore some counterfactual suppositions to shed light on major issues that determined the outcome of the war.

What if Truman had accepted a provision in the Potsdam ultimatum allowing the Japanese to retain a constitutional monarchy? This alternative was supported by Stimson, Grew, Forrestal, Leahy, McCloy and possibly Marshall. Churchill also favored this provision, and it was part of Stimson's original draft of the Potsdam Proclamation. Undoubtedly, a promise to retain the monarchy would have strengthened the peace party's receptivity of the Potsdam ultimatum. It would have led to intense discussion much earlier among Japanese policymakers on whether or not to accept the Potsdam terms, and it would have considerably diminished Japan's reliance on Moscow's mediation.

Nevertheless, the inclusion of this provision would not have immediately led to Japan's surrender, since those who adhered to the mythical notion of the *kokutai* would have strenuously opposed the acceptance of the Potsdam terms, even if it meant the preservation of the monarchy. Certainly, the three war hawks in the Big Six would have objected on the grounds that the Potsdam Proclamation would spell the end of the armed forces. But peace advocates could have accused the war party of endangering the future of the imperial house by insisting on additional conditions. Thus, the inclusion of this provision would have hastened Japan's surrender, though it is doubtful that Japan would have capitulated before the atomic bomb was dropped on Hiroshima and the Soviet Union entered the war. The possibility of accepting the Potsdam terms might have been raised immediately after the atomic bombing on

Hasegawa, Tsuyoshi. From *Racing the Enemy: Stalin, Truman, and the Surrender of Japan* (Belnap Press, 2005), pp. 290–303. Copyright © 2005 by The President and Fellows of Harvard College. Reprinted by permission of The Belnap Press of Harvard University Press.

Hiroshima. This provision might have tipped the balance in favor of the peace party after the Soviet invasion, thus speeding up the termination of the war.

Why, then, didn't Truman accept this provision? One explanation was that he was concerned with how the public would react to a policy of appeasement. Domestic public opinion polls indicated an overwhelmingly negative sentiment against the emperor, and inevitably Archibald McLeish, Dean Acheson, and others would have raised strident voices of protest. Byrnes had warned that a compromise with the emperor would lead to the crucifixion of the president.

But would it have? Although public opinion polls were overwhelmingly against the emperor, newspaper commentaries were evenly split between those who advocated the abolition of the emperor system and those who argued that the preservation of the monarchical system could be compatible with eradication of Japanese militarism. Truman could have justified his decision on two powerful grounds. First, he could have argued that ending the war earlier would save the lives of American soldiers. Second, he could have explained that this decision was necessary to prevent Soviet expansion in Asia, though he would have had to present this argument carefully so as not to provoke a strong reaction from the Soviet Union.

Truman's refusal to include this provision was motivated not only by his concern with domestic repercussions but also by his own deep conviction that America should avenge the humiliation of Pearl Harbor. Anything short of unconditional surrender was not acceptable to Truman. The buck indeed stopped at the president. Thus, as long as Truman firmly held to his conviction, this counterfactual supposition was not a real alternative.

But the story does not end here. Another important, hidden reason motivated Truman's decision not to include this provision. Truman knew that the unconditional surrender demand without any promise to preserve a constitutional monarchy would be rejected by the Japanese. He needed Japan's refusal to justify the use of the atomic bomb. Thus so long as he was committed to using the atomic bomb, he could not include the provision promising a constitutional monarchy.

What if Truman had asked Stalin to sign the Potsdam Proclamation without a promise of constitutional monarchy? In this case, Japanese policymakers would have realized that their last hope to terminate the war through Moscow's mediation was dashed. They would have been forced to confront squarely the issue of whether to accept the Potsdam surrender terms. The ambiguity of the emperor's position, however, still remained, and therefore the division among policymakers was inevitable, making it likely that neither the cabinet nor the Big Six would have been able to resolve the differences.

Japan's delay in giving the Allies a definite reply would surely have led to the dropping of the atomic bombs and Soviet participation in the war. Would Japan have surrendered after the first atomic bomb? The absence of a promise to preserve the monarchical system in the Potsdam terms would have prevented the peace party, including Hirohito and Kido, from acting decisively to accept surrender. Ultimately, the Soviet invasion of Manchuria would still have provided the coup de grace.

What if Truman had invited Stalin to sign the Potsdam Proclamation and included the promise to allow the Japanese to maintain a constitutional monarchy? This would have forced Japanese policymakers to confront the issue of whether to accept the Potsdam terms. Undoubtedly, the army would have insisted, if not on the continuation of the war, at least on attaching three additional conditions to the Potsdam Proclamation in order to ensure its own survival. But the promise of preserving the monarchical system might have prompted members of the peace party to intercede to end the war before the first atomic bomb, although there is no guarantee that their argument would have silenced the war party. The most crucial issue here is how the emperor would have reacted to the Potsdam terms had they contained the promise of a constitutional monarchy and been signed by Stalin in addition to Truman, Churchill, and Chiang Kai-shek. Undoubtedly, he would have been more disposed to the Potsdam terms, but the promise of a constitutional monarchy alone might not have induced the emperor to hasten to accept the ultimatum. A shock was needed. It is difficult to say if the Hiroshima bomb alone was sufficient, or whether the combination of the Hiroshima bomb and Soviet entry into the war was needed to convince the emperor to accept surrender. Either way, surrender would have come earlier than it did, thus shortening the war by several days.

Nevertheless, these counterfactual suppositions were not in the realm of possibility, since Truman and Byrnes would never have accepted them, for the reasons stated in the first counterfactual. The atomic bomb provided them with the solution to previously unsolvable dilemmas. Once the solution was found to square the circle, Truman and Byrnes never deviated from their objectives. An alternative was available, but they chose not to take it.

This counterfactual was dubious for another reason. If Stalin had been asked to join the ultimatum, he would never have agreed to promise a constitutional monarchy. Stalin's most important objective in the Pacific War was to join the conflict. The promise of a constitutional monarchy might have hastened Japan's surrender before the Soviet tanks crossed the Manchurian borders— a disaster he would have avoided at all costs. This was why Stalin's own version of the joint ultimatum included the unconditional surrender demand. Had Stalin been invited to join the ultimatum that included the provision allowing Japan to retain a constitutional monarchy, he would have fought tooth and nail to scratch that provision. Ironically, both Stalin and Truman had vested interests in keeping unconditional surrender for different reasons.

What if Hiranuma had not made an amendment at the imperial conference on August 10, and the Japanese government had proposed accepting the Potsdam Proclamation "with the understanding that it did not include any demand for a change in the status of the emperor under the national law"? Hiranuma's amendment was an egregious mistake. Although the three war hawks in the Big Six attached three additional conditions to acceptance, they lacked the intellectual acumen to connect their misgivings to the fundamental core of the *kokutai* debate. Without Hiranuma's amendment the emperor would have supported the one-conditional acceptance of the Potsdam terms as formulated at the first imperial conference; this condition was compatible, albeit narrowly, with a constitutional monarchy that Stimson, Leahy, Forrestal, and Grew would have accepted. If we believe Ballantine, Byrnes and Truman might have accepted the provision. But Hiranuma's amendment made it impossible for the American policymakers to accept this condition without compromising the fundamental objectives of the war.

On the other hand, given Truman's deep feelings against the emperor, even the original one condition—retention of the emperor's status in the national laws—or even the Foreign Ministry's original formula (the preservation of the imperial house) might have been rejected by Truman and Byrnes. Nevertheless, either formula might have been accepted by Grew, Dooman, and Ballantine, and would have strengthened the position advocated by Stimson, Leahy, Forrestal, and McCloy that Japan's first reply should be accepted.

What if the Byrnes Note had contained a clear indication that the United States would allow the Japanese to retain a constitutional monarchy with the current dynasty? The rejection of Japan's conditional acceptance of the Potsdam terms as amended by Hiranuma was not incompatible with the promise of a constitutional monarchy. The lack of this promise triggered the war party's backlash and endangered the peace parry's chances of ending the war early. Had the Byrnes Note included the guarantee of a constitutional monarchy under the current dynasty, Suzuki would not have temporarily defected to the war party, and Yonai would not have remained silent on August 12. War advocates would have opposed the Byrnes Note as incompatible with the *kokutai*. Nevertheless, a promise to preserve the monarchy would have taken the wind out of their sails, especially, given that the emperor would have more actively intervened for the acceptance of the Byrnes Note. Stalin would have opposed the Byrnes Note if it included the provision for a constitutional monarchy, but Truman was prepared to attain Japan's surrender without the Soviet Union anyway. This scenario thus might have resulted in Japan's surrender on August 12 or 13 instead of August 14.

Without the atomic bombs and without the Soviet entry into the war, would Japan have surrendered before November 1, the day Operation Olympic was scheduled to begin? The *United States Strategic Bombing Survey,* published in 1946, concluded that Japan would have surrendered before November 1 without the atomic bombs and without Soviet entry into the war. This conclusion has become the foundation on which revisionist historians have constructed their argument that the atomic bombs were not necessary for Japan's surrender. Since Barton Bernstein has persuasively demonstrated in his critique of the *Survey* that its conclusion is not supported by its own evidence, I need not dwell on this supposition. The main objective of the study's principal author, Paul Nitze, was to prove that conventional bombings, coupled with the naval blockade, would have induced Japan to surrender before November 1. But Nitze's conclusion was repeatedly contradicted by the evidence provided in the *Survey* itself. For instance, to the question, "How much longer do you think the war might have continued had the atomic bomb not been dropped?" Prince Konoe answered: "Probably it would have lasted all this year." Bernstein introduced numerous other testimonies by Toyoda, Kido, Suzuki, Hiranuma, Sakomizu, and others to contradict the *Survey's* conclusion. As Bernstein asserts, the *Survey* is "an unreliable guide."

The Japanese leaders knew that Japan was losing the war. But defeat and surrender are not synonymous. Surrender is a political act. Without the twin shocks of the atomic bombs and Soviet entry into the war, the Japanese would never have accepted surrender in August.

Would Japan have surrendered before November 1 on the basis of Soviet entry alone, without the atomic bomb? Japanese historian Asada Sadao contends that without the atomic bombs but with Soviet entry into the war, "there was a possibility that Japan would not have surrendered before November 1." To Asada the shock value was crucial. Whereas the Japanese anticipated Soviet entry into the war, Asada argues, the atomic bombs came as a complete shock. By contrast, Bernstein states: "In view of the great impact of Soviet entry . . . in a situation of heavy conventional bombing and a strangling blockade, it does seem quite probable—indeed, far more likely than not—that Japan would have surrendered before November without the use of the A-bomb but after Soviet intervention in the war. In that sense . . . there may have been a serious 'missed opportunity' in 1945 to avoid the costly invasion of Kyushu without dropping the atomic bomb by awaiting Soviet entry."

The importance to Japan of Soviet neutrality is crucial in this context. Japan relied on Soviet neutrality both militarily and diplomatically. Diplomatically, Japan pinned its last hope on Moscow's mediation for the termination of the war. Once the Soviets entered the war, Japan was forced to make a decision on the Potsdam terms. Militarily as well, Japan's Ketsu-go strategy was predicated on Soviet neutrality; indeed, it was for this reason that the Military Affairs Bureau of the Army Ministry constantly overruled the intelligence section's warning that a Soviet invasion might be imminent. Manchuria was not written off, as Asada claims; rather, the military was confident that Japan could keep the Soviets neutral, at least for a while. When the Soviets invaded Manchuria, the military was taken by complete surprise. Despite the bravado that the war must continue, the Soviet invasion undermined the confidence of the army, punching a fatal hole in its strategic plan. The military's insistence on the continuation of war lost its rationale.

More important, however, were the political implications of the Soviet expansion in the Far East. Without Japan's surrender, it is reasonable to assume that the Soviets would have completed the occupation of Manchuria, southern Sakhalin, the entire Kurils, and possibly half of Korea by the beginning of September. Inevitably, the Soviet invasion of Hokkaido would have been raised as a pressing issue to be settled between the United States and the Soviet Union. The United States might have resisted the Soviet operation against Hokkaido, but given the Soviets' military strength, and given the enormous casualty figures the American high command had estimated for Olympic, the United States might have conceded the division of Hokkaido as Stalin had envisaged. Even if the United States succeeded in resisting Stalin's pressure, Soviet military conquests in the rest of the Far East might have led Truman to concede some degree of Soviet participation in Japan's postwar occupation. Whatever the United States might or might not have done regarding the Soviet operation in Hokkaido or the postwar occupation of Japan, Japanese leaders were well aware of the danger of allowing Soviet expansion to continue beyond Manchuria, Korea, Sakhalin, and the Kurils. It was for this reason that the Japanese policymakers came together at the last moment to surrender under the Potsdam terms, that the military's insistence on continuing the war collapsed, and that the military accepted surrender relatively easily. Japan's decision to surrender was above all a political decision, not a military one. Therefore, even without the atomic bombs, the war most likely would have ended shortly after Soviet entry into the war—before November 1.

Would Japan have surrendered before November 1 on the basis of the atomic bomb alone, without the Soviet entry into the war? The two bombs alone would most likely not have prompted the Japanese, to surrender, so long as they still had hope that Moscow would mediate peace. The Hiroshima bombing did not significantly change Japan's policy, though it did inject a sense of urgency into the peace party's initiative to end the war. Without the Soviet entry into the war, it is not likely that the Nagasaki bomb would have changed the situation. Anami's warning that the United States might have 100 atomic bombs and that the next target might be Tokyo had no discernible impact on the debate. Even after the Nagasaki bomb, Japan would most likely have still waited for Moscow's answer to the Konoe mission.

The most likely scenario would have been that while waiting for the answer from Moscow, Japan would have been shocked by the Soviet invasion in Manchuria sometime in the middle of August, and would have sued for peace on the Potsdam terms. In this case, then, we would have debated endlessly whether the two atomic bombs preceding the Soviet invasion or the Soviet entry would have had a more decisive impact on Japan's decision to surrender, although in this case, too, clearly Soviet entry would have had a more decisive impact.

Richard Frank, who argues that the atomic bombings had a greater impact on Japan's decision to surrender than Soviet involvement in the war, relies exclusively on contemporary sources and discounts postwar testimonies. He emphasizes especially the importance of Hirohito's statement at the first imperial conference, the Imperial Rescript on August 15, and Suzuki's statements made during cabinet meetings. This methodology, though admirable, does not support Frank's conclusion. Hirohito's reference to the atomic bomb at the imperial conference comes from Takeshita's diary, which must be based on hearsay. None of the participants who actually attended the imperial conference remembers the emperor's referring to the atomic bomb. The Imperial Rescript on August 15 does refer to the use of the "cruel new bomb" as one of the reasons for the termination of the war, with no mention of Soviet entry into the war. But during his meeting with the three marshals on August 14, the emperor referred to both the atomic bomb and Soviet entry into the war as the decisive reasons for ending the war. Moreover, the Imperial Rescript to the Soldiers and Officers issued on August 17 refers to Soviet entry as the major reason for ending the war and makes no reference to the atomic bomb. In contemporary records from August 6 to August 15 two sources (the Imperial Rescript on August 15 and Suzuki's statement at the August 13 cabinet meeting) refer only to the impact of the atomic bomb, three sources only to Soviet entry (Konoe on August 9, Suzuki's statement to his doctor on August 13, and the Imperial Rescript to Soldiers and Officers on August 17), and seven sources both to the atomic bomb and Soviet involvement. Contemporary evidence does not support Frank's contention.

Without Soviet participation in the war in the middle of August, the United States would have faced the question of whether to use the third bomb sometime after August 19, and then the fourth bomb in the beginning of September, most likely on Kokura and Niigata. It is hard to say how many atomic bombs it would have taken to convince Japanese policymakers to abandon their approach to Moscow. It is possible to argue, though impossible to prove, that the Japanese military would still have argued for the continuation of the war after a third or even a fourth bomb.

Could Japan have withstood the attacks of seven atomic bombs before November 1? Would Truman and Stimson have had the resolve to use seven atomic bombs in succession? What would have been the impact of these bombs on Japanese public opinion? Would the continued use of the bombs have solidified or eroded the resolve of the Japanese to fight on? Would it have hopelessly alienated the Japanese from the United States to the point that it would be difficult to impose the American occupation on Japan? Would it have encouraged the Japanese to welcome the Soviet occupation instead? These are the questions we cannot answer with certainty.

On the basis of available evidence, however, it is clear that the two atomic bombs on Hiroshima and Nagasaki alone were nor decisive in inducing Japan to surrender. Despite their destructive power, the atomic bombs were not sufficient to change the direction of Japanese diplomacy. The Soviet invasion was. Without the Soviet entry into the war, the Japanese would have continued to fight until numerous atomic bombs, a successful allied invasion of the home islands, or continued aerial bombardments, combined with a naval blockade, rendered them incapable of doing so.

Legacies

The Bomb in American Memory

After the war was over, each nation began constructing its own story about how the war ended. Americans still cling to the myth that the atomic bombs dropped on Hiroshima and Nagasaki provided the knockout punch to the Japanese government. The decision to use the bomb saved not only American soldiers but also the Japanese, according to this narrative. The myth serves to justify Truman's decision and ease the collective American conscience. To this extent, it is important to American national identity. But as this book demonstrates, this myth cannot be supported by historical facts. Evidence makes clear that there were alternatives to the use of the bomb, alternatives that the Truman administration for reasons of its own declined to pursue. And it is here, in the evidence of roads not taken, that the question of moral responsibility comes to the fore. Until his death, Truman continually came back to this question and repeatedly justified his decision, inventing a fiction that he himself later came to believe. That he spoke so often to justify his actions shows how much his decision to use the bomb haunted him.

On August 10 the Japanese government sent a letter of protest through the Swiss legation to the United States government. This letter declared the American use of the atomic bombs to be a violation of Articles 22 and 23 of the Hague Convention Respecting the Laws and Customs of War on Land, which prohibited the use of cruel weapons. It declared "in the name of the Japanese Imperial Government as well as in the name of humanity and civilization" that "the use of the atomic bombs, which surpass the indiscriminate cruelty of any other existing weapons and projectiles," was a crime against humanity, and demanded that "the further use of such inhumane weapons be immediately ceased." Needless to say, Truman did not respond to this letter. After Japan accepted the American occupation and became an important ally of the United States, the Japanese government has never raised any protest about the American use of the atomic bombs. The August 10 letter remains the only, and now forgotten, protest lodged by the Japanese government against the use of the atomic bomb.

To be sure, the Japanese government was guilty of its own atrocities in violation of the laws governing the conduct of war. The Nanking Massacre of 1937, biological experiments conducted by the infamous Unit 731, the Bataan March, and the numerous instances of cruel treatment of POWs represent only a few examples of Japanese atrocities. Nevertheless, the moral lapses of the Japanese do not excuse those of the United States and the Allies. After all, morality by definition is an absolute rather than a relative standard. The forgotten letter that the Japanese government sent to the United States government on August 10 deserves serious consideration. Justifying Hiroshima and Nagasaki by making a historically unsustainable argument that the atomic bombs ended the war is no longer tenable. Our self-image as Americans is tested by how we can come to terms with the decision to drop the bomb. Although much of what revisionist historians argue is faulty and based on tendentious use of sources, they nonetheless deserve credit for raising an important moral issue that challenges the standard American narrative of Hiroshima and Nagasaki.

The Stalinist Past

Soviet historians, and patriotic Russian historians after the collapse of the Soviet Union, justify the Soviet violation of the Neutrality Pact by arguing that it brought the Pacific War to a close, thus ending the suffering of the oppressed people of Asia and the useless sacrifices of the Japanese themselves. But this book shows that Stalin's policy was motivated by expansionist geopolitical designs. The Soviet leader pursued his imperialistic policy with Machiavellian ruthlessness, deviousness, and cunning. In the end he managed to enter the war and occupy those territories to which he felt entitled. Although he briefly flirted with the idea of invading Hokkaido, and did violate the provision of the Yalta Agreement to secure a treaty with the Chinese as the prerequisite for entry into the war, Stalin by and large respected the Yalta limit. But by occupying the southern Kurils, which had never belonged to Russia until the last days of August and the beginning of September 1945, he created an intractable territorial dispute known as "the Northern Territories question" that has prevented rapprochement between Russia and Japan to this day. The Russian government and the majority of Russians even now continue to cling to the myth that the occupation of the southern Kurils was Russia's justifiable act of repossessing its lost territory.

Stalin's decisions in the Pacific War are but one of many entries in the ledger of his brutal regime. Although his imperialism was not the worst of his crimes compared with the Great Purge and collectivization, it represented part and parcel of the Stalin regime. Certainly, his conniving against the Japanese and the blatant land-grabbing that he engaged in during the closing weeks of the war are nothing to praise. Although the crimes committed by Stalin have been exposed and the new Russia is making valiant strides by shedding itself of the remnants of the Stalinist past, the Russians, with the exception of a few courageous historians, have not squarely faced the historical fact that Stalin's policy toward Japan in the waning months of the Pacific War was an example of the leader's expansionistic foreign policy. Unless the Russians come to this realization, the process of cleansing themselves of the Stalinist past will never be completed.

The Mythology of Victimization and the Role of Hirohito

It took the Japanese a little while to realize that what happened to the Kurils during the confused period between August 15 and September 5 amounted to annexation of Japan's inherent territory, an act that violated the Atlantic Charter and the Cairo Declaration. But the humiliation the Japanese suffered in the four-week Soviet-Japanese War was not entirely a result of the Soviet occupation of the Kurils. The Soviet occupation of the Kurils represented the last of many wrongs that the Soviets perpetrated on the Japanese, beginning with the violation of the Neutrality Pact, the invasion of Manchuria, Korea, southern Sakhalin, and the deportation and imprisonment of more than 640,000 prisoners of war. The "Northern Territories question" that the Japanese have demanded be resolved in the postwar period before any rapprochement with the Soviet Union (and Russia after 1991) is a mere symbol of their deep-seated resentment of and hostility toward the Russians who betrayed Japan when it desperately needed their help in ending the war.

Together with the Soviet war against Japan, Hiroshima and Nagasaki have instilled in the Japanese a sense of victimization. What Gilbert Rozman calls the Hiroshima syndrome and the Northern Territories syndrome are an inverted form of nationalism. As such they have prevented the Japanese from coming to terms with their own culpability in causing the war in Asia. Before August 14, 1945, the Japanese leaders had ample opportunities to surrender, for instance, at the German capitulation, the fall of Okinawa, the issuance of the Potsdam Proclamation, the atomic bomb on Hiroshima, and Soviet entry into the war. Few in Japan have condemned the policymakers who delayed Japan's surrender. Had the Japanese government accepted the Potsdam Proclamation unconditionally immediately after it was issued, as Sato and Matsumoto argued, the atomic bombs would not have been used, and the war would have ended before the Soviets entered the conflict. Japanese policymakers who were in the position to make decisions—not only the militant advocates of war but also those who belonged to the peace party, including Suzuki, Togo, Kido, and Hirohito himself—must bear the responsibility for the war's destructive end more than the American president and the Soviet dictator.

In postwar Japan, Hirohito has been portrayed as the savior of the Japanese people and the nation for his "sacred decisions" to end the war. Indeed, without the emperor's personal intervention, Japan would not have surrendered. The cabinet and the Big Six were hopelessly divided, unable to make a decision. Only the emperor broke the stalemate. His determination and leadership at the two imperial conferences and his steadfast support for the termination of the war after the decisive meeting with Kido on August 9 were crucial factors leading to Japan's surrender.

This does not mean, however, that the emperor was, in Asada's words, "Japan's foremost peace advocate, increasingly articulate and urgent in expressing his wish for peace." He was, as all other Japanese leaders at that time, still pinning his hope on Moscow's mediation, rejecting the unconditional surrender demanded by the Potsdam Proclamation until the Soviet entry into the war. After the Soviets joined the fight, he finally changed his mind to accept the Potsdam terms. In Japan it has been taboo to question the motivation that led Hirohito to accept surrender. But the findings of this book call for a reexamination of his role in the ending of the Pacific War. His delay in accepting the Allied terms ensured the use of the bomb and Soviet entry into the war.

Although Hirohito's initiative after August 9 should be noted, his motivation for ending the war was not as noble as the "sacred decision" myth would have us believe. His primary concern was above all the preservation of the imperial house. He even flirted with the idea of clinging to his political role. Despite the myth that he said he did not care what happened to him personally, it is likely that he was also in fact deeply concerned about the safety of his family and his own security. At the crucial imperial conference of August 10, Hiranuma did not mince words in asking Hirohito to take responsibility for the tragedy that had befallen Japan. As Konoe, some of the emperor's own relatives, and Grew, the most ardent supporter of the Japanese monarchy, argued, Hirohito should have abdicated at the end of the war to make a clean break with the Showa period that marked anything but what "Showa" meant: enlightened peace. His continuing reign made Japan's culpability in the war ambiguous and contributed to the nation's inability to come to terms with the past.

Thus this is a story with no heroes but no real villains, either—just men. The ending of the Pacific War was in the last analysis a human drama whose dynamics were determined by the very human characteristics of those involved: ambition, fear, vanity, anger, and prejudice. With each successive decision, the number of remaining alternatives steadily diminished, constraining ever further the possibilities, until the dropping of the bomb and the destruction of the Japanese state became all but inevitable. The Pacific War could very well have ended differently had the men involved made different choices. But they did not.

So they left it for us to live with the legacies of the war. The question is, Do we have the courage to overcome them?

EXPLORING THE ISSUE

Was It Necessary to Drop the Atomic Bomb to End World War II?

Critical Thinking and Reflection

1. Professor Maddox makes a strong case for the military reasons why the atomic bomb was dropped.

   a. Discuss his central argument.
   b. Describe how he counters revisionist arguments that there were viable alternatives to dropping the bomb.
   c. Critically evaluate his analysis of June 18, 1945, that the invasion of Kyushu and Honshu would cost approximately 40,000 deaths and 193,500 casualties and not the 500,000 deaths projected by Truman in his *Memoirs*.
   d. Evaluate Maddox's analysis of the attempts by Japan to negotiate surrender via the Russians. How realistic were the Japanese proposals?

2. Professor Hasegawa argues that dropping the atomic bombs was unnecessary because the Russian declaration of war against the Japanese was the primary reason why the Japanese surrendered. Critically analyze this argument and evaluate his evidence.

3. Critically evaluate the following counterfactual (what if) propositions advanced by Professor Hasegawa:

   a. What if Truman had accepted a provision in the Potsdam ultimatum allowing the Japanese to retain a constitutional monarchy?
   b. What if Truman had asked Stalin to sign the Potsdam proclamation without a promise of a constitutional monarchy?
   c. What if the Japanese government had accepted the Potsdam proclamation without trying to increase the Emperor's power under national law?
   d. What if the Byrnes note had contained a clear indication that the United States would allow the Japanese to retain a constitutional monarchy with the current dynasty?
   e. Without the atomic bombs and without Soviet entry into the war, would Japan have surrendered before November 1, the day Operation Olympic was scheduled to begin?
   f. Would Japan have surrendered before November 1 on the basis of Soviet entry alone, without the atomic bomb?
   g. Would Japan have surrendered before November 1 on the basis of the atomic bomb alone, without the Soviet entry into the war?

4. Professor Hasegawa attributes realistic assessments to the aims of Truman, Stalin, and the emperor. What were their goals for ending

the war? How do they differ from the legacies and patriotic memories of the bomb as viewed by Americans, Russians, and the Japanese?

5. Compare and contrast and critically evaluate the arguments of Professors Maddox and Hasegawa as regards the events ending World War II in the Pacific.

Is There Common Ground?

Historians continue to differ over the motives for dropping the atomic bomb—political or military. Should there have been a test demonstration on a deserted island for the officials from Japan and the United States to observe? Should a specific warning have been given as to the time and target which was going to be bombed? Should the United States have continued more conventional bombing raids until Japan surrendered? Should American government officials have considered a land invasion of Japan as an alternative to the bomb? Should President Truman have accepted earlier the Japanese request not to treat Emperor Hirohito as a war criminal?

Additional Resources

Hasegawa and Maddox's books deserve to read in their entirety. See also Sadao Asadu, "The Shock of the Atomic Bomb and Japan's Decision to Surrender —A Reconsideration," *Pacific Historical Review* (vol. 67, November 1998).

In addition to the Bernstein essay and Hogan collection, J. Samuel Walker has provided two useful essays: "The Decision to Use the Bomb: A Historiographical Update," *Diplomatic History* (vol. 14, Winter 1990) and "Recent Literature on Truman's Atomic Bomb Decision: The Search for Middle Ground," *Diplomatic History* (vol. 29, April 2005). Useful collections of primary sources include Robert H. Ferrell, ed., *Truman and the Bomb: A Documentary History* (High Plains Publishing, 1996) and Michael B. Stoff, Jonathan F. Fanton, and R. Hal Williams, eds., *The Manhattan Project: A Documentary Introduction to the Atomic Age* (Temple University Press, 1991), which contains facsimiles of original documents.

Hasegawa moves beyond the seminal research of his former teacher, Robert J.C. Butow, *Japan's Decision to Surrender* (Stanford University Press, 1954) written over 50 years ago, which discussed conflicts between the extreme militarists and the Japanese moderates who wanted to pursue a surrender with the condition of keeping the emperor as the nominal leader of the country. Butow basically substantiates the arguments of Professor Maddox. Hasegawa's interpretation conflicts with Richard B. Frank's *Downfall: The End of the Imperial Japanese Empires* (Random House, 1999), which argues that when the emperor announced his decision in the early morning hours to surrender, he gave three reasons: (1) the fear of a domestic upheaval; (2) inadequate defense preparations to resist the invasion; and (3) the vast destructiveness of the atomic bomb and the air attacks. The emperor, says Frank, did not refer to Soviet intervention.

Internet References . . .

CWIHP: Cold War International History Project

Scholarship on the Cold War has been written primarily by Westerners without access to sources in Soviet archives. This extensive collection seeks to remedy the gap in Cold War historiography by presenting sources from the former Communist bloc.

www.wilsoncenter.org/index.cfm?fuseaction=topics.home&topic_id=14

http://legacy.wilsoncenter.org/coldwarfiles/index.html

Central Intelligence Agency (CIA) Electronic Reading Room

The CIA has digitized thousands of formerly secret documents declassified to comply with Freedom of Information Act requests. Keyword search capabilities are provided for the complete website. In addition, there are eight collections designated as "frequently requested records," which total nearly 8,000 documents. These collections cover a number of Cold War topics.

www.foia.cia.gov/default.asp

www.foia.cia.gov/

The American Experience: Vietnam Online

Vietnam Online was developed to accompany "Vietnam: A Television History," the award-winning television series produced by WGBH Boston.

www.pbs.org/wgbh/amex/vietnam

Vietnam Center and Archive

This massive web furnishes several large collections. The "Oral History Project" presents full transcriptions of more than 475 audio oral histories conducted with U.S. men and women who served in Vietnam. The "Virtual Vietnam Archive" offers more than 408,000 pages from more than 270,000 documents regarding the Vietnam War.

http://Vietnam.ttu.edu/

Teach Women's History Project

These teaching and reference materials focus on the women's rights movement of the past 50 years and its opposing forces.

www.feminist.org/research/teachersguide/teach1.html

The Cold War and Beyond

World War II ended in 1945, but the peace that everyone had hoped for never came. In 1949, China came under communist control, the Russians developed an atomic bomb, and communist subversion of high-level officials in the State and Treasury Departments of the U.S. government was uncovered. By 1950 a "Cold War" between the Western powers and the Russians was in full swing, and American soldiers were fighting a hot war in Korea to "contain" communist expansion. In September 1962, the Soviets attempted to bring offensive missile sites onto the island of Cuba. By the end of the crisis, Kennedy and Premier Nikita Khrushchev had developed a respect for one another, but not without bringing the world to the brink of nuclear war. Another hot spot was Southeast Asia, where President Lyndon Johnson escalated America's participation in the Vietnam War in 1965. President Nixon negotiated a peace in January 1973 to bring troops home, but sixteen months later the South Vietnamese government surrendered to the Communists.

Over the course of the 1960s, the United States experienced challenges to traditional institutions and values from political and cultural rebels who comprised a countercultural protest. This movement began to fall apart by the end of the decade, and the momentum for social reform centered in the Women's Liberation Movement, an effort that extended well into the 1970s.

In the 1970s, Presidents Nixon, Ford, and Carter were unable to manage an economy whose major problem was to balance the trade-off between low levels of unemployment and acceptable levels of inflation. The economy of the 1980s, however, exploded with new high tech jobs and created a growing gap not only between the rich and the poor but also between the wealthy and the American middle class.

- Was President Truman Responsible for the Cold War?
- Did President John F. Kennedy Cause the Cuban Missile Crisis?
- Did the Activism of the 1960s Produce a Better Nation?
- Did President Nixon Negotiate a "Peace with Honor" in Vietnam in 1973?
- Has the Women's Movement of the 1970s Failed to Liberate American Women?
- Were the 1980s a Decade of Affluence for the Middle Class?

ISSUE 13

Was President Truman Responsible for the Cold War?

YES: Arnold A. Offner, from "Another Such Victory": President Truman, American Foreign Policy, and the Cold War, *Diplomatic History* (Spring 1999)

NO: John Lewis Gaddis, from *We Now Know: Rethinking Cold War History* (Oxford University Press, 1997)

Learning Outcomes

After reading this issue, you should be able to:

- List the major events leading to the Cold War from 1945 to 1950.
- Identify and give the significance of the following terms: "atomic diplomacy" and "containment."
- Discuss the orthodox interpretation as to who caused the Cold War.
- Evaluate Stalin's responsibility for the Cold War?
- Assess President Truman's role as a "parochial nationalist."
- Discuss the revisionist interpretation as to who caused the Cold War.

ISSUE SUMMARY

YES: Arnold A. Offner argues that President Harry S Truman was a parochial nationalist whose limited vision of foreign affairs precluded negotiations with the Russians over Cold War issues.

NO: After a half century of scholarship, John Lewis Gaddis argues that Joseph Stalin was uncompromising and primarily responsible for the Cold War.

Less than a month before the war ended in Europe the most powerful man in the world, President Franklin Delano Roosevelt, died suddenly from a brain embolism. A nervous, impetuous, and inexperienced Vice President Harry S.

Truman became the president. Historians disagree whether Truman reversed Roosevelt's relationship with Stalin or whether the similarities in policy were negated by Truman's blunt negotiating style compared with FDR's suave, calm approach. But disagreements emerged over issues such as control over the atomic bomb, Germany, Poland, and the economic reconstruction of Europe.

The question of Germany was paramount. During the war it was agreed that Germany would be divided temporarily into zones of occupation with the United States, Great Britain, and the newly liberated France controlling the western half of Germany, whereas the Russians would take charge of the eastern half. Berlin, which was 90 miles inside of the Russian zone, would also be divided into zones of occupation. Arguments developed over boundaries, reparations, and transfers of industrial equipment and agricultural foodstuffs between zones. In May 1946, the Americans began treating the western zones as a separate economic unit because the Russians were transferring the food from their zone back to the Soviet Union. In September 1946, Secretary of State James Byrnes announced that the Americans would continue to occupy their half of Germany indefinitely with military troops. By 1948, a separate democratic West German government was established. The Russians protested by blocking ground access to the western zones of Berlin, but the Americans continued to provide the West Berliners with supplies through an airlift. After 10 months, because of the bad publicity, the Russians abandoned the Berlin blockade and created a separate, Communist East German government.

Roosevelt and Churchill had conceded Russian control over Eastern Europe during the World War II conferences. The question was how much control. Stalin was not going to allow anti-Communist governments to be established in these countries. He had no understanding of how free elections were held. Consequently, when the Cold War intensified in 1947 and 1948, Russian-dominated Communist governments were established in Hungary, Poland, and Czechoslovakia.

In February 1946, Stalin delivered a major speech declaring the incompatibility of the two systems of Communism and Capitalism. The next month, Winston Churchill, now a retired politician, delivered his famous speech at a commencement ceremony at Westminster College in Fulton, Missouri, with the Truman administration's consent, in which he complained about the "iron curtain" that Russia was imposing on Eastern Europe. At the same time, George Kennan, a bright multi-linguist American diplomat who had spent years in Germany and Russia and who would become the head of Truman's policy planning staff, wrote a series of telegrams and articles that set the tone for the specific policies the Truman administration would undertake. Kennan had coined the phrase "containment," a word that would be used to describe America's foreign policy from Truman to the first President Bush. Containment would assume various meanings and would be extended to other areas of the globe besides Europe in ways Kennan claims were a misuse of what his original intentions were. Nevertheless the Truman administration took steps to stop further Russian expansionism.

In 1947, a series of steps was undertaken both to "contain" Russian expansionism and to rebuild the economies of Europe. On March 12, in an address in front of a Republican-controlled Congress, Truman argued in somewhat inflated rhetoric that "it must be the policy of the United States to support free peoples who are resisting attempted subjugation by armed minorities or by outside pressures." In the same speech, in what became known as the "Truman Doctrine," the President requested and received $400 million in economic and military assistance to Greece and Turkey. Almost as an afterthought, American military personnel were sent to oversee the reconstruction effort, a precedent that would later be used to send advisers to Vietnam.

In June 1947, Secretary of State George C. Marshall announced a plan to provide economic assistance to all European nations. This included the Soviet Union, which rejected the offer and formed its own economic recovery group. In April 1948, Congress approved the creation of the Economic Cooperation Administration, the agency that would administer the program. The Marshall Plan would be remembered as America's most successful foreign aid program, where 17 billion dollars was channeled to the Western European nations. By 1950, industrial production had increased 64 percent since the end of the war, whereas the communist parties declined in membership and influence.

When did the Cold War begin? Was it inevitable? Should one side take most of the blame for the anxiety and occasional hysteria that this conflict created? In the YES selection, Arnold Offner takes issue with President Truman's recent biographers Robert H. Ferrell, *Harry S Truman: A Life* (University of Missouri Press, 1994), Alonzo L. Hamby, *Man of the People: A Life of Harry S Truman* (Oxford, 1995), and especially David McCullough's *Truman* (Simon & Schuster, 1992), all of whom rank Truman among the near-great presidents. Offner describes Truman as a "parochial nationalist" whose outlook on foreign policy was ethnocentric and who made rash and quick decisions to cover his insecurities. Offner also accuses the Truman administration with practicing "atomic diplomacy" at the end of the war, when the United States was the sole possessor of the A-bomb, to make the Russians more manageable in Europe.

In the NO selection, Professor John Gaddis accepts the fact that Truman was insecure. He also believes that throughout 1945 up to early 1946, the Truman administration was responding to the political and economic uncertainties of the post–World War II environment. Although the United States took the lead in creating the World Bank and the International Monetary Fund to supply money for rebuilding Europe's destroyed infrastructure, these institutions were woefully inadequate to the task. It was also unclear whether the United States was going to re-enter a recession, as had occurred at the end of the World War I. Gaddis insists that the United States created its Western European empire by invitation through the implementation of the Truman Doctrine, the Marshall Plan, the rebuilding of West Germany, and the formation of NATO. On the other hand, Russia created its empire by force. Starting in Romania in 1945 and in Poland and Hungary in 1947 and ending with the takeover in Czechoslovakia in 1948, the Russians imposed totalitarian governments on its citizens.

Gaddis, therefore, places most of the blame for the Cold War on Stalin, an authoritarian imperialist who "equated world revolution with the expanding influence of the Soviet state." Truman was constrained by the democratic electoral system of checks and balances and a Republican-controlled Congress from 1946 to 1948, but Stalin had no such constraints. He purged all his real and potential revolutionary opponents in the 1930s and late 1940s and pursued foreign policy objectives as a romantic revolutionary. In summary, according to Gaddis, if Mikhail Gorbachev had been the Soviet leader in 1945, there might have been alternate paths to the Cold War, but with Stalin in charge, "there was going to be a cold war whatever the West did."

YES

Arnold A. Offner

"Another Such Victory": President Truman, American Foreign Policy, and the Cold War

As the twenty-first century nears, President Harry S. Truman's reputation stands high. This is especially true regarding his stewardship of foreign policy although, ironically, he entered the Oval Office in 1945 untutored in world affairs, and during his last year in the White House, Republicans accused his administration of having surrendered fifteen countries and five hundred million people to communism and sending twenty thousand Americans to their "burial ground" in Korea. Near the end of his term, Truman's public "favorable" rating had plummeted to 23 percent.

Within a decade, however, historians rated Truman a "near great" president, crediting his administration with reconstructing Western Europe and Japan, resisting Soviet or Communist aggression from Greece to Korea, and forging collective security through NATO. In the 1970s the "plain speaking" Truman became a popular culture hero. Recently, biographers have depicted him as the allegory of American life, an ordinary man whose extraordinary character led him to triumph over adversity from childhood through the presidency, and even posited a symbiotic relationship between "His Odyssey" from Independence to the White House and America's rise to triumphant superpower status. Melvyn P. Leffler, in his *A Preponderance of Power*, has judged Truman to have been neither a naif nor an idealist but a realist who understood the uses of power and whose administration, despite serious, costly errors, prudently preserved America's national security against real or perceived Soviet threats.

Collapse of the Soviet Union and Europe's other Communist states, whose archives have confirmed Truman's belief in 1945 that their regimes governed largely by "clubs, pistols and concentration camps," has further raised the former president's standing. This has encouraged John Lewis Gaddis and others to shift their focus to Stalin's murderous domestic rule as the key determinant of Soviet foreign policy and the Cold War. As Gaddis has contended, Stalin was heir to Ivan the Terrible and Peter the Great, responsible for more state-sanctioned murders than Adolf Hitler, and treated world politics as an extension of domestic politics: a zero sum game in which his gaining security meant depriving all others of it. For Gaddis and others, that is largely the answer to the question of whether Stalin sought or caused the Cold War.

From *Diplomatic History*, Spring 1999, pp. 127–143, 153–155 (excerpts). Copyright © 1999 by Society for Historians of American Foreign Relations. Reprinted by permission of Wiley-Blackwell via Rightslink.

But as Walter LaFeber has said, to dismiss Stalin's policies as the work of a paranoid is greatly to oversimplify the Cold War. Indeed, historians of Stalin's era seem to be of the preponderant view that he pursued a cautious but brutal realpolitik. He aimed to restore Russia's 1941 boundaries, establish a sphere of influence in border states, provide security against a recovered Germany or Japan or hostile capitalist states, and gain compensation, notably reparations, for the ravages of war. Stalin calculated forces, recognized America's superior industrial and military power, put Soviet state interests ahead of Marxist–Leninist ideology, and pursued pragmatic or opportunistic policies in critical areas such as Germany, China, and Korea.

Thus, the time seems ripe, given our increased knowledge of Soviet policies, to reconsider President Truman's role in the Cold War. As Thomas G. Paterson has written, the president stands at the pinnacle of the diplomatic-military establishment, has great capacity to set the foreign policy agenda and to mold public opinion, and his importance, especially in Truman's case, cannot be denied. But contrary to prevailing views, I believe that his policymaking was shaped by his parochial and nationalistic heritage. This was reflected in his uncritical belief in the superiority of American values and political-economic interests and his conviction that the Soviet Union and communism were the root cause of international strife. Truman's parochialism also caused him to disregard contrary views, to engage in simplistic analogizing, and to show little ability to comprehend the basis for other nations' policies. Consequently, his foreign policy leadership intensified Soviet–American conflict, hastened the division of Europe, and brought tragic intervention in Asian civil wars.

In short, Truman lacked the qualities of the creative or great leader who, as James MacGregor Burns has written, must broaden the environment in which he and his citizenry operate and widen the channels in which choices are made and events flow. Truman, to the contrary, narrowed Americans' perception of their world political environment and the channels for policy choices and created a rigid framework in which the United States waged long-term, extremely costly global cold war. Indeed, before we celebrate America's victory in this contest we might recall that after King Pyrrhus's Greek forces defeated the Romans at the battle of Asculum in 280 B.C., he reflected that "another such victory, and we are undone."

II

Truman's parochialism and nationalism, and significant insecurity, were rooted in his background, despite his claim to have had a bucolic childhood of happy family, farm life, and Baptist religiosity. In fact, young Harry's poor eyesight, extended illness, and "sissy" piano playing alienated him from both his peers and his feisty father and fostered ambivalence in him toward powerful men. On the one hand, Truman deferred to "Boss" Thomas Pendergast, his dishonest political benefactor, and to Secretaries of State George Marshall and Dean Acheson, whose manner and firm viewpoints he found reassuring. On the other hand, he denounced those whose style or ways of thinking were unfamiliar. This included the State Department's "striped pants boys," the military's "brass hats" and "prima donnas," political "fakirs" [sic] such as Teddy and Franklin Roosevelt, and "professional liberals." For Truman, Charles de Gaulle, Josef Stalin, Ernest Bevin, and Douglas MacArthur were each, at one time or another, a "son of a bitch."

Truman's need to demonstrate his authority underlay his upbraiding of both Soviet Foreign Minister Vyacheslav Molotov in April 1945 for Russia's alleged failure to keep its agreements and his secretary of state, James Byrnes, for allegedly exceeding his authority at the Moscow Conference of Foreign Ministers (CFM) that December. Truman naively likened Stalin to Pendergast, who, like Harry's father, always kept his word, but then took great umbrage at the thought that the Soviet leader had broken his word over Poland, Iran, or Germany. Truman also blamed MacArthur for misleading him at their Wake Island meeting in 1950 about Chinese intentions in the Korean War, but this was equally Truman self-deception.

Truman's self-tutelage in history derived largely from didactic biographies of "great men" and empires. This enhanced his vision of the globe but provided little sense of complexity or ambiguity and instilled exaggerated belief that current events had exact historical analogues that provided the key to contemporary policy. The new president was "amazed" that the Yalta accords were so "hazy" and fraught with "new meanings" at every reading, which probably contributed to his "lackluster" adherence to them. Shortly, Truman uncritically applied analogues about 1930s appeasement of Nazi Germany to diplomacy with the Soviet Union and crises in Iran, Greece, Turkey, and Korea.

Further, young Harry's Bible reading and church going did not inspire an abiding religiosity or system of morals so much as a conviction that the world was filled with "liars and hypocrites," terms he readily applied to his presidential critics, and a stern belief, as he wrote in 1945, that "punishment always followed transgression," a maxim that he applied to North Korea and the People's Republic of China (PRC).

Truman's early writings disdained non-Americans and minorities ("Chink doctor," "dago," "nigger," "Jew clerk," and "bohunks and Rooshans"), and in 1940 he proposed to deport "disloyal inhabitants." As president in 1945 he questioned the loyalty of "hyphenate" Americans, and in 1947 he signed Executive Order 9835, creating an unprecedented "loyalty" program that jettisoned basic legal procedural safeguards and virtually included a presumption of guilt.

Truman's command of men and bravery under fire in World War I were exemplary but not broadening. He deplored Europe's politics, mores, and food and sought only to return to "God's country." He intended never to revisit Europe: "I've nearly promised old Miss Liberty that she'll have to turn around to see me again," he wrote in 1918, and in 1945 he went reluctantly to Potsdam to his first and only European summit.

Nonetheless, Truman identified with Wilsonian internationalism, especially the League of Nations, and as a senator he supported President Franklin Roosevelt on the World Court, neutrality revision, rearmament, and Lend Lease for Britain and Russia. He rightfully said "I am no appeaser." But his internationalism reflected unquestioned faith in American moral superiority, and his foreign policy proposals largely comprised military preparedness. He was indifferent to the plight of Republican Spain and too quickly blamed international conflict on "outlaws," "savages," and "totalitarians." After Germany invaded the Soviet Union in 1941, he hastily remarked that they should be left to destroy one another—although he opposed Germany's winning—and he likened Russian leaders to "Hitler and Al Capone" and soon inveighed against the "twin blights—atheism and communism." Hence, while Truman supported the fledgling United Nations and the liberalization of world trade, the man who became president in April 1945 was less an incipient internationalist than a parochial nationalist given to excessive fear that appeasement, lack of preparedness, and enemies at home and abroad would thwart America's mission (the "Lord's will") to "win the peace" on its terms.

President Truman inherited an expedient wartime alliance that stood on shaky ground at Yalta in February 1945 and grew more strained over Soviet control in Romania and Poland and U.S. surrender talks with German officials at Bern that aroused Stalin's fears of a separate peace. Truman lamented that "they didn't tell me anything about what was going on." He also had to depend on advisers whose views ranged from Ambassador Averell Harriman's belief that it was time to halt the Russians' "barbarian invasion" of Europe to counsel from FDR emissaries Joseph Davies and Harry Hopkins to try to preserve long-term accord. Truman's desire to appear decisive by making quick decisions and his instinct to be "tough" spurred his belief that he could get "85 percent" from the Russians on important matters and that they could go along or "go to hell."

Initially, the president's abrupt style and conflicting advice produced inconsistent policy. His mid-April call for a "new" government in Poland and his "one-two to the jaw" interview with Molotov brought only a sharp reply from Stalin, after which the United States recognized a predominantly Communist Polish government. In May, Truman approved "getting tough" with the Russians by suddenly curtailing Lend Lease shipments, but Anglo-Soviet protests caused him to countermand the cutoffs. He then refused Prime Minister Winston Churchill's proposal to keep Anglo-American troops advanced beyond their agreed occupation zones to bargain in Germany and soon wrote that he was "anxious to keep all my engagements with the Russians because they are touchy and suspicious of us."

Still, Truman determined to have his way with the Russians, especially in Germany. Tutored in part by Secretary of War Henry L. Stimson, he embraced the emergent War-State Department position that Germany was key to the balance of power in Europe and required some reconstruction because a "poor house" standard of living there meant the same for Europe, and might cause a repeat of the tragic Treaty of Versailles history. Truman replaced Roosevelt's reparations negotiator, Isador Lubin, with conservative oil entrepreneur Edwin Pauley, who brushed off both Soviet claims to Yalta's $20 billion in reparations and State Department estimates that Germany could pay $12–14 billion. Truman also said that when he met with Churchill and Stalin he wanted "all the bargaining power—all the cards in my hands, and the plan on Germany is one of them."

The other card was the atomic bomb, which inspired Truman and Byrnes to think that they could win their way in Europe and Asia. Byrnes told the president in April that the bomb might allow them to "dictate our terms" at the war's end and in May indicated his belief that it would make the Russians more "manageable." Stimson counseled Truman that America's industrial strength and unique weapon comprised a "royal straight flush and we mustn't be a fool about how we play it," that it would be "dominant" in any dispute with Russia over Manchuria, and a "weapon" or "master card" in America's hand in its "big stakes" diplomacy with the Russians.

The president readily analogized diplomacy with his poker playing and, as Martin J. Sherwin has shown, believed that use of his atomic "ace-in-the-hole" would allow him to wrest concessions from Stalin. Truman had incentive to delay a summit meeting until the bomb was ready and to take no steps to obviate its use. In late spring he passed over proposals to modify unconditional surrender that sought to induce Japan's quick capitulation, and he would not give the Japanese or Russians notice of the atomic bomb.

Truman set sail for Potsdam highly disposed to atomic diplomacy, albeit not "blackmail." His nationalist perspective shaped his thinking. He aimed to advance American interests only: "win, lose, or draw—and we must win." En route, he approved Pauley's policy to give "first charge" priority to German occupation and maintenance costs over reparations. "Santa Claus is dead," Truman wrote, and the United States would never again "pay reparations, feed the world, and get nothing for it but a nose thumbing." Further, after Stimson brought word on 16 July of the successful atomic test in New Mexico and urged an early warning and offer to retain the Emperor as means to induce Japan's rapid surrender, Truman and Byrnes refused. That ended the last, brief chance at atomic restraint.

After meeting Stalin on 17 July, Truman wrote that he was unfazed by the Russian's "dynamite" agenda because "I have some dynamite too which I'm not exploding now." The following day he asserted that the "Japs will fold up" before Russia entered the Pacific war, specifically "when Manhattan appears over their homeland." Truman agreed with Byrnes that use of the bomb would permit them to "out-maneuver Stalin on China," that is, negate the Yalta concessions in Manchuria and guarantee that Russia would "not get in so much on the kill" of Japan or its occupation. Assured by 24 July that the bomb would be ready before Russia's entry, the president had to be persuaded even to hint to Stalin that he had a new weapon and afterward exulted in the mistaken belief that the Russian leader had not caught on to the bomb. Truman then hastened to issue the Potsdam Declaration without Soviet signature on 26 July and signed his "release when ready" order on the bombs on the 31st.

News of the bomb's power also greatly reinforced Truman's confidence to allow Byrnes to press European negotiations to impasse by refusing the Russians access to the Ruhr, rejecting even their low bid for $4 billion in industrial reparations, and withdrawing the Yalta accords. Convinced that the New Mexico atomic test would allow the United States to "control" events, Byrnes pushed his famous 30 July tripartite ultimatum on German zonal reparations, Poland's de facto control over its new western border (including Silesia) with Germany, and Italy's membership in the UN. "Mr. Stalin is stallin'," Truman wrote hours before the American-set deadline on 31 July, but that was useless because "I have an ace in the hole and another one showing," aces that he knew would soon fall upon Japan.

Truman won his hand, as Stalin acceded to zonal reparations. But Truman's victory was fraught with more long-term consequences than he envisioned. He had not only equated his desire to prevent use of taxpayer dollars to help sustain occupied Germany with the Russians' vital need for reparations, but also given them reason to think, as Norman Naimark has written, that the Americans were deaf to their quest for a "paltry" $10 billion or less to compensate for Germany's having ravaged their nation. Further, America's insistence on zonal reparations would impede development of common economic policy for all of Germany and increase likelihood of its East–West division.

In addition, use of two atomic bombs on Hiroshima and Nagasaki—the second was not militarily necessary—showed that for Truman and Byrnes, the prospect of political gain in Europe and Asia precluded serious thought not to use the bombs. And this may have led the Russians to conclude that the bombs were directed against them, or their ability to achieve their strategic interests. But Stalin would not be pressured; he was determined to pursue a Russian atomic bomb.

Shortly, Truman backed Byrnes's "bomb in his pocket" diplomacy at the London CFM, which deadlocked over Russian control in Eastern Europe and American control in Japan. Truman told Byrnes to "stick to his guns" and tell the Russians "to go to hell." The president then agreed with "ultranationalist" advisers who opposed international atomic accord by drawing misleading analogies about interwar disarmament and "appeasement" and by insisting that America's technological-industrial genius assured permanent atomic supremacy. Truman held that America was the world's atomic "trustee"; that it had to preserve the bomb's "secret"; and that no nation would give up the "locks and bolts" necessary to protect its "house" from "outlaws." The atomic arms race was on, he said in the fall of 1945, and other nations had to "catch up on their own hook."

In the spring of 1946, Truman undercut the Dean Acheson-David Lilienthal plan for international control and development of atomic resources by appointing as chief negotiator Bernard Baruch, whose emphasis on close inspections, sanctions, no veto, and indefinite American atomic monopoly virtually assured Russian refusal. Despite Acheson's protests, Truman analogized that "if Harry Stimson had been backed up in Manchuria [in 1931] there would have been no war." And as deadlock neared in July 1946, the president told Baruch to "stand pat."

Ultimately the UN commission weighing the Baruch Plan approved it on 31 December 1946. But the prospect of a Soviet veto in the Security Council precluded its adoption. Admittedly, Stalin's belief that he could not deal with the United States on an equal basis until he had the bomb and Soviet insistence on retention of their veto power and national control of resources and facilities may have precluded atomic accord in 1946. Still, Baruch insisted that the United States could get its way because it had an atomic monopoly, and American military officials sought to preserve a nuclear monopoly as long as possible and to develop a strategy based on air power and atomic weapons. As

David Holloway has written, neither Truman nor Stalin "saw the bomb as a common danger to the human race."

Meanwhile, Byrnes's diplomacy in Moscow in December 1945 had produced Yalta-style accords on a European peace treaty process, Russian predominance in Bulgaria and Romania and American primacy in China and Japan, and compromise over Korea, with Soviet disputes with Iran and Turkey set aside. But conservative critics cried "appeasement," and in his famous but disputed letter of 5 January 1946, an anxious president charged that Byrnes had kept him "completely in the dark"; denounced Russian "outrage[s]" in the Baltic, Germany, Poland, and Iran and intent to invade Turkey; and said that the Russians understood only an "iron fist" and "divisions" and that he was tired of "babying" them. In fact, Truman knew of most of Byrnes's positions; they had hardly "babied" Russia since Potsdam; and no Russian attack was imminent. The letter reflected Truman's new "get tough" policy, or personal cold war declaration, which, it must be emphasized, came six weeks before George Kennan's Long Telegram and Churchill's Iron Curtain speech.

Strong American protests in 1946 caused the Russians to withdraw their troops from Iran and their claims to joint defense of the Turkish Straits. In the latter case, Truman said he was ready to follow his policy of military response "to the end" to determine if Russia intended "world conquest." Once again he had taken an exaggerated, nationalist stance. No one expected a Russian military advance; America's action rested on its plans to integrate Turkey into its strategic planning and to use it as a base of operations against Russia in event of war. And in September, Truman approved announcement of a Mediterranean command that led to the United States becoming the dominant naval power there by year's end.

Meanwhile, Truman ignored Secretary of Commerce Henry Wallace's lengthy memoranda during March–September 1946 that sought to promote economic ties with Russia and questioned America's atomic policies and global military expansiveness. The president then fired Wallace after he publicly challenged Byrnes's speech on 6 September in Stuttgart propounding West German reconstruction and continued American military presence there. The firing was reasonable, but not the rage at Wallace as "a real Commy" and at "parlor pinks and soprano-voiced men" as a "national danger" and "sabotage front" for Stalin.

Equally without reason was Truman's face value acceptance of White House special counsel Clark Clifford's "Russian Report" of September 1946 and accompanying "Last Will of Peter the Great." Clifford's report rested on a hasty compilation of apocalyptic projections of Soviet aim to conquer the world by military force and subversion, and he argued that the United States had to prepare for total war. He wrote in the "black and white" terms that he knew Truman would like and aimed to justify a vast global military upgrade and silence political critics on the left and right. Tsar Peter's will was an old forgery purporting to show that he had a similar design to conquer Eurasia. Truman may have found the report so "hot" that he confined it to his White House safe, but he believed the report and the will and soon was persisting that the governments of the czars, Stalin, and Hitler were all the same. Later he told a mild critic of American policy to read Tsar Peter's will to learn where Russian leaders got their "fixed ideas."

It was a short step, Clifford recalled, from the Russian Report to Truman's epochal request in March 1947 for military aid to Greece and Turkey to help "free peoples" fight totalitarianism. Truman vastly overstated the global-ideological aspects of Soviet–American conflict. Perhaps he sought to fire "the opening gun" to rouse the public and a fiscally conservative Republican Congress to national security expenditures. But he also said that this was "only the beginning" of the "U.S. going into European politics," that the Russians had broken every agreement since Potsdam and would now get only "one language" from him. He added in the fall of 1947 that "if Russia gets Greece and Turkey," it would get Italy and France, the iron curtain would extend to western Ireland, and the United States would have to "come home and prepare for war."

Truman's fears were excessive. Stalin never challenged the Truman Doctrine or Western primacy in Turkey, now under U.S. military tutelage, and Greece. He provided almost no aid to the Greek rebels and told Yugoslavia's leaders in early 1948 to halt their aid because the United States would never allow the Greek Communists to win and break Anglo-American control in the Mediterranean. When Marshal Josip Broz Tito balked, Stalin withdrew his advisers from Yugoslavia and expelled that nation from the Cominform. Tito finally closed his borders to the Greek rebels in July 1949.

Perhaps U.S. officials feared that Britain's retreat from Greece might allow Russia to penetrate the Mediterranean, or that if Greek Communists overthrew the reactionary Greek regime (Turkey was not threatened) they might align Athens with Moscow. Still, the Truman administration's costly policy never addressed the causes of Greece's civil war; instead, it substituted military "annihilation of the enemy for the reform of the social and economic conditions" that had brought civil war. Equally important, Truman's rhetorical division of the world into "free" versus "totalitarian" states, as Gaddis once said, created an "ideological straitjacket" for American foreign policy and an unfortunate model for later interventions, such as in Korea—"the Greece of the Far East," as Truman would say—and in French Indochina.

The Truman Doctrine led to the Marshall Plan in June 1947, but they were not "two halves of the same walnut," as Truman claimed. State Department officials who drew up the European Recovery Plan (ERP) differentiated it from what they viewed as his doctrine's implications for "economic and ultimately military warfare." The Soviets likened the Truman Doctrine to retail purchase of separate nations and the Marshall Plan to wholesale purchase of Europe.

The Soviet view was narrow, although initially they had interest in participating and perhaps even harbored dreams that the United States would proffer a generous Lend Lease-style arrangement. But as the British quickly saw, Soviet participation was precluded by American-imposed financial and economic controls and, as Michael J. Hogan has written, by the integrated, continental approach to aid rather than a nation-by-nation basis that would have benefited war-devastated Russia. Indeed, in direct talks in Paris, U.S. officials refused concessions, focused on resources to come from Russia and East Europe, and insisted on German contributions to the ERP ahead of reparations payments or a peace treaty—and then expressed widespread relief when the Soviets rejected the ERP for themselves and East Europe.

The Marshall Plan proved to be a very successful geostrategic venture. It helped to spur American–European trade and Western European recovery, bring France into camp with Germany and satisfy French economic and security claims, and revive eastern Germany industrially without unleashing the 1930s-style "German colossus" that Truman's aides feared. The Marshall Plan was also intended to contain the Soviets economically, forestall German–Soviet bilateral deals, and provide America with access to its allies' domestic and colonial resources. Finally, as the British said, the Truman administration sought an integrated Europe resembling the United States, "God's own country."

The Marshall Plan's excellent return on investment, however, may have cost far more than the $13 billion expended. "The world is definitely split in two," Undersecretary of State Robert Lovett said in August 1947, while Kennan forewarned that for defensive reasons the Soviets would "clamp down completely on Czechoslovakia" to strengthen their hold on Eastern Europe. Indeed, the most recent evidence indicates that Stalin viewed the Marshall Plan as a "watershed" event, signaling an American effort to predominate over all of Europe. This spurred the Soviets into a comprehensive strategy shift. They now rigged the elections in Hungary, proffered Andrei Zhdanov's "two camps" approach to world policy, created the Cominform, and blessed the Communist coup in Czechoslovakia in February 1948. Truman, in turn, concluded that the Western world confronted the same situation it had a decade earlier with Nazi Germany, and his bristling St. Patrick's Day speeches in March 1948 placed sole onus for the Cold War on the Soviet Union. Subsequently, Anglo-American talks at the Pentagon would culminate in NATO in April 1949.

Meanwhile, the U.S. decision to make western Germany the cornerstone of the ERP virtually precluded negotiations to reunify the country. In fact, when Secretary of State Marshall proposed during a CFM meeting in the spring of 1947 to offer current production reparations to the Russians to induce agreement to unify Germany, the president sternly refused. Marshall complained of lack of "elbow room" to negotiate. But Truman would not yield, and by the time of the next CFM in late 1947 the secretary showed no interest in Russian reparations or Ruhr access. Despite America's public position, Ambassador to Moscow Walter Bedell Smith wrote, "we really do not want nor intend to accept German unification on any terms that the Russians might agree to, even though they seemed to meet most of our requirements."

The Americans were by then onto their London Conference program to create a West German state and, as Stalin said in February 1948, "The West will make Western Germany their own, and we shall turn Eastern Germany into our own state." In June, the Soviet dictator initiated the Berlin blockade to try to forestall the West's program, but Truman determined to "stay, period." He believed that to withdraw from Berlin would seriously undermine U.S. influence in Europe and the ERP and destroy his presidential standing, and he remained determined to avert military confrontation.

But Truman saw no connection between the London program and the blockade, as Carolyn Eisenberg has written. Further, his belief that "there is nothing to negotiate" and accord with General Lucius Clay's view that to withdraw from Berlin meant "we have lost everything we are fighting for" exaggerated the intent of Stalin's maneuver and diminished even slim chances for compromise on Germany, including Kennan's "Plan A" for a unified, neutralized state with American and Soviet forces withdrawn to its periphery. As Marshall said in August 1948, there would be "no abandonment of our position" on West Germany.

Eventually, Truman and the airlift prevailed over Stalin, who gave in to a face-saving CFM in May 1949 that ended the blockade, with nothing else agreed. The new secretary of state, Acheson, said that the United States intended to create a West German government "come hell or high water" and that Germany could be unified only by consolidating the East into the West on the basis of its incipient Bonn Constitution. Likewise Truman said in June 1949 that he would not sacrifice West Germany's basic freedoms to gain "nominal political unity."

Long convinced that the United States was locked in "a struggle with the USSR for Germany," the president showed no interest when Stalin made his most comprehensive offer on 10 March 1952, proposing a Big Four meeting to draft a peace treaty for a united, neutral, defensively rearmed Germany free of foreign troops. Whether Stalin was seeking a settlement to reduce great power conflict over a divided Germany has been debated. His note came only after the United States and its allies were near contractual accord on West German sovereignty and Acheson had just negotiated his "grand slam" providing for German forces to enter a proposed European Defense Community (EDC) linked to NATO. Acheson held that Stalin had thrown a "golden apple" of discord over the iron curtain to forestall a sovereign, industrially strong, and rearmed West Germany joining an American-led alliance system.

Truman gave full sway to Acheson, who hesitated to reject Stalin's offer out of hand. But he insisted that the allies "drive ahead" with the German contractuals and EDC. He also got support from West German Chancellor Konrad Adenauer to shape uniform allied replies, with conditions, such as UN-supervised elections in all of Germany prior to negotiations and unified Germany's right to join any "defensive European community," that he knew Stalin would reject. Further, although Truman and Acheson had just coaxed Kennan to become ambassador to Moscow, they never asked his advice or gave him a policy clue despite meeting with him three times in April. This confirmed Kennan's view that "we had no interest in discussing the German problem with the Soviet Government in any manner whatsoever."

Stalin, meanwhile, told East German leaders in April 1952 that the West would never accept any proposal they made and that it was time to "organize your own state" and protect its border. The United States won the so-called battle of the notes, although exchanges continued. But the allies concluded the German contractuals and the EDC in late May. And when the French then reverted to proposing a four power meeting on Germany, Acheson said that four power control was long past. He then shaped the note so that it "puts onus on Sovs sufficiently to make it unlikely that Sovs will agree to mtg on terms proposed." He was right, and in September the note writing drew to its anticlimactic closure.

Prospect for accord based on Stalin's note was remote, but not just because Stalin wanted, as Vojtech Mastny has written, either a unified "pro-Soviet though not necessarily communist" Germany or a full-fledged East German satellite. Truman had no interest in a unified, neutral, or demilitarized Germany and now believed that a rearmed FRG was as vital to NATO as West Germany was to ERR German unity was possible only on the basis of West over East. Thus, Ambassador Kennan said after talking to U.S. officials linked to NATO in the fall of 1952 that they saw no reason to withdraw U.S. forces from Germany "at any time within the foreseeable future under any conceivable agreement with Russia." This meant that the "split of Germany and Europe" would continue. And it did, for the next forty years. . . .

<hr />

No one leader or nation caused the Cold War. The Second World War generated inevitable Soviet–American conflict as two nations with entirely different political-economic systems confronted each other on two war-torn continents. The Truman administration would seek to fashion a world order friendly to American political and economic interests, to achieve maximum national security by preventing any nation from severing U.S. ties to its traditional allies and vital areas of trade and resources, and to avoid 1930s-style "appeasement." Truman creditably favored creation of the UN, fostered foreign aid and reconstruction, and wished to avert war, and, after he recognized his "overreach" in Korea, he sought to return to the status quo ante.

Nonetheless, from the Potsdam Conference through the Korean War, the president contributed significantly to the growing Cold War and militarization of American foreign policy. He assumed that America's economic-military-moral superiority assured that he could order the world on its terms, and he ascribed only dark motives to nations or leaders who resisted America's will. Monopoly control of the atomic bomb heightened this sense of righteous power and impelled his use of atomic bombs partly to outmaneuver the Russians in China and over Japan. Truman also drew confidence from the bombs that he could deny the Soviets any fixed sum of German reparations despite their feasibility, the Yalta accords, and the apparent disregard of Russia's claim to compensation for its wartime suffering. American-imposed zonal reparations policy only increased the East–West divide and diminished prospects to reunite Germany, although Stalin evidently remained open to the idea of a united and neutralized Germany until 1949 and conceivably as late as 1952. But Truman, as Marshall learned in the spring of 1947, had little interest in negotiating such an arrangement, and his administration's decision that year to make western Germany the cornerstone of the Marshall Plan and Western Europe's reconstruction virtually precluded German unification except by melding East into West. Formation of NATO and insistence that a unified Germany be free to join a Western military alliance reinforced division of Germany and Europe.

It is clear that Truman's insecurity with regard to diplomacy and world politics led him to seek to give the appearance of acting decisively and reinforced his penchant to view conflict in black and white terms and to divide nations into free or totalitarian societies. He shied from weighing the complexities of historic national conflicts and local or regional politics. Instead, he attributed nearly every diplomatic crisis or civil war—in Germany, Iran, Turkey, Greece, and Czechoslovakia—to Soviet machination and insisted that the Russians had broken every agreement and were bent on "world conquest." To determine his response he was quick to reach for an analogy, usually the failure of the Western powers to resist Germany and Japan in the 1930s, and to conclude that henceforth he would speak to the Russians in the only language that he thought they understood: "divisions." This style of leadership and diplomacy closed off both advocates and prospects for more patiently negotiated and more nuanced or creative courses of action.

Truman also viscerally loathed the Chinese Communists, could not comprehend Asian nationalism, demonized Asian opponents, and caused the United States to align itself with corrupt regimes. He was unable to view China's civil war apart from Soviet–American conflict. He brushed off criticism of America's intervention on behalf of the frightful GMD, refused to open channels of communication with the emergent PRC, and permitted the American-armed, Taiwan-based GMD to wage counterrevolutionary war against China's new government, whose sovereignty or legitimacy he never accepted. The Korean War then overtook his administration. The president decided to preserve South Korea's independence but set an unfortunate if not tragic precedent by refusing to seek formal congressional sanction for war. His decision to punish North Korea and implement "rollback," and his disdain for the PRC and its concerns before and after it entered the war, brought unnecessary, untold destruction and suffering to Asians and Americans and proved fatal to his presidency. Still, in his undelivered farewell address Truman insisted that "Russia was at the root" of every problem from Europe to Asia, and that "Trumanism" had saved countless countries from Soviet invasion and "knocked the socks off the communists" in Korea.

In conclusion, it seems clear that despite Truman's pride in his knowledge of the past, he lacked insight into the history unfolding around him. He often could not see beyond his immediate decision or visualize alternatives, and he seemed oblivious to the implications of his words or actions. More often than not he narrowed rather than broadened the options that he presented to the American citizenry, the environment of American politics, and the channels through which Cold War politics flowed. Throughout his presidency, Truman remained a parochial nationalist who lacked the leadership to move America away from conflict and toward detente. Instead, he promoted an ideology and politics of Cold War confrontation that became the modus operandi of successor administrations and the United States for the next two generations.

We Now Know:
Rethinking Cold War History

[Joseph] Stalin appears to have relished his role, along with [Franklin D.] Roosevelt and [Winston] Churchill, as one of the wartime Big Three. Such evidence as has surfaced from Soviet archives suggests that he received reassuring reports about Washington's intentions: "Roosevelt is more friendly to us than any other prominent American," Ambassador Litvinov commented in June 1943, "and it is quite obvious that he wishes to cooperate with us." Whoever was in the White House, Litvinov's successor Andrei Gromyko predicted a year later, the Soviet Union and the United States would "manage to find common issues for the solution of . . . problems emerging in the future and of interest to both countries." Even if Stalin's long-range thinking about security did clash with that of his Anglo-American allies, common military purposes provided the strongest possible inducements to smooth over such differences. It is worth asking why this *practice* of wartime cooperation did not become a *habit* that would extend into the postwar era.

The principal reason, it now appears, was Stalin's insistence on equating security with territory. Western diplomats had been surprised, upon arriving in Moscow soon after the German attack in the summer of 1941, to find the Soviet leader already demanding a postwar settlement that would retain what his pact with Hitler had yielded: the Baltic states, together with portions of Finland, Poland, and Romania. Stalin showed no sense of shame or even embarrassment about this, no awareness that the *methods* by which he had obtained these concessions could conceivably render them illegitimate in the eyes of anyone else. When it came to territorial aspirations, he made no distinction between adversaries and allies: what one had provided the other was expected to endorse. . . .

On the surface, this strategy succeeded. After strong initial objections, Roosevelt and Churchill did eventually acknowledge the Soviet Union's right to the expanded borders it claimed; they also made it clear that they would not oppose the installation of "friendly" governments in adjoining states. This meant accepting a Soviet sphere of influence from the Baltic to the Adriatic, a concession not easily reconciled with the Atlantic Charter. But the authors of that document saw no feasible way to avoid that outcome: military necessity required continued Soviet cooperation against the Germans. Nor were they themselves prepared to relinquish spheres of influence in Western Europe and the Mediterranean, the Middle East, Latin America, and East Asia. Self-determination was a sufficiently malleable concept that each of the Big Three could have endorsed, without sleepless nights, what the Soviet government had said about the Atlantic Charter: "practical application of these principles will necessarily adapt itself to the circumstances, needs, and historic peculiarities of particular countries."

That, though, was precisely the problem. For unlike Stalin, Roosevelt and Churchill would have to defend their decisions before domestic constituencies. The *manner* in which Soviet influence expanded was therefore, for them, of no small significance. Stalin showed little understanding of this. Having no experience himself with democratic procedures, he dismissed requests that he respect democratic proprieties. "[S]ome propaganda work should be done," he advised Roosevelt at the Tehran conference after the president had hinted that the American public would welcome a plebiscite in the Baltic States. "It is all nonsense!" Stalin complained to [Soviet Foreign Minister V. M.] Molotov. "[Roosevelt] is their military leader and commander in chief. Who would dare object to him?" When at Yalta F.D.R. stressed the need for the first Polish election to be as pure as "Caesar's wife," Stalin responded with a joke: "They said that about her, but in fact she had her sins." Molotov warned his boss, on that occasion, that the Americans' insistence on free elections elsewhere in Eastern Europe was "going too far." "Don't worry," he recalls Stalin as replying, "work it out. We can deal with it in our own way later. The point is the correlation of forces."

The Soviet leader was, in one sense, right. Military strength would determine what happened in that part of the world, not the enunciation of lofty principles. But unilateral methods carried long-term costs Stalin did not foresee: the most significant of these was to ruin whatever prospects existed for a Soviet sphere of influence the East Europeans themselves might have accepted. This possibility was not as far-fetched as it would later seem. . . . [Stalin] would, after all, approve such a compromise as the basis for a permanent settlement with Finland. He would initially allow free elections in Hungary, Czechoslovakia, and the Soviet occupation zone in Germany. He may even have *anticipated an enthusiastic response* as he took over Eastern Europe. "He was, I think, surprised and hurt," [W. Averell] Harriman [one of Roosevelt's closest advisors] recalled, "when the Red Army was not welcomed in all the neighboring countries as an army of liberation." "We still had our hopes," [Nikita] Khrushchev remembered, that "after the catastrophe of World War II, Europe, too, might become Soviet. Everyone would take the path from capitalism to socialism." It could be that there was another form of romanticism at work here, quite apart from Stalin's affinity for fellow authoritarians: that he was unrealistic enough to expect ideological solidarity and gratitude for liberation to override old fears of Russian expansionism as well as remaining manifestations of nationalism among the Soviet Union's neighbors, perhaps as easily as he himself had overridden the latter—or so it then appeared—within the multinational empire that was the Soviet Union itself.

If the Red Army could have been welcomed in Poland and the rest of the countries it liberated with the same enthusiasm American, British, and Free French forces encountered when they landed in Italy and France in 1943 and

1944, then some kind of Czech–Finnish compromise might have been feasible. Whatever Stalin's expectations, though, this did not happen. That nonevent, in turn, removed any possibility of a division of Europe all members of the Grand Alliance could have endorsed. It ensured that an American sphere of influence would arise there largely by consent, but that its Soviet counterpart could sustain itself only by coercion. The resulting asymmetry would account, more than anything else, for the origins, escalation, and ultimate outcome of the Cold War.

*

. . . It has long been clear that, in addition to having had an authoritarian vision, Stalin also had an imperial one, which he proceeded to implement in at least as single-minded a way [as the American]. No comparably influential builder of empire came close to wielding power for so long, or with such striking results, on the Western side.

It was, of course, a matter of some awkwardness that Stalin came out of a revolutionary movement that had vowed to smash, not just tsarist imperialism, but all forms of imperialism throughout the world. The Soviet leader constructed his own logic, though, and throughout his career he devoted a surprising amount of attention to showing how a revolution and an empire might coexist. . . .

Stalin's fusion of Marxist internationalism with tsarist imperialism could only reinforce his tendency, in place well before World War II, to equate the advance of world revolution with the expanding influence of the Soviet state. He applied that linkage quite impartially: a major benefit of the 1939 pact with Hitler had been that it regained territories lost as a result of the Bolshevik Revolution and the World War I settlement. But Stalin's conflation of imperialism with ideology also explains the importance he attached, following the German attack in 1941, to having his new Anglo-American allies confirm these arrangements. He had similar goals in East Asia when he insisted on bringing the Soviet Union back to the position Russia had occupied in Manchuria prior to the Russo-Japanese War: this he finally achieved at the 1945 Yalta Conference in return for promising to enter the war against Japan. "My task as minister of foreign affairs was to expand the borders of our Fatherland," Molotov recalled proudly many years later. "And it seems that Stalin and I coped with this task quite well." . . .

*

From the West's standpoint, the critical question was how far Moscow's influence would extend *beyond* whatever Soviet frontiers turned out to be at the end of the war. Stalin had suggested to Milovan Djilas that the Soviet Union would impose its own social system as far as its armies could reach, but he was also very cautious. Keenly aware of the military power the United States and its allies had accumulated, Stalin was determined to do nothing that might involve the USSR in another devastating war until it had recovered sufficiently to be certain of winning it. "I do not wish to begin the Third World War over the Trieste question," he explained to disappointed Yugoslavs, whom he ordered to evacuate that territory in June 1945. Five years later, he would justify his decision not to intervene in the Korean War on the grounds that "the Second World War ended not long ago, and we are not ready for the Third World War." Just how far the expansion of Soviet influence would proceed depended, therefore, upon a careful balancing of opportunities against risks. . . .

Who or what was it, though, that set the limits? Did Stalin have a fixed list of countries he thought it necessary to dominate? Was he prepared to stop in the face of resistance within those countries to "squeezing out the capitalist order"? Or would expansion cease only when confronted with opposition from the remaining capitalist states, so that further advances risked war at a time when the Soviet Union was ill-prepared for it?

Stalin had been very precise about where he wanted Soviet boundaries changed; he was much less so on how far Moscow's sphere of influence was to extend. He insisted on having "friendly" countries around the periphery of the USSR, but he failed to specify how many would have to meet this standard. He called during the war for dismembering Germany, but by the end of it was denying that he had ever done so: that country would be temporarily divided, he told leading German communists in June 1945, and they themselves would eventually bring about its reunification. He never gave up on the idea of an eventual world revolution, but he expected this to result—as his comments to the Germans suggested—from an expansion of influence emanating from the Soviet Union itself. "[F]or the Kremlin," a well-placed spymaster recalled, "the mission of communism was primarily to consolidate the might of the Soviet state. Only military strength and domination of the countries on our borders could ensure us a superpower role."

But Stalin provided no indication—surely because he himself did not know—of how rapidly, or under what circumstances, this process would take place. He was certainly prepared to stop in the face of resistance from the West: at no point was he willing to challenge the Americans or even the British where they made their interests clear. . . . He quickly backed down when confronted with Anglo-American objections to his ambitions in Iran in the spring of 1946, as he did later that year after demanding Soviet bases in the Turkish Straits. This pattern of advance followed by retreat had shown up in the purges of the 1930s, which Stalin halted when the external threat from Germany became too great to ignore, and it would reappear with the Berlin Blockade and the Korean War, both situations in which the Soviet Union would show great caution after provoking an unexpectedly strong American response.

What all of this suggests, though, is not that Stalin had limited ambitions, only that he had no timetable for achieving them. Molotov retrospectively confirmed this: "Our ideology stands for offensive operations when possible, and if not, we wait." Given this combination of appetite with aversion to risk, one cannot help but wonder what would have happened had the West tried containment earlier. To the extent that it bears partial responsibility for the coming of the Cold War, the historian Vojtech Mastny has argued, that responsibility lies in its failure to do just that. . . .

Stalin's policy, then, was one of imperial expansion and consolidation differing from that of earlier empires only in the determination with which he pursued it, in the instruments of coercion with which he maintained it, and in the ostensibly anti-imperial justifications he put forward in support of it. It is a testimony to his skill, if not to his morality, that he was able to achieve so many of his imperial ambitions at a time when the tides of history were running against the idea of imperial domination—as colonial offices in London, Paris, Lisbon, and The Hague were finding out—and when his own country was recovering from one of the most brutal invasions in recorded history. The fact that Stalin was able to *expand* his empire when others were contracting and while the Soviet Union was as weak as it was, requires explanation. Why did opposition to this process, within and outside Europe, take so long to develop?

One reason was that the colossal sacrifices the Soviet Union had made during the war against the Axis had, in effect, "purified" its reputation: the USSR and its leader had "earned" the right to throw their weight around, or so it seemed. Western governments found it difficult to switch quickly from viewing the Soviet Union as a glorious wartime ally to portraying it as a new and dangerous adversary. President Harry S. Truman and his future Secretary of State Dean Acheson—neither of them sympathetic in the slightest to communism—nontheless tended to give the Soviet Union the benefit of the doubt well into the early postwar era. . . .

Resistance to Stalin's imperialism also developed slowly because Marxism–Leninism at the time had such widespread appeal. It is difficult now to recapture the admiration revolutionaries outside the Soviet Union felt for that country before they came to know it well. . . . Because the Bolsheviks themselves had overcome one empire and had made a career of condemning others, it would take decades for people who were struggling to overthrow British, French, Dutch, or Portuguese colonialism to see that there could also be such a thing as Soviet imperialism. European communists—notably the Yugoslavs—saw this much earlier, but even to most of them it had not been apparent at the end of the war.

Still another explanation for the initial lack of resistance to Soviet expansionism was the fact that its repressive character did not become immediately apparent to all who were subjected to it. . . .

One has the impression that Stalin and the Eastern Europeans got to know one another only gradually. The Kremlin leader was slow to recognize that Soviet authority would not be welcomed everywhere beyond Soviet borders; but as he did come to see this, he became all the more determined to impose it everywhere. The Eastern Europeans were slow to recognize how confining incorporation within a Soviet sphere was going to be; but as they did come to see this, they became all the more determined to resist it, even if only by withholding, in a passive but sullen manner, the consent any regime needs to establish itself by means other than coercion. Stalin's efforts to consolidate his empire therefore made it at once more repressive and less secure. Meanwhile, an alternative vision of postwar Europe was emerging from the other great empire that established itself in the wake of

World War II, that of the United States, and this too gave Stalin grounds for concern. . . .

❧◈❧

What is there new to say about the old question of responsibility for the Cold War? Who actually started it? Could it have been averted? Here I think the "new" history is bringing us back to an old answer: that *as long as Stalin was running the Soviet Union, a cold war was unavoidable.*

History is always the product of determined and contingent events: it is up to historians to find the proper balance between them. The Cold War could hardly have happened if there had not been a United States and a Soviet Union, if both had not emerged victorious from World War II, if they had not had conflicting visions of how to organize the postwar world. But these long-term trends did not in themselves *ensure* such a contest, because there is always room for the unexpected to undo what might appear to be inevitable. *Nothing* is ever completely predetermined, as real triceratops and other dinosaurs discovered 65 million years ago when the most recent large asteroid or comet or whatever it was hit the earth and wiped them out.

Individuals, not asteroids, more often personify contingency in history. Who can specify in advance—or unravel afterwards—the particular intersection of genetics, environment, and culture that makes each person unique? Who can foresee what weird conjunctions of design and circumstance may cause a very few individuals to rise so high as to shape great events, and so come to the attention of historians? Such people may set their sights on getting to the top, but an assassin, or a bacillus, or even a carelessly driven taxicab can always be lurking along the way. How entire countries fall into the hands of malevolent geniuses like Hitler and Stalin remains as unfathomable in the "new" Cold War history as in the "old."

Once leaders like these do gain power, however, certain things become highly probable. It is only to be expected that in an authoritarian state the chief authoritarian's personality will weigh much more heavily than those of democratic leaders, who have to share power. And whether because of social alienation, technological innovation, or economic desperation, the first half of the twentieth century was particularly susceptible to great authoritarians and all that resulted from their ascendancy. It is hardly possible to imagine Nazi Germany or the world war it caused without Hitler. I find it increasingly difficult, given what we know now, to imagine the Soviet Union or the Cold War without Stalin.

For the more we learn, the less sense it makes to distinguish Stalin's foreign policies from his domestic practices or even his personal behavior. Scientists have shown the natural world to be filled with examples of what they call "self-similarity across scale": patterns that persist whether one views them microscopically, macroscopically, or anywhere in between. Stalin was like that: he functioned in much the same manner whether operating within the international system, within his alliances, within his country, within his party, within his personal entourage, or even within his family. The Soviet leader waged cold wars on all of these fronts. The Cold War we came to know was only one of many from *his* point of view.

Nor did Stalin's influence diminish as quickly as that of most dictators after their deaths. He built a *system* sufficiently durable to survive not only his own demise but his successors' fitful and half-hearted efforts at "de-Stalinization." They were themselves its creatures, and they continued to work within it because they knew no other method of governing. Not until [Mikhail] Gorbachev was a Soviet leader fully prepared to dismantle Stalin's structural legacy. It tells us a lot that as it disappeared, so too did the Cold War and ultimately the Soviet Union itself.

This argument by no means absolves the United States and its allies of a considerable responsibility for how the Cold War was fought—hardly a surprising conclusion since they in fact won it. Nor is it to deny the feckless stupidity with which the Americans fell into peripheral conflicts like Vietnam, or their exorbitant expenditures on unusable weaponry: these certainly caused the Cold War to cost much more in money and lives than it otherwise might have. Nor is it to claim moral superiority for Western statesmen. None was as bad as Stalin—or Mao—but the Cold War left no leader uncorrupted: the wielding of great power, even in the best of times, rarely does.

It is the case, though, that if one applies the always useful test of counterfactual history—drop a key variable and speculate as to what difference this might have made—Stalin's centrality to the origins of the Cold War becomes quite clear. For all of their importance, one could have removed Roosevelt, Churchill, Truman, Bevin, Marshall, or Acheson, and a cold war would still have probably followed the world war. If one could have eliminated Stalin, alternative paths become quite conceivable. For with the possible exception of Mao, no twentieth-century leader imprinted himself upon his country as thoroughly and with such lasting effect as Stalin did. And given his personal propensity for cold wars—a tendency firmly rooted long before he had even heard of Harry Truman—once Stalin wound up at the top in Moscow and once it was clear his state would survive the war, then it looks equally clear that there was going to be a Cold War whatever the west did. Who then was responsible? The answer, I think, is authoritarianism in general, and Stalin in particular.

EXPLORING THE ISSUE

Was President Truman Responsible for the Cold War?

Critical Thinking and Reflection

1. Define "containment" as a policy. How did it originate? How did the Truman administration use it? Why was diplomat George F. Kennan critical of its long-term application?
2. Critically examine what Gaddis means by arguing that the United States created an "Empire by invitation" in Europe after World War II. Also examine what Offner means when he argues that Truman was a "parochial nationalist." How did Truman's perception of the world affect the decisions he made during the years from 1945 to 1950?
3. Compare and contrast and critically evaluate the interpretation of the Cold War of Gaddis and Offner in regards to the following:

   a. The Munich analogy
   b. New strategic thinking (Atomic diplomacy; containment)
   c. America's global interests
   d. Russia's global interests
   e. A combination of America's and Russia's military and economic power 1945–1950
   f. The lend-lease controversy
   g. Atomic diplomacy (threats or sincere arms control offers)
   h. Iran and Middle East issues
   i. Truman Doctrine
   j. Marshall Plan
   k. Korean War
   l. Truman's personality
   m. Stalin's personality

4. Do you think that if FDR had lived into 1948 that the Cold War could have been avoided? Was the Cold War the fault of Truman's "parochial nationalist" outlook?
5. Do you agree or disagree with Gaddis, who argues that the Cold War was inevitable because of Stalin's personality? Critically evaluate.

Is There Common Ground?

Both sides have hardened their positions in assessing blame for the Cold War. Revisionists believe that Americans did not recognize the legitimate concerns of the Soviet Union regarding its security. Understanding that Russia had suffered enormous casualties on the eastern front, the United States should have granted more concessions for Russian territorial control over Eastern Europe in order to prevent a third invasion from France or Germany through that weakened frontier. Meanwhile, after attempts to negotiate the Yalta agreements laid down by his predecessor FDR, President Truman recognized how difficult it would be to work with Stalin. There is a tendency among many Americans to lay blame for the Cold War at the feet of the Soviet Union whose leaders were captive to Communist ideology. What is ignored is the degree to which the United States was equally driven by a competing ideology of democracy and free market capitalism. Consequently, both sides viewed each other as a threat.

Additional Resources

The literature on the Cold War is enormous. Students who wish to study this topic in greater detail should consult *Containment: Documents on American Policy and Strategy, 1945–1950* edited by Thomas H. Etzold and John Lewis Gaddis (Columbia University Press, 1978). Another comprehensive work is Melvyn P. Leffler, *A Preponderance of Power: National Security, the Truman Administration, and the Cold War* (Stanford University Press, 1992). The two best readers to excerpt the various viewpoints on the Cold War are Thomas G. Paterson and Robert J. McMahon, eds., *The Origins of the Cold War*, 3rd ed. (D C. Heath, 1991) and Melvyn P. Leffler and David S. Painter, eds., *Origins of the Cold War: An International History* (Routledge, 1994). Finally, David Reynolds has edited a useful series of essays in *The Origins of the Cold War: International Perspectives* (Yale University Press, 1994).

Two recent major books published on the Cold War are Campbell Craig and Frederick Logwall, *America's Cold War: The Politics of Insecurity* (The Belknap Press of Harvard University Press, 2009, 2012), a moderate revisionist treatment, and Gaddis' recent biography of *George F. Kennan: An American Life* (Penguin, 2011), which spawned two interesting review essays: Frank Cortigliola, "Is This George Kennan," *The New York Review of Books* (December 8, 2011); and Louis Menand, "Getting Real: George F. Kennan's Cold War," *The New Yorker*, November 14, 2011. Gaddis' argument with the revisionists is nicely summarized in Karen J. Winkler, "Scholars Refight the Cold War," *The Chronicle of Higher Education* (March 2, 1994, pp. 8–10). See also Tony Judt, "Why the Cold War Worked," *The New York Review of Books* (October 9, 1997) and "A Story Still to be Told," *The New York Review of Books* (March 23, 2006) for critical reviews of Gaddis' *We Now Know: Rethinking Cold War History* (Oxford University Press, 1997). Perhaps the best critiques of Gaddis are three of his earlier books: *The United States and the Origins of the Cold War, 1941–1947* (Columbia University Press, 1972); *Russia, the Soviet Union and the United States: An Interpretative History*, 2nd ed. (McGraw Hill, 1990); and *Strategies of Containment: A Critical Appraisal of America's Postwar Foreign Policy* (Oxford, 1978). Valuable bibliographies are contained in all the previous books. The most up-to-date is Melvin P. Leffler, "Cold War and Global Hegemony, 1945–1991," *OAH Magazine of History* (March 2005).

ISSUE 14

Did President John F. Kennedy Cause the Cuban Missile Crisis?

YES: Thomas G. Paterson, from "When Fear Ruled: Rethinking the Cuban Missile Crisis," *New England Journal of History* (vol. 52, Fall 1995)

NO: Robert Weisbrot, from *Maximum Danger: Kennedy, the Missiles, and the Crisis of American Confidence* (Ivan R. Dee, 2001)

Learning Outcomes

After reading the essays, the student will be able to:

- Understand Premier Khrushchev's reasons for putting Soviet missiles in Cuba in the summer of 1962.
- Understand President Kennedy's response to the missiles placed in Cuba.
- Understand the traditional and revisionist interpretations of the Cuban Missile Crisis.
- Understand the impact of the newly declassified documents—such as minutes of the meetings and conferences between former American and Soviet officials—in changing our perceptions about decision making in the Oval Office.
- Understand the impact of the concepts of "crisis management" and "nation building" in the formation of our foreign/policy.

ISSUE SUMMARY

YES: Professor Thomas G. Paterson believes that President Kennedy, even though he moderated the American response and compromised in the end, helped precipitate the Cuban missile crisis by his support for both the failed Bay of Pigs invasion in April 1961 and the continued attempts by the CIA to assassinate Fidel Castro.

NO: Historian Robert Weisbrot argues that the new sources uncovered in the past 20 years portray Kennedy as a president who had not only absorbed the values of his time as an anti-Communist cold warrior but who nevertheless acted as a rational leader and was conciliatory toward the Soviet Union in resolving the Cuban missile crisis.

In 1959, the political situation in Cuba changed drastically when Fulgencio Batista y Zaldi'var was overthrown by a 34-year-old revolutionary named Fidel Castro, who led a guerilla band in the Sierra Maestra mountain range. Unlike his predecessors, Castro refused to be a lackey for American political and business interests. The new left-wing dictator seized control of American oil refineries and ordered a number of diplomats at the U.S. embassy in Havana to leave the country. President Dwight D. Eisenhower was furious and responded shortly before he left office by imposing economic sanctions on the island and breaking diplomatic ties.

Eisenhower's successor, John F. Kennedy, supported an invasion of Cuba by a group of disaffected anti-Castro Cuban exiles that had been planned by the previous administration to foster the overthrow of Castro. The April 1961 Bay of Pigs invasion was a disaster as Castro's army routed the invaders, killing many and imprisoning others. The Kennedy administration responded by securing Cuba's removal from the Organization of American States (OAS) in early 1962, imposed an economic embargo on the island, and carried out threatening military maneuvers in the Caribbean.

The isolation and possibility of a second invasion of this Caribbean Communist client state probably influenced Soviet Premier Nikita Khrushchev to take a more proactive stance to defend Cuba. In the summer of 1962, he sent troops and conventional weapons to the island; by September 1962, missile launching pads had been installed. President Kennedy confronted criticism from Republicans, such as Senator Kenneth Keating of New York, who charged that the Russians were bringing not only troops but also nuclear weapons to Cuba. At first, Kennedy was concerned with the political implications of the charges for the 1962 congressional races, and on September 11, 1962, he assured reporters that the Cuban military buildup was primarily defensive in nature.

President Kennedy was probably caught off-guard with Khrushchev's bold actions in Cuba in the fall of 1962. Did Khrushchev want to compensate for the Russian "missile gap"? Did he want to trade Russia's withdrawal from Cuba with the American withdrawal from Berlin? Did Khrushchev wish to provide Cuba with military protection from another U.S. invasion? Forty years later, with much more evidence available from the Cuban and Russian participants in these events, Khrushchev's motives are still the subject of debate. President Kennedy, like most policymakers, had to make his decision to blockade Cuba on the basis of the best available information at the time.

The situation changed drastically on the morning of October 16, 1962, when National Security Council adviser McGeorge Bundy informed the president that photographs from U-2 reconnaissance flights over Cuba revealed that the Russians were building launching pads for 1,000-mile medium-range missiles as well as 2,200-mile intermediate-range missiles. The president kept the news quiet. He ordered more U-2 flights to take pictures and had Bundy assemble a select group of advisers who became known as the Executive Committee of the National Security Council (Ex-Comm). For six days and nights, the president favored a blockade, or what he called a "quarantine," of the island. On October 22, 1962, Kennedy revealed his plans for the quarantine over national television.

Mark J. White has succinctly summarized the resolution of the Cuban missile crisis in the introduction to his edited collection of documents entitled *The Kennedys and Cuba: The Declassified Documentary History* (Ivan R. Dee, 1999). "During the second week of the crisis," writes White, "from JFK's October 22 address to the achievement of a settlement six days later, Kennedy and Khrushchev initially fired off messages to each other, defending their own positions and assailing their adversary's. But a series of developments from October 26 to 28 suddenly brought the crisis to an end." Khrushchev offered to remove the missiles if the American president promised not to invade Cuba and removed the Jupiter missiles that the United States had installed along the Soviet border in Turkey. Kennedy publically promised not to invade Cuba and privately agreed to withdraw the missiles in Turkey, an arrangement that satisfied Khrushchev and brought an end to the most dangerous episode of the entire Cold War era.

Was President Kennedy responsible for the Cuban missile crisis? Professor Thomas Paterson, one of the best known revisionist diplomatic historians, has authored numerous books and articles critical of America's Cold War policies in Europe and Cuba, and is quite critical of what he sees as JFK's fumbling efforts to resolve the crisis via diplomacy. First he challenges the "Camelot image" of Kennedy as the hero who avoided nuclear war by negotiating a settlement with the Russians to take the missiles out of Cuba, thereby avoiding a military confrontation. In Paterson's view, Kennedy's reckless personal behavior was also carried out in his professional life. The president, according to Paterson, was looking for a way to manage the crisis. Rejecting the choices of Eisenhower who wavered between threats of nuclear retaliation or doing nothing, Kennedy believed a third way involved the use of "special forces" like the Green Berets might alter the balance of power in the attempt to "nation build" third world countries to favor the western way over the communist alternative. (The reader is not far off the mark if he perceives similar policies being pursued in Iraq and Afghanistan today.) Paterson admits that the Khrushchev–Castro decision to place missiles in Cuba "ranks as one of the most dangerous in the Cold War." Yet, he blames the policies of the Eisenhower–Kennedy administrations for this decision. As Paterson writes, "Had there been no exile expeditions at the Bay of Pigs, no destructive covert activities, no assassination plots, no military maneuvers and plans, and no economic and diplomatic steps to harass, isolate and destroy the Castro government, there would not have been a Cuban missile crisis." Was Kennedy's response a triumph of effective crisis management? Not in Paterson's view. "In the end," he says, "the two superpowers, frantic to avoid nuclear war and scared by the prospects of doomsday, stumbled toward a settlement."

In the NO selection, Professor Robert Weisbrot rejects both the earlier portraits of Kennedy partisans that JFK was an "effective crisis manager" and the assessments of critics who discern in the president's foreign policy "a dismal amalgam of anti-Communist hysteria, reckless posturing, and a disturbing gleeful crisis orientation." Relying on new evidence made available over the past 20 years, such as the declassified Ex-Comm conversations and the transcripts of several conferences involving Soviet and American scholars and former officials (including Cuba's Castro), Weisbrot sees Kennedy not as a cold warrior but as a rational leader who defused the crisis. Concluding that Kennedy was neither the lone crisis hero as his chief speech writer Ted Sorenson portrayed him in *The Kennedy Legacy* (Macmillan, 1969) nor a macho anti-Communist counterrevolutionary as many revisionists have insisted, Weisbrot credits a number of other participants for softening the crisis. Secretary of State Dean Rusk, for example, was not the "silent Buddha" as portrayed in the writings of earlier Kennedy admirers. It was Rusk who revealed that Kennedy's fall-back plan was to have U.N. Secretary General U. Thant propose a swap of missiles in Turkey and Cuba. It was Llewellyn Thompson, the former ambassador to the Soviet Union, and not Robert Kennedy who suggested accepting Khrushchev's tacit proposals and not the harsher terms of his public demands. Then there was Kennedy's National Security Adviser McGeorge Bundy who acknowledged: "The most important part of crisis management is not to have a crisis, because there's no telling what will happen once you're in one." Scott D. Sagan's, *Limits of Safety: Organizations, Accidents and Nuclear Weapons* (Princeton University, 1985), lists a number of potential disasters, which Professor Weisbrot recounts, that occurred during the Cuban missile crisis, some of which even President Kennedy was not aware. The real failure of crisis management occurred later, Weisbrot believes, when the Kennedy–Johnson team, full of exuberance over their success in Cuba, believed they could manage similar crises in Southeast Asia.

YES

Thomas G. Paterson

When Fear Ruled: Rethinking the Cuban Missile Crisis

Nikita Khrushchev cried and then rushed to the American Embassy in Moscow to sign the book of condolence. Fidel Castro remarked, again and again, "This is bad news," and then turned silent. In Bremen, Germany, a "sea of flowers" engulfed the U.S. consulate, and in Nice, France, construction crews stopped working. A Czech citizen asked: "Who will lead us now?" Europeans were left, said one of them, "Like children in the darkness."

"He glittered when he lived," wrote one of John F. Kennedy's admiring assistants and biographers, Arthur M. Schlesinger, Jr. "Everyone around him thought he had the Midas touch and could not lose." "It can be said of him," eulogized one editorial, "that he did not fear the weather, and did not trim his sails, but instead challenged the wind itself . . . to cause it to blow more softly and more kindly over the world and its people." "The man was magic," a congressman recalled, "He lit up a room. He walked in, and the air was lighter, the light was brighter."

In a time of wrenching turmoil at home and abroad, President John F. Kennedy, for people everywhere, represented hope, youthful energy, courage, determination, compassion, and innovative leadership. He envisioned a new order to pry America out of its doldrums, to get it moving again, as he so often put it. He had won popular approval from the American people and he had touched people abroad, becoming for many a legitimate hero. His wit, eloquent oratory, self-confident style, athleticism, and handsome looks captivated a generation seeking the light at the end of the tunnel. "Though I never met him, I knew him just the same," went the words of a song by the musical group, The Byrds. "He was a friend of mine."

Some thirty years after Kennedy's death, such words still resonate among Americans who feel the anguish of dashed hopes—their slain leader losing his chance to make a difference, taking with him the promise of a better future. Yet, now, we also have more perspective on the tumultuous decade of the sixties. We have had the terrible experience of Vietnam, many frightening Cold War confrontations, and the Watergate and Iron-Contra scandals to make us more skeptical of our leaders and more searching in our assessments. Most important, we now have what must undergird any careful account of the Kennedy era—declassified documents from the Kennedy Library in Boston,

From *New England Journal of History,* Fall 1995, pp. 12–37. Copyright © 1995 by New England Journal of History. Reprinted by permission of New England History Teachers Association (NEHTA).

the Central Intelligence Agency, and East German and Soviet archives, among others. The massive documentary record, although incomplete, has generated scholarly studies that peel back the layers of once hidden stories, expose complexities, separate image from reality, and compel us to contend with a less satisfying past than the one we would prefer and have imagined. The positive images Kennedy's advisers so skillfully broadcast—the cosmetic cream of celebration that covered his blemishes—have not altogether disappeared but they have faded. We have more balance, more insight, more evidence. Our portrait of John F. Kennedy has become necessarily less flattering. Such is the nature of always evolving historical research and interpretation, although we can take no comfort from it.

We now have an unadorned Kennedy, a whole Kennedy, a very human Kennedy, whose character, judgment, and accomplishments have been called into question. The demythologizing of John F. Kennedy, for example, includes a reconsideration of the image of the family man. Although Kennedy genuinely loved his children, he was a brazen, reckless womanizer who named the women he wanted for sex and usually got them, including Hollywood starlets and Judith Campbell Exner, mistress to crime bosses as well as to the President. This is the stuff of sensationalism, of course, but these sexual indiscretions also endangered national security, his presidency, and his health. Kennedy, moreover, was gravely ill. Had the voting public known the extent of his ailments in 1960—especially his Addison's disease and severe back pain, for which he took injections of concoctions of amphetamines, steroids, calcium, and vitamins administered by a discredited doctor—had the public known, they may not have taken the risk of sending him to the White House. His reputation as a writer has also encountered the test of evidence. His book, *Profiles in Courage*, published in 1955, for which he took personal credit and won a Pulitzer Prize, was actually written for him by an aide and a university professor.

The 1960 presidential candidate who criticizing the Eisenhower Administration for permitting the Soviets to gain missile superiority—the famed charge of a "missile gap"—became the President who learned that the United States held overwhelming nuclear supremacy—yet he nonetheless tremendously expanded the American nuclear arsenal. CIA officers, believing that they were carrying out presidential instructions, tried to assassinate Cuba's Fidel Castro and send sabotage teams to destroy life and property on the island. For a President who said that Americans should "never fear to negotiate," Kennedy seemed more enamored with military than with diplomatic means: defense expenditures increased thirteen percent in the Kennedy years, counter-insurgency training and warfare accelerated, and U.S. intervention in Vietnam deepened.

Given the disparity between image and reality and the inevitable reinterpretation that new documentation and distance from events stimulate, it is not surprising that ambiguity now marks Kennedy scholarship. He appears as both confrontationist and conciliator, hawk and dove, decisive leader and hesitant improviser, hyperbolic politician and prudent diplomat, poor crisis preventer but good crisis manager, idealist and pragmatist, glorious hero and flawed man of dubious character. On the one hand he sponsored the Peace

Corps, and on the other he attended personally to the equipment needs of the Green Berets. On the one hand he called for an appreciation of Third World nationalism, and on the other he intervened in Vietnam and Cuba to try to squash nationalist movements he found unacceptable. He said that the United States respected neutralism, yet he strove to persuade important neutrals such as India, Indonesia, and Egypt to shed their non-alignment for alliance with the United States in the Cold War.

Kennedy preached democracy, but sent military aid to oppressive Latin American regimes, and the Alliance for Progress did not meet its goals because it shored up elites, who took the money for their own purposes. He said he knew that the Sino-Soviet split compelled a new policy toward the People's Republic of China, but he spoke often about a monolithic Communism and rejected options to improve relations with the PRC. On the one hand he created the Arms Control and Disarmament Agency, and on the other expanded the number of American intercontinental ballistic missiles from some 60 to more than 420. On the one hand, seeing Eastern Europe as the "Achilles heel of the Soviet empire" and discarding John Foster Dulles' provocative and failed policy of "liberation," he strove for improved relations with Soviet Russia's neighbors. But on the other he signed a trade bill that denied most-favored-nation treatment to Yugoslavia. On the one hand he called for a new Atlantic community, and on the other he refused to share decision-making power with increasingly disgruntled Western European allies.

Some analysts have argued that had Kennedy lived and won reelection in 1964, he would have withdrawn from Vietnam and transformed the Cold War from confrontation to peace and disarmament. Some Kennedy-watchers have emphasized that the President was evolving as a leader; that is, through education imposed by crises, Kennedy grew and began to temper his ardent Cold War anti-Communism, learning the limits of American power. "The heart of the Kennedy legend," the journalist James Reston has aptly noted, "is what might have been." We can never be sure about what Kennedy might have done, but we do know what he *did*. And that is were we must focus our attention—on the Kennedy *record*. Was it "stunningly successful," as one writer has claimed, or was it something quite less—high on image, but mixed if not low on results?

The centerpiece in the Kennedy record is his handling of the Cuban missile crisis. His role in this disturbing crisis—the closest the United States and the Soviet Union ever came to nuclear war—has especially undergone scrutiny in the last few years. Recent international conferences, featuring Kennedy-era decisionmakers, and the declassification of documents in Russia, Cuba, and the United States give us a new, more textured view of Kennedy and the missile crisis. It may be true, as Secretary of State Dean Rusk remembered, that "President Kennedy had ice water in his veins," but serious doubts have emerged about whether this event ranks as his "finest hour."

This dangerous moment in world history should not be championed as a supreme display of crisis management, calculated control, and statesmanship, but rather explored as a case of near misses that scared the crisis managers on both sides into a settlement because, in the words of National Security Affairs Adviser McGeorge Bundy, the crisis was "so near to spinning out of control."

New evidence also prompts us to investigate the Cuban missile crisis not as a simple good guys–bad guys drama foisted on the United States by an aggressive Soviet Union and crazed Castroite Cuba, but as a crisis for which Kennedy policies must bear some responsibility. This article plumbs the origins of the crisis, Kennedy's management of it, and the outcome, the "narrow squeak" that it was.

Those hair-trigger days of October 1962, stand out in the drama of the Cold War. Before that quaking month, the Soviets had boldly and recklessly placed medium-range missiles in Cuba—missiles that could carry nuclear warheads and destroy American cities. On October 14, an American U-2 spy-plane snapped photographs which revealed the construction of several missile sites. Determined to force the missiles from Cuba, Kennedy soon convened a council of wise men called the Executive Committee or ExComm. ExComm considered four policy options: "talk them out," "squeeze them out," "shoot them out," or "buy them out." Ultimately the committee advised the president to surround Cuba with a naval blockade as the best means to resolve the crisis. Kennedy went on television the evening of October 22 to explain the crisis and the U.S. response.

An international war of nerves soon began. More than sixty American ships went on patrol to enforce the blockade. The Strategic Air Command went on nuclear alert, moving upward to Defense Condition (DEFCON) 2 for the first time ever—the next level being deployment. B-52 bombers, packed with nuclear weapons, stood ready, while soldiers and equipment moved to the southeastern United States to prepare for an invasion of Cuba. Thousands of road maps of the island were distributed to anxious troops. Nail-biting days followed as Soviet ships steamed toward the U. S. armada. Grabbing a few hours of sleep on cots in their offices and expecting doomsday, Kennedy's advisers wondered if they would ever see their families again. And then, finally, with great relief, on October 28, Khrushchev appealed for restraint and the Americans and Soviets settled. In return for a Kennedy pledge not to invade Cuba and to withdraw U.S. Jupiter missiles from Turkey, Khrushchev promised to "dismantle," "crate, and return" his SS-4 missiles to the Soviet Union, and he fulfilled his pledge.

Kennedy's handling of the crisis, Arthur Schlesinger had effusively written, constituted a "combination of toughness and restraint, of will, nerve and wisdom, so brilliantly controlled, so matchlessly calibrated." "We've won a great victory," Kennedy himself told congressional leaders." In private, the President crowed to friends, "I cut his balls off."

"We have been had," growled Admiral George Anderson, in a quite different view. The no invasion pledge, complained Cuban exiles, "was another Bay of Pigs for us." "It's the greatest defeat in our history," snapped General Curtis LeMay. These statements about "victory" and "defeat" actually set the question too narrowly. A more revealing question is this: How did we get into the crisis in the first place?

Cuba and the United States had been snarling at one another ever since Fidel Castro came to power in early 1959 and vowed to reduce U.S. power on the island. While Cuba accelerated a bitterly anti-American revolution, the

Eisenhower Administration imposed economic sanctions and initiated covert CIA actions. A defiant Castro moved Cuba steadily toward Communism and military alliance with the Soviet Union. Just before Kennedy's inauguration, President Eisenhower broke diplomatic relations with Cuba. Kennedy soon accelerated a multitrack program of covert, economic, diplomatic, and propagandistic elements designed to bring Castro down. Secretary of Defense Robert McNamara later remarked: "If I had been in Moscow or Havana at that time [of 1961–1962], I would have believed the Americans were preparing for an invasion."

Essential to understanding the frightening missile crisis of fall 1962, in fact, is the relationship between U.S. activities and Soviet/Cuban decisions. The time of events is critical, and there is no doubt that Castro saw Cuba's acceptance of the missiles as the formation of a military alliance with the Soviet Union, similar to membership in the Warsaw Pact. In May 1962, the Soviets and Cubans first discussed the idea of placing nuclear-tipped missiles on the island; in early July, during a trip by Raul Castro to Moscow, a draft agreement was initialed; in late August, during a trip by Che Guevara to Moscow, the final touches were put on the accord.

What was the United States doing during those critical months before August? By 1962, more than two hundred anti-Castro Cuban exile organizations operated in the United States. After the failed Bay of Pigs invasion of early 1961, Cuban exiles chafed at the bit in Florida, eager to avenge their losses. Many of them banded together under the leadership of Jose Miro Cardona, the former prime minister. Miro Cardona met with President Kennedy in Washington on April 10, 1962, and the Cuban exile left the meeting persuaded that Kennedy intended to use U. S. armed forces against Cuba. Indeed, after Miro Cardona returned to Miami, he and his Revolutionary Council began to identify recruits for a Cuban unit in the U.S. military.

If Havana worried about such maneuverings, it grew apprehensive too about the alliance between the exile groups and the CIA, whose commitment to the destruction of the Castro regime knew few bounds. Hit-and-run saboteurs burned cane fields and blew up oil depots and transportation facilities. In May, one group attacked a Cuban patrol boat off the northern coast of the island. The Revolutionary Student Directorate, another exile organization, used two boats to attack Cuba in August. Alpha 66 attacked Cuba on numerous occasions, as did other CIA saboteurs. CIA officers and "assets" were at the same time plotting to assassinate Fidel Castro.

Some of these activities came under the wing of Operation Mongoose, the covert effort engineered by Attorney General Robert Kennedy to disrupt the Cuban economy and stir unrest on the island. As General Maxwell Taylor recalled, after the Bay of Pigs "a new urgency" was injected into "Kennedy's concern for counterinsurgency. . . . Robert Kennedy told counterinsurgency specialist Colonel Edward Lansdale that the Bay of Pigs "insult needed to be redressed rather quickly."

Intensified economic coercion joined covert activities. The Kennedy Administration, in February 1962, banned most imports of Cuban products. Washington also pressed its NATO allies to support the "economic isolation" of Cuba. Soon Cuba was forced to pay higher freight costs, enlarge its foreign debt, and suffer factory shut-downs due to the lack of spare parts once [brought] in the United States. The effect on Cuba was not what Washington intended: more political centralization and repression, more state management, closer ties to the Soviet Union.

In early 1962, as well, Kennedy officials engineered the eviction of Cuba from the Organization of American States. The expulsion registered loudly in Havana; which interpreted it as "political preparation for an invasion."

At about the same time, the American military planning and activities, some public, some secret, demonstrated U.S. determination to cripple the Castro government. Mongoose director Lansdale noted in a top secret memorandum to the President that he designed his schemes to "help the people of Cuba overthrow the Communist regime from within Cuba. . . ." And if the revolt proved successful, the United States would have to sustain it. That is, he said, the United States would likely have to "respond promptly with military force. . . ." Indeed, "the basic plan requires complete and efficient support of the [U.S.] military." The chairman of the Joint Chiefs of Staff, General Taylor, explained in the spring of 1962 that "indigenous resources" would carry out the Operation Mongoose plan to overthrow the Cuban government, but, he added, the plan "recognizes that final success will require decisive U.S. military intervention." Because the scheme also required close cooperation with Cuban exiles, it is likely that Castro's spies picked up from the leaky Cuban community in Miami at least vague suggestions that the U. S. military was plotting action against Cuba. As CIA agents liked to joke, there were three ways to transmit information rapidly: telegraph, telephone, and tell-a-Cuban.

Actual American military maneuvers heightened Cuban fears. One well publicized U.S. exercise, staged during April—also in 1962—included 40,000 troops and an amphibious landing on a small island near Puerto Rico. Some aggressive American politicians, throughout 1962, were calling for the real thing: an invasion of Cuba. In the summer of 1962, finally, the U. S. Army began a program to create Spanish-speaking units; the Cuban exiles who signed up had as their "primary" goal, as they put it, a "return to Cuba" to battle the Castro government.

By late spring/summer 1962, then, at the very time that Havana and Moscow were contemplating defensive measures that included medium-range missiles, Cuba felt besieged from several quarters. Havana was eager for protection. The Soviet Union had become its trading partner; and the Soviets, after the Bay of Pigs, had begun military shipments that ultimately included small arms, howitzers, armored personnel carriers, patrol boats, tanks, MIG jet fighters, and surface-to-air missiles. Yet all of this weaponry, it seemed, had not deterred the United States. And, given the failure of Kennedy's multitrack program to unseat the Cuban leader, "were we right or wrong to fear direct invasion" next, asked Fidel Castro. As he said in July 1962, shortly after striking the missile-deployment agreement with the Soviets: "We must prepare ourselves for that direct invasion." He welcomed the Soviet missiles to deter the United States. And the Soviet Union grabbed at any opportunity to notch up its position in the nuclear arms race.

The Khrushchev-Castro decision to place missiles in Cuba ranks as one of the most dangerous in the Cold War. Yet had there been no exile expedition at the Bay of Pigs, no destructive covert activities, no assassination plots, no military maneuvers and plans, and no economic and diplomatic steps to harass, isolate and destroy the Castro government, there would not have been a Cuban missile crisis. "We'd carried out the Bay of Pigs operation, never intending to use American military force—but the Kremlin didn't know that," a pensive Robert McNamara recalled some twenty-five years after the event. "We were running covert operations against Castro" [and] "people in the Pentagon were even talking about a first strike [nuclear policy]. . . . So the Soviets may well have believed we were seeking Castro's overthrow *plus* a first strike capability." The former Defense Secretary concluded: "This may have led them to do what they did in Cuba."

To stress only the global dimension—Soviet–American competition, as is commonly done, is to slight the local or regional sources of the conflict. As somebody put it, we have looked too much at the international climate and too little at the local weather. To slight the local conditions is to miss the central point that Premier Nikita Khrushchev would never have had the opportunity to install dangerous missiles in the Caribbean if the United States had not been attempting to actively to overthrow the Cuban government.

If Kennedy's war against Cuba helped initiate the crisis, Kennedy must also bear responsibility for how the crisis unfolded so dangerously—how the crisis began to spin out of control. Kennedyites prided themselves on a calculated, well managed foreign policy; they believed that they could control events through the rational use of force and wise deciphering of the intentions and capabilities of friends and foes alike.

The sources for such confidence in "control" were many. First, the popularity of the concept of "control accounting" or "management control" in business and government, popularized by think tanks such as the RAND Corporation and personified in Secretary McNamara, who believed that numbers told much if not all and that almost everything could be reduced to fine-tuned plans and balances—including a "balance of terror."

Second, the Kennedy people admired a strong presidency. Critical of Dwight Eisenhower for weak leadership in the 1950s, the Kennedyites extolled a strong, activist executive who would generate policy, command the bureaucracy, and lead Congress—in short, a chief executive in firm control.

Third, at work were popular Clausewitzian notions of disciplined war—that "war in all its phases must be rationally guided by meaningful political purposes." Yet another source of the control mentality was the "can-do" style of the Kennedy team and its exaggerated sense of U.S. power and the American ability to right a world gone wrong, to remake other societies, to face down adversaries. The United States, McGeorge Bundy once remarked, "was the locomotive at the head of mankind, and the rest of the world [was] the caboose." Arthur Schlesinger captured the mood this way: "Euphoria reigned; we thought for a moment that the world was plastic and the future unlimited."

Last, Kennedy officials had a faddish fascination with anti-revolutionary, counter-insurgency doctrines, modernization theories, and covert methods, which suggested that the application of limited power could produce desired results; that violence could be managed; and that through nation-building, the United States could guide countries toward peace and prosperity, if not replicate itself abroad and win allies."

In the early 1960s, this faith in control did not go unchallenged within the administration. Schlesinger himself grew alarmed by the Administration's fervent embrace of counterinsurgency. As he wrote later, it became a "mode of warfarer . . . which nourished an American belief in the capacity and right to intervene in foreign lands, and which was both corrupting in method and futile in effect." Ambassador Adlai Stevenson remarked to a friend that "they've got the damndest bunch of boy commandos running around [here] . . . [that] you ever saw." Under Secretary of State George Ball never warmed to what he called the "high priests, who talked a strange, sacerdotal language" with a quaintly Madison Avenue ring." He criticized the nation-building ideas of Walt Rostow as a "most presumptuous undertaking," for Ball doubted that "American professors could make bricks without the straw of experience and with indifferent and infinitely various kinds of clay." This calls to mind Sam Rayburn's remark after Vice President Johnson came back from a White House meeting thoroughly excited about the brainpower of Kennedy's young assistants: "Well, Lyndon," Rayburn said, "they may be every bit as intelligent as you say, but I'd feel a whole lot better about them if just one of them had run for sheriff once."

As it turned out, the world was not malleable, events could not be predicted or controlled with pinpoint accuracy, and the rather heady people in the Kennedy entourage proved fallible. Recent studies of the Berlin crisis, for example, reveal just how difficult it is to control local leaders or commanders, be they General Lucius Clay in West Germany or Walter Ulbricht in East Germany. Clausewitz himself had warned about "uncertainty." The "general unreliability of all information," he wrote, "presents a special problem"—"all action takes place . . . in a kind of twilight, which, like fog or moonlight, often tends to make things seem grotesque and larger than they really are."

Still, the control mentality dominated the Kennedy Administration. Exploration of its place during the missile crisis helps scholars test the question of crisis management. What emerges from the mounds of documents is not so much an enviable exercise in crisis management, but rather a study in near misses, imperfect instructions, confusions, miscalculations, and exhaustion. These negative traits gained life because President Kennedy, at the start, ruled out negotiations with either the Soviet Union or Cuba. He decided to inform the Soviets of U.S. policy through a television address rather than through diplomatic channels. The stiff arming of diplomacy seriously raised the level of danger.

Some ExComm participants recommended that negotiations be tried first. In the beginning, McGeorge Bundy urged consideration not only of military plans but of a "political track" or diplomacy. But Kennedy showed little interest in negotiations. When McNamara mentioned that diplomacy might precede military action, for example, the President immediately switched the discussion to another question: How long would it take to get air strikes organized? Conspicuously absent from the first meeting of the crisis was a serious probing of Soviet and Cuban motivation or any reflection on how U.S. actions may have helped trigger the crisis. At the second ExComm meeting of October 16, Secretary of State Dean Rusk argued against the surprise air strike that General Taylor had bluntly advocated. Rusk recommended instead "a direct message to Castro." At the close of Rusk's remarks, Kennedy once again derailed such thoughts and returned to the military option, immediately asking: "Can we get a little idea about what the military thing *is*?

During the tense days that followed, former Ambassador to the Soviet Union Charles Bohlen advised that Moscow would have to retaliate against the United States if American bombs killed its technicians. A stern letter to Khrushchev should be "tested" first as a method to gain withdrawal of the missiles. Joined by former ambassador to the Soviet Union Llewellyn Thompson, Bohlen favored opening "talks" with Moscow—a "diplomatic approach." Bohlen told the President: "I don't see the urgency of military action." And a grim Ambassador to the United Nations, Adlai Stevenson, appealed to Kennedy: "The existence of nuclear missile bases anywhere is negotiable before we start anything." But, after helping to initiate the crisis, Kennedy bypassed diplomacy in favor of confrontation.

During the hair-trigger days after the October 22 speech, much went wrong, the level of danger constantly went up, and weary and irritable decisionmakers sensed that they were losing their grip. "A high risk of uncontrollable escalation" dogged the crisis. Robert Kennedy remembered that, on October 25, "we were on the edge of a precipice with no way off. . . . President Kennedy had initiated the course of events, but he no longer had control over them." So much unraveled, so much could not be reigned in. First, there was the possibility that what Robert Kennedy called a "crackpot" exile group would attempt to assassinate Castro or raid the island. Operation Mongoose sabotage teams were actually already inside Cuba; they had been dispatched there before the missile crisis and now they could not be reached by their CIA handlers. What if this "half-assed operation," the Attorney General worried, ignited trouble. One of these teams actually did blow up a Cuban factory on November 8. To cite another mishap: not until the 27th of October did the administration think to inform the Soviets that the quarantine line was an arc measured at 500 nautical miles around Cuba. What if a Soviet captain inadvertently piloted his ship into the blockade zone?

The legendary feud between McNamara and his admirals during the crisis revealed trouble. This exchange between the Defense Secretary and Admiral George Anderson could not have been reassuring at the time:

> McNamara: "When that ship reaches the line, how are you going to stop it?"
> Anderson: "We'll hail it."
> McNamara: "In what language—English or Russian?"
> Anderson: "How the hell should I know?"
> McNamara: "What will you do if they don't understand?"
> Anderson: "I suppose we'll use flags."

McNamara: "Well, what if they don't stop?"

Anderson: "We'll send a shot across the bow."

McNamara: "Then what if that doesn't work?"

Anderson: "Then we'll fire into the rudder."

McNamara: "You are not going to fire a single shot at anything without my express permission, is that clear?". . .

Anderson: "Don't worry, Mr. Secretary, we know what we are doing here."

The Soviet ships, fortunately, stopped and returned home.

The Navy's anti-submarine warfare activities also carried the potential of escalating the crisis. Soviet submarines prowled near the quarantine line, and, following the standing rules of engagement, Navy ships forced several of them to surface. In one case, a Navy commander exercised the high-risk option of dropping a depth charge on a Soviet submarine. As one specialist on crisis management has written, the President and McNamara "may not have fully understood the operational implications of their authorization of ASW [Anti-submarine warfare] operations."

Another opportunity for trouble occurred when the commander of the Strategic Air Command, General Thomas S. Power, issued DEFCON 2 alert instructions in the clear. Alerts serve to prepare American forces for war, but they also carry the danger of escalation, because movement to a high category might be read by an adversary as American planning for a first strike. Under such circumstances, the adversary might be tempted to launch a preemptive strike. The Soviets, feeling their way cautiously through the crisis, chose not to read it that way.

Two serious episodes in the air on October 27 also saw the breakdown of crisis management. In the morning, a U-2 was shot down over Cuba by a surface-to-air missile. Who did it? Did *Cubans*, after having fought Soviet soldiers to take over the SAM sites? Or did a Soviet general in Cuba, on his own, without Khrushchev's knowledge or authorization but perhaps with Castro's, order the shootdown? It seems that the senior Soviet officer, apparently following standing orders to shoot if an American invasion occurred—an invasion he apparently judged to be underway—made the decision during a time when "the psychological climate was . . . ripe for panic" and when "the United States was doing its best to flex its muscles in the region as visibly as possible." In any case, American decisionmakers assumed that Soviets manned the SAM batteries; thus, the shoot-down constituted a dangerous escalation.

General LeMay readied for a massive air strike. McNamara now thought "invasion had become almost inevitable." But President Kennedy hesitated to retaliate, surely scared, now increasingly timid about taking another step toward nuclear war. The President decided to seek an accommodation with Khrushchev. He bypassed ExComm and dispatched his brother to deliver an ultimatum—and a compromise—to Soviet Ambassador Anatoly Dobrynin: start pulling out the missiles within forty-eight hours or U.S. forces would remove them. After Dobrynin asked about a trade (a trade Khrushchev had requested)—the U. S. Jupiter missiles in Turkey for the Soviet missiles in Cuba—Robert Kennedy offered an important American concession: the Jupiters would be dismantled if the problem in Cuba were resolved. As the President said in an ExComm meeting, "we can't very well invade Cuba with all its toil . . . when we could have gotten them out by making a deal on the same missiles in Turkey."

The White House also learned on the 27th of October that an American U-2 plan overflew the northeastern part of the Soviet Union, probably because equipment malfunctioned. Soviet fighters scrambled to intercept it, and American jets from Alaska took flight to rescue the errant aircraft. Although the spy plane flew home without having unleashed a dog fight, Moscow might have read the incident as provocative—a prelude to a bombing attack. As in so many of these examples, decisionmakers in Washington lost control of the crisis to personnel at the operational level. That same afternoon, Cuban anti-aircraft batteries hit a low-flying U.S. reconnaissance aircraft. Castro savored more.

Another aspect of the control issue raises doubts about Kennedy's handling of the crisis. ExComm members represented considerable intellectual talent and experience, but a mythology of cool calculation has grown up around their role. ExComm actually debated alternatives under "intense strain," often in a "state of anxiety and emotional exhaustion." Some advisers suffered such stress that they seemed to become passive or unable to perform their responsibilities.

An assistant to Adlai Stevenson recalled that he had had to become an ExComm "back-up" for the ambassador because, "while he could speak clearly, his memory wasn't very clear . . ." Why? Vice Admiral Charles Wellborn explained that the "emotional state and nervous tension that was involved in [the missile crisis] had this effect." Stevenson, said Wellborn, was feeling "pretty frightened." So apparently was Dean Rusk. Robert Kennedy remembered that the Secretary of State "frequently could not attend our meetings," because "he had a virtually complete breakdown mentally and physically." Once, when Rusk's eyes swelled with tears, Dean Acheson barked at him: "Pull yourself together, Dean, you're the only Secretary of State we have." We cannot determine how stress affected the advice ExComm gave Kennedy, or whether the President himself was speeding on his amphetamines, but at least we know that the crisis managers struggled against time, sleep, exhaustion, and themselves, and they did not always think clearheadedly at a time when the stakes were very high. Had Stevenson and Rusk, both of whom recommended diplomacy and compromise, been steadier, the option of negotiations at the start might have received a better hearing and the world might have been spared so grueling a confrontation. In any case, as McNamara has recalled, there was always the danger that "people may crack" and become "quivering, panicky, irrational people" if "you just keep piling it on."

As for the Soviets, they too sensed that the crisis was spinning out of control. Khrushchev's rambling letter of October 26 to Kennedy betrayed desperation, if not disarray, in the Kremlin. "You and I should not now pull on the ends of the rope in which you have tied a knot of war, because the harder you and I pull, the tighter the knot will become," the Soviet premier wrote. When the knot becomes too tight, Khrushchev observed, it will have to be cut, unleashing the "dread forces our two countries possess." Khrushchev also had to worry about his field commanders. Russian accounts indicate that Soviet forces in Cuba possessed short-range tactical nuclear missiles with warheads. Although the Soviet commander apparently did not have predelegated authority to fire the missiles, Kremlin decisionmakers had to worry about possible mishap, miscommunication or panic that might lead to a firing. These circumstances and the shootdown of the U-2 over Cuba meant that Khrushchev, too, was experiencing the failure of control and the possible ascendancy of accident.

Add to these worries his trouble with Fidel Castro, who demanded a bold Soviet response to U.S. actions and who might provoke an incident with the United States that could escalate the crisis. Castro was pressing the Soviets to use nuclear weapons to save Cuba should the United States attack. "Such adventurists," remarked a Soviet decisionmaker. Khrushchev sternly told his advisers: "You see how far things can go. We've got to get those missiles out of there before a real fire starts." He sensed that time was running out, that events were outpacing the wits of leaders. The United States might invade, and then what? Like Kennedy, to head off disaster, he appealed for a settlement—and the two men and nations compromised. Khrushchev did not consult Castro, but rather informed him, because "we did not have time." That Khrushchev was nervous and fearful about another dangerous twist in the crisis seems clear, because he took the unusual step of announcing the withdrawal of the missiles via Radio Moscow. He did not want to waste the precious time that would have been required to encode, transmit, decode, and translate a diplomatic message. "You see," McNamara has said, "from beginning to end, fear ruled." Khrushchev "shitted in his pants," crudely remarked one Soviet official."

A triumph of American and Kennedy prudence? A triumph of crisis management? Historians no longer think so. In the end, the two superpowers, frantic to avoid nuclear war and scared by the prospects of doomsday, stumbled toward a settlement. "We were in luck," remarked Ambassador John Kenneth Galbraith, "but success in a lottery is no argument for lotteries." If the crisis had lasted more than thirteen days, remembered a U.S. adviser, "the whole thing would have begun to unravel."

President Kennedy helped precipitate the missile crisis by harassing Cuba through his multi-track program. Then he reacted to the crisis by suspending diplomacy in favor of public confrontation. In the end, he frightened himself. In order to postpone doomsday, or at least to prevent a high-casualty invasion of Cuba, he moderated the American response and compromised. Khrushchev withdrew his mistake, while gaining what Ambassador Llewellyn Thompson thought was the "important thing" all along for the Soviet leader: being able to say, "I saved Cuba. I stopped an invasion."

After the missile crisis, Castro sought better relations with Washington, and he made gestures toward detente. He sent home thousands of Soviet military personnel. He publicly called for rapprochement. But, after Castro returned from a trip to the Soviet Union, where he patched up relations with Khrushchev and won promises of more foreign aid, Robert Kennedy asked the CIA to crank up another anti-Castro campaign. The National Security Council soon approved a new sabotage program, and the CIA devised new dirty tricks.

The agency also revitalized its assassination option by making contact with a traitorous Cuban official, Rolando Cubela. Codenamed AM/LASH, he and the CIA plotted to kill Fidel Castro. On the very day that President Kennedy died, AM/LASH rendezvoused with CIA agents in Paris, where he received a ball-point pen rigged with a poisonous hypodermic needle intended to produce Castro's instant death.

Months before, in June of 1963, President Kennedy had delivered an unusual speech at American University that seemed to mark a break with the past. He asked Americans to reexamine their hard-line, anti-Soviet attitudes and he appealed for negotiations with the Soviet Union. He also revealed his uneasiness with a strategic policy so dependent upon nuclear weapons. And the president urged the Soviets to join him in reducing nuclear-arms stockpiles.

This high-minded, conciliatory speech, coming just months before his assassination and at a time when he was preparing the country and the Senate for a limited test ban treaty, has persuaded some that Kennedy was shedding his Cold Warriorism. Yet, as the father of the containment doctrine and Kennedy's Ambassador to Yugoslavia, George F. Kennan, sadly remarked, "one speech is not enough." We can, for example, contrast the American University address with two speeches that Kennedy was prepared to deliver in Texas on November 22, 1963, had he not been killed. In the first, Kennedy boasted about his administration's high military buildup. The United States, he said, had to blunt the "ambitions of international Communism." As for Vietnam in particular, the United States "dare not weary of the task." Neither in this undelivered Dallas speech nor in another planned for Austin did Kennedy speak of negotiations. Indeed, the Cold War rhetoric that Kennedy had asked citizens to tone down just months earlier at American University had become revitalized in these two speeches.

Kennedy's foreign policy legacy, then, is mixed, his direction at the end of his life uncertain. Escalation in Vietnam, an arms race of massive proportion and fear, greater factionalism in the Atlantic alliance, and a globalism of overcommitment that ensured crises and weakened the American economy stand beside the Peace Corps and an end to the Berlin crisis. Kennedy surely had doubts about the cliches of the Cold War, but he never shed them. Despite the rhetoric of the bold, new thinking, Kennedy and his advisers never fundamentally reassessed American foreign policy assumptions. Instead, they endowed them with more vigor because they believed that they, unlike those before them, could control—could manage—events.

As historians digging into the documents, we have learned that the world was not plastic, that magic means not only enchantment but sleight of hand, and that President Kennedy did not have the Midas touch. We must reckon with a past colored more with subtle grays than with the extremes of blacks and whites. With such enlightenment comes much discomfort.

Robert Weisbrot    **NO**

Maximum Danger: Kennedy, the Missiles, and the Crisis of American Confidence

The Missile Crisis in Historical Perspective

In his history of nuclear policy, *Danger and Survival*, McGeorge Bundy acknowledged, "Forests have been felled to print the reflections and conclusion of participants, observers, and scholars" on the Cuban missile crisis. The first great wave of coverage occurred in the mid-1960s, as the nation savored a cold war triumph and saluted a martyred leader of untold promise. A second wave peaked in the 1970s, as critics dissected the episode not to extol President Kennedy's supreme feat but to expose his feet of clay. Beginning in the mid-1980s the deforestation again accelerated, as declassified sources and meetings by former officials from America, Russia, and Cuba provided a wealth of factual corrections to early, long unchallenged recollections. Yet this crisis, perhaps the most intensely scrutinized fortnight in American history, is just beginning to come into historical focus.

1. Early Histories: Kennedy's Matchless "Crisis Management"

Kennedy's admirers were first to the ramparts in the battle over the president's historical reputation. The president's speech writer and special counsel Theodore Sorensen, historian Arthur Schlesinger, Jr., columnists and presidential intimates Joseph Alsop and Charles Bartlett, NBC correspondent Elie Abel, and the president's brother and attorney general, Robert Kennedy (in his posthumously published memoir *Thirteen Days*), all depicted the Soviet placement of missiles in Cuba as a brazen, nuclear-tipped challenge that the president could not decline without compromising credibility and tempting still bolder provocations. Brimming with insiders' revelations of tense national security meetings, their narratives formed a paradigm of successful crisis management that, they suggested, future policymakers should study and emulate.

The early histories lauded President Kennedy for cool judgement "in steering a safe course between war and surrender." Although he had discounted diplomacy alone as inadequate to dislodge the missiles and, in any case, a poor answer to nuclear blackmail, Kennedy had rejected urgings to bomb the missile sites (possibly followed by an invasion of Cuba), which would likely have killed many Russians. According to Robert Kennedy, at least six of twelve top aides, both civilian and military, had pressed this doubtful "surgical" solution, prompting him to muse that had any of them been president, "the world would have been very likely plunged in a catastrophic war."

Kennedy drew further praise for conjuring a diplomatic miracle from an unpromising and increasingly volatile standoff. Elie Abel reported that Khrushchev's public demand that America remove its Jupiter missiles from Turkey was "a doubled sense of shock" to Kennedy, who "distinctly remembered having given instructions, long before" to remove the obsolete Jupiters. Now the president "reflected sadly on the built-in futilities of big government," for "not only were the missiles still in Turkey but they had just become pawns in a deadly chess game." Still, Sorensen observed, "The President had no intention of destroying the Alliance by backing down."

As the story was told: After much wrangling and confusion among Ex Comm members, Robert Kennedy offered "a thought of breathtaking simplicity and ingenuity: why not ignore the second Khrushchev message and reply to the first?" With his brother's approval, he informed the Soviet ambassador that while "there could be no quid pro quo or any arrangement made under this kind of threat or pressure. . . . President Kennedy had been anxious to remove those missiles" and still hoped to do so "within a short time after this crisis was over." The attorney general served this carrot on a stick, adding that either the Soviets must remove the missiles promptly or the Americans would do so. The next morning Khrushchev publicly acceded to these terms.

In the heady aftermath of the crisis, President Kennedy saluted the Soviet premier for his "statesmanlike" decision and privately cautioned aides that there should be "no boasting, no gloating, not even a claim of victory. We had won by enabling Khrushchev to avoid complete humiliation—we should not humiliate him now." Robert Kennedy recalled, "What guided all [the president's] deliberations was an effort not to disgrace Khrushchev," to leave the Soviets a path of graceful retreat.

For a nation emerging from a week of terror of the missile crisis, Henry Pachter wrote in the book *Collision Course,* the "style" and "art" of Kennedy's leadership had "restored America's confidence in her own power." Sorensen, haggard from two weeks of stress and fatigue, recalled pondering the president's achievement as he leafed through a copy of *Profiles in Courage* and read the introductory quotation from Burke's eulogy of Charles James Fox: "He may live long, he may do much. But here is the summit. He never can exceed what he does this day."

2. Revisionist Histories: Reckless Kennedy Machismo

Whether or not history moves in cycles, historians typically do, and by the 1970s the once-standard odes to President Kennedy had given way to hard-edged, often hostile studies. As portrayed by the new histories, the "brief shining moment" of Kennedy's Camelot was illumined by nothing more magical than the beacons of modern public relations. From his youth Kennedy had flaunted a reckless self-indulgence encouraged by the family's founding tyrant, Joseph P. Kennedy, who imparted to his male children his own ambition, opportunism, and a shameless *machismo* toward women. A succession of affairs unencumbered by emotional involvement; publication of an intelligent but amateurish senior thesis courtesy of family friends; embellishment of a war record marked by heroism but also by some unexplained lapses in leadership; and reception of a Pulitzer Prize for *Profiles in Courage,* written in significant part by his aide, Sorensen, all reflected a pursuit of expedience more than excellence.

Critics found that Kennedy's performance as president confirmed and extended rather than overcame this pattern of flamboyant mediocrity. They discerned in his conduct of foreign policy a dismal amalgam of anti-Communist hysteria, reckless posturing, and a disturbingly gleeful crisis orientation. The results were accordingly grim, ranging from the early disaster at the Bay of Pigs to the placement—or misplacement—of more than fifteen thousand U.S. military personnel in Vietnam by the time of Kennedy's death. Scarcely learning from his early mistakes, Kennedy ignored legitimate Cuban concerns for defense against American intervention and needlessly flirted with the apocalypse in order to force the removal of missiles that scarcely affected the world military balance. To judge from their skeptical recounting, this harrowing superpower confrontation might better be termed the "misled crisis," for it stemmed from Kennedy's perception of a threat to his personal and political prestige rather than (as Americans were misinformed) to the nation's security.

No crisis existed, then, until Kennedy himself created one by forgoing private diplomacy for a public ultimatum and blockade. Considering that the United States had already planned to remove its obsolete missiles from Turkey, Kennedy should have heeded Adlai Stevenson's advice to propose immediately a trade of bases, rather than rush into a confrontation whose outcome he could neither foresee nor fully control. Instead, "From the first, he sought unconditional surrender and he never deviated from that objective." "He took an unpardonable mortal risk without just cause," Richard J. Walton wrote. "He threatened the lives of millions for appearances' sake."

The prime historical mystery to the revisionists was why any American president would needlessly play Russian roulette in the nuclear age. Critics conceded that the president may have felt "substantial political pressures" over Cuba but blamed him for having largely created those pressures with shrill, alarmist speeches. "He had been too specific about what the United States would and would not tolerate in Cuba, and his statements reduced his options," Louise FitzSimons wrote. Garry Wills also saw Kennedy as a prisoner of his own superheated rhetoric about Khrushchev, Communists, and missiles, which aroused a false sense of crisis; "If he was chained to a necessity for acting, he forged the chains himself. . . . Having fooled the people in order to lead them, Kennedy was forced to serve the folly he had induced."

Revisionist writers detected a sad consistency in Kennedy's anti-Communist hyperbole, so that the missile crisis appeared to be a logical by-product of his style rather than simply a grisly aberration. During his bid for the presidency in 1960 Kennedy had stirred voters by charging his Republican opponent, Vice President Richard Nixon, with failing to "stand up to Castro" and to Khrushchev, or to prevent a potentially lethal "missile gap" with the Soviets (in fact Americans had a vast lead). Such ideological zeal remained evident in the Ex Comm, where, David Detzer claimed, Kennedy was "more Cold Warrior" than many, "worrying about America's reputation (and maybe his own) for toughness. . . ."

Scholars in the rising genre of psychohistory traced the nation's "perilous path" in the missile crisis to "the neuroticism of Kennedy's machismo." According to Nancy Gager Clinch, the president viewed the Cuban missiles "as a personal challenge to [his] courage and status," and "In the Kennedy lexicon of manliness, not being 'chicken' was a primary value." This interpretation radiated to other fields: Sidney Lens, in his study of the military-industrial complex, found in Kennedy's "willingness to gamble with the idea of nuclear war . . . a loss of touch with reality, almost a suicidal impulse."

The more judicious of the new historians, like Richard J. Walton, tempered their personal indictments by depicting the president as "an entirely conventional Cold Warrior." Still, in addition to "his fervent anti-communism, and his acceptance of the basic assumptions of American postwar foreign policy," "the *machismo* quality in Kennedy's character" pushed him to embark on "an anti-communist crusade much more dangerous than any policy Eisenhower ever permitted." Burdened by both personal flaws and political pressures, Kennedy failed during the missile crisis to keep American policy from exhibiting, in his own words, "a collective death-wish for the world."

Like traditional historians of the missile crisis, the revisionists identified a hero, but it was the Soviet premier, Nikita Khrushchev, who withdrew the missiles at risk to his prestige. "Had Khrushchev not done so, there might well have been no later historians to exalt Kennedy," for then Kennedy and his aides, so set on victory at any cost, "would burn the world to a cinder." In effect the new histories inverted the earlier images of Kennedy as a sentry for international order standing firm against a ruthless Soviet Union. To the revisionists, Kennedy's belligerence itself posed the chief threat of global annihilation, and only the belated prudence of his counterpart in the Kremlin salvaged the peace.

3. New Evidence, Old Myths

For more than two decades after the missile crisis, scholarship churned along these two interpretive poles, grinding ever finer a limited cache of primary sources. Denied access to most records of the Ex Comm meetings, historians continued to rely on memoirs by several of President Kennedy's aides. As for the Soviets, a commentator for *Izvestia* later lamented that their press "treated the episode with socialist surrealism," refusing even to concede Khrushchev's placement of nuclear weapons in Cuba. "The word 'missiles' never appeared in the newspapers, though later, in the Kennedy-Khrushchev letters, the phrase 'weapons the United States considers offensive' was used."

As late as 1982 a writer surveying the historical literature could reasonably assert, "There are no new facts about the Kennedys, only new attitudes." Seldom has an insight aged more rapidly or spectacularly. Beginning in the mid-to-late eighties the volcanic flow of information and inquiry in the era of *glasnost* enabled several conferences on the missile crisis in which Soviet and American scholars and former officials shared facts and feelings long guarded like vital national secrets. These exchanges, coinciding with the declassification of various Ex Comm conversations, overturned much of what both traditional and revisionist scholars had long believed, extending even to shared assumptions about the basic facts of the crisis.

The entire twenty-five-year debate over whether Kennedy was warranted in not pledging to withdraw the Turkish missiles was abruptly exposed as based on a faulty record of events. In 1987 former Secretary of State Dean Rusk revealed that Kennedy had secretly prepared a fallback plan to have UN Secretary General U Thant propose a mutual dismantling of missiles in Cuba and Turkey. This would have let the president appear to comply only with a UN request rather than a Soviet demand. Whether Kennedy would have resorted to this gambit is uncertain, but clearly he had been seeking ways to defuse the risk of war.

Kennedy's back-channel efforts to end the crisis went further still. At a conference in Moscow in 1989, the former Soviet ambassador to the United States, Anatoly Dobrynin, recalled an explicit American agreement to withdraw the missiles from Turkey, not simply a vague expression of hope that this might eventually occur. Robert Kennedy had asked him not to draw up any formal exchange of letters, saying it was important not to publicize the accord, for it could show the administration to be purveying a falsehood to the American public. Sorensen deepened the panelists' astonishment by confirming that Robert Kennedy's diaries, which formed the basis of the posthumously published book *Thirteen Days*, were indeed explicit on this part of the deal. But at the time it was still a secret even on the American side, except for the president and a few officials within the Ex Comm. Sorensen explained that in preparing *Thirteen Days* for publication, "I took it upon myself to edit that out of his diaries."

As a result of Sorensen's editing discretion, Kennedy's conciliatory policy on the Turkish missiles was distorted by histories of the crisis into a symbol of either his valiant resolve or his confrontational bent. Similarly historians had long emphasized the imminent danger of a U.S. attack on the Cuban missile sites, whether to highlight the president's grave choices or to further indict him for war-mongering. Yet McNamara insisted in 1987, "There was no way we were going to war on Monday or Tuesday [October 29 or 30]. No way!" McNamara had suggested in the Ex Comm an intermediate step of tightening the quarantine to include petroleum, oil, and lubricants, and felt "very certain" that the president would have preferred this step to authorizing an attack.

Some of the new evidence is considerably less flattering to President Kennedy's image as a peacemaker. Records of the first day of Ex Comm meetings, October 16, show both John and Robert Kennedy inclined, with most other participants, to a quick air strike. The president's vaunted containment of the risks of war also appears less reassuring than in the idealized portrayals of early histories and memoirs. The perennial boast that he only modestly opened a Pandora's box of nuclear dangers lost much of its luster as scholars inventoried what had nearly escaped. The president never learned that U.S. destroyers might have crippled a Soviet submarine with depth charges near the quarantine line, an episode that could have triggered a wider naval clash. Kennedy also did not know of a series of false nuclear alerts that, in combination with the Strategic Air Command's heightened combat readiness, DEFCON (Defense Condition) 2, posed risks of inadvertent escalation.

Still more alarming, on October 27 a U.S. reconnaissance pilot strayed into Soviet territory, a violation that Khrushchev indignantly likened to a preparation for a preemptive nuclear strike. "There's always some son of a bitch who doesn't get the word," the president said on learning of this provocation. Kennedy would have been still more displeased had he known that because of the heightened military alert, U.S. fighter planes scrambling to protect the lost pilot from Russian MiGs were armed not with conventional weapons but with nuclear missiles. Scott D. Sagan, whose resourceful study *The Limits of Safety* discloses various military miscues and malfunctions during the crisis that might have led to a wider conflict, concludes that while "President Kennedy may well have been prudent," he lacked "unchallenged final control over U.S. nuclear weapons."

Nor did the danger of unwanted escalation stem entirely from U.S. nuclear forces. According to Anatoli Gribkov, who headed operational planning for the Soviet armed forces in 1962, the Russians had placed in Cuba not only medium-range missiles but also twelve *Luna* tactical missiles with nuclear warheads designed for ground combat support. Had Kennedy ordered an invasion, the Soviet commander in Cuba, General Issa Pliyev, in the event he lost contact with Moscow, had authority to fire the *Lunas* at the American landing force. On hearing this in 1992, a stunned McNamara exclaimed, "No one should believe that a U.S. force could have been attacked by tactical nuclear warheads without the U.S. responding with nuclear warheads. And where would it have ended? In utter disaster."

Even Ex Comm veterans who had long exalted the Kennedy administration's "rational crisis management" have renounced the very notion as romantic—and dangerous. President Kennedy's National Security Adviser, McGeorge Bundy, acknowledged, "The most important part of crisis management is not to have a crisis, because there's no telling what will happen once you're in one." McNamara agreed, "'Managing' crises is the wrong term; you don't 'manage' them because you *can't.* . . ." On the twenty-fifth anniversary of the missile crisis, Sorensen, Kennedy's loyal aide and biographer, termed the confrontation "unwise, unwarranted and unnecessary."

The new scholarship has further chipped at the Kennedys' larger-than-life image by crediting the much maligned foreign policy establishment with contributions hitherto unknown or attributed wholly to the president and his brother. Secretary of State Dean Rusk, belying later charges that he was ineffectual in the Ex Comm and nearing a breakdown, originated the contingency plan to have UN Secretary General U Thant request the withdrawal of missiles in both Turkey and Cuba. With the president's approval, Rusk prepared Andrew Cordier, the president of Columbia University and a former UN parliamentarian, to approach U Thant. Had Khrushchev not accepted an earlier American offer, Rusk's idea might have served as the basis for a settlement under UN auspices.

The administration's celebrated "acceptance" of Khrushchev's tacit proposals on October 26 rather than his sterner public demands the next day—a ploy once credited to Robert Kennedy alone—in fact had a complex patrimony, Llewellyn Thompson, the former ambassador to the Soviet Union, whom Robert Kennedy's memoir credits generously but generally for "uncannily accurate" advice that was "surpassed by none," may have first suggested the outlines of this strategy. Bundy, Assistant Secretary of State for Latin American Affairs Edwin Martin, and others also offered variations on this gambit in informal discussions. Robert Kennedy formally proposed the idea in an Ex Comm meeting and drafted a response with Sorensen. But the view that this was his exclusive brainchild—a view nurtured by his own seemingly definitive account—underscores that memoirs seldom reveal an author's limitations other than a selective memory.

The very machinery of government, long viewed as a cumbersome, bumbling foil to a dynamic chief executive, now appears to have been a responsive (if not fully respected) partner. Contrary to early accounts, the failure to remove American missiles from Turkey before the crisis did not stem from unwitting bureaucratic sabotage of a presidential directive. Rather, Kennedy himself had acquiesced in the delay to avoid embarrassing a Turkish government that had only recently hinged its prestige on accepting the missiles. The president may well have been dismayed by their continued presence, but he was in no way surprised by it in the Ex Comm meetings. Rusk dismissed reports of the president's alleged betrayal by a lazy State Department, saying, "He never expressed any irritation to me because he had been fully briefed by me on that situation."

These and other discoveries all augur a far richer, more precise understanding of Kennedy's role in the missile crisis. But they have yet to produce an interpretive framework to encompass them. Should historians conclude that the president was less militant than once thought because he sanctioned a trade of missile bases? Or more militant because he initially leaned toward bombing Cuba? Does he now appear more adept at crisis management, given his elaborate fallback plans for a possible settlement through the UN? Or simply lucky to survive his own ignorance of swaggering American officers, false nuclear alerts, and nuclear-equipped Soviet forces in Cuba? Was the president more dependent on the Ex Comm in light of contributions by unsung heroes such as Llewellyn Thompson? Or did he treat the Ex Comm as having limited relevance, as in his concealment from most members of the private deal on the Turkish missiles? On these and other issues, the additions to our knowledge have been individually striking but cumulatively chaotic.

A way to make sense of these seemingly disparate and even conflicting pieces of evidence is to view President Kennedy as a moderate leader in a militant age. His vision at all times extended beyond the Ex Comm's deliberations, encompassing the formidable national consensus that the Soviet base in

Cuba should be challenged militarily. Honing his policies on the grindstone of political necessity, Kennedy ordered a blockade of the island and considered still bolder action because he knew that Soviet leaders and the American public alike would otherwise view him as fatally irresolute. Yet within his circumscribed political setting, he proved more willing than most Americans, both in and outside his circle of advisers, to limit bellicose displays and to offer the Russians timely, if covert, concessions.

Despite a growing awareness of Kennedy's political constraints, the revisionist image of a man driven by both insecurity and arrogance to rash policies has proven extraordinarily resilient. Thomas G. Peterson, who incisively recounts the covert war against Castro waged by two administrations, judges Kennedy's brand of cold war leadership more dangerous than Eisenhower's. "Driven by a desire for power," Paterson writes, "Kennedy personalized issues, converting them into tests of will." Far from simply continuing "his predecessor's anti-Castro policies," Kennedy "significantly increased the pressures against the upstart island" out of an obsession with Castro. "He thus helped generate major crises, including the October 1962 missile crisis. Kennedy inherited the Cuban problem—and he made it worse."

In *The Dark Side of Camelot* (1997) the award-winning journalist Seymour Hersh cranks up to full strength the assault on Kennedy's character that had stamped revisionist writings of the 1970s. Contrasting Khrushchev's "common sense and dread of nuclear war" with Kennedy's "fanaticism" during the missile crisis, Hersh concludes: "For the first time in his presidency, Kennedy publicly brought his personal recklessness, and his belief that the normal rules of conduct did not apply to him, to his foreign policy. . . . The Kennedy brothers brought the world to the edge of war in their attempts to turn the dispute into a political asset."

Textbooks too have incorporated into their "objective" look at American history the notion that Kennedy's belligerence is the key to understanding his foreign policy. In a leading work, *Promises to Keep: The United States Since World War II* (1999), Paul Boyer finds that "Kennedy's approach to Cold War leadership differed markedly from Eisenhower's. Shaped by an intensely competitive family and a hard-driving father whom he both admired and feared, he eagerly sought to prove his toughness to the Soviet adversary."

The focus on Kennedy's supposed confrontational bent to explain his policies reaches its fullest—and most problematic—development in the aptly titled study by Thomas C. Reeves, *A Question of Character*. Reeves's Kennedy was "deficient in integrity, compassion, and temperance," defects that clearly influenced his Cuban policy, from the decision [in 1961] to ignore the moral and legal objections to an invasion, and through the creation of Operation Mongoose." During the missile crisis too, "Kennedy at times seemed unduly militant, and his aggressive and competitive instincts led him to grant the [diplomatic] initiative to the Soviets at critical points where more skilled diplomacy might have avoided it." Reeves dismisses claims that the president sought never to "challenge the other side needlessly," with the comment, "Neither, of course, were the Kennedys prepared to accept anything short of victory." Faced with the mounting evidence of Kennedy's prudence, Reeves allows that the president's "personal agony over the conflict, his several efforts to avoid bloodshed, and his willingness to make a trade of Turkish for Cuban missiles, revealed a deeper concern for the nation and the world than many who knew him well might have suspected." But little else leavens Reeves's generally dour portrait of a president whose personal failings compounded the risks of war. Like other revisionist scholars, Reeves dutifully ingests the new scholarship on the missile crisis but cannot easily digest it.

The hazards of treating presidential character as the Rosetta stone to make sense of policies in the missile crisis should by now give pause to even the most confirmed of Kennedy's admirers or detractors. The emergence of contributions by Rusk, Thompson, Bundy, Martin, and other establishment figures has made it more difficult to portray the Kennedys as lonely titans striding across the political stage with ideas and policies uniquely their own. And, granted that Kennedy was "the key decisionmaker," he nonetheless acted within tightly defined parameters that had little to do with the character of the chief executive.

The amplified record of decision-making has also recast or removed issues that long galvanized and framed debates over Kennedy's character. Interpretations of the president's supposedly tough policy on the Jupiter missiles now appear to have rested on accounts that, by embellishment and concealment alike, exaggerated his brinkmanship. The puncturing of those distortions should deflate as well the images of Kennedy as either a surpassingly valiant leader or a Neanderthal cold warrior.

Traditional historians, it is now clear, both sanitized and romanticized the historical record in portraying President Kennedy as an ideal fusion of hawkish resolve and dovish reserve, who forced out the Cuban missiles without making needless concessions or taking heedless risks. In fact Kennedy resolved the crisis not simply through toughness and diplomatic legerdemain but by pledging to remove the missiles from Turkey, a deal he publicly spurned and his partisans long proudly but wrongly denied. And while Kennedy's defenders lauded his rejection of calls for air strikes and invasion, they overlooked the provocation of his actual policies, including the plots against Castro, the push for ever greater American nuclear superiority, and, of course, the blockade of Cuba.

The historical record is even more resistant to revisionist portraits of a president whose psychological deformities impelled him to risk peace for the sake of personal glory or catharsis. These accounts were from the first suspect, whether in drawing tortured connections between Kennedy's womanizing and his foreign policy or deriding him for sharing the beliefs of his own generation rather than a later one. They simply collapse under the weight of evidence that, during the gravest crisis of the cold war, Kennedy repeatedly proved more prudent than many aides, both civilian and military. As he told his brother Robert on October 26, "If anybody is around to write after this, they are going to understand that we made every effort to find peace and every effort to give our adversary room to move. I am not going to push the Russians an inch beyond what is necessary."

Ernest May and Philip Zelikow, editors of an invaluable annotated record of the Ex Comm sessions, marvel that "[Kennedy] seems more alive to the possibilities and consequences of each new development than anyone else." On October 27, with pressure mounting for decisive action, the president "is the only one in the room who is determined not to go to war over obsolete missiles in Turkey." May and Zelikow acknowledge Kennedy's partial responsibility for this superpower clash but deem it "fortunate" that "[he] was the president charged with managing the crisis."

The most telling dismissal of revisionist rhetoric comes from Kennedy's adversaries themselves. Shortly after the crisis ended, Khrushchev admitted to an American journalist, "Kennedy did just what I would have done if I had been in the White House instead of the Kremlin." In his memoirs the former Soviet leader lamented Kennedy's death as "a great loss," for "he was gifted with the ability to resolve international conflicts by negotiation, as the whole world learned during the so-called Cuban crisis. Regardless of his youth he was a real statesman." As for those "clever people" who "will tell you that Kennedy was to blame for the tensions which might have resulted in war," Khrushchev said, "You have to keep in mind the era in which we live." Castro, for his part, believed Kennedy "acted as he did partly to save Khrushchev, out of fear that any successor would be tougher."

The misrepresentations of Kennedy's leadership go deeper than the debates over whether he was heroic or merely reckless, idealistic or expedient, poised or impulsive. Scholars have so focused on Kennedy's style, aura, temperament, and character as to slight, if not obscure, the crucial framework of national values that he necessarily accommodated and largely shared. The missile crisis, as much as anything, is the story of how Kennedy faithfully reflected a remarkable consensus in political institutions and public opinion regarding America's role as Free World champion in the nuclear age.

Contrary to the impression left by Kennedy's partisans, the Executive Committee he formed to advise him during the missile crisis was never a sealed laboratory for reinventing American policy. Nor was it, as the revisionists later had it, a forum for venting personal demons at public expense. Rather, like any leader in a democracy, Kennedy self-consciously labored under constraints imposed by public opinion, the Congress, the military, the CIA, and a host of civilian constituencies. To argue that he could or should have disdained these pressures is to imply a preference for philosopher kings over accountable presidents. Whatever the appeal of such arguments, they leave little room for either the ideal or the reality of American democracy.

Americans in the early sixties overwhelmingly regarded the prospect of missiles in Cuba as intolerably threatening and judged leaders by their firmness against Soviet encroachments. Whoever occupied the Oval Office would therefore have faced intense pressures to demand removal of the missiles, direct low-level military action against Cuba, and avoid apparent concessions to the Russians. Buffeted by partisan sniping, public opinion, and the force of inherited policies, President Kennedy pursued all of these options. Throughout he sought to minimize confrontation with the Soviet Union to a degree consistent with his political survival.

Accounting for the full political weight of entrenched national attitudes can help resolve the central paradox of Kennedy's policies during the missile crisis, which reflected elements of both recklessness and restraint. Considered against the background of his times, Kennedy appears a rational leader, conciliatory and even empathetic towards his counterpart in the Kremlin. Yet he also represented a political culture marked by fear and bluster, qualities stoked by an uncontrolled arms race and Manichen visions of the East-west divide. To ask which was the "real" Kennedy is to speak of a chimera: a leader somehow extricable from his era.

Kennedy embodied the and–Soviet, anti-Communist values—and obsessions–of his day, though with more skepticism and caution than most contemporaries. His relative detachment from cold war dogmas was not enough to avoid a crisis caused by mutual misjudgments. Still, it allowed for a crucial modicum of flexibility and restraint that helped keep this crisis from spiraling toward war.

It may be tempting to conclude that Kennedy's avoidance of a wider conflict warrants cynicism rather than celebration, as the bare minimum one should expect of any sane leader in the nuclear age. Yet the obstacles to military restraint between states are no less daunting simply because the dangers are so great. Whatever Kennedy's missteps, he proved—together with Soviet Premier Khrushchev—that leaders can resist the lures of unchecked escalation even while mired in a climate of mutual suspicion, fear, and hostility. This achievement may yet gain new luster as nuclear weapons spread to other nations steeped in their own bitter rivalries, a development auguring two, three, many missile crises to come.

EXPLORING THE ISSUE

Did President John F. Kennedy Cause the Cuban Missile Crisis?

Critical Thinking and Reflection

1. Critically analyze the disparity between the image of President Kennedy's foreign policy versus the reality.
2. Critically analyze the strengths and weaknesses of the new sources about the Cuban missile crisis—such as declassified government memos, transcriptions of the Ex-Comm meetings, and transcriptions of several conferences held in Moscow and Havana where participants and their children recalled the roles they played during the crisis.
3. Compare and contrast the traditional view, the revisionist view, and the post-revisionist view of the roles of Kennedy and Khrushchev in resolving the Cuban missile crisis.
4. Compare and contrast and critically evaluate the interpretations of Paterson and Weisbrot as to the causes and solutions of the Cuban missile crisis.

Is There Common Ground?

All writers agree on the timing of the events. Khrushchev started the crisis in the summer of 1962 when Russian ships brought offensive Intercontinental Ballistic Missiles (IBMs) to the island. Kennedy responded in a nontraditional way in the beginning by announcing over radio and television that the United States was establishing a "quarantine" or "blockade" around the island. After several attempts at back door diplomacy with Robert Kennedy, the Attorney General and the President's brother, pledging not to invade Cuba and privately to withdraw obsolete missiles in Turkey and Italy within the next six months, Khrushchev's negotiator agreed to take the missiles out of Cuba immediately.

The basic question asked is which national leader was most responsible for bringing the post–World War II superpowers to the brink of nuclear war. Both Kennedy and Khrushchev wanted to work out a compromise. Both were pressured by hard liners on their respective advising committees. Suppose the Russian ships crossed the blockade line and refused to turn back? Did the Russian commander have the right to start a war without checking with Khrushchev? If the United States had invaded Cuba, how much damage would American ships ships have suffered? If troop losses mounted because the CIA underestimated the number of Russian soldiers and ICBMs on the island, would the war have escalated to a full-scale nuclear one?

Two random incidents occurred, which might have led to war had more belligerent leaders other than the two Ks been in power. First, on October 27 a U-2 was shot down over Cuba by a surface-to-air missile. Who did it? Cubans? Russians? Kennedy decided to bypass his own committee and have his brother go behind the scenes to negotiate with Khrushchev's aide. Meanwhile, Khrushchev ignored a U-2 flight whose pilot accidentally overflew the northeastern portion of the Soviet Union and was rescued by American planes without incident.

Managing a crisis such as the showdown in Cuba demonstrates that there is a lot of luck to keep events from spinning out of control. The reader need only study America's crisis over the Pearl Harbor attack, the escalation of the Vietnam War, and the 9/11 attacks, which led to the war on terror to realize the value of peacefully resolving the Cuban missile crisis.

Additional Resources

The literature on the Cuban missile crisis is enormous. In addition to the comprehensive footnotes and bibliography in Weisbrot, start with Mark J. White, ed., "The Cuban Imbroglio: From the Bay of Pigs to the Missile Crisis and Beyond," *Kennedy: The New Frontier Revisited* (New York University Press, 1998). All the selections in this volume strive for an alternative to the Camelot and counter-Camelot interpretations of the Kennedy presidency. The same may be said of White's *Missiles in Cuba: Kennedy, Khrushchev, Castro and the 1962 Crisis* (Ivan R. Dee, 1997). Thomas Paterson's scathing analysis in "Fixation with Cuba: The Bay of Pigs, Missile Crisis and Covert War against Castro," in Thomas Paterson, ed., *Kennedy's Quest for Victory: American Foreign Policy, 1961–1963* (Oxford University Press, 1989) reinforces the interpretation presented in this issue.

A superb collection of articles can be found in Robert A. Divine, ed., *The Cuban Missile Crisis* (Quadrangle Books, 1971), which contains older but still useful essays. Divine also reviews a number of books and collections of primary sources, secondary articles, and roundtable discussions in "Alive and Well: The Continuing Cuban Missile Crisis Controversy," *Diplomatic History* (Fall 1994). See the articles by Barton J. Bernstein, Richard Ned Lebow, Philip Brenner, and the editor himself in James A. Nathan, ed., *The Cuban Missile Crisis Revisited* (St. Martin's Press, 1992), all of which are based on research in the records opened by the American, former Soviet, and Cuban governments and collected by the independent National Security Archive.

There are a number of primary sources that students can explore without visiting the archives. See, for example, Laurence Chang and Peter Kornbluh, eds., *The Cuban Missile Crisis. 1962: A National Security Archive Documents Reader,* rev. ed. (New Press, 1998). Students are fortunate to have tape recordings of the Ex-Comm meetings. They have been transcribed, along with some other meetings, by Ernest R. May and Philip D. Zelikow in their edited book, *The Kennedy Tapes; Inside the White House During the Cuban Missile Crisis* (Harvard University, 1997). A number of excellent summaries of the crisis have appeared in the twenty-first century. In 2001, James A. Nathan provided an up-to-date concise *Anatomy of the Cuban Missile Crisis* in the Greenwood Press Guides Series to Historic Events of the Twentieth Century. Sheldon M. Stern has corrected some of the transcripts of the Ex-Comm meetings and has used those tapes to construct a favorable interpretation of JFK, who "often stood virtually alone against war-like council from the Ex-Comm, the Joint Chiefs of Staff, and Congress during these historic thirteen days." See Stern's *Averting "The Final Failure": John F. Kennedy and the Secret Cuban Missile Crisis Meetings* (Stanford University Press, 2003) and a shortened paperback version for students, *The Week the World Stood Still: Inside the Secret Cuban Missile Crisis Meetings* (Stanford University Press, 2005). Alice L. George's *Awaiting Armageddon: How Americans Faced the Cuban Missile Crisis* (University of North Carolina Press, 2003) points out how unprepared the public was for civil defense in the eight days the public was aware of the crisis.

Other references include a superb recent account from Michael Dobbs, *One Minute to Midnight: Kennedy, Khrushchev, and Castro on the Brink of Nuclear War* (New York: Knopf 2008); Max Frankel, *High Noon in the Cold War* (New York: Presidio Press, 2004); and Graham Allison and Philip D. Zelikow, *Essence of Decision,* rev. ed. (Reading, MA: Longman, 1999). Two authoritative brief accounts are Don Munton and David A. Welch, *The Cuban Missile Crisis: A Concise History* (New York: Oxford University Press, 2007); and James G. Hershberg, "The Cuban Missile Crisis," in Melvyn P. Leffler and Odd Arne Westad, eds., *The Cambridge History of the Cold War* (New York: Cambridge University Press, 2009).

There also are a number of videos for classroom use on the Cuban missile crisis. In 1992, NBC aired a two-hour documentary *The Cuban Missile Crisis: 30 Years Later;* in the same year, PBS produced a 30-year retrospective in the "Front Line" series on *The Cuban Missile Crisis.*

For Internet sources, see the following:

CNN and BBC produced a 24-hour documentary on the Cold War in 1998. The website has valuable interviews, documents, and transcripts of the 50-minute videos, as well as some material not included in the films that aired. The work on the Cuban missile crisis was the 10th in this series. See http://cnn.com/SPECIALS/cold.war/episodes/10/

For transcripts of Ex-Comm meetings in streaming audio, see www.hpol.org//jfk/cuban//

The Cold War History Project, a joint effort of George Washington University and the National Security Archive, has especially good documents on the Cuban missile crisis. See http://cwihp.si.edu/pdj.htm

C-SPAN Online provides RealAudio clips and transcripts from tapes that President Kennedy secretly recorded in the White House, RealAudio newsreels from 1962, an image gallery of the major players and surveillance photos, and RealAudio archives. See www.c-spall.org/guide/society/cuba

The Department of State's definitive volumes relating to the Cuban missile crisis are available online: Foreign Relations of the United States, "Cuba," vol. X, 1961–1963; and Foreign Relations of the United States, "Cuban Missile Crisis and Aftermath," vol. XI, 1961–1963. See www.state.gov/

Documents Relating to American Foreign Policy: The Cuban Missile Crisis is a website maintained by Mount Holyoke College. The collection includes documents, links, and other historical materials concerning the Cuban missile crisis. See www.mtholyoke.edu/acad/intrel/cuba.htm

ISSUE 15

Did the Activism of the 1960s Produce a Better Nation?

YES: Terry H. Anderson, from *The Sea Change* (Oxford University Press, 1995)

NO: Peter Clecak, from *The New Left* (Harper & Row, 1973)

Learning Outcomes

After reading this issue, you should be able to:

- Define the term "New Left" as it applies to the 1960s.
- Summarize the main goals of the Port Huron Statement.
- Evaluate the legacy of the Students for a Democratic Society (SDS) and the Youth International Party ("Yippies").
- Discuss the strengths and weaknesses of the New Left critique of American society.
- Compare and contrast the political and cultural rebels of the 1960s in terms of their leadership, goals, strategies, and level of success in affecting change.

ISSUE SUMMARY

YES: Terry H. Anderson concludes that the activism of the 1960s inspired citizens of all types to demand changes that produced a transformation of American politics, society, culture, and foreign power and made the United States a more democratic and inclusive nation.

NO: Peter Clecak contends that the political and cultural revolutionaries of the 1960s failed to revolutionize themselves or American society and quickly discovered that, without a clear program, viable organizations, or a significant constituency, they were essentially powerless against the prevailing social order.

In the summer of 1960, a University of Michigan undergraduate named Tom Hayden, who served as an editor for his campus newspaper, the *Michigan Daily,* made a trip to California. He paid a visit to the University of California at Berkeley before making his way to Los Angeles to cover the Democratic National Convention. In Los Angeles, Hayden was captivated by the idealistic energy and enthusiasm for change articulated by young Massachusetts Senator John Kennedy, who became the Democratic Party's nominee for president of the United States. Only a few months before, Hayden had joined with a handful of his campus associates in Ann Arbor to resurrect an almost defunct student organization—the Student League for Industrial Democracy—that traced its roots to an early twentieth-century student group founded by the Socialist writer Upton Sinclair. Changing the name of their organization to Students for a Democratic Society, these young campus activists established connections with participants of the ongoing college student sit-ins, whom they admired for the ferocity of their commitment to eliminating segregation in southern public accommodations in order to bring racial democracy to Dixie. Following his Michigan graduation in 1961, Hayden headed south to represent SDS in support of the newly established and largely African American Student Nonviolent Coordinating Committee's (SNCC) organizing efforts, and he was beaten and jailed while participating in civil rights activities. (Hayden eventually served for nearly two decades in the California legislature and is currently a political activist and writer for *The Nation*.)

The creators of SDS envisioned their organization as a think tank comprising talented activists from the nation's elite universities and colleges. Many of the early members were "red-diaper babies"—the children of American Communist parents who had comprised the Old Left of the 1930s and 1940s, whose support of the Soviet Union, however, had diminished in the wake of news reports of the Stalinist purges in which millions of Russians perished at the hands of the totalitarian state, as well as in response to the firestorm of anti-Communist hysteria associated with the early years of the Cold War. Propelled by family ideologies along with encouragement from intellectuals such as C. Wright Mills, who insisted that a "new left" should be led by students on the nation's campuses, SDS members sought to champion radical democratic values, and Tom Hayden took up the task of outlining the group's purpose and goals. At a conference convened at a United Auto Workers' educational camp in Port Huron, Michigan, in June 1962, Hayden penned a manifesto that expressed concern over the inconsistencies between ideals and reality that he observed in the United States: racial discrimination in a country dedicated to equality; growing affluence while millions resided in poverty; discussion of the benefits of nuclear power amidst fears of nuclear destruction; and presidential statements about America's peaceful intentions while the Kennedy Administration poured more and more dollars into the nation's military budget. This "Port Huron Statement" presented a clarion call for a new ideology of change, demanding that college students abandon the apathy of the 1950s and seek to transform society through the application of participatory democracy and mass protest emanating from college campuses. The university, after all, was a place where ideas should be openly debated. Or was it?

In 1964, the Free Speech Movement erupted on the Berkeley campus when the university's administration attempted to prohibit students from handing out fliers encouraging participation in voter registration projects in the South. Mario Savio, a graduate student who had recently returned from the Mississippi Freedom Summer, emerged as one of the key leaders of this California campus protest, which resulted in the occupation of administrative offices and mass arrests, activities that would be repeated at Berkeley and on many other campuses over the course of the decade.

These challenges to university policies reflected a broader rejection of authority by members of the "baby boom" generation, many of whom, like the members of SDS, were questioning the legitimacy of The Establishment in a variety of forms: the university; the family; the federal government; and corporate America. In his book, *The Making of a Counter Culture: Reflections on the Technocratic Society and Its Youthful Opposition* (Doubleday, 1968), historian Theodore Roszak attempted to articulate a context for what was going on. Targeting what he labeled the "technocracy," which seemed arbitrarily to restrain individual initiative and imagination, Roszak concluded that "the primary project of our counter culture is to proclaim a new heaven and a new earth so vast, so marvelous that the inordinate claims of technical expertise must of necessity withdraw to a subordinate and marginal status in the lives of men." In addition, Roszak contributed to our understanding of the counter culture by describing two groups of rebels: the political rebels of the New Left and the sociocultural rebels (or "hippies") whose alienation from mainstream culture was leading them to drop out of society and to seek solace in a parallel lifestyle of hallucinogenic drugs and communal living.

Many Americans insisted that this youth rebellion was little more than people behaving very badly, and these attitudes were reinforced as the protesters took to the streets in response to the expanding involvement of the United States in the Southeast Asian conflict. Scholars continue to debate the extent to which antiwar activists influenced the Vietnam policies of either the Johnson or Nixon administrations, but there is little doubt that the opposition to the war began to draw to a close once the protests returned to campus in 1970. First, at Kent State University, Ohio National Guardsmen were summoned by Governor James Rhodes to quell an uprising that had led to the burning of the campus ROTC building—fueled by media reports about "secret" extensions of the Vietnam conflict. On May 4, the soldiers opened fire on students, killing four and wounding nine others—some but not all of them involved in a protest against escalation of the war into Cambodia. Almost four months later, four young domestic terrorists bombed the Army Math Research Center at the University of Wisconsin-Madison, killing a postdoctoral physicist and causing $6 million damage. Columnist George Will characterized the incident as "the Hiroshima of the New Left."

For many who came of age during the 1960s, there is a tendency to idealize the decade as one in which young Americans sought to remake the lethal culture of their parents. Critics of the counter cultural rebellion see little to applaud. In the YES and NO selections, Terry Anderson and Peter Clecak offer sharply different appraisals of the activism of the 1960s. Anderson believes that the 1960s produced a positive transformation of American politics, society, culture, and foreign policy resulting in a more democratic and tolerant society. Minority groups benefited from a legal and political revolution that destroyed Jim Crow, and women gained far greater access to political and economic power.

He concludes that the New Left effectively destroyed the Cold War political culture by challenging its authority and inspiring Americans to demand change in many areas of life.

Clecak, on the other hand, argues that radicals in the 1960s failed to revolutionize themselves or their society and largely remained powerless to shape the prevailing social order. Organizations like Students for a Democratic Society fell far short of realizing their egalitarian ideals, demonstrating that it is easier to craft a statement of political goals than to carry those goals to fruition. In the end, according to Clecak, these activists had little to offer in terms of ethical or political insight into contemporary American problems.

YES

Terry H. Anderson

The Sea Change

. . . **W**hatever one thinks of the sixties, the tumultuous era cracked the cold war culture and the nation experienced a sea change—a significant transformation in politics, society, culture, and foreign policy. The legacies of that era are worthy of another book, one that would detail recent trends in the nation's history, and thus be as controversial as the popular debate over whether the sixties were "good or bad" or the academic arguments over race, gender, and equality. Since that book is not possible here, this chapter will offer some generalizations about the legacies of the movement and the sixties.

The political legacies of the sixties were apparent to anyone watching the 1976 Democratic National Convention in New York City. African American Congresswoman Barbara Jordan of Houston gave a stirring opening address, and black Mayor Tom Bradley of Los Angeles and Chicano Governor Jerry Apodaca of New Mexico were selected as two co-chairs of the convention. Grace Olivarez, a Chicana feminist from New Mexico, presented the welfare reform plank to the platform. Cesar Chavez delivered the nominating speech for youthful California Governor Jerry Brown, and also from that state was delegate Tom Hayden. The eventual nominee, Governor Jimmy Carter of Georgia, represented the end of Jim Crow—in the November election both white and black southerners voted for the same candidate for the first time, delivering the presidency to the first man from the Deep South since before the Civil War.

That bicentennial year also revealed the impact of the new left, although those activists had been grumbling since the 1968 election that they had failed to bring about a "revolution," a New America. In 1962 they had set a course for the nation in *The Port Huron Statement,* which condemned racial bigotry, anti-Communist paranoia, popular complacency, corporate irresponsibility, and a remote control government and economy controlled by power elites. Those activists failed to interest the majority in long-term efforts to reduce poverty, reform welfare, or curtail the military-industrial complex. Nevertheless, they succeeded in destroying cold war political culture. Americans no longer live in a society that fears change, that suspects dissent. Activists buried McCarthyism. Demonstrations have become routine. Authorities are questioned, scrutinized, and that has changed official behavior. Government offices are open for public inspection, and activists altered police tactics. No longer are protesters beaten.

From *The Movement and the Sixties: Protest in America from Greensboro to Wounded Knee* by Terry H. Anderson (1995), pp. 412–415, 416–423. Copyright © 1995 by Terry H. Anderson. Reprinted by permission of Oxford University Press, Ltd.

Police are more educated and integrated; they are trained in crowd control, and they work at improving their relations with all in the community. Because of political activists, empowerment is taken for granted.

The new left also influenced the Democratic party. In 1896, William Jennings Bryan co-opted the Populist party platform of 1892 and thus transformed the Democrats into the party of reform. Eighty years later the Democrats did the same, embracing ideas expressed in *The Port Huron Statement*. Since then, they have become the party of civil rights, personal freedom, environmentalism, corporate responsibility, and a foreign policy emphasizing human rights. Moreover, political activists of the 1960s pried open democracy, which earlier reformers had done by extending the vote during the Jacksonian and progressive eras. This time, the movement wrestled political control from white males who for years had been negotiating alone behind closed doors. Activists revived the old progressive idea, You *can* fight city hall, and what activist Bo Burlingham noted in 1976 will remain pertinent for some years: "The convulsions of the last decade have produced something that has fundamentally altered the terms of American politics . . . change is both possible and necessary."

The movement inspired citizens of all types to express their democratic rights, to demand change, and that included conservatives. The backlash began as a response to blacks marching for their civil rights and to students making demands on campus. The struggle raised issues of integration and equal employment opportunity, and that contributed to white flight to the suburbs and charges of "reverse discrimination." Because of race issues, many white working men deserted the party that had boosted and represented them, the Democratic, and became conservatives who voted Republican. The counterculture and women's movement shocked other citizens and they joined the backlash: Phyllis Schlafly and her campaign Stop ERA; Anita Bryant and her crusade against sexual liberation; and a host of others who appeared as televangelists on the "700 Club," "Praise the Lord Club," and "The Old-Time Gospel Hour"—conservatives who reached the zenith of their popularity during the first administration of the "Reagan Revolution."

Ronald Reagan's triumph in 1980 did not overturn the 1960s; there was no return to 1950s America. While the president was very popular, the majority of citizens did not honor his call for traditional social roles or support his environmental views, cold war foreign policy, or attempts to dismantle civil rights legislation and defeat the Equal Rights Amendment.

In fact, sixties political values marched on during the 1980s, and a central theme since has been inclusion. Every primary campaign and convention since has included delegates representing all Americans. Jimmy Carter named more women and minorities to his administration than any previous president, and by 1984 civil rights activist Jesse Jackson had formed his Rainbow Coalition and was running for the Democratic nomination for president. That year female Representative Geraldine Ferraro accepted the party's vice presidential nomination. Republican presidents during the 1980s named Hispanics, African Americans, and women to their Cabinets and to the Supreme Court, and a member of the sixties generation, Bill Clinton, pledged and then appointed a Cabinet that would "look more like America." The long era of white men exclusively controlling the body politic was over.

America became multicultural—a legacy of the struggle. For minorities, the sixties were a legal and political revolution. In just a few years minorities overturned centuries of legal inferiority and discrimination and obtained their rights guaranteed by the Constitution—an astounding achievement for any society. President Johnson proposed and Congress passed the Civil Rights Act of 1964, Voting Rights Act of 1965, Fair Housing Rights Act of 1968. With the support of the Supreme Court, the nation integrated politic facilities, ended all voting restrictions, and accepted the idea that men and women charged with a crime should be judged by a jury of their peers. The 1960s killed the legal system called Jim Crow, and since then citizens have witnessed the unprecedented election of people of all races and the rise of minority political power, from mayors and police chiefs of predominately white cities, to governors, Congress, the Cabinet, and the Supreme Court. Furthermore, Black Power advocates stimulated a flourishing of cultural pride that spread to Hispanics, Native Americans, and other ethnic groups, all of whom have embraced empowerment. The federal government answered ethnic demands by ruling against discriminatory practices by businesses and agencies and by enforcing bilingual ballots and education. Ultimately, the struggle challenged Anglo America, and the result was a new definition of "American."

The struggle also diminished stereotyping and racism. That was apparent as early as 1975 when a Cabinet member, Earl Butz, made a racist joke and was forced to resign. Since then, a black leader who was hated by millions, mistrusted by presidents, harassed by the FBI, and assassinated—Martin Luther King, Jr.—has become a national icon. Congress established a federal holiday observing his birthday, placing him on equal footing with Washington, Jefferson, and Lincoln. Numerous opinion polls since have demonstrated that racism as measured by slurs and stereotypes has declined, especially among the young. Compare white racial convictions before and after the 1960s. Attitudes that had been held for centuries have changed considerably, have become more tolerant. Television programs and movies today depicting minorities would not have been possible without the struggle, and school textbooks are more inclusive than at any time in our history. Opinion polls in the 1990s demonstrated that whites and blacks, three to one, felt that race relations have improved since the 1960s and two-thirds felt that the nation has made significant progress. "There's room for improvement," stated black restaurant owner W. A. Mathis in 1994 about race relations in Mississippi, "but it's 99 percent better than it used to be." . . .

The legacy of the struggle is clouded by the issue of race, but the impact made by student activism on the American university is more apparent. The sixties generation of students raised fundamental questions: Who controls the university? What rights do students have? What are appropriate courses for a college degree? Activism disrupted and then changed campus life, and at most colleges, gone are the days of *in loco parentis,* the barracks regimented dormitory life, the mandate that the administration rules and the students are ruled. What Mount Holyoke College activist Julie Van Camp stated in 1969 remains valid: "After Columbia a lot of administrators got a rude awakening, but they also realized that many of the student grievances were valid. So now when we want change we a aren't going up against a stone wall any more. It's more like a mattress." Administrators became more flexible, students received more choice, and activism has been apparent whenever moral issues arise, as demonstrated by the anti-apartheid crusades of the 1980s.

Furthermore, students in the various power movements challenged an education based on male European civilization, provoking administrators to develop new classes on African American, Chicano, Native American, Jewish, and women's studies. That prompted a debate. "About the sixties it is now fashionable to say that although there were indeed excesses, many good things resulted," wrote professor Allan Bloom in 1987. "But, so far as universities are concerned, I know of nothing positive coming from that period; it was an unmitigated disaster for them." Conservatives complain about a seemingly endless debate over what is and what is not politically correct. Others, however, note that the debate demonstrates that the movement brought about more sensitivity about language, and they note that activists forced changes in the educational experience that resulted in new scholarship on new topics for a multicultural America. Whatever the case, students of the sixties confronted the educational establishment, and the result was more personal freedom on campus, and a broader college curriculum, than at any time in history.

The legacies of the antiwar movement also are mired in debate. As North Vietnamese tanks rolled into Saigon in 1975, Americans sank into resentment, cynicism, the willed attempt to forget the long nightmare. Depression and denial. "The United States did not lose the war," proclaimed Hubert Humphrey in 1975. "The South Vietnamese did." Within a few years neo-conservatives were adopting a new approach. Actually, the war was, President Reagan declared in 1982, a "noble cause," and a few years later Richard Nixon reinterpreted his own policy: "On January 27, 1973, when Secretary of State William Rogers signed the Paris peace agreements, we had won the war in Vietnam. We had attained the one political goal for which we had fought the war: The South Vietnamese people would have the right to determine their own political future." He and many conservatives claimed that the United States lost the war because wimpy liberals forced his administration to end aid to South Vietnam. Our troops were stabbed in the back by cowardly congressmen, an idea popularized after every defeat, and one boosted this time by actors in numerous "Rambo" and "missing in action" movies. Although these actors and almost all of the young neo-conservatives avoided service in Vietnam, their ideas were warmly received by many who wanted someone to blame and by those who desired to accept another nationalistic myth instead of cruel fact. But in fact, by 1970 two-thirds of citizens wanted to withdraw from South Vietnam even if that nation fell to the North, a figure that increased to 80 percent as the last U.S. troops came home in 1973. Congress was only representing the views of the electorate. Furthermore, after the Cambodian invasion there were no Rambos in the U.S. Army in Vietnam. "By 70," recalled General Norman Schwartzkopf, "it was over. . . . Everyone wanted to get out." Indeed, antiwar activism inside the military was rampant. Americans at home did not want to continue the conflict, and G.I.s in the war zone had little desire to risk their lives. Eventually, even to the great silent majority, Vietnam was not a noble cause, but a lost one. "Nobody was sorry to hear the war was over," wrote Jerry Rubin. "And even more amazing, nobody asked, 'Who won?' Nobody gave a fuck."

But citizens did care about future foreign policy, for Vietnam taught two lessons: America is not invincible; in that sense, the Vietnamese killed the John Waynes. Second, the presidents and their wise men who direct foreign policy cannot be trusted. While Americans have supported the commander-in-chief in short military operations, they also have continually expressed skepticism about intervention in foreign lands. Citizens had cast aside the 1950s ideas of containment and the Domino Theory even before the demise of the Soviet Union. Despite Ronald Reagan's popularity, citizens two to one opposed his attempts to overthrow the Sandinista government in Nicaragua and his stationing of only 55 army advisers in El Salvador. George Bush understood the popular mood, promising that the *allied* intervention to liberate Kuwait was "not another Vietnam," and then withdrawing U.S. troops as soon as feasible, ending Desert Storm.

The antiwar movement alone did not end U.S. participation in Vietnam, but it did provoke citizens out of cold war allegiance, it generated and focused public opposition, and influenced presidents Johnson and Nixon. After all, LBJ quit his job and Nixon withdrew from Vietnam, actions incompatible with their personalities and inconceivable without the antiwar movement. Protesters also prompted citizens to raise questions about their nation's foreign policy, and so, the sixties killed the Imperial Presidency. The commander-in-chief since has not had the power to order U.S. troops to fight in foreign lands without citizens asking, Why? Is U.S. involvement necessary, is it in the national interest? True, the quick Desert Storm war was popular. It also had international support and was approved by Congress, itself a legacy of the movement. But one wonders how much activism and counterculture behavior would have resurfaced if the desert campaign would have forced the reintroduction of the draft and lasted three years, just a third of the length of Vietnam. In this sense then, the antiwar movement was victorious, for as historian George Herring stated: "The conventional wisdom in the military is that the United States won every battle but lost the war. It could be said of the antiwar movement that it lost every battle but *eventually* won the war—the war for America's minds and especially for its soul."

The movement also won a new armed force. The resistance publicized a discriminatory Selective Service, and that along with an unpopular war, forced Nixon to abolish the system and establish a lottery, eventually leading to a volunteer armed forces that has freed young men from a staple of cold war culture—two years of military service. On campus, ROTC training is no longer mandatory. Because of G.I. resistance within the services, the brass tossed out numerous "Mickey Mouse regulations" and erected a more flexible and especially professional U.S. military. The Old Army became the New Army.

The movement changed other American institutions. Many religious denominations today are more concerned about social ills, more active in their communities, and more integrated, while the number of alternative beliefs has expanded and is more accepted. Sixties activists raised old questions concerning business: What is more important, personal and community or private and corporate rights? What is legitimate corporate behavior? By challenging the establishment, the movement provoked a return to business social responsibility. Corporations since have increased their visibility in communities, and their advertisements often attempt to convince the public that they are environmentally aware and good citizens. Executives of old companies and some new businesses have become involved in progressive politics, from Ben and Jerry's to Working Assets. Finally, companies have changed their hiring patterns. Giving applicants an equal opportunity was a fundamental change in business practices, affecting many occupations, and according to one business journal, new positions for minorities and women were "clearly a response to social protest."

The establishment today includes more women than ever before—a legacy of the women's movement. At the beginning of the new wave of feminism, editor John Mack Carter of *Ladies' Home Journal* published a statement that raised eyebrows. "The point is: this is 1970. All peoples and both sexes are free to reexamine their roles. They are free to grow where they have been stunted, to move forward where they have been held back, to find dignity and self-fulfillment on their own terms." Radical as it seemed then, the statement now is taken for granted. Since then, a "woman's place" is *her* decision. On television, gone are the days of June Cleaver. Sitcoms since have portrayed numerous career females, from "Hill Street Blues" to "Murphy Brown." Heroines can be as complex as heroes. Feminists confronted sexism, provoked men to reconsider their views, and along the way brought about men's liberation. Men have the freedom to choose whether to be the provider, the decision-maker, to stay at home with the children, or to remain single. Roles shifted, as demonstrated by polls in the 1980s that a majority of citizens agreed that men and women should share housework and child-rearing equally. Feminists also changed the family. In the 1950s about 70 percent of families were traditional: a dad who was the breadwinner, and a mom who was the wife, mother, and homemaker. By 1990 only 15 percent of families fit that description. More women than ever before are working, and while the economy was significant in pushing them out of the house and into the office, contemporary opinion polls demonstrate that a majority of females want marriage, children, *and career.* Naturally, that strained the family. Divorce rates have doubled since 1970, but another view is that people no longer feel obligated to spend their entire lives in loveless marriages. "It now appears," pollster Louis Harris noted in 1987, "that the country is witnessing a radical and even revolutionary change in the basic role of women within the family unit." Sex roles have not ended, of course, but because of the movement, America has become a more androgynous society with more flexible views on those roles than at any time, and of any nation.

Activists also were successful in winning legal and political power. Although feminists did not succeed in getting the Equal Rights Amendment ratified, they utilized civil rights acts and decimated discriminatory state and federal laws. During the 1970s most states revised divorce laws, established the idea of common property and no-fault divorce, and accepted the notion that women were full and equal partners in marriage, not subordinate to the husband. Women also revolutionized American politics. While very few had been elected before 1970, by 1990 women had become mayors, governors, congresswomen, senators, and Supreme Court Justices. Two decades after the Strike for Equality, Texas elected a female governor and senator, California elected two such senators, and they had become prime ministers in nations such as Britain, Canada, Norway, Poland, and Turkey. By the time a female becomes president, few will be concerned about the question, "Would you vote for a woman?"

Feminists liberated occupations and the professions. Females sued states, universities, and corporations, resulting in major victories and job opportunities. Almost all states and hundreds of local governments legalized the concept of equal pay for comparable worth, and since then the amount females make compared with males, the earnings gap, has been slowly narrowing. While critics charge that there is a "glass ceiling," that most top positions still are held by white men, feminists nevertheless punched open the door of opportunity. Quotas keeping women out of colleges and professional schools have been abolished, and clearly, women—not minorities—were the main beneficiaries of affirmative action and equal opportunity; they are the ones competing against white males for appointments in colleges and professional schools and for jobs. Between 1970 and 1990 the percentage of female attorneys, professors, physicians, and business managers increased from approximately 5 percent to one-third. Supreme Court Justice Ruth Bader Ginsburg noted: "When I began teaching law in 1963, few women appeared on the roster of students, no more than four of five in a class of over one hundred. . . . Law school textbooks in that decade contained such handy advice as 'land, like women, was meant to be possessed.' . . . The changes we have witnessed since that time are considerable. Women are no longer locked out, they are not curiosities in any part of the profession."

The argument here is not that the women's movement brought about complete equality, a condition reserved for utopia. In fact, as feminist scholars note, liberation generally helped white, middle-class women, having much less impact on the poor, and it contributed to the feminization of poverty since new laws made it easier for husbands to abandon their families. The number of single mothers living in poverty has soared. Since liberation, women do more, often receiving the double burdens of home and work, while they listen to the media discuss the so-called burdens of being independent.

Nevertheless, activists exposed private matters long suppressed—abortion, harassment, incest, lesbianism, rape, wife and child beating—forcing public discussion that resulted in a more open society. They challenged the traditional system of education and brought about more sensitivity in the classroom and in textbooks, and they inspired female writers who flooded the nation with new, exciting literature and scholarship. Moreover, in a relatively short time, feminists revolutionized the legal status of women while they changed relations between males and females that had existed for centuries, resulting in more freedom to define their own lives. Because of feminists, women have more opportunities, more equality, more freedom, than at any time. "It changed my life," Betty Friedan simply wrote. The women's movement resulted in changes so profound, and so accepted, that to the ire of many older activists, young females today often take their rights for granted and have to be reminded of their mothers' status. Women's liberation was the most successful social movement of the sixties—and of American history.

Feminists changed the meaning of "traditional values," and that also is the legacy of the counterculture. Since the first hippies walked down the streets of Haight-Ashbury, critics have castigated them, blaming them for everything from the decline of the American family, to the drug and venereal disease epidemics, even for AIDS. Sex, drugs, rock and roll. To most citizens since, the word "hippie" is similar to "Communist" in the 1950s—anyone undesirable. Freaks filled the void in the great American pastime: the search for a scapegoat. No doubt some of their values and behavior did contribute to social problems. But that topic demands a balanced monograph, not a brief chapter, and not another polemic.

The counterculture first subverted, and then with the aid of other movements, significantly altered the cold war culture. Coming out of the Great Depression, the older generation saved for the future, worked for the family, and followed the roles and the rules. The counterculture challenged that, encouraged experimentation, and provoked millions to consider, or reconsider, their lives. As one middle-aged journalist wrote about his two years visiting communes, "My route criss-crossed the country, leading me into the centers of great cities, far into the backwoods and wilderness, and up a great many mountains. It also took me—sometimes to my great surprise and distress—off the external roadmap into uncharted areas of my own consciousness, where I negotiated for the first time a bewildering tangle of fears, prejudices, and longings."

The counterculture resulted in a value system that has survived with the baby boomers. Surveys by Daniel Yankelovich Group in the early 1970s were confirmed in the late 1980s by Peter Hart Research Associates. The ethics of about 30 million people were altered in a meaningful way by the 1960s events, especially by civil rights struggle, women's liberation, and the war. Some 16 million also stated that personal changes were the result of the counterculture. Those who participated in some aspect of the movement are different from their parents. These sixties people are more skeptical about experts, leaders, politicians, and about institutions—the church, government, and military. They are more flexible, introspective, and tolerant, especially concerning race, living arrangements, and personal behavior. They are more open about their feelings, compassionate, and more liberated sexually. Women feel that they have the same right to sexual satisfaction as men, as demonstrated by a revolution of opinion about premarital sex: The double standard has been buried. Even during the conservative 1980s, numbers soared of interracial marriages, gay and lesbian couples, and single men and women living together. Cohabitation and other alternative living arrangements are common. Being "normal" is no longer a mandate for behavior: Be yourself. Sixties people are more interested in self-fulfillment, defining their own lives, and they often question authority and do their own thing: Let it be.

Most of the counterculture values that since have become clichés still influence behavior. America is more casual in dress and behavior than ever before, and the daily diet includes a wide variety of health foods as corporations proclaim on their packages, "No Artificial Flavors or Preservatives." States have repealed laws prohibiting various forms of sexual behavior between consenting adults, and they have decreased penalties for personal use of drugs. Gone are the days when a court would sentence Timothy Leary to years in prison for half an ounce of marijuana, a drug that still is the most common illegal one in the nation. Youth is not necessarily defined by age, as demonstrated by a legion of middle-aged joggers, hikers, swimmers, rock stars, and others participating in behavior that in the 1950s would not have been appropriate. The result is more personal freedom than at any time in the history of the Republic—so much in fact that youth since has had little to protest, and some have become bewildered with all their options. As James Reston wrote about the graduating class of 1985, there was "nothing to confuse them but freedom." More than ever, America is the land of the free.

Most likely, the sixties will remain for some time as the benchmark for the way sixties people behave and think, just as their parents were influenced by the Great Depression and World War II. Regardless of the barrage from the press declaring that another former hippie or radical has seen the light and accepted a position on Wall Street, opinion polls and surveys have demonstrated that sixties people continue to live their lifestyles. In the 1970s Michael Rossman tried to explain that to journalists who asked him what happened to radicals "when they grow up." "How can I tell them," he remarked, that "it is a process, not a state?" And in the 1990s Bernadine Dohrn added, "You can't win for losing. Either you fulfill their stereotype of being a radical 60's person or you've sold out." Most have not sold out, and evidence is supplied at college reunions. "There's no going back," stated Michigan alumna Julia Wrigley, and at the twentieth anniversary of the Columbia uprising Morris Dickstein noted that instead of describing careers in law, medicine, or banking, the former students "talked about working as labor organizers, peace activists, or campaigners for abortion rights or gay liberation." In Madison, a sociology professor surveyed 300 former civil rights activists and found that most of them had become teachers, lawyers, writers, and consultants: "None voted for Nixon. Two voted for Reagan." Studies have demonstrated that the protest generation remains quite distinctive in its views on civil rights, equality, politics, and lifestyle, a phenomenon *Newsweek* called "The Graying of Aquarius."

Since the sixties, all of the various movements have diminished. That is natural, for the activists succeeded in bringing about a sea change, a different America. Like their predecessors during the Jacksonian period, progressive era, and 1930s, sixties activists were provoked by the inconsistencies between the Founding Fathers' noble ideals and the disappointing realities for many citizens. They responded by holding demonstrations that raised questions. The first wave asked about the rights of black citizens, the rights of students, about their obligation to fight a distant and undeclared war. They provoked the nation to look in the mirror. The second wave expanded the issues to include all minorities and women, and broadened the attack against the establishment. Since, liberation and empowerment have become threads in the nation's multicultural social and political fabric. By confronting the status quo, activists inspired a debate that since has taken place in Congress, courts, city halls, board rooms, streets, and even bedrooms. The debate involves the political and the personal, and it asks the central question of this democracy: What is the meaning of "America"? Like reformers before, provoking a re-evaluation of that question was the most significant legacy of [the movement and the sixties.]

Peter Clecak  **NO**

The New Left

As the stultifying fifties drew to a close, a new generation of radicals promised fresh directions in American politics. Idealistic, bright, and energetic, these young people revived the confidence of weary men on the Left. Of course the new radicals had obvious limitations: they possessed no clear program, no viable organization, not even a formidable constituency. And they were innocent of the disastrous potentialities of moral vision insufiiciently tempered by political realism. But these were the inseparable strengths and weaknesses of youth. Vision would be modified by experience, it was supposed. What counted was their idealism and their enormous energy—indeed, their very existence after an arid season on the Left. . . .

After a decade of movement, however, . . . the hopes of a generation of radicals soured; their visions took on disturbing shapes; their politics turned into fantasies of an impossible revolution. Born in the optimistic climate of the New Frontier, the movement reenacted "the tragic rhythm of American radicalism" within the brief span of a decade. The two most publicized styles of radicalism at the end of the sixties—Students for a Democratic Society and the Yippies—revealed the intense frustration and impotence of those who thoroughly reject the present social order. If the political revolutionaries acquired the usual symptoms of exhaustion—sectarianism, dogmatism, and elitism—the cultural revolutionaries displayed the opposite marks of radical incoherence. Both groups exchanged the complexities of history for simplistic myths. . . .

The Political Revolutionaries

Although largely repudiated by later leaders of SDS factions, "The Port Huron Statement" is in many respects a remarkable document, a powerful record of the dominant moods of an articulate minority of the young in the early sixties. The wide disparities between the rhetoric and the realities of American life stirred them into radical action. Everywhere they looked, students confronted specific manifestations of radical paradoxes: the American creed of racial equality and the grim facts of bigotry; the celebration of domestic progress and the aimlessness of much work and most leisure; the myth of affluence and the realities of poverty; the rhetorical commitment to assisting underdeveloped nations and the ever more lopsided global polarization of wealth; and most ominously, the proclamations of peaceful intentions amid furious preparations for a catastrophic nuclear war.

At the outset, then, the young Left displayed a partial awareness of the chief dilemmas of contemporary American radicalism: the paradox of power-lessness and the moral ambiguities of politics. Their youth allowed them fresh, vivid perceptions of the intolerable dilemmas that parents and teachers had distanced through a variety of perspectives, best summarized in Daniel Bell's concept of "the end of ideology." Since the chance of total revolution-ary change in advanced nations of the West had vanished, Bell contended, progress would henceforth come about less dramatically, in slow, relatively even stages. By emphasizing the enormous complexity of modern societies and the unavailability of revolutionary levers of change, the "end of ideol-ogy" theorists—Bell, Seymour Martin Lipset, and others—also tended to mini-mize the moral dimensions of domestic and international injustices, and the urgency of acting against them. In the end, these intellectuals "resolved" the dilemmas by obliterating the paradox of radical powerlessness; they came to accept the basic features of the American system, if only because there seemed to be no politically viable alternative.

A political conflict between the generations became imminent as the new radicals focused on what their elders no longer wanted to look at directly. The young had no good reason to accept the resignation of the intellectuals, for their own radical odyssey had just begun. And older, ex-Left intellectuals were still adjusting to the crushing losses of an earlier radicalism. For a variety of reasons, then, neither group could accept the basic position of the other. The fresh, unmediated perceptions of American dilemmas reinforced the mood of urgency among the young radicals at Port Huron: "Our work is guided by the sense that we may be the last generation in the experiment with living." Still, they understood that most of their fellow citizens did not care—or had learned not to care—about the drift toward apocalypse. "We are," they frankly admit-ted, "a minority. . . . In this is perhaps the outstanding paradox: we ourselves are imbued with urgency, yet the message of our society is that there is no viable alternative. . . ." The received wisdom of resignation struck the young as a counsel of despair that they sought to exorcise with hope, with a "yearning to believe there *is* an alternative to the present."

To reestablish radical vision after its virtual disappearance in the 1950s, activists formulated an optimistic though tentative statement of their values. They asserted that man is "infinitely precious and possessed of unfulfilled capacities for reason, freedom, and love." But in America the myth of unlimited consumption had dehumanized everyone—the affluent who had too much and the poor who had too little. The expression of man's dormant capacities required a new social setting, "a democracy of individual participation, gov-erned by two central aims: that the individual share in those social decisions determining the quality and direction of his life; that society be organized to encourage independence in men and provide the media for their common participation."

Recognizing the initial need for enlarging their campus constituencies, founders of the movement cast about for political equivalents of the existential moods of students. In the early phases, it was assumed that success could not be measured by political victories or even by "the intellectual 'competence' or 'maturity' of the students involved. . . ." The leaders harbored no illusions about prevalent student attitudes or the dismal state of higher education. After portraying the defensive ennui and the flight into private life by the vast majority, "The Port Huron Statement" provisionally traced individual frustrations to structural causes, noting that "apathy is not simply an attitude" but rather "a product of social institutions and of the structure and organization of higher education itself." Hence the primary opportunity of the new movement lay "in the fact [that] the students are breaking the crust of apathy and overcoming the inner alienation that remain the defining characteristics of American college life."

Within this general framework, specific targets were brought into focus: the outmoded character of the *in loco parentis* theory, the excessive specialization and compartmentalization of knowledge, the alienating effects of value-free social science, and a cumbersome "academic bureaucracy" that contributes "to the sense of outer complexity and inner powerlessness." University authorities now openly acknowledge the validity of nearly every criticism of higher education in "The Port Huron Statement." And the beginnings of reform are evident in the abandonment of *in loco parentis* by major institutions, in the development of interdisciplinary curricula, and in the search for new modes of teaching and learning. But in 1962 few academics understood (or would acknowledge) the breadth and depth of student discontent. It is probably not too cynical to assume that the guardians of higher education would have accelerated their drive toward specialized undergraduate programs of study as long as students remained outwardly docile (and funds for rapid expansion remained available). The most impassioned critics of the new radicalism frequently display notoriously bad memories; whatever SDS was to become, it played a serious part in nudging the complacent into an awareness of the profound conflicts that were to dominate colleges and universities throughout the sixties.

Though sketchy, the radicals' analysis of the larger political scene had the solid virtues of identifying the primary problems that would haunt the nation throughout the decade, and of outlining the intricate social, psychological, and political dimensions of a fresh departure from the pace and direction of American life. Drawing heavily on the work of [C. Wright] Mills, they clearly identified the dominant trend toward increasing private power under the public façade of democracy. American politics was sinking into an "organized . . . stalemate: calcification dominates flexibility as the principle of parliamentary organization, frustration is the expectancy of legislators intending liberal reform, and Congress becomes less and less central to national decision-making, especially in the area of foreign policy."

To rescue the essential values of American liberalism from the complacency of intellectuals and from the crude deformations of philistines, the founders charted a vague politics of radical reform that included protest and confrontation as well as electoral activity. In general, the early SDS advocated a Left-liberal coalition of students, civil-rights and peace groups, labor, the poor, and the conscience constituency of affluent professionals. Since the wide range of available tactics was to serve the larger ends of their vision, they ruled out violence, which "requires generally the transformation of the target, be it a human being or a community of people, into a depersonalized object of hate."

Though flawed by strains of pretentious romanticism, "The Port Huron Statement" generally struck a balance between the articulation of ideals and the recognition of social realities. The founders intended to combine the best elements of the liberal tradition—its sense of the fragility of democracy and of the complexity of modern social problems—with a critique of its failures. They fused an awareness of the problematic with their passionate determination to solve radical paradoxes by embarking upon a sweeping politics of reform. But it was far easier to draw up a statement of political intentions than to execute it. The founders of SDS did not anticipate the devastating effects that the impending clash with the larger society would have on their efforts to develop a radical analysis, vision, and politics. Unable to calculate the narrow range of American politics, they could not know how quickly their activity would dramatize the inherent weaknesses and limitations of a radical youth movement in an advanced capitalist society. This interplay between their own expectations and the resistance of society propelled the drive toward sectarianism. . . .

Unable to chart the historical present accurately, incapable of developing a politics of transition, the new Left of the sixties also failed to imagine the outlines of a decent future. The social vision of young revolutionaries was essentially a simplistic negation of the worst features of the present. It proceeded from the fundatmentalist premise of the absolute depravity of a world where, under capitalism, each man bears the marks of the Original Sin of alienation, which turns him away from himself and against others. Dehumanized people continually reproduce a dehumanized world of bureaucracy, technology, and centralized control over ever wider areas of public and private life. Blind to their own unfreedom, the vast majority of the people do not even consciously desire liberation. Overadministered and ceaselessly manipulated individuals do not want what they need, and they generally do not need what they want. Since the disease of alienation resides both in contemporary social structures and in individuals, the movement's theorists had to posit a new society and a new man. . . .

The vague images of a new man and society vacillated between the revolutionaries' desire for total liberation and their need to submit to tightly structured collectives. . . . Liberation turned into a growing charter of "freedom from": it signified release from stultifying work and enervating leisure; from social convention; from corrupt, media-dominated politics; from sexual inhibitions; and from the culture of the past. In the widest sense, then, it represented a quasi-religious yearning to be free from "the things of earth," which is to [stay] free from the complexities and ironies of history.

The loss of historical perspective implied by these images seriously subverted the political potentialities of the movement. Despite individual exceptions, those who controlled the organizations of the new Left tended toward ever more bizarre notions of liberation, until at last the distinction between capitalism and civilization blurred. Every institution, value, and social convention fell short of the simplistic criterion of egalitarianism. All notions of order, rank, hierarchy, and distinction came under sustained attack—along with the gross economic, social, political and cultural inequities built into monopoly capitalist society. . . .

How could it have been otherwise? The seemingly opposed notions of liberation actually met on common ground. Both were politically impossible in the American context. And both were profoundly antidemocratic. . . . But the concept of liberation, conceived as a charter of total freedoms from existing forms of civilization, presupposed a Marcusean context of a communist community in which all genuine needs of individuals would be met. Yet the political revolutionaries obviously could not enact this version of liberation in contemporary society: they could not become the new men they vaguely imagined. Nor could they, in the early stages, create an egalitarian, democratic political organization without leaders. Moreover, many radicals used this utopian concept of freedom, deduced from an impossible social vision, to judge and condemn the present. In the process, the idea of socialism as a goal lost whatever power it had, or might have gained. And the idea of democracy, both as a political means of inducing change and as an intrinsically important component of a fully developed socialist society, was deprived of much of its force.

This ideological pattern alone would have guaranteed political marginality and intensified feelings of alienation. But the final impetus toward sectarianism and organizational collapse was provided by the complementary notion of liberation considered as submission to the rigid dictates of an obviously repressive collective, a false community. The authoritarian version of liberation was repressive in practice, since it entailed the reduction of individual needs and potentialities to the narrow demands of the whole. Though such a diminished image of man was at least historically possible on a small scale, the dominant cultural pattern of individualism quickly blunted its main thrust. No amount of collectivist rhetoric could dispel the pervasive emotional attachment of large numbers of young radicals to the cluster of notions summarized in the concept of individualism.

Thus utopian radicals of the sixties ensured their own political powerlessness by refusing to accept the disparity between emotional individualism and collectivist rhetoric of community as a pervasive fact of American life. This fundamental paradox, I believe, illuminates the main internal cause of the organizational demise of the political "revolutionaries." Despite its many ambiguous meanings and mythical connotations, the central impulse of individualism survived, thwarting the efforts of utopian Marxists to establish disciplined political organizations. Individualism functions as a self-selecting mechanism by which people attracted to utopian ideologies leave—or never join—organizations based on authoritarian notions of "liberation." Or else it becomes a centrifugal force within vanguard parties, promoting splintering and, in many instances, total disintegration. This, at least, was the experience of the sixties.

The Cultural Revolutionaries

Plagued by similar frustrations, political and cultural revolutionaries shared a spirit of unremitting opposition to American society. This is not surprising, considering their common backgrounds: predominantly young, white, middle-class, and disillusioned, they demanded full release from the dull, affluent settings of their childhoods, no less than from the prefabricated adult roles in what they regarded as the same meaningless rituals of production and consumption. Of course no clear line separates political from cultural revolutionaries; their moods, tactics, and personal styles were responses to the same society and culture. Though few people held a pure form of either position in the sixties, the extremes illuminate much of the interior social and psychic territory. On the continuum of liberation, cultural revolutionaries stand to the left of their political counterparts who cling (however tenuously) to language and logic, theory and political action as means of shaping men and history. The Yippies, representing the most flamboyant semipolitical force in the cultural revolution, found these lingering commitments a source of new frustrations, new orthodoxies, new prisons of the mind.

Unencumbered by the idea of reason and history, Yippies did not need to establish political priorities, to mediate between utopian desires and genuine historical options. Jerry Rubin, a leading spokesman, experienced the futility of sectarian politics at first hand: "For years I went to left-wing meetings trying to figure out what the hell was going on. Finally I started taking acid, and I realized what was going on: nothing. I vowed never to go to another left-wing meeting again. Fuck left-wing meetings!" By submitting wholly to the spirit of liberation through total opposition to American culture and society, they evaded the radical paradoxes of independent Left intellectuals and the radical problems of the new revolutionaries. "The Yippies are Marxists," Rubin declared facetiously: "We follow in the revolutionary tradition of Groucho, Chico, Harpo and Karl."

The accent was on direct, unmeditated, frenetic action against every actual and imagined form of repression. *Do It!*, Rubin's bestseller, provided the cultural revolutionary's reply to the perennial question, "What Is to Be Done?" The vague parody of Lenin was sufficiently precise for Rubin's purpose: "Previous revolutions aimed at seizure of the state's highest authority, followed by the takeover of the means of production. The Youth International Revolution will begin with mass breakdown of authority, mass rebellion, total anarchy in every institution in the Western world. Tribes of longhairs, blacks, armed women, workers, peasants and students will take over." The subtitle—*Scenarios for Revolution*—is equally revealing. For the cultural revolutionaries sought to bypass radical paradoxes by obliterating distinctions between life (in particular, the categories of reason, history, and politics) and art, turning everything in sight into a gigantic set for a musical comedy in a violent key: "language," Rubin contends, "does not radicalize people—what changes people is the emotional involvement of action. What breaks through apathy and complacency are confrontations and actions, the creation of new situations which previous mental pictures do not explain, polarizations which define people into rapidly new situations."

Personal and social salvation—and the two cannot be distinguished in this gestalt—begin when one externalizes his frustrations, dreams, hopes, and anxieties. Conformity and isolation turn into creative conflict and community. Once large numbers enlisted as revolutionary actors, it was claimed, old structures would crumble and power would pass into the hands of the people. . . .

Whereas theorists of the political Left were obsessively scholastic (however mad their points of departure), the Yippies regarded reason as a trap. As Hoffman put it: "It's only when you get to the End of Reason can you begin to enter WOODSTOCK NATION." Antitheoretical and antirational, the Yippies searched for new modes of expressing their revulsion against the PIG NATION. Since reason and language had been appropriated by the enemy, Yippies sought the only uncorrupted modes of expression—sensations and feelings. In their attempts to constitute new worlds, they thus begin with severe, partially self-imposed limitations. Through spokesmen such as Hoffman, the Yippies registered their opposition in concrete, intensely personal terms. Insofar as they depended upon language at all, they avoided alienating abstractions, sticking to a language of the nerves.

Since the aim was to make an instant cultural revolution rather than to define a long-range political one, Hoffman rejected theory and politics, relying instead on a self-consciously fashioned social myth to account for his revulsion against contemporary America. Like the political revolutionaries, he divided the world simplistically into two camps—the PIG NATION and the WOODSTOCK NATION, one perishing, the other rising out of its ruins. For Hoffman, the gathering at Woodstock in the summer of 1969 was not merely a rock festival but the birth of a nation, the formation of another country where the diseases of civilization would disappear. Let the tribe gather together, let everyone do "what the fuck he wants," and then the details of government can be worked out. There is in this comic-strip perspective no need for elaborate theory, no need for social vision, and no need for a politics of transition. The cultural revolution is NOW, and the only "politics" of this transformation is self-defense against the "fascist pigs," he declares, sweeping the details of strategy aside with the grandiose phrase "by any means necessary." According to Hoffman, the flower children of the middle sixties were beginning to rise above their early innocence and passiveness. Like the political militants who graduated from liberalism to uncompromising revolutionary postures, Yippies had to drop their pacific fantasies in order to resist actively the harsh repression of the larger society.

The Yippies' primitivism obviously had little to offer in the way of ethical or political insight into contemporary dilemmas. The idea of doing one's own thing is not the culmination of ethics but its obvious precondition and cause. And the political and social consequences of everyone's pursuing his whims were predictably disastrous. Hoffman ... romanticizes the pathetic scene at Woodstock that provided the content for his fantasies. But the new "nation" survived only three days before paralysis set in. As the *New York Times* observed, "What kind of culture is it that can produce so colossal a mess: one youth dead and at least three others in hospitals from overdoses of drugs; another dead from a mishap while sleeping in an open field. The highways for twenty miles around made completely impassable, not only for the maddened youth but for local residents and ordinary travelers." Had the *Times* reporter been able to go beyond the perspective of a foreign correspondent and drop his mask of moral arrogance, he might have been able to recognize the responsible culture as his own.

For Hoffman, an insider, the tragic aspects of Woodstock disappeared into his fantasy of a new nation taking shape. He was as blind as most petty chieftains to the agony of the lower castes, of those who form the writhing backdrop to his own flamboyant fantasies. Except for a few media figures such as Joan Baez and Jerry Rubin, Hoffman revealingly portrayed Woodstock as a faceless nation. He saw only the incredible energy of the young, not the massive waste of human potential that such gatherings of aimless people exemplify. As one participant in Woodstock West observed: "I kept thinking we are so stupid, so unable to cope with anything practical. Push forward, smoke dope. But maintain? Never. We don't know how. We've been coddled, treadmilled, straight-teethed and vitamin-pilled, but we don't know what to do on our own. Reports of a revolution are vastly premature. We don't like the power structure. But we have to live together. We will be governed by others until we learn how to govern ourselves. . . ."

At bottom, then, the Yippie quest is for authenticity, for a believable sense of self. Since the prevailing culture has appropriated and distorted rationality through its language and values, no less than through its disorienting pace of technological change, the search centers on feelings as the only remaining mode of authenticity. In *Woodstock Nation*, Hoffman presents himself as a representative character in revolt (though he makes it quite clear that he is cleverer and more intense than others). . . .

What renders the total performance unconvincing, however, is Hoffman's steady refusal to take himself seriously. All the confident pronouncements become tentative by virtue of his self-conscious comic pose. By disclaiming accountability for his fantasies, his thoughts, and his actions, he ultimately denies any responsibility for himself. The external and internal sense of reality he frantically tries to construct turns out to be no more than an illusion. Protesting that he's "only in it for kicks and stuff," he nevertheless emerges as the sad butt of his own elaborate gag. None of the roles he tries on so cavalierly fit—nor do all of them at once. They are so many unconvincing media images that fail to provide satisfying forms for the amorphous flow of energy. And so the endless cycle of expending himself continuously exposes his own emptiness. . . .

In the end, after the brief appeal of the Yippies had been exhausted by the media, Rubin and Hoffman cut their hair. And when the Democratic Party held its 1972 convention in Miami, they were there, inside the hall. Facing the television cameras once again, they looked rather like their former selves—innocent, ambitious high-school seniors of the middle fifties. Meanwhile, remnants of the Yippies, camping out in a nearby park, complained that Jerry and Abbie had sold out. Actually they were only looking for new ways to buy in, to retain their tenuous roles as prophets of a new culture.

Like many leaders of the new Left, Rubin and Hoffman could not succeed in their quest for authenticity if only because they were individualists who rejected conventional ways of making it without ever really abandoning the aim of personal success. Their revolt against alienation demanded the establishment of community. Yet through savage caricatures of other revolutionaries who sought political roads to utopia, Yippies rejected the very idea of organization. As the underground writer Paul Krassner put it, "The Crazies have a rule that in order to become a member one must first destroy his membership card." Lacking both the desire and the capacity for organization, Yippie leaders could not hope to retain the attention of would-be followers, who quickly dispersed, seeking new modes of metapolitical expression. . . .

Like other packaged entertainment figures without disciplined talent, however, new Left leaders could not hold an audience for long. Doubtless the media, as some claim, corrupted many ambitious young Leftists. But most turned out to be willing victims who sought publicity as avidly as publicists sought them. Having been weaned on such cultural fare as *Howdy Doody Time* and the *Mickey Mouse Club* in the fifties, Hoffman, Rubin, and others easily fell into their comic roles in the sixties. The cultural distance only seemed greater than it was. The leaders of leaderless groups committed to total change could not resist the most fundamental American, imperative of making it.

Conclusion

As a major expression of the wider cultural revolt, Yippies articulated the antipolitical implications of the new Left's search for utopia. Each grouping exposed the utopian and apocalyptic character of the other. And though there is an endless variety to the themes, moods, and styles of metapolitical criticism, the underlying perspectives and social implications remain fairly constant. Insofar as contemporary visionaries reject social criticism and politics for modes of spiritual salvation from alienation, they join with multitudes of more conventional secular and religious figures in the American tradition. The basic paradigm of personal salvation experienced in small communities has a long heritage: the critic-preacher or prophet articulates hopes, fears, and frustrations, and, then prescribes a means of personal relief, often with the stipulation that if everyone were to accept his prescription, the world would be quickly delivered from evil. This formula links the tracts of vegetarians, the sermons of Billy Graham, and the latest techniques of transcendental meditation imported from remote Indian villages.

Thus it was not surprising that by the early seventies, when Yippies and the political revolutionaries had passed from the center of the public stage, the Jesus movement was flourishing, along with a plethora of exotic religious fantasies that furthered the formation of small communities, or the establishment by fiat of "communities" of solipsists unable to distinguish their own from other worlds. As long as the disparity between the cultural aim of ending alienation through the enactment of community and the political aims of achieving full democracy and social justice persists, temporary, unstable groups of hippies, Yippies, and Jesus freaks will form colonies in the interstices of advanced industrial society. The rank and file will reject its pressures and the ethic of private material gain only to magnify the private virtues of passivity and self-involvement. As antipolitical minorities, however, these groups will be as harmless to the establishment as sanctified members of tiny fundamentalist sects: both renounce certain values of society only to legitimize and perpetuate them by acquiescing in the status quo.

By the end of the sixties, SDS and the Yippies emerged as the most extreme symbols of white protest and revolt in American society; they were at the same time among the most impotent radical groups, with their encounter with power ending in powerlessness. In their distinctive ways, political and cultural revolutionaries reinforce antipolitical attitudes in the wider society. Though not without some political importance, they exercise virtually no control over the uses of their public activity. Their analyses, visions, and politics preclude a coherent synthesis of motive and act, intention and execution. Hence, in addition to being self-defeating, the revolutionaries have become potentially dangerous insofar as they threaten less apocalyptic radical constituencies, intensifying political repression across the Left, and contributing to the erosion of civil rights and liberties. . . .

The most disheartening failure of the new Left, however, was one of omission. Revolutionaries not only repelled the majority of Americans: they also disillusioned a majority on the Left who refused to go over the psychological brink into holistic fantasies of total change. There is a terrible irony here: the new radicals who contributed in important ways to the emergence of anticapitalist modes of consciousness in the sixties were unable to organize the energies they helped to unleash. Driven to mythical modes of understanding that symbolically united their incompatible desires to establish social justice and end alienation, they could neither anticipate nor control the antipolitical consequences of their activity. Isolating themselves even as they were isolated by others, the new revolutionaries could revolutionize neither themselves nor society.

As a youth movement, the new Left quickly reached its predictable political limits, though not before having helped to shake the country out of the complacency of the Eisenhower years. Many of its graduates, and countless others whose outlooks have been influenced by the movement, will move into society, mainly as members of the service professions—law, medicine, teaching, social work, urban planning. Even though they temper the utopian visions of their youth, they will also retain their distrust of received ideology. Some will pursue experimental attitudes toward the questions of how to live within the dominant society. Others will drop out to pursue even more fluid alternative patterns of work and leisure. . . .

The most obvious—and most modest—lesson of the radicalism of the sixties, then, is a negative one that was implicit in the theory of plain Marxists and explicit in the practice of the new revolutionaries: visions of a *Gemeinschaft* community in twentieth-century America are "romantic and utopian in theory, oppressive and reactionary in practice." Mounting social problems may in fact lead to an apocalyptic seizure. But that real possibility ought not to license an uninhibited play of subjective visions of disaster. It is one thing to possess the capacity for imagining an apocalypse and quite another to succumb to the apocalyptic imagination. Those who looked forward to the greening of America, whether through the evolution of a new consciousness or after a destructive revolution, hopelessly blurred this distinction. Instead of evading radical paradoxes, the new revolutionaries submitted to ahistorical versions of them. They quickly discovered their powerlessness against the prevailing social order. . . .

EXPLORING THE ISSUE

Did the Activism of the 1960s Produce a Better Nation?

Critical Thinking and Reflection

1. What was the Port Huron Statement? To what extent were the goals of this document realized by the radical activists of the 1960s?
2. According to Terry Anderson, what were the key contributions of young activists to American society in the 1960s?
3. Compare and contrast the leaders, goals, strategies, and accomplishments of both the political and cultural revolutionaries in the 1960s.
4. According to Peter Clecak, what factors prevented 1960s' activists from accomplishing their goals?

Is There Common Ground?

Most Americans would agree that the decade of the 1960s was a divisive period in which youthful rebels launched an assault against the traditional values of twentieth-century America. A prominent target appeared to be authority in any form, whether parental, educational, political, or cultural. Many young people obviously found these protest activities exhilarating, ideologically meaningful, and politically essential to move the United States toward a more consistently progressive path. Many of their elders were more liable to judge the revolt as nonsensically self-indulgent and immature at best and dangerous and destructive at worst.

The larger question posed by this issue, however, is whether or not this activism produced beneficial results. Those who view the decade from a more positive perspective can point to the improved pattern of race relations, a more inclusive society in general that extends rights broadly, a system of higher education in which the tradition of *in loco parentis* was dislodged by a recognition that students deserve a voice in curricular and policy matters that concern them, and a more self-conscious environmentalist movement bent on protecting the planet from the carelessness of human behavior. Critics of the activism very often contend that whatever problems exist in the United States today can be placed at the feet of a "sixties generation" that was more determined to tear down than to build up and whose protest generated incivility that has infected most of the nation's institutions. Perhaps the only issue upon which all can agree is that the music was really great.

Additional Resources

Students interested in knowing more about the 1960s have many sources to choose from. The six-hour television documentary "Making Sense of the Sixties" is magnificent. Three of the best scholarly studies of the period are: Allen J. Matusow, *The Unraveling of America: A History of Liberalism in the 1960s* (Harper & Row, 1984); John Patrick Diggins, *The Rise and Fall of the American Left* (W. W. Norton, 1992); and David Farber, *The Age of Great Dreams: America in the 1960s* (Hill and Wang, 1994). Valuable autobiographical accounts include Tom Hayden, *Reunion: A Memoir* (Random House, 1988); Todd Gitlin, *The Sixties: Years of Hope, Days of Rage* (Bantam, 1993); and Bill Ayers, *Fugitive Days: Memoirs of An Antiwar Activist* (Beacon Press, 2001). Kirkpatrick Sale, *SDS* (Random House, 1973) is the most comprehensive work on the Students for a Democratic Society. James Miller, *"Democracy is in the Streets": From Port Huron to the Siege of Chicago* (Simon & Schuster, 1987) is written by a former SDS member but is generally balanced. Mark Rudd's *Underground: My Life With SDS and the Weathermen* (William Morrow, 2009) follows the path of the leader of the 1969 Columbia University strike into the terrorist Weather Underground Organization. For an unabashedly critical assessment of student activism written by former radicals, see Peter Collier and David Horowitz, *Destructive Generation: Second Thoughts About the '60s* (Summit Books, 1989).

Radicalism on the campus of the University of California at Berkeley is covered impressively in W. J. Rorabaugh, *Berkeley at War: the 1960s* (Oxford University Press, 1989) and David Lance Goines, *The Free Speech Movement: Coming of Age in the 1960s* (Ten Speed Press, 1993). Michael Rossman, *The Wedding within the War* (Doubleday, 1965) provides first-hand observations from one of the key participants in the Free Speech Movement. The impact of the antiwar protest on the conflict in Vietnam is argued from opposing perspectives by Melvin Small, *Antiwarriors: The Vietnam War and the Battle for America's Hearts and Minds* (Scholarly Resources, 2002) and Adam Garfinkle: *Telltale Hearts: The Origins and Impact of the Vietnam Antiwar Movement* (St. Martin's Press, 1995). Tom Bates, *Rads: The 1970 Bombing of the Army Math Research Center at the University of Wisconsin and Its Aftermath* (Harper Collins, 1992) is the most comprehensive account of that tragedy.

For an explanation of youthful alienation and dissent from a psychological perspective, see three important studies by Kenneth Keniston: *Youth and Dissent: The Rise of a New Opposition* (Harcourt Brace Jovanovich, 1960); *Young Radicals: Notes on Committed Youth* (Harcourt Brace Jovanovich, 1960); and *The Uncommitted: Alienated Youth in American Society* (Dell, 1968). The classic account of the counter culture in the Haight-Ashbury District in San Francisco is Nicholas von Hoffman's *We Are the People Our Parents Warned Us Against* (Ivan R. Dee, 1968).

ISSUE 16

Did President Nixon Negotiate a "Peace with Honor" in Vietnam in 1973?

YES: Richard Nixon, from *The Vietnam Syndrome* (Warner Books, 1980)

NO: Larry Berman, from *No Peace, No Honor: Nixon, Kissinger, and Betrayal in Vietnam* (The Free Press, 2001)

Learning Outcomes

After reading this issue, you should be able to:

- Describe the major events that led to the United States' involvement in Vietnam from 1954 through 1975.
- Discuss President Nixon's policy of "Vietnamization" of the war.
- Critically analyze the Nixon–Kissinger theory that the U.S. Congress allowed South Vietnam to collapse.
- Critically analyze the "decent internal" theory.
- Critically analyze the "peace with honor" that Professor Larry Berman says Nixon negotiated with the North Vietnamese.

ISSUE SUMMARY

YES: Former President Richard Nixon believes that the South Vietnamese government would not have lost the war to North Vietnam in 1975 if Congress had not cut off aid.

NO: According to Professor Larry Berman, President Nixon knew that the Paris Peace Accords of January 1973 were flawed, but he intended to bomb North Vietnamese troops to prevent the collapse of South Vietnam until he left office.

$\mathbf{A}$t the end of World War II, imperialism was coming to a close in Asia and anti-imperialist movements emerged all over Asia and Africa, often producing chaos. The United States faced a dilemma. On the one hand, America was a nation conceived in revolution and was sympathetic to the struggles of the developing nations. On the other hand, the United States was afraid that many of the revolutionary leaders in those countries were Communists who would place their people under the control of the expanding empire of the Soviet Union. By the late 1940s, the Truman administration decided that it was necessary to stop the spread of communism. The policy that resulted was known as "containment."

The first true military test of the "containment" doctrine came soon. Korea, previously controlled by Japan, had been temporarily divided at the 38th parallel at the end of World War II. Communists gained control of North Korea, whereas anticommunist revolutionaries established a government in South Korea. When neither side would agree to a unified government, the temporary division became permanent. After North Korea attacked South Korea in late June 1950, President Truman led the nation into an undeclared war under the auspices of the United Nations. The Korean War lasted three years and was fought to a stalemate.

Vietnam provided the second test of the "containment" doctrine in Asia. Vietnam had been a French protectorate from 1885 until Japan took control during World War II. Shortly before the war ended, the Japanese gave Vietnam its independence, but the French were determined to reestablish their influence in the area. Conflicts emerged between the French-led nationalist forces of South Vietnam and the Communist-dominated provisional government of the Democratic Republic of Vietnam (DRV) established in Hanoi in August 1945. Ho Chi Minh was the president of the DRV. An avowed Communist since the 1920s, Ho had also become the major nationalist figure in Vietnam. As the leader of the anti-imperialist movement against French and Japanese colonialism for over 30 years, he managed to tie together the Communist and nationalist movements in Vietnam.

A full-scale war broke out in 1946 between the Communist government of North Vietnam and the French-dominated country of South Vietnam. The war lasted eight years. After the Communists had inflicted a disastrous defeat on the French at the battle of Dienbienphu in May 1954, the latter decided to pull out. At the Geneva Conference the following summer, Vietnam was divided at the 17th parallel pending elections.

The U.S. involvement in Vietnam came after the French withdrew. In 1955, the Republican President Dwight Eisenhower refused to recognize the Geneva Accords but supported the establishment of the South Vietnamese government whose leader was Ngo Dinh Diem. In 1956 Diem refused to hold elections that would have provided a unified government for Vietnam in accordance with the Geneva agreement. The Communists in the South responded by again taking up the armed struggle. The war continued unabated for another 19 years.

Both President Eisenhower and his Democratic successor, John F. Kennedy, were anxious to prevent South Vietnam from being taken over by the Communists. Economic assistance and military aid were given to the South Vietnamese government. A major problem for President Kennedy lay in the unpopularity of the South Vietnamese government. Kennedy supported the overthrow of the Diem regime (though not his murder) in October 1963 and hoped that the successor government would establish an alternative to communism. His hopes were unrealized. Kennedy himself was assassinated three weeks later. His successor Lyndon Johnson changed the character of American policy in Vietnam by escalating the air war and increasing the number of ground forces from 21,000 in 1965, to a full fighting force of 550,000 at its peak in 1968.

The next president, Richard Nixon, wanted to get America out of Vietnam but, like former President Lyndon Johnson, he did not want to be the first U.S. president to lose a war. He, therefore, adopted a new policy of "Vietnamization" whereby aid to the Republic of South Vietnam was increased to ensure the defeat of the Communists, whereas more responsibility was given to the South Vietnamese military. At the same time, American troops were gradually withdrawn from Vietnam. Guerilla raids into Cambodia in the spring of 1970 to overthrow the left-wing government and destroy the enemy's sanctuaries along the border led to massive antiwar protests at home. In March 1972, American and South Vietnamese troops repelled a massive North Vietnamese invasion. Nixon ordered intensified bombing near Hanoi and mined seven North Vietnamese harbors to stop supplies from China to the Soviet Union.

The Christmas bombings of 1972 probably broke the stalemate in negotiations at Paris between the three sides, which had begun in the spring of 1968 when President Lyndon Johnson had announced he was no longer running for re-election. The Paris Peace Accords of January 1973 were militarily one-sided in favor of North Vietnam. Although the remaining 60,000 American troops would be withdrawn within several months, the North Vietnamese would be allowed to keep 150,000 troops in the South. A cease-fire was declared, and several hundred American prisoners of war (POW) flew home to be greeted warmly by family and friends.

The Paris Peace Accords were barely signed before the terms were broken as North Vietnamese and Vietcong troops started fighting again with the South Vietnamese. President Nixon, embroiled in the Watergate scandal, was unable to come to the aid of President Thieu. Following Nixon's forced resignation on August 9, 1974 (to avoid impeachment proceedings), the problem of Vietnam fell to his successor Gerald Ford. In the spring of 1975, the North Vietnamese army overran South Vietnam. A corrupt, poorly led South Vietnamese army received no help from the United States because Congress refused President Ford's pleas for air power and military assistance. On April 30, the last American helicopter flew out of the American embassy in Saigon onto a ship in the South China Sea. The embarrassingly massive airlift, which left many loyal South Vietnamese behind, was over. So was the Vietnam War. The price was catastrophic. According to Professor Alan Brinkley, "More than 1.2 million Vietnamese soldiers had died in combat, along with countless civilians throughout the region. The United States paid a heavy price as well. The war had cost the nation almost $150 billion in direct costs and much more indirectly. It had resulted in the deaths of over 55,000 young Americans and the injury of 300,000 more. And the nation had suffered a heavy blow to its confidence."

Both Nixon and his Secretary of State, Henry Kissinger, have given their own accounts of the president's handling of the Southeast Asia crisis. See Nixon's *No More Vietnams* (Arbor House, 1985) and his autobiography *RN: The Memoirs of Richard Nixon* (Warner Books, 1978). Kissinger has condensed his two volumes of memoirs pertaining to Vietnam into *Ending the Vietnam War* (Simon and Schuster, 2003) and even further in *Diplomacy* (Simon and Schuster, 1994). Although both men argue that South Vietnam could have been saved, they give different accounts of the peace negotiations leading to the withdrawal of American troops in the winter of 1973. The rivalry between the two is fully explored in Robert Dallek, *Nixon and Kissinger: Partners in Power* (Harper Collins, 2007).

In the YES selection, former President Nixon presents his own version of the Vietnam fiasco. His contention is that, despite policy failure by prior presidents, his administration stemmed the tide. When the last U.S. troops were withdrawn and the Paris Peace Accords were signed in January 1973 between the two Vietnams, the South Vietnamese had achieved military victory. Although the victory was short-lived, Nixon argues that South Vietnam would have been saved but for the United States Congress, under the influence of antiwar protestors and the liberal press, which refused to send further aid or to support any U.S. bombing missions in Vietnam.

In the NO selection, Larry Berman, professor of history at the University of California, Davis, has challenged the Nixon–Kissinger version of the ending of the Vietnam War. Through a careful use of declassified notes of key presidential advisers located in the National Archives or presidential libraries, as well as translations of transcript-like narratives of documents from the Hanoi archives, Berman describes a story of "diplomatic deception and public betrayal" regarding the Paris Peace Accords that supposedly brought an honorable end to the Vietnam War in January 1973. Berman accepts the "decent interval" interpretation first advanced by CIA agent Frank Snepp in a book of the same title published in 1973 and argues that Kissinger and Nixon realized that once American troops were withdrawn, both sides would violate the cease-fire agreements, and South Vietnam would lose the war within two years. Berman, however, adds a new twist to this view. Both Nixon and Kissinger knew that the South Vietnamese government was doomed to fail, but Nixon expected to resume bombing the North Vietnamese military to prevent the collapse of South Vietnam, at least until he left office at the end of his second term in January 1977.

The Vietnam Syndrome

The final chapters have yet to be written on the war in Vietnam. It was a traumatizing experience for Americans, a brutalizing experience for the Vietnamese, an exploitable opportunity for the Soviets. It was also one of the crucial battles of World War III. . . .

Vietnam was partitioned in 1954, with a communist government in the North under Ho Chi Minh and a noncommunist government in the South with its capital in Saigon. Between the two was a demilitarized buffer zone—the DMZ. Soon Ho's government in Hanoi was infiltrating large numbers of agents into the South, where they worked with guerrilla forces to set up networks of subversion and terrorism designed to undermine the Saigon government.

The interim premier of South Vietnam, Ngo Dinh Diem, became its first president In 1955. He proved to be a strong and effective leader, particularly in containing the communist guerrilla forces that were directly supported by the North in violation of the 1954 Partition Agreement. The Eisenhower administration provided generous economic assistance and some military aid and technical advisers, but Eisenhower rejected proposals to commit American combat forces.

Large-scale infiltration from the North began in 1959, and by 1961 the communists had made substantial gains. Sir Robert Thompson arrived in Vietnam that year to head the British Advisory Mission. Thompson had been Secretary of Defense of the Malayan Federation when the communist insurgency had been defeated there. He and the CIA people on the scene understood the importance of local political realities in guerrilla war. In putting down the rebellion in Malaya over the course of twelve years, from 1948 to 1960, the British had learned that local, low-level aggression was best countered by local, low-level defense. Britain had used only 30,000 troops in Malaya, but had also employed 60,000 police and 250,000 in a home guard.

With the excellent advice he was getting, Diem was able to reverse the momentum of the war and put the communists on the defensive. Just as the war in Malaya had been won, the war in Vietnam was being won in the early 1960s. But then three critical events occurred that eventually turned the promise of victory into the fact of defeat.

The first took place far from Vietnam, in Cuba, in 1961: the Bay of Pigs invasion. That disastrous failure prompted President John F. Kennedy to order

From *The Real War* by Richard Nixon (Warner Books, 1980). Copyright © 1980 by Richard Nixon. Reprinted by permission of Grand Central Publishing/Hachette Book Group. All rights reserved.

a postmortem, and General Maxwell Taylor was chosen to conduct it. He concluded that the CIA was not equipped to handle large-scale paramilitary operations and decided that the American effort in Vietnam fit into this category. He therefore recommended that control of it be handed over to the Pentagon, a decision that proved to have enormous consequences. The political sophistication and on-the-spot "feel" for local conditions that the CIA possessed went out the window, as people who saw the world through technological lenses took over the main operational responsibility for the war.

Another key turning point came the next year, in 1962, in Laos. At a press conference two months after his inauguration Kennedy had correctly declared that a communist attempt to take over Laos "quite obviously affects the security of the United States." He also said, "We will not be provoked, trapped, or drawn into this or any other situation; but I know that every American will want his country to honor its obligations." At the Geneva Conference in July 1962 fifteen countries signed an agreement in which those with military forces in Laos pledged to withdraw them and all agreed to stop any paramilitary assistance. All the countries complied except one: North Vietnam. North Vietnam never took any serious steps to remove its 7,000-man contingent from Laos—only 40 men were recorded as leaving—and the United States was therefore eventually forced to resume covert aid to Laos to prevent the North Vietnamese from taking over the country.

North Vietnam's obstinacy in keeping its forces in Laos—which had increased to 70,000 by 1972—created an extremely difficult situation for the South Vietnamese. The communists used the sparsely inhabited highlands of eastern Laos, and also of Cambodia, as a route for supplying their forces in South Vietnam. These areas also gave them a privileged sanctuary from which to strike, enabling them to concentrate overwhelmingly superior forces against a single local target and then slip back across the border before reinforcements could be brought in. The "Ho Chi Minh Trail" through Laos enabled the communists to do an end run around the demilitarized zone between North and South and to strike where the defenders were least prepared.

If South Vietnam had only had to contend with invasion and infiltration from the North across the forty-mile-long DMZ, it could have done so without the assistance of American forces. In the Korean War the enemy had to attack directly across the border; North Korea could hardly use the ocean on either side of South Korea as a "privileged sanctuary" from which to launch attacks. But Hanoi was able to use sanctuaries in Laos and Cambodia as staging grounds for its assault on South Vietnam. In addition to making hit-and-run tactics possible, these lengthened the border the South had to defend from 40 to 640 miles, not counting indentations. Along these 640 miles there were few natural boundaries. The North Vietnamese were free to pick and choose their points of attack, always waiting until they had an overwhelming local advantage, in accordance with the strategy of guerrilla warfare. Our failure to prevent North Vietnam from establishing the Ho Chi Minh Trail along Laos' eastern border in 1962 had an enormous effect on the subsequent events in the war.

The third key event that set the course of the war was the assassination of Diem. Diem was a strong leader whose nationalist credentials were as solid as Ho Chi Minh's. He faced the difficult task of forging a nation while waging a war. In the manner of postcolonial leaders, he ran a regime that drew its inspiration partly from European parliamentary models, partly from traditional Asian models, and partly from necessity. It worked for Vietnam, but it offended American purists, those who inspect the world with white gloves and disdain association with any but the spotless. Unfortunately for Diem, the American press corps in Vietnam wore white gloves, and although the North was not open to their inspection, the South was. Diem himself had premonitions of the fatal difference this might make when he told Sir Robert Thompson in 1962, "Only the American press can lose this war."

South Vietnam under Diem was substantially free, but, by American standards, not completely free. Responsible reporting seeks to keep events in proportion. The mark of irresponsible reporting is that it blows them out of proportion. It achieves drama by exaggeration, and its purpose is not truth but drama. The shortcomings of Diem's regime, like other aspects of the war, were blown grossly out of proportion.

"The camera," it has been pointed out, "has a more limited view even than the cameraman and argues always from the particular to the general." On June 11, 1963, the camera provided a very narrow view for the television audience in the United States. On that day, in a ritual carefully arranged for the camera, a Buddhist monk in South Vietnam doused himself with gasoline and set himself on fire. That picture, selectively chosen, seared a single word into the minds of many Americans: repression. The camera's focus on this one monk's act of self-immolation did not reveal the larger reality of South Vietnam; it obscured it. Even more thoroughly obscured from the television audience's view were the conditions inside North Vietnam, where unfriendly newsmen were not allowed.

Recently, in the Soviet Union, a Crimean Tartar set himself on fire to protest the thirty-five-year exile of his people from their ancestral homeland. A picture of this did not make the network news; it did not even make the front pages; I saw a story about it, with no pictures, buried on page twenty-one of the Los Angeles *Times*.

Communist regimes bury their mistakes; we advertise ours. During the war in Vietnam a lot of well-intentioned Americans got taken in by our well-advertised mistakes.

Some Buddhist temples in Vietnam were, in effect, headquarters of political opposition, and some Buddhist sects were more political than religious. The fact that Diem was a devout Catholic made him an ideal candidate to be painted as a repressor of Buddhists. They also played very skillful political theater; the "burning Buddhist" incident was an especially grisly form. But the press played up the Buddhists as oppressed holy people, and the world placed the blame on their target, Diem. The press has a way of focusing on one aspect of a complex situation as "the" story; in Vietnam in 1963 "the" story was "repression."

President Kennedy grew increasingly, unhappy at being allied with what was being portrayed as a brutal, oppressive government. Apparently without seriously considering the long-term consequences, the United States began putting some distance between itself and Diem.

On November 1, 1963, Diem was overthrown in a coup and assassinated. Charges that the U.S. government was directly involved may be untrue and unfair. However, the most charitable interpretation of the Kennedy administration's part in this affair is that it greased the skids for Diem's downfall and did nothing to prevent his murder. It was a sordid episode in American foreign policy. Diem's fall was followed by political instability and chaos in South Vietnam, and the event had repercussions all over Asia as well. President Ayub Khan of Pakistan told me a few months later, "Diem's murder meant three things to many Asian leaders: that it is dangerous to be a friend of the United States; that it pays to be neutral; and that sometimes it helps to be an enemy."

The months of pressure and intrigue preceding the coup had paralyzed the Diem administration and allowed the communists to gain the initiative in the war. Once Diem was disposed of, the gates of the Presidential Palace became a revolving door. Whatever his faults, Diem had represented "legitimacy." With the symbol of legitimacy gone, power in South Vietnam was up for grabs. Coup followed coup for the next two years until Nguyen Van Thieu and Nguyen Cao Ky took over in 1965. The guerrilla forces had taken advantage of this chaotic situation and gained a great deal of strength in the interim.

President Kennedy had sent 16,000 American troops to Vietnam to serve as combat "advisers" to the regular South Vietnam units, but after Diem's assassination the situation continued to deteriorate. In 1964 Hanoi sent in troops in order to be in a position to take over power when the government of South Vietnam fell. By 1965 South Vietnam was on the verge of collapse. In order to prevent the conquest by the North, President Johnson, in February started bombing of the North, and in March the first independent American combat units landed in Danang. As our involvement deepened, reaching a level of 550,000 troops by the time Johnson left office, fatal flaws in the American approach became manifest.

In World War II we won basically by out producing the other side. We built more and better weapons, and we were able to bombard the enemy with so many of them that he was forced to give up. Overwhelming firepower, unparalleled logistical capabilities, and the massive military operations that our talent for organization made possible were the keys to our success. But in World War II we were fighting a conventional war against a conventional enemy. We also were fighting a total war, and therefore, like the enemy, we had no qualms about the carnage we caused. Even before Hiroshima an estimated 35,000 people were killed in the Allied firebombing of Dresden; more than 80,000 perished in the two-day incendiary bombing of Tokyo a month later.

Vietnam, like Korea, was a limited war. The United States plunged in too impulsively in the 1960s, and then behaved too indecisively. We tried to wage a conventional war against an enemy who was fighting an unconventional war. We tried to mold the South Vietnamese Army into a large-scale conventional force while the principal threat was still from guerrilla forces, which called for the sort of smaller-unit, local-force response that had proved so successful in Malaya. American military policy-makers tended to downplay the subtler political and psychological aspects of guerrilla war, trying instead to win by throwing massive quantities of men and arms at the objective. And then, the impact even of this was diluted by increasing American pressure gradually rather than suddenly, thus giving the enemy time to adapt. Eisenhower, who refrained from publicly criticizing the conduct of the war, privately fumed about the gradualism. He once commented to me: "If the enemy holds a hill with a battalion, give me two battalions and I'll take it, but at great cost in casualties. Give me a division and I'll take it without a fight."

In Vietnam during that period we were not subtle enough in waging the guerrilla war; were too subtle in waging the conventional war. We were too patronizing, even contemptuous, toward our ally, and too solicitous of our enemy. Vietnamese morale was sapped by "Americanization"of the war; American morale was sapped by perpetuation of the war.

Democracies are not well equipped to fight prolonged wars. A democracy fights well after its morale is galvanized by an enemy attack and it gears up its war production. A totalitarian power can coerce its population into fighting indefinitely. But a democracy fights well only as long as public opinion supports the war, and public opinion will not continue to support a war that drags on without tangible signs of progress. This is doubly true when the war is being fought half a world away. Twenty-five years ago the ancient Chinese strategist Sun Tzu wrote, "There has never been a protracted war from which a country had benefited. . . . What is essential in war," he went on, "is victory not prolonged operations." Victory was what the American people were not getting.

We Americans are a do-it-yourself people. During that period we failed to understand that we could not win the war for the South Vietnamese: that, in the final analysis, the South Vietnamese would have to win it for themselves. The United States bulled its way into Vietnam and tried to run the war our way instead of recognizing that our mission should have been to help the South Vietnamese build up their forces so that they could win the war.

When I was talking with an Asian leader before I became President, he graphically pointed out the weakness in what was then the American policy toward South Vietnam: "When you are trying to assist another nation in defending its freedom, U.S. policy should be to help them fight the war but not to fight it for them." This was exactly where we had been going wrong in Vietnam. As South Vietnam's Vice President Ky later said, "You captured our war."

When I took office in 1969 it was obvious the American strategy in Vietnam needed drastic revision. My administration was committed to formulating a strategy that would end American involvement in the war and enable South Vietnam to win.

Our goals were to:

—Reverse the "Americanization" of the war that had occurred from 1965 to 1968 and concentrate instead on Vietnamization.
—Give more priority to pacification so that the South Vietnamese could be better able to extend their control over the countryside.
—Reduce the invasion threat by destroying enemy sanctuaries and supply lines in Cambodia and Laos.
—Withdraw the half million American troops from Vietnam in a way that would not bring about a collapse in the South.

—Negotiate a cease-fire and a peace treaty.

—Demonstrate our willingness and determination to stand by our ally if the peace agreement was violated by Hanoi, and assure South Vietnam that it would continue to receive our military aid as Hanoi did from its allies, the Soviet Union and, to a lesser extent, China.

En route to Vietnam for my first visit as President, I held a press conference in Guam on July 25, 1969, at which I enunciated what has become known as the Nixon Doctrine. At the heart of the Nixon Doctrine is the premise that countries threatened by communist aggression must take the primary responsibility for their own defense. This does not mean that U.S. forces have no military role; what it does mean is that threatened countries have to be willing to bear the primary burden of supplying the manpower. We were already putting the Nixon Doctrine into effect in Vietnam by concentrating on Vietnamization. This meant, as Secretary of Defense Melvin Laird put it, helping South Vietnam develop "a stronger administration, a stronger economy, stronger military forces and stronger police for internal security."

The most important aspect of Vietnamization was the development of South Vietnam's army into a strong, independent fighting force capable of holding its own against the communists—both the guerrilla forces and the main-force units from the north that were then waging conventional war.

In October 1969 I sent Sir Robert Thompson to Vietnam as my special adviser, with instructions to give me a candid, first-hand, independent evaluation of the situation. He reported that he was able to walk safely through many villages that had been under Vietcong control for years. He was so impressed with the progress that had been made that he thought we were in "a winning position" to conclude a just peace if we were willing to follow through with the efforts we were making.

After giving sharply increased emphasis to Vietnamization and pacification, the first order of military business was to hit at the enemy sanctuaries and supply lines in Laos and Cambodia. . . .

Cambodia

In March 1969, in response to a major new offensive that the North Vietnamese had launched against our forces in South Vietnam, I ordered the bombing of enemy-occupied base areas in Cambodia. The bombing was not publicly announced because of our concern that if it were, Sihanouk would be forced to object to it. However, even after it was disclosed by leaks to the New York *Times* in April, Sihanouk did not object. On the contrary, in May 1969, two months after the bombing had started, he said, "Cambodia only protests against the destruction of the property and lives of Cambodians. . . . If there is a buffalo or any Cambodian killed, I will be informed immediately . . . (and) I will protest."

In June 1969, Sihanouk said at a press conference that one of Cambodia's northeast provinces was "practically North Vietnamese territory," and the next month he invited me to visit Cambodia to mark the improvement of relations between our two countries. But Sihanouk's tilt toward the United States did not satisfy Cambodian public opinion. The Cambodians strongly objected to North Vietnam's violation of their sovereignty. In a series of rapidly moving events in March 1970, demonstrations against North Vietnamese occupation of Cambodian territory led to the sacking of the North Vietnamese and Vietcong embassies in Phnom Penh. Within a matter of days the North Vietnamese were given forty-eight hours' notice to vacate the country. Tiring of Sihanouk's careful balancing act, the Cambodian Parliament voted unanimously to depose him. . . .

Throughout April we showed restraint while the Vietnamese communist forces ran rampant through Cambodia. Our total military aid delivered to Cambodia consisted of 3,000 rifles provided covertly. The communists did not show similar restraint; they made it clear that their sole objective was domination of Cambodia.

Finally, on April 30, I announced our decision to counter the communist offensive by attacking North Vietnamese-occupied base areas in Cambodia bordering on South Vietnam. Our principal purpose was to undercut the North Vietnamese invasion of that country so that Vietnamization and plans for the withdrawal of American troops could continue in South Vietnam. A secondary purpose was to relieve the military pressure exerted on Cambodia by the North Vietnamese forces that were rapidly overrunning it. The North Vietnamese had been occupying parts of eastern Cambodia for over five years and returned there after we left; in contrast we limited our stay to two months and advanced only to a depth of twenty-one miles. It is obvious to any unbiased observer who the aggressor was. . . .

The joint operations by the U.S. Army and ARVN wiped out huge stores of North Vietnamese equipment—15 million rounds of ammunition (a full year's supply), 14 million pounds of rice (four months' supply), 23,000 weapons (enough for seventy-four full-strength North Vietnamese battalions), and much more.

Thanks to this and the following year's Lam Son operation in Laos by the South Vietnamese forces, Hanoi was unable to stockpile enough supplies for a full-scale attack on South Vietnam until two years later—in 1972. Valuable time had been won with which to complete the task of Vietnamization. And even when the 1972 offensive came, it was weakest and easiest to contain from the direction of the sanctuaries in Cambodia, a testimony to the effectiveness of our measures. . . .

The 1972 Invasion

The American and South Vietnamese operations in Cambodia and Laos in 1970 and 1971 successfully prevented major North Vietnamese and Vietcong offensives in South Vietnam during those years and made it possible for the United States to continue to withdraw its forces on schedule.

By the spring of 1972 Hanoi recognized that it could not conquer South Vietnam through guerrilla war tactics, even with the help of conventional units, and that it could not win the support of the South Vietnamese people. There was no creditable way for Hanoi to claim any longer that the war in the South was a civil war between the Saigon government and the Vietcong, so North Vietnam dropped the facade of "civil war" and launched a full-scale conventional invasion of the South. Fourteen divisions and twenty-six independent regiments invaded the South. This left only one division and four independent regiments in Laos and no regular ground forces at all in North Vietnam.

As Sir Robert Thompson put it, "It was a sign of the times that this Korean-type communist invasion, which twenty years before would have prompted united Western action and ten years before a Kennedy crusade, immediately put in doubt American resolve and probably won the Wisconsin primary for Senator George McGovern."

U.S. mining of Haiphong Harbor and the use of our airpower against targets in North Vietnam helped save the day, but the fighting on the ground was done exclusively by South Vietnamese forces. North Vietnam lost an estimated 130,000, killed and disabled. The invasion was a failure. . . .

[Our] actions in 1972 strengthened rather than weakened our new relationship with the Soviets and the Chinese. They both could see that we had power, the will to use it, and the skill to use it effectively. This meant that we were worth talking to. We could be a reliable friend or a dangerous enemy. This did not mean that they could publicly abandon their communist allies in Hanoi. However, their support for Hanoi noticeably cooled, which increased the incentive for Hanoi's leaders to make a peace agreement.

As a result of their decisive defeat in the 1972 offensive and their growing concern about the reliability of their Soviet and Chinese allies, the North Vietnamese finally began to negotiate seriously. But they were as stubborn at the conference table as they were on the battlefield. They wanted victory more than they wanted peace. Despite the overwhelming defeat of the peace-at-any-price candidate in the U.S. November elections, they continued to balk at our minimum terms.

On December 14, I made the decision to renew and increase the bombing of military targets in North Vietnam. The bombing began on December 18. It was a necessary step, and it proved to be the right decision. Although it was a very difficult choice, the realities of war, and not the wishful thinking of the ill-informed, demanded this action. The bombing broke the deadlock in negotiations. The North Vietnamese returned to the negotiating table, and on January 23, 1973, the long-waited peace agreement was finally achieved.

After their decisive defeat on the ground by South Vietnamese forces in the spring offensive and the destruction of their war-making capabilities by the December bombing, the North Vietnamese knew that militarily they were up against almost impossible odds. As the South Vietnamese economy continued to prosper far more than that of the North, Hanoi's communist ideology had less and less appeal. Thieu's Land to the Tiller program, for example, had reduced tenancy from 60 to 7 percent by 1973, a truly revolutionary development that undercut the communists' argument that the government allied itself with the rich and oppressed the people. Also, the North Vietnamese knew that both the Soviets and the Chinese had a stake in their new relationship with us and might not be willing to endanger that relationship by providing military supplies in excess of those allowed by the Paris peace agreement of January 1973.

From Victory to Defeat

We had won the war militarily and politically in Vietnam. But defeat was snatched from the jaws of victory because we lost the war politically in the United States. The peace that was finally won in January 1973 could have been enforced and South Vietnam could be a free nation today. But in a spasm of shortsightedness and spite, the United States threw away what it had gained at such enormous cost. . . .

On January 2, 1973, the House Democratic Caucus voted 154-75 to cut off all funds for Indochina military operations as soon as arrangements were made for the safe withdrawal of U.S. troops and the return of our prisoners of war. Two days later a similar resolution was passed by the Senate Democratic Caucus, 36-12. This, it should be noted, was before Watergate began to weaken my own position as President, and only three months before withdrawal of American forces was completed, and the last of the 550,000 American troops that were in Vietnam when I took office in 1969 were brought back. . . .

If the peace agreement was to have any chance to be effective, it was essential that Hanoi be deterred from breaking it. In a private letter to Thieu I had stated that "if Hanoi fails to abide by the terms of this agreement, it is my intention to take swift and severe retaliatory action." At a news conference on March 15, with regard to North Vietnamese infiltration into South Vietnam and violation of the agreement, I stated, "I would only suggest that based on my actions over the past four years, the North Vietnamese should not lightly disregard such expressions of concern, when they are made with regard to a violation."

In April, May, and June of 1973, with my authority weakened by the Watergate crisis, retaliatory action was threatened but not taken. Then Congress passed a bill setting August 15 as the date for termination of U.S. bombing in Cambodia and requiring congressional approval for the funding of U.S. military action in any part of Indochina. The effect of this bill was to deny the President the means to enforce the Vietnam peace agreement by retaliating against Hanoi for violations.

Once Congress had removed the possibility of military action against breaches of the peace agreement, I knew I had only words with which to threaten. The communists knew it too. By means of the bombing cutoff and the War Powers resolution passed in November 1973, Congress denied to me and to my successor, President Ford, the means with which to enforce the Paris agreement at a time when the North Vietnamese were openly and flagrantly violating it. It is truly remarkable that, for two years after the signing of the peace agreement in January 1973, the South Vietnamese held their own against the well-supplied North, without American personnel support either in the air or on the ground and with dwindling supplies.

Throughout 1974 the Russians poured huge amounts of ammunition, weaponry, and military supplies into North Vietnam, and the North in turn poured them into the South. In March 1974 Hanoi was estimated to have 185,000 men, 500 to 700 tanks, and 24 regiments of antiaircraft troops in the South. With the threat of American air power gone, the North Vietnamese built new roads and pipelines to move their armies and supplies about. At the same time, that the Soviet Union was arming Hanoi for the final assault, the United States Congress was sharply curtailing the flow of aid to South Vietnam. U.S. aid to South Vietnam was halved in 1974 and cut by another third in 1975. The United States ambassador to South Vietnam, Graham Martin, warned the Senate foreign Relations Committee that such cuts in military aid would "seriously tempt the North to gamble on an all-out military offensive." His warning was tragically prophetic.

The original plan of the North Vietnamese was to launch their final offensive in 1976. But then they stepped up their timetable. At the start of 1975 Phuoc Long province fell to the communists, the first province South Vietnam had lost completely since 1954. There was relatively little reaction in the United States. Hanoi decided to make larger attacks in 1975 in preparation for the final offensive in 1926. On March 11, Ban Me Thout fell, and on the same day the U.S. House of Representatives refused to fund a $300 million supplemental military aid package that President Ford had proposed. Together with the earlier cutback of aid, this had a devastating effect on the morale of the South Vietnamese, as well as denying them the means with which to defend themselves; they were desperately short of military supplies and dependent for them on the United States. It also gave a tremendous psychological boost to the North. The North threw all of its remaining troops into the battle. Thieu tried to regroup his undersupplied forces in more defensible perimeters, and the hastily executed maneuver turned into a rout. By the end of April it was all over. Saigon became Ho Chi Minh City.

Hanoi had suffered an overwhelming defeat when it launched a conventional attack on the South in 1972. Then the North Vietnamese had been stopped on the ground by the South Vietnamese, while bombing by our air force and mining by our navy crippled their efforts to resupply their forces in the South. B-52 strikes could have had a devastating effect on the large troop concentrations that Hanoi used in its final offensive, but in 1975 Hanoi did not have to reckon with our air and naval forces, and thanks to ample Soviet military aid they had overwhelming advantages in tanks and artillery over South Vietnam's ground forces. After North Vietnam's victory General Dung, Hanoi's field commander in charge of the final offensive, remarked that "The reduction of U.S. aid made it impossible for the puppet troops to carry out their combat plans and build up their forces. . . . Thieu was then forced to fight a poor man's war. Enemy firepower had decreased by nearly 60 percent because of bomb and ammunition shortages. Its mobility was also reduced by half due to lack of aircraft, vehicles and fuel."

Our defeat in Vietnam can be blamed in part on the Soviets because they provided arms to Hanoi in violation of the peace agreement, giving the North an enormous advantage over the South in the final offensive in the spring of 1975. It can be blamed in part on the tactical and strategic mistakes made by President Thieu and his generals. It is grossly unfair to put the blame on South Vietnam's fighting men, the great majority of whom fought bravely and well against overwhelming odds. A major part of the blame must fall on the shoulders of those members of the Congress who were responsible for denying to the President, first me and then President Ford, the power to enforce the peace agreements, and for refusing to provide the military aid that South Vietnamese needed in order to meet the North Vietnamese offensive on equal terms.

But Congress was in part the prisoner of events. The leaders of the United States in the crucial years of the early and mid-1960s failed to come up with a strategy that would produce victory. Instead, first they undermined a strong regime, and then simply poured more and more U.S. troops and materiel into South Vietnam in an ineffective effort to shore up the weaker regimes that followed. They misled the public by insisting we were winning the war and thereby prepared the way for defeatism and demagoguery later on. The American people could not be expected to continue indefinitely to support a war in which they were told victory was around the corner, but which required greater and greater effort without any obvious signs of improvement.

By following the strategy I initiated in 1969, we and the South Vietnamese were able to win the war militarily by the time of the Paris accords of January 27, 1973. The 550,000 American troops that were in Vietnam when I came into office in 1969 had been withdrawn and South Vietnam was able to defend itself—if we supplied the arms the Paris accords allowed.

But the public had been so misinformed and misled by unwise government actions and the shallow, inflammatory treatment of events by the media that morale within the United States collapsed just when the North was overwhelmingly defeated on the battlefield. We won a victory after a long hard struggle, but then we threw it away. The communists had grasped what strategic analyst Brian Crozier said is the central point of revolutionary war: "that it is won or lost on the home front." The war-making capacity of North Vietnam had been virtually destroyed by the bombings in December of 1972, and we had the means to make and enforce a just peace, a peace with honor. But we were denied these means when Congress prohibited military operations in or over Indochina and cut back drastically on the aid South Vietnam needed to defend itself. In the final analysis, a major part of the blame must be borne by those who encouraged or participated in the fateful decisions that got us into the war in the 1960's, and who then by their later actions sabotaged our efforts to get us out in an acceptable way in the 1970's.

By inaction at the crucial moment, the United States undermined an ally and abandoned him to his fate. The effect on the millions of Cambodians, Laotians, and South Vietnamese who relied on us and have now paid the price of communist reprisals is bad enough. But the cost in terms of raising doubts among our allies as to America's reliability, and in terms of the encouragement it gives to our potential enemies to engage in aggression against our friends in other parts of the world, will be devastating for U.S. policy for decades to come. . . .

Larry Berman

 **NO**

No Peace, No Honor: Nixon, Kissinger, and Betrayal in Vietnam

To date, there have been two quite different explanations for the failure of the Paris Accords and the subsequent end of the country known as South Vietnam.

Richard Nixon and Henry Kissinger have always maintained that they won the war and that Congress lost the peace. The treaty itself, they said, although not perfect, was sound enough to have allowed for a political solution if North Vietnam had not so blatantly violated it. North and South Vietnam could have remained separate countries. When the North did violate the agreement, Watergate prevented the president from backing up his secret guarantees to President Thieu. Kissinger goes even further, insisting there was nothing secret about the promises Nixon made to Thieu. In any case, by mid-1973 Nixon was waging a constitutional battle with Congress over executive privilege and abuse of powers; he could hardly start a new battle over war powers to defend South Vietnam. "By 1973, we had achieved our political objective: South Vietnam's independence had been secured," Nixon later told Monica Crowley, former foreign policy assistant and confidante, "But by 1975, the Congress destroyed our ability to enforce the Paris agreement and left our allies vulnerable to Hanoi's invading forces. If I sound like I'm blaming Congress, I am."

Kissinger has put it this way: "Our tragedy was our domestic situation. . . .

In April [1973], Watergate blew up, and we were castrated. . . . The second tragedy was that we were not permitted to enforce the agreement. . . . I think it's reasonable to assume he [Nixon] would have bombed the hell out of them during April."

The other explanation for the failure of the Paris Accords is known as the "decent interval." This explanation is far less charitable to Nixon or Kissinger because it is premised on the assumption that by January 1973, U.S. leaders cared only about securing the release of American POWs and getting some type of accounting on MIAs, especially in Laos. The political future of South Vietnam would be left for the Vietnamese to decide; we just did not want the communists to triumph too quickly. Kissinger knew that Hanoi would eventually win. By signing the peace agreement, Hanoi was not abandoning its long-term objective, merely giving the U.S. a fig leaf with which to exit. In his book *Decent Interval,* Frank Snepp wrote: "The Paris Agreement was thus a cop-out of sorts, an American one. The only thing it definitely guaranteed was an American withdrawal from Vietnam, for that depended on American action alone. The rest of the issues that had sparked the war and kept it alive were left essentially unresolved—and irresolvable."

Kissinger was asked by the assistant to the president, John Ehrlichman, "How long do you figure the South Vietnamese can survive under this agreement?" Ehrlichman reported that Kissinger answered, "I think that if they're lucky they can hold out for a year and a half." When Kissinger's assistant John Negroponte opined that the agreement was not in the best interests of South Vietnam, Kissinger asked him, "Do you want us to stay there forever?"

Nixon yearned to be remembered by history as a great foreign policy president; he needed a noncommunist South Vietnam on that ledger in order to sustain a legacy that already included détente with the Soviets and an opening with China. If South Vietnam was going down the tubes, it could not be on Nixon's watch. "What really matters now is how it all comes out," Nixon wrote in his diary in April 1972. "Both Haldeman and Henry seem to have an idea—which I think is mistaken—that even if we fail in Vietnam we can survive politically. I have no illusions whatsoever on that score, however. The U.S. will not have a credible policy if we fail, and I will have to assume responsibility for that development."

⋘◉⋙

No Peace, No Honor draws on recently declassified records to show that the true picture is worse than either of these perspectives suggests. The reality was the opposite of the decent interval hypothesis and far beyond Nixon's and Kissinger's claims. The record shows that the United States *expected* that the signed treaty would be immediately violated and that this would trigger a brutal military response. Permanent war (air war, not ground operations) at acceptable cost was what Nixon and Kissinger anticipated from the so-called peace agreement. They believed that the only way the American public would accept it was if there was a signed agreement. Nixon recognized that winning the peace, like the war, would be impossible to achieve, but he planned for indefinite stalemate by using the B-52s to prop up the government of South Vietnam until the end of his presidency. Just as the Tonkin Gulf Resolution provided a pretext for an American engagement in South Vietnam, the Paris Accords were intended to fulfill a similar role for remaining permanently engaged in Vietnam. Watergate derailed the plan.

The declassified record shows that the South Vietnamese, North Vietnamese, and the United States disregarded key elements of the treaty because all perceived it was in their interest to do so. No one took the agreement seriously because each party viewed it as a means for securing something unstated. For the United States, as part of the Nixon Doctrine, it was a means of remaining permanently involved in Southeast Asia; for the North Vietnamese, it was the means for eventual conquest and unification of Vietnam; for the South Vietnamese, it was a means for securing continued support from the United States.

The truth has remained buried for so long because Richard Nixon and Henry Kissinger did everything possible to deny any independent access to the historical record. As witnesses to history, they used many classified top-secret documents in writing their respective memoirs but later made sure that everyone else would have great difficulty accessing the same records. They have limited access to personal papers, telephone records, and other primary source materials that would allow for any independent assessments of the record pertaining to the evolution of negotiating strategies and compromises that were raised at different stages of the protracted process. The late Admiral Elmo "Bud" Zumwalt, Jr., former chief of naval operations, said that "Kissinger's method of writing history is similar to that of communist historians who took justifications from the present moment and projected backwards, fact by fact, in accounting for their country's past. Under this method, nothing really was as it happened." This is how the administration's history of "peace with honor" was written.

The personal papers of Henry Kissinger are deposited in the Library of Congress with a deed of gift restricting access until five years after his death. For years we have been denied access to the full transcripts of Kissinger's negotiations. Verbatim hand-written transcripts of the secret meetings in Paris were kept by Kissinger's assistants, Tony Lake, Winston Lord, and John Negroponte. Negroponte gave a complete set of these meeting notes to Kissinger for writing his memoirs, but they were never returned. In his deposition to the Kerry Committee investigation, which examined virtually all aspects of the MIA issue and gave special attention to the Paris negotiations, Winston Lord stated that there were "verbatim transcripts of every meeting with the Vietnamese. I'm talking now about the secret meetings, because I took, particularly toward the beginning, and we got some help at the end, the notes as did Negroponte or Smyser or Rodman and so on." Only now have notes of these secret back-channel meetings become available. Furthermore, the North Vietnamese have published their own narrative translation of the Kissinger-Tho negotiations.

This is the story of a peace negotiation that began with Lyndon Johnson in 1968 and ended with the fall of South Vietnam in 1975. Many secret meetings were involved. The principal sources include transcript-like narratives of documents from Hanoi archives that have been translated by Luu Van Loi and Nguyen Anh Vu and published as *Le Duc Tho-Kissinger Negotiations in Paris;* declassified meeting transcripts from a congressional investigation of MIAs in Southeast Asia; declassified meeting notes from the papers of Tony Lake and memoranda of conversations from recently declassified materials in the National Archives or presidential libraries. These three have been triangulated to connect minutes as well as linkages between events. In many cases, I have been able to fill in classified sections through materials in back-channel cables from Kissinger to Ambassador Ellsworth Bunker or President Nixon.

Here, then, is the emerging story of what Nixon called "peace with honor" but was, in fact, neither. This story of diplomatic deception and public betrayal has come to the light only because of the release of documents and tapes that Richard Nixon and Henry Kissinger sought to bury for as long as possible. Prior to these declassifications, we knew only what Nixon or Kissinger wanted us to know about the making of war and shaping of the so-called honorable peace in Vietnam. . . .

⋅⋖⊙⋗⋅

It has been over thirty years since the United States and Vietnam began talks intended to end the Vietnam War. The Paris Peace Talks began on May 13, 1968, under the crystal chandeliers in the ballroom of the old Majestic Hotel on Avenue Kleber and did not end until January 27, 1973, with the signing of the Agreement on Ending the War and Restoring Peace in Vietnam at the International Conference Center in Paris. Despite the agreement, not a moment of peace ever came to Vietnam. This book uses a cache of recently declassified documents to offer a new perspective on why the country known as South Vietnam ceased to exist after April 1975.

Since the very first days of his presidency in January 1969, Richard Nixon had sought an "honorable peace" in Vietnam. In January 1973 he characterized the Paris agreement as having achieved those lofty goals: "Now that we have achieved an honorable agreement, let us be proud that America did not settle for a peace that would have betrayed our allies, that would have abandoned our prisoners of war, or that would have ended the war for us, but would have continued the war for the 50 million people of Indochina."

A speakers' kit assembled within the White House on the evening of the president's announcement of the cease-fire described the final document as "a vindication of the wisdom of the President's policy in holding out for an honorable peace—and his refusal to accept a disguised and dishonorable defeat. Had it not been for the President's courage—during four years of unprecedented vilification and attack—the United States would not today be honorably ending her involvement in the war, but would be suffering the consequences of dishonor and defeat. . . . The difference between what the President has achieved and what his opponents wanted, is the difference between peace with honor, and the false peace of an American surrender."

A White Paper drafted for distribution to members of Congress offered more barbed attacks on his critics.

> For four agonizing years, Richard Nixon has stood virtually alone in the nation's capital while little, petty men flayed him over American involvement in Indochina. For four years, he has been the victim of the most vicious personal attacks. Day and night, America's predominantly liberal national media hammered at Mr. Nixon, slicing from all sides, attacking, hitting, and cutting. The intellectual establishment—those whose writings entered America into the Vietnam war—pompously postured from their ivy hideaways, using their inordinate power to influence public opinion. . . . No President has been under more constant and unremitting harassment by men who should drop to their knees each night to thank the Almighty that they do not have to make the same decisions that Richard Nixon did. Standing with the President in all those years were a handful of reporters and number of newspapers—nearly all outside of Washington. There were also the

courageous men of Congress who would stand firm beside the President. But most importantly there were the millions upon millions of quite ordinary Americans—the great *Silent Majority* of citizens—who saw our country through a period where the shock troops of leftist public opinion daily propagandized against the President of the United States. *They were people of character and steel.*

Meanwhile, the North Vietnam heralded the Paris agreement as a great victory. Radio Hanoi, in domestic and foreign broadcasts, confined itself for several days to reading and rereading the Paris text and protocols. From the premier's office in Hanoi came the declaration that the national flag of the Democratic Republic of Vietnam (DRV) should be flown throughout the country for eight days, from the moment the cease-fire went into effect on January 28 through February 4. For three days and nights, Hanoi's streets were filled with crowds of people celebrating the fact that in 60 days there would be no foreign troops in Vietnam.

The *Nhan Dan* editorial of January 28, titled "The Great Historic Victory of Our Vietnamese People," observed, "Today, 28 January, the war has ended completely in both zones of our country. The United States and other countries have pledged to respect our country's independence, sovereignty, reunification, and territorial integrity. The United States will withdraw all U.S. troops and the troops of other foreign countries and their advisors and military personnel, dismantle U.S. military bases in the southern part of our country and respect our southern people's right to self-determination and other democratic freedoms."

Premier Pham Van Dong was more forthcoming to American broadcaster Walter Cronkite that "the Paris Agreement marked an important victory of our people in their resistance against U.S. aggression, for national salvation. For us, its terms were satisfactory. . . . The Paris agreement paved the way for our great victory in the Spring of 1975 which put an end to more than a century of colonial and neo-colonial domination over our country and restored the independence, freedom and unity of our homeland."

Perhaps the most honest response came from a young North Vietnamese cadre by the name of Man Duc Xuyen, living in Ha Bac province in North Vietnam. In a postcard, he extended Tet New Year wishes to his family. "Dear father, mother and family," the letter began. "When we have liberated South Viet-Nam and have unified the country, I will return."

Only in South Vietnam was there no joy or celebration over the signing of the Paris agreement. By the terms of the deal, over 150,000 North Vietnamese troops remained in the South, whereas the United States, over the course of Nixon's presidency, had unilaterally withdrawn over 500,000 of its own troops. President Nguyen Van Thieu and his fellow countrymen understood that the diplomatic battle had been won by Le Duc Tho. President Thieu was agreeing to nothing more than a protocol for American disengagement. True, President Nixon had guaranteed brutal retaliation if the North resumed any aggression. But could these guarantees be trusted? The fate of his country depended on them. Twenty-eight months later, South Vietnam would disappear. . . .

James Reston wrote on March 18 that, "once the withdrawal of American prisoners and troops is complete—and it will be within a few weeks—there will be an interesting legal question: what legal authority would the President then have to order American men and bombers back into battle?" The administration was quick to respond. Secretary of Defense Richardson stated that the president retained "residual authority" to bomb in order to maintain the peace and that such bombing was merely a "mopping up exercise." He provided an elaboration on this crucial point: "If he had the authority up to the moment the documents were signed, he has the authority in the following weeks to see that those agreements are lived up to."

But there would be no strikes in March after all. Nixon decided he did not want to jeopardize the return of the final group of American POWs, which finally occurred on March 29, 1973.

By April 1973 Nixon and Kissinger were again considering bombing Khe Sanh. On April 16, Bunker tried to talk Kissinger and Nixon out of it because it would "effectively destroy the cease-fire. I question whether the ICCS would survive bombing attacks in SVN or Laos. . . . Our resuming the bombing of SVN or Laos would also destroy the cease-fire in the minds of the South Vietnamese." Besides, in Bunker's view, the rainy season was about to start and there was no need to restart the bombing in South Vietnam. "In fact, the communists may regard this infiltration effort as compensating for our Enhance and Enhance Plus."

On April 17, Bunker backed off a bit: "I have no problem with 'massive strikes' in Laos and Cambodia. . . . I question the effectiveness of bombing the Trail in Laos and the advisability of bombing either the Trail or Khe Sanh before your meeting with Le Duc Tho." (Kissinger was scheduled to meet again with Le Duc Tho in order to hammer out problems in the agreement.) Kissinger cabled right back with his long-held belief that "it is our judgment that the North Vietnamese will break the cease-fire whenever and however it suits their purpose. They need no provocation. We are therefore considering massive strikes in Laos [to] leave no doubt as to their chances of getting away with flagrant disregard of the agreements."

•◀◉▶•

Five days before he had been sworn in for his second term as the nation's thirty-seventh president, Nixon had written in his diary, "It is ironic that the day the news came out stopping the bombing of North Vietnam, the Watergate Four plead guilty." Unbeknown to anyone, as Henry Kissinger was negotiating with Le Duc Tho in Paris, "Watergate was changing from amber to red," recalled Admiral Zumwalt. "The private commitments made by Nixon to Thieu were unraveling alongside Nixon's presidency."

More than a private commitment was at stake; a secret plan was being overtaken by events. By April 30, Nixon had told the country that he accepted responsibility for the Watergate incident, but he also denied any personal involvement in either the break-in or cover-up. He said that he had been misled by subordinates who had made an "effort to conceal the facts." Nixon announced the nomination of Elliot Richardson as attorney general and that Richardson would have authority to appoint a special prosecutor. The White House also announced that the president had accepted the resignations of Ehrlichman, Haldeman, Attorney General Richard Kleindienst, and the president's counsel, John Dean. As Kissinger later told Stanley Karnow, "After June 1973 I did not believe that the cease-fire would hold. I certainly did not after July 1973. Watergate was in full strength. We had intelligence documents from North Vietnam decoded that Nixon could not honor his pledge and do what he had done in 1972 because of domestic situations."

Watergate would have another effect. Kissinger later stated that this was a "different Nixon. He approached the problems of the violations in a curiously desultory fashion. He drifted. He did not hone in on the decision in the single-minded, almost possessed manner that was his hallmark. The rhetoric might be there, but accompanied this time with excuses for inaction. In retrospect, we know that by March, Watergate was boiling."

There is no question now, nor was there then, that Watergate sapped any resolve that Nixon may have had to bomb again. For decades, Henry Kissinger has used that fact to justify his argument that the administration—including himself—never intended to abandon South Vietnam. Yet something is hard to swallow in that argument. Nixon, the die-hard anticommunist, may have convinced himself that the American people would support South Vietnam in the face of the new—and newly illegal—Northern aggression no matter what. But most Americans were weary of the war, and the public no longer held the same zeal for anticommunism that it had had in the late 1940s and 1950s.

Could Kissinger, the realist, the pragmatist, have failed to see this? Indeed, two newly released records of conversations at meetings suggest a more devious plan. The first, a meeting with Lee Quan Yew, prime minister of Singapore, on August 4,1973, reveals, in Kissinger's own words, the belief that bombing was the only way to make certain that the South would not fall.

The secret meeting occurred in the Captain's Conference Room of the New York Port Authority Policy Building at Kennedy Airport. The euphoria of January's peace with honor was now a distant memory. Lee had just returned from meeting Nha.

Kissinger told Lee that "[Nha] dislikes me intensely!"

"That is not important—personal likes and dislikes. The important thing is the job to be done. I told him it would be useful if Thieu met me. He said, 'why not just meet me?'"

"What is your impression of Nha?" asked Kissinger.

"He is bright, ambitious. With full confidence that what he says will carry weight with the President," said Lee.

"That is true. He is also immature. Emotional," concluded Kissinger.

But Kissinger had come to talk about Watergate and Vietnam, not Mr. Nha. "Our objectives are still the same. We have suffered a tragedy because of Watergate. . . . We were going to bomb North Vietnam for a week, then go to Russia, then meet with Le Duc Tho. Congress has made it impossible." Then Kissinger made the tell-tale confession of his dashed hopes: "In May and June I drew the conclusion that the North Vietnamese were resigning themselves to a long pull of 5-to-6 years. . . . And it would have been a cer tainty if we had given them one blow." In other words, a little bombing now might have slowed them down, which would be a decent interval before losing the South. Nixon and Kissinger would not be directly tied to it.

One more blow was a far more realistic expectation on Kissinger's part. Kissinger told Lee that "the last three months were the most difficult period for us. We couldn't say anything because we could never be sure what some junior aide would say next. But as soon as the hearings are over, we will go on the counter-offensive. We are already in the process. While we are in these difficulties, we have to stay cool. But we won't give up our foreign policy. We will regain the initiative. In Southeast Asia, we haven't gone through all this for four years to abandon it. Sixty-one percent voted in November 1972 not to abandon Southeast Asia. It was a clear issue."

The meeting ended with Lee Kuan Yew's saying how important it was that South Vietnam survive through 1976. "My concern is to have it last through 1976 so that you will have a strong President. If it falls, you will have a new President who says, 'that's what tore American society apart.'"

Kissinger must have been reassured, because he told Lee, "You are an asset to us in that part of the world and we have no interest in destroying you. We won't leave any documents around. They stay in my office."

A little more than a month later, on September 26, Kissinger met with Nguyen Phu Duc in the Waldorf Towers in New York. Kissinger was now secretary of state, and Duc asked Kissinger what the United States planned to do with respect to the North's violations of the Paris Accord. "If it were not for domestic difficulties, we would have bombed them. This is now impossible. Your brothers in the North only understand brutality," said Kissinger. The secretary then spoke about how the Congress had acted "irresponsibly" by cutting off support for bombing, but North Vietnamese "suspiciousness is playing into our hands. They don't completely understand the restrictions placed on us by Congress. President Nixon has fooled them so often that they are probably more concerned that you believe. It is important that you show confidence and behave strongly." He ended with a joke: "Treat them like you treat me."

The conversation then got much more revealing. Kissinger made a startling admission: "I came away from the January negotiations with the feeling that we would have to bomb the North Vietnamese again in early April or May." He did not say, "If the North violated the accord, we would bomb." He confirmed what Haig had told Phouma, what Nixon had said to Thieu and what Zumwalt had concluded in November 1972 at the JCS meeting: it was a sham peace held together with a plan to deceive the American public with the rhetoric of American honor. He knew the North would cheat and was planning on resuming the bombing.

As Kissinger toasted Le Duc Tho with words of peace in January 1973, and as Richard Nixon addressed the nation with news of an honorable peace in Vietnam, both men knew that as soon as the last American POW was home, the bombing would be renewed. For Nixon, the bombing would continue right through 1976, and for Kissinger, just long enough to pick up his Nobel Peace Prize.

Writing in the *Wall Street Journal* on April 27, 1975, William Buckley noted that Watergate had derailed the president's plan to pulverize Hanoi and that Nixon at the time was too emotionally unstable to renew the bombing: "What would Nixon, under Kissinger's prodding, have done, if his reactions had been healthy, when only a few weeks after the Paris Accord was executed, North Vietnam began its blatant disregard of it. My own information is that it was planned, sometime in April, to pulverize Hanoi and Haiphong," wrote Buckley. Indeed, the plans were made even earlier.

One final question remains: Would even short-term bombing support for the South have been accepted by the public? In interviewing done on the day of the Vietnam agreement, a Gallup Poll asked the following questions:

- "When United States troops are withdrawn from Vietnam, do you think a strong enough government can be maintained in South Vietnam to withstand Communist political pressure, or not?" Fifty-four percent believed that government in the South would not survive; 27 percent believed South Vietnam would last; 19 percent had no opinion.
- "After United States troops are withdrawn from Vietnam, do you think North Vietnam in the next few years is likely to try to take over South Vietnam again, or not?" Seventy percent thought that the North would try to take over the South, 16 percent thought no, and 14 percent had no opinion.
- "Suppose when the United States troops are withdrawn, North Vietnam does try to take over South Vietnam again, do you think the United States should send war materials to South Vietnam, or not?" Fifty percent believed the U.S. should not send war materials, while 38 percent said yes, and 12 percent had no opinion.
- "If North Vietnam does try to take over South Vietnam again, do you think the United States should bomb North Vietnam, or not?" Seventy-one percent said no to bombing, while 17 percent said yes, and 12 percent had no opinion.
- "If North Vietnam does try to take over South Vietnam again, do you think the United States should send troops to help South Vietnam, or not?" Seventy-nine percent were opposed to sending troops, while 13 percent favored such an action, and 8 percent had no opinion.

Kissinger later acknowledged that he had misjudged the willingness of the American people to defend the agreement. "But I admit this: we judged wrong. And what we judged wrong above all was our belief that if we could get peace with honor, that we would unite the American people who would then defend an agreement that had been achieved with so much pain. That was our fundamental miscalculation. It never occurred to me, and I'm sure it never occurred to President Nixon, that there could be any doubt about it, because an agreement that you don't enforce is a surrender; it's just writing down surrender terms."

Twenty-five Years Later

On the occasion of the twenty-fifth anniversary of the Paris agreement, the Nixon Center in Washington, D.C., convened a conference, "The Paris Agreement on Vietnam: 25 Years Later." Noticeable by their absence were those who in the intervening years had questioned "peace with honor." Kissinger attended and spoke about the many letters and private assurances given by Nixon to Thieu in which he promised to enforce the agreement: "I would simply ask some honest researcher sometime to compare the letters that President Nixon wrote to Thieu with the letters that still have not been published that President Kennedy or Johnson wrote to other leaders to see who made the bigger commitments. Or even other Presidents, in other circumstances. These were never treated as national commitments. These were expressions of the intentions of the President. Every senior member of the administration—including myself, the Secretary of Defense, the Secretary of State—is represented in compendiums of statements that said publicly every week that we intended to enforce the agreement. There was nothing new about that. . . . If I had any idea that all this was possible, I would not have participated in, and President Nixon would never have authorized, any sort of agreement. I believe it could otherwise have been maintained for a long enough period of time to give the South Vietnamese an opportunity, as the South Koreans were given, to develop their own future."

With respect to consultations with President Thieu, Kissinger's position remained unchanged: "There were all kinds of proposals that we made during that period—the last one made publicly in January 1972 by President Nixon when he disclosed the secret talks which had been going on, and which had been preceded by a secret proposal in May 1971 (all of which, incidentally, President Thieu, approved, probably thinking they would never be accepted). It was not as if we just slipped a proposal to the North Vietnamese that the South Vietnamese had never seen. In fact, I believe that Al Haig took every proposal to Saigon before we made it, and that was approved—although I will admit that the speed with which we moved at the end undoubtedly surprised the South Vietnamese."

The records that Kissinger and Nixon chose to omit from their respective memoirs offer a far more devious explanation. Hoang Duc Nha once employed a Vietnamese proverb to describe his dealings with Kissinger, translated as, "We are like frogs looking up from the darkness at the bottom of the well," meaning that the Vietnamese were in the dark about Kissinger's motives and intentions. Even today, almost three decades since the Paris Accords were signed, Kissinger would prefer that we all remain, like the South Vietnamese, in the dark.

EXPLORING THE ISSUE

Did President Nixon Negotiate a "Peace with Honor" in Vietnam in 1973?

Critical Thinking and Reflection

1. Trace the events from the Eisenhower years through the Nixon years (1954–1973) leading to the United States' involvement and withdrawal from Vietnam. In your answer, consider the following:

   a. Geneva Accords (1954)
   b. Diem Regime (1955–1963)
   c. 1956: a year of no elections
   d. Kennedy's policy of counterinsurgency
   e. Johnson's escalation
   f. Nixon Doctrine
   g. Paris Peace Accords (1973)

2. Critically evaluate President Nixon's view of the Vietnam War. Did his policies succeed in bringing a true peace to Vietnam? Could Congress have saved Vietnam in 1974 and 1975? Did Nixon and Kissinger really expect Vietnam to fall after a decent interval?

3. Critically examine Professor Larry Berman's thesis that President Nixon and Secretary of State Kissinger negotiated a peace settlement that was doomed to fail and that U.S. bombing raids should have prevented the collapse of South Vietnam once the cease fire was violated. Does Berman provide new evidence for his interpretation? If so, what are his sources? Are his sources subject to a different interpretation?

4. Compare Nixon's and Berman's interpretation as to how the Vietnam War ended. Did Nixon withhold evidence that supports Berman's contention that he and Kissinger expected South Vietnam to collapse after a "decent interval"?

5. What lessons can President Obama learn from the Vietnam War in making policy in Iraq, Iran, and Afghanistan?

Is There Common Ground?

Both today's Republicans and today's Democrats claim to have learned lessons from the Vietnam War. In the presidential election of 2004, the war came back to haunt both candidates. The then President George Bush had to prove he served in the Alabama National Guard during the war, whereas Senator John Kerry had to defend his patriotism as a former leader of the Vietnam Veterans against the War. In the summer of 2009, President Obama was weighing his options in Afghanistan. Should he send troops there? Republicans were reading former CIA agent Lewis Sorley's *A Better War, the Unexamined Victories and Final Tragedy of America's Last Years in Vietnam* (Harcourt Brace, 1999), which argues that Nixon's policymakers, particularly General Creighton Abrams, "dropped General Westmoreland's war of attrition and search-and-destroy missions in favor of a holistic approach aimed at 'pacifying' the population of South Vietnam," for lessons on how to win, whereas Democrats, including Obama, were reading Gordon M. Goldstein's *Lessons in Disaster: McGeorge Bundy and the Path to War in Vietnam* (Henry Holt, 2008). Bundy was head of the National Security Council under both Presidents Kennedy and Johnson and, like former Secretary of Defense Robert F. McNamara, had second thoughts about escalating the war in 1965. See "A Battle of Two Books Rages," *The Wall Street Journal* (October 7, 2009).

Additional Resources

There are thousands of books on the Vietnam War. The two best overviews are George C. Herring, *America's Longest War: The United States and Vietnam, 1950–1975*, 3rd ed. (McGraw-Hill, 1996) and David L. Anderson, ed., *Shadows on the White House: Presidents and the Vietnam War, 1945–1975* (University Press of Kansas, 1993), which provides historical essays on the role of every president from Truman through Ford as regards the Vietnam War. See also Jeff T. Hay, *The Greenhaven Encyclopedia of the Vietnam War* (Greenhaven Press, 2004). Another military historian and former Vietnam War military commander, James H. Willbanks, supports some of Sorley's interpretation. In *Abandoning Vietnam: How America Left and South Vietnam Lost Its War* (University Press of Kansas, 2004), Willbanks argues that the South Vietnamese, with the aid of U.S. advisers and air power, held off the North Vietnamese military advances in 1972. But the Paris Peace Accords, negotiated by a politically weakened Nixon along with corrupt South Vietnamese political leaders and incompetent senior military leadership, caused the demise of South Vietnam. Other important military perspectives are available in Harry G. Summers, Jr., *On Strategy: A Critical Analysis of the Vietnam War* (Presidio Press, 1982), Bruce Palmer, Jr., *The Twenty-Five Year War: America's Military Role in Vietnam* (University Press of Kentucky, 1984), and H.R. McMaster, *Dereliction of Duty: Lyndon Johnson, Robert McNamara, the Joint Chiefs of Staff, and the Lies That Led to Vietnam* (HarperCollins, 1997).

Professor Berman's interpretation is also challenged by Jeffrey Kimball in his comprehensive *Nixon's Vietnam War* (University Press of Kansas, 1998). Furthermore, in an article for *The SHAFR Newsletter* (September 2001) entitled "The Case of the 'Decent Interval': Do We Now Have a Smoking Gun?" Kimball insists that Berman misinterpreted some of his evidence. The "decent interval" was adopted in the fall of 1970 after Nixon's initial plan for a quick victory and withdrawal had failed, and not in 1973 at the Paris Peace Talks as Berman claims. Perhaps we will have a better assessment of Nixon's policies when all of his tapes along with Kissinger's correspondence are opened for researchers at the National Archives or the Nixon Presidential Library.

The 13-part television documentary first broadcast on PBS has long been available for classroom use. Stanley Karnow, *Vietnam: A History* (Viking Penguin, 1983) and Stephen Cohen, ed., *Vietnam: Anthology and Guide to a Television History* (Alfred A. Knopf, 1983) are printed supplements to the televised series. Francis Fitzgerald's Pulitzer Prize-winning *Fire in the Lake: The Vietnamese and the Americans in Vietnam* (Little, Brown, 1972) places the war against the backdrop of the culture of Indochina, whereas Myra MacPherson, *Long Time Passing: Vietnam and the Haunted Generation* (Doubleday, 1984) analyzes the war's impact on American society.

A number of anthologies examine the conflict in Southeast Asia from a number of different perspectives. Three of the best are Harrison E. Salisbury, ed., *Vietnam Reconsidered: Lessons From a War* (Harper & Row, 1984); Jeffrey P. Kimball, ed., *To Reason Why: The Debate About the Causes of U. S. Involvement in the Vietnam War* (McGraw-Hill, 1990); and Andrew J. Rotter, ed., *Light at the End of the Tunnel: A Vietnam War Anthology* (St. Martin's Press, 1991).

ISSUE 17

Has the Women's Movement of the 1970s Failed to Liberate American Women?

YES: F. Carolyn Graglia, from *Domestic Tranquility* (Spence, 1998)

NO: Sara M. Evans, from "American Women in the Twentieth Century," in Harvard Sitkoff, ed., *Perspectives on Modern America: Making Sense of the Twentieth Century* (Oxford University Press, 2001)

Learning Outcomes

After reading this issue, you should be able to:

- List six main events in the history of American women.
- Identify and give the significance of the "cult of motherhood" and its major components.
- Describe the impact of the Women's Suffrage Movement.
- Describe the impact of World War II on American women.
- Describe what is meant by the Women's Movement in the 1960s.
- Describe the impact of Betty Freidan's book, *The Feminine Mystique* (1963) on American middle-class women.
- Distinguish between the mainstream and radical wings of the Women's Liberation Movement.
- List and discuss the major accomplishments of the Women's Movement between 1968 and 1975.
- Describe and explain the reasons for the backlash in the 1980s.
- Compare the first and second women's liberation movements.

ISSUE SUMMARY

YES: Writer and lecturer F. Carolyn Graglia argues that women should stay at home and practice the values of "true motherhood" because contemporary feminists have discredited marriage, devalued traditional homemaking, and encouraged sexual promiscuity.

NO: According to Professor Sara M. Evans, despite class, racial, religious, ethnic, and regional differences, women in the United States experienced major transformations in their private and public lives in the twentieth century.

In 1961, President John F. Kennedy established the Commission on the Status of Women to examine "the prejudice and outmoded customs that act as barriers to the full realization of women's basic rights." Two years later, Betty Friedan, a closet leftist from suburban Rockland County, New York, wrote about the growing malaise of the suburban housewife in her best-seller *The Feminist Mystique* (W.W. Norton, 1963).

The roots of Friedan's "feminine mystique" go back much earlier than the post–World War II "baby boom" generation of suburban America. Women historians have traced the origins of the modern family to the early nineteenth century. As the nation became more stable politically, the roles of men, women, and children became segmented in ways that still exist today. Dad went to work, the kids went to school, and mom stayed home. Women's magazines, gift books, and religious literature of the period ascribed to these women a role that Barbara Welter has characterized as the "Cult of True Womanhood," in which the ideal woman upheld four virtues—piety, purity, submissiveness, and domesticity. (See Welter's essay in *American Quarterly* (Summer 1996), as well as Barbara Berg's earlier work *The Remembered Gate: Origins of American Feminism: The Woman & the City, 1800–1860* (Oxford University Press, 1978).

In nineteenth-century America, most middle-class white women stayed home. Those who entered the workforce as teachers or became reformers were usually extending the values of the Cult of True Womanhood to the outside world. This was true of the women reformers in the Second Great Awakening and the peace, temperance, and abolitionist movements before the Civil War. The first real challenge to the traditional value system occurred when a handful of women showed up at Seneca Falls, New York, in 1848 to sign the Women's Declaration of Rights.

At the beginning of the twentieth century, a number of middle-class women from elite colleges in the Northeast were in the vanguard of a number of progressive reform movements—temperance, anti-prostitution, child labor, and settlement houses. Working in tandem with the daughters of first-generation immigrants employed in the garment industry, the early feminists realized that laws affecting women could be passed only if women had the right to vote. After an intense struggle, the Nineteenth Amendment was ratified on August 26, 1920. The "suffragettes" overcame the arguments of male and female antisuffragists who associated women voters with divorce, promiscuity, and neglect of children and husbands with the ratification of the Nineteenth Amendment in 1920. Once the women's movement obtained the right to vote, however, there was no agreement on future goals. The movement stalled between the two world wars for a variety of reasons: women pursued their own individual freedom in a consumer-oriented society in the 1920s; and the Great Depression of the 1930s placed the economic survival of the nation at the forefront. But the World War II had long-range effects on women. Minorities—African Americans and Hispanics, in particular—worked at high wages for over three years in factory jobs traditionally reserved for white males; so did married white females, often in their 30s.

World War II brought about major changes for working women. Six million women entered the labor force for the first time, many of whom were married. "The proportion of women in the labor force," writes Lois Banner, "increased from 25 percent in 1940 to 36 percent in 1945. This increase was greater than that of the previous four decades combined." Many women moved into high-paying, traditionally men's jobs as police officers, firefighters, and precision toolmakers. Steel and auto companies that converted over to wartime production made sure that lighter tools were made for women to use on the assembly lines. The U.S. federal government also erected federal childcare facilities.

When the war ended in 1945, many of these women lost their nontraditional jobs. The federal day-care program was eliminated, and the government told women to go home even though a 1944 study by the Women's Bureau concluded that 80 percent of working women wanted to continue in their jobs after the war. Most history texts emphasize that women did return home, moved to the suburbs, and created a baby boom generation, which reversed the downward size of families in the years from 1946 to 1964. What is lost in this description is the fact that after 1947 the number of working women again began to rise, reaching 31 percent in 1951. The consciousness of the changing role of women during World War II would reappear during the 1960s. When Friedan wrote *The Feminine Mystique* in 1963, both working-class and middle-class college-educated women experienced discrimination in the marketplace. When women worked, they were expected to become teachers, nurses, secretaries, and airline stewardesses—the lowest paying jobs in the workforce. In the turbulent 1960s, this situation was no longer accepted, and by 1973, at the height of the Women's Liberation Movement, women comprised 42 percent of the American workforce. By the beginning of the twenty-first century, middle-class women had made substantial gains in the professions compared with 1960. They represented 43 percent of law school classes as opposed to 2 percent in 1960, 35 percent of students in MBA programs as compared to 4 percent in 1960, 38 percent of all physicians and dentists in contrast to 6 percent and 1 percent, respectively, in those categories in 1960, and 39 percent in doctoral programs today, up from 11 percent in 1960. Working-class women, on the other hand, have been much less successful in breaking into traditional blue collar jobs such as truck driving and construction.

In the YES selection, F. Carolyn Graglia's critique of contemporary feminism is a throwback to attitudes toward women of the late nineteenth and early twentieth centuries, which opposed the woman social workers and suffragists who appeared to be intruding upon the man's world and applauded the "Cult of True Womanhood." Graglia argues that contemporary feminism ignores women's primary role in raising children and preserving the moral character of the family. She blames "second-wave" feminists, along with the

Great Society's social programs, for promoting a sexual revolution that has destroyed the American family by fostering a high divorce rate and sexually transmitted diseases.

Historian and feminist Sara M. Evans takes a long-range view of the women's liberation movement and concludes that women in the United States have experienced major positive transformations in their private and public lives in the twentieth century. By comparing the political, legal, and domestic situation of women in 1900 with the present, Evans charts the successes and failures that were achieved by the two waves of feminist protest movements in the twentieth century. She describes the two streams that formed the women's liberation movement from the mid-1960s. First were the professional women like Betty Freidan, who created the National Organization for Women (NOW) in 1966 and who worked with women leaders in labor unions, government, and consciousness-raising groups to demand enforcement of Title VII of the 1965 Civil Rights Act, which banned discrimination in employment and wages. A second wing of feminist activists emerged from the civil rights and antiwar New Left protest groups from the elite universities. Many of these women felt like second-class citizens in these movements and decided they had their own issues that they had to confront.

Evans dubs the period from 1968 to 1975 "the golden years" because of Congress' passage of the Equal Rights Amendment in Congress in 1972, the 1973 Supreme Court decision (*Roe v. Wade*) legalizing abortion, Title IX of the Higher Education Act, which opened intercollegiate athletics to women, the Women's Equity Education Act, and the Equal Credit Opportunity Act. She recognizes that the women's movement suffered a "backlash" in the 1980s as American society became much more conservative. The New Right blamed the increases in divorce, single parenthood, out-of-wedlock births, abortions, and open homosexuality for the cultural values of the 1960s.

Both the antifeminist Graglia and to a much less extent the profeminist Evans have been critiqued by moderate feminists such as Elizabeth Fox-Genovese and Cathy Young, who contend that contemporary feminists have not spoken to the concerns of married women, especially women from poor to lower–middle-class families who must work in order to support the family. Fox-Genovese's *Feminism Is Not the Story of My Life: How Today's Feminist Elite Have Lost Touch with the Real Concerns of Women* (Doubleday, 1996) is peppered with interviews of whites, African Americans, and Hispanic Americans of different classes and gives a more complex picture of the problems women face today. Young, author of *Cease Fire! Why Women Must Join Forces to Achieve True Equality* (Free Press, 1999), asserts that Graglia denies the real discrimination women faced in the job market in the 1950s. Furthermore, Graglia's critique of the sexual revolution, Young contends, is an attempt to restore a view of female sexuality as essentially submissive.

YES

F. Carolyn Graglia

Domestic Tranquility

Introduction

Since the late 1960s, feminists have very successfully waged war against the traditional family, in which husbands are the principal breadwinners and wives are primarily homemakers. This war's immediate purpose has been to undermine the homemaker's position within both her family and society in order to drive her into the work force. Its long-term goal is to create a society in which women behave as much like men as possible, devoting as much time and energy to the pursuit of a career as men do, so that women will eventually hold equal political and economic power with men. . . .

Feminists have used a variety of methods to achieve their goal. They have promoted a sexual revolution that encouraged women to mimic male sexual promiscuity. They have supported the enactment of no-fault divorce laws that have undermined housewives' social and economic security. And they obtained the application of affirmative action requirements to women as a class, gaining educational and job preferences for women and undermining the ability of men who are victimized by this discrimination to function as family breadwinners.

A crucial weapon in feminism's arsenal has been the status degradation of the housewife's role. From the journalistic attacks of Betty Friedan and Gloria Steinem to Jessie Bernard's sociological writings, all branches of feminism are united in the conviction that a woman can find identity and fulfillment only in a career. The housewife, feminists agree, was properly characterized by Simone de Beauvoir and Betty Friedan as a "parasite," a being something less than human, living her life without using her adult capabilities or intelligence, and lacking any real purpose in devoting herself to children, husband, and home.

Operating on the twin assumptions that equality means sameness (that is, men and women cannot be equals unless they do the same things) and that most differences between the sexes are culturally imposed, contemporary feminism has undertaken its own cultural impositions. Revealing their totalitarian belief that they know best how others should live and their totalitarian willingness to force others to conform to their dogma, feminists have sought to modify our social institutions in order to create an androgynous society in which male and female roles are as identical as possible. The results of the feminist juggernaut now engulf us. By almost all indicia of well-being, the institution of the American family has become significantly less healthy than it was thirty years ago.

Certainly, feminism is not alone responsible for our families' sufferings. As Charles Murray details in *Losing Ground,* President Lyndon Johnson's Great Society programs, for example, have often hurt families, particularly black families, and these programs were supported by a large constituency beyond the women's movement. What distinguishes the women's movement, however, is the fact that, despite the pro-family motives it sometimes ascribes to itself, it has actively sought the traditional family's destruction. In its avowed aims and the programs it promotes, the movement has adopted Kate Millett's goal, set forth in her *Sexual Politics,* in which she endorses Friedrich Engels's conclusion that "the family, as that term is presently understood, must go"; "a kind fate," she remarks, in "view of the institution's history." This goal has never changed: feminists view traditional nuclear families as inconsistent with feminism's commitment to women's independence and sexual freedom.

Emerging as a revitalized movement in the 1960s, feminism reflected women's social discontent, which had arisen in response to the decline of the male breadwinner ethic and to the perception—heralded in Philip Wylie's 1940s castigation of the evil "mom"—that Western society does not value highly the roles of wife and mother. Women's dissatisfactions, nevertheless, have often been aggravated rather than alleviated by the feminist reaction. To mitigate their discontent, feminists argued, women should pattern their lives after men's, engaging in casual sexual intercourse on the same terms as sexually predatory males and making the same career commitments as men. In pursuit of these objectives, feminists have fought unceasingly for the ready availability of legal abortion and consistently derogated both motherhood and the worth of full-time homemakers. Feminism's sexual teachings have been less consistent, ranging from its early and enthusiastic embrace of the sexual revolution to a significant backlash against female sexual promiscuity, which has led some feminists to urge women to abandon heterosexual sexual intercourse altogether.

Contemporary feminism has been remarkably successful in bringing about the institutionalization in our society of the two beliefs underlying its offensive: denial of the social worth of traditional homemakers and rejection of traditional sexual morality. The consequences have been pernicious and enduring. General societal assent to these beliefs has profoundly distorted men's perceptions of their relationships with and obligations to women, women's perceptions of their own needs, and the way in which women make decisions about their lives.

Traditional Homemaking Devalued

The first prong of contemporary feminism's offensive has been to convince society that a woman's full-time commitment to cultivating her marriage and rearing her children is an unworthy endeavor. Women, assert feminists, should treat marriage and children as relatively independent appendages to their life of full-time involvement in the workplace. To live what feminists assure her is the only life worthy of respect, a woman must devote the vast bulk of her time and energy to market production, at the expense of marriage and children. Children, she is told, are better cared for by surrogates, and marriage, as these feminists perceive it, neither deserves nor requires much attention; indeed, the very idea of a woman's "cultivating" her marriage seems ludicrous. Thus, spurred on by the women's movement, many women have sought to become male clones.

But some feminists have appeared to modify the feminist message; voices—supposedly of moderation—have argued that women really are different from men. In this they are surely right: there are fundamental differences between the average man and woman, and it is appropriate to take account of these differences when making decisions both in our individual lives and with respect to social issues. Yet the new feminist voices have not conceded that acknowledged differences between the sexes are grounds for reexamining women's flight from home into workplace. Instead, these new voices have argued only that these differences require modification of the terms under which women undertake to reconstruct their lives in accordance with the blueprint designed by so-called early radicals. The edifice erected by radical feminism is to remain intact, subject only to some redecorating. The foundation of this edifice is still the destruction of the traditional family. Feminism has acquiesced in women's desire to bear children (an activity some of the early radicals discouraged). But it continues steadfast in its assumption that, after some period of maternity leave, daily care of those children is properly the domain of institutions and paid employees. The yearnings manifested in women's palpable desire for children should largely be sated, the new voices tell us, by the act of serving as a birth canal and then spending so-called quality time with the child before and after a full day's work.

Any mother, in this view, may happily consign to surrogates most of the remaining aspects of her role, assured that doing so will impose no hardship or loss on either mother or child. To those women whose natures make them less suited to striving in the workplace than concentrating on husband, children, and home, this feminist diktat denies the happiness and contentment they could have found within the domestic arena. In the world formed by contemporary feminism, these women will have status and respect only if they force themselves to take up roles in the workplace they suspect are not most deserving of their attention. Relegated to the periphery of their lives are the home and personal relationships with husband and children that they sense merit their central concern.

Inherent in the feminist argument is an extraordinary contradiction. Feminists deny, on the one hand, that the dimension of female sexuality which engenders women's yearning for children can also make it appropriate and satisfying for a woman to devote herself to domestic endeavors and provide her children's full-time care. On the other hand, they plead the fact of sexual difference to justify campaigns to modify workplaces in order to correct the effects of male influence and alleged biases. Only after such modifications, claim feminists, can women's nurturing attributes and other female qualities be adequately expressed in and truly influence the workplace. Manifestations of these female qualities, feminists argue, should and can occur in the work-place once it has been modified to blunt the substantial impact of male aggression and competitiveness and take account of women's special requirements.

Having launched its movement claiming the right of women—a right allegedly denied them previously—to enter the workplace on an *equal* basis with men, feminism then escalated its demands by arguing that female differences require numerous changes in the workplace. Women, in this view, are insufficiently feminine to find satisfaction in rearing their own children, but too feminine to compete on an equal basis with men. Thus, having taken women out of their homes and settled them in the workplace, feminists have sought to reconstruct workplaces to create "feminist playpens" that are conducive to female qualities of sensitivity, caring, and empathy. Through this exercise in self-contradiction, contemporary feminism has endeavored to remove the woman from her home and role of providing daily care to her children—the quintessential place and activity for most effectively expressing her feminine, nurturing attributes.

The qualities that are the most likely to make women good mothers are thus redeployed away from their children and into workplaces that must be restructured to accommodate them. The irony is twofold. Children—the ones who could benefit most from the attentions of those mothers who do possess these womanly qualities—are deprived of those attentions and left only with the hope of finding adequate replacement for their loss. Moreover, the occupations in which these qualities are now to find expression either do not require them for optimal job performance (often they are not conducive to professional success) or were long ago recognized as women's occupations—as in the field of nursing, for example—in which nurturing abilities do enhance job performance.

Traditional Sexual Morality Traduced

The second prong of contemporary feminism's offensive has been to encourage women to ape male sexual patterns and engage in promiscuous sexual intercourse as freely as men. Initially, feminists were among the most dedicated supporters of the sexual revolution, viewing female participation in casual sexual activity as an unmistakable declaration of female equality with males. The women in our society who acted upon the teachings of feminist sexual revolutionaries have suffered greatly. They are victims of the highest abortion rate in the Western world. More than one in five Americans are now infected with a viral sexually transmitted disease which at best can be controlled but not cured and is often chronic. Sexually transmitted diseases, both viral and bacterial, disproportionately affect women because, showing fewer symptoms, they often go untreated for a longer time. These diseases also lead to pelvic infections that cause infertility in 100,000 to 150,000 women each year.

The sexual revolution feminists have promoted rests on an assumption that an act of sexual intercourse involves nothing but a pleasurable physical sensation, possessing no symbolic meaning and no moral dimension. This is an understanding of sexuality that bears more than a slight resemblance to sex as depicted in pornography: physical sexual acts without emotional involvement. In addition to the physical harm caused by increased sexual promiscuity, the denial that sexual intercourse has symbolic importance within a framework of moral accountability corrupts the nature of the sex act. Such denial necessarily makes sexual intercourse a trivial event, compromising the act's ability to fulfill its most important function after procreation. This function is to bridge the gap between males and females who often seem separated by so many differences, both biological and emotional, that they feel scarcely capable of understanding or communicating with each other.

Because of the urgency of sexual desire, especially in the male, it is through sexual contact that men and women can most easily come together. Defining the nature of sexual intercourse in terms informed by its procreative potentialities makes the act a spiritually meaningful event of overwhelming importance. A sexual encounter so defined is imbued with the significance conferred by its connection with a promise of immortality through procreation, whether that connection is a present possibility, a remembrance of children already borne, or simply an acknowledgment of the reality and truth of the promise. Such a sex act can serve as the physical meeting ground on which, by accepting and affirming each other through their bodies' physical unity, men and women can begin to construct an enduring emotional unity. The sexual encounter cannot perform its function when it is viewed as a trivial event of moral indifference with no purpose or meaning other than producing a physical sensation through the friction of bodily parts.

The feminist sexual perspective deprives the sex act of the spiritual meaningfulness that can make it the binding force upon which man and woman can construct a lasting marital relationship. The morally indifferent sexuality championed by the sexual revolution substitutes the sex without emotions that characterizes pornography for the sex of a committed, loving relationship that satisfies women's longing for romance and connection. But this is not the only damage to relationships between men and women that follows from feminism's determination to promote an androgynous society by convincing men and women that they are virtually fungible. Sexual equivalency, feminists believe, requires that women not only engage in casual sexual intercourse as freely as men, but also that women mimic male behavior by becoming equally assertive in initiating sexual encounters and in their activity throughout the encounter. With this sexual prescription, feminists mock the essence of conjugal sexuality that is at the foundation of traditional marriage.

Marriage as a Woman's Career Discredited

Even academic feminists who are considered "moderates" endorse doctrines most inimical to the homemaker. Thus, Professor Elizabeth Fox-Genovese, regarded as a moderate in Women's Studies, tells us that marriage can no longer be a viable career for women. But if marriage cannot be a woman's career, then despite feminist avowals of favoring choice in this matter, homemaking cannot be a woman's goal, and surrogate child-rearing must be her child's destiny. Contrary to feminist claims, society's barriers are not strung tightly to inhibit women's career choices. Because of feminism's very successful efforts, society encourages women to pursue careers, while stigmatizing and preventing their devotion to child-rearing and domesticity.

It was precisely upon the conclusion that marriage cannot be a viable career for women that *Time* magazine rested its Fall 1990 special issue on "Women: The Road Ahead," a survey of contemporary women's lives. While noting that the "cozy, limited roles of the past are still clearly remembered, sometimes fondly," during the past thirty years "all that was orthodox has become negotiable." One thing negotiated away has been the economic security of the homemaker, and *Time* advised young women that "the job of full-time homemaker may be the riskiest profession to choose" because "the advent of no-fault and equitable-distribution divorce laws" reflect, in the words of one judge, the fact that "[s]ociety no longer believes that a husband should support his wife."

No-fault divorce laws did not, however, result from an edict of the gods or some force of nature, but from sustained political efforts, particularly by the feminist movement. As a cornerstone of their drive to make women exchange home for workplace, and thereby secure their independence from men, the availability of no-fault divorce (like the availability of abortion) was sacrosanct to the movement. *Time* shed crocodile tears for displaced homemakers, for it made clear that women must canter down the road ahead with the spur of no-fault divorce urging them into the workplace. Of all *Time*'s recommendations for ameliorating women's lot, divorce reform—the most crying need in our country today—was not among them. Whatever hardships may be endured by women who would resist a divorce, *Time*'s allegiance, like that of most feminists, is clearly to the divorce-seekers who, it was pleased to note, will not be hindered in their pursuit of self-realization by the barriers to divorce that their own mothers had faced.

These barriers to divorce which had impeded their own parents, however, had usually benefited these young women by helping to preserve their parents' marriage. A five-year study of children in divorcing families disclosed that "the overwhelming majority preferred the unhappy marriage to the divorce," and many of them, "despite the unhappiness of their parents, were in fact relatively happy and considered their situation neither better nor worse than that of other families around them." A follow-up study after ten years demonstrated that children experienced the trauma of their parents' divorce as more serious and long-lasting than any researchers had anticipated. *Time* so readily acquiesced in the disadvantaging of homemakers and the disruption of children's lives because the feminist ideological parameters within which it operates have excluded marriage as a *proper* career choice. Removing the obstacles to making it a *viable* choice would, therefore, be an undesirable subversion of feminist goals.

That *Time* would have women trot forward on life's journey constrained by the blinders of feminist ideology is evident from its failure to question any feminist notion, no matter how silly, or to explore solutions incompatible with the ideology's script. One of the silliest notions *Time* left unexamined was that young women want "good careers, good marriages and two or three kids, and they don't want the children to be raised by strangers." The supposed realism of this expectation lay in the new woman's attitude that "I don't want to work 70 hours a week, but I want to be vice president, and *you* have to change." But even if thirty hours were cut from that seventy-hour workweek, the new woman would still be working the normal full-time week, her children would still be raised by surrogates, and the norm would continue to be the feminist version of child-rearing that *Time* itself described unflatteringly as "less a preoccupation than an improvisation."

The illusion that a woman can achieve career success without sacrificing the daily personal care of her children—and except among the very wealthy, most of her leisure as well—went unquestioned by *Time*. It did note, however, the dissatisfaction expressed by Eastern European and Russian women who had experienced, as a matter of government policy, the same liberation from home and children that our feminists have undertaken to bestow upon Western women. In what *Time* described as "a curious reversal of Western feminism's emphasis on careers for women," the new female leaders of Eastern Europe would like "to reverse the communist diktat that all women have to work." Women have "dreamed," said the Polish Minister of Culture and Arts, "of reaching the point where we have the choice to stay home" that communism had taken away. But blinded by its feminist bias, *Time* could only find it "curious" that women would choose to stay at home; apparently beyond the pale of respectability was any argument that it would serve Western women's interest to retain the choice that contemporary feminism—filling in the West the role of communism in the East—has sought to deny them.

Nor was its feminist bias shaken by the attitudes of Japanese women, most of whom, *Time* noted, reject "equality" with men, choosing to cease work after the birth of a first child and later resuming a part-time career or pursuing hobbies or community work. The picture painted was that of the 1950s American suburban housewife reviled by Betty Friedan, except that the American has enjoyed a higher standard of living (particularly a much larger home) than has the Japanese. In Japan, *Time* observed, being "a housewife is nothing to be ashamed of." Dishonoring the housewife's role was a goal, it might have added, that Japanese feminists can, in time, accomplish if they emulate their American counterparts.

Japanese wives have broad responsibilities, commented *Time,* because most husbands leave their salaries and children entirely in wives' hands; freed from drudgery by modern appliances, housewives can "pursue their interests in a carefree manner, while men have to worry about supporting their wives and children." Typically, a Japanese wife controls household finances, giving her husband a cash allowance, the size of which, apparently, dissatisfies one-half of the men. Acknowledging that Japanese wives take the leadership in most homes, one husband observed that "[t]hings go best when the husband is swimming in the palm of his wife's hand." A home is well-managed, said one wife, "if you make your men feel that they're in control when they are in front of others, while in reality you're in control." It seems like a good arrangement to me.

Instead of inquiring whether a similar carefree existence might appeal to some American women, *Time* looked forward to the day when marriage would no longer be a career for Japanese women, as their men took over household and child-rearing chores, enabling wives to join husbands in the workplace. It was noted, however, that a major impediment to this goal, which would have to be corrected, was the fact that Japanese day-care centers usually run for only eight hours a day. Thus, *Time* made clear that its overriding concern was simply promoting the presence of women in the work force. This presence is seen as a good *per se,* without any *pro forma* talk about the economic necessity of a second income and without any question raised as to whether it is in children's interest to spend any amount of time—much less in excess of eight hours a day—in communal care. . . .

The Awakened Brünnhilde

. . . Those who would defend anti-feminist traditionalism today are like heretics fighting a regnant Inquisition. To become a homemaker, a woman may need the courage of a heretic. This is one reason that the defense of traditional women is often grounded in religious teachings, for the heretic's courage usually rests on faith. The source of courage I offer is the conviction, based on my own experience, that contemporary feminism's stereotypical caricature of the housewife did not reflect reality when Friedan popularized it, does not reflect reality today, and need not govern reality.

Feminists claimed a woman can find identity and fulfillment only in a career; they are wrong. They claimed a woman can, in that popular expression, "have it all"; they are wrong—she can have only some. The experience of being a mother at home is a different experience from being a full-time market producer who is also a mother. A woman can have one or the other experience, but not both at the same time. Combining a career with motherhood requires a woman to compromise by diminishing her commitment and exertions with respect to one role or the other, or usually, to both. Rarely, if ever, can a woman adequately perform in a full-time career if she diminishes her commitment to it sufficiently to replicate the experience of being a mother at home.

Women were *never* told they could *not* choose to make the compromises required to combine these roles; within the memory of all living today there were always some women who did so choose. But by successfully degrading the housewife's role, contemporary feminism undertook to force this choice upon all women. I declined to make the compromises necessary to combine a career with motherhood because I did not want to become like Andrea Dworkin's spiritual virgin. I did not want to keep my being intact, as Dworkin puts it, so that I could continue to pursue career success. Such pursuit would have required me to hold too much of myself aloof from husband and children: the invisible "wedge-shaped core of darkness" that Virginia Woolf described as being oneself would have to be too large, and not enough of me would have been left over for them.

I feared that if I cultivated that "wedge-shaped core of darkness" within myself enough to maintain a successful career, I would be consumed by that career, and that thus desiccated, too little of me would remain to flesh out my roles as wife and mother. Giving most of myself to the market seemed less appropriate and attractive than reserving myself for my family. Reinforcing this decision was my experience that when a woman lives too much in her mind, she finds it increasingly difficult to live through her body. Her nurturing ties to her children become attenuated; her physical relationship with her husband becomes hollow and perfunctory. Certainly in my case, Dr. James C. Neely spoke the truth in *Gender: The Myth of Equality:* "With too much emphasis on intellect, a woman becomes 'too into her head' to function in a sexual, motherly way, destroying by the process of thought the process of feeling her sexuality."

Virginia Woolf never compromised her market achievements with motherhood; nor did the Brontë sisters, Jane Austen, or George Eliot. Nor did Helen Frankenthaler who, at the time she was acknowledged to be the most prominent living female artist, said in an interview: "We all make different compromises. And, no, I don't regret not having children. Given my painting, children could have suffered. A mother must make her children come first: young children are helpless. Well, paintings are objects but they're also helpless." I agree with her; that is precisely how I felt about the briefs I wrote for clients. Those briefs were, to me, like helpless children; in writing them, I first learned the meaning of complete devotion. I stopped writing them because I believed they would have been masters too jealous of my husband and my children.

Society never rebuked these women for refusing to compromise their literary and artistic achievements. Neither should it rebuke other kinds of women for refusing to compromise their own artistry of motherhood and domesticity. Some women may agree that the reality I depict rings truer to them than the feminist depiction. This conviction may help them find the courage of a heretic. Some others, both men and women, may see enough truth in the reality I depict that they will come to regret society's acquiescence in the status degradation of the housewife. They may then accept the currently unfashionable notion that society should respect and support women who adopt the anti-feminist perspective.

It is in society's interest to begin to pull apart the double-bind web spun by feminism and so order itself as not to inhibit any woman who *could* be an awakened Brünnhilde. Delighted and contented women will certainly do less harm—and probably more good—to society than frenzied and despairing ones. This is not to suggest that society should interfere with a woman's decision to follow the feminist script and adopt any form of spiritual virginity that suits her. But neither should society continue to validate destruction of the women's pact by the contemporary feminists who sought to make us all follow their script. We should now begin to dismantle our regime that discourages and disadvantages the traditional woman who rejects feminist spiritual virginity and seeks instead the very different delight and contentment that she believes best suits her.

Sara M. Evans

 **NO**

American Women in the Twentieth Century

In 1900, our foremothers predicted that the twentieth century would be the "century of the child." It might be more accurate, however, to call it the "century of women." Among the many dramatic changes in American society, it is hard to find an example more striking than the changes in women's lives on every level.

At the beginning of the twentieth century, women were challenging the confines of an ideology that relegated them to the private realm of domesticity. Despite the reality that thousands of women could be found in factories, offices, and fields—not to mention in a wide variety of political and reform activities—those ideas still held powerful sway both in law and in dominant notions of propriety. Over the course of the twentieth century, however, women in America emerged fully (though still not equally) into all aspects of public life—politics, labor force participation, professions, mass media, and popular culture. As they did so, they experienced a transformation in the fundamental parameters of their private lives as well—marriage, family, fertility, and sexuality. In complex ways, women transformed the landscapes of both public and private life so that at century's end we are left with a deeply puzzling conundrum about just what we mean by the terms *public* and *private*.

Women, of course, are part of every other social group. Deeply divided by race, class, religion, ethnicity, and region, they don't always identify with one another, and as a result women's collective identity—their sense of solidarity as women—has waxed and waned. Twice in this century, however, there has been a massive wave of activism focused on women's rights. We can trace the surges of change in women's status that accompanied each of these, one at the beginning and another near the end of the century.

Changes in women's lives were certainly driven by large structural forces such as the emergence of the postindustrial service economy, rising levels of education, and the exigencies of two world wars. Yet they have also been due to women's own self-organized activism in two great waves and in numerous ripples in between. In some instances, women fought for the right to participate in public life. In other instances, already present in public spaces, they struggled for equity. As a result of these struggles, American political and public life has undergone a series of fundamental transformations. Not only are women in different places at the end of the century then they were at the beginning, but also all Americans enter a new century shaped by the complexities of women's journey.

1900—Dawn of the Twentieth Century

At the beginning of the twentieth century, women's lives were defined primarily by their marital status, linked to race and class. If we take a snapshot (understanding that we are capturing a moment in a dynamic process of change), the normative adult woman—both statistically and in the images that pervaded popular culture—was married, middle class, and white. On average, women lived to 48.3 years; they married around age 22 and bore approximately four children. The vast majority of households consisted of male-headed married couples and their children.

In 1900 women's legal standing was fundamentally governed by their marital status. They had very few rights.

- A married woman had no separate legal identity from that of her husband.
- She had no right to control of her reproduction (even conveying information about contraception, for example, was illegal); and no right to sue or be sued, since she had no separate standing in court.
- She had no right to own property in her own name or to pursue a career of her choice.
- Women could not vote, serve on juries, or hold public office. According to the Supreme Court, Women were not "persons" under the Fourteenth Amendment to the Constitution that guarantees equal protection under the law.

These realities reflected an underlying ideology about women and men that allocated the public realms of work and politics to men and defined the proper place of women in society as fundamentally domestic. Confined to the realm of the home, women's duty to society lay in raising virtuous sons (future citizens) and dutiful daughters (future mothers). Over the course of the nineteenth century, however, women had pushed at the boundaries of their domestic assignment, both by choice and by necessity. They invented forms of politics outside the electoral arena by forming voluntary associations and building institutions in response to unmet social needs. In the 1830s, when women like Sarah and Angelina Grimké began to speak publicly against slavery, the mere appearance of a woman as a public speaker was considered scandalous. By 1900, however, women appeared in all manner of public settings, setting the stage for change in the twentieth century.

Signs of Change

A closer look at women's status in 1900 reveals trends that signal imminent change particularly in the areas of education, labor force participation, and sexuality. The coexistence of new possibilities alongside ongoing restrictions and discrimination laid the groundwork for challenges to the norms of female subordination.

Education Women in 1900 had achieved a high degree of literacy. In fact, more girls than boys actually graduated from high school, probably because boys had access to many jobs that did not require significant education. When it came to higher education, however, women were seriously disadvantaged. They were overtly excluded from most professional education: only about 5 percent of medical students were women, and women's exclusion from legal education shows up in the fact that in 1920 only 1.4 percent of lawyers in the United States were female.

It is crucial to note, however, that in 1900 women constituted about 30 percent of students in colleges and universities, including schools for the growing female professions of nursing, teaching, librarianship, and social work. In the long run, this was a potent mix, as thousands of middle-class women embraced the opportunity to pursue higher education, which in turn generated new expectations. Education was a crucial force in creating the key leadership as well as a highly skilled constituency for the feminist mobilizations at either end of the century.

Labor Force Participation In 1900, though wage labor was defined as a fundamentally male prerogative, women could be found in many parts of the labor force. Women's work outside the home, however, was framed by their marital status and overt discrimination based on race as well as sex.

- Approximately one in five women worked outside the home, a figure that was sharply distinguished by race: 41 percent nonwhite; 17 percent white.
- The average working woman was single and under age 25.
- Only 11 percent of married women worked outside the home (up to 15% by 1940), though the proportion among black women (26%) was considerably higher because discrimination against black men made it much harder for blacks to secure a livable income from a single wage.
- Available occupations were sharply limited. Most women who worked for wages served as domestics, farm laborers, unskilled factory operatives, or teachers. In fact, one in three women employed in nonagricultural pursuits worked in domestic service.
- Some new female-dominated professions, such as nursing, social work, and librarianship, were emerging. In addition, the feminization of clerical work, linked to the new technology of the typewriter and the record-keeping needs of growing corporate bureaucracies, signaled a dramatic trend that made the "working girl" increasingly respectable. By 1920 the proportion of women engaged in clerical work (25.6%) had surpassed the number in manufacturing (23.8), domestic service (18.2%), and agriculture (12.9%).

Sexuality and the Body Late Victorians presumed (if they thought about it at all) that female sexuality should be confined entirely to marriage. Compared with today, there was very little premarital sex, and women were understood not to have much in the way of sexual desire. It was illegal to transmit information about contraception, though women clearly conveyed it anyway through networks of rumor and gossip. Within the dominant middle class even the simplest acknowledgments of female sexuality were suppressed into euphemism and other forms of denial. Body parts could not be named in polite company, so chicken "legs" and "breast," for example, became "dark meat" and "white meat." Female attire covered women's bodies with clothing that revealed some shape but very little skin.

Yet, as the twentieth century dawned with its emerging consumer culture, sexuality could no longer be so easily contained. Popular culture included vaudeville, dance halls, and a growing variety of public amusements (such as the brand-new movie theaters). In the past, women who frequented such places risked having a "bad reputation." Yet the growing popularity of public amusements within the "respectable middle class" was beginning to challenge such perceptions.

Women's bodies were also finding new visibility in athletics. In the wildly popular arenas of public competition such as baseball and boxing, athletics were virtually synonymous with masculinity. And yet women were beginning to play lawn tennis, field hockey, and gymnastics. Some even rode bicycles.

Race, Class, and Gender Ideals   Within the gender ideology of the urban middle class that emerged over the course of the nineteenth century, the "good woman" (and her antithesis) took on distinct characteristics associated with race and class. "Good" (white, Protestant, middle class) women embodied private virtues. They were chaste, domestic, pious, and submissive. "Bad" women were "low class"—immigrants, racial minorities—presumed to be promiscuous, bad mothers, and improper housewives largely on the basis of their presence in previously male-only public spaces (factories, saloons, dance halls). Such perceptions multiplied in the case of southern black women subjected to a regime of racial/sexual domination that included the constant threat of rape and the public humiliations of segregation. Yet, the denigration of lower-class and minority women on the basis of their presence in public was getting harder to sustain as growing numbers of supposedly "respectable" women showed up in the same, or similar, spaces.

The First Wave

This brief sketch of women's condition at the beginning of the century points to several forces for change that would bear fruit in the first few decades. The growth in women's education, their move into a wide variety of reform efforts as well as professions, laid the groundwork for a massive suffrage movement that demanded the most basic right of citizenship for women. The claim of citizenship was in many ways a deeply radical challenge to the ideology of separate spheres for men and women. It asserted the right of the individual woman to stand in direct relation to the state rather than to be represented through the participation of her husband or father. The growing power of the women's suffrage movement rested both on women's collective consciousness, born in female associations, and on increased individualism among women in an urbanizing industrializing economy.

While a small but crucial number of upper-middle-class women attended college, where they developed a transformed awareness of their own potential as women both individually and collectively, working-class immigrant and African-American women experienced both individualism and collectivity in very different ways. Forced to work outside the home in the least-skilled, lowest paying jobs, both they and their employers presumed that women's labor force participation was temporary. Unions objected to their presence and blocked them from apprenticeship and access to skilled jobs. Despite these obstacles, when wage-earning women organized their own unions, often in alliance with middle-class reformers, they exhibited awesome courage and militancy. In the garment district of New York, for example, the "uprising of the twenty thousand" in 1909 confounded the garment industry and led to a new kind of industrial unionism.

By 1910, middle-class white reformers had formed increasingly effective alliances with black and working-class women around the issue of women's suffrage. The massive mobilization of American women in the decade before the Nineteenth Amendment was ratified in 1920 included rallies of thousands of "working girls" and the organization of numerous African-American women's suffrage clubs. Shared exclusion from the individual right of civic participation symbolized their common womanhood. Following their victory, leaders of the National American Woman Suffrage Association joyfully dismantled their organization and reassembled as the newly formed League of Women Voters. Their new task, as they defined it, was to train women to exercise their individual citizenship rights.

Such a reorientation seemed congruent with the popular culture of the 1920s, which emphasized individual pleasures along with individual rights. The development of a consumer economy, emphasizing pleasure and using sexuality to sell, offered women other paths out of submissive domesticity and into more assertive forms of individualism, paths that did not require solidarity, indeed, undermined it. The female subculture that relied on a singular definition of "woman" eroded. Female reform efforts remained a powerful force in American politics—laying much of the groundwork for the emergence of a welfare state—but a broad-based movement for women's rights no longer existed after 1920. The pace of change in areas like education and labor force participation also reached a plateau and remained relatively unchanged for several decades after 1920. Modern women were individuals. And "feminism" became an epithet.

The loss of female solidarity meant that women's organizations in subsequent decades drew on narrow constituencies with very different priorities. Professional women, lonely pioneers in many fields, felt the continuing sting of discrimination and sought to eradicate the last vestiges of legal discrimination with an Equal Rights Amendment (ERA). The National Women's Party, one of the leading organizations in the struggle, first proposed the ERA in

1923 for the vote. But they were opposed by former allies, social reformers who feared that the protections for working women, which they had won during the Progressive era, would be lost. Though fiercely opposed to the ERA, reformers continued to advocate a stronger role for government in responding to social welfare. Many of them—with leaders like Eleanor Roosevelt—assumed key positions in the 1930s and shaped the political agenda known as the New Deal. In particular, their influence on the Social Security Act laid the foundations of the welfare state. Even among female reformers, however, alliances across racial lines remained rare and fraught with difficulty. As the progressive female reform tradition shaped an emergent welfare state, African-American voices remained muted, the needs of working women with children unaddressed.

The Second Wave

By mid-century the conditions for another surge of activism were under way. During the Second World War women joined the labor force in unprecedented numbers. Most significant, perhaps, married women and women over age 35 became normative among working women by 1950. Yet cold war culture, in the aftermath of World War II, reasserted traditional gender roles. The effort to contain women within the confines of the "feminine mystique" (as Betty Friedan later labeled this ideology), however, obscured but did not prevent rising activism among different constituencies of women. Under the cover of popular images of domesticity, women were rapidly changing their patterns of labor force and civic participation, initiating social movements for civil rights and world peace, and flooding into institutions of higher education.

The President's Commission on the Status of Women, established in 1961, put women's issues back on the national political agenda by recruiting a network of powerful women to develop a set of shared goals. They issued a report in 1963, the same year that Friedan published *The Feminine Mystique*. That report documented in meticulous detail the ongoing realities of discrimination in employment and in wages, numerous legal disabilities such as married women's lack of access to credit, and the growing problems of working mothers without adequate child care. In 1964, Title VII of the Civil Rights Act gave women their most powerful legal weapon against employment discrimination. An opponent of civil rights introduced Title VII, and many members of Congress treated it as a joke. But Title VII passed because the small number of women then in Congress fiercely and effectively defended the need to prohibit discrimination on the basis of "sex" as well as race, religion, and national origin.

The second wave emerged simultaneously among professional women and a younger cohort of social activists. Professionals, with the leadership of women in labor unions, government leaders, and intellectuals like Friedan, created the National Organization for Women (NOW) in 1966 to demand enforcement of laws like Title VII. A second branch of feminist activism emerged from younger women in the civil rights movement and the student new left. Civil rights offered a model of activism, an egalitarian and visionary language, an opportunity to develop political skills, and role models of courageous female leaders. Young women broke away in 1967 to form consciousness-raising groups and build on the legacy of the movements that had trained them.

The slogan, "the personal is political," became the ideological pivot of the second wave of American feminism. It drove a variety of challenges to gendered relations of power, whether embodied in public policy or in the most intimate personal relationships. The force of this direct assault on the public/private dichotomy has left deep marks on American politics, American society, and the feminist movement itself. Issues like domestic violence, child care, abortion, and sexual harassment have become central to the American political agenda, exposing deep divisions in American society that are not easily subject to the give-and-take compromises of political horse-trading.

From 1968 to 1975, the "Women's Liberation Movement," using the techniques of consciousness-raising in small groups, grew explosively. The synergy between different branches of feminist activism made the 1970s a very dynamic era. Feminist policymakers dubbed the years 1968 to 1975 "the golden years" because of their success in courtrooms and legislatures. These included the Equal Rights Amendment, which passed Congress in 1972 and went to the states; the 1973 Supreme Court decision legalizing abortion (*Roe v. Wade*); Title IX of the Higher Education Act, which opened intercollegiate athletics to women; the Women's Equity Education Act; and the Equal Credit Opportunity Act.

Women formed caucuses and organizations in most professional associations and in the labor movement. By the mid-1970s there were feminist organizations representing a broad range of racial groups as well—African-American women, Chicanas and Hispanic women, Asian-American women, Native American women. Women also built new organizations among clerical workers to challenge the devaluation and limited opportunities of traditional women's work.

With their new strength, women challenged barriers to the professions (law, medicine), to ordination within mainstream Protestant and Jewish denominations, and to the full range of traditionally male blue-collar occupations, from carpenters to firefighters and police. They filed thousands of complaints of discrimination, mounted hundreds of lawsuits, and also built thousands of new institutions—day-care centers, shelters for battered women, bookstores, coffeehouses, and many others. The new feminism drew on women's stories to rethink the most intimate personal aspects of womanhood including abortion rights, sexual autonomy, rape, domestic violence, and lesbian rights.

The second wave of feminism also changed the American language both through its own publications (of which there were hundreds, the largest of them being *Ms.*, first published in 1972) and through pressure on commercial publishing houses and mass media. New words entered the American lexicon—"Ms.," "firefighter," "sexism"—while uses of the generic masculine (mankind, brotherhood, policeman) suddenly seemed exclusive. In Women's Studies programs, which grew rapidly in the early 1970s, young scholars rethought the paradigms of their disciplines and initiated new branches of knowledge.

The second wave provoked a strong reaction, of course, revealing not only male hostility but also deep fissures among women themselves. Antifeminism became a strong political force by the late 1970s with the mobilization of Phyllis Schlafley's Stop-ERA and antiabortion forces. In the face of widespread cultural anxiety about equality for women and changing gender roles, the Equal Rights Amendment stalled after 1975 and went down to defeat in 1982 despite an extension of the deadline for ratification. Antifeminism drew on the insecurities of a declining economy in the wake of the Vietnam War and on the growing political power of the New Right which made cultural issues (abortion, the ERA, "family values," and homophobia) central. The 1980s, framed by the hostile political climate of the Reagan administration, nourished a growing backlash against feminism in the media, the popular culture, and public policy. As public spending shifted away from social programs and toward the military, female poverty increased sharply. The Reagan boom after 1983 did not touch the poorest, disproportionately female and racial minority, segments of the population.

At the same time, the 1980s witnessed the continued growth of women's presence in positions of public authority: Supreme Court justice, astronaut, arctic explorer, military officer, truck driver, carpenter, Olympic star, bishop, rabbi. Mainstream religious denominations began to rewrite liturgies and hymn books to make them more "inclusive." Despite regular announcements of the "death" of feminism, it would be more accurate to say that in the 1980s feminism entered the mainstream with new levels of community activism, sophisticated political fundraisers like EMILY's List, and broad political alliances on issues like comparable worth. Experimental "counterinstitutions" started in the 1970s (battered women's shelters, health clinics, bookstores, etc.) survived by adopting more institutionalized procedures, professionalized staff, and state funding. Women's Studies took on the trappings of an academic discipline.

Feminism was broad, diffuse, and of many minds in the 1980s. Legal and cultural issues grew more complex. Feminist theorists wrestled with the realities of differences such as race, class, age, and sexual preference, asking themselves whether the category "woman" could withstand such an analysis. The multifaceted activities that embraced the label "feminist"—policy activism, research think tanks, literary theory, music, art, spirituality—signaled the fact that the women's movement had lost some cohesiveness.

The testimony of Anita Hill during the 1991 hearings on the nomination of Clarence Thomas to the Supreme Court, however, catalyzed a new round of national conversation, complicated by the deep fissures of race and sex. The sight of a genteel black woman being grilled by a committee of white men who made light of this "sexual harassment crap" mobilized thousands of women to run for office and contribute to campaigns. In 1992 an unprecedented number of women were elected to public office.

2000—Dawn of a New Millennium

If we return to our original categories to describe women's situation at the end of the twentieth century, the contrast with 1900 could hardly be more dramatic. The average woman now can expect to live 79.7 years (65% longer than her great-grandmother in 1900), marry at age 24.5, and bear only about two children (if any at all). There are now decades in women's lives—both before and after the years of childbearing and child care—which earlier generations never experienced. As a result of the second wave of women's rights activism in the final decades of the twentieth century, in politics and law, labor force participation, education, and sexuality, women live in a truly different world. Yet, in each instance equity remains an elusive goal, suggesting the need for continued and revitalized activism in the twenty-first century.

Politics and Law

No longer defined by their marital status, women enjoy virtually the full range of formal legal rights. In addition to winning the right to vote in 1920, they achieved equal pay (for the same work) in 1963 and guarantees against discrimination in housing and employment in 1964 (Title VII of the Civil Rights Act). Since 1970 women have won the right to a separate legal identity; privacy rights regarding reproduction and bodily integrity; and rights to sue for discrimination in employment, to work when pregnant, to equal education, and to equal access to athletics. Whole new bodies of law have developed since the 1970s on issues like domestic violence and sexual harassment. Nonetheless, the failure of the Equal Rights Amendment (ERA) in 1982 means that women still have no constitutional guarantee of equality.

In the last twenty-five years we have also seen a dramatic growth in the numbers of female elected officials. In 1997 there were 60 women in Congress (11.2%)—14 of them women of color; 81 statewide executive officials (25%); 1,597 state legislators (21.5%); and 203 mayors of cities with population over 30,000 (20.6%). There are two women on the Supreme Court, 30 female circuit court judges (18.6%), and 107 female district court judges (17.2%).

Education

At the end of the twentieth century, 88 percent of young women ages 25 to 34 are high-school graduates. The transformations in primary and secondary education for girls cannot be captured in graduation numbers, however. They also reside in the admission of girls to shop and other vocational classes (and boys to cooking and sewing courses), in girls' participation in athletics, in curricula that—at least sometimes—emphasize women's achievements in the past, and in school counselors who no longer single-mindedly socialize girls for domesticity and/or nonskilled stereotypically female jobs.

In the arena of higher education women are closing in on equity. Today, 54 percent of all bachelor of arts degrees go to women; 25 percent of women aged 25 to 34 are college graduates. Most striking, the proportion of women in professional schools is now between 36 and 43 percent. The revolution of the late twentieth century is evident in these figures, as most of the change occurred in the last three decades. Compare current numbers with those of 1960, when the proportion of women in law school was 2 percent (today 43%); medicine 6 percent (today 38%); MBA programs 4 percent (today 36%); Ph.D. programs 11 percent (today 39%), and dentistry 1 percent (today 38%).

Labor Force Participation

In stark contrast to a century ago, more than 61 percent of all women are in the labor force, including two-thirds of women with preschoolers and three-fourths of women with school-age children. Though African-American women continue to work at a higher rate than average (76% overall), the gap is clearly shrinking as the patterns that they pioneered are becoming the norm. With overt discrimination now outlawed, women practice virtually every occupation on the spectrum from blue collar to professional.

Yet alongside change, older patterns persist. Women remain concentrated in female-dominated, low-paid service occupations despite their presence in many professions and in traditionally male blue-collar occupations such as construction or truck driving. Although the exceptions are highly visible (tracked in the popular media frequently as interesting and unusual phenomena), 70 percent of women work either in the services industry (health and education) or in wholesale or retail trade. Women's median weekly earnings are still only 75 percent those of men—though there has been a dramatic gain since 1970 when they were 62.2 percent. (Note, however, that this change represents a combined gain for women of 17% and a 3% decline for men.)

Sexuality, Fertility, and Marriage

The late twentieth century has witnessed a sharp increase in single motherhood even as overall fertility has declined. One birth in three is to an unmarried woman; in 1970, that proportion was only one in ten. Sixty-nine percent of children live with two parents; 23.5 percent with mother only (for African Americans this is 52%).

Some of this single parenthood is due to divorce, something that was relatively rare in 1900 and today affects nearly one in every two marriages. The divorce rate seems to have peaked in 1980, however, and has declined somewhat since that time (in 1980 there were 5.2 divorces/1,000 population; today there are 4.4). Single motherhood is not the source of shame that it was in 1900, but it remains highly correlated with poverty.

If female sexuality was suppressed in 1900 (even though incompletely), at the end of the century sexual references and images saturate American culture. It was not until the 1930s that birth control became legal in most states. In 1961 the birth control pill introduced the possibility of radically separating sexual experience from the likelihood of procreation. Then in 1973, the Supreme Court's *Roe v. Wade* decision legalized abortion. Today, premarital sex is common, even normative. According to the Alan Guttmacher Institute, in the early 1990s, 56 percent of women and 73 percent of men had sex by age 18.

As dramatic, homosexuality has become an open subject of public discourse, and lesbians—once completely hidden, even to one another—are creating new public spaces and organizations, fields of intellectual inquiry and theory, and families that rely on voluntary ties in the absence of any legal sanction. Lesbians have been a major constituency and source of leadership in the second feminist wave. Twenty years of visibility, however, is just a beginning. American society remains deeply, and emotionally, divided on the issue of homosexuality. Opposition to gay rights marks a key issue for the religious right, and open violence against lesbians and gay men continues.

Race and Class

The second wave grew directly from and modeled itself on the civil rights movement in the 1950s and 1960s. That movement, itself, relied heavily on the grass-roots (if relatively invisible) leadership of African-American women. In the last decades of the century, the voices of minority women have become increasingly distinct and powerful. Diversity among women, as in the society at large, has taken on new dimensions with a surge of immigration since the 1960s from Southeast Asia, East Africa, Central America, and other parts of the Third World. Predictions based on immigration and fertility suggest that by the middle of the next century whites will be only half the U.S. population. Women of color will become the new norm. Women remain deeply divided on racial grounds, but race is no longer defined as black and white.

Challenges to traditional conceptions of gender have also shaken the previous consensus on what constitutes a "good woman" (except perhaps to the right-wing traditionalists who still hold to a set of ideals quite similar to those that dominated American culture a century ago). Yet discomfort with women's move into public life is still widespread, and race and class stigmas remain. The massive growth of a welfare system whose clients are disproportionately women and children combines racial and gender stereotypes to create a new category of "bad women": single, minority, poor mothers. And wherever women appear in previously male-dominated environments, they remain suspect. In particular, the sharply polarized emotional response to Hillary Rodham Clinton during her time as first lady illustrates the undercurrent of anger at powerful, professional women. Radio talk shows have filled thousands of hours with hosts and callers venting their hostility toward this woman who, in their view, did not stay "in her place." But, of course, that is the open question at century's end: just what is "woman's place"?

Conclusion

This brief discussion of women in the twentieth century does not trace a smooth arc from the beginning of the century to the end. It is not simply about "progress" toward "equality." But it is, indeed, about a kind of sea change with unanticipated consequences and with dramatic acceleration in the last thirty years.

In the nineteenth century women created much of what today we call civil society. In the twentieth century they used that layer of society—which lies between formal governmental structures and private familial life—in an amazing variety of ways to reshape the landscape of American life. Virtually all of the public spaces previously presumed to belong properly to men—paid labor, higher education, electoral politics and public office, athletics—now incorporate a large and visible proportion of women. This theme of participation in public life, and the concomitant politicization of issues previously considered personal, runs through the entire century.

Such spectacular shifts have clearly been driven by large structural forces: the emergence of a postindustrial service economy, rising levels of education, two cataclysmic world wars, global power and national wealth on a level never imagined, changing patterns of marriage, fertility, and longevity. Yet the most dramatic changes can clearly be traced in equal measure to two large waves of women's activism.

The suffrage movement, by the 1910s, involved hundreds of thousands of women, branching out both tactically with the use of massive public parades and street corner speeches (females occupying public, political spaces) and in composition as it reached out to working women, immigrants, and minorities. That movement won for women the fundamental right of citizenship, the right to vote. And the Progressive movement on which it built laid the groundwork and provided many key players for the subsequent emergence of the welfare state. The impact of the second wave shows up in the astonishing acceleration of change in the last three decades of the century.

Each of these waves continued to surge forward in the decades after cresting. But each was also followed by a period in which the multiplicity of women's voices reasserted itself along with debates over the real meaning of equality. And each left much work undone for subsequent generations that face new issues and new dilemmas.

In the twenty-first century women will have choices that have never before been available, but they will not be easy. The twentieth century challenged our very definitions of male and female. Many of the signs of manhood and womanhood no longer function effectively. Work is no longer a manly prerogative and responsibility. Families are no longer constituted around a male breadwinner, a wife, and their children. More often they are two-income households (same or different sexes) or single-parent households. Large numbers of single men and women live alone. Yet "family values" have become a political code for attacks on welfare mothers, homosexuals, and nontraditional families (which, in fact, far outnumbered traditional ones). In the absence of significant societal or governmental support for women's traditional responsibilities, women assume a double burden. They participate in the labor force almost to the same degree as men, and yet work outside the home is still organized as though workers had wives to take care of household work, child care, and the myriad details of private life. Work outside the home makes few accommodations to the demands and priorities of family life.

The pioneering work of the twentieth century—as women made their way into hostile, male-dominated public spaces—remains unfinished. Most of the barriers have been broken at least once. But equity remains a distant goal. Achieving that goal is complicated by the fact that for the moment women are not a highly unified group. The contemporary struggles within feminism to deal with the differences among women are the essential precursor to any future social movement that claims to speak for women as a group. The very meanings of masculinity and femininity and their multiple cultural and symbolic references are now overtly contested throughout the popular culture.

Another legacy of the feminist movement that proclaimed that "the personal is political" is an unresolved ambiguity about just where the boundary between the personal and the political properly lies, and the dilemmas resulting from politicizing private life. At the end of the century, Americans faced a constitutional crisis rooted in the strange career of personal politics. For an entire year virtually everyone in the United States was riveted by the scandal concerning President Clinton, Monica Lewinsky, Kenneth Starr, and the American Congress. Behaviors that once would have been considered purely private (and gone unremarked by political reporters, for example) became the basis for impeachment. Who defended the distinction between public and private and who assaulted it? The tables seem to have turned with a vengeance as the right wing pried into intimate details about the president's sexual activities in a consensual relationship while the liberals (including feminist leaders) protested. The politicization of private life is indeed a double-edged sword. This should be no surprise, as conservative backlash since the 1970s has evidenced a clear willingness to use the power of the state to enforce its vision of proper private relationships on issues such as abortion, homosexuality, divorce, prayer in the schools, and the content of textbooks.

The recent history of feminism calls to our attention a number of dimensions in this crisis that should not go unnoticed. First, there have always been many members of society (racial and sexual minorities, welfare recipients, and women, to name only the most obvious) whose private behaviors have been scrutinized and regulated by those in power. By forcing these issues into public debate and evolving laws that might protect such groups (for example laws against sexual harassment) feminists have also removed the cover of silence that protected powerful men from public scrutiny for their private behaviors. That such laws were subsequently used in a campaign to unseat a president whose election was directly due to the votes of politically mobilized women resonates with irony.

Women's solidarity has waxed and waned across the twentieth century. It will certainly continue to do so in the twenty-first. The next wave of feminist activism will no doubt take a shape we cannot envision, just as no one at the dawn of the twentieth century could have imagined the battles that awaited them. That there will be another wave, however, is a safe prediction, given the unfinished agendas of the last century and the still unforeseen contradictions that future changes will create. The next wave will shape the new century.

Bibliography

William H. Chafe, *The American Woman: Her Changing Social, Economic, and Political Roles, 1920–1970* (New York: Oxford University Press, 1972), laid the groundwork for subsequent studies of twentieth-century women. Peter Filene examines the implications of changing definitions of womanliness and manliness on both sexes in *Him/Her Self: Sex Roles in Modern America*, 2nd ed. (Baltimore: Johns Hopkins University Press, 1986). Sara M. Evans, *Born for*

Liberty: A History of Women in America, 2nd ed. (New York: Free Press, 1996) provides a general overview of women in American history.

The "first wave" of women's rights activism in the twentieth century is chronicled by Nancy F. Cott, *The Grounding of Modern Feminism* (New Haven, Conn.: Yale University Press, 1987); and Mari Jo Buhle and Paul Buhle, eds., *The Concise History of Woman Suffrage: Selections from the Classic Work of Stanton, Anthony, Gage, and Harper* (Urbana: University of Illinois Press, 1978). On women's role in the New Deal see Susan Ware, *Beyond Suffrage: Women in the New Deal* (Cambridge, Mass.: Harvard University Press, 1981). The critical eras of the 1940s and the cold war are examined in Susan Hartmann, *The Homefront and Beyond: American Women in the 1940s* (Boston: Twayne Publishers, 1982); and Elaine Tyler May, *Homeward Bound: American Families in the Cold War Era* (New York: Basic Books, 1988). There is a growing literature on the "second wave" of feminism. Some starting points would be Sara Evans, *Personal Politics: The Roots of Women's Liberation in the Civil Rights Movement and the New Left* (New York: Vintage, 1980); Alice Echols, *Daring to Be Bad: Radical Feminism in America, 1967–1975* (Minneapolis: University of Minnesota Press, 1989); and Donald Mathews and Jane De Hart, *Sex, Gender, and the Politics of ERA* (New York: Oxford University Press, 1990).

For more depth on the history of sexuality see John D'Emilio and Estelle B. Freedman, *Intimate Matters: A History of Sexuality in America* (New York: Harper & Row, 1988); on education see Barbara Solomon, *In the Company of Educated Women: A History of Women and Higher Education in America* (New Haven, Conn.: Yale University Press, 1985); on women in the labor force see Julia Blackwelder, *Now Hiring: The Feminization of Work in the United States, 1900–1995* (College Station: Texas A&M University Press, 1997). Some excellent starting points on racial minority and immigrant ethnic women include Vicki L. Ruíz, *From Out of the Shadows: Mexican Women in Twentieth-Century America* (New York: Oxford University Press, 1999); on African-American women see Jacqueline Jones, *Labor of Love, Labor of Sorrow: Black Women, Work, and the Family from Slavery to the Present* (New York: Basic Books, 1985); and on Chinese women Judy Yung, *Unbound Feet: A Social History of Chinese Women in San Francisco* (Barkeley: University of California Press, 1995); Donna Gabaccia, *From the Other Side: Women, Gender, and Immigrant Life in the U.S., 1920–1990* (Bloomington: Indiana University Press, 1994).

For the most recent descriptions of women's status in all aspects of American life, see the series sponsored by the Women's Research and Education Institute in Washington, D.C., *The American Woman* (New York: W. W. Norton). This series has been updated biannually from its inception in 1987.

EXPLORING THE ISSUE

Has the Women's Movement of the 1970s Failed to Liberate American Women?

Critical Thinking and Reflection

1. Discuss the role that women should fulfill in American society in the twenty-first century, according to Graglia. Critically analyze her views of contemporary feminism.
2. List and describe the characteristics of the nineteenth-century "Cult of True Womanhood." Compare the similarities and differences of Graglia's views of what women's roles should be today with the nineteenth-century ideal of womanhood.
3. Compare and contrast the similarities and differences between the first (1900–1920) and second (1968–1975) women's liberation movements. Be sure to discuss the racial and class backgrounds of these movements, their respective goals, their accomplishments and failures, and the reasons why each of these movements declined.
4. The 1980s was a decade of both successes and failures for the women's movement. Critically analyze.
5. According to Professor Sara M. Evans, the phrase "the personal is political" has been used by conservatives against the women's movement. Her examples are the Anita Hill testimony before the Senate Judiciary Committee in 1991, President Clinton's sex scandal with intern Monica Lewinsky, and the conservative talk show diatribes against Senator Hilary Rodham Clinton. Critically analyze this paradox.
6. Compare the analyses of Graglia and Evans on the impact of the women's movement on American society. Where do they agree, and where do they disagree?

Is There Common Ground?

Both women on the left and women on the right would deny there is common ground between the two movements. Upon closer inspection, however, an interesting study would be to see how many conservative women active in business and politics took advantage of the Equal Rights Amendment in 1972 and the Higher Education Act (especially Title IX), which opened the doors of collegiate athletics and higher educational opportunities in traditional male fields such as law, medicine, and scientific research. One should also study the number of conservative woman politicians such as Michelle Bachman and

Sara Palin. Imagine if Governor Palin had been elected Vice-President, how would "family values" traditionalists within the Republican Party have related to a woman whose daughter was pregnant during the campaign? How much does Palin embody both the liberated women and the traditional mother?

Additional Resources

The best starting point is Ruth Rosen, *The World Split Open: How the Modern Woman's Movement Changed America* (Viking, 2000), written by a former Berkeley activist for her students who were born in the 1980s. In 1988 Harvard University Press reprinted Betty Friedan's two later books—*The Second Stage* and *It Changed My Life*, both with new introductions with suggestions for the twenty-first century—which are critical of some of the directions that the women's movement has taken. Important books and articles by activists with a historical perspective include Sara Evans, *Personal Politics: The Roots of Women's Liberation in the Civil Rights Movement and the New Left* (Vintage, 1979). This book is nicely summarized in "Sources of the Second Wave: The Rebirth of Feminism," in Alexander Bloom, ed., *Long Time Gone: Sixties America Then and Now* (Oxford, 2001).

For a general overview of women's history, see Evans, *Born for Liberty: A History of Women in America*, 2nd ed. (Free Press, 1996) and Roger Adelson's "Interview with Sara Margaret Evans," *The Historian* (vol. 63, Fall 2000); Donna Gabaccia, *From the Other Side: Women, Gender and Immigrant Life in the U.S., 1920–1990* (Indiana University Press, 1994); and John D'Emilio and Estelle B. Freedman, *Intimate Matters: A History of Sexuality in America* (Harper & Row, 1988).

Review essays from various journals reflect the continuous battle over the importance of the women's movement. The neoconservative magazine *Commentary* is constantly critical of feminism. See Elizabeth Kristol, "The Sexual Revolution" (April 1996) and Elizabeth Powers, "Back to Basics" (March 1999). Also critical is Daphne Patai, "Will the Real Feminists in Academe Stand Up," *The Chronicle of Higher Education* (October 6, 2000, pp. B6-B9). Sympathetic to the movement are Christine Stansell, "Girlie Interrupted: The Generational Progress of Feminism," *The New Republic* (January 15, 2001) and Andrew Hacker, "How are Women Doing," *The New York Review of Books* (Fall 2000). See also Jo Freeman, "The Women's Liberation Movement: Its Origins, Structure, Activities, and Ideas," in Jo Freeman, ed., *Women: A Feminist Perspective*, 3rd ed. (Mayfield, 1984); Estelle B. Freedman, *No Turning Back: The History of Feminism and the Future of Women* (Ballantine, 2001); and Susan Brownmiller, *In Our Time: Memoir of a Revolution* (Dial Press, 2000).

Books that deal with the impact of the movement on specific groups include Johnnetta B. Cole and Beverly Gray-Sheftall, *Gender Talk: The Struggle for Women's Equality in African American Communities* (Balantine, 2003); Jacqueline Jones, *Labor of Love, Labor of Sorrow: Black Women, Work, and the Family from Slavery to the President* (Basic Books, 1985); Vicki L. Ruiz, *From Out of the Shadows: Mexican Women in Twentieth-Century Books* (April 11, 2002); and Kim France's review of Phyllis Chesler, *Letters to a Young Feminist* (Four Walls Eight Windows, 1998) in *The New York Times Book Review* (April 26, 1998, pp. 10–11).

ISSUE 18

Were the 1980s a Decade of Affluence for the Middle Class?

YES: J. David Woodard, from *A Rising Tide* (Praeger, 2006)

NO: Thomas Byrne Edsall, from "The Changing Shape of Power: A Realignment in Public Policy," in Steve Fraser and Gary Gerstle, ed., *The Rise and Fall of the New Deal Order, 1930–1980* (Princeton University Press, 1980)

Learning Outcomes

After reading this issue, you should be able to:

- Critically examine "Keynesian" economics.
- Critically examine "supply-side" economics.
- Compare and contrast the strength and weaknesses of both economic philosophies.
- Describe the cultural and economic changes in the United States in the 1980s.
- Describe and critically analyze the political, social, and economic changes that Edsall argues took place in the 1980s.

ISSUE SUMMARY

YES: According to Professor J. David Woodard, supply-side economics unleashed a wave of entrepreneurial and technological innovation that transformed the economy and restored America's confidence in the Golden Age from 1983 to 1992.

NO: Political Journalist Thomas Byrne Edsall argues that the Reagan Revolution brought about a policy realignment that reversed the New Deal and redistributed political power and economic wealth to the top 20 percent of Americans.

I n 1939, after six years of the New Deal, unemployment in the United States remained at an unacceptably high rate of 17 percent. World War II bailed

America out of the Great Depression. When 20 million workers entered the armed forces, married American women, along with African American and Hispanic men and women, filled the void in the high-paying factory jobs. Everyone not only made money but also poured it into war bonds and traditional savings accounts. Government and business cemented their relationship with "cost plus" profits for the defense industries.

By the end of 1945, Americans had stashed away $134 billion in cash, savings accounts, and government securities. This pent-up demand meant there would be no depression akin to the end of World War I or the 1930s. Following initial shortages before industry completed its conversion to peacetime production, Americans engaged in the greatest spending spree in the country's history. Liberals and conservatives from both political parties had developed a consensus on foreign and domestic policies.

The president's Council of Economic Advisers was comprised of Keynesians, who believed that government spending could increase employment even if it meant that budget deficits would be temporarily created. For nearly 25 years, they used fiscal and monetary tools to manipulate the economy so that inflation would remain low while employment would reach close to its maximum capacity. Around 1968, the consensus surrounding domestic and foreign policy broke down for three reasons: (1) the Vietnam imbroglio, (2) the oil crises of 1974 and 1979, and (3) the decline of the smokestack industries.

Lyndon Johnson's presidency was ruined by the Vietnam War. He believed that he could escalate the war and his Great Society programs at the same time. His successor, Richard Nixon, attempted to solve the Vietnam dilemma by bringing the American troops home and letting Asians fight Asians. The process of withdrawal was slow and costly. Also expensive were many of the Great Society programs, such as Social Security, Aid to Families with Dependent Children, environmental legislation, and school desegregation, which Nixon continued to uphold. In August 1971, Nixon acknowledged that he had become a Keynesian when he imposed a 90-day wage and price control freeze and took the international dollar off the gold standard and allowed it to float. With these bold moves, Nixon hoped to stop the dollar from declining in value. He was also faced with a recession that included both high unemployment and high inflation. "Stagflation" resulted, leading to the demise of Keynesian economics.

In early 1974, shortly before Nixon was forced to resign from office, the major oil-producing nations of the world—primarily in the Middle East—agreed to curb oil production and raise oil prices. The OPEC cartel, protesting the pro-Israeli policies of the western nations, brought these countries to their knees. In the United States, gasoline went from $0.40 to $2.00 per gallon in a matter of days. In the early 1980s, President Jimmy Carter implored the nation to conserve energy, but he appeared helpless as the unemployment rate approached double digits and as the Federal Reserve Board raised interest rates to 18 percent in a desperate attempt to stem inflation.

The Reagan administration introduced a new economic philosophy: supply-side economics. Its proponents, led by economists Martin Anderson and Arthur Laffer, believed that if taxes were cut and spending on frivolous social programs were reduced—even while military spending increased—businesses would use the excess money to expand. More jobs would result, consumers would increase spending, and the multiplying effect would be a period of sustained growth and prosperity. Two books that explain the rise of the post–World War II conservative movement in which Reagan became the major player are Lee Edwards' sympathetic *The Conservative Revolution: The Movement that Remade America* (Free Press, 1999) and Godfrey Hodgson's more critical *The World Turned Right Side Up: A History of the Conservative Ascendancy in America* (Houghton Mifflin, 1996). Gregory L. Schneider's essay "Conservatism and the Reagan Presidency," in Richard S. Conley, ed., *Reassessing the Reagan Presidency* (University Press of America, 2003) is a sympathetic but objective account with a full bibliography.

In the YES selection, Professor J. David Woodard argues that the 1980s was a decade of affluence for all classes. Supply-side economics, he says, unleashed a wave of entrepreneurial and technological innovation that transformed the economy and restored American's confidence between 1983 and 1992. He notes with approval the increased participation of the middle class in the stock market. He also points out the risks taken by new investors who saw a 22 percent dip in the market in mid-October 1987. While disapproving of the insider trading tactics that landed multimillionaire Wall Street dealers Michael Milken and Ivan Boesky in jail, Woodard approves of the free-market rational actor model espoused by Milton and Rose Friedman in their book *Free to Choose* (Avon Books, 1985), which "effectively" rebutted the government-as-manager thesis.

Although Woodard argues that "a rising tide" raised the income level of 90 percent of Americans, he does not counter the statistical arguments of Thomas Edsall, who believes the boat leaked for those blue collar urban whites and minorities who found themselves in poverty and the lower middle class. Woodard admits that inequalities existed between "the knowledge practitioners" who controlled the new economy and the noneducated blue collar workers who saw their well-paid union-protected jobs in steel, automobiles, and oil refining fall victim to increasing automation and the practice of foreign outsourcing.

Woodard also criticizes the manner in which capitalism has been portrayed by the movie industry in such films as *Wall Street* and *Bonfire of the Vanities*, and he finds distasteful the nonrational "deconstructionist" views of the social science and humanities scholars and critics at the nation's elite universities. Interestingly, he views President Ronald Reagan as both a premodern and a postmodern figure, claiming that while Reagan's convictions were of an earlier time, "his style of image politics, [were] carefully crafted and orchestrated for mass consumption."

Political Journalist Thomas Byrne Edsall's disagrees with Woodard's analysis. Yes, there was prosperity in the 1980s, but only for a few groups. The Reagan revolution, Edsall says, brought about a policy alignment as well as a political one that redistributed political and economic wealth to the top 20 percent of Americans. His description of the changing landscape of political and economic power in the 1970s and 1980s could just as easily be applied to the present conditions in the United States. Political parties declined in influence; members of Congress received the bulk of their money from economic interest groups and political action committees (PACS), in spite of reforms to curb their influence; and presidential candidates and presidential office holders operated their campaigns and policy considerations independent of Congress. Edsall believes that the Republican Party attained power because of the defection of the white male working class, both in the South and in the North. He argues that the Wallace third-party movements in 1968 and 1972 capitalized on the consequences of the civil rights and women's movement, which produced affirmative action jobs for women and minorities in areas previously held by white males. The defection of well-paid union jobs in steel, coal, automobiles, and clothing manufacturing to foreign countries also contributed to the income decline of the noncollege-educated white male, who had to settle for low-wage jobs in the service industries.

A Rising Tide

The Reagan Revolution, as the times came to be called, followed the economic growth in real income from 1983 through the end of the president's second term in 1988, to the recession that concluded the Bush presidency in 1992. During this time the gross domestic product (GDP) doubled. In the expansion through the two Reagan terms, "real-after-tax income per person rose by 15.5 percent, [and] the real median income of families, before taxes, went up 12.5 percent." Measured in constant 1990 dollars, the percentage of families earning between $15,000 and $50,000 fell by 5 points, and the percentage earning more than $50,000 in constant dollars rose by 5 points. Millions of families moved up the ladder from the lower class to the middle class. America had gone from "stagflation" and the highest prices in thirty years to galloping capitalism, and everyday citizens were investing in the stock market.

The middle-class market sought the deposits of ordinary savers and young people just beginning to accumulate assets. Wall Street had previously ignored these customers, but now it sought them out. Prudential-Bache, an aggressive firm, was quoted in *Barron's* as saying it "sees its clients as the $40,000-a-year young professional on the fast track." As the market expanded, more individuals placed their money in funds to balance risk and profit. Suddenly the stock market report was of interest to everyone.

Stockbrokers assured investors that their money was safe, but in late 1987 they discovered the real meaning of risk. The market was doing quite well for the first nine months of the year; it was up more than 30 percent and reaching unprecedented heights. Then, in the days between October 14 and October 19, the market fell off a cliff. On October 19, subsequently known as "Black Monday," the Dow Jones Industrial Average plummeted 508 points, losing 22.6 percent of its total value. This was the greatest loss Wall Street had ever suffered on a single day, even worse than the crash of 1929. It took two years for the Dow to recover completely; not until September of 1989 did it regain all the value it lost in the 1987 crash.

One important lesson came out of the crash: investors who sold took a bath. Those who held on and continued a disciplined and systematic program received rewards. The American economy continued as the greatest wealth producer the world had ever seen. The consequence of all this was a standard of living beyond the comprehension of the rest of the world, and a cause for envy by peer nations. While $200,000 was enough to make the top 1 percent of American income in 1980, a family might need well over $300,000 to be in that category a decade later. The Congressional Budget Office estimated that it would take more than $550,000 to be in the top 1 percent in 1992. No sooner had a survivor of the 1970s comprehended what was happening than he became obsolete. Reagan's supply-side ideas unleashed a wave of entrepreneurial and technological innovation that transformed the economy and restored the country's self-confidence. Economic prosperity had been the impossible dream of youth, and now it was everywhere.

The vast majority of the population experienced substantial gains in real income and wealth. With millions of people earning more money, much higher incomes were required to make it to the top 5 percent, or the top 1 percent of the nation's income bracket. At the time, the rising tide of economic prosperity lifted at least 90 percent of the American family boats. For those who lived through it, the 1983–1992 period would be remembered as an uncomplicated golden time, mourned as lost, and remembered as cloudless.

The spending began at home, where people purchased new homes and remodeled older ones. Declining interest rates made mortgages affordable, and the number of single-family homes expanded each year from 1980 to 1988. Consumers also had more cars to drive as the two-income, two-car family became the norm. From 1980 to 1988, the number of new car models increased by half, the most popular being the minivans for suburban families. Lower air fares and discount packages allowed passengers to travel to previously unheard-of places, and the number of people flying overseas rose by 40 percent during the 1980s.

Much of this expense for the new lifestyle was charged to credit cards. Americans took three-, four-, and five-day trips and the amount of credit card debt more than doubled. Specialty chain stores like the Gap, Limited, and Banana Republic targeted upscale, professional customers who wanted to take advantage of their new standing and credit to add the latest styles to their wardrobes. Shopping malls proliferated in suburban settings, and the consumption ethic gave birth to Wal-Mart, destined in the next decade to become the nation's largest company. While American life was becoming more affluent, it was also becoming more complex.

Of course there were critics, and for them the era was never that splendid; it was derided for its inbred conformity, flatulent excesses, and materialistic binges. The "me" decade of the 1970s turned into the "my" decade of the 1980s. The faultfinders saw the surge of abundance as a joyless vulgarity. In 1987, filmmaker Oliver Stone released the movie *Wall Street*. The story involved a young stockbroker, Bud Fox, who becomes involved with his hero, Gordon Gekko, an extremely successful, but corrupt, stock trader. In the most memorable scene of the movie. Gekko makes a speech to the shareholders of a company he was planning to take over. Stone used the scene to give Gekko, and by extension corporate America at the time, the characteristic trait of economic success.

Gekko: Teldar Paper, Mr. Cromwell, Teldar Paper has 33 different vice presidents, each making over 200 thousand dollars a year. Now, I have spent the last two months analyzing what all these guys do, and I still can't figure it out. One thing I do know is that our paper company lost 110 million dollars last year, and I'll bet that half of that was spent in all the paperwork going back and forth between all these vice presidents.

The new law of evolution in corporate America seems to be survival of the unfittest. Well, in my book you either do it right or you get eliminated.

In the last seven deals that I've been involved with, there were 2.5 million stockholders who had made a pretax profit of 12 billion dollars. Thank you.

I am not a destroyer of companies. I am a liberator of them!

The point is, ladies and gentlemen, is that greed—for lack of a better word—is good.

Greed is right.

Greed works.

Greed clarifies, cuts through, and captures the essence of the evolutionary spirit.

Greed in all its forms—greed for life, for money, for love, knowledge—has marked the upward surge of mankind.

And greed—you mark my words—will not only save Teldar Paper, but that other malfunctioning corporation called the USA.

Thank you very much.

The same theme was addressed in literature. In 1990, one of America's foremost writers, Tom Wolfe, released a blockbuster bestseller entitled *The Bonfire of the Vanities*. The book dealt with what Wolfe called the "big, rich slices of contemporary life," in this case the heady materialism of the 1980s. The plot followed the life of Sherman McCoy, a prodigiously successful bond trader at a prestigious Wall Street firm. One night Sherman, accompanied by his mistress, fatally injures a black man in a car accident. As a result of this accident, all the ennui of metropolitan life, race relations, instant affluence and gratification, and the class structure of the city afflict the lead character.

As a member of the new ruling class, Sherman McCoy and other bond traders were allied with opportunistic politicians in speculative excesses. Sherman was supremely confident that he would escape his fate. The 1980s were critiqued as the epitome of American decline and the triumph of finance capitalism spurred by Wall Street bond and stock manipulators, like McCoy's employer, Eugene Lopwitz. Sherman McCoy had to pay for his greed and irresponsibility; he lost his job, his wife and his child, his mistress, his home, and his class standing. But in the end he lied to escape prosecution, and got even with every institution—the courts, the media, and the economic system—which were also built on a foundation of lies.

American capitalism, and its excesses, had long been a topic of intellectual and literary criticism. Theodore Dreiser wrote the novel *An American Tragedy* in 1925 as a critique of business practices at the time. The story followed a bellboy who sets out to gain success and fame, only to slip into murder and death by execution. Dreiser declared that the materialistic society was as much to blame as the murderer himself. What was new in the *Bonfire* plot was that the perpetrators escaped capture and conviction. In the new world people could be evil and—if they had enough money—bear no consequences for their actions.

During the 1980s, the power and influence of American corporations expanded to exorbitant heights. General Motors had revenues greater than 90 percent of the world's nations. The Reagan administration eased restrictions on the stock market and on antitrust laws so some of the more massive corporate takeovers in American history happened in the decade. The largest one was between R. J. Reynolds, the tobacco company, and Nabisco, the maker of cookies, crackers, and cereals, for $24.9 billion.

Other companies were taken over in what was known as a leveraged buy-out, where investors joined forces with the managers of a company to buy it. The funds came from the managers themselves, but most were borrowed. The money for takeovers was raised through the sale of so-called junk bonds. Junk bonds were high-risk investments by securities rating agencies, such as Standard and Poor's and Moody's, marked as such because they had a potential for higher yield and failure. If the people who bought the bonds were successful in the takeover, then they were handsomely rewarded; but if they failed, then there was the possibility that the bonds would not be repaid.

Companies with low debt loads were attractive targets for leveraged buy-outs, which meant that successful businessmen found themselves the object of "corporate raiders." Benjamin Franklin's age-old virtues of thrift and frugality resulted in business success, so much so that the entrepreneurial founders lost control of their companies. Sometimes, to prevent these unwanted effects, recently acquired companies bought back their stock at higher than market prices—in effect, paying raiders to go away. The practice was known as "green-mail" for its resemblance to blackmail. More than $12 billion in green-mail was paid by corporations such as Texaco, Warner, and Quaker State in the first few months of 1984.

The business of mergers required dozens of brokers, lawyers, and bankers. A new class of business people known as "young, urban professionals," or "yuppies," emerged as experts in the takeover game. They were stereotyped as college-educated men and women, who dressed well, lived in expensive apartments, drove expensive cars, exercised in gyms, and worked twelve-hour days. "An MBA (Masters of Business Administration), a condo and a BMW" became the mantra of the age. One woman interviewed on television unabashedly declared, "I aspire to materialism." "Big spender" became a term of approbation. A writer at the time described it this way: "People saw money as power . . . [they went to] 'power lunches' while wearing fashionable 'power suits' . . . designer fashions bloated egos and fattened the cash registers of swank stores." The spenders were living on credit and buying on margin, but they did not seem to mind. Spending and mergers were fueling the boom, and any tendency to go slow was seen as alarming.

Leveraged buyouts were risky, but legal, transactions. As in any business, a few successful corporate raiders operated outside the law. On May 12, 1986, Dennis Levine, who had made $12.6 million on insider-trading deals, implicated two well-known Wall Street traders: Michael Milken and Ivan Boesky.

Both men were charged with violations of federal securities law. Boesky agreed to pay $100 million in forfeitures and penalties, and Michael Milken admitted to six felonies and agreed to pay $600 million in fines. The amount of the fines was staggering, but more revealing was the corporate raider lifestyle the investigations uncovered. In the early 1980s Milken was reportedly making $550 million a year.

Overall, the freeing of the market for corporate control had important benefits for women in the workforce. College-educated women moved into fields like business, engineering, medicine, and law. "The result was that women as a whole, whose average earnings had been 58 percent of those of men in 1979, earned 68 percent ten years later." Professional women began moving into managerial positions where they soon faced the problem of how to combine motherhood and career. In the 1980s work itself was changing. The computer and instant communication enabled more people to work at home, and women soon learned that part-time, or maternity leave, arrangements allowed them to close the income gap with their male counterparts.

The boom arose from numerous springs: the new government economic philosophy, technological innovation, an altered world economy, and a changing labor market. The latter trend would have political consequences well into the next century. For example, immigration had a dramatic influence on the labor pool and the expansion of entry-level jobs. In the 1970s, 4.5 million immigrants were legally admitted into the country, and many more came illegally. In the 1980s legal immigration swelled to 7.4 million, with additional millions of illegal entrants. The vast majority of immigrants from Central and South America, who made up about half the total, had considerably lower levels of schooling than native-born Americans. Their presence resulted in higher wages for college graduates and depressed wages for those who had lower levels of schooling.

The immigration trends caused increases in wage and income inequality, because of the demand for skilled labor due to technological changes and new trade patterns. Sophisticated new technologies flourished in the aerospace, defense, electronics, and computer industries. Sprawling scientific complexes raised the standard of living for millions of Americans. Research funds for technology, or R & D (research and development), which were practically insignificant in the 1950s, amounted to an estimated $100 billion a year at the end of the 1980s. Americans were making money with their minds, and not on the assembly line.

Little of this was new. Sociologist Daniel Bell wrote in 1973 that there was a natural progression from a traditional society, based on agriculture, to an industrial one based on manufacturing. Then there was a subsequent transition from an industrial to a postindustrial society, which culminated in a service economy. This progression to a postindustrial society occurred when the emphasis on the production of goods was overtaken by a service economy. The postindustrial society meant an extension of scientific rationality into the economic, social, and political spheres. By the late 1970s only 13 percent of American workers were involved in the manufacture of goods, whereas a full 60 percent were engaged in the production of information. The new "knowledge society" was run by university-trained employers. In this society technical skill was the base of power, and education the means of access to power. Individuals who exercised authority through technical competence, called "technocrats," dominated society.

The birth years of the postindustrial society were in the 1950s, but it came to fruition in the 1980s. The 1950s saw great technological developments such as the atomic bomb and the digital computer, but the character of knowledge itself began to change thirty years later. Workers had to be taught how to think, not how to do routine tasks. Change was so prevalent that knowledge of any specific task was quickly washed away by a new wave of innovation. Theoretical knowledge of abstract principles was central in the postindustrial society, and the key organization of the future was the university, along with think tanks and research centers.

During the 1980s the academy itself was changing. The number of professors at American universities in 1980 was four times what it was in 1960. As faculties grew, so too did the specialization of their disciplines. Student enrollments in fields like business, computer science, engineering, and mathematics soared, while the liberal arts and social sciences lost out in comparison. It was the age of the computer chip, which made everything smaller and faster.

Universities were only the tip of the iceberg of culture producers that included not only the creators of the new society, but also its transmitters. Labor in the postindustrial context involved those in journalism, publishing, magazines, broadcast media, theater, and museums and anyone who was involved in the influence and reception of serious cultural products. The growth of cultural output was a fact in the knowledge industry. Consider what happened to those Daniel Bell called "the cultural mass" of art producers. New York had only a handful of galleries in 1945, and no more than a score of known artists; by the 1980s the city had some 680 galleries and more than 150,000 artists. Add to these artists producers of books, printers, serious music recordings, writers, editors, movie makers, musicians, and so forth and the size of just one part of the mass culture was exposed.

Bell argued that the postindustrial society would change politics, as well as culture and economics. In his view, government would increasingly become instrumental in the management of the economy; less control would be left to market forces. Instead of relying on the invisible hand, Bell saw that the postindustrial society would work toward directing and engineering society. He could not have been more wrong. The spirit of the 1980s was against the command decision views of Daniel Bell. Conservatives had long denounced Keynesian economics as a fraud, and expanding government as a threat, but their ideas were unpopular in the period of post-World War II prosperity. When liberalism's troubles began to mount in the 1970s, free market alternatives re-emerged.

Milton and Rose Friedman effectively rebutted the government as manager thesis, and replaced it with the free market-rational actor model. Their book, *Free to Choose,* was as clear an exposition of free market economics as anything since Adam Smith, and it showed how good intentions in Washington often had deplorable results in practice. Friedman made conservative economic ideas available and attractive to the mass public. To quote their thesis on the power of a free market idea: "If an exchange between two parties is voluntary, it will not take place unless both believe that they will benefit from it," or "the price system is the mechanism that performs this task without central direction, without requiring people to speak to one another or like one another." This was the book that explained how freedom had been eroded, and prosperity undermined, by the runaway spending and growth of government in Washington. *Free to Choose* was very influential on the thinking of Ronald Reagan and millions of ordinary Americans.

As strange as it may seem, by the 1980s the modern postindustrial society was itself becoming old fashioned. The period after World War II was characterized by three things: (1) the power of reason over ignorance, (2) the power of order over disorder, and (3) the power of science over superstition. These features were regarded as universal values, and were inculcated into the fabric of American culture. They were also the basis for Ronald Reagan's view of the world. His time with General Electric convinced him that American technology was second to none, and he wedded that faith to the national experience. After he left office he said, "There are no such things as limits to growth, because there are no limits on the human capacity for intelligence, imagination and wonder."

In the decade of the 1980s, the faith in reason, order, and the power of science, so dear to Reagan, was coming in for criticism. The command and control center for the criticism was the universities, the very postindustrial leaders Daniel Bell had identified years earlier. Much of Reagan's initial political success in his California gubernatorial race was based on criticism of antagonistic college students and their teachers, and his belief that America was a nation of technological might that outproduced and advanced knowledge to win a rightful place on the world stage. For example, Reagan regularly recalled American production in World War II, and his belief that the nation was a "bastion of freedom," and "a city set on a hill."

The problem was that universities were questioning everything Reagan said and stood for. The best known of these criticisms was labeled as deconstruction, a French import that questioned rationality and definitions. Deconstruction held that written words could never have fixed meanings, and, as a result, any text revealed ambiguities, contradictions, hidden meanings, and repressive political relationships. The modern world, according to these new thinkers, had expanded industrial capitalism and scientific thinking, but it also brought the world Auschwitz, the possibility of nuclear war, the horrors of Nazism and Stalinism, neocolonialism, racism, and world hunger. The critics believed that modernism had run its course, and society had entered a new age—the age of postmodernism.

Postmodernism is a complicated term because the concept appears in a wide variety of disciplines and areas of study, including art, architecture, music, film, literature, fashion, and technology. In general, postmodernism rejects the uncritical acceptance of the power of reason, order, and science. According to postmodernists, the assumption that there is such a thing as objective truth is at base a modern fallacy. For them there is no linear progress in society, no ideal social order, and no standardization of knowledge. Instead the world was a picture of fragmentation, indeterminacy, and chaos. Postmodernists held that culture should affirm this fragmented reality, and consider order to be only provisional and varying from person to person.

The contrast between modern and postmodern is seen in a comparison of professions. In several of them, such as medicine, law, and engineering, mastery of a specific body of knowledge and the application of an intrinsic logic led to something known as progress. When a doctor diagnosed and treated a disease, or when an engineer designed a bridge, their work assumed a rational understanding of the world and a logical means of dealing with it. In short, these professions presupposed an objective order in existence. Different medical doctors, using the same objective science and trained in a standard methodology, could examine the same patient and arrive at an identical diagnosis and course of treatment. They exemplify modernism.

A host of new professions arose by the 1980s that had no universally recognized body of knowledge, and no generally accepted methods, although they invoked the jargon of science. The social sciences were shining examples of new postmodern professions. For example, someone in need of "mental health" could be treated by a Freudian, a Jungian, a humanist, or a behaviorist. A political scientist could be a behaviorist, a formal theorist, one trained in classical political thought, or an area specialist with no training other than language skills, and then there were those who believed politics could not be a science. The philosophies behind the psychological analysis and the political analysis were incompatible, and the methodologies conflicted and were oftentimes incomplete and sometimes untested. They exemplify postmodern professions.

The conflict between modern and postmodern surfaced in Reagan's appointment of William Bennett as chairman of the National Endowment for the Humanities. Bennett had a Ph.D. in philosophy from the University of Texas and a law degree from Harvard. He was a conservative academic who spoke movingly about the threat deconstruction and postmodernism posed to the teaching of the Western classics. "We must give greater attention to a sound common curriculum emphasizing English, history, geography, math, and science . . . [and] we have to understand why these subjects were thrown out or weakened in the cultural deconstruction of our schools of the last twenty-five years." The very thing Bennett warned against was taking place at one of America's premier universities. The curriculum of Stanford became an issue in 1988, when the faculty voted to reform the Western Civilization course away from a "European-Western and male bias." The revision became an issue for discussion not only on college campuses, but also in newspapers and television talk shows across the country.

The education debate was part of a national one on the modernist/ postmodernist divide. The society had not moved beyond modernity; there were still plenty of people who thought America was the hope of the world and believed in its technological future as well. But there were others who had their doubts, and they delighted in the period of transition. The character of the change was seen in the new pop culture.

The baby boomers, usually defined as those born between 1946 and 1964, left the world a legacy of rock and roll. In the 1980s "rock became a reference point for a splintered culture." The most important outlet for 1980s music was MTV, or Music Television, that began broadcasting on August 1, 1981. It brought music videos into American homes, and criticism of the dominant modern culture to a new generation. Some immediately saw that the new medium, which exulted in "fast cuts, slow motion, and artsy black-and-white photography—all selling sex and violence—defined the visual style of the decade, spreading to movies, prime time series, advertising and magazines."

The end of the peace and love generation of music came on December 8, 1980, when John Lennon was shot seven times outside the Dakota, an apartment building where he lived in New York City. Lennon's murder, by twenty-five-year-old Mark David Chapman, was made more horrifying because the assassin was a self-confessed fan. The paranoid fear by pop starts of their audiences was epitomized in Lennon's death, which was a prelude to the era's approaching fragmentation and cult of personality.

Michael Jackson was the most important pop rock star of the decade. When Jackson recorded *Off the Wall* with Quincy Jones as producer in 1979, it sold 6 million copies. That achievement made it the best-selling album ever recorded by an African American. His next album, *Thriller,* entered the Billboard Top Ten on January 3, 1983, where it stayed for seventy-eight weeks, remaining at number one for thirty-seven weeks. At the end of the decade, *Thriller* had sold over 40 million copies, making it the best-selling record album of all time.

By the mid-1980s, African American artists dominated the Top Ten music list. Lionel Richie, Tina Turner, Rick James, Billy Ocean, and Stevie Wonder all had number one hits in 1984. The most flamboyant artist of the time was Prince Rogers Nelson, whose shocking lyrics on the album *Dirty Mind* (1980) led Tipper Gore to form the Parents Music Resource Center in 1984 to protest sexually explicit lyrics. That protest would eventually result in "Parental Advisory" labels on album covers. Prince's flamboyant style led to questions about his personal life, especially if he was gay or bisexual. His response was classically postmodern: "Who cares?"

The popularity of rock music, and musicians, became a global experience in the 1980s. Renowned rock figures embarked on world tours, and the performances were experienced through enormous video screens and television broadcasts. Technology blurred the distinction between live events and reproduced videos and recordings. "From rock music to tourism to television and even education, advertising imperatives and consumer demand are no longer for goods, but for experiences." A rock music concert became the ultimate postmodern experience, proof with manufactured reality that all claims to truth—and even truth itself—were socially constructed.

In July 1985, one of the biggest events in rock history, the Live Aid concert, was held simultaneously in London and Philadelphia. The concert was attended by 160,000 fans while another 1.5 billion watched it on television or listened on the radio in 130 countries. The two simultaneous all-day concerts involved pretty much anybody who was anybody in the rock-and-roll world, and Phil Collins caught the supersonic Concord to play in both cities on two different continents. Hundreds of thousands of people raised their voices together to end the show by singing, "We are the World." The Live Aid concert raised over $80 million in foreign aid that went to seven African nations: Ethiopia, Mozambique, Chad, Burkina Faso, Niger, Mali, and Sudan.

MTV opened opportunities for women to flaunt their personality and sexuality on the screen in ways, and at an age, their parents could never have imagined. Tina Turner, Cyndi Lauper, and Madonna Ciccone emerged as singing, sexual icons of the time. The latter's album *Like a Virgin* created a stir when she took the woman-as-sex-object ploy to new public heights. She found herself singing to prepubescent audiences dressed in layered gypsy blouses, bangled necklaces, and an exposed midriff. In true postmodern style, Madonna changed her public image many times, going from dance queen to "boy toy," to the "Material Girl," to trashy on-stage exhibitionist. Each time, she influenced popular fashion and the style of pop music.

Rock music was becoming an index of cultural capital, and a telltale revelation of social change. Older Americans, who had invented the youth culture, stood by speechless as their children adopted rebellious fashions at increasingly younger ages. Girls as young as eleven or twelve found themselves on the cover of beauty magazines. A 1989 article in the *New York Times* described a new marketing drive of cosmetics for little girls, six years old, "painted to the hilt." Preadolescent dieting was rampant in the fourth and fifth grades, and in a survey of schoolgirls in San Francisco, more than half described themselves as overweight, while only 15 percent were so by medical standards.

American adolescence in the 1980s was prolonged, enjoyed, and catered to by a host of advertisers offering instant gratification. None of this was new, but the scale of the assault was unprecedented. The television suggested a morality far different from what most Americans were used to. Little girls wore leg warmers and wanted to be like Jennifer Beals, the dancing heroine in *Flashdance*. Patrick Swayze crossed the line from courtship to seduction in *Dirty Dancing*. The top movie in 1986 was *Top Gun* starring Tom Cruise as Lt. Pete "Maverick" Mitchell, a U.S. Navy fighter pilot who seduces his flight instructor. At some time every kid saw, or played with, a *Ghostbuster* product. The 1984 science fiction comedy starred three parapsychologists who were fired from New York University and started up their own business investigating and eliminating ghosts.

The 1980s were a time when the "Cola Wars" between Coke and Pepsi reached new heights—or lows, depending on your perspective. Coke was losing market share to its competitor, so on April 23, 1985, "New Coke," a sweeter variant on the original, was released with great fanfare. By the middle of June, people were saying "no" to New Coke. The reaction was nationwide, with the recent product called "furniture polish" and "sewer water." Within weeks "Coke Classic" returned to the market, and the company stock jumped 36 percent. Only in America could a marketing disaster turn into company profit. For entertainment, Americans fooled with Rubik's Cube, a plastic square with its surface subdivided so that each face consisted of nine squares. Rotation of each face allowed the smaller cubes to be arranged in different ways. The challenge, undertaken by millions of addicts, was to return the cube from any given state to its original array with each face consisting of nine squares of the same color.

Kids still rode bicycles around the neighborhood, swam in local pools, and used little CB radios to talk to each other. Schools were discussing twelve-month sessions, but summer for most was still from Memorial Day to Labor Day. They did not yet have 100 channels to flip through on television, or cell phones to flip open, email, or instant messengers. If they wanted to visit with friends they still went home and gave them a call.

Television aired a number of shows with black stars, the most successful of which was the *Bill Cosby Show*. It was the top-rated show of the decade, and showed African Americans as economically successful, middle-class professionals. *Miami Vice* made a star of Don Johnson. *The Golden Girls* made its premier in 1985 and featured stars well into their fifties and sixties. The best night on television from 1984 to 1986 was Thursday, when *The Cosby Show, Family Ties, Cheers, Night Court,* and *Hill Street Blues* dominated. *St. Elsewhere,* along with shows like *Hill Street Blues, L.A. Law,* and *Thirtysomething* were a result of demographic programming at a time when cable television was experiencing spectacular growth. The shows earned comparatively low ratings, but were kept on the air because they delivered highly desirable audiences of young affluent viewers whom advertisers wanted to reach. In 1987, a fourth network, Fox, went on the air to compete with CBS, NBC, and ABC. Before the end of the decade, 90 percent of American homes were able to tune into Fox.

Talk shows flooded onto the airways in the 1980s. David Letterman got his start in 1982, and by 1989 Oprah Winfrey, Geraldo Rivera, Sally Jessey Raphael, Pat Sajak, Arsenio Hall, and Larry King hosted popular shows. The Reagan appointees on the Federal Communications Commission (FCC) revolutionized broadcasting when they voted to abolish the agency's long-standing fairness doctrine, which required broadcasters to provide a balanced presentation of public issues. With FM radio stations given over to rock and country music, older, more conservative listeners turned to AM radio, where right-wing hosts like Rush Limbaugh, Pat Buchanan, and G. Gordon Liddy entertained them with criticisms of women, liberals, Democrats, and environmentalists.

In the burgeoning suburbs, kids collected and traded Garbage Pail Kids, and had to have as many Cabbage Patch Kids as possible. They wore Swatch watches and Izod shirts, and spent time in shopping malls where they found their every need: music stores, clothing stores, fast food courts, movie theaters, and all their friends. On their first kiss they heard "Take Your Breath Away" on the radio, they danced like an Egyptian, and they did the "moonwalk," The Challenger explosion was broadcast live, and a viewer never heard a curse word used on television.

The combination of technological change and more consumer outlets led to a growth in pornography. Cheap video technology allowed the industry to grow to an estimated $7 billion in 1984, as three-quarters of the nation's video stores carried the tapes for rental. In May of 1985, Attorney General Ed Meese appointed a commission to study the effects of pornography and suggest ways to control it. The recommendations had little effect because the individualistic ethic of the time valued choice and consumption over any standard of government control of cultural morality.

For most Americans, the return of economic prosperity was tacit proof that an improvement of black and white relations was imminent. An expanding economy meant gains for everyone. Discussions of race revolved around the place of affirmative action, but the nation was occasionally treated to sensational stories of scandal, and introduced to new leaders. In November 1987, a black teenager covered in dog excrement with racial slurs written on her body was discovered crawling in the garbage of a town south of Poughkeepsie, New York. The girl, Tawana Brawley, was soon represented by the Reverend Al Sharpton of New York City and two lawyers. Sharpton had no congregation, but did have a reputation as a community activist and spokesman for dissident causes. Brawley claimed to have been abducted by several white men who held her for four days and repeatedly raped her while in captivity. The Sharpton team turned the sensational incident into a national media feeding frenzy.

Before the press, Sharpton claimed that Brawley was the victim of a racist judicial system, and the legal team recommended she not cooperate with the police conducting the investigation. Eventually, Tawana Brawley's story fell apart, and an official examination found that she had never been assaulted and had smeared the excrement and written the epithets herself. Once the truth came out, the two lawyers were subject to legal discipline, but Al Sharpton suffered no repercussions and continued his race-baiting activities. He ran for the New York Senate seat in 1992 and 1994, for mayor of New York City in 1997, and for the Democratic presidential nomination in 2004. Throughout his career he never apologized or explained his activities in the Tawana Brawley case.

The Brawley case showed the power of the new mass media. The "age of publicity," as Louis Kronenberger called it, began in the 1920s when flagpole sitting and goldfish swallowing became ways to get attention. Conspicuous ballyhoo became fashionable after World War II, when couples took their marriage vows on carnival carousels and spent their honeymoons in department store windows. As television grew, so too did the Barnum spirit. World records were set for domino toppling, frankfurter eating, and kazoo playing, and all of it was seen on television. The problem was that no one could predict what was likely to become news or why it would occupy public attention or for how long. More importantly, fame in America not only lasted for just fifteen minutes; it often left devastating results in its wake.

In October of 1987 the country fixated on the rescue of "Baby Jessica" McClure, who fell down an eight-inch-wide, twenty-two-foot-deep hole in her backyard in Midland, Texas. For the next fifty-eight hours the country watched spellbound as rescuers left jobs and worked nonstop to save the baby. On the evening of October 16, paramedics Steve Forbes and Robert O'Donnell wriggled into a passageway drilled through rock to save "Baby Jessica."

When it was over, the gifts sent to her would provide a million-dollar trust fund. Twenty years later, hardened West Texas roughnecks would wipe tears from their cheeks as they talked about the rescue and the media coverage it inspired. The child's parents, Chip and Cissy McClure, subsequently divorced, and one of the rescuers, Robert O'Donnell, killed himself in 1995. His brother, Ricky, said O'Donnell's life fell apart because of the stress of the rescue. In the new media age fame was fleeting and suffocating at the same time.

In 1941 Henry Luce wrote an article for *Life* magazine entitled "The American Century." Luce was the most powerful and innovative mass communications person of his era, and the purpose of his essay was twofold: (1) to urge American involvement in World War II, and (2) to put forth the idea that the American principles of democracy and free enterprise would eventually come to dominate the world. The idea of American preeminence was dangerous in the eyes of some, but the basis of the piece bespoke what most people acknowledged whether they liked Luce's formulation or not.

"We have some things in this country which are infinitely precious and especially American," wrote Luce, "a love of freedom, a feeling for the equality of opportunity, a tradition of self-reliance and independence." Forty-two years later, the editors of *Time* magazine, the sister publication to *Life,* updated Luce's vision with an essay entitled "What Really Mattered." In the essay the *Time* editors evaluated the meaning of America and what values were most precious to its citizens in 1983. They concluded the fundamental idea America represented was freedom, but it was different from what Luce had in mind: "America was merely free: it was freed unshackled. . . . To be free was to be modern: to be modern was to take chances. . . . The American Century was to be the century of unleashing."

During the 1980s the limits of freedom were explored in the political, social, and personal realm. In the 1930s, scientists freed the atom, and fifty years later doctors were trying to free the body from its genetic dictates. Could organ transplants, sex change operations, and genetic manipulation make us immortal? Could the nation be free of superstition, so that Americans could indulge their passions for personal peace and affluence? Freedom was one of the prime conditions of postmodernity, and the cultural preoccupation with it a prelude for change. The advent of a global communications system meant that the world was coming together at one level, and falling apart at another. At the end of the decade the United States was the world's only superpower, yet it would be held captive by countries with only a fraction of its political power, but united by television to worldwide religious followers across the globe.

Postmodernism came of age in this climate in the decade of the 1980s. The election and re-election of ex-actor Ronald Reagan put a new gloss on the possibility of politics shaped by images alone. The convictions of the president were a throwback to an earlier time, but his style of image politics, carefully crafted and orchestrated for mass consumption, was of a newer era. The world was changing, and the older language of genres and forms was becoming obsolete.

Thomas Byrne Edsall  **NO**

The Changing Shape of Power:
A Realignment in Public Policy

The past twenty years in America have been marked by two central political developments. The first is the continuing erosion of the political representation of the economic interests of those in the bottom half of the income distribution. The second is the growing dominance of the political process by a network of elites that includes fund-raisers, the leadership of interest groups, specialists in the technology and manipulation of elections, and an army of Washington lobbyists and law firms—elites that augment and often overshadow political officeholders and the candidates for office themselves.

This shift in the balance of power has not been accompanied by realignment of the electorate, although the shape and relative strength of the Republican and Democratic Parties have changed dramatically.

Twice during the past twenty years, the Republican party has had the opportunity to gain majority status: in the early 1970s, and again after the 1980 election. The first opportunity emerged when the fragile Democratic coalition was fractured by the independent presidential bid of Alabama governor George G. Wallace in 1968. The Democratic party then amplified its own vulnerability four years later with the nomination of Sen. George S. McGovern, Democrat of South Dakota, whose candidacy alienated a spectrum of traditional Democrats from Detroit to Atlanta. This potential Republican opportunity crumbled, however, when the web of scandals known as Watergate produced across-the-board setbacks for the GOP in campaigns ranging from city council contests to the presidency in the elections of 1974 and 1976.

The period from 1978 to 1981 offered even more fertile terrain for the Republican party. Not only had Democratic loyalties dating back to the depression of the 1930s been further weakened during the presidency of Jimmy Carter, with the emergence of simultaneous inflation and high unemployment, but the candidacy of Ronald Reagan provided the Republican party with its first substantial opportunity to heal the fissures that had relegated the GOP to minority status for two generations. In Reagan, the party long identified with the rich found a leader equipped to bridge divisions between the country club and the fundamentalist church, between the executives of the Fortune 500 and the membership of the National Rifle Association. Just

From *The Rise and Fall of the New Deal Order, 1930–1980,* by Steve Fraser, and Gary Gerstle, eds., pp. 269–279, 281–289. © 1989 Princeton University Press. Reprinted by permission.

as Watergate halted Republican momentum in the early 1970s, however, the severe recession of 1981–82 put the brakes on what had the earmarks of a potential Republican takeover, for the first time since 1954, of both branches of Congress. In the first two years of the Reagan administration, the Republican party captured the Senate by a six-vote margin and, with a gain of thirty-two House seats, acquired de facto control of the House in an alliance with southern Democratic conservatives. The recession, however, resulted in the return of twenty-six House seats to the Democrats in 1982, and with those seats went the chance to establish Republican dominance of the federal government.

As the two parties have gained and lost strength, the underlying alteration of the balance of political power over the past decade has continued in a shift of power among the rich, the poor, and the middle class; among blacks and whites; among regions in the country; and among such major competitors for the federal dollar as the defense and social services sectors.

The past twenty years have, in effect, produced a policy realignment in the absence of a political realignment. The major beneficiaries of this policy realignment are the affluent, while those in the bottom half of the income distribution, particularly those whose lives are the most economically marginal, have reaped the fewest rewards or have experienced declines in their standard of living.

A major factor contributing to this development is the decline of political parties: In the United States, as well as in most democratic countries, parties perform the function of representing major interests and classes. As parties erode, the groups that suffer most are those with the fewest resources to protect themselves. In other words, the continued collapse of the broad representation role of political parties in the United States has direct consequences for the distribution of income.

As the role of parties in mobilizing voters has declined, much of the control over both election strategy and issue selection—key functions in defining the national agenda—has shifted to a small, often interlocking, network of campaign specialists, fund-raisers, and lobbyists. While this element of politics is among the most difficult to quantify, there are some rough measures. For example, there are approximately thirty Republican and Democratic consultants and pollsters, almost all based in Washington, who at this writing are the principal strategists in almost every presidential and competitive Senate race, in addition to playing significant roles in gubernatorial, House, and local referenda contests.

At another level, the years from 1974 to 1984 show a steady growth in the financial dependence of House and Senate candidates on political action committees (PACS), vehicles through which money is transferred from organized interest groups to elected officeholders. In that decade, the PAC share of the total cost of House campaigns went from 17 percent to 36 percent, while individual contributions fell from 73 percent to 47 percent, with the remainder coming from parties, loans, and other sources. For House Democratic incumbents, 1984 marked the first year in which PACS were the single most important source of cash; they provided 47 percent of the total, compared with 45 percent from individuals.

This shift has, in turn, magnified the influence of a group of lobbyists who organize Washington fund-raisers for House and Senate incumbents, among whom are Thomas Hale Boggs, Jr., whose clients include the Trial Lawyers Association, the Chicago Board of Options Exchange, and Chrysler; Edward H. Forgotson, whose clients include Enserch Corp., the Hospital Corp. of America, and the Texas Oil and Gas Corp.; Robert J. Keefe, whose clients include Westinghouse and the American Medical Association; and J. D. Williams, whose clients include General Electric Co. and the National Realty Committee. The Washington consulting-lobbying firm of Black, Manafort, Stone, Kelly and Atwater provides perhaps the best example of the range of political and special interests one firm can represent. In 1987, one partner, Charles Black, managed the presidential bid of Rep. Jack Kemp (R—N.Y.); another, Lee Atwater, managed the campaign of Vice-President George Bush; and a third, Peter Kelly, was a principal fund-raiser for the campaign of Sen. Albert Gore (D—Tenn.). At the same time, the firm's clients have included the Dominican Republic, the anti-Communist insurgency in Angola run by Jonas Savimbi, Salomon Brothers, the government of Barbados, the Natural Gas Supply Association, and, briefly, the Marcos government in the Philippines. In addition, the firm has served as principal political consultant to the Senate campaigns of Phil Gramm (R—Tex.), Jesse Helms (R—N.C) and Paula Hawkins (formerly R—Fla.).

A few general indicators of the scope of lobbying and political party bureaucracies point to the sizable influence small elites can exercise over public policy. In 1986, there were almost 10,000 people employed as registered Washington lobbyists, with 3,500 of these serving as officers of 1,800 trade and professional organizations, including labor unions; another 1,300 were employed by individual corporations, and approximately 1,000 represented organizations ranging from the National Right to Life Association to the Sierra Club. The six major political party committees headquartered in Washington now employ roughly 1,200 people. The creation and expansion of such ideological think tanks as the Heritage Foundation, the Center for National policy, the Urban Institute, the American Enterprise Institute, the Cato Institute, and the Hoover Institution have established whole networks of influential public policy entrepreneurs specializing in media relations and in targeted position papers. Within a general framework of increasingly monopolized American mass media—both print and electronic—the growth of the Gannett and Los Angeles Times—Mirror chains are examples of an ever greater concentration of power within the media, just as the acquisition of NBC by General Electric has functioned to submerge a major network within the larger goals of the nation's sixth biggest corporation. Staffers acquiring expertise and influence on Capitol Hill, in the executive branch, and throughout the regulatory apparatus routinely travel to the private sector—and sometimes back again—through the so-called revolving door. In effect, an entire class of public and private specialists in the determination of government policy and political strategy has been created—a process replicated in miniature at the state level.

The rise to authority of elites independent of the electorate at large, empowered to make decisions without taking into direct account the economic interests of voters, is part of a much larger shift in the balance of power involving changed voting patterns, the decline of organized labor, a restructuring of the employment marketplace, and a transformed system of political competition. This power shift, in turn, has produced a policy realignment most apparent in the alteration of both the *pre-tax* distribution of income and the *after-tax* distribution of income. In both cases, the distribution has become increasingly regressive. The alteration of the pretax distribution of income is the subject of a broad debate in which there are those, particularly critics on the left, who argue that growing regressivity emerges from government policies encouraging weakened union representation and a proliferation of low-wage service industry jobs. On the other side, more conservative analysts contend that changes in the pre-tax distribution result from natural alterations of the marketplace and the workplace, as the United States adjusts to a changing economic and demographic environment. The figures in table 1, derived from Census Bureau data, indicate changes in the distribution of pretax household income from 1980 through 1985. . . .

The data clearly show a growing disparity in the distribution of income. Of the five quintiles, all but those in the top 20 percent have seen their share of household income decline. In addition, most of the gains of the top 20 percent have, in fact, been concentrated in the top 5 percent of the income distribution. The gain of 1.1 percent for the top 5 percent translates into a total of $38.8 billion (in 1987 dollars) more for this segment of the population than if the income distribution had remained constant after 1980. These regressive

Table 1

Shares of Pre-Tax Household Income, by Income Distribution

Income group	Year 1980 (%)	1985 (%)
Quintile[a]		
Bottom	4.1	3.9
Second	10.2	9.7
Third	16.8	16.3
Fourth	24.8	24.4
Top	44.2	45.7
Top 5%	16.5	17.6

Sources: Bureau of the Census, *Estimating After-Tax Money Income Distribution,* Series P-23, no. 126, issued August 1983; and ibid., *Household After-Tax Income: 1985,* Series P-23, no. 151, issued June 1987.

[a] A quintile is a block of 20% of the population.

Table 2

Shares of After-Tax Household Income, by Income Distribution

	Year	
Income group	1980 (%)	1985 (%)
Quintile[a]		
Bottom	4.9	4.6
Second	11.6	11.0
Third	17.9	17.2
Fourth	25.1	24.7
Top	40.6	42.6
Top 5%	14.1	15.5

Sources: Bureau of the Census, *Estimating After-Tax Money Income Distribution,* Series P-23, no. 126, issued August 1983; and ibid., *Household After-Tax Income: 1985,* Series P-23, no. 151, issued June 1987.

[a] A quintile is a block of 20% of the population.

trends were, moreover, intensified by the tax policies enacted between 1980 and 1985, as demonstrated in table 2, based on Census Bureau data.

What had been a $38.8 billion improvement in the status of the top 5 percent in pre-tax income over these six years becomes a $49.5 billion gain in after-tax income, while the bottom 80 percent of the population saw larger losses in its share of after-tax income between 1980 and 1985 than it had seen in the case of pre-tax income. These findings are even more sharply delineated in a November 1987 study by the Congressional Budget Office showing that from 1977 to 1988, 70 percent of the population experienced very modest increases in after-tax income or, for those in the bottom 40 percent, net drops, when changes over that period in the federal income tax, the Social Security tax, corporate tax, and excise taxes are taken into account. In contrast, those in the seventy-first to ninetieth percentiles experienced a modest improvement, and those in the top 10 percent significantly improved their standard of living. For those at the very top, the gains have been enormous. Table 3, developed from Congressional Budget Office data, shows that distribution.

What these tables point to is a major redistribution of economic power in the private marketplace and of political power in the public sector, which, in turn, has been reflected in very concrete terms in family income patterns. One of the major characteristics, then, of the post–New Deal period in American politics has been a reversal of the progressive redistribution of income that underlay the policies of the administrations of Franklin Roosevelt and Harry Truman.

Table 3

Changes in Estimated Average After-Tax Family Income, by Income Distribution (In 1987 Dollars)

Income group	1977 average income ($)	1988 average income ($)	Percentage change (+or −)	Dollar change (+ or −)
Decile[a]				
First (poor)	3,528	3,157	−10.5	−371
Second	7,084	6,990	−1.3	−94
Third	10,740	10,614	−1.2	−126
Fourth	14,323	14,266	−0.4	−57
Fifth	18,043	18,076	+0.2	+33
Sixth	22,009	22,259	+1.1	+250
Seventh	26,240	27,038	+3.0	+798
Eighth	31,568	33,282	+5.4	+1,718
Ninth	39,236	42,323	+7.9	+3,087
Tenth (rich)	70,459	89,793	+27.4	+19,324
Top 5%	90,756	124,651	+37.3	+33,895
Top 1%	174,498	303,900	+74.2	+129,402
All groups	22,184	26,494	+9.6	+2,310

Sources: Congressional Budget Offices, *The Changing Distributi on of Federal Taxes: 1975–1990,* October 1987.

[a]A decile is a block of 1096 of the population.

In the competition between the defense and social welfare sectors, the outcome of a parallel, although more recent, shift in the balance of power can be seen in the years from 1980 through 1987. During this period, the share of the federal budget going to national defense grew from 22.7 percent in 1980 to 28.4 percent in 1987. At the same time, the share of federal dollars collectively going to education, training, employment, social services, health, income security, and housing dropped from 25.5 percent in 1980 to 18.3 percent in 1987.

In many respects, these policy changes reflect the rising strength of the Republican party. In terms of tax policy and the balance of spending between defense and social programs, the Republican party under Ronald Reagan has been the driving force pushing the country to the right. During the past ten years, the Republican party has made substantial gains in the competition for the allegiance of voters, gaining near parity by 1987, reducing what had been a 20- to 25-point Democratic advantage in terms of self-identification to a six- or seven-point edge.

The income distribution trends and the shifts in budget priorities began, however, before the Republican party took over the presidency and the U.S. Senate in 1980. The emergence of a vital, competitive Republican party is less a cause of the changed balance of power in the country than a reflection of the underlying forces at work in the post-New Deal phase of American politics.

Together, these forces—which include the deterioration of organized labor, the continued presence of divisive racial conflict, the shift from manufacturing to service industries, the slowing rates of economic growth, the threat of international competition to domestic production, the replacement of political organization with political technology, and the growing class-skew of voter turnout—have severely undermined the capacity of those in the bottom half of the income distribution to form an effective political coalition.

In tracing the erosion of the left wing of the Democratic party in the United States, it is difficult to overestimate the importance of the collapse of the labor movement. In 1970, the continuing growth in the number of labor union members came to a halt. Unions represented 20.7 million workers that year, or 27.9 percent of the nonagricultural work force. Through 1980, the number of workers represented by unions remained roughly the same, dropping slightly to 20.1 million employees by 1980. At the same time, however, the total work force had grown, so that the percentage of workers who were represented by unions fell to 23 percent in 1980. With the election of Ronald Reagan, however, the decline of organized labor began to accelerate sharply, a process encouraged by Reagan's firing of 11,500 striking patco air traffic controllers, and by the appointment of pro-management officials to the National Labor Relations Board and to the Department of Labor. From 1980 to 1986, not only did the share of the work force represented by unions drop from 23 percent to 17.5 percent, but the number of workers in unions began to fall precipitously for the first time in fifty years, dropping by 3.1 million men and women, from 20.1 million to 17 million, in 1986. During the first half of the 1980s, almost all the decline in union membership was among whites employed in private industry.

The decline of organized labor dovetailed with a continuing shift from traditional manufacturing, mining, and construction employment to work in the technology and service industries. From 1970 to 1986, the number of jobs in goods-producing industries, which lend themselves to unionization, grew only from 23.8 million to 24.9 million, while employment in the service industries, which are much more resistant to labor organizing, shot up from 47.3 million to 75.2 million.

The difficulties of organized labor were compounded by the unexpected decision on the part of many of the major corporations in the early 1970s to abandon what had been a form of tacit détente between labor and management, in which Fortune 500 companies kept labor peace through agreements amounting to a form of profit sharing by means of automatic cost-of-living pay hikes. Faced with growing competition from foreign producers—in 1968, car imports exceeded exports for the first time in the nation's history, an unmistakable signal that domestic producers of all goods faced serious foreign competition—major American companies dropped the fundamentally cordial relations that had characterized the largest part of postwar union negotiations. Catching the leaders of organized labor entirely unprepared, these corporations adopted a tough, adversarial approach regarding both pay and fringe benefits, willing to break union shops and to relocate facilities either abroad or in nonunion communities in the South and Southwest.

The decline of organized labor was particularly damaging to the Democratic party because unions represent one of the few remaining institutional links between working-class voters and the Democratic party. The decline of political parties has resulted in the end of the clubhouse tie between the party of Franklin Delano Roosevelt and the blue-collar voters of row- and tract-house neighborhoods throughout the Northeast and Midwest. In addition, it is among these white, blue-collar workers that the racial conflicts within the Democratic party have been the most divisive. Interviews with whites in Dearborn, Michigan, the west-side suburbs of Birmingham, Chicago, Atlanta, and New Orleans—all communities that have suffered major industrial layoffs and that are either part of or adjoin cities now run by Democratic black mayors—reveal voters who are disenchanted with the unions that failed to protect their jobs, and with a local Democratic party no longer controlled by whites. Race, which previously severed the tie between the white South and the Democratic party, has, in cities with black mayors, served to produce white Republican voting, not only for president but for local offices that once were unchallenged Democratic bastions.

These developments, in the 1970s, contributed significantly to the creation of a vacuum of power within the Democratic party, allowing the party to be taken over, in part, by its most articulate and procedurally sophisticated wing: affluent, liberal reformers. This faction capitalized first on the public outcry against police violence at the Chicago presidential convention in 1968, and then on the Watergate scandals in the mid-1970s, to force priority consideration of a series of reforms involving campaign finance, the presidential nominating process, the congressional seniority system, the congressional code of ethics—and an expansion of the federal role in regulating the environment, through creation of the Environmental Protection Agency and new water- and air-pollution standards. The strength of this wing of the Democratic party subsided during the 1980s, although its leverage within the party has been institutionalized through the creation of a host of primaries and caucuses in the presidential selection process, giving disproportionate influence to middle- and upper-middle-class voters and interests in a party that claims to represent the nation's working and lower-middle classes. The turnout in primaries and in caucuses is skewed in favor of the affluent and upper-middle class. In addition, these delegate selection processes have been contributing factors in the acceleration of the decline of political organizations in working-class communities.

The Democratic agenda set in the 1970s by the reform wing of the party was, however, more important for what it omitted and neglected than for what was included. The ascendancy of the reformers took place just when the fissures within the Democratic party had become most apparent. In 1968, 9.9 million mostly Democratic voters turned to George C. Wallace, the segregationist-populist governor of Alabama, and they strayed off the Democratic reservation in 1972 when Nixon beat McGovern by a margin of 47.2 million votes to 29.2 million. The cultural and ideological gulf that had steadily widened between these voters and the wings of the Democratic party supporting the antiwar movement, gay rights, women's rights, and civil rights had reached such proportions in the early and mid 1970s that rapprochement between warring factions was difficult, if not impossible.

The rise to prominence within the Democratic party of a well-to-do liberal-reform wing worked in other ways to compound the divisions in the party Relatively comfortable in their own lives, reformers failed to recognize the growing pressure of marginal tax rates on working- and lower-middle-class voters. The progressive rate system of the federal income tax remained effectively unchanged from the early 1950s through the 1970s, so that the series of sharply rising marginal tax rates that had originally been designed to affect only the upper-middle class and rich, began to directly impinge on regular Democratic voters whose wages had been forced up by inflation. By neglecting to adjust the marginal rate system to account for inflation, in combination with repeated raising of the highly regressive Social Security tax, Democrats effectively encouraged the tax revolt of the 1970s which, in turn, provided a critically important source of support to the conservative movement and to the rise of the Republican party. . . .

On the Republican side, the same developments that debilitated the Democratic coalition served to strengthen ascendant constituencies of the Right. For a brief period in the late 1970s and early 1980s, the constituencies and interests underpinning the Republican party had the potential to establish a new conservative majority in the electorate. The tax revolt, the rise of the religious right, the mobilization of much of the business community in support of the Republican party, renewed public support for defense spending, the political-financial mobilization of the affluent, and the development of a conservative economic theory promising growth through lower taxes—all combined to empower the political right to a degree unprecedented since the 1920s.

Proposed tax cuts provided an essential common ground for the right-of-center coalition that provided the core of the Reagan revolution. The combination of corporate tax reductions and individual tax cuts embodied in the 1981 tax bill served to unify a divided business community by providing a shared legislative goal, to strengthen the commitment of the affluent to the Republican party, and to attract white working- and lower-middle-class former Democrats who had seen their paychecks eaten away by inflation-driven higher marginal rates. The tax cut theme was adopted as a central element of the speeches of such religious-right figures as the Rev. Jerry Falwell of the Moral Majority, Ed McAteer of the Religious Roundtable, and the Rev. Marion G. (Pat) Robertson of the Christian Broadcast Network. . . .

This growing political tilt in favor of the affluent is further reflected in voting turnout patterns over the past twenty years. During this period, the class-skewing of voting in favor of the affluent has grown significantly. In the presidential election year of 1964, the self-reported turnout among members of professions associated with the middle and upper classes was 83.2 percent, compared with 66.1 percent among those employed in manual jobs, including skilled crafts, a difference of 17.1 points; by 1980, the spread between the two had grown to 25 points, 73 percent to 48 percent. In the off-year election of 1966, the percentage-point spread in terms of voter turnout between middle-to-upper-class job holders and those employed in manual jobs was 18.1 percent; by 1978, this had grown to a 23.8-percent spread. While overall turnout has been declining, the drop has been most severe among those in the bottom third of the income distribution.

For the Republican party, these turnout trends were a political bonanza, accentuated by trends in the correlation between income and both voting and partisan commitment. Through the 1950s, 1960s, and into the early 1970s, the sharp class divisions that characterized the depression-era New Deal coalition structure gave way to diffuse voting patterns with relatively little correlation between income and allegiance to the Democratic or Republican party. By 1980 and 1982, with the election of Reagan and then the enactment of the budget and tax bills of 1981, the correlation between income and voting began to reemerge with a vengeance. By 1982, the single most important determinant of probable voting, aside from membership in either the Republican or Democratic party, became income, with the Democratic margin steadily declining as one moved up the ladder. . . .

In other words, the Reagan years polarized the electorate along sharp income lines. While income made almost no difference in the partisan loyalties of 90 percent of the population in 1956, by 1984 income became one of the sharpest dividing lines between Democrats and Republicans. In 1956, the very poor were only 5 percentage points more likely to be Democratic than the upper-middle class, and 40 points more likely than the affluent top 10 percent of the income distribution. By 1984, however, the spread between the poor and the upper-middle class reached 36 points, and between the poor and affluent, 69 points. . . .

These figures accurately describe an electorate polarized by income, but what they mask are the effects of black and white voter participation on the figures. The civil rights movement, and civil rights legislation enacted in the 1960s, enfranchised millions of blacks who, in 1956, were barred from voting. During the twenty-eight years from 1956 to 1984, roughly 4.2 million blacks entered the electorate. During the same period, blacks' allegiance to the Democratic party, which in 1956 held their loyalty by a 34-percentage-point edge, increased to provide an overwhelming 72-percentage-point Democratic edge in 1984. This infusion of black Democratic support sharply increased the low-income tilt of the party: in 1984, the median family income for whites was $28,674, while for blacks it was $15,982.

The Reagan revolution was, at its core, a revolution led by the affluent. The class polarization of voters . . . cut across the country, but nowhere were the trends stronger than in the South, where a realignment in miniature took place among the white elite. In the 1950s, Democratic allegiance in the South was strongest among the most well-to-do whites, for whom the Democratic party was the vehicle for maintaining the pre-civil rights social structure of the Confederate states. These voters gave the Democratic party their support by a 5 to 1 margin, higher than that of any other income group in the South. By the 1980s, in the aftermath of a civil rights movement supported by the Democratic party, these same voters had become the most Republican in the South. "The class cleavage had reversed itself," John R. Petrocik, of UCLA, noted. Whites, particularly white men, have become increasingly Republican as blacks have become the most consistent source of Democratic votes. In the five presidential elections from 1968 to 1984, only one Democrat, Jimmy Carter, received more than 40 percent of the white vote, and by 1984, white, male Protestants voted for Reagan over Mondale by a margin of 74 to 26.

The Reagan revolution would, however, have been a political failure if it had not gained extensive support from voters outside the upper-middle class. In addition to the deep inroads made in previously Democratic working-class communities in northern urban areas, perhaps the single most important source of new support for the Republican party has been the religious Right.

In a far shorter period, voters identifying themselves as born-again Christians radically shifted their voting in presidential elections. Between 1976 and 1984, these voters went from casting a 56-to-44 margin for the Democratic candidate, Jimmy Carter, to one of the highest levels of support of any group for the reelection of President Reagan in 1984: 81 to 19, according to *New York Times*/CBS exit polls. This shift represents, in effect, a gain of eight million voters for the GOP.

As a political resource, support among born-again Christians represents not only a loyal core of voters, but a growing core. In contrast with such main-line churches as the United Methodist Church, the United Church of Christ, and the United Presbyterians, which experienced membership losses from 1970 to 1980, the fundamentalist, evangelical, and charismatic churches have seen their congregations grow at an explosive rate: the Southern Baptist Convention by 16 percent, the Assemblies of God by 70 percent, and Seventh Day Adventists by 36 percent.

The Republican party has, in turn, been the major beneficiary of an internal power struggle taking place within the Southern Baptist Convention, now the largest Protestant denomination. During a ten-year fight, the denomination has been taken over by its conservative wing, believers in the "absolute inerrancy" of the Bible. This wing of the denomination, in turn, has been a leading force within the broader religious Right, as such pastors as Adrian Rogers, James T. Draper, Jr., and Charles F. Stanley—all outspoken conservatives—have won the denomination's presidency. The move to the right has been reflected in the ranks of the denomination, producing what amounts to a realignment of the ministry of the Southern Baptist Convention. James L. Guth, of Furman University, found that in just three years, surveys of Southern Baptist ministers showed a remarkable shift from a strong majority in 1981 favoring the Democratic party 41 to 29, to nearly 70 percent in 1984 favoring the GOP, 66 to 26.

The growth of Republican strength is not, however, confined to evangelical and charismatic Christians, and the party appears to be developing a much broader religious base as part of its core constituency. In one of the most interesting recent analyses of voting trends, Frederick T. Steeper, of Market Opinion Research, and John Petrocik, of UCLA, have found that since 1976, one of the sharpest partisan cleavages emerging among white voters in the electorate is between those who attend church regularly and those who never go to church. This represents a major change from past findings. In the period from 1952 to 1960, there was no statistical difference between the Democratic and Republican loyalties of white churchgoers and nonchurchgoers. By the elections of 1972 and 1976, a modest difference began to appear, with non-churchgoers 7 percentage points more likely to be Democrats than regular churchgoers. By 1986, however, the spread had grown to a striking 35-point difference, with regular churchgoers identifying themselves as Republicans by a 22-point margin, and with nonchurchgoers identifying themselves as Democrats by a 13-point edge. The partisan spread between churchgoers and nonchurchgoers was most extreme among white Northern Protestants (51 points) and Catholics (52 points). These findings dovetail with studies showing that the memberships of such Establishment, nonevangelical denominations as the Methodists, Episcopalians, Lutherans, and Presbyterians were significantly more supportive of the election of Ronald Reagan than the electorate at large. . . .

Cumulatively, developments over the past twenty years—the deterioration of the labor movement; economically polarized partisanship; the skewing of turnout patterns by income; stagnation of the median family income; the rising importance of political money; the emergence of a Republican core composed of the well-to-do and the religious; the globalization of the economy; and competition from foreign producers—have combined to disperse constituencies and groups seeking to push the country to the left, and to consolidate those on the right. The consequences of that shift are most readily seen in the figures in table 3, which show that 80 percent of the population has experienced a net loss in after-tax income between 1977 and 1988, while the top 5 percent has seen average family income grow by $26,134, and the top 1 percent, by $117,222.

In the long run the prospects are for the maintenance of a strong, conservative Republican party, continuing to set the national agenda on basic distributional issues, no matter which party holds the White House. Barring a major economic catastrophe, or a large-scale international conflict, the basic shift from manufacturing to service industry jobs is likely to continue to undermine the political left in this country, not only for the reasons outlined earlier in this essay, but also by weakening economically—and therefore politically—those in the bottom 40 percent of the income distribution.

In the thirty-year period spanning 1949 to 1979, the number of manufacturing jobs grew by an average of three million a decade, from 17.6 million in 1949, to 20.4 million in 1959, to 24.4 million in 1969, and finally to a high of 26.5 million in 1979. This growth in no way kept pace with the increase in service industry jobs, which shot up from 26.2 million in 1949 to 63.4 million in 1979, but the continuing, if modest, manufacturing expansion provided a partial cushion in an economy going through a major restructuring—a restructuring involving the loss of 950,000 jobs in steel and other metals industries, automobiles, food production, and textiles from 1972 to 1986. From 1979 to 1986, however, the absolute number of manufacturing jobs began to decline, dropping from 26.5 million to 24.9 million, a loss of 1.6 million jobs.

These employment shifts have been particularly damaging to blacks and Hispanics. From 1970 to 1984, in major northern cities, there has been a massive decline in the number of jobs requiring relatively little education—the kind of jobs that provide entry into the employment marketplace for the poor—and a sharp increase in the number of jobs requiring at least some higher education: "Demographic and employment trends have produced a serious mismatch between the skills of inner-city blacks and the opportunities available to them . . . substantial job losses have occurred in the very industries in which urban minorities have the greatest access, and substantial employment gains have occurred in the higher-education-requisite industries that are beyond the reach of most minority workers," according to William Julius Wilson, of the University of Chicago (see table 4).

While blacks and Hispanics will, at least for the time being, disproportionately bear the burden of this shift in job requirements, the altered structure of the marketplace will work to the disadvantage of the poorly educated of all races. In 1985, there were 30.6 million whites over the age of twenty-five without a high school education—five times the number of blacks without high school degrees (5.9 million) and seven times the number of poorly educated Hispanics (4.4 million). These job market trends will intensify throughout the rest of this century. According to estimates by the Department of Labor, 21.4 million jobs will be created between 1986 and the year 2000, all of which will be in service industries or government, as losses in traditional goods manufacturing industries are unlikely to be fully offset by gains in the technology manufacturing sector. In terms of educational requirements, there will be a significant increase in the proportion of jobs requiring at least one year of college education, no change in the proportion of jobs requiring a high school degree, and a sharp decline in the percentage of jobs requiring no high school education.

In effect, trends in the job market through the next ten years will in all likelihood exacerbate the regressive distribution of income that has taken place over the past decade. Under American democracy, those who are unemployed or marginally employed are weakest politically. The decline of traditional political organizations and unions has made significantly more difficult the political mobilization of the working poor, the working class, and the legions of white-collar workers making from $10,000 to $25,000 a year—a universe roughly containing 24.6 million white households, 3.4 million black households, and 2 million Hispanic households. Within this group, providing a political voice becomes even more difficult for those workers with poor educations who have been dispersed from manufacturing employment into cycles of marginal work. While most of those who have lost manufacturing jobs have found full-time employment, such workers have, in the main, seen wages fall and fringe benefits, often including medical coverage, decline or disappear, leaving them even further outside of the American mainstream and

Table 4

Changes in the Combined Number of Jobs, by Employee Education Level, in New York, Philadelphia, Boston, Baltimore, St. Louis, Atlanta, Houston, Denver, and San Francisco, 1970 and 1984

	Number of Jobs		
Mean level of employee education	1970	1984	Change, 1970–84
Less than high school	3,068,000	2,385,000	−683,000
Some higher education	2,023,000	2,745,000	+722,000

Sources: Computed from William Julius Wilson, *The Truly Disadvantaged: The Inner City, the Underclass, and Public Policy* (Chicago: University of Chicago Press, 1987), table 2.6, p. 40. The table, in turn, is taken from John D. Kasarda, "The Regional and Urban Redistribution of People and Jobs in the U.S." (Paper presented to the National Research Council Committee on National Urban Policy, National Academy of Sciences, 1986).

even less well equipped to ensure adequate educational levels for their children. When combined with the declining voter turnout rates associated with falling income, these workers have fallen into what amounts to a new political underclass.

The major forces at work in the last two decades of the post-New Deal period are, then, cumulatively functioning to weaken the influence and power of those in the bottom half of the income distribution, while strengthening the authority of those in the upper half, and particularly the authority of those at elite levels. Trends in political competition and pressures in the private marketplace have combined to create a whipsaw action, reversing New Deal policies that empowered the labor movement and reduced disparities between rich and poor. Recent forces, both in the marketplace and in the political arena, have not produced a realignment of the electorate, but, in terms of outcomes, there has been a realignment in public policy—with few forces, short of a downturn in the business cycle, working against the continuing development of a political and economic system in which the dominant pressures will be toward increased regressively in the distribution of money and in the ability to influence the outcome of political decisions.

EXPLORING THE ISSUE

Were the 1980s a Decade of Affluence for the Middle Class?

Critical Thinking and Reflection

1. Discuss and critically evaluate the following statement by Political Journalist Thomas B. Edsall:

   Together these forces—which include the deterioration of organized labor, the continued presence of divisive racial conflict, the shift from manufacturing to service industries, the slowing rates of economic growth, the threat of international competition to domestic production, the replacement of political organization with political technology, and the growing class-skew of voter turnout—have severely undermined the capacity of those in the bottom half of the income distribution to form an effective political coalition.

2. Critically evaluate the reasons why white males defected from the Democratic Party. How much can be attributed to job replacement from companies outside the United States or from competition from women and African American and Hispanics?

3. The Republican Party has increased its membership and influence equal to the Democratic Party since the 1970s. Critically analyze and discuss the importance of economic, cultural, and religious factors in this shift. In your discussion evaluate whether cultural or economic issues are more important in explaining this transformation.

4. Professor Woodard entitles his chapter on the 1980s "A Rising Tide." Explain what he means by this. Woodard argues that the values of reason, order, and science conflicted with the criticisms of postindustrial society under the labels of "deconstruction or post modernism." Critically analyze what he means by this contradiction.

5. Critically analyze the following two statements by Professor Woodard: "The vast majority of the population experienced substantial gains in real income of wealth"; and "The rising tide of economic prosperity lifted at least 90 percent of the American family boats." Is it possible to reconcile these statements with Edsall's view that the lower middle class and the poor were hurt by Reaganomics?

6. Explain who the "knowledge workers" are. How did they attain economic power in the United States? Define the following terms:

   a. Me decade
   b. My decade
   c. Yuppie

d. Leveraged Buyout
e. Greenmail

Is There Common Ground?

It is difficult to find common ground between the critics of "supply-side" economics who believe the 1980s widened the income gap between the rich and the middle class and supporters of "supply-side" economics who maintain that all classes benefited from the prosperity of the era. Edsall's major thesis is that in the 1980s, a policy rather than a political alignment was led by the upper middle and upper classes. This view is supported by Frederick Strobel, a former senior business economist at the Federal Reserve Bank of Atlanta in *Upward Dreams, Downward Mobility: The Economic Decline of the American Middle Class* (Rowman & Littlefield, 1993). The reasons that Strobel gives for the economic decline include an increased supply of workers (baby boomers, housewives, and immigrants), a decline in union membership, a strong dollar, an open import dollar that destroyed many U.S. manufacturing jobs, corporate merger mania, declining government jobs, energy inflation, high interest rates, and the corporate escape from federal, state, and local taxes.

Unexpected criticism also comes from President Reagan's own director of the Office of Management and Budget, David A. Stockman. His *Triumph of Politics: Why the Revolution Failed* (Harper & Row, 1986) details the "ideological hubris" that surrounded Reagan's advisers, who, in conjunction with a spendthrift Congress beholden to outside interest groups, ran up massive budget deficits by implementing a theory known as supply-side economics. More critical from the left are a series of academic articles in Michael A. Bernstein and David E. Adler, ed., *Understanding America's Economic Decline* (Cambridge University Press, 1994). Also critical are the writings of Kevin Phillips, especially *The Politics of Rich and Poor: Wealth and the American Electorate in the Reagan Aftermath* (Random House, 1990) and Joseph J. Hogan "Reganomics and Economic Policy" in Dilys M. Hill, et al., eds., *The Reagan Presidency: An Incomplete Revolution?* (St. Martin's Press, 1990), which argues, "while constantly disavowing government interventionism and proclaiming the virtues of a free market economy, the Reagan administration continually pursued economic expansionist policies based upon massive government deficits, periods of maintained monetary expansionism and unprecedented high levels of international borrowing."

For dissenting views that support supply-side economics was the key policy leading to America's economy since the early 1980s, see almost any issue of *Commentary, the National Review, The Weekly Standard, Barron's*, and editorial pages of *The Wall Street Journal*. For example, see "The Real Reagan Record," *The National Review* (August 31, 1992, pp. 25–62), especially the essays by Alan Reynolds in *Upstarts and Downstarts*, who asserts that all income groups experienced significant gains in income during the 1980s, and Paul Craig Roberts, "What Everyone 'Knows' about Reaganomics," *Commentary* (February 1992), which is critical of the Keynesian explanation for the economic downturn in the early 1990s. Two books that fully support Reagan's positive contribution to the prosperity of the 1980s (in addition to Woodard) are John Ehrman, *The*

Eighties: America in the Age of Reagan (Yale University Press, 2005) and Cato Institute economist Richard B. McKenzie, *What Went Right in the 1980s* (Pacific Research Institute for Public Policy, 1994). Karl Zinsmeister, "Summing Up the Reagan Era," *Wilson Quarterly* (Winter 1990) is similar to Woodard and Ehrman in its interpretation.

Additional Resources

James D. Torr provides balanced treatments in the edited volumes, *Ronald Reagan* (Thomson Gale, 2001) and *The 1980s: America's Decades* (Greenhaven Press, 2000). The two most recent and important collections of essays by historians and political scientists are Richard S. Conley, ed., *Reassessing the Reagan Presidency* (University Press of America, 2003) and W. Elliot Brownlee and Hugh Davis Graham, eds., *The Reagan Presidency: Pragmatic Conservatism and Legacies* (University Press of Kansas, 2003). In the essay on taxation, authors Brownlee and C. Eugene Steuerle argue that Reagan's commitment to the extreme version of the Laffer curve came in 1977, two or three years earlier than the version given by David Stockman, just before Reagan's victory in the 1980 New Hampshire primaries where supposedly, Laffer drew his famous curve on a dinner napkin. The two authors claim that Reagan had been reading economist Jude Wanniski's *Wall Street Journal* editorials supporting Laffer's ideas. Finally, worth consulting for the worldwide perspective is Bruce J. Schulman, "The Reagan Revolution in International Perspective: Conservative Assaults on the Welfare State across the Industrialized World in the 1980s," in Conley, ed., *Reassessing the Reagan Presidency*. For Reagan's impact on the 2008 presidential race, see Karen Tumulty, "How the Right Went Wrong: What Would Ronnie Do? And Why the Republican Candidates Need to Reclaim the Reagan Legacy," *Time* (March 26, 2007).

Contributors to This Volume

EDITORS

LARRY MADARAS is a professor of history emeritus at Howard Community College in Columbia, Maryland. He received a B.A. from the College of Holy Cross in 1959 and an M.A. and a Ph.D. from New York University in 1961 and 1964, respectively. He has also taught at Spring Hill College, the University of South Alabama, and the University of Maryland at College Park. He has been a Fulbright Fellow and has held two fellowships from the National Endowment for the Humanities. He is the author of dozens of journal articles and book reviews.

JAMES M. SoRELLE is a professor of history and former chair of the Department of History at Baylor University in Waco, Texas. He received a B.A. and M.A. from the University of Houston in 1972 and 1974, respectively, and a Ph.D. from Kent State University in 1980. In addition to introductory courses in United States and world history, he teaches advanced undergraduate classes in African American history, the American civil rights movement, and the 1960s, as well as a graduate seminar on the civil rights movement. His scholarly articles have appeared in the *Houston Review, Southwestern Historical Quarterly,* and *Black Dixie: Essays in Afro-Texan History and Culture in Houston* (Texas A&M University Press, 1992), edited by Howard Beeth and Cary D. Wintz. He also has contributed entries to *The New Handbook of Texas, The Oxford Companion to Politics of the World, Encyclopedia of African American Culture and History, The Encyclopedia of the Confederacy,* and *The Encyclopedia of African American History.*

AUTHORS

TERRY H. ANDERSON is a professor of history at Texas A & M University. He is the author of *The United States, Great Britain, and the Cold War, 1944–1947* (University of Missouri Press, 1981); *The Pursuit of Fairness: A History of Affirmative Action* (Oxford University Press, 2005); *The Sixties,* 4th ed. (Prentice Hall, 2011); and *Bush's Wars* (Oxford University Press, 2011).

EDWARD L. AYERS is an American historian who has been serving as the president of the University of Richmond since 2007, and winner of the Bancroft Prize. Prior to his appointment, he had been a professor of history at the University of Virginia since 1980 where he also served as the Buckner W. Clay Dean of the College and Graduate School of Arts and Sciences. Some of his other books include *Vengeance and Justice: Crime and Punishment in the Nineteenth-Century American South* (Oxford University Press, 1984); *In the Presence of Mine Enemies: War in the Heart of America, 1859–1863* (W. W. Norton, 2003), and *What Caused the Civil War? Reflections on the South and Southern History* (W. W. Norton, 2005).

LARRY BERMAN, professor and director of the University of California Washington Center, has written two previous books on Vietnam, *Planning a Tragedy* and *Lyndon Johnson's War,* and has appeared in several major television documentaries on the war. He lives in Davis, California, and Washington, DC.

ROGER BILES is a professor in and chair of the history department at East Carolina University in Greenville, North Carolina. He is the author of *The South and the New Deal* (University Press of Kentucky, 1994) and *Richard J. Daly: Politics, Race, and the Governing of Chicago* (Northern Illinois Press, 1994).

WILLIAM G. CARLETON (1903–1982) was a professor emeritus at the University of Florida and author of the widely used textbook, *The Revolution in American Foreign Policy.*

PETER CLECAK is a professor emeritus of social ecology at the University of California, Irvine. He is also the author of *Crooked Paths, Reflections on Socialism, Conservatism, and the Welfare State* (Harper & Row, 1977) and *America's Quest for the Ideal Self: Dissent and Fulfillment in the 60's and 70's* (Oxford University Press, 1984).

JOHN M. COOPER, JR., Professor of History at the University of Wisconsin is the author of numerous books on World War I and Versailles including the definitive biography, *Woodrow Wilson: A Biography* (Alfred A. Knopf, 2009).

RICHARD M. DALFIUME is a professor emeritus of history and the author of *The Desegregation of the U.S. Armed Forces: Fighting on Two Fronts, 1939–1953* (University of Missouri Press, 1969).

CARL N. DEGLER is the Margaret Byrne professor emeritus of American history at Stanford University in Stanford, California. He is a member of the editorial board for the Plantation Society, and he is a member and former president of the American History Society and the Organization of American

Historians. His book *Neither Black nor White: Slavery and Race Relations in Brazil and the United States* (University of Wisconsin Press, 1972) won the 1972 Pulitzer Prize for history.

THOMAS BYRNE EDSALL is a widely respected political journalist who has written numerous books and articles for *The New Republic, The Atlantic Monthly, The Washington Post,* and *The New York Times.*

SARA M. EVANS is the distinguished McKnight University professor of history at the University of Minnesota, where she has taught women's history since 1976. She is the author of several books including *Personal Politics: The Roots of Women's Liberation in the Civil Rights Movement and the New Left* (1979) and *Born for Liberty: A History of Women in America,* 2nd ed. (1997). Born in a Methodist parsonage in South Carolina, she was a student activist in the civil rights and antiwar movements in North Carolina and has been an active feminist since 1967.

BURTON W. FOLSOM is a professor of history at Hillsdale College in Michigan and senior historian at the Foundation for Economic Education in Irvington, New York. He is a regular columnist for *The Freeman* and has written articles for *The Wall Street Journal* and *American Spectator,* among other publications. He lives in Michigan.

JOHN LEWIS GADDIS is the Robert A. Lovett professor of history at Yale University in New Haven, Connecticut. He has also been distinguished professor of history at Ohio University, where he founded the Contemporary History Institute, and he has held visiting appointments at the United States Naval War College, the University of Helsinki, Princeton University, and Oxford University. He is the author of many books, including *We Now Know: Rethinking Cold War History* (Oxford University Press, 1997).

JOHN S. GORDON is a specialist in business and financial history whose articles have appeared in numerous prominent magazines and newspapers for the past 20 years. He is a contributing editor to *American Heritage* and since 1989 has written the "Business of America" column. His other books include *Hamilton's Blessing: The Extraordinary Life and Times of Our National Debt* (Walker, 1997), *The Great Game: The Emergence of Wall Street as a World Power, 1653–2000* (Scribner, 1999), and *A Thread Across the Ocean: The Heroic Story of the Transatlantic Cable* (Walker, 2002).

F. CAROLYN GRAGLIA is a trained lawyer, writer, and lecturer whose articles and books challenge the viewpoint of the modern women's movement.

HERBERT G. GUTMAN (1928–1985) was internationally recognized as America's leading labor and social historian. He taught at many colleges and universities, including Stanford University, William and Mary College, and the Graduate Center of the City University of New York, where he founded the American Working Class History Project.

OSCAR HANDLIN was the Carl M. Loeb professor of history at Harvard University in Cambridge, Massachusetts, where he has been teaching since 1941. A Pulitzer Prize–winning historian, he has written or edited more than 100 books, including *Liberty in Expansion* (Harper & Row, 1989), which he coauthored with Lilian Handlin, and *The Distortion of America,* 2nd ed. (Transaction Publishers, 1996).

TSUYOSHI HASEGAWA is a professor in the Department of History and the co-director of the Center for Cold War Studies at the University of California at Santa Barbara. Born in Tokyo in the year the Pacific War began, he received his BA in international relations at Tokyo University and his MA in Soviet area studies, and PhD in history at the University of Washington. He taught at the State University of New York at Oswego and at the Slavic Research Center of Hokkaidō University before he moved to the University of California at Santa Barbara in 1990. Specializing both in the Russian Revolution and in Russo-Japanese relations, he has written *The February Revolution: Petrograd 1917* (1981); *Daily Life of Petrograd during the Russian Revolution* (1989; in Japanese); *The Northern Territories Dispute and Russo-Japanese Relations,* 2 vols. (1998), which received the Ohira Masayoshi Memorial Prize for 1999; *Racing the Enemy: Stalin, Turman, and the Surrender of Japan* (2005), which received the Robert Ferrell Book Prize from the Society of Historians of American Foreign Relations in 2006, and its revised translation into Japanese: *Antō: Sutarin, Toruman to Nihon no kōfuku* (2006), which received the seventh Yomiuri Sakuzō Prize in 2006.

RICHARD HOFSTADTER (1916–1970) was a professor of history at Columbia University and is considered to be among the best American historians of the post–World War II generation. His books *The American Political Tradition and the Men Who Made It* (Alfred A. Knopf, 1948) and *The Age of Reform: From Bryan to F.D.R.* (Alfred A. Knopf, 1955) are considered classics.

LEEANNA KEITH earned her PhD at the University of Connecticut and currently teaches history at Collegiate School, a boys' day school in New York City, which is the oldest independent school in the United States.

ROBERT JAMES MADDOX is a professor emeritus of history at Penn State University and is the author of two dozen books and articles on recent American history with a specialty on Cold War diplomacy.

JAMES TICE MOORE (1946–2009) was a professor of history and former departmental chair at Virginia Commonwealth University where he taught for 31 years. His scholarly works focused on the American South, especially Virginia and include *Two Paths to the New South: Virginia Debt Controversy, 1870–83* (University Press of Kentucky, 1974) and (with Edward Younger) *The Governors of Virginia* (University of Virginia Press, 1982).

RICHARD NIXON was America's 37th president who was twice elected and ended America's participation in the Vietnam War. In August 1974, he resigned the presidency after the Judiciary Committee of the House of Representatives voted to present articles of impeachment against him before the full House. He wrote almost a dozen books in retirement.

ARNOLD A. OFFNER is Cornelia F. Hugel professor of history and head of the history department at Lafayette College. He is the author of *American*

Appeasement: United States Foreign Policy and Germany, 1933–1938 (1969) and *Origins of the Second World War: American Foreign Policy and World Politics, 1917–1941* (1975); and with Theodore A. Wilson coedited *Victory in Europe, 1945: The Allied Triumph over Germany and the Origins of the Cold War* (1999). He has recently completed a book-length study of President Harry S. Truman and the origins of the Cold War.

GILMAN M. OSTRANDER was author of over a dozen books on American intellectual and cultural history. He taught at Reed College, Ohio State University, the University of Missouri, and Michigan State University before taking a teaching position at the University of Waterloo in Canada, where he served as a professor of history from 1971 until the time of his death. Some of his most important books include *American Civilization in the First Machine Age, 1890–1940* (Harper & Row, 1970) and *Republic of Letters: The American Intellectual Community, 1775–1865* (Rowman & Littlefield, 1999).

THOMAS G. PATERSON is a professor of history at the University of Connecticut in Storrs, CT. His articles have appeared in *Journal of American History* and *Diplomatic History* (where he has served upon the editorial boards) and *American Historical Review.* A past president of the Society for Historians of American Foreign Relations, he has authored, coauthored, or edited many books, including *Contesting Castro* (Oxford University Press, 1994) and *On Every Front,* 2nd ed. (W. W. Norton, 1993).

CHARLES POSTEL is an assistant professor of history at San Francisco University where he specializes in politics, reform movements, populism, and the Gilded Age and Progressive Era. His first book was *Power and Progress: Populist Thought in America* (University of California Press, 2002). His most recent book on *The Populist Vision,* excerpted in this reader, won the Bancroft Prize and Frederick Jackson Turner Award in 2008.

HEATHER COX RICHARDSON is a professor of history at the University of Massachusetts, Amherst. Her other books include *The Greatest Nation of the Earth: Republican Economic Policies during the Civil War* (Harvard University Press, 1997) and *West from Appomattox: The Reconstruction of America after the Civil War* (Yale University Press, 2007).

DAVID A. SHANNON taught at the University of Maryland and is the author of *Twentieth Century America,* 4th ed. (Houghton Mifflin, 1977) and the editor of *Southern Business: The Decades Ahead* (MacMillan, 1981).

HARVARD SITKOFF is a professor of history at the University of New Hampshire and is the author of *A New Deal for Blacks: The Emergence of Civil Rights as a National Issue: The Depression Decade,* 30th anniversary edition (Oxford University Press, 1979, 2009); *The Struggle for Black Equality, 1954–1980* (Hill and Wang, 1981); and *King: Pilgrimage to the Mountaintop* (Hill & Wang, 2008).

TED STEINBERG is a professor of history at Case Western University and is the author of several books on the history of the American environment.

T.H. WATKINS, a former senior editor of *American Heritage,* has been editor of *Wilderness,* the magazine of the Wilderness Society, since 1982. He is the author or coauthor of 19 books, including the recently published *Righteous Pilgrim: The Life and Times of Harold L. Ickes,* which has been nominated for a National Book Award.

ROBERT WEISBROT is a professor of history at Colby College in Waterville, Maine, where he is also on the advisory committee for the African American Studies Program. He is the author of *From the Founding of the Southern Christian Leadership Conference to the Assassination of Malcolm X (1957–65)* (Chelsea House, 1994).

J. DAVID WOODARD is a professor of history and political science at the University of South Carolina and is the author of a number of books and articles about the modern conservative movement.

MARK WYMAN is a professor of history at Illinois State University and the author of *Round-Trip to America: The Immigrant Returns to Europe, 1880–1930* (Cornell University Press, 1993).

HOWARD ZINN was a civil rights protester and peace activist with a PhD from Columbia University. He taught for many years at Spelman College and Boston University and was immensely popular with the students. He has written hundreds of articles, but *A People's History of the United States* (HarperCollins, 1980, 1999) has sold enough copies to make a millionaire out of a Socialist.